BOND DEFAULT MANUAL

2nd Edition

Duncan L. Clore, Editor

Fidelity and Surety Law Committee
Tort and Insurance Practice Section
American Bar Association

The materials contained herein represent the opinions of the authors and editors and should not be construed to be the action of either the American Bar Association or the Tort and Insurance Practice Section unless adopted pursuant to the bylaws of the Association.

Nothing contained in this book is to be considered as the rendering of legal advice for specific cases, and readers are responsible for obtaining such advice from their own legal counsel. This book and any forms and agreements herein are intended for educational and informational purposes only.

Permission from the American Institute of Architects to reprint the forms on pages 421-425 is gratefully acknowledged.

Printed in the United States of America.

Library of Congress Catalog Card Number 95-76558
ISBN 1-57073-169-1

00 99 98 97 5 4 3 2

CONTENTS

CONTRIBUTORS

HUGH N. ANDERSON • Partner in the Madison, Wisconsin law firm of Wickwire Gavin, P.C. Mr. Anderson attended the University of Wisconsin (B.A. and M.S.), and received his J.D. degree from Stanford Law School.

GEORGE J. BACHRACH • Partner in the Baltimore, Maryland law firm of Whiteford, Taylor & Preston. He received his Bachelor of Arts degree, *cum laude*, from Harvard University in 1971 and his Juris Doctor degree from Georgetown University Law Center in 1974. He is a Vice-Chair of the ABA/TIPS Fidelity & Surety Law Committee.

JAMES H. BAUMGARTNER, JR. • Managing partner in the Dallas, Texas law firm of Vial, Hamilton, Koch & Knox, L.L.P. He is a graduate of the University of California at Berkeley, B.S. 1965, and the University of Texas, L.L.B. 1968.

PHILIP L. BRUNER • Head of the Fidelity & Surety/Construction Law Practice Group in the Minneapolis, Minnesota law firm of Faegre & Benson. He received his B.A. degree from Princeton University, M.B.A. degree from Syracuse University, and J.D. degree from the University of Michigan Law School. He is a fellow of the American College of Construction Lawyers, the National Contract Management Association, and is currently Chair of the ABA/TIPS Fidelity & Surety Law Committee.

DUNCAN L. CLORE • Partner in the Dallas, Texas law firm of Strasburger & Price, L.L.P. He is a graduate of Centre College, B.A. 1970, and Southern Methodist University School of Law, J.D. 1976. Mr. Clore is a Vice-Chair of the ABA/TIPS Fidelity & Surety Law Committee.

MARTHA CRANDALL COLEMAN • Partner in the Dallas, Texas law firm of Strasburger & Price, L.L.P. She is a graduate of Grinnell College, B.A. 1982, and the University of Texas School of Law, J.D. 1985.

GAVIN P. CRAIG • Partner in the Minneapolis, Minnesota law firm of Wickwire Gavin, P.C. Mr. Craig attended the University of Southern California (B.S.), and received his J.D. degree from McGeorge School of Law, University of the Pacific.

F. MALCOLM CUNNINGHAM, JR. • Managing partner in the West Palm Beach, Florida law firm of Cunningham & Self. Mr. Cunningham is a graduate of Fisk University, B.S. 1977, and Howard University School of Law, J.D. 1980. After graduation, he served as a law clerk for the Honorable Joseph W. Hatchett, Circuit Judge, United States Court of Appeals for the Fifth Circuit.

DAVID C. DREIFUSS • Partner in the Livingston, New Jersey law firm of Nagel, Rice & Dreifuss. He received his undergraduate degree, *cum laude*, from the University of Connecticut in 1974, his Juris Doctor from Rutgers School of Law (Newark) in 1977, and his L.L.M. from New York University School of Law in 1983. Mr. Dreifuss is a Vice-Chair of the ABA/TIPS Fidelity & Surety Law Committee. He has also served as Chair of other Committees of TIPS, including the Membership Involvement Committee.

DONALD G. GAVIN • Partner in the Washington, D.C. and Vienna, Virginia law firm of Wickwire Gavin, P.C. He is a graduate of the law school of the University of Pennsylvania, J.D. 1967, and has a degree in Government Procurement Law from the National Law Center of George Washington University, L.L.M. 1972. He is a past Chair of the Public Contract Law Section of the American Bar Association and is a Vice-Chair of the ABA/TIPS Fidelity & Surety Law Committee.

KENNETH M. GIVENS, JR. • Manager of the Fidelity & Surety Department of the Claim Division of the Fidelity & Deposit Company of Maryland, Baltimore, Maryland. Mr. Givens received his undergraduate degree from Hamilton College, Clinton, New York, and his law degree from Villanova University School of Law.

Deborah S. Griffin • Partner in the Boston, Massachusetts law firm of Peabody & Arnold. She received her A.B. degree, *cum laude*, in 1971 from Bryn Mawr College and her J.D. degree in 1974 from Boston University School of Law. She is a past Chair of the American Bar Association's Forum on the Construction Industry and a Vice-Chair of the ABA/TIPS Fidelity & Surety Law Committee. She has served as liaison between the ABA Forum on the Construction Industry and the National Association of Women in Construction (NAWIC) and as a Director of Boston Chapter 15 of NAWIC. In 1989, she was elected a charter member of the American College of Construction Lawyers.

James J. Hartnett, IV • Associate in the Minneapolis, Minnesota law firm of Faegre & Benson. He received his B.A. degree from Williams College and his J.D. degree, *magna cum laude*, from New York University.

Todd C. Kazlow • Western Region Manager, Fidelity/Surety Claim Department of United States Fidelity & Guaranty Company in Baltimore, Maryland. He is a graduate of the University of Maryland at College Park, B.A. 1979, and New England School of Law, Boston, Massachusetts, J.D. 1982.

Richard A. Kowalczyk • Manager, Recovery Unit and Northeast Claims, Fidelity and Surety Claim Department, United States Fidelity & Guaranty Company. He received his J.D. degree from the University of Maryland Law School in 1973.

T. Scott Leo • Partner in the Chicago, Illinois law firm of Sedgwick, Detert, Moran & Arnold. He is a graduate of the University of Illinois, B.A. 1976, and the Washington University School of Law in St. Louis, J.D. 1980. He is a Vice-Chair of the ABA/TIPS Fidelity & Surety Law Committee.

Lawrence Lerner • Member of the Board of Directors of the Kansas City, Missouri law firm of Sandler, Balkin, Hellman & Weinstein, Professional Corporation. He received a B.S. in Civil Engineering from the City College of the City University of New York in 1971, and his J.D. degree from the Pepperdine University School of Law in 1980. Mr.

Lerner became a licensed Professional Engineer in the State of Colorado in 1977.

Patrick J. O'Connor, Jr. • Partner in the Minneapolis, Minnesota law firm of Faegre & Benson. Mr. O'Connor is a graduate of Hamline University, B.A. 1975, and Washington College of Law, American University, J.D. 1981. He is a Vice-Chair of the ABA/TIPS Fidelity & Surety Law Committee.

William S. Piper • Illinois attorney associated with the Law Offices of Alan I. Boyer and engaged with Viceroy Management, Inc., a surety claims management company serving various surety companies. He is a graduate of Loyola University of Chicago, B.A. and J.D.

Gary J. Rouse • Partner in the New Orleans, Louisiana law firm of Koch and Rouse. He obtained his J.D. in 1970 from the Louisiana State University Law Center. After graduation he worked as Senior Law Clerk for The Honorable Nauman S. Scott, Chief Judge, United States District Court, Western District of Louisiana. Mr. Rouse is a Vice-Chair of the ABA/TIPS Fidelity & Surety Law Committee.

Keith Witten • Member of the Board of Directors of the Kansas City, Missouri law firm of Sandler, Balkin, Hellman & Weinstein, Professional Corporation. He is a graduate of Auburn University, B.A. 1968, and the University of Kansas School of Law, J.D. 1971.

INTRODUCTION

The Fidelity & Surety Law Committee of the American Bar Association Tort and Insurance Practice Section is pleased to publish this second edition of the *Bond Default Manual*, which updates and expands the first edition published in 1987. The Committee extends its special thanks to the editor of this second edition, Duncan L. Clore, Dallas, Texas, and to the respective authors for their significant contributions. We also recognize our indebtedness to the editor of the first edition, Richard S. Wisner, Chicago, Illinois, and to his authors for their seminal contributions.

The *Bond Default Manual* itself is an outgrowth of the myriad papers presented to the Fidelity & Surety Law Committee at its mid-winter and summer meetings over many decades. The footnotes of the *Bond Default Manual*, which cite dozens of published and unpublished papers, stand in testimony to the outstanding contributions of our committee members and long-standing traditions of our committee in the development and analysis of the law of suretyship.

This second edition of the Bond Default Manual is a worthy successor to the first edition, and should be studied carefully by all practitioners in the field.

Philip L. Bruner
Minneapolis, Minnesota
Chair, Fidelity & Surety Law Committee

INTRODUCTION

From *Bond Default Manual* (original edition)

On January 23, 1987, the Fidelity and Surety Law Committee of the Tort and Insurance Practice Section of the American Bar Association presented its Annual Mid-Winter Surety Program at the Waldorf Astoria Hotel in New York City. The program was entitled "Performance Bond Default: Four Directions Compared and Contrasted." The format consisted of a panel discussion by eight experienced surety claim attorneys divided into four two-man teams (one a company representative and one a private practitioner). Each team was assigned one of the four traditional options of a surety upon default of its performance bond principal: 1) Financing the Contractor; 2) Completion by the Surety; 3) Tendering of a New Contractor by the Surety; and 4) Completion of Contract by the Owner.

The quality of the program led to the Committee's decision to videotape it for training and educating new attorneys and surety claims personnel. Although many scholarly papers have been prepared and delivered on these topics, the Committee perceived a need among its members for a single comprehensive resource which would provide the insight and address the basic information and techniques involved in performance bond claims handling.

The video program and the manual were designed and produced to be used together. The video program consists of five tapes, each of approximately 50 minutes duration. The tapes correspond generally with chapters 2 through 5 of the manual. The first chapter is devoted to the surety's investigation procedures. It is recommended that the corresponding chapter in the manual be read before viewing any of the videotapes. A further suggestion is to use the videotapes during seminar training sessions, stopping the tapes at selected intervals to stimulate discussion.

The Committee is greatly indebted to those who participated in this endeavor. The team concept to compare and contrast the four directions originated with Thomas G. Ottenweller of San Francisco, who not only moderated the original January 23, 1987 New York Surety Program, but also worked tirelessly to complete the manual and the videotaping program. The panel discussion format was the brainchild of Richard S. Wisner of Chicago. Dick arranged several meetings of the panelists and convinced them all it could be done. The videotape preservation of this inspired panel for training of future generations of surety claims attorneys was the idea of James A. Black of Baltimore, Maryland. Jim put together the budget and worked with Liz Williamson, Associate Director of the ABA Consortium for Professional Education, in setting up the actual taping session at KTCA, Public Television, in Minneapolis-St. Paul on April 27, 1987. Without the efforts of each, this project would never have succeeded.

Our special thanks go of course to the authors and panel members: William F. Haug of Phoenix, Arizona and Thomas A. Joyce of Hartford, Connecticut ("Financing the Bond Principal"), Richard S. Wisner of Chicago, Illinois and Wayne S. Jensen of Seattle, Washington ("Takeover and Completion by the Surety"), James A. Knox of Dallas, Texas and Robert D. Carnaghan of Baltimore, Maryland ("Tender of a New Contractor by the Surety"), and Patrick E. Hartigan, Kansas City, Missouri, John B. Hayes of Oklahoma City, Oklahoma and Andrew J. Ruck of Philadelphia, Pennsylvania ("Owner Completion").

James F. Crowder, Jr.
Chairman, Fidelity and
Surety Law Committee

CHAPTER 1

BOND, CONTRACTUAL AND STATUTORY PROVISIONS AND GENERAL AGREEMENT OF INDEMNITY

David C. Dreifuss

I. Introduction

This chapter presents the circumstances a surety faces when a default occurs. These circumstances are analogous to stormy weather conditions confronting a ship's captain. Just as the captain has no control over the ocean or inclement weather conditions, the surety often has little control over the circumstances surrounding a default. This manual focuses on how the surety can successfully "weather" the storm, and like the skillful captain maneuver its way through the pitfalls which confront it.

When a default occurs, the surety is presented with the provisions of the bond or bonds issued by the surety, the provisions in the contract or contracts which its principal entered into, as well as the applicable statutory provisions. Furthermore, the general agreement of indemnity contains the provisions included by the underwriters when the indemnity agreement was executed. Thus, as with the ship's captain, the surety claims professional is presented with conditions through which he or she must maneuver. The purpose of this chapter is to focus on those provisions.

II.
Bond Provisions

While the underwriters may have input with respect to the language of the bond prior to issuance, generally the bond provisions are drafted by the obligee or a consultant retained by the obligee. Usually, these provisions are not negotiable, and either the bond is issued or the underwriters decline issuance. While some obligees draft bond provisions that are extremely favorable to the obligee, most of the bonds issued contain relatively standard provisions.

One series of bond forms that are fairly commonplace are those published by The American Institute of Architects, which sells forms of bid bonds, performance bonds and payment bonds. Since architects often prepare the specifications, including the bond forms, these forms are fairly commonplace.

Other bond forms often utilized are those prescribed by or designed consistent with an applicable statute. Certain statutes expressly provide forms for bonds consistent with their requirements.[1]

However, some obligees, especially sophisticated non-public obligees, have attempted to impose upon sureties obligations that have not traditionally been assumed by sureties. As one author has recently written:

> The surety's liability does not include damages for tort injuries, criminal penalties against contractors, the results of the obligee's negligence, or any number of other types of damages which are not the completion of the work or payment of subcontractors and suppliers. In many cases recently, however, owners and obligees have attempted to expand the liability of the surety by drafting bond forms which add these types of damages to those traditionally covered by the surety.[2]

Therefore, assumptions should not be made as to the likely bond form. Rather, it is crucial that the bond form issued by the surety be carefully

---

1 *See, e.g.*, FLA. STAT. ANN. § 255.05(3) (West 1994); N.J. STAT. ANN. 2A:44-147 (West 1994); N.C. GEN. STAT. § 44A-33 (1994) and OHIO REV. CODE ANN. § 153.571 (Anderson 1993).

2 Lynn M. Schubert, *Modern Contract Bonds—An Overview*, *in* THE LAW OF SURETYSHIP, 3-1, at 3-7 (Edward G. Gallagher ed., 1993).

reviewed. See Appendix, Exhibits 1.1-1.4 for examples of commonly used bond forms.

The bond is the contract executed by the surety; it establishes the extent of the surety's liability. It is subject to the general law of contracts, and a reviewing court "should consider the language in the contract, subject matter of the contract, and the object and purpose of the [bond] contract" to determine the intent of the parties.[3] In most jurisdictions, sureties are liable only in accordance with the strict terms of their undertaking.[4] As one court has declared:

> [T]he obligation of a surety is measured by the contract of surety. The surety's obligation cannot be extended by implication or enlarged by construction beyond the terms of the suretyship agreement, in a way to include any subject or person other than expressed or necessarily implied from the suretyship contract. In other words, a surety in Florida is bound to the extent and in the manner indicated in the undertaking, and no further. The Courts of Florida will not presume that the contracting parties intended to include in their agreement a provision other than, or different from, those indicated by the language used.[5]

This doctrine of interpretation is substantially different from that applicable to insurance policies where, generally, all ambiguities are construed against the carrier. This is one of the reasons why it is important to emphasize to claimants as well as judges and adversaries that the surety, even if also an insurance company, is acting in its capacity as a surety.

The bond may include provisions that operate as a complete defense to any suit or claim. For example, where the bond contains a provision

---

3 See *American Home Assurance Co. v. Larkin General Hospital, Ltd.*, 593 So.2d 195, 197 (Fla. 1992).

4 *See, e.g., United States v. Seaboard Sur. Co.*, 817 F.2d 956, 963 (2d Cir.), *cert. denied*, 484 U.S. 855 (1987); *Monmouth Lumber Co. v. Indemnity Ins. Co. of N. America*, 21 N.J. 439, 452, 122 A.2d 604, 611 (N.J. 1956) and *Mendel-Mesick-Cohen-Architects v. Peerless Ins. Co.*, 426 N.Y.S.2d 124, 126 (N.Y. App. Div. 1980).

5 *State of Florida ex rel. Westinghouse Elec. Supply Co. v. Wesley Constr. Co.*, 316 F. Supp. 490, 497 (S. D. Fla. 1970), *aff'd by* 453 F.2d 1366 (5th Cir. 1972).

that limits the time to file suit to a period shorter than the relevant statute-of-limitations period, the shorter period will generally be enforced even when a claimant had no knowledge of this bond provision.[6]

A. Bid Bond

Succinctly stated, a bid bond provides that if the bidder submitting the bid that the owner intends to accept does not enter into a contract and provide other documents required by the contract (such as performance and payment bonds) the surety may be called upon to pay some amount to the obligee. Since the bid that the owner intends to accept has generally been submitted by the lowest responsible bidder, the bid bond provides protection to the obligee that is forced to enter into a higher contract amount as a result of the lowest responsible bidder failing to fulfill the requirements necessary to enter into the contract itself. As to public construction, bid bonds are often required by statute and generally provide either for a fixed amount to be forfeited to the obligee or for the surety to pay the difference between the amount bid by its principal and the contract price ultimately awarded to another bidder. This difference may rise up to the penal sum of the bond.

B. Performance Bond

Generally, a performance bond is conditioned upon the principal's faithful and complete performance of the contract. These bonds often contain provisions regarding the time period for institution of suit against the surety under the bond, the relevant venue for any such suit, the timing for notice to be provided to the surety as well as the surety's maximum liability—the penal sum—for damages under the bond. These provisions can be very significant to the surety's decision-making process. For example, where the cost to complete a project is substantially greater than the penal sum, sureties will generally not undertake completion of the project in question.

---

6 *See, e.g.*, *Ribeira & Lourenco Concrete Constr., Inc. v. Jackson Health Care Assocs.*, 554 A.2d 1350, 1353 (N.J. Super. Ct. App. Div. 1989) *aff'd*. 571 A.2d 1311 (N.J. 1990) and cases cited therein.

Certain bonds also set forth either the conduct required of the surety in the event of a termination for default or, in the alternative, the options available to the surety in the event of a termination for default. For example, completion bonds may require the surety to complete the project in the event of a default. The performance bond form published by The American Institute of Architects (A312)[7] expressly sets forth the options available to the surety issuing such bonds in the event of a termination for default. The options set forth are relatively extensive in that the surety may:

1. arrange for the principal, with the obligee's consent, to complete the contract;
2. undertake to perform and complete the contract;
3. arrange for the tender of a new contractor acceptable to the owner with performance and payment bonds and pay to the owner the amount of the owner's damages; or
4. waive the aforesaid rights and pay the owner the damages incurred by the owner calculated after investigation or deny liability and notify the owner of its reasons.

Most performance bonds also incorporate by reference the underlying contract between the principal and the obligee. Thus, the surety must thoroughly review all contractual provisions before considering its options. Significant contractual provisions will be reviewed later in this chapter.

C. Payment Bond

Succinctly stated, the payment bond provides that the surety shall make payment to subcontractors, laborers and/or materials suppliers who are not paid by the principal. However, as is true with the performance bond, the payment bond generally includes provisions that can prove to be of great significance. These provisions may relate to the time for submission of a claim to the surety, the earliest point at which suit may be instituted, the limitations period beyond which suit may not be instituted, venue for any litigation and the penal sum. Often, the language of the payment bond is based upon relevant statutory provisions, which will be addressed later in this chapter. Since the surety's liability should not

---

7 American Institute of Architects Document A312, Performance Bond and Payment Bond, December 1984 Edition.

exceed that of its principal, the surety should have all of the defenses of its principal (as well as surety defenses, where applicable), and the subcontract may be incorporated into the bond by reference, it is imperative that the subcontract and/or applicable purchase order be carefully examined. Again, such provisions will be considered later in this chapter.

Since many claimants and/or their attorneys are unaware of the statutory and/or bond provisions relative to the timing of suits or actions pursuant to payment bonds, such provisions may often provide valuable defenses to sureties. In any event, all of the bond provisions should be carefully examined and considered with respect to each payment bond claim.

III.
Contractual Provisions

The provisions set forth in the contract by and between the principal and the obligee are significant for a number of reasons. First, they are often expressly incorporated into the bond by language contained in the bond itself. Secondly, even if the contract is not incorporated into the bond, the contract provisions often significantly impact the options that a surety is likely to select. For example, where the contractual provisions set forth in the contract between the obligee and the principal are especially onerous or include provisions regarding responsibility for any contamination on the site, a surety may elect not to undertake completion but to undertake another option. Furthermore, where a tender is being considered, any relet bid package must incorporate all applicable provisions set forth in the underlying contract between the principal and the obligee unless the surety and obligee negotiate to the contrary.

Whereas the underwriters profess to review the contracts and may do so in order to evaluate whether or not a contractor possesses the expertise to perform the general scope of work set forth therein, they are generally not equipped to thoroughly review all legal and technical aspects of the contract. With respect to public construction, the terms and conditions of the contract are dictated exclusively by the owner/obligee and its consultant(s). The same is also generally true with respect to private construction where the project is placed for bidding amongst a number of contractors. However, the principal may have input, even substantial input, when it negotiates the contract with the owner/obligee in connection with private construction.

Contractual provisions are also often dictated, in part, by funding sources. For example, where federal funding has been provided with respect to a project let for bid by a state or local government or agency, certain provisions, such as minority hiring, shall be required. In fact, some funding sources, generally with respect to private construction, will require in the bid specifications that the contractor provide dual obligee bonds whereby they are included as an obligee, together with the owner, on the bond itself.

The length and/or complexity of the contract varies and is often totally unrelated to the size or complexity of the project. For example, some contracts are short and straightforward whereas others are thousands of pages long. In other instances, the contract itself may be one or two pages but then incorporate by reference hundreds if not thousands of pages of general and special conditions, including the technical specifications.

Often, the drafter incorporates provisions from other contracts or contract forms. The American Institute of Architects publishes general and supplemental conditions, which are used frequently, perhaps because the drafter is often an architect.

The special conditions generally set forth how the work will be completed from a technical standpoint. In a design build situation where the principal is serving as the designer as well as the general contractor, such provisions may not be incorporated, or, more likely, they may set forth general parameters as to performance requirements or methods of construction. In a multi-prime situation in which the owner enters into different contracts with different trades, the special conditions vary by contract. However, regardless whether the project is a multi-prime project or one in which the principal serves as the general contractor with respect to all aspects of construction, the details of special conditions can vary widely by contract.

While general and/or supplemental conditions also tend to vary widely by contract, there are common issues which they generally address. The following is a cursory review of some of those issues. Again, the importance of the contract, regardless of whether general, supplemental or special conditions are involved, cannot be overstated for it is the alleged breach of the contract that resulted in the termination for default in the first place. It is also the decision whether or not to complete that contract and, if so, which mechanism to utilize that is addressed in the later chapters.

A. Termination

Since this book pertains to bond defaults which, stated differently, are terminations for default, the termination provisions set forth in the contract provide a good starting point. Generally, the contract may contain provisions for termination for the convenience of the owner as well as provisions for termination for cause. Where the termination is for convenience, the owner/obligee is generally not in a position to call upon the surety to complete the contract and/or to assume responsibility for any damages incurred by the owner/obligee. However, when a principal is experiencing financial difficulties and/or payment bond claims have been asserted with respect to a project being terminated for convenience, the surety may take interest in the financial resolution of a termination for convenience and may seek to protect itself by utilizing the consent of surety requirement. (Most owners seek the consent of the surety before releasing the retainage provided for in the contract.)

Furthermore, the contract often imposes certain obligations upon the owner and/or its representatives. This is important since the failure of the owner to comply with those requirements may constitute breach of the contract by the owner and may also provide defenses to the surety.

Bases for a termination for cause often include the following:

1. the contractor's commission of a substantial violation of the contract and, after notice from the owner, architect, or construction manager, failure to cure the violation within the time period set forth in the contract;
2. failure to supply adequate materials and/or properly skilled workers;
3. failure to promptly pay subcontractors and/or materials suppliers and/or its workers;
4. persistent failure to comply with applicable laws, regulations, directives, etc., of a public agency or authority with jurisdiction over the project;
5. failure to complete the project in a timely fashion; and
6. adjudication of the principal to be a bankrupt or general assignment by the principal for the benefit of its creditors or appointment of a receiver due to the principal's insolvency.

Contracts often provide that, when a contractor has been terminated for cause, the owner may take possession of all materials and equipment on the site and may proceed to finish the remaining work and to withhold any further funds from the contractor until the work has been completed. Often, the contracts provide for what I will characterize as the general breach-of-contract remedy, namely that the principal/contractor shall be liable for any excess costs to complete over and above those set forth in the contract. However, if excess funds remain after the owner has completed the contract and incurred any and all expenses in connection with it, then the excess shall be paid to the contractor/principal. Some contracts define such expenses, which may include interest charges, consultant fees, legal fees and other charges in addition to the cost to complete. Other contracts do not define these expenses.

Often, contracts provide for liquidated damages; these may or may not be set forth in the termination provisions of the general conditions. Generally, under a liquidated-damages clause, the contractor must pay the owner a fixed amount for every day that the contract work is not completed beyond the completion date in the contract, or any approved extensions. When a contractor has been terminated for cause, and the delay in completion by others and/or the owner extends well beyond the contract completion date, liquidated damages may prove to be substantial. The surety may determine that there is a basis for granting an extension of time to its principal and thus reducing or eliminating liquidated damages. Furthermore, when the surety is called upon to complete and it agrees to do so, the owner/obligee may still seek to withhold the amount of liquidated damages from payment requisitions submitted by the surety. The same may be true with respect to a tender situation in that the amount tendered by the surety may need to compensate for liquidated damages, which the owner/obligee may intend to withhold from the completing contractor. Obviously, this issue would need to be the subject of negotiation.

B. Disputes

Many general conditions provide for a method to resolve disputes. These methods vary widely by contract. Contracts may provide for an initial method to resolve disputes, such as a decision by the architect, meeting of representatives of the two parties, or a formal decision by a contracting officer or a designated public official (with respect to public projects). When one of these initial procedures does not resolve the dispute, the disputes clause may then provide for resolution by means of mediation, arbitration or litigation.

Where mediation or arbitration are set forth, the contracts generally designate a certain association or organization, such as the American Arbitration Association, as the binding decision maker. Where litigation is designated, the general conditions often set forth requirements such as venue and whether or not a jury may be requested.

Regardless of which mode of dispute resolution is designated, often notice and other requirements are set forth as well. These requirements may include time parameters with respect to dispute resolution. Failure to adhere to these provisions can result in a waiver of rights.

These conditions and requirements are of great concern to the surety when the principal has been terminated for default. As noted above, when the terms and provisions of the contract are incorporated into the bond, those terms and conditions are generally binding upon the surety. In some instances, the general conditions provide specifically that the dispute resolution provisions will apply to the surety in the event of a termination for default.

Where the general conditions do not expressly address that issue and the bond does not incorporate the provisions, the surety still must focus upon this clause primarily for two reasons. First, even when the contract provisions are not incorporated into the bond, the courts may seek to do so. Second, the dispute between the principal and the obligee may be very significant to the surety. For example, some courts have indicated that an arbitration or litigation as to which the surety has notice may be binding upon the surety regardless whether the surety participates.[8] Further, when the bond provides for one mechanism for dispute resolution and the contract provides for a different mechanism, the surety that prefers the dispute resolution mechanism may be able to avail itself of that provision when the obligee either does not focus upon the issue or does not object. In contrast, at least one court has held that when a bond

8 *See*, *e.g.*, *Raymond Int'l Builders v. First Indem. of Am. Ins. Co.*, 516 A.2d 620, 622 (N.J. 1986) and cases cited therein.

provides for dispute resolution in court and a contract provides for arbitration, the surety may be compelled to arbitrate.[9]

C. Payment Provisions

Virtually all contracts between principals and owners/obligees provide when the owner/obligee shall make payments to the principal. Usually, the contracts provide for periodic payments based on the progress of the principal. Often the payments are to be provided on a monthly basis with the principal submitting monthly requisitions or requests for payment. The surety should consider the amount of contract funds remaining versus the cost of completion after the principal has been terminated for default in evaluating its completion options. The surety also should carefully review the owner/obligee's compliance with the contract's payment provisions, since overpayment to the principal by the obligee may provide a partial or complete defense for the surety.

Many payment provisions require that the contractor utilize or certify that it has utilized the contract funds paid by the owner to pay subcontractors and/or materials suppliers. These provisions are often consistent with trust fund acts enacted in some states relative to public construction. Falsified certifications and/or violations of a trust fund act may result in personal liability of the principal's responsible officer or officers.

Most contracts provide for a review procedure with respect to the principal's requests for payment. The surety may have some defenses/ affirmative claims if it is determined that the principal's work for which the principal has been paid was not performed properly. However, the majority of contracts, including those published by The American Institute of Architects, exculpate the architect-engineer from any responsibility for determining the quality or propriety of the work performed by the principal. Nevertheless, the actions of the architect or engineer can still be addressed during disputes in which the architect/engineer assumed

---

9 *See Cianbro Corp. v. Empresa Nacional De Ingenieria y Technologia, S.A.*, 697 F. Supp. 15 (D. Me. 1988) (holding that contract is incorporated by reference into surety's bond). *But see, e.g., In re Interactive Video Resources, Inc.*, 170 B. R. 716 (S. D. Fla. 1994) and *Travelers Indem. Co. v. Hayes Contractors, Inc.*, 389 N.W. 2d 257 (Minn. Ct. App. 1986).

responsibility for coordination, supervision and/or inspection or the contract is silent as to the architect's/engineer's liability.

D. Duties Relative to Protection of Persons and Property

Generally speaking, after issuance of the notice to proceed through the date of final acceptance, most contracts provide that the principal/contractor shall be responsible for the worksite and all materials, equipment and other property there as well as all employees and other persons involved or affected by the worksite. These provisions may concern the surety when the principal has been terminated for default because the project site, as of that time, may be unsafe or vulnerable to weather conditions or vandalism. During its investigation, the surety may either attempt to secure the site, based upon an express and full reservation of rights, or it may require the owner/obligee to secure the site and to minimize or mitigate damages in so doing.

E. Insurance

Most contracts require the principal/contractor to obtain various kinds of insurance, including comprehensive general liability coverage, contractual liability insurance, workers compensation insurance and other forms of insurance. These provisions should be considered by the surety in two respects. First, any completing contractor either tendered by the surety or retained by the surety to complete must comply with these provisions unless the obligee agrees to reduce or waive these requirements. Secondly, the surety may benefit from pursuing a claim or claims against one of these carriers. For example, damage to property caused by defective workmanship (not the cost to correct the defective workmanship itself) may be covered by a comprehensive general liability policy. Again, this is an area that the surety should consider during its investigation.

F. Changes in the Work to be Performed by the Principal/Contractor

Most contracts provide mechanisms to change the scope of work. These are commonly referred to as "change orders." A request for issuance of a change order often must be submitted within a short period of time after the contractor learns that there are bases for a change order, or this option is deemed waived. These requests are usually reviewed by the owner's consultant(s). Some contracts also provide a procedure for appeal from the denial of a change order.

At one time sureties could exculpate themselves from liability when a significant change in the scope of work had been agreed upon by the principal and the obligee. But now many bond forms expressly provide that the surety shall remain liable under the bond irrespective of any changes in the work. If the bond has no such provision, a significant change in the scope of the work may prove to be either a partial or complete release of the surety's obligations under the bond. In most states the release is partial; therefore, the surety is discharged only to the extent it has been prejudiced by the change.

Furthermore, changes in the work are important to the surety when investigating whether or not to complete or tender a completing contractor. Changes in the scope of work may also result in incomplete work and/or payment bond claims in excess of the penal sum of the bonds.

G. Subcontract Provisions

The precise provisions incorporated into a subcontract and/or purchase order depend on which party drafted the document. If the subcontractor is sophisticated and/or is a specialty subcontractor or materials supplier, its form subcontract and/or purchase order may be utilized. Generally, these contracts and/or purchase orders treat the transaction as separate and distinct from the relationship between the general contractor and the owner. When the materials have been provided and/or the subcontract work performed, the materials supplier/subcontractor is to be paid.

In contrast, the larger or more sophisticated general contractors require that their forms be utilized. These forms often incorporate the general and special conditions of the general contractor's contract with the owner as well as technical specifications that relate to the work performed or materials provided by the subcontractor/materials supplier. Often, they provide that, with respect to change orders, the general contractor will be responsible only for payments indicated on written change orders and only for the quantities and/or amounts approved by the owner.

Other provisions may address the timing of payments, amounts of retainage withheld and a variety of other issues, such as those addressed above. Familiarity with these provisions is important for several reasons. First, of course, when the principal is a subcontractor or materials supplier, the subcontract and/or purchase order shall be incorporated into the performance bond by reference and sets forth the scope of the principal's obligations and those of any completing contractor. When the principal is the general contractor, subcontracts may address important provisions regarding (1) assignment of the subcontracts to the surety by its principal, (2) agreement of the subcontractor/material supplier to adhere to the terms and conditions of the subcontract/purchase order in connection with completion efforts by the surety or its tendered contractor, and (3) payment bond claims in general.

IV.
Statutory Provisions

The federal government and virtually every state have enacted legislation pertaining to contract surety bonds. When a bond or contract provision conflicts with a statutory provision, the statutory provision usually controls. These statutory provisions are not, however, the only statutory provisions relevant to the surety. Numerous other statutory provisions, such as the applicable construction codes and environmental laws, may be significant. These other provisions are too numerous and extensive to address here.

In addition, various regulations, ordinances, orders and directives may be applicable to the work to be performed. Even when the contract does not expressly incorporate these items by reference, the courts usually deem them incorporated and rely on them when applicable.

Some statutes require the successful bidder on a public project to provide performance and payment bonds.[10] Others set forth specific

---

10 *See, e.g.*, ALA. CODE §§ 39-1-1 and 39-2-8 (1994); ARIZ. REV. STAT. ANN. § 34-222 (1994); CAL. CIV. CODE § 3247 (West 1994); CAL. PUB. CONT. CODE § 10821 (West 1994); COLO. REV. STAT. § 24-105-202 (1994); GA. CODE ANN. § 36-10-4 (1994); IDAHO CODE § 54-1926 (1994); IND. CODE § 36-1-12-14 (1994); KAN. STAT. ANN. § 60-1111 (1993); LA. REV. STAT. ANN. § 38:2216 (West 1994); MICH. COMP. LAWS ANN. § 129.201 (1994); MISS. CODE ANN. § 31-5-51 (1994); NEV. REV. STAT. § 339.025 (1993); N.M. STAT. ANN. § 13-4-18 (1994); 8 PA. CONS. STAT. § 193 (1994); TEX. GOV'T. CODE ANN. § 2253.021 (West 1994);

requirements as to the timing and venue of suits on the bonds.[11] Perhaps the best known of these statutes is the Miller Act, which provides, in part:

> § 270a. Bonds of contractors for public buildings or works; waiver of bonds covering contract performed in foreign country
>
> (a) Type of bonds required
>
> Before any contract for the construction, alteration, or repair of any public building or public work of the United States is awarded to any person, such person shall furnish to the United States the following bonds, which shall become binding upon the award of the contract to such person, who is hereinafter designated as 'contractor':
>
> (1) A performance bond with a surety or sureties satisfactory to the officer awarding such contract, and in such amount as he shall deem adequate, for the protection of the United States.
>
> (2) A payment bond with a surety or sureties satisfactory to such officer for the protection of all persons supplying labor and material in the prosecution of the work provided for in said contract for the use of each such person. Whenever the total amount payable by the terms of the contract shall be not more than $1,000,000 the said payment bond shall be in a sum of one-half the total amount payable by the terms of the contract. Whenever the total amount payable by the terms of the contract shall be more than $1,000,000 and not more than $5,000,000, the said payment bond shall be in a sum of 40 per centum of the total amount payable by the terms of the contract. Whenever the total amount payable by the terms of the contract shall be more than $5,000,000 the said payment bond shall be in the sum of $2,500,000.
>
> (b) Waiver of bonds for contracts performed in foreign countries

---

VA. CODE ANN. § 11-58 (Mich. 1994).

11 *See*, *e.g.*, ARK. CODE ANN. § 22-9-403 (1994); IND. CODE ANN. § 36-1-12-14(g) (West 1994); KAN. STAT. ANN. § 60-1111(b) (1993); DEL. CODE ANN. tit. 29, § 6909(d) (1994); S.C. CODE ANN. § 57-5-1660 (b) (Law. Co-op. 1993).

The contracting officer in respect of any contract is authorized to waive the requirement of a performance bond and payment bond for so much of the work under such contract as is to be performed in a foreign country if he finds that it is impracticable for the contractor to furnish such bonds.

(c) Authority to require additional bonds

Nothing in this section shall be construed to limit the authority of any contracting officer to require a performance bond or other security in addition to those, or in cases other than the cases specified in subsection (a) of this section.

(d) Coverage for taxes in performance bond

Every performance bond required under this section shall specifically provide coverage for taxes imposed by the United States which are collected, deducted, or withheld from wages paid by the contractor in carrying out the contract with respect to which such bond is furnished. However, the United States shall give the surety or sureties on such bond written notice, with respect to any such unpaid taxes attributable to any period, within ninety days after the date when such contractor files a return for such period, except that no such notice shall be given more than one hundred and eighty days from the date when a return for the period was required to be filed under Title 26. No suit on such bond for such taxes shall be commenced by the United States unless notice is given as provided in the preceding sentence, and no such suit shall be commenced after the expiration of one year after the day on which such notice is given.[12]

The statute further provides as to payment bond claimants:

§ 270b. Rights of persons furnishing labor or material

(a) Every person who has furnished labor or material in the prosecution of the work provided for in such contract, in respect of which a payment bond is furnished under sections 270a to 270d of this title and who has not been paid in full therefor before the expiration of a period of ninety days after the day on which the last of the labor was

12 40 U.S.C. § 270a (1995).

> done or performed by him or material was furnished or supplied by him for which such claim is made, shall have the right to sue on such payment bond for the amount, or the balance thereof, unpaid at the time of institution of such suit and to prosecute said action to final execution and judgment for the sum or sums justly due him: *Provided, however*, That any person having direct contractual relationship with a subcontractor but no contractual relationship express or implied with the contractor furnishing said payment bond shall have a right of action upon the said payment bond upon giving written notice to said contractor within ninety days from the date on which such person did or performed the last of the labor or furnished or supplied the last of the material for which such claim is made, stating with substantial accuracy the amount claimed and the name of the party to whom the material was furnished or supplied or for whom the labor was done or performed. Such notice shall be served by mailing the same by registered mail, postage prepaid, in an envelope addressed to the contractor at any place he maintains an office or conducts his business, or his residence, or in any manner in which the United States marshal of the district in which the public improvement is situated is authorized by law to serve summons.
>
> (b) Every suit instituted under this section shall be brought in the name of the United States for the use of the person suing, in the United States District Court for any district in which the contract was to be performed and executed and not elsewhere, irrespective of the amount in controversy in such suit, but no such suit shall be commenced after the expiration of one year after the day on which the last of the labor was performed or material was supplied by him. The United States shall not be liable for the payment of any costs or expenses of any such suit.[13]

This statute has been the basis for many of the state statutes, commonly referred to as "Little Miller Acts." This statute has also been referred to in numerous published opinions.

As exemplified by the above quoted provisions, many statutory provisions either impose obligations upon a surety or, in the alternative, provide defenses for and/or limitations of liability on the surety. For example, if a subcontractor or materials supplier has not instituted suit within one year of when it last provided materials or ceased work on a

---

13 40 U.S.C. § 270b (1995).

project, and the Miller Act or a comparable state statute applies, the surety may be relieved of liability to the payment bond claimant.[14]

The investigating surety should avoid actions that may lead a claimant to believe it will be paid and should constantly reserve its rights and defenses. Otherwise, the claimant may successfully argue that the surety is estopped from asserting some defenses, such as the failure of the claimant to adhere to the applicable statutory time limitation.

While the courts generally construe the statutes relative to bonds in connection with public projects broadly to protect those that the legislature intended to benefit, it is important to impress upon the courts the difference between surety bonds and insurance policies. In other words, while the legislation may be broadly construed, where a bond is consistent with the legislation, it is important to indicate that the bond language itself is to be construed strictly in accordance with the surety's undertaking as clearly set forth in the bond.

Many states have also enacted trust fund acts. This legislation requires that a contractor receiving public funds in connection with a public project utilize those funds to pay its subcontractors and/or materials suppliers. Some of the statutory provisions impose liability (for fraud) upon the officers of the corporation; this liability may not be dischargeable in bankruptcy.[15] These provisions, while not relevant to interpretation of the bond or the surety's obligations, can be effective in securing the cooperation of the principal and/or its officers. This is especially true given the fact that indemnification obligations are generally dischargeable in bankruptcy.

---

14 *See, e.g., Kiva Constr. and Eng'g, Inc. v. Int'l Fidelity Ins. Co.*, 749 F. Supp. 753 (W.D.La. 1990), *aff'd by* 961 F.2d 213 (5th Cir. 1992).

15 *In re Piercy*, 140 B.R. 108 (Bankr. D. Md. 1992); *In re Holmes*, 117 B.R. 848 (Bankr. D. Md. 1990). *See also In re Englund*, 20 B.R. 957 (Bankr. E.D. Mich. 1982) (holding that the Michigan Building Contract Fund Act creates a fiduciary relationship that comes within the section of the Bankruptcy Code excepting from discharge any debt of the individual debtor for fraud or defalcation while acting in a fiduciary capacity).

V.
General Agreement of Indemnity

Another document that a surety should consider when its principal has been terminated for default is the general agreement of indemnity. Underwriters obtain a general agreement of indemnity when they initially establish a relationship or bonding line with the principal. The underwriters will thoroughly analyze the principal's finances before establishing such a relationship. Often, the underwriters also analyze the financial position of the shareholders of a privately held corporation and require these shareholders and their spouses to sign a general agreement of indemnity as indemnitors.

The indemnification relationship is probably most indicative of the conceptual differences between surety bonds and insurance policies. Surety bonds are intended to serve as credit instruments, somewhat similar to letters of credit. As with letters of credit posted by a bank on behalf of a client, a surety, conceptually, should not incur a loss since, in the event the surety makes payment, its principal is to indemnify the surety. Indemnity "arises from contract, either express or implied, and is the right of a person who has been compelled to pay what another should have paid to require complete reimbursement."[16] A general agreement of indemnity includes rights of the surety under common law, such as the right to indemnification and/or exoneration from its principal, and also includes rights that extend beyond those at common law. Courts have upheld indemnity agreements that authorize the surety to charge the principal for payments the surety made in good faith and under the belief that it was liable for the sums disbursed, regardless of whether liability existed.[17]

An important way a general agreement of indemnity expands the rights of the surety beyond the common law is by giving the surety the right to pursue the individual indemnitors. When the corporate principal is insolvent or bankrupt, the surety's right of indemnification against the individual and his/her spouse can be extremely important for cooperation as well as reimbursement for losses and expenses. The importance of a

---

16 *Four Seasons Envtl., Inc. v. Westfield Cos.*, 638 N.E. 2d 91, 92 (Ohio Ct. App. 1994).

17 *International Fidelity Ins. Co. v. Spadafina*, 192 A.D.2d 637 (N.Y. App. Div. 1993).

spouse's execution of a general agreement of indemnity cannot be overemphasized since savvy contractors often place ownership of assets over the years with their spouses or, in the alternative, own assets jointly with their spouses. In many states, the surety can recover from the spouse in these situations only when the spouse dies (assuming the indemnitor outlives the spouse) or the asset is sold (at which time the surety may be able to obtain the net amount of the indemnitor's share).

The precise wording of general agreements of indemnity vary by company. However, certain provisions are common. Some of those provisions follow:

A. Indemnification

An example of an indemnification provision is as follows:

> Indemnitor(s) jointly and severally agree to indemnify Surety from and against any and all Loss and to this end Indemnitor(s) promise:
>
> (a) To promptly reimburse Surety for all Loss and it is agreed that (1) originals or photocopies of claim drafts or payment records kept in the ordinary course of business, including computer print-outs, verified by affidavit, shall be prima facie evidence of the fact and amount of such Loss; (2) Surety shall be entitled to reimbursement for any and all disbursements made by it in good faith, under the belief that it was liable, or that such disbursement was necessary or prudent.
>
> (b) To deposit with Surety on demand the amount of any reserve against Loss which Surety is required or deems it prudent to establish, whether on account of an actual liability or one which is, or may be asserted against it.

The courts generally uphold these provisions and enforce the surety's rights to indemnification pursuant thereto unless the surety made the underlying payment fraudulently or in bad faith.[18] Even when not

---

18 *See, e.g.*, *Fidelity & Deposit Co. v. Bristol Steel & Iron Works, Inc.*, 722 F.2d 1160 (4th Cir. 1983); *Commercial Ins. Co. v. Pacific-Peru Constr. Corp.*, 558 F.2d 948 (9th Cir. 1977); *Transamerica Ins. Co. v. Bloomfield*, 401 F.2d 357 (6th Cir. 1968); *Engbrock v. Federal Ins. Co.*, 370 F.2d 784 (5th Cir. 1967).

imperative to do so, most sureties place the principal and indemnitors on notice of claims for two reasons. First, if the principal/indemnitors are aware of any reason why the surety should not make the payment or should pay less than the amount claimed, they may provide that information to the surety and enable the surety to reduce its loss. Secondly, if the principal and/or indemnitors are provided with the information and they do not respond, then they may be deemed to have waived any opportunity to object to the payment made by the surety. Generally, where a surety makes payment in spite of the objection of the principal/indemnitors, it is based upon the surety's investigation and conclusion that the amount to be paid is appropriate. In fact, it has been held by some courts that even where payment of a claim rests, according to the indemnification agreement, within "the sole discretion of the surety, [it is anticipated] that the surety will settle only after reasonable investigation of the claims, counterclaims, and possible defenses."[19]

B. Security

An example of a security provision is as follows:

> As security for the performance of this Agreement Indemnitor(s) grant to Surety a security interest in (1) all Equipment and Material and (2) all sums due or to become due to Indemnitor(s) or any of them in connection with any Contract. The security interests are effective in the case of each Contract as of the date of the Contract. Indemnitor(s) authorize Surety at its discretion and at any time to file or serve this instrument or a true copy hereof as a Financing Statement or other notice under the Uniform Commercial Code or any similar law, and Indemnitor(s) authorize Surety to complete this instrument in any manner required for such use, and to prepare and attach schedules describing items of security covered hereunder. Indemnitor(s) hereby appoint Surety as Attorney-in-Fact for each of them to endorse and to deposit or negotiate checks, drafts, warrants and all similar instruments payable to Indemnitor(s), such Power of Attorney to be invoked and exercised by Surety as stated herein.

---

19 *See, e.g., United States ex rel. Trustees of Elec. Workers Local Pension Fund v. D Bar D Enterprises, Inc., et al.*, 772 F. Supp. 1167, 1170 (D. Nev. 1991).

While this provision grants the surety a security interest in equipment, materials and contract funds, most sureties do not record the general agreement of indemnity until after a problem has arisen. However, recording the general agreement of indemnity shortly after executing it is helpful in the event that claims are asserted against the surety since the date of recording often establishes priority amongst creditors under the law. However, from an underwriter's perspective, recording early may present problems for the principal when obtaining financing from banks or other financial institutions.

Often the general agreement of indemnity is not, in and of itself, in recordable form. In that regard, it may be preferable to have the indemnitors execute a UCC-1 that refers to all equipment and materials as well as contract sums and that incorporates the general agreement of indemnity by reference.

In addition to the rights granted by this provision, the surety possesses important equitable subrogation rights. An analysis of those rights is beyond the scope of this chapter. Given the scope of the security interest provided above, this provision can be very important to the surety when its principal has been terminated for default.

C. Other Provisions

Other provisions may provide for the surety to undertake and enforce its full panoply of rights in the event of a termination for default or some other event. An example of these provisions follows:

> Indemnitor(s) agree that any of the following shall constitute an Act of Default hereunder:
>
> (a) Failure to perform the work of any Contract in timely and proper fashion, or to make payment when due of bills in connection therewith.
>
> (b) A declaration of default by any Contract Owner.
>
> (c) The sustaining of Loss by Surety under any Bond.
>
> (d) The establishment by Surety in good faith of reserve(s) against Loss.
>
> Indemnitor(s) agree that in the event of an Act of Default:

(a) Surety may enforce the security interests granted hereby and may take any action necessary to obtain possession of the funds and property subject thereto, including the use of its Power of Attorney, and in this connection all persons and organizations from whom funds subject to this Agreement are or may become payable are directed to pay such funds to Surety on its demand.

(b) Surety is authorized at its option to take over or arrange completion of any Contract by any means it deems appropriate and may under the assignment herein and/or as trust beneficiary exercise all right, title and interest of Indemnitor(s) in Equipment and Material and Sub-Contract(s).

(c) All funds realized by Surety under this Agreement may at its option be applied in reimbursement of Loss or used for the performance of any Contract. Any surplus remaining in Surety's hands after the reimbursement of all Loss, completion of all Contracts, and the exoneration of all Bonds shall be paid to Indemnitor(s) as their interests may appear.

As indicated, the general agreement of indemnity expressly permits the surety to undertake certain options. While sureties must be careful to avoid prejudicing the rights of their principals, they also must be aggressive in protecting their own rights and minimizing their losses. While many sureties enter into other agreements depending upon the option they elect after the principal has been terminated for default, provisions such as these enable the surety to undertake aggressive enforcement of its rights.

Other provisions that may be incorporated into the general agreement of indemnity include:

1. providing for the indemnitors to pay all premiums and charges of the surety with respect to bonds which it issues on behalf of the principal;
2. the rights of the surety pursuant to the agreement are in addition to the surety's legal and equitable rights at law;
3. definitional provisions, such as defining the word Loss above to include counsel fees and consultant fees;
4. surety need not notify the indemnitors of and it may proceed to engage in the release of security, collateral and/or release indemnitor;

5. surety need not provide notice and may refuse to provide any bond even where it has already furnished the bid bond and need not provide notice as to any changes in any bond or contract;
6. the liability of the indemnitors is joint and several;
7. standard provisions such as the law pursuant to which the agreement shall be construed, venue of any disputes by and between the surety and the indemnitors and that all other provisions shall remain in effect if one provision is declared illegal by any court.

Another issue that may arise, especially when one shareholder in a closed corporation has sold his/her interest to another shareholder, is termination of an indemnitor's involvement as indemnitor. Generally, the agreements provide that the indemnitor shall be liable with respect to all bonds issued prior to the termination of his/her involvement as an indemnitor but that the indemnitor shall not be liable for any losses attributable to any bonds issued after the indemnitor provides notice to the surety that he/she no longer wishes to be an indemnitor. However, by terminating his/her involvement, an indemnitor may impact the creditworthiness of the principal, which is based on the indemnification granted the surety.

Succinctly stated, the general agreement of indemnity provides the surety with important rights where there has been a termination for default or a voluntary default by the principal. The surety should carefully study the general agreement of indemnity when the surety has been advised of any claims and/or termination of a principal.

VI.
Conclusion

This Chapter is intended to be a relatively brief review of significant bond, contractual and statutory provisions, as well as provisions set forth in the general agreement of indemnity, which the surety should review and consider when determining its course of action. Hopefully, this book will help sureties to weather the storm.

CHAPTER 2, SECTION A

THE SURETY'S INVESTIGATION

William S. Piper

I. Introduction

Although facts giving rise to a contract default and bond claim are unique and can be complex, they often follow a similar pattern. The decisions made by a surety are primarily fact driven which underscores the need to properly investigate any bond claim. The focus of this chapter is not on the right decision in a given circumstance. Instead, this chapter addresses the need to gain information and how one generally goes about gathering it. Specifically, this chapter will focus on the objectives of the investigation, the responsibility to investigate, the information required to make appropriate decisions, the significance of such information, and the source from which such information is obtainable.

A. The Investigation as a Foundation for Decision Making

Decision making generally flows from the facts and careful weighing of the risks involved when the facts are not entirely known. If decisions are difficult to make, it is generally because not all of the relevant facts have been learned. The difficulty in decision making for a surety following a contract default often stems from the need to make immediate decisions to avoid compounding delays on a project and increasing the surety's exposure, without the time to fully investigate or obtain cooperation of the parties. As a general rule, promptness, thoroughness, and communication are important guidelines for any surety investigation, as the speed with which the surety reacts and the extent to which it understands the situation, will, in the end, greatly assist the surety in controlling and mitigating its loss.

B. Objectives of the Investigation

The primary objective of any surety claim investigation is to gather sufficient relevant facts to make appropriate assessments and decisions regarding the surety's exposure, obligation and liability. Initially, it may be difficult to distinguish a real bond claim involving a material default from a typical construction dispute which the parties can resolve on their own. During the course of construction, the goal of an underwriter or producing agent is to monitor the progress of work performed by the principal and to promptly identify a potential bond claim that may then trigger additional responsibilities on the part of the surety to respond and/or investigate. Accordingly, the surety may wish to periodically monitor the status and progress of construction by making status inquiries of the obligee. Such inquiries may serve an added purpose by giving the obligee an obligation to put the surety on notice that a problem exists. A failure to do so may afford the surety a defense based upon a lack of prompt notice should a claim later arise and the obligee delayed notifying the surety.

As the claim situation develops and is presented, the surety must focus on how and when it should respond to the claim. Further, the surety must assess the financial exposure for the claim so that appropriate initial reserves are promptly established to cover a loss should liability later be determined and the surety becomes obligated to fulfill its obligation.

The surety does not provide its contract guarantee with the expectation that it will incur a loss on any given bond. Accordingly, and notwithstanding the assessment of any financial exposure, it is an appropriate objective for the investigation to find out why the claim situation arose and what defenses are available to discharge the surety in whole or in part. Finally, the goal of any investigation is to explore and determine how the loss or exposure can be controlled or mitigated through the recovery of indemnity or other salvage.

II.

A. Identifying the Claim and the Initial Response

Any typical construction project has its problems, including technical, financial and personnel conflicts. Plans change, hidden conditions are encountered, and the weather prevents work. There are good project managers and poor ones. Some contractors make profits and others underestimate. Back charges are incurred and change orders granted during any significant project. Work cannot be completed unless there is cash flow to pay the bills as they accrue. Not every problem that arises on a project, however, requires the involvement and investigation of a surety.

Identifying when a default is a bond claim is important as it triggers the surety's obligations under the bond to investigate and possibly to perform. As the recent case of *L & A Contracting Co. v. Southern Concrete Services, Inc.*[1] suggests, not every breach is a material default that triggers the surety's liability and obligations under a bond. A typical performance bond generally predicates the surety's liability to respond upon a clause which states:

> "...whenever principal shall be declared by obligee to be in default under the subcontract, the obligee having performed obligee's obligations thereunder..."[2]

Such a clause recognizes that a surety is secondarily liable to the obligee and cannot be expected to intervene and act until the principal, who is primarily liable, is no longer permitted to perform. As the court stated:

> "a declaration of default sufficient to invoke the surety's obligations under the bond must be made in clear, direct, and unequivocal language. The declaration must inform the surety that the principal has committed a material breach or series of material breaches of the subcontract, that the obligee regards the subcontract as terminated, and that the surety must immediately commence performing under the bond."[3]

---

1 17 F.3d 106 (5th Cir. 1994).

2 *See also*, American Institute of Architects Document No. A312, December 1984 edition.

3 17 F.3d at 111.

By comparison, the California Insurance Department went so far as to define "notice of claim" as part of its Unfair Claims Settlement Practices Regulation.[4] Under the regulations, the obligation to investigate is triggered by a "notice of claim" which is defined as

> (2) for purposes of surety claims, any written notification by a claimant to an insurer or its agent that reasonably apprises the insurer the claimant wishes to make a claim under the bond and;
> (A) the principal has defaulted in the bonded obligation; or,
> (B) a condition giving rise to the insurer's obligation under the bond has arisen.[5]

Once a default and termination of the contract is declared, a surety may want to examine the procedure set forth in the contract to assess whether the principal was properly terminated. A failure to properly terminate, particularly on a government project, may give both the principal and the surety a basis to appeal the termination and deny coverage for the claim asserted.

More problematic for the surety are those situations where the principal has been declared in default, but not terminated, or where the bond form does not expressly require a declaration of default for triggering the liability of the surety. A surety will find that the term "default" is often used loosely and with the intent to cover every minor or technical breach of the specifications. While the holding of *L & A Contracting* appears to invoke common sense by requiring there to be a notice of default, some courts have found that absent express requirements in the bond, there is no absolute duty to give notice of default.[6] Regardless of the bond terms, the risk of being accused of interfering in the principal's contractual relationship will often lead the surety to insist the obligee terminate the contract (i.e. terminate the principal's rights to

---

4 CAL. CODE OF REGS., tit. 10, §§ 2695.1-.17 (1993). The regulations specifically include surety claim investigations.

5 CAL. CODE OF REGS., tit. 10, § 2695.2(o)(2) (1993).

6 *See*, *Winston Corp. v. Continental Casualty*, 361 F. Supp. 1023 (S.D. Ohio 1973), *rev'd on other grounds*, 508 F.2d 1298 (6th Cir.) *cert. denied*, 423 U.S. 914 (1975); *Peachtree Roxboro Corp. v. United States Casualty Co.*, 114 S.E.2d 49 (Ga. Ct. App. 1960).

proceed) so that the surety can freely respond to the claim.[7] In those situations where disputes exist and the contractor continues or wants to perform, the surety must also consider carefully the extent to which it will intervene or finance the operations of the principal.[8]

During a default stage prior to termination, a surety's representatives can pursue several goals. One goal is encouraging the principal to properly complete as much of its work as possible before a termination occurs, as the more work that is properly completed, the less exposure the surety will theoretically have at the time a demand is made upon the bond.

Some bond forms may require the obligee to demand and require the surety to attend a pre-default meeting presumably intended to address the concerns of the obligee and give the surety time to commence an investigation or arrange a cure of the principal's default. The role of the surety at this stage can be that of a mediator in an effort to resolve disputes and encourage continued progress on the project.

Prior to a declaration of default and/or a direct demand upon the surety to perform under its bond, communications from the obligee noting disputes or performance problems involving the surety's principal should always be acknowledged by the surety and referred to the principal for response. See Exhibit 2.1. In doing so, it would be prudent for the surety to ask for its principal's position regarding such a claim and insist that the principal respond in writing directly to the obligee with a copy to the surety. See Exhibit 2.2.

By insisting that a principal respond and document its position, a surety takes an important step toward preserving evidence that it may

---

7 The California Regulations would appear to support this position as a "notice of claim" must not only apprise the surety of a wish to make a claim, but also that the principal has defaulted or a condition giving rise to the insurer's obligation has arisen. CAL. CODE OF REGS., tit. 10, § 2695.2(o)(2) (1993).

8 Courts have recognized the potential risk of liability claims from a principal or defense to indemnity claims faced by a surety if it interferes with the principal's contract, pays a claim too quickly or prejudices any defenses the principal may have against the obligee. *Dodge v. Fidelity & Deposit Co.*, 778 P.2d 1240 (1989); *Board of Directors of the Ass'n. of Apartment Owners of the Discovery Bay Condominium v. United Pacific Ins. Co.*, 884 P.2d 1134 (Haw. 1994); B.C. Hart, *Bad Faith Litigation Against Sureties*, 24 TORT & INS. L. J. 18, 19 (1988).

eventually need to evaluate a bond claim. Undoubtedly, the principal often will offer conflicting information, color its story differently, lie, or even ignore the surety and the problem. During this phase, as well as after default and a demand upon the surety, how the principal responds and the extent to which the principal can prove its position may tell the surety claims investigator a lot about the veracity of the principal, the merits of any claim or defense and the principal's ability to continue managing a project. Even if the principal appears right, lack of substantiation may affect a surety's ultimate evaluations and decisions if it appears the principal is not in a position to prove the point should the matter lead to litigation.

At the same time the surety is directing the principal to respond to a complaint and is evaluating the veracity of the principal and the merits of its position, the surety is also cognizant that the allegations of the obligee may be suspect. All too often the surety is notified of disputes by the obligee as leverage to extract concessions or as inducement to the principal to perform, knowing that the involvement of the surety may interfere with the principal's ability to secure bonds from the surety for other jobs. Following an initial investigation, it would be appropriate for a surety to observe that the principal's position has merit and encourage the parties to resolve the dispute between themselves or through some form of mediation or arbitration.

As many typical construction complaints are first received by a local producing agent or underwriter for the surety, such persons should be aware of their limits in addressing problems and not overstep such limits by direct intervention, committing the surety to action or positions or admitting liability without a thorough investigation. Any notice of claim should be immediately transmitted to the surety. During the initial stages of a claim, the surety's claim representative may experience a common situation where small disputes and claims are only the tip of a problem and that a much bigger problem looms on the horizon, requiring prompt and thorough investigation by the surety.

Generally, the relationships between the principal and obligee can be strained, which places additional pressure upon the surety to act as the problems are not addressed and resolved. Sometimes interim solutions or decisions can be offered to keep a project progressing while the surety continues its investigation of the default. In doing so, the surety may invite the good will and further cooperation of the obligee in resolving the ultimate dispute. The surety should be careful to reserve rights and defenses while taking such interim action.

B. The Duty to Conduct an Independent Investigation

Once a direct demand or claim is made upon the surety, certain duties arise.[9] The surety has an obvious and justifiable responsibility to protect itself from loss. Over-riding the relationship between the surety and the obligee, however, is what is commonly referred to as the "implied covenant of good faith and fair dealing" which a surety satisfies by acting reasonably in response to a claim by its obligee.[10] Hence, it is commonly recognized that once a claim arises, surety has a duty to independently investigate the claim.[11]

The duty to investigate does not stand alone as there are duties and responsibilities imposed upon the principal and obligee as well which give rise to a tripartite relationship among all the parties. The covenant of good faith and fair dealing imposes the obligation to cooperate on both the principal and obligee which is essential if the surety is to conduct an independent investigation.

As one court stated, the surety's duty to investigate the facts does not mean a surety has a duty to "create the claim," i.e., substantiate mere allegations.[12] Clearly any claimant has a responsibility to document its claim (i.e. submit a proof of claim) before a duty to corroborate the accuracy of a properly documented claim arises.[13] After receiving a mere notice of a claim, it would be advisable for a surety to both acknowledge

---

9 This chapter is not intended to cover contract or tort liability for damages to any party by reason of breach of any duty of good faith or violation of any statutory or regulatory obligations. Whether any cause of action exists must be examined on a state by state basis.

10 *Loyal Order of Moose, Lodge 1392 v. Int'l Fidelity Ins. Co.*, 797 P.2d 622 (Alaska 1990).

11 *Dodge v. Fidelity & Deposit Co.*, 778 P.2d 1240 (Ariz. 1989).

12 *Farmer's Union Cent. Exch., Inc. v. Reliance Ins. Co.*, 675 F. Supp. 1534 (D. N.D. 1987).

13 *Id.* at 1542.

it and request further documentation to substantiate the claim.[14] By doing so, the surety properly shifts the burden of substantiating the claim back to the claimant or obligee. Until the claim is documented, further corroboration is not required although it may be desirable from the surety's standpoint.[15] See Exhibit 2.3.

While proceeding with its investigation, a surety must consider its duties toward its principal. Clearly, an independent investigation not only requires a surety to corroborate the accuracy of a properly documented claim, but also to consider the legal and factual positions of its principal and the effect the surety's actions and decisions will have upon the principal's legal rights against the obligee. As one court put it, the duty of good faith owed to the obligee does not require the surety to act in bad faith toward its principal.[16]

An effort should be made to bring the principal into the investigation. Liability under a General Agreement of Indemnity may be the only inducement a principal or indemnitor may have to cooperate. At the onset of a default or claim, the surety needs to notify the principal that a claim

---

14 By comparison, California Insurance Regulations require a surety to provide necessary claim forms, instructions, and reasonable assistance within 21 days upon receiving a notice of claim except in cases where the first notice of claim the insurer receives is a notice of legal action. CAL. CODE OF REGS., tit. 10, § 2695.5(h) (1993). Section 2695.5(a) also requires an acknowledgment of a notice of claim immediately and in no event later than 15 days. *Id.* at § 2695.5(a).

15 Again, by comparison, Section 2695.10(b) of the California Regulations which govern "Standards for Prompt, Fair and Equitable Settlements Applicable to Surety Insurance", provides following receipt of a notice of claim *and* a proof of claim, the surety has sixty days in which to "accept or deny the claim, in whole or in part, *and* affirm or deny liability." *Id.* § 2695.10(b). Presumably, if a notice of claim is received and a proof of claim requested but is not submitted properly for the surety to decide whether the claim falls within the scope of the bond, the sixty days to act on the claim does not commence. After a proof of claim is submitted, if the surety cannot decide within sixty days whether to "accept or deny the claim," the surety must keep the claimant apprised of the need for additional time to decide, the reasons for it, what additional information may be needed and how long it might take to consider the claim. Thereafter, the claimant must be kept apprised every thirty days.

16 *Dodge v. Fidelity & Deposit Co.*, 778 P.2d 1240 (Ariz. 1989).

has been made for which the surety is required to investigate. The principal needs to be reminded of its indemnity obligations including its obligation to indemnify not only against loss, but also the expense of investigation. Finally, the principal should be encouraged to cooperate with the surety in the surety's investigation since it is only through such cooperation that liability for any loss or expenses can be kept to a minimum. See Exhibit 2.4.

Quite often, too, the surety is faced with a principal who is uncooperative for any number of reasons, not the least of which pertains to a desire by the principal to resolve its own problems and not incur two sets of attorney's fees in responding to a claim. This last reason is particularly difficult for the surety when it is collateralized and the principal demands that the defense be tendered to it. If the defense appears to have merit, the surety may feel inclined to permit such a tender and avoid a dispute over whether the cost of any investigation and/or defense of the claim is recoverable. While the principal may not be affected by the obligee's threat of "bad faith," the surety should be cautious and may have to educate its principal that the surety has a duty to "independently" investigate which requires a reasonable level of inquiry and evaluation by the surety, all of which cannot be simply tendered. Accordingly, the principal cannot expect that the surety's obligation of good faith requires the surety to act in bad faith towards its obligee by tendering a defense with no questions asked. Whatever the meritorious defense, effort should be made to document the defense in the claim file as protection against a charge that the surety did not investigate.

A surety's right of indemnity can be protected if it investigates a claim in good faith and attempts to resolve the claim (or mitigate its loss) without prejudicing the rights the principal may have to seek recourse from the obligee or claimant.[17] The principal also has corresponding obligations under the agreement of indemnity (such as a duty to collateralize or exonerate the surety from liability) which, if breached, may give the surety greater latitude in establishing its good faith for compromising claims and mitigating the loss exposure.

While balancing the duties owed to the obligee and principal, the surety should keep in mind that the duty to investigate does not obligate

---

17 *Fidelity & Deposit Co. v. Bristol Steel & Iron Works, Inc.*, 722 F.2d 1160 (4th Cir. 1983).

the surety to resolve legitimately disputed issues of fact.[18] Some have suggested that if the evidence produced by either side creates a fact issue with regard to the validity of the claim so as to preclude the entry of a directed verdict or summary judgment, there cannot be bad faith.[19] The surety's investigation need merely show a reasonable basis for the failure to pay the claim.

Whether the foregoing concepts of good faith and fair dealing are consistent with statutory and regulatory provisions in each state needs to be examined and considered by the surety.[20] Having a general understanding of the objectives of a surety investigation as well as the general obligations to conduct such an investigation, the surety representative is then prepared to go forward and investigate the facts.

III.

A. Sources of Information

The surety will gather the facts and relevant information from many sources and will often find the information to be incomplete, inaccurate and/or inconsistent. Generally, the surety will look to the following sources of information:

1. Underwriting, including the producing agent;
2. The bond and contract documents;
3. The principal and its records;
4. The obligee and its records;
5. Subcontractors and suppliers;
6. Current credit or asset reports on the principal and bankruptcy schedules;

---

18 *Farmer's Union Cent. Exch. Inc. v. Reliance Ins. Co.*, 675 F. Supp. 1534 (D. N.D. 1987).

19 *Id.* at 1539.

20 The California regulations specifically require that the regulations be set forth and incorporated into any claims manual. Other states take different approaches and do not necessarily treat "contract guarantees" as traditional insurance. Such states may impose time limits to act upon claims after which interest, and possible penalties or attorney fees, may be imposed for delay.

7. The opinions of any architect, consultants, and experts.

B. The Review of Underwriting, Bond and Contract

The underwriting file, the underwriter and any producing agent will generally provide the investigator with background information on the principal including a general understanding of the character and competence of the contractor, its job history, its financial condition (at least at the time the bond was written), the circumstances under which the bond was written, and a list of other bonded projects. In addition, important documents such as the General Agreement of Indemnity, copies of any bonds, contracts, and status reports can be obtained.

A thorough review of the bond and contract documents is critical. These documents will define the scope of work and undertaking of each of the parties at the time the bond was issued. Of particular importance is the penal sum of the bond, a description of what contract is covered by the bond, what event may trigger the surety's liability, what options are available to the surety in responding to a claim, and other types of damages such as delay damages, for which the surety may be liable.

The surety will review the bond to determine the named parties and those that may assert claims against the bond. Rights may be afforded to other parties through dual obligee riders or the surety may be faced with claims by parties that do not have a "right of action" as expressed under the terms of the bond.

Where the principal has multiple contracts or phased work, it is essential for the surety to determine which contract and scope of work is covered by the bond. Typically, the penal sum of the bond is equal to the amount of the contract, but not always. At the time of an initial bond application, the parties may represent to the underwriter a certain scope of work that is later expanded through subsequent change orders. The surety investigator needs to compare the original scope of work to the scope of work now claimed to exist at the time of default as it may suggest possible defenses involving a material change in the contract that is prejudicial to the rights of surety.

Occasionally, bonds are issued after work has commenced. Generally, the underwriter has investigated the status and possibly relied upon a letter from the obligee indicating no problems with the work or in payment of bills. Should a claim later develop, the surety will want to examine the history of the claim in relation to original underwriting information since it may reveal a failure to disclose information material to the underwriting decision and afford the surety a defense based upon fraud in the inducement of the bond.

The bond form may not clearly set forth all of the obligations of the surety, particularly where there is a clause incorporating the contract by reference. The contract should be reviewed for provisions that attempt to impose additional obligations upon the surety, such as insurance requirements and indemnity obligations. The contract documents will, in all likelihood, contain provisions relating to important issues involving liquidated damages, warranty obligations, design responsibilities, payment application and the approval process.

The bond form may indicate what triggers a claim and what obligations are then placed upon the surety to respond as well as when and how to respond. There may also be clauses waiving notice and/or affecting the rights and defenses of the surety pertaining to changes, payments, or the administration of the contract. Each of these will have to be evaluated and considered as to their legal effect and validity based upon the facts and the law in each jurisdiction.

C. Reviewing the Principal's Records

Assuming the principal maintained job records, the surety will want to examine these to shed light on several issues. Documents to be obtained include:

1. Complete contract documents that govern the construction, including a full copy of the contract, change orders, pending change orders, general and special conditions, specifications and drawings;
2. Copies of all progress estimates and/or pay applications;
3. A list of all subcontract and purchase orders for suppliers and, if appropriate, copies of the subcontracts and purchase orders;
4. Accounts payable and accounts receivable ledgers;
5. Other information pertaining to tax obligations, union obligations, insurance obligations and bank debt;
6. The original bid estimate file; and
7. Job correspondence.

Efforts should be made to obtain the contractor's own original estimate for the work as well as any estimate to complete the work.

D. Reviewing the Obligee's Records

With respect to the obligee's records, efforts should be made to obtain and review the following:

1. Contract documents, including the plans and specifications;
2. Change orders and back charges, whether they relate to the principal or other contractors on the project;
3. Job minutes, progress reports, and punchlists;
4. Pay applications and certifications for payment and canceled checks;
5. Job schedules (both original and revised) and any notice to proceed;
6. Notices of nonpayment from subcontractors and suppliers of the principal;
7. A list of all original bidders with the amounts of their bids; and
8. Correspondence with the principal.

E. General Investigation and Assessments

As the obligee may not wait for the surety to respond, the surety should also consider visiting the job site and photographing the site to depict the general state of completion and any items claimed to be deficient at the time of notice of default. Material stored on the premises can be noted and taken into account when considering a cost to complete.

The potential for environmental liability should be noted either from an inspection of the work site or examination of the scope of work such as asbestos abatement, demolition work or lead paint abatement. Such environmental exposure under CERCLA[21] or state laws may significantly

---

21 Comprehensive Environmental Response, Compensation, and Liability Act, 42 U.S.C. § 9601 *et. seq.* (1994).

affect whether the surety will takeover, tender or even finance the principal.[22]

In reviewing the status of construction, the architect may be helpful in identifying the remaining scope of work, the quality of the work in place as well as preliminary estimates of the cost to complete. If financing of the principal is contemplated, opinions may be generated from the architect regarding the technical ability and qualifications of the principal's work force. Further, inquiry should determine the percentage of completion of the work and lead to a contract accounting of the funds. More likely than not, the surety will receive differing or conflicting opinions from the obligee, principal, and consultant.

In general, a surety will seek the following information pertaining to the status of contract funds:

1. Original contract price;
2. Net change orders (plus or minus);
3. Adjusted contract price;
4. The amount paid contractor to date;
5. Contract balance;
6. Earned but unpaid progress payments;
7. Retainage; and
8. Unearned contract balance.

Disputes over contract balances may require the examination of canceled checks. Consideration should also be given to all change orders and back charges, including those that are pending as well as those previously rejected or now claimed by the principal but not yet documented and submitted.

Approved pay applications in the hands of the obligee can assist the surety in evaluating the percentage of completion. However, a site visit by a consultant may be necessary to confirm that the obligee or its architect has properly evaluated and approved the work in place and made

---

22 *See also*, William S. Piper, *Environmental Risk Management on Construction Projects: A Surety's Perspective, Environmental Construction: Market or Minefield?* (unpublished paper submitted at the A.B.A. Forum on the Construction Industry/Tort and Insurance Practice Section Fidelity & Surety Law Committee joint meeting in New York, N.Y. on January 27, 1994).

payments accordingly. Significant discrepancies may suggest to the surety the possibility of overpayment defenses to any default claim or, alternatively, a possible breach of contract for non-payment by the obligee.

If the job has been substantially completed, evidence of substantial completion should be obtained and the date noted as it may affect the ability of an obligee or payment bond claimant to assert claims. Such dates may also trigger warranty periods. If the principal has left the job uncompleted, the last date the principal was on the job should be noted as, under some bond forms, this date triggers a time limitation period in which to commence a suit.

Finally, the surety must be aware of any schedules or delay impacts upon other contractors or subcontractors as a result of the principal's default. The scheduled date of completion should be noted with a preliminary assessment of exposure for liquidated damages. At the same time, consideration should be given to obtaining evidence of waiver of liquidated damages or any other basis for time extensions.

As will be noted in a subsequent section of this chapter, the use of a consultant can be extremely beneficial in evaluating a performance bond claim and deciding how to respond. The consultant may inspect the job site and prepare an estimate of the cost to complete. See Exhibit 2.5. In doing so, the consultant may be required to develop a scope of remaining work and seek concurrence, where possible, from the obligee. The solicitation of bids to complete can be done by the surety alone or in conjunction with the obligee and perhaps should be done in such a way as to allow the surety to choose various options in resolving the performance bond claim, such as tendering a contractor or taking over and completing.

IV.
Protecting Salvage

The contract balance, whether earned or unearned, should be available to the surety to cover the cost of satisfying its obligations under the performance bond as the surety is ordinarily subrogated to the rights of the obligee. However, the surety must recognize that, in all likelihood there will be other creditors such as the Internal Revenue Service, a secured lender or a bankruptcy trustee, all of whom may claim an interest or right in the contract balances. The surety must prepare to defend its equitable interest in the funds.

Although not necessarily required under the Uniform Commercial Code,[23] many sureties consider filing the General Agreement of Indemnity as a financing statement in order to further secure its interest in contract balances. Generally, such a filing is required to secure the surety's interest in other contract funds and assets of the principal besides the bonded receivable.[24] As part of its initial acknowledgement of the default to the obligee, the surety needs to put the obligee on notice that the contract funds are first applied to completion costs and should not be released to the principal or any other creditor. A release of contract funds after default prejudices the surety's equitable interest in said funds.

As part of an initial investigation, many sureties will conduct credit or asset searches of the principal and indemnitors to identify assets available for indemnity, the financial condition of the principal, other creditors that may interfere with completion of the work, or the surety's interest in the funds, etc. Depending upon the circumstances, sureties may also wish to consider filing actions for exoneration, specific performance of the General Agreement of Indemnity, or an equitable action for *quia timet* before a claim is resolved.

V.
Conclusion

Depending upon the complexity of the facts surrounding the default, the surety investigation can be dynamic and multi-faceted. As one gains experience in the field of surety claims, a keen sense of where to look, what to ask and what to consider is developed. The success of the investigation will ultimately depend upon skill and a proper assessment of the risks involved with the decisions to be made in each case.

---

23 U.C.C. § 9-104(6).

24 *Transamerica Ins. Co. v. Barnett Bank*, 540 So.2d 113 (Fla. 1989).

CHAPTER 2, SECTION B

THE SURETY'S USE OF CONSULTANTS IN CONNECTION WITH CONTRACT BOND DEFAULTS

Kenneth M. Givens, Jr.[1]

I. Introduction

The important auxiliaries of the surety in its unceasing contract bond default campaigns are the legions of outside consultants that, for a price, come to the aid of the surety and its in-house troops. For purposes of this section, a consultant is anyone who guides, advises or assists the surety in the handling of a contract bond default, including, without limitation, attorneys, accountants, architects, engineers, and construction managers.

The high cost of the employment of consultants is notorious among surety company underwriting executives. The surety industry does not maintain figures on the aggregate cost of the use of consultants in contract surety cases, but, based on an extrapolation from data compiled by the Surety Association of America, a surety industry organization, the sureties

1 The author gratefully acknowledges the assistance of his colleague at the Fidelity and Deposit Company of Maryland, W. Dean Highcove, for his help in the preparation of this Section. The author also wishes to thank Thomas J. Burke, P.E., an associate of Forcon International Corporation, Tampa, FL, for his insights and comments on the types and functions of consultants.

may have paid consultants as much as $100,000,000, or possibly more than that, in 1993 in connection with contract bond claims.[2] Needless to say, surety claim executives and their staffs are under constant, severe pressure to control and contain, if not reduce, the cost of outside consultants. The fact of the matter is, however, that surety companies have a need for consultants, a need that is dictated by the complexities of the typical bond default, let alone the mega-loss defaults that have occurred since the early 1980's. A surety simply does not have the in-house human resources to deal with the issues presented by many bond defaults. Ideally, the surety needs consultants to assist it in meeting its obligations fairly and in a manner that protects the surety's assets.

The original edition of the *Bond Default Manual* did not contain a section on the use of consultants. There has not been much writing on the subject.[3] The inclusion of this Section in this revision of the *Bond Default*

---

2 The Surety Association of America reported that net premiums for all lines of surety business, including contract, judicial and miscellaneous, written in 1993 totaled $1,925,713,243. Allocated loss expense, which consists for the most part of the amounts paid to consultants, totaled 6.7%, or $129,022,787, of net premiums. Contract surety represents about 70% of all surety business. Since loss expense on contract surety claims generally exceeds loss expense on non-contract surety claims, the author assumes that more than 70% of the aggregate loss expense on surety lines is related to contract surety—hence the estimate of $100,000,000.

3 The surety program of the 1992 mid-winter meeting of the A.B.A. Tort and Insurance Practice Section's Fidelity & Surety Law Committee was titled "Reducing Costs and Improving Results in Surety Cases." Papers presented in this program that are recommended reading on the subject of the surety's use of consultants are: Thomas J. Acchione, *Selecting and Managing Outside Counsel* (unpublished paper submitted at the A.B.A. Tort and Insurance Practice Section Fidelity & Surety Law Committee mid-winter meeting in New York, N.Y. on January 24, 1992); Michael T. Sugar, Jr., *Selecting and Managing Outside Consultants* (unpublished paper submitted at the A.B.A. Tort and Insurance Practice Section Fidelity & Surety Law Committee mid-winter meeting in New York, N.Y. on January 24, 1992); H. Bruce Shreves, *Reducing Costs and Improving Results in Surety Cases* (unpublished paper submitted at the A.B.A. Tort and Insurance Practice Section Fidelity & Surety Law Committee mid-winter meeting in New York, N.Y. on January 24, 1992); P.K. Wright, *Developing a Case Budget* (unpublished paper submitted at the A.B.A. Tort

Manual is a recognition of the importance of the role and impact of consultants in the handling of contract bond defaults, not only financially but also functionally.

The purpose of this Section is to discuss a number of important issues that confront the surety that seeks to employ the services of a consultant relative to a bond default. What types of consultants are available to the surety? When does a surety need a consultant? How does a surety find the consultants it needs? How does a surety select a consultant? How does a surety interact with its consultant to achieve the best and most cost-effective results?

II.
Types Of Consultants—Who They Are And What They Do

As the issues that might arise from a default on a bonded construction project are potentially myriad, so, at least in theory, are myriad the types of consultants that may be available to help the surety deal with those issues. The types of consultants the surety will encounter in connection with a bond default may be grouped in the following five general categories:

1. legal consultants;
2. accounting consultants;
3. construction consultants;
4. technical consultants; and
5. other consultants.

The ensuing sections elaborate on these categories of consultants.

---

and Insurance Practice Section Fidelity & Surety Law Committee mid-winter meeting in New York, N.Y. on January 24, 1992). The papers presented at the surety program of the A.B.A. Tort and Insurance Practice Section's Fidelity & Surety Law Committee 1988 mid-winter meeting titled "Practical Considerations in the Selection of and Use of Construction Consultants" are also helpful. Finally, many articles have appeared in trade and professional journals on the general topic of managing the expense of outside counsel; *see, e.g.*, Martin Teicher, *Perspectives on the Relationship between Corporate and Outside Litigation Counsel*, 36 FOR THE DEFENSE, Dec. 1994 at 2.

A. Legal Consultants

These are lawyers—men and women trained in the law and licensed to practice law in one or more jurisdictions in the United States. To be of general use to a surety relative to a bond default, a lawyer must have sound knowledge of and experience in suretyship and construction law. The lawyer should also have substantial trial experience. Lawyers provide guidance, advice and services to the surety in the following areas:

1. the identification and evaluation of defenses which may be available to the surety under the contract, the bond or applicable law;
2. the interpretation of the legal effect of documents;
3. legal guidance on areas that require factual, technical or financial investigation;
4. the drafting of documents related to the bond default, such as financial assistance agreements, takeover agreements and completion agreements;
5. the handling of litigation that arises from the bond default, such as claims against the performance and payment bonds and recovery actions against the principal and indemnitors; and
6. participation in meetings and negotiations related to the bond default.

Lawyers also provide counsel and advice to a surety in any number of specialized areas of the law that may apply to a particular bond default. Several specialties that pertain to many defaults are bankruptcy, secured transactions and environmental law.

By virtue of the fact that legal issues are often central to a bond default, it is obvious that a lawyer—the legal consultant—is capable of being deeply involved in almost all aspects of the default, from beginning to end. Sureties without well-staffed claim departments may be compelled to include outside counsel in the process of handling the default to a pervasive extent. Many sureties, however, have claim departments that are staffed by experienced claims attorneys. These surety companies are inclined to use outside counsel on a more limited basis, especially in view of the current corporate emphasis on controlling and containing expenses.

B. Accounting Consultants

The surety's accounting consultant is generally a certified public accountant (CPA) who specializes in construction accounting. Other accounting consultants include non-CPA's who, nevertheless, have had extensive experience in the accounting aspect of the construction business.

Accounting consultants collect and assemble the data the surety requires to obtain a reasonably accurate picture of a principal's financial condition. This data is needed, along with information supplied by other consultants, so that the surety can determine its exposure to loss from the bond default and so that the surety can assess which option it should choose to respond to the default. Primarily, accounting consultants assist a surety in the following ways:

1. ascertaining the financial status of the principal's contracts;
2. determining the amounts of current payables on the principal's projects, as well as for general and administrative expenses;
3. determining the amounts of earned retainages on the principal's projects;
4. discovering the status of the principal's liability for federal, state and local payroll, sales and income taxes;
5. ascertaining whether the principal is current in the payment of insurance premiums for liability, property and workers' compensation insurance; and
6. determining the status of any outstanding loans owed by the principal to banks or other lenders.

C. Construction Consultants

The construction consultant is an engineer or a construction manager who specializes in project and construction management. In many bond default cases, management issues are of central importance, and it is the construction consultant who aids the surety in handling these issues. The construction consultant enables the surety to perform its investigation of the bond default and to decide upon the course of action it will take. Some of the information the construction consultant furnishes at this preliminary stage of the bond default process includes:

1. the percentage of completion of the principal's work;
2. the quality of the work;
3. the projected completion date;

4. estimates of the cost to complete the work, either with the principal's forces or by using a replacement contractor; and
5. the identification and analysis of claims of the principal, obligee or subcontractors.

The construction consultant needs to have the ability to bring all of this diverse information together and fashion it into a coherent whole that is understandable by the surety.

If the surety decides to procure bids for the completion of the bonded work, the construction contractor will assist in putting together the bid package and the evaluation of the bids. If the surety takes over the completion of the work, the construction consultant will monitor the completion of the work by the surety's contractor, approving requisitions for payment from the completion contractor and acting as liaison between the surety and the obligee's project representative, who is typically an engineer or architect.

It should be clear from the foregoing that, when we say that the construction consultant must specialize in project and construction management, the emphasis is on people who have actually been in charge of those activities. The skills that are required to be a competent construction consultant are many. There are no licenses applicable to a construction consultant. The skills of the construction consultant are not included *per se* in the practice of engineering. Therefore, a professional engineer's license is not mandatory.

The construction consultant must have a broad range of skills. These skills are usually not found in individuals who do not have substantial, long-term experience as project managers or construction managers on large projects. The following listing of the essential skills required of a construction consultant will demonstrate the breadth of the range of which we are speaking:

- contract administration;
- scheduling;
- estimating;
- procurement;
- site office administration;
- home office administration;
- drawing and specification interpretation;
- contract accounting;
- labor relations; and
- dispute resolution.

In summary, the surety's construction consultant needs to be a construction management generalist who has had substantial practical experience.

D. Technical Consultants

Distinguished from the generalist construction consultant is the technical consultant. The technical consultant advises the surety on specialized issues of engineering or science that may arise in connection with a bond default. For example, there may have been a structural failure on a project. The surety may need to retain a structural engineer with a professional engineer's license to address the adequacy of the design. If the sufficiency of the materials used in the construction are in question in the failure, the surety may need to employ a materials specialist, such as a metallurgist. A surety would employ an architect as a technical consultant to review the competency with which the plans and specifications for a project were prepared.

Technical consultants are the experts that the surety needs from time to time to deal with a particular construction problem. Occasionally, technical consultants are needed to testify as experts in legal proceedings. Sometimes they are retained expressly for that purpose. It is generally not necessary that a technical consultant possess a college degree or a license in order to qualify as an expert, but the surety should consult with its trial counsel before choosing a technical consultant for the purpose of providing expert testimony.

E. Other Consultants

This is the catchall category that is necessary because of the infinite number of issues and problems that challenge the surety on a bond default and for which the surety may need guidance and assistance. Consultants who appraise assets and prepare property for sale, such as auctioneers, fit in this category. Another example is the former surety company claims representative whose experience may be helpful to the surety with a staffing shortage.

III.
Determining The Need To Hire A Consultant

A. Generally

Circumstances vary widely from default to default, and it is difficult to describe how a surety determines that it needs a consultant. As a general proposition, a surety needs a consultant whenever the surety cannot conduct the investigation or some other aspect of the bond default process that is critical to the surety's fulfillment of its obligations with its own personnel, because of a lack of skill, knowledge, expertise, or staffing problems. In this regard, it must be remembered that a surety not only has the obligation to obligees and claimants to handle claims fairly and promptly, but also has the responsibility to its shareholders and reinsurers to handle claims as cost-effectively and as cost-efficiently as possible. A surety must consider these duties in determining whether it needs the services of a consultant. Used properly, the consultant helps the surety discharge both of these duties.

B. Cost Considerations in Determining Need

In large surety bond default cases, cases involving many projects and millions of dollars of potential loss, the question of expense does not come into play in deciding whether a consultant is needed. In other cases, where the exposure to loss is small relative to the cost of a consultant, the issue may be difficult to resolve. However, cost should not determine whether the surety has the capability to investigate the claim. If the surety does not want to incur the cost of a consultant, then the surety must either perform as demanded or not perform and risk exposure from claims for having performed an improper investigation.

C. Timeliness in Making the Decision

It is fundamental that a surety must recognize its need to retain a consultant as soon as possible in the development in the bond default. This is a corollary of the surety's duty to its obligees and claimants to handle claims promptly and fairly and its duty to its shareholders and reinsurers to mitigate loss. The surety that procrastinates in the retention of a consultant usually pays a severe price for its delay. Time is money in the construction industry.

IV.
Finding A Consultant

The surety industry has at its disposal a large pool of consultants available to assist it in connection with a bond default. When a surety decides that it needs a consultant, where does it look to find those who are best suited for the task?

A. The Surety's Own Files

This may be the best and most frequently used source for finding a consultant. Surety's tend to engage those consultants with whom they have had success. Some sureties complete evaluations of consultants at the conclusion of an assignment and place these evaluations in files that are maintained on each consultant that is used.

B. Other Consultants

Sureties frequently solicit recommendations for consultants from other consultants. Outside counsel is also a good and reliable source of information on all types of consultants. Consultants who are truly concerned with the best interests of their surety clients will also make recommendations to the surety concerning their competitors, when, because of conflicts of interest, the nature of the default, the geographical location, or the unavailability of personnel, the consultant is unable to accept an assignment.

C. Other Sureties

It is not uncommon for one surety to contact another to obtain information on consultants. This source of information is usually tapped when the surety is confronted with a problem in a geographical location strange to it ("Do you know any lawyers in Guam?").

D. Publications

Numerous publications exist which list the names of consultants in various fields. These include compilations of consultants by state, such as the *Martindale-Hubbell Law Directory*,[4] *Hine's Insurance Counsel*[5] and *Best's Directory of Recommended Insurance Attorneys*.[6] All of these publications, which are updated annually, indicate whether a firm's practice includes certain specialties, such as surety and construction law and bankruptcy. There are also periodical publications, such as professional and trade journals, in which advertisements, especially those of construction and technical consultants, appear.

E. Marketing

Hardly a day or week passes that a surety claims representative does not receive marketing materials in the mail from consultants. These materials often consist of resumes, project histories, sample reports, billing rates and client lists. A surety would be well served to save this information, storing it for future reference in files, organized by type of consultant and geographic region. Many consultants follow up on their mailings with telephone calls to the claims representative, requesting the opportunity to meet to discuss business opportunities. Surety claims representatives are notoriously busy, but it is not a waste of the claims representative's time to set aside a few minutes to see and hear what a new consultant may have to offer. Such a meeting affords the surety the chance to explain its expectations of consultants and, perhaps more importantly, to assess, at least at first blush, whether the consultant is the kind of individual with whom the surety can establish a good working relationship.

---

4 MARTINDALE-HUBBELL LAW DICTIONARY (Martindale-Hubbell, 1992 ed.).

5 HINE'S INSURANCE COUNSEL (James R. Collins et al. eds., 86th ed. 1994).

6 BEST'S DIRECTORY OF RECOMMENDED INSURANCE ATTORNEYS (A.M. Best Co., 1995 ed.).

V.
Selecting A Consultant

The surety's selection of a consultant may be the most crucial decision the surety makes with respect to a bond default. The factors in the decision process can be many, but perhaps the considerations can be reduced to a basic few.

A. Cost

The surety may think that cost is *the* most important factor in selecting a consultant. This is natural because of the pressures surety claim departments are under to control expenses. However, cost is not of preeminent importance in the selection process. Consultants usually bill by the hour, although some now offer some form of alternative billing, such as flat fee or blended fee arrangements. A fee rate which appears to be too high may cause a surety to eliminate a consultant from consideration. This knee jerk reaction is generally not in the surety's best interest. The true measure of a consultant is not the hourly cost of the services. The true measure is the value that the surety receives for the services that are performed. Did the benefits derived from the cost exceed the cost itself by acceptable margin? This determination need not wait until the conclusion of the assignment. Continuous monitoring of the results of the consultant's services in conjunction with a review of the consultant's billings should inform the surety during the progress of the case as to whether it is getting its moneys' worth.

B. Competence and Qualifications

This involves making sure that you have the right person for the job and is perhaps the key to the successful employment of a consultant. Consequently, the surety should place the highest priority on this aspect. The surety must match the competency and qualifications of the consultant with the assignment.

It is sometimes most difficult to match the right construction consultant with the job. There is a great proliferation of construction consultants in today's market, and the constituents of this expanding group come from diverse construction industry backgrounds. There are basically three types of construction: residential, commercial and industrial. Commercial construction includes heavy construction. Most surety bond defaults occur in commercial construction, involving the building of schools, prisons, office buildings, hotels, heavy construction projects such as roads and bridges, and other infrastructure projects. While consultants seem to address similar issues in all types of construction, there are enough unique characteristics in the types of building construction mentioned above that the surety will want the consultant it chooses to have some familiarity with the type of construction involved in the default.

In order to ensure itself that it is selecting a consultant fit for the task, the surety needs to receive resumes of the individuals proposed for the assignment. The resumes must be replete with details of practical experience, as well as with educational and other professional credentials. If possible, the surety should interview the consultant in order to explore the resume, discuss the consultant's approach to the issue of the default and inform the consultant of the surety's expectations.

C. The Subjective Element

This is something that can be discerned only through actual personal experience. A consultant may have an impressive resume, showing just the right kind of expertise for the work related to the default. The more important question is whether the consultant possesses the other attributes that are critical for success: common sense, good judgment, trustworthiness, creativity, and persuasiveness. As Martin Teicher, Assistant General Counsel and Chief Litigation Counsel for Ciba-Geigy Corporation, wrote in an article that appeared in a recent edition of *For The Defense*, "The real world isn't a multiple choice test, and corporate clients don't want important matters handled by rote."[7]

D. The Organizational Element

The surety needs to know that the consultant has the organizational resources to handle the assignment. The consultant should have the facilities and personnel commensurate with the size of the task. There is nothing more frustrating or, in some cases, dangerous than the consultant who is too busy with other matters so that the surety's telephone calls are

---

7 Teicher, *supra*, note 3 at 4.

regularly unanswered or who does not have the technology to produce timely and comprehensible reports.

A factor that sureties do not often consider when selecting construction consultants is whether the consultant has property and liability insurance to protect the surety adequately. Construction projects are hazardous places. Construction consultants are the representatives of the surety on construction projects and may subject the surety to great exposure through their actions. The surety should request from the construction consultant an insurance certificate that names the surety as additional named insured. Sureties assume that lawyers and accountants have professional liability insurance but give little thought as to whether other consultants have it or need it. A surety may consider it appropriate to inquire as to whether consultants other than lawyers and accountants have professional liability insurance, particularly consultants who will provide expert testimony in legal proceedings.

E. Compatibility Among Consultants

Sureties will often employ more than one type of consultant on a case. Because of the great diversity of issues present in a bond default, legal, financial, management, and technical, it is not unusual to find lawyers, accountants, construction managers, and engineers, working with the surety as a team. The surety has to be cognizant of the ability of these disparate units of the team to work cooperatively. Some consultants do not work together well for one reason or another—egotism, arrogance, etc.—and the surety must be sensitive to these conflicts of personality in making its selections of consultants. Alas, knowledge of incompatibility between consultants is chiefly acquired only by making the wrong choice.

VI.
The Surety's Interaction With Consultants

The surety looks to the consultant for guidance, advice and assistance on those aspects of the bond default that the surety is not able to handle itself. Although the surety depends on the expertise of the consultant, the surety cannot simply hire the consultant and then retire to the office and await the results. The successful, cost-beneficial use of a consultant demands that the surety interact constantly with the consultant. The surety, through its claims representative, must be an active participant throughout the course of the resolution of the bond default. The more the surety's claim representative is involved in the default, the better he or she will understand the issues. This involvement includes personal visits to job sites and attendance at important meetings with obligees and claimants.

Interaction does not mean that the surety is the dictator of everything that is done in the case. Remember, the surety uses the consultant for guidance. Interaction implies real cause and effect upon each other, a reciprocity of action and influence on the conduct of the case. The consultant must know what the surety wants; the surety has to know what the consultant can do to help the surety achieve its goals. What follows are some devices a surety can use to develop a program to cultivate and bring to fruition optimum interaction with its consultants.

A. Establish Engagement Policies for Consultants

This involves the surety's thinking about what it generally expects from its consultants. What is the surety's concept of the ideal relationship with a consultant? The surety should set out this concept in writing, along with any terms and conditions of the relationship that the surety believes will apply to any assignment that the surety may make to the consultant. In the Appendix is a form of written engagement policy for outside counsel. See Exhibit 2.6. This kind of policy can be used for other types of consultants. The policy's preamble states that the relationship is a partnership. The policy continues to cover general terms and conditions of the relationship, such as the furnishing of budgets and plans of action, the kinds of expenses for which the surety will reimburse outside counsel and the frequency and format of billings. Other issues that might be covered in a policy for outside counsel are the prior review of pleadings, discovery procedures, the retention of experts, and the furnishing of periodic status reports. The surety should review the engagement policy with the consultant face to face as soon as a consulting relationship is contemplated or as soon as the policy is promulgated. If the consultant has any problems with the policy, it is incumbent upon both surety and consultant to resolve the problems. The surety and the consultant need to have an open and frank relationship, and the written engagement policy serves as the foundation of such a relationship.

B. The Scope of Services Letter

As soon as practicable after the surety has selected a consultant for an assignment, the surety has to sit down with the consultant and determine what it is that the consultant is going to do for surety. The obligee has declared a default and demanded performance of the remaining work by the surety. There are dozens of subcontractors and suppliers screaming for payment; several have already filed lawsuits. The principal argues that it can finish and ultimately hold the surety harmless, if only the surety will provide some interim financial assistance. At this point the surety and consultant, or consultants, must decide upon a course of action as to how the surety is to meet its objective, which is, of course, the satisfaction of its obligations at minimum loss and expense. The details of this course should be worked out jointly and, after all alternatives have been explored, set down in writing. This document, called the scope of services letter, delineates the duties of the consultant and expectations of the consultant with respect to the specific assignment. It should be clear that the consultant is to perform only those services that are set out in the letter, but that the consultant should advise the surety if the consultant believes that additional services should be undertaken (or, for that matter, services eliminated) in order to fulfill the surety's objectives. Regular discussion should occur between the surety and the consultant and the surety regarding the scope of services. The scope of services should be a working document. Any changes to the scope of services letter should be reduced to writing.

C. Budgets

The surety should require that the consultant furnish budgets as soon as possible after the surety and the consultant have established a course of action. Budgets help the surety decide whether the course of action will be cost effective. Once the surety receives the budget, the surety may decide that the benefits to be derived from the pursuit of it are not worth it. In that event, the surety should go back to the drawing board with the consultant. The players will have to make adjustments in the game plan. The budget forms are task-oriented. Therefore, the surety will be able to follow the course of the budgets as it receives and evaluates the consultant's periodic billings. The surety, and the consultant for that matter, can track the adequacy of the budget of the case as it progresses.

The consultant will need to explain any deviations. Has the character of the case changed? Does the plan need revision? Is the surety getting value for its money? A form of budget designed for use with construction consultants appears in the Appendix. See Exhibit 2.7.

All of these devices result in constant communication between the surety and the consultant. Without such communication it is the rare bond default that does not assume a monstrous life of its own that seems to consume the surety's assets without any intelligible basis.

VII.
Conclusion

Sureties have needed and continue to need consultants to assist them in making decisions about their obligations, asserting defenses and performing their obligations in a manner that will mitigate any loss. In recent years, the surety industry has focused on the high cost of using consultants. The cost is acceptable, indeed it is beneficial, if the surety uses the services of consultants wisely. The focus of the surety industry must not be on the cost but rather on what can be gained by the use of consultants. This can be accomplished by knowledge of the types of consultants, how to use the various types of consultants, how to select the right consultant, and how to interact productively with the consultant.

CHAPTER 3

THE SURETY'S ANALYSIS OF INVESTIGATIVE RESULTS: "TO PERFORM OR NOT TO PERFORM—THAT IS THE QUESTION"

Philip L. Bruner
Patrick J. O'Connor, Jr.
James J. Hartnett, IV

I. Introduction

The most difficult decision, bar none, for the performance bond surety is whether to admit or deny liability under its performance bond after receipt of a demand from the obligee. No other decision in the field of suretyship is made under the intense "battlefield" pressures generated collectively by the complexities of the construction process, the limited time available for investigation, the frequency of competing contentions between obligees and principals, the high stakes of a wrong decision, and the real risk of "second-guessing" in future litigation.[1]

---

1 A good perspective on the environment in which the surety's decision is made was articulated by the District of Columbia Court of Appeals in *Blake Constr. Co. v. C.J. Coakley Co., Inc.*, 431 A.2d 569 (D.C. 1981), as follows:

> [E]xcept in the middle of a battlefield, nowhere must men coordinate the movement of other men and all materials in the midst of such chaos and with such limited certainty of present

The horns of the surety's dilemma stand in sharp relief. The wrong decision to *admit* liability can lead to unnecessary expenditures, to rupture of long-standing profitable bonding relationships with the contractor and its indemnitors, and to invariable claims seeking relief from indemnity obligations and recovery of tortious extra-contractual damages. The wrong decision to *deny* liability, although saving the immediate expenditure of money, ultimately can cost more money due to the surety's lack of control over the completion process, and can lead to the rupture of business relationships with the obligees and to the assertion of contract claims for breach of the bond and tort claims seeking extra-contractual damages. Two immutable absolutes in the surety's tripartite relationship with its obligee and principal are: (1) rarely can a wrong decision be reversed, and (2) any decision frequently is second-guessed in courts years after the decision is made. To aid the surety in reaching the correct decision is the purpose of this chapter.[2]

> facts and future occurrences as in a huge construction project such as the building of this $100 million hospital. Even the most painstaking planning frequently turns out to be mere conjecture and accommodation to changes must necessarily be of the rough, quick, and *ad hoc* sort, analogous to ever-changing commands on the battlefield. Further, it is a difficult task for a court to be able to examine testimony and evidence in the quiet of a courtroom several years later concerning such confusion and then extract from them a determination of precisely when the disorder and constant readjustment, which is to be expected by any subcontractor on a job site, become so extreme, so debilitating and so unreasonable as to constitute a breach of contract between a contractor and a subcontractor. This was the formidable undertaking faced by the trial judge in the instant case....

2 Any surety who repeatedly decides incorrectly ultimately will confront Hamlet's immortal challenge: "To be or not to be that is the question." Many fine articles have been written about aspects of the surety's decision. *See, e.g.*, J. William Ernstrom, et al., *Pivotal Legal Precedent Affecting Underwriting and Claim Handling by a Surety: II. Investigation of Claims* (unpublished paper submitted at the A.B.A. Tort and Insurance Practice Section Fidelity & Surety Law Committee mid-winter meeting in New York, N.Y. on January 27, 1995); M. Michael Egan, *Discharge of the Performance Bond Surety*, *in* THE LAW OF SURETYSHIP 12-1 (Edward G. Gallagher ed., 1993); Marilyn Klinger & James P. Diwik, *The Contract*

It is important that surety representatives recognize that the surety is not alone in having to make critical decisions. The most critical decision, bar none, for the performance bond obligee is whether to terminate for default the contractor's performance under the bonded contract. The wrong decision to terminate results in the obligee's completion of the contract without recourse against the contractor or surety for its excess costs of completion, and with liability to the contractor for recovery of its lost profits for breach of contract and even of tort claims for extra-contractual damages. The wrong decision not to terminate may result in

---

Performance Bond, *in* THE LAW OF SURETYSHIP 7-1 (Edward G. Gallagher ed., 1993); James A. Knox, *Representing the Private Owner*, *in* CONSTRUCTION DEFAULTS: RIGHTS, DUTIES, AND LIABILITIES § 9.3, at 201 (Robert F. Cushman and Charles A. Meeker eds., 1989); Kevin L. Lybeck, *Scope of the Performance Bond Surety's Obligation*, *in* THE LAW OF SURETYSHIP 10-1 (Edward G. Gallagher ed., 1993); Steven B. Kaplan, *Performance Bond Claims: The Surety's Defenses—An Update* (unpublished paper submitted at the A.B.A. Tort and Insurance Practice Section Fidelity & Surety Law Committee mid-winter meeting in New York, N.Y. on January 25, 1991); B. Davenport, Jr., *To What Extent May the Surety of a Defaulting But Solvent Principal Accede to the Principal's Request that It Be Permitted to Remedy the Default and Complete the Project?* (unpublished paper submitted at the A.B.A. Tort and Insurance Practice Section Fidelity & Surety Law Committee annual meeting in New York, N.Y. on August 12, 1986); J. Hinchey, *Surety's Performance Over Protest of Principal: Considerations and Risks* (unpublished paper submitted at the A.B.A. Tort and Insurance Practice Section Fidelity & Surety Law Committee annual meeting in New York, N.Y. on August 12, 1986); H. Meyer, *The Nonperforming Surety* (unpublished paper submitted at the A.B.A. Tort and Insurance Practice Section Fidelity & Surety Law Committee annual meeting in New York, N.Y. on August 12, 1986); J. Smirz, *Takeover Agreement and Maintaining Existing Subcontractors and Suppliers for the Takeover Contract* (unpublished paper submitted at the A.B.A. Tort and Insurance Practice Section Fidelity & Surety Law Committee annual meeting in New York, N.Y. on August 12, 1986); Britt, *The Surety's Investigation*, 17 FORUM 1151 (1982); Schroeder, *Providing Financial Support to the Contractor*, 17 FORUM 1190 (1982); Thompson, *Completion Options Available to a Performance Bond Surety Other Than Financing Its Principal*, 17 FORUM 1215 (1982); Webster, *The Surety's Decision on What to Do*, 17 FORUM 1168 (1982).

unsatisfactory completion, as to time or quality or both, with recourse limited to the contractor and not the surety.[3] The obligee's wrong decisions, like those of the surety, rarely are reversible.

It is the obligee who must make the first move. The surety's liability under standard performance bonds is triggered only if (1) the contractor *is* in default under the bonded contract, (2) the contractor has been *declared* by the obligee to be in default under the bonded contract, and (3) the obligee has performed (*i.e.*, not materially breached) its obligations under the bonded contract. The obligee's analysis of whether or not to terminate the bonded contract, and the surety's analysis of whether or not to respond to the obligee's notice of default under the performance bond, is often made in the face of conflicting claims, potentially catastrophic financial consequences, and under intense time pressures. These three cardinal conditions to the triggering of the surety's liability demand careful analysis by both the obligee and surety amid the myriad of facts and contractual provisions pertinent to the rights and obligations of the parties under the bonded contract and under the performance bond. The analysis also must consider the "judicial gloss" provided by the precedential effect of court decisions upon the facts and relevant contractual provisions.

II.
Interpreting the Results of the Investigation: The Objective of Analysis

The surety's first objective is to review the results of its investigation to decide whether it owes the obligee an obligation to perform under its bond: Is the principal in default? Is the owner in default? Does the surety have any contract or bond defenses? In many cases this decision will not be difficult if the surety's principal acknowledges default or, while not

3 A surety has been afforded relief due to the obligee's failure to terminate the contractor earlier than it did. In *Ohio Casualty Ins. Co. v. U.S.*, 12 Cl. Ct. 590 (1987), the court found that had the government terminated the contractor within a reasonable time, there would have been sufficient contract funds available to the surety to perform the contract without loss. Due to the government's failure to timely terminate the contract, the surety was entitled to damages to cover its out-of-pocket losses. Moreover, as noted in section VI.A, substantial performance of the bonded contract may discharge the surety.

acknowledging default, is unable to offer any credible justification or excuse for its non-performance.

Even if the principal's default is not in question, however, the surety must still inquire into whether the obligee has performed its obligations under the bonded contract. Obviously, if the principal's default was caused by the obligee's material breach of the construction contract, the surety has a defense to performance.[4] In many cases, the principal will be of the opinion that the obligee breached the agreement, and will not acknowledge default, claiming instead that its non-performance was the result of the obligee's defalcations.[5] Because it is possible for the obligee as well as the principal to be in default, a review of the performance of both parties should precede the surety's determination of whether it owes an obligation under its bond.

Should the surety conclude that its principal is in default while the obligee has performed its contractual commitments, the surety still may not be obligated to perform due to one or more surety defenses. Some common surety defenses include the obligee's failure to provide adequate or timely notice pursuant to the applicable bond language or governing statute,[6] and failure to commence suit within the time prescribed in the bond or prevailing law.[7] If the surety's investigation reveals that no surety defenses exist then, in light of the conclusion that the principal is in default while the obligee has performed, the surety's inquiry shifts to the next stage; *i.e.*, deciding the manner in which to perform its bond obligations.

Achieving a familiarity with the principal's records and the contract documents is crucial to determining the threshold question of whether to perform and, if so, what to do. The investigation should yield such

---

4 *See, e.g., Chicago College of Osteopathic Medicine v. George A. Fuller Co.*, 719 F.2d 1335 (7th Cir. 1983) (owner's failure to disclose information and to make timely payment discharged surety).

5 It is not uncommon for principals and indemnitors to argue that the surety acted too hastily in accepting the obligee's declaration of default. *See Windowmaster Corporation v. Morse-Diesel, Inc.*, 722 F. Supp 1532 (N.D. Ill. 1988).

6 *See, e.g., Dockendorf v. Orner*, 293 N.W.2d 395 (Neb. 1980).

7 *See, e.g., State Board of DeSoto County v. Safeco Ins. Co.*, 434 So. 2d 38 (Fla. Dist. Ct. App. 1983); *Yeshiva University v. Fidelity & Deposit Co. of Maryland*, 500 N.Y.S.2d 24 (1986).

contract documents as the principal's contract, plans and specifications, change orders, progress payments, construction schedules, submittals, subcontracts and purchase orders. The surety should also have available to it the principal's records, such as receivables; outstanding payables to suppliers and subcontractors, including retainage due subcontractors; job cost ledgers; analyses of the cost to complete the unearned portion of the contract; and insurance policies. In addition, the surety should review the principal's original bid summary and work papers, in relation to the principal's job cost ledger and job records to verify important claim events having financial impact.

Upon an examination of the job site to determine quantities of work in place and whether the work is acceptable for its intended use, the surety may be in a position, upon review of the contract documents, to calculate the cost to complete the work. The surety may also have information available to it regarding the principal's other contracts, both bonded and unbonded. The surety should also have obtained sufficient financial information from its principal to determine the principal's overall financial condition. With this information, the surety can begin to analyze which particular performance option is most appropriate for the situation. Obviously, this analysis must take into account the language of the bond or governing statute as certain restrictions may be placed upon the surety with respect to which performance options it might be able to employ.

The surety's investigation frequently begins before a default has been declared. During the surety's routine practice of collecting information regarding its principals and the status of bonded jobs, concerns may develop over whether a principal will be able to successfully complete a particular bonded project. Financial information obtained by the surety may suggest that the principal is in a precarious financial condition. Nevertheless, the principal is not in default. Nor has the obligee declared the principal to be in default. In cases where a default has yet to occur but the surety is fearful that one might occur, one of the primary concerns often is the preservation of the bonded contract funds. In this pre-default stage, the surety's rights of subrogation have not yet matured and, therefore, the surety's remedy is in the nature of seeking injunctive relief based upon a reasonable fear that it will be called upon to perform due to an eventual default by its principal. This anticipatory or preventive relief is in the form of a *quia timet* action.[8] Like most court proceedings, *quia timet* actions can be cumbersome and time-consuming.

Rarely do the investigative results lead to "black and white" conclusions. The all too common scenario in which the principal and obligee blame each other for problems associated with the project usually presents the issue of which party is more right than the other. It is not uncommon for the obligee to complain that the principal is not making progress with the work, and the principal to respond that progress has been impeded by the owner's demand for work outside the scope of the contract or failure to pay for extra work caused by a differing site condition. The list of possible disagreements is limitless. It is these difficult situations that are the focus of this chapter.

III.
The Bond

Determining whether the surety has an obligation to perform requires a careful review of the language of the bond. The bond language will describe the conditions of the surety's obligation and may enumerate the surety's performance options. There are five basic types of performance bonds: standard private performance bonds, statutory performance bonds, indemnity bonds, manuscript bonds, and completion bonds, each of which may contain different conditions for performance and different performance options. The five types of bonds are briefly described below.

A. Standard Private Performance Bonds

Most private performance bonds are issued as standardized bond forms utilized by the construction industry. These bonds typically provide the surety with well-defined conditions of performance and a number of options in the event of the principal's default. Two of the most commonly

---

8 *See* Mann & Jennings, *Quia Timet: A Remedy for the Fearful Surety,* 29 FORUM 685 (1985); Mann, *Enforcing the Surety's Rights Prior to Actual Payment of Claims*, Defense Research Institute Special Publication, *The Pursuit of Subrogation and Indemnity Claims*, vol. 1991 no. 3; Downs, *Quia Timet as a Preventer of Anticipated Mischief,* 1956 A.B.A. SEC. INS., NEG. & COMP. L. PROC. 173; *Moreley Construction v. Maryland Casualty Co.*, 90 F.2d 976 (8th Cir. 1937).

used standardized bond forms are the American Institute of Architects' A311 bond, published in 1970, and A312 bond published in 1984.[9]

Under the A311 bond, the surety is obligated to perform "whenever [the principal] shall be, and declared by [the obligee] to be in default under the Contract, the [obligee] having performed [obligee's] obligations thereunder...."[10] Thus, the three necessary conditions for the surety's performance under the A311 bond are: (1) a default by the principal; (2) a declaration of default by the obligee; and (3) no breach of contract by the obligee. The surety must conclude that all three conditions are satisfied before performance is required. The A311 bond provides the surety with three options upon default of the principal: (1) to promptly remedy the default; (2) to take over and complete the contract; or (3) to arrange for another contractor to complete the contract, with the surety paying the obligee the difference between the cost of completion and the remaining contract funds.[11]

Under the A312 bond, the surety's obligation to perform does not arise until after (1) the obligee has notified the surety and its principal of its intent to declare a default; (2) the obligee has, in fact, declared the principal to be in default and has terminated the principal's rights under the contract; (3) the obligee has agreed to pay the contract balances to the surety; and (4) the obligee is not itself in default of its obligations under the contract. The A312 bond expressly states what is implicit in the A311 bond, namely, that the obligee has a recognized legal obligation to terminate the principal's contract before calling upon the surety.[12] Under the A312 bond, the surety has five options upon the principal's default: (1) to arrange for the principal, with consent of the obligee, to complete the contract; (2) to undertake to complete the contract itself; (3) to arrange for another contractor to complete contract; (4) to tender to the obligee

---

9 Other organizations such as the Engineer's Joint Contract Documents Committee also have created standardized performance bond forms. *See* EJCDC Doc. No. 1910-28A (1984).

10 *Id.*

11 *See* American Institute of Architects Document A311, February 1970 edition.

12 *L&A Contracting v. Southern Concrete Services*, 17 F.3d 106, 111 (5th Cir. 1994).

an amount of money sufficient to satisfy the surety's obligations; or (5) to deny liability to the obligee in whole or in part.[13]

B. Statutory Performance Bonds

Most public construction projects, including all federal construction projects in excess of $100,000,[14] require contractors to provide performance bonds and labor and material payment bonds. Because the bonding requirements for public projects are typically established by statute, the surety's liability under its performance bond will likewise be defined by statute.[15] This is true regardless of language in the bond which purports to limit the surety's liability or expand its performance options beyond what is permitted by the express terms of the statute.[16]

Standard Form 25 of the Federal Acquisition Regulations is the statutory performance bond required for all federal government contracts in excess of $100,000.[17] Unlike private bonds, the SF-25 bond does not give the surety any options in the event of the principal's default. To the contrary, the bond provides that the surety is bound "for payment of the penal sum" unless the principal "performs and fulfills all the undertakings, covenants, terms, conditions, and agreements in the contract during the original term of the contract and any extensions thereof that are granted by the Government ... and pays to the Government the full amount of the taxes imposed by the Government...."[18] Thus, the SF-25 bond does not impose any substantial conditions on the government to invoke the surety's

---

13 *See* American Institute of Architects Document A312, December 1984 edition.

14 Federal performance bond requirements are established by the Miller Act, 40 U.S.C. § 270a, *et seq.*

15 *See United States for the use of Hill v. American Surety Co.*, 200 U.S. 197 (1906); *Maricopa Turf, Inc. v. Sunmaster, Inc.*, 842 P.2d 1370 (Ariz. Ct. App. 1992).

16 *See id.*; *see also Florida Keys Community College v. Insurance Co. of North America*, 456 So. 2d 1250 (Fla. Dist. Ct. App. 1984); *Fenetz v. Stine*, 407 So. 2d 1381 (La. Ct. App. 1981); *City of Marshall v. American General Ins. Co.*, 623 S.W.2d 445 (Tex. Ct. App. 1981).

17 *See* 48 C.F.R. § 53.301-25.

18 *Id.*

obligation, other than declaring a valid default, and does not allow the surety to select its manner of performance.

Many states that require statutory bonds do not have their own standard bond forms. Nevertheless, the bonding statutes often set forth specific conditions for the surety's performance and specify the required penal sum. Bond language which conflicts with these statutory requirements is simply disregarded unless the language affords coverage greater than that required by statute.[19] Thus, to determine a surety's performance obligations under a statutory bond, both the bond language and the applicable statute need to be consulted.

C. Indemnity Bonds

As the name suggests, indemnity bonds require the surety to indemnify the obligee for any losses which the obligee may suffer as a result of the principal's failure to perform the underlying contract. One advantage of this type of bond is that it does not require the surety to complete the contract upon default of the principal. Instead, the obligee completes the project, and then the surety later indemnifies the obligee for the cost of completion. However, the surety should not wait until after the obligee completes the contract to evaluate the nature and scope of its indemnity obligation. This should be done immediately upon default of the principal and, if possible, before any completion work begins.

The bond language describing the conditions of the surety's performance under an indemnity bond can be quite broad. The following is a typical example:

> NOW, THEREFORE, the condition of this obligation is such that, if the Principal shall faithfully perform the work as specified in the contract on his part, and shall fully indemnify and save harmless the Obligee, from all costs and damage which the Obligee may suffer by reason of

---

19 *See, e.g., Waterworks, Gas & Sewer Bd. v. P.A. Buchanan Contracting Co.*, 318 So. 2d 267 (Ala. 1975); *Nelson Roofing Co. v. United Pacific Ins. Co.*, 245 N.W.2d 866 (Minn. 1976); *Paul Schoonover, Inc. v. Ram Constr., Inc.*, 630 P.2d 27 (Ariz. 1981); *South Carolina Pub. Serv. Comm'n v. Colonial Constr. Co.*, 266 S.E.2d 76 (S.C. 1980); *City of San Antonio v. Argonaut Ins. Co.*, 644 S.W.2d 90 (Tex. Ct. App. 1982); *Valliant v. Dept. of Trans.*, 437 So. 2d 845 (La. 1983).

> failure to so do and shall fully reimburse and repay the Obligee all outlay and expense which the Obligee may incur in making good any such default, and shall pay all persons who have contracts directly with the Principal for labor or materials, then this obligation shall be null and void, otherwise it shall remain in full force and effect.[20]

Indemnity bonds can create substantial risks for the surety, because the surety may have little or no control over the manner in which the obligee completes the contract and, hence, little or no control over the cost of completion. Furthermore, broad indemnity language sometimes found in these bonds will, in all likelihood, require the surety to indemnify the obligee for a variety of consequential damages, including lost profits.[21] One clear advantage of the indemnity bond is that the surety is not exposed to liability to third-party beneficiaries.[22] Thus, indemnity bond obligations should be considered carefully before the surety agrees to undertake them.

D. Manuscript Bonds

Although many performance bonds are standardized, sureties often will draft their own bond form or prepare specialized bonds to address specific concerns or deal with unusual situations. These manuscript bonds may contain special provisions relating to the surety's obligation to perform and/or manner of performance. A manuscript bond might be used in situations where multiple sureties are underwriting portions of the same risk or where the risks of performance are unusually high, such as projects

---

20 *Bossier Medical Properties v. Abbott & Williams Constr. Co.*, 557 So. 2d 1131, 1134 (La. Ct. App. 1990) (note that this bond language also includes labor and material payment bond obligations).

21 *See Bossier Medical Properties*, 557 So. 2d at 1135 (La. Ct. App. 1990) (holding that surety was obligated to compensate obligee for lost rents caused by construction delays where bond contained broad indemnity language); *Capua v. W.E. O'Neil Constr. Co.*, 367 N.E.2d 669, 670-71 (Ill. 1977); *People v. Westchester Colprovia Corp.*, 147 N.Y.S.2d 185, 187 (N.Y. App. Div. 1955).

22 *Bourrett v. Bride Constr. Co.*, 84 N.W.2d 4 (Iowa 1959); *compare Camelot Excavating v. St. Paul Fire & Marine*, 301 N.W.2d 275 (Mich. 1981).

which involve the cleanup and disposal of toxic waste or nuclear material. Obviously, it is important to examine the language of such specialized bonds to determine the surety's obligations.

E. Completion Bonds

Completion bonds are a rare type of performance bond which give the surety only one option upon default of the principal: To take over and complete the contract work. Completion bonds often name a lending institution as the obligee and a builder-developer as the principal.[23] Under a completion bond, the surety guarantees that the principal can complete the work by the specified date.[24]

Completion bonds are rarely entered into by sureties, because they create substantial open-ended risks, and because there is no obligation on the part of the obligee and lender to advance funds for completion. A surety may also be held liable for substantial consequential damages under a completion bond.[25] As a result, completion bonds are anathema to the modern commercial surety.

In summary, a surety's performance obligations will depend, to a great extent, upon an analysis of the language of the bond and any applicable statutes in the context of the underlying facts. But, regardless of the bond form, the fundamental question that each surety must address before deciding whether and how to perform is: Has the principal defaulted on its contractual obligations? Defining what constitutes a valid default will be addressed in the next section.

IV.
What Constitutes a Default?

A "default" that triggers a surety's obligation to perform under its performance bond must rise to the level of a *material breach* of the

---

23 *See Prudence Co. v. Fidelity & Deposit Co.*, 297 U.S. 198, 204 (1935); Trainor Co. v. Aetna Casualty & Surety Co., 290 U.S. 47, 52 (1933).

24 *See Prudence*, 297 U.S. at 204; *Trainor*, 290 U.S. at 52.

25 *See Prudence*, 297 U.S. at 205-07.

bonded contract warranting termination by the owner.[26] Ordinary items of uncompleted or non-conforming work, endemic to every construction project and routinely completed or corrected later in the construction process or as "punchlist" or "warranty" work, rarely constitute *material* breaches.[27] The same is true for delays in completion where the contract did not designate "time is of the essence,"[28] or where the parties contracted for exclusive remedies for delay.[29] The existence of a material breach ordinarily is a question of fact for the jury to decide.[30] In determining whether any failure of performance is a material breach, the following circumstances are significant:

1. the extent to which the injured party will be deprived of the benefit which he reasonably expected;
2. the extent to which the injured party can be adequately compensated for the part of that benefit of which he will be deprived;
3. the extent to which the party failing to perform or to offer to perform will suffer forfeiture;
4. the likelihood that the party failing to perform or to offer to perform will cure his failure, taking account of all the circumstances including any reasonable assurances;

---

26 *See L&A Contracting v. Southern Concrete Services*, 17 F.3d 106, 110 (5th Cir. 1994):

> Although the terms "breach" and "default" are sometimes used interchangeably, their meanings are distinct in construction suretyship law. Not every breach of a construction contract constitutes a default sufficient to require the surety to step in and remedy it. To constitute a legal default, there must be a (1) material breach or series of breaches (2) of such magnitude that the obligee is justified in terminating the contract.

27 *Miree Painting Co. v. Woodward Constr. & Design, Inc.*, 627 So. 2d 389 (Ala. Civ. App. 1992), *rev. on other grounds*, 627 So. 2d 393 (Ala. 1993).

28 *Wilmett Partners v. Hamel*, 594 N.E.2d 1177 (Ill. App. Ct. 1992); *Wright v. Stevens*, 445 So.2d 791 (Miss. 1984); *String v. Steven Dev. Corp.*, 307 A.2d 713 (Md. 1973).

29 *Vermont Marble Co. v. Baltimore Contractors, Inc.*, 520 F. Supp. 922 (D.D.C. 1981); *Wright v. Stevens*, 443 So. 2d 791 (Miss. 1984); *String v. Steven Dev. Corp.*, 307 A.2d 713 (Md. 1973).

30 *Olin Corp. v. Central Industries, Inc.*, 576 F.2d 642 (5th Cir. 1978).

5. the extent to which the behavior of the party failing to perform or to offer to perform comports with standards of good faith and faith dealing.[31]

Typical examples of material breaches by construction contract obligees are analyzed under Section VI below.

Virtually all construction contracts contain a termination clause that defines the grounds and procedures for termination. Two standard termination clauses widely used in construction are contained in contract documents promulgated by the American Institute of Architects and the federal government:

14.2 TERMINATION BY THE OWNER FOR CAUSE[32]

14.2.1 The Owner may terminate the Contract if the Contractor:

.1 *persistently or repeatedly* refuses to supply enough properly skilled workers or proper materials;
.2 fails to make payment to Subcontractors for materials or labor in accordance with the respective agreements between the Contractor and the Subcontractors;
.3 *persistently* disregards laws, ordinances, or rules, regulations or orders of a public authority having jurisdiction; or
.4 otherwise is guilty of *substantial breach* of a provision of the Contract Documents.

14.2.2 When any of the above reasons exist, *the Owner upon certification by the Architect that sufficient cause exists to justify such action*, may without prejudice to any other rights or remedies of the Owner and after giving the Contractor and the Contractor's surety, if any, *seven days' written notice*, terminate employment of the Contractor and may, subject to any prior rights of the surety:

---

31 RESTATEMENT (SECOND) OF CONTRACTS, § 241 (1981); *Marshall Constr. Ltd. v. Coastal Sheet Metal & Roofing, Inc.*, 569 So. 2d 845 (Fla. Dist. Ct. App. 1990); *see* Corbin, *Contracts*, § 946.

32 American Institute of Architects Document A201 (1987).

.1 take possession of the site and of all materials, equipment tools, and construction equipment and machinery thereon owned by the Contractor;
.2 accept assignment of subcontracts pursuant to Paragraph 5.4; and
.3 finish the Work by whatever reasonable method the Owner may deem expedient.

14.2.3 When the Owner terminates the Contract for one of the reasons stated in Subparagraph 14.2.1, the Contractor shall not be entitled to receive further payment until the Work is finished.

14.2.4 If the unpaid balance of the contract Sum exceeds costs of finishing the Work, including compensation for the Architect's services and expenses made necessary thereby, such excess shall be paid to the Contractor. If such costs exceed the unpaid balance, the Contractor shall pay the difference to the Owner. The amount to be paid to the Contractor or Owner, as the case may be, shall be certified by the Architect, upon application, and this obligation for payment shall survive termination of the Contract. (Emphasis added.)

DEFAULT (FIXED-PRICE CONSTRUCTION) (APR 1984)[33]

(a) If the Contractor *refuses or fails* to prosecute the work or any separable part, with the diligence that will insure its completion within the time specified in this contract including any extensions, or *fails* to complete the work within this time, the Government may, by *written notice* to the Contractor, terminate the right to proceed with the work (or the separable part of the work) that has been delayed. In this event, the Government may take over the work and complete it by contract or otherwise, and may take possession of and use any materials, appliances, and plant on the work site necessary for completing work. *The Contractor and its sureties shall be liable* for any damage to the Government resulting from the Contractor's refusal or failure to complete the work within the specified time, whether or not the Contractor's right to proceed with

33 Federal Acquisition Regulation 52.249-10.

the work is terminated. This liability includes any increased costs incurred by the Government in completing the work.

(b) The Contractor's right to proceed *shall not be terminated nor the Contractor charged with damages under this clause, if—*

(1) *The delay in completing the work arises from unforeseeable causes beyond the control and without the fault or negligence of the Contractor*. Examples of such causes include (i) acts of God or of the public enemy, (ii) acts of the Government in either its sovereign or contractual capacity, (iii) acts of another Contractor in the performance of a contract with the Government, (iv) fires, (v) floods, (vi) epidemics, (vii) quarantine restrictions, (viii) strikes, (ix) freight embargoes, (x) unusually severe weather, or (xi) delays of subcontractors or suppliers at any tier arising from unforeseeable causes beyond the control and without the fault or negligence of both the Contractor and the subcontractors or suppliers; *and*

(2) *The Contractor, within 10 days from the beginning of any delay* (unless extended by the Contracting Officer), *notifies* the Contracting Officer in writing of the causes of delay. The Contracting Officer shall ascertain the facts and the extent of delay. If, in the judgment of the Contracting Officer, the findings of fact warrant such action, the time for completing the work shall be extended. The findings of the Contracting Officer shall be final and conclusive on the parties, but subject to appeal under the Disputes clause.

(c) If, after termination of the Contractor's right to proceed, it is determined that the Contractor was not in default, or that the delay was excusable, the rights and obligations of the parties will be the same as if the termination had been issued for the convenience of the Government.

(d) The rights and remedies of the Government in this clause are in addition to any other rights and remedies provided by law or under this contract. (Emphasis added.)

Termination clauses are carefully scrutinized by courts to ensure their enforceability. Clauses found to be against public policy will be deemed to be unenforceable.[34] A termination clause may be found to be against public policy if it allows the defaulting party to reap a windfall, provides the terminating party with an incentive to breach the agreement, or discourages the terminating party from mitigating its damages.[35] Even if a contract does not contain a termination clause, the non breaching party may rescind the contract and recover in *quantum meruit* for the reasonable value of services rendered, or may affirm the contract and recover costs of performance plus lost profits.[36]

Because construction disputes invariably involve complex technical questions, and because the owner and its design professional are in the best position to articulate the contractor's alleged "defaults" that justify termination of the bonded contract, contract termination clauses typically require the owner to give the contractor notice containing sufficient information about any alleged "default" to permit the contractor to take steps to "cure" the default prior to termination. Only if the contractor fails to take steps to cure the default within the time provided by the termination clause may the owner terminate the contract and call upon the surety to complete the work under its performance bond.[37]

The "notice of default" must clearly and unequivocally notify the contractor and surety of the specific material breaches of contract upon

---

34 *See, e.g., Saxon Constr. & Management Corp. v. Master Clean of North Carolina, Inc.*, 641 A.2d 1056 (N.J. Super. Ct. App. Div. 1994). In *Saxon*, a termination clause in a subcontract was declared void as against public policy, because the clause simply said that upon termination for default the contractor would complete the work out of the balance of subcontract funds and the subcontractor would receive any balance remaining after the subcontract work had been completed. The court found that this type of clause, which did not require the contractor to establish any specific grounds for default, was too vague and allowed the contractor to reap a windfall since it could replace the subcontractor with a cheaper competitor at will.

35 *Id.*

36 *Pacific Coast Engineering Co. v. Merritt Chapman & Scott Corp.*, 411 F.2d 889 (9th Cir. 1969); *Wilmett Partners v. Hamel*, 594 N.E.2d 1177 (Ill. App. Ct. 1992).

37 Even in the absence of express cure language an owner may have an implied duty to provide the contractor adequate notice and opportunity to cure defects prior to termination of the contract. *See McClain v. Kimbrough Constr. Co.*, 806 S.W.2d 194 (Tenn. Ct. App. 1990).

which the owner relies in terminating the bonded contract and in calling upon the surety to perform.[38] The notice of default also should identify and substantiate just which events on the construction project the obligee deems to constitute material breaches of contract, as distinguished from mere routine complaints and assertive efforts short of termination attempting to direct the contractor's attention to improve some aspect of contract performance.[39]

V.
Analysis of the Obligee's Termination of the Bonded Contract

The obligee's wrongful termination of the bonded contract is itself a breach of contract that relieves the surety of liability under its performance bond.[40] Because termination of the bonded contract for default is judicially recognized as a draconian measure resulting in forfeiture, courts carefully scrutinize the obligee's motives and the underlying facts to ensure that grounds for termination fairly exist and that the termination procedures have been properly complied with. The

---

38 *See L&A Contracting v. Southern Concrete Services*, 17 F.3d 106, 111 (5th Cir. 1994):

> A declaration of default sufficient to invoke the surety's obligations under the bond must be made in clear, direct, and unequivocal language. The declaration must inform the surety that the principal [contractor] has committed a material breach or series of material breaches of the [contract], that the obligee regards [the contract] as terminated, and that the surety must immediately commence performing under the terms of its bond.

39 *Id.* at 111 note 18:

> It is not asking too much of obligees to require that when they wish to give up on a principal and look to the surety for satisfaction, rather than merely to urge the principal to what they hope will be better performance, they must say so to the surety *in clear, unequivocal terms*.

40 *Miller v. City of Broken Arrow*, 660 F.2d 450 (10th Cir. 1981); *U.S. Home Corp. v. Suncoast Utilities*, 454 So. 2d 601 (Fla. 1984).

burden of proof of default is upon the obligee, even if designated a defendant in litigation.[41]

The obligee's termination of the principal under the termination clause of a bonded contract can be upheld only if the obligee sustains its burden of proof that (1) the principal materially breached its contract, (2) the principal's breaches were not induced or preceded by the obligee's own supervening material breaches of contract, such as nonpayment, maladministration of the construction process, or refusal to grant proper time extensions or other recognized "contract defenses," (3) the obligee's termination was not improperly motivated or conceived in bad faith and was made independently and with the exercise of discretion by its representative having authority to terminate the contract, (4) the principal was given ample notice of deficiencies so as to understand what needed to be "cured," (5) the obligee properly followed its contractually-specified termination procedure, (6) the contract was not "substantially performed," and (7) the obligee did not "waive" any contract completion dates or requirements upon which it relied to support its termination. A detailed analysis of the termination procedure is as follows:

A. The Importance of Good-Faith Motive

An obligee's default termination of a bonded contract may be invalidated by the owner's wrongful motive. A termination for default based on motives other than legitimate and well-documented concerns over the principal's inability to perform may cause the termination action to be deemed to be wrongful.[42]

---

41 *See Lisbon Contractors, Inc. v. United States*, 828 F.2d 759 (Fed. Cir. 1987).

42 Illustrative of this point is *Paul Hardeman, Inc. v. Arkansas Power & Light Co.*, 380 F. Supp. 298 (E.D. Ark. 1974). In *Hardeman*, the owner's "subjective, emotional, and visceral" response to a contractor's claim for additional costs was a termination for default to get the contractor off the job. Although the court found that there had been "some technical breaches of contract by both parties," and that "neither party was totally without blame," the court concluded:

> [The owner] was not justified in dealing with the problem in this draconic manner. Its action in doing so was wrongful and

Termination clauses frequently provide that the decision to terminate will be made by the "owner's representative" designated under the contract after issuance of a certificate by the design professional. To encourage the exercise of the right of termination for default only for fair and proper reasons, courts have rigorously enforced the procedural requirements of the termination clause. Issuance of the specified architect's certificate stating that sufficient cause exists to terminate the contract is a condition precedent to termination.[43] The decision to terminate for default must be reached through the exercise of independent discretion by the person designated under the contract. If that person follows the direction of a superior or others to terminate the contractor for default or simply fails to make an independent inquiry and decision, the termination may be set aside.[44]

> constituted an overriding breach of the agreement which not only prevents it from obtaining judgment for the costs of the completion of the work, but, to the contrary, forms a legal basis for [the contractor] to obtain monetary relief against [the owner].

See also Darwin Constr. Co. Inc. v. United States, 811 F.2d 593, 596 (Fed. Cir. 1987) ("The contractor's status of technical default served only "as a useful pretext for taking the action found necessary on other grounds unrelated to the [contractor's] performance or to the propriety of the extension of time."); *Ballenger Corp. v. City of Columbia*, 331 S.E.2d 365 (S.C. Ct. App. 1985); *Torncello v. United States* , 681 F.2d 756 (Ct. Cl. 1982); *Green Island Contracting Corp. v. State*, 458 N.Y.S.2d 828 (Ct. Cl. 1983).

43 *American Continental Life Ins. Co. v. Rainier Const. Co.*, 607 P.2d 372 (Ariz. 1980); *Peter Kiewit Sons Co. v. Summit Const. Co.*, 422 F.2d 242 (8th Cir. 1969); *Oden Constr. Co. v. Hecton*, 65 So. 2d 442 (Miss. 1953).

44 Illustrative of this point is *Schlesinger v. United States*, 390 F.2d 702 (N.Y. Ct. Cl. 1968). In *Schlesinger*, a default termination was set aside because no one in the government contracting office exercised independent discretion in the termination decision. The court set aside the termination with this admonition:

> The record affirmatively shows that nobody in the Navy, neither the Contracting Officer nor his superiors, exercised the discretion they possessed under the [termination for default clause]. The [contractor's] status of technical default served only as a useful

B. The Importance of a Proper "Cure" Notice

Virtually all termination for default clauses require the owner to give the contractor "notice of default." The purpose of this notice is to give the contractor an opportunity to "cure" the defaults and thereby preclude termination. Even where the contract does not contain an express provision to furnish the contractor with a "cure notice," the contract may be deemed to include an implied obligation on the part of the owner to give a contractor fair notice and a reasonable opportunity to correct deficiencies or nonconformances prior to termination of the contract.[45]

> pretext for the taking of action felt to be necessary on other grounds unrelated to the [contractor's] performance or the propriety of an extension of time ... Such abdication of responsibility we have always refused to sanction where there is administrative discretion under the contract.... This protective rule should have special application for default-termination which has the drastic consequence of leaving the contractor without any further compensation.

Id. at 709; *see also John A. Johnson Constr. Corp. v. United States*, 132 F. Supp. 698 (Ct. Cl. 1955) (holding that "ulterior motives" involving possible litigation do not constitute a valid ground for termination in the exercise of independent discretion).

45 *See McClain v. Kimbrough Constr. Co., Inc.*, 806 S.W.2d 194 (Tenn. Ct. App. 1990), in which the Tennessee Court of Appeals ruled that the owner's implied obligation to give the contractor a cure notice would be read into every construction contract:

> Requiring notice is a sound rule designed to allow the defaulting party to repair the defective work, to reduce the damages, to avoid additional defective performance, and to promote the informal settlement of disputes [case citations omitted]. Thus, even when the parties have not included a "take over" clause in their contract, courts have imposed on contractors the duty to give subcontractors notice and an opportunity to cure before terminating the contract for faulty performance.

Id. at 198; *see also Pollard v. Saxe & Yolles Development Co.*, 515 P.2d 88, 92 (Cal. 1974) (holding that, "[t]he requirement of notice of breach

Termination of a contract for default without giving the required "cure notice" is a material breach of contract.[46]

The owner's "cure notice" must fairly apprise the contractor of the specific defaults upon which the owner intends to rely in terminating the contract if the defaults are not cured.[47] The notice should "describe the inadequate performance and must fairly advise [the contractor] that [the

---

is based on a sound commercial rule designed to allow the defendant opportunity for repairing the defective item, reducing damages, avoiding defective products in the future, and negotiating settlements").

46 Illustrative of this point is *Cuddy & Mountain Concrete v. Citadel Constr.*, 824 P.2d 151 (Idaho App. 1992). In *Cuddy*, an owner became frustrated with the contractor's poor production due to bad weather, made arrangements to hire a successor contractor, and then terminated the contractor for default without providing the contractually-required seven-day written notice. The owner also had his project manager "supplement" previously written daily project logs to provide a "more specific record of [the contractor's] work in case something happened after the termination." The jury not only found the contract to have been breached by the owner's failure to give a "cure notice," but awarded punitive damages as compensation for the owner's heavy-handed conduct. *See also Bruning Seeding Co. v. McArdle Grading*, 439 N.W.2d 789 (Neb. 1989); *United States for the Use of Cortolano & Barone v. Morano Constr.*, 724 F. Supp. 88 (S.D.N.Y. 1989); and *Burras v. Canal Constr. & Design Co.*, 470 N.E.2d 1362 (Ind. Ct. App. 1984).

47 *See Blaine Economic Development Auth. v. Royal Elec. Co., Inc.*, 520 N.W.2d 473 (Minn. Ct. App. 1994). In *Blaine*, an owner was found to have wrongfully terminated a construction contract without having first given a proper "cure notice." Although the owner claimed that project correspondence and agendas constituted adequate notice of performance deficiencies, the Court of Appeals of Minnesota ruled that those documents neither informed the contractor that the problems were jeopardizing the contract nor directed the contractor to do anything about them within a specific time. *See also Miree Painting Co. v. Woodward Constr. & Design, Inc.*, 627 So. 2d 389 (Ala. Ct. App. 1992), *rev. on other grounds,* 627 So. 2d 393 (Ala. 1993) (holding that a "punch list" is neither a cure notice nor a termination notice, and that in the absence of a proper "cure notice," the termination was wrongful); *Hannon Elec. Co. v. United States*, 31 Fed. Cl. 135, 148 (1994) (holding that a "cure notice" that "thoroughly defined the parameters of the problem" was adequate).

owner] considers the inadequate performance serious enough that, without prompt correction, the contract will be terminated."[48]

A fundamental question relating to the adequacy of any "cure notice" is whether the "cure" of a material condition of performance is ascertainable by a contractor of ordinary competence, or must be analyzed and defined by the owner's design professional of record. The necessity and reasonableness of any "cure" involving construction defects of a material nature necessarily must take into consideration the intent of the plans and specifications as evidenced by the underlying design calculations and criteria, and the legal doctrines of substantial performance and economic waste.

The owner's insistence upon a construction defect "cure" in strict compliance with contract plans and specifications, without regard to design criteria, economic waste, or substantial performance, is unreasonable and may constitute a breach of contract. Whether a construction defect "cure" must strictly comply with the contract plans and specifications, and even the necessity for any "cure" at all, are determinations that the design professional of record properly should make. The design professional also is the proper party to advise the contractor of the specific "fix" necessary to "cure" the nonconformance so as to meet the intent of the plans and specifications. A contractor justifiably may look to the owner and design professional of record for direction as to just what repair or replacement work is necessary. Consideration of design safety factors, usually known only by the design professional, is fundamental to both the materiality of a construction defect and the need for and extent of the "cure."[49] For this and other reasons, most standard termination clauses provide that the architect or engineer of record must certify that "sufficient cause exists" to justify termination.

C. The Owner's Waiver of the Right to Terminate for Default

A material breach by the contractor may be waived by the owner by failure to take timely action to terminate the contract for default and by

48 *Id.* at 477.

49 *See Granite Constr. Co. v. United States*, 962 F.2d 998 (Fed. Cir. 1992) (holding that the government was wrong in insisting upon replacement of a nonconforming water stop that in fact provided a safety factor substantially greater than that required by the government's design).

owner encouragement to the contractor to continue performance.[50] However, waiver will not be inferred by a failure of the owner to terminate while the owner takes a reasonable time to investigate conditions under a reservation of rights.[51]

Waiver of the specifications also may arise as a result of the owner's failure to take timely action to terminate the contract for default and by owner "course of dealing."[52] A default termination based upon noncom-

---

50 *See Devito v. United States*, 413 F.2d 1147 (Ct Cl. 1969). In *Devito*, the government's failure to exercise its right of termination for 48 days, together with its knowledge of the contractor's continued performance, constituted a waiver of the contractor's breach:

> Time is of the essence in any contract containing fixed dates for performance. When a due date is passed and a contract has not been terminated for default within a reasonable time, the inference is created that time is no longer of the essence so long as the constructive election not to terminate continues and the contractor proceeds with performance. The proper way thereafter for the time to again become of the essence is for the government to issue a notice under the default clause setting a reasonable but specific time for performance upon pain of default termination. The election to waive performance remains in force until the time specified in the notice, and thereupon time is reinstated as being of the essence. The notice must set a new time for performance that is both reasonable and specific from the standpoint of the performance capabilities of the contractor at the time that the notice is given.

Id. at 1154; *see also Structural Systems, Inc. v. Borg-Warner Health Products*, 654 S.W.2d 300 (Mo. 1983); *Martin J. Simko Constr. Inc. v. United States*, 11 Cl. Ct. 257 (1986), *vacated in part on other grounds*, 852 F.2d 540 (Fed. Cir. 1988); *Sun Cal Inc. v. United States*, 21 Cl. Ct. 31 (1990); *Gamm Constr. Co. v. Townsend*, 336 N.E.2d 592 (Ill. App. Ct. 1975).

51 *See Indemnity Ins. Co. of North America v. United States*, 14 Cl. Ct. 219 (1988).

52 *See Hannon Elec. Co. v. United States*, 31 Fed. Cl. 135 (1994), in which the court addressed this issue as follows:

pliance with waived contract terms or specifications constitutes a breach of contract.

VI.
Analysis of the Surety's "Contract Defenses"

The surety, upon termination, steps into the shoes of its principal under the bonded contract and is entitled to assert against the obligee its principal's claims for additional compensation and defenses against liability arising out of or related to the contract. The surety therefore must analyze the terms of the bonded contract and the facts surrounding the contract to determine whether the owner and contractor each have performed their respective material obligations. If the obligee is found to have materially

---

> The government's unprotesting observation or acceptance of performance that it later contends was incorrect can have one of two legal consequences. [Citation omitted.] First, if the interpretation of ambiguous specifications is in dispute, such actions serve to show that the contractor's interpretation is reasonable and that the government shared the contractor's interpretation of the specifications before the dispute arose. [Citation omitted.] In this context, the contractor need prove little more than the fact that such conduct occurred. It need not show that it relied on the government's conduct, or that the actions were those of a government official with the authority to waive contract requirements.... A contractor also can use the government's unprotesting observation or acceptance of noncontractual performance to demonstrate that the government has waived a contract requirement. Professor John Cibinic has named this argument the "constructive waiver of specifications" [citation omitted]. A constructive waiver of specifications occurs not where the contract is ambiguous, but rather, where the government "has administered an initially unambiguous contract in such a way as to give a reasonably intelligent and alert opposite party the impression that a contract requirement has been suspended or waived.

Id. at 146 (citing *Gresham & Co. v. United States*, 470 F.2d 542, 555 (Ct. Cl. 1972)); *see also Miller Elevator Co. v. United States*, 30 Fed. Cl. 662 (1994).

breached the bonded contract prior to any breach by the principal, or to have induced the principal's breach, the obligee's termination of the bonded contract is itself a material breach that may exonerate both the principal and the surety from liability, and will allow the contractor to recover damages either under the contract or in *quantum meruit*.

It is a fundamental principle of law that an owner's material breach of contract relieves a contractor of its obligation to perform and precludes a termination by the owner for default.[53] Some of the events in the construction process that may constitute either an excuse for contractor nonperformance or an outright material breach by the owner are described below:

A. Substantial Performance

The owner may not terminate for default a construction contract that has been substantially performed.[54] Substantial performance of a construction contract is typically defined as that degree of performance which provides the owner with construction suitable for the purpose for which

---

53 *See Marathon Oil Co. v. Hollis*, 305 S.E.2d 864 (Ga. Ct. App. 1983). In *Marathon*, the court allowed a contractor to recover, notwithstanding arguments that the contractor failed to complete on time. Among other things, the court concluded that: (1) the contractor "did perform the majority of the work properly pursuant to the contract and that it stood ready to correct any defects," (2) the contractor was not able to complete its work according to the original schedule because of owner-caused interruptions or other delays for which the contractor was not responsible, and (3) the owner waived the contract completion date. *See also, D.E.W., Inc. v. Depco Forms, Inc.*, 827 S.W.2d 379 (Tex. Ct. App. 1992); *Horton Industrial, Inc. v. Village of Moweaqua*, 492 N.E.2d 220 (Ill. App. Ct. 1986).

54 The term "substantial performance" is used throughout the cases interchangeably with the term "substantial completion." *See, e.g., Worthington Corp. v. Consolidated Aluminum Corp.*, 544 F.2d 227, 230-31 (5th Cir. 1976) (using substantial completion and substantial performance interchangeably); *Husar Industries Inc. v. A.G. Huber & Sons, Inc.*, 675 S.W.2d 565, 572-73 (Mo. Ct. App. 1985) (same).

it is intended.[55] Failure of the contractor to complete all work under a substantially performed contract allows the owner merely to utilize any retained contract funds to complete the remaining work if the contractor fails to do so.[56]

In essence, substantial performance means that the contractor has completed its work to such an extent that it cannot be said to have *materially* breached the contract.[57] Absent a material breach of contract,

---

55 *See, e.g., O & M Constr., Inc. v. State, Div. of Admin.*, 576 So. 2d 1030, 1035 (La. Ct. App.) (substantial performance ... means that the construction is fit for the purpose intended...."), *cert. denied*, 581 So. 2d 691 (La. 1991); *Husar Industries, Inc. v. A.G. Huber & Sons, Inc.*, 674 S.W.2d 565 (Mo. Ct. App. 1984) ("a building is substantially complete when it has reached the state in its construction so that it can be put to the use for which it was intended"); *Dittmer v. Nokleberg*, 219 N.W.2d 201, 206 (N.D. 1974) ("there is substantial performance ... when all the essentials necessary to the full accomplishment of the [building's intended] purposes ... are performed").

56 *See O & M Constr., Inc. v. State*, 576 So. 2d at 1035 ("a building contractor is entitled to recover the contract price even though defects or omissions are present when he has substantially performed the building contract"); *Huget v. Musso Partnership*, So. 2d 91, 93 (La. Ct. App.), *cert. denied*, 509 So. 2d 462 (La. 1987) ("[t]he law is clear that a building contract may not be dissolved after substantial performance has been rendered"); *Prudential Ins. Co. v. Stratton*, 685 S.W.2d 818 (Ark. Ct. App. 1985) ("[A] contractor who has substantially performed is entitled to recover the contract price, less the difference in value between the work as done and as contracted to be done, or less the cost of correcting defective work where this can be done without great expense or material injury to the structure as a whole"); *Dixon v. Nelson*, 107 N.W.2d 505, 507 (S.D. 1961) (holding that a contractor who has rendered substantial performance is entitled to the contract price with a deduction for minor defects and nonperformance).

57 *See J.M. Beeson Co. v. Sartori*, 553 So. 2d 180 (Fla. Dist. Ct. App. 1989). In *Beeson*, a contractor who accepted a contract for the construction of a shopping center, which included several anchor tenants and out-parcels, completed all but one anchor tenant facility within the contract time. The owner alleged that the contractor was in default and sought to assess liquidated damages. The court, however, ruled in favor of the contractor as follows:

the contractor may not be terminated for default and thereby deprived of its contact price as adjusted to compensate the owner for any uncompleted work. In view of judicial dislike for the forfeiture aspects of default terminations, courts frequently have rejected owner allegations of material breaches in the face of substantial performance.[58]

> The doctrine of "substantial performance" is held by this court in *Ocean Rich Development Corp. v. Quality Plastering, Inc.*, 247 So. 2d 72, 75 (Fla. 4th D.C.A. 1971): "Substantial performance is that performance of a contract which, while not full performance, is so nearly equivalent to what was bargained for that it would be unreasonable to deny the promisee the full contract price subject to the promisor's right to recover whatever damages have been occasioned him by the promisee's failure to render full performance. *See* 3A *Corbin on Contracts*, § 702 et seq." To say that substantial performance is performance which is nearly equivalent to what is bargained for, as the case law defines the term, in essence means that the owner can use the property for the use for which it is intended....

Id. at 182.

58 *See Campagna v. Smallwood*, 428 So. 2d 1343 (La. Ct. App. 1983) ("substantial performance by a contractor is readily found, despite the existence of a large number of defects in both material and workmanship, unless the structure is totally unfit for the purpose for which it was originally intended"); *United States for the Use of M. Maltese & Sons v. Juneau Constr.*, 759 F.2d 253 (2d Cir. 1985) ("Maltese had complied sufficiently with American Institute of Steel Construction Standards insofar as tolerances were concerned and the root openings in the majority of the connections between the columns and beams fell within acceptance mill tolerances"); *Radiation Technology v. United States*, 366 F.2d 1003 (Ct. Cl. 1966) ("It is our view that even where time is of the essence, *i.e.*, where performance must occur by a given date, this factor must not demand that performance be measured in terms of strict conformity. It does require that performance be timely, but assuming this, there would thereafter remain for inquiry the question as to whether performance was substantial in other respects."); *Wilson v. Kapetan, Inc.*, 595 A.2d 369 (Conn. App. Ct. 1976) ("Under Louisiana law, substantial performance is a question of fact and a primary factor is whether the plant can be put to the use for which it was originally intended."); *M&W Masonry Constr., Inc. v. Head*, 562 P.2d 957 (Okla. Ct. App. 1976) ("We hold under the

Since the owner may not terminate the contract for default after it has been substantially performed, the owner necessarily is not permitted to pursue the surety under the performance bond. In recognition of this rule, owners sometimes require contractors at the time of substantial completion to provide separate "maintenance" or "warranty" bonds to ensure completion of punch list work or subsequently discovered latent defects, or may state expressly in the performance bond that the surety's obligations will extend to incomplete or defective work remaining after substantial completion. Whether a surety ultimately will be held liable under its performance bond for latent defects discovered after substantial performance depends upon a variety of factors including: (1) whether the precise language of the bond affords coverage; (2) if the bond affords coverage, the amount of time which has passed between the date of substantial completion and the date of discovery of the latent defects; (3) the extent and nature of the defects; and (4) the case law of the relevant jurisdiction.[59]

B. The Owner's Duties Incident to Project Design

It has long been a fundamental principle of law that the party in control of preparing and furnishing the detailed design documents is responsible for design inadequacies. Thus, where the owner issues detailed design documents found to be defective, fails to disclose critical

---

evidence plaintiff substantially performed its agreement and therefore had a right to quit for lack of an installment progress payment."); *Husar Indust., Inc. v. A.L. Huber & Son, Inc.*, 674 S.W.2d 565 (Mo. Ct. App. 1984) ("A building is substantially complete when it has reached the state in its construction so that it can be put to the use for which it was intended even though comparatively minor items remain to be furnished or performed ..."); *Patco Homes v. Rochetti*, 522 N.Y.S.2d 903 (N.Y. App. Div. 1987).

59 *See, e.g., Hunters Pointe Partners v. United States Fidelity & Guaranty Co.*, 486 N.W.2d 136 (Mich. Ct. App. 1992); *School Board v. St. Paul Fire & Marine Ins. Co.*, 449 So. 2d 872 (Fla. Dist. Ct. App. 1984); *Florida Board of Regents v. Fidelity & Deposit Co.*, 416 So. 2d 30 (Fla. Dist. Ct. App. 1982); *Vitenas v. Centanni*, 381 So. 2d 531 (La. Ct. App. 1980); *Regents of the University of California v. Hartford Accident & Indemnity Co.*, 131 Cal. Rptr. 112 (Cal. Ct. App. 1976).

information to the contractor, or maintains control over the contractor's construction methods, the contractor's nonperformance will be excused.

1. The owner's implied warranty of design adequacy

The owner's implied warranty of the adequacy of its detailed design documents furnished to the contractor is a firmly established principle of construction law,[60] which has been adopted in virtually all American jurisdictions.[61] This obligation has been held to extend from a general

---

60 *See United States v. Spearin*, 248 U.S. 132 (1918). In *Spearin*, a construction site was flooded by a break in a sewer line constructed in conformance with government design documents. The government took the position that the contractor was responsible for the site clean-up because the project had not been completed and accepted and the contract required the contractor to assume responsibility for the site and examine the site and the plans. The contractor showed that it had complied fully with the government's plans and specifications in constructing the broken sewer line. In a lucid opinion written by Justice Brandeis, the Court held as follows:

> [I]f the contractor is bound to build according to plans and specifications prepared by the owner, the contractor will not be responsible for the consequences of defects in the plans and specifications.... [T]he insertion of the articles prescribing the character, dimensions, and location of the sewer imported a warranty that if the specifications were complied with, the sewer would be adequate. This implied warranty is not overcome by the general clauses requiring the contractor to examine the site, to check the plans, and to assume responsibility for the work until completion and acceptance. The obligation to examine the site did not impose him the duty of making a diligent inquiry into the history of the locality, with a view to determining, at his peril, whether the sewer specifically prescribed by the government would prove adequate. The duty to check the plans did not impose the obligation to pass upon their adequacy to accomplish the purpose in view.

Id. at 135.

61 *See* 6 A.L.R.3d 1394 (citing authorities from various jurisdictions which have adopted the implied warranty of design specifications).

contractor to its subcontractors, even though the general contractor simply passed on the design information received from the owner.[62] The owner's approval of shop drawings and submittals has been held to incorporate their details into the owner's design for implied warranty purposes.[63] The implied warranty may be invoked only insofar as the contractor reasonably relies upon the owner's detailed design information. Absent reasonable reliance upon the owner's defective design, the contractor's non-performance is not excused.[64]

2. *The owner's implied warranty of commercial availability of specified construction materials*

A corollary to the owner's implied warranty of design adequacy is that, when the owner specifies a single-source product, the owner also impliedly warrants the commercial availability of the product.[65] If the

---

62 *See APAC Carolina, Inc. v. Town of Allendale*, 41 F.3d 157 (4th Cir. 1994).

63 *See Northeastern Plate Glass Corp. v. Mary Walter, Inc.*, 537 N.Y.S.2d 657 (N.Y. App. Div. 1989). In *Northeastern*, the owner was held responsible for a defective window wall panel anchorage system that resulted in four panels falling off a state university dormitory building within two years of their installation. The defective anchoring details were suggested and furnished by the contractor's wall panel supplier. In imposing responsibility upon the owner, the court concluded that improper design rather than improper materials or installation was the cause of the failure and ruled that the owner retained responsibility for the loss because "the owner and its architects retained all ultimate control over and responsibility for" the construction plans and specifications. *See also Toombs & Co. v. United States*, 4 Cl. Ct. 535 (1984).

64 *Al Johnson Constr. Co. v. United States*, 854 F.2d 467 (Fed. Cir. 1988); *Tyger Constr. Co. Inc. v. United States*, 31 Fed. Cl. 177 (1994).

65 *See Edward M. Crough, Inc. v. Department of General Services*, 572 A.2d 457 (D.C. 1990). In this case, the school district issued a re-roofing specification that required the contractor to install roofing materials manufactured by a single company. When the manufacturer later refused to sell the materials except at an exorbitant price, the owner allowed the contractor to substitute different materials after an extensive delay. Upon completion, the contractor sued the owner for its extra costs of performance based upon the owner's alleged breach of its implied warranty

product is not commercially available, the contractor and surety cannot be held responsible for delays or damages caused by the product's unavailability.

3. *The government contractor defense*

A variant to the owner's implied warranty of the adequacy of its design is the "government contractor" defense. Under this defense, a contractor who performs work or furnishes materials pursuant to the government's detailed design documents is exonerated from liability to both the government and injured third persons.[66]

4. *The owner's implied duty of disclosure*

Implied in every contract is a duty on the part of the owner to disclose information material to the contractor's performance that is not available from other sources.[67] Failure by the owner to disclose material

---

of commercial availability. The court upheld the implied warranty of commercial availability but concluded, however, that the warranty did not extend to specified materials which were in fact available but at an exorbitant price.

66 *See Board of Education v. W.R. Grace Corp.*, 609 A.2d 92 (N.J. Super. Ct. Law Div. 1992). In this case, the school district's claim against the contractor for installation of construction materials containing asbestos was denied because the materials had been specified in detail by the owner and its project architect, and the contractor had merely complied with the architect's plans and specifications. In reaching this decision, the court followed long-standing precedent. *See also Boyle v. United Technologies*, 487 U.S. 500 (1988); *Yearsley v. W. A. Ross Constr. Co.*, 309 U.S. 18 (1940); *Ryan v. Feeny & Sheehan Building Co.*, 145 N.E. 321 (N.Y. 1924).

67 *See City of Indianapolis v. Twin Lakes Enterprises, Inc.*, 568 N.E.2d 1073 (Ind. Ct. App. 1991). In this case, the City was found to have breached its implied duty of disclosure by failing to inform a dredging contractor about large obstructions previously dumped by the City into the reservoir to be dredged:

> [T]he City did not inform Twin Lakes about the extent of the dumping but insisted that Twin Lakes continue to dredge the site,

information is a breach of contract which can result in both the contractor and the surety being exonerated from liability for damages resulting from the breach.

5. *Blended design and performance specifications*

Owners and designers frequently prepare specifications containing both design details and performance requirements to be satisfied by the contractor. Sometimes these performance requirements take the form of performance acceptance tests. When design details and performance acceptance tests requirements are incompatible, the issue of liability must be carefully analyzed.[68]

> which it did. The contract and the circumstances in this case were of such a nature that Twin Lakes could only partly perform its obligations. In fact, Twin Lakes continued to perform the dredging after the money provided under the original contract and change orders had been expended until it was expelled from the site. The failure to inform Twin Lakes of the nature and extent of the obstructions, in the face of assumed obligations to the contrary, went to the very heart of the agreement to dredge the site. As such, the breach of that obligation constituted a material breach of contract.

Id. at 1080.

68 Illustrative of this point is *W.H. Lyman Constr. Co. v. Village of Gurnee*, 403 N.E.2d 1325 (Ill. Ct. App. 1980). In this case, the Village's contract documents for construction of a sewer (1) contained both detailed plans and specifications describing the work, and (2) imposed an infiltration test which the completed sewer was required to pass before the Village would accept the work and make final payment to the contractor. The contract also contained a disclaimer of responsibility by the owner and engineer regarding the contractor's inability to meet the infiltration test. After the sewer was completed in conformance with the contract documents, the contractor was unable to pass the infiltration test and the owner refused to pay. The court resolved the subsequent suit in favor of the contractor as follows:

> We construe this provision [the acceptance test and disclaimer] as an impermissible attempt on the part of the Village to shift the

6. *The owner's approval of contractor plant and equipment or "work plan"*

Contract documents frequently include provisions that require the owner to approve the contractor's plant and equipment or "work plan" prior to the owner's issuance of a notice to proceed. By approving the contractor's work plan, the owner implicitly accepts as reasonable the assumptions which underlie the plan (such as assumptions relating to expected site conditions) and may later be precluded from arguing that the plan was inadequate to complete the work.[69]

> responsibility for the sufficiency and adequacy of the plans to the contractor without providing the contractor the corresponding benefit of having something to say about the plans he is strictly bound to follow. The contractor's duty is to perform his part of the contract in a workmanlike manner, not to evaluate the suitability of the specifications or, in the language of *Spearin*, "to pass upon their adequacy to accomplish the purpose in view."

Id. at 1332; *see also Chantilly Constr. Corp. v. Dept. of Highways*, 369 S.E.2d 438 (Va. Ct. App. 1988); *Fruin-Colnon Corp. v. Niagara Frontier Transportation Authority*, 585 N.Y.S.2d 248 (N.Y. App. Div. 1992).

69 *See United States v. Atlantic Dredging Co.*, 253 U.S. 1 (1919). In this case, a dredging contractor encountered compacted sand and gravel with cobbles and complained that these materials were different from conditions represented in the plans and specifications to be "mainly mud or mud with an admixture of sand" (*i.e.*, non-compacted). The contract documents had reserved to the owner the right to inspect and approve the contractor's plant and equipment prior to allowing the contractor to proceed with the work. The owner had exercised this right and given approval. The significance of the owner's approval was explained by the court as follows:

> [T]he government's care of its interests extended to the inspection of the instrumentalities of the contractor, and required the character and capacity of the plant which was to be used, to be submitted for inspection and approval. In fulfillment of the requirement, the company submitted its plan. It was only efficient for dredging material of the character mentioned in the specifications and described on the map, and it was so approved. The significance of the submissions and approval is manifest. The character and

Extensive owner "field control" over products furnished by the contractor also may excuse the contractor's non-performance.[70] The same is true with respect to construction methods specified by the owner that prove unsuitable due to unanticipated conditions.[71] Similarly, a

---

> capacity of the plant conveyed to the [government] the fact that the company was accepting as true the representation of the specifications and the map of the materials to be dredged; and reciprocally the approval of the plant by the [government] was an assurance to the company of the truth of the representation, and the justification of reliance upon it.

Id. at 5.

70 *See C.J. Langenfelder & Son, Inc. v. Pennsylvania DOT*, 404 A.2d 745 (Pa. 1979). In this case, the owner was held to have impliedly warranted that the contractor's concrete was adequate for the owner's intended purposes, even though the concrete mix design was designed and furnished by the concrete supplier. The owner had exercised detailed inspection and control in approving the concrete mix design, inspecting the ingredients prior to mixing and testing the concrete prior to placement. The court recognized the owner's extensive field control over the concrete in reaching this conclusion:

> When the [DOT] seeks to exert such *close control* over the source, the formulation, and the production of the material to be used in the construction project, it cannot disclaim responsibility for delays caused by defects in that material.

Id. at 751 (emphasis added).

71 *See McCree & Co. v. State*, 91 N.W.2d 713 (Minn. 1958). In *McCree*, a highway embankment specification required that embankment fill be compacted to the specified density. The contractor, using compaction methods dictated by the owner's design, failed to achieve the desired density. The owner argued that contractor workmanship was the cause of the problem. The Supreme Court of Minnesota, however, sided with the contractor as follows:

> [T]he owner's actions in furnishing detailed plans and specifications control not only the particular result to be accomplished, but also the particular construction methods to be followed and used and supports an implied warranty in keeping with the intention

"methods" specification also may shift liability for delayed completion from the contractor to the owner.[72]

7. *The owner's implied warranty of design versus the contractor's warranty of materials*

Contract documents usually contain clauses under which the contractor warrants its construction materials against defects. Owners frequently argue that the contractor's express warranty against material defects overrides the owner's implied warranty of design where the product fails as a result of design considerations. The cases, however, suggest that both warranties are equally effective and the determination of which warranty has been breached is a question of fact for the jury.[73]

> and expectation of the parties that the plans, specifications, and soils conditions were such as would permit successful conclusion of the work. The State was the party in control who dictated the entire contract and retained control from start to finish.

Id. at 725.

72 *See Midwest Dredging Co. v. McAninch Corp.*, 424 N.W.2d 216 (Iowa 1988). In this case, the state specified that the contractor should use a 22-inch transfer pipe to hydraulically transfer highway embankment fill material from a borrow site to the embankment site, but then sought to hold the contractor responsible for failure to complete the contract when the contractor encountered a significant number of boulders in the borrow site material larger than the transfer pipe diameter. The Iowa Supreme Court held as follows:

> DOT drew up plans based on its tests and required that a specific dredging and piping technique be employed. By doing so, DOT impliedly represented that the material from Borrow C could be hydraulically dredged and piped in accordance with its plans and [specifications]. DOT went beyond mere presentation of boring results and an implied warranty consequently arose.

Id. at 222.

73 *See Trustees of Indiana University v. Aetna Casualty & Surety Co.*, 920 F.2d 429 (7th Cir. 1990). In this case, the owner and architect had approved the use of "courthouse blend" bricks as the face material for four

8. *The owner's responsibility for latent ambiguities in its design*

Arguments over the intent of the owner's design documents are frequent in construction. Contractor non-performance due to latent ambiguities or conflicts in design remain the responsibility of the owner. Courts will apply various rules of construction in an effort to resolve ambiguity.[74] These rules include consideration of "reasonable logical interpretation," the "whole agreement," the "principal apparent purpose," "trade custom and usage," "concurrent interpretation and practice," "course of dealing" under prior contracts, "silent acquiescence" to the other party's interpretation, and, as a last resort, "construing against the drafter."[75]

---

buildings being constructed at Indiana University's Southeast Regional Campus in Albany, Indiana. Under the contract, the contractor warranted its work to be free of defects. When the bricks began to "spall" and deteriorate two years after installation, the bricks were tested and found to be excessively porous and with a high rate of water absorption. At trial, the owner claimed that the porous condition was due to the bricks being "under-fired during the manufacturing process," and thus defective. The contractor argued, however, that the "courthouse blend" bricks, as properly manufactured, were not "suited to the environmental conditions [severe freeze/thaw conditions] in which they were used." A jury decided in favor of the contractor and its surety and against the owner. On appeal, the United States Court of Appeals for the Seventh Circuit affirmed that the jury could find that the owner's design specification requiring installation of courthouse blend bricks was defective rather than the bricks themselves and was not "trumped" by the contractor's express warranty of its materials.

74 *See* RESTATEMENT (SECOND) OF CONTRACTS, §§ 212-223 (1981); 17A AM. JUR. 2d, *Contracts* §§ 336-420 (1991).

75 *See Darwin Constr. Co. v. United States*, 31 Fed. Cl. (1994). In *Darwin*, a specialized trade meaning was used to interpret the contractor's obligations under a landscaping contract. The question was whether a "plant list" and a "planting by lots" provision were intended to be synonymous or separate. The court ruled that the ambiguity was to be construed in accordance with specialized trade usages which indicated that the "plantings by lots" list was intended only to designate plant locations, rather than additional plants to be furnished.

C. The Owner's Implied Duty of Cooperation

American jurisprudence applies in all contracts the obligation to cooperate in the performance of the contract and not to delay, hinder, or interfere with the performance of other parties.[76] Over the years, owners have been found on numerous occasions to have breached their implied duty of cooperation in the context of construction contracts. Such instances have included failure to provide timely site access,[77] failure to complete other work necessary to allow the contractor to proceed,[78] and failure to reasonably schedule and coordinate the work.[79]

Owners frequently seek to hold contractors responsible for non-performance over which contractors have no control. Unless contractual language expressly provides that contractors will be responsible to complete on time without regard to cost, contractors ordinarily are entitled to extensions of time for delays beyond their control and may even be entitled to compensation for delay within the owner's control. "Excusable" causes of delay have included unusually severe weather, strikes and labor disturbances, acts of God, acts of government, and other events beyond the control of both the owner and contractor. "Compensable" delays, which excuse contractor non-performance and entitle the contractor to be compensated for the delay, include the entire gamut of delays within the exclusive control of the owner under typical construction contracts:

---

76 *See Gulf M & O Railway Co. v. Illinois Railway Co.*, 128 F. Supp. 311 (N.D. Ala. 1954) in which this doctrine was articulated as follows:

> A contracting party impliedly obligates himself to cooperate in the performance of his contract and the law will not permit him to take advantage of an obstacle to performance which he has created or which lies within his power to remove.

Id. at 324.

77 *See Douglas Northwest Inc. v. Bill O'Brien & Sons Constr. Inc.*, 828 P.2d 565 (Wash. Ct. App. 1992); *Capital City Drywall Corp. v. DC Smith Constr. Co.*, 270 N.W.2d 608 (Iowa 1978); *R.G. Pope Constr. Co., Inc. v. Guardrail of Roanoke, Inc.*, 244 S.E.2d 774 (Va. 1978).

78 *See J.J. Brown Co. v. J.L. Simmons Co.*, 118 N.E.2d 781 (Ill. 1954).

79 *See Tribble & Sons Co. v. Consolidated Services*, 744 S.W.2d 945 (Tex. Ct. App. 1988).

providing contract "direction," making timely and proper inspections, providing timely review and approval of shop drawings, furnishing timely owner materials and equipment, providing adequate design documents, furnishing proper coordination of other contractors on site, making changes in the work, and a host of other similar responsibilities.

Owner allegations that the contractor is behind schedule must be analyzed carefully to determine whether the contractor in fact is responsible for the delays or is entitled to more time (and perhaps money) because the delays were caused either by the owner or by supervening events beyond the control of both the owner and contractor. An owner's failure to grant proper time extensions may preclude the owner for terminating the contractor for default based upon delay.[80] An owner's inclusion in the contract of exclusive remedies for contractor delay, such as a "claim submission" clause or "liquidated damages" clause, also may preclude termination for delay.[81]

D. The Owner's Responsibility for Differing Site Conditions

Unless expressly disclaimed in the contract, the owner ordinarily is responsible for non-performance due to conditions at the site that differ materially from those represented in the contract documents or otherwise ordinarily encountered. Most contracts today contain an explicit "differing site conditions" clause under which the owner assumes the risk of such conditions. The purpose of such a clause is to make it unnecessary for contractors to include large contingencies in their bids to cover the risk of encountering unanticipated adverse subsurface conditions or concealed conditions in existing structures.[82]

Even in the absence of an express clause, however, owners have been held liable for differing site conditions under various theories including

---

80 *See J.D. Hedin Constr. Co. v. United States*, 408 F.2d 424 (Ct. Cl. 1969); *W.F. Magann Corp. v. Diamond Mfg. Co., Inc.*, 580 F. Supp. 1299 (D.S.C. 1984).

81 *See Vermont Marble Co. v. Baltimore Contractors, Inc.*, 520 F. Supp. 922 (D.D.C. 1981); *Construction Contracting & Mgmt. v. McConnell*, 815 P.2d 1161 (N.M. 1991).

82 *See Metropolitan Sewage Commission v. R.W. Constr.*, 241 N.W.2d 371 (Wis. 1976).

(1) breach of implied warranty;[83] (2) owner misrepresentation of conditions in the contract documents;[84] (3) owner failure to disclose material information;[85] and (4) mutual mistake.[86]

E. Owner Failure To Properly Administer The Contract

Contractors have been excused for non-performance caused by owner mal-administration of the contract in the following situations:

1. Change orders

Virtually all construction contracts contain a clause allowing the owner unilaterally to issue written change orders during contract performance to change contract requirements without being in breach of contract. The clause enables the owner to order desired changes within the general scope of the contract, to take advantage of new or improved construction methods and techniques, to correct errors and plans, to amend the construction schedule to deal with unforeseen circumstances or field conditions, or to address changed owner needs. Upon issuance of a change order, the owner has an obligation to pay the contractor for the extra work and to extend extra time needed for performance.[87]

---

83 *See Big Chief Drilling Co. v. United States*, 26 Cl. Ct. 1276 (1992).

84 *See Hollerbach v. United States*, 233 U.S. 165 (1914).

85 *See PT&L Constr. Co. v. New Jersey DOT*, 531 A.2d 1330 (N.J. 1987).

86 *See John Burns Constr. Co. v. Hiderlake, Inc.*, 433 N.E.2d 1126 (Ill. App. Ct. 1982); *S.J. Groves & Sons Co. v. State*, 273 S.E.2d 465 (N.C. Ct. App. 1980).

87 *See Bagwell Coatings, Inc. v. Middle South Energy, Inc.*, 797 F.2d 1298 (5th Cir. 1986) (holding that a contractor was entitled to a "total cost" recovery for the owner's breach of contract, where the owner's construction manager, after giving a contractor "assurances that it would work out its cost problems" related to change orders, continued to "haggle over minutia" and refused to authorize additional compensation for changes because of "alleged documentation inadequacies").

2. *Owner nonpayment*

Owner nonpayment has served as the basis for setting aside default terminations in numerous cases.[88] The obligation to pay will be considered in the context of surrounding circumstances, even where contract language makes it discretionary.[89]

---

88 *See, e.g., Sage Street Assoc. v. Northgate Constr. Co.*, 809 S.W.2d 775 (Tex. Ct. App. 1991) (holding that an owner's nonpayment of change orders billed according to the terms of the contract excused the contractor's performance and relieved the performance bond surety of all liability to the owner); *Darrell J. Didericksen & Sons v. Magna Water*, 613 P.2d 1116 (Utah 1980) ("It was only when Magna refused to provide acceptable change orders that the work stopped, as the contractor refused to proceed further without written direction or authorization as required."); *White River Dev. Co. v. Meco Systems, Inc.*, 806 S.W.2d 735 (Mo. Ct. App. 1991) ("When a progress payment due is not made, a builder is entitled to suspend performance and await either other assurances satisfactory to it or actual payment."); *Blake Constr. Co., Inc. v. C.. Coakley Co., Inc.*, 431 A.2d 569 (D.C. 1981) ("When Blake failed to assure Coakley that it would be compensated for the additional expenses it incurred beyond those contemplated in the subcontract, Blake also breached the implicit terms of the subcontract and Coakley acted properly in discontinuing performance under the subcontract."); *John W. Johnson, Inc. v. Basic Constr. Co.*, 429 F.2d 764 (D.C. Cir. 1970) ("We accordingly decide that Basic was required to give Johnson a commitment for payment for the extra painting even though it received none from [the owner], that it breached the contract when it refused to do so, that Johnson's abandonment was fully justified and that it was entitled to be compensated for the work it performed."); *Tennessee Asphalt Co. v. Purcell Enterprises*, 631 S.W.2d 439 (Tenn. Ct. App. 1982) (substantial delay in payment constituted a material breach); *U.S. ex rel Endicott Enterprises v. Star Bright Constr. Co.*, 848 F. Supp. 1161 (D. Del. 1994).

89 *U.S. v. Lennox Metal Mfg. Co.*, 225 F.2d 302 (2d Cir. 1955) (surrounding circumstances dictated that the government was required to make progress payments even though the contract language made them discretionary).

3. *"Cardinal" changes*

A truly fundamental change by the owner in the nature of the bonded contract is a breach of contract which discharges the contractor from its obligation to further perform.[90] This type of change is usually referred to in the case law as a "cardinal" change. Although the case law provides some guidance in determining whether a cardinal change has occurred, courts routinely caution that "each case must be analyzed on its own facts and in light of its own circumstances."[91]

There are two distinct tests for cardinal changes. First, a cardinal change is said to occur when the obligee affects an alteration of the work so drastic that it effectively requires the contractor to perform duties materially different from those originally bargained for.[92] This expression of the cardinal change doctrine is sometimes referred to as the "scope of the contract" test.[93] Second, in the context of projects awarded through a competitive bidding process, a cardinal change can occur when the contract is modified in such a way so as to materially change the field of competition.[94] This expression of the doctrine is sometimes referred to as the "scope of the competition" test, and requires an analysis of the substance of the change rather than its magnitude.[95]

---

90 *See Norman Peterson Co. v. Container Corp. of America*, 172 Cal. App. 3d 628 (1985); *Airprep Technology, Inc. v. United States*, 30 Fed. Cl. 488 (1994) (holding that the contractor's alleged default was excused because that the contractor's failure of performance arose from the government's insistence upon additional requirements that constituted a cardinal change to the contract).

91 *Wunderlich Contracting Co. v. United States*, 351 F.2d 956, 966 (Ct. Cl. 1965); *Edward R. Marden Corp. v. United States*, 442 F.2d 364, 369 (Ct. Cl. 1971).

92 *See General Dynamics Corp. v. United States*, 585 F.2d 457, 462 (Ct. Cl. 1978).

93 *See Aragona Constr. Co. v. United States*, 165 Ct. Cl. 382, 391 (1964).

94 *See Cray Research, Inc. v. Dept. of Navy*, 556 F. Supp. 201, 203 (D.D.C. 1982).

95 *See, e.g., Webcraft Packaging.*, Comp. Gen. Dec. B-194087, 79-2 CPD 120 (holding that post-bid change in requisition requirement, permitting use of standard paper rather than specialized paper, constituted a cardinal change, because a large number of potential suppliers of standard paper were prevented from bidding).

The surety should check for cardinal changes by applying the scope of the contract test or the scope of the competition test in the following situations:

a. where the dollar value of the work to be performed under the contract increases substantially, *i.e.*, by more than one hundred percent;[96]
b. where the method of performing the contract changes, so that the risks of performance are significantly altered;[97]
c. in the competitive bidding context, where the method of performance changes in a way that potential bidders could not reasonably have anticipated;[98] or
d. where the method of payment to or financing of the contractor changes in such a way so as to expose the surety to greater risk of loss.[99]

---

96 *See, e.g., Edward R. Marden Corp.*, 442 F.2d at 370 (cardinal change found where cost of completing construction more than doubled due to structural design errors); *Peter Kiewit Sons' Co. v. Summit Constr. Co.*, 442 F.2d 242 (8th Cir. 1969) (cardinal change found where cost of backfilling operation increased from $600,000 to approximately $2 million); *Employers Ins. of Wausau v. Construction Management Engineers, Inc.*, 377 S.E.2d 119 (S.C. Ct. App. 1989) (cardinal change occurred where contract value increased from $2.3 million to $6.2 million).

97 *See, e.g., Memorex Corp.*, 61 Comp. Gen. 42, B-200722, 81-2 CPD ¶ 334 (change in procurement method from outright purchase to a lease-to-ownership plan shifted substantial risks from the government to contractor and, therefore, constituted a cardinal change).

98 *See, e.g., American Air Filter Co.*, Comp. Gen. B-188408, 78-1 CPD ¶ 36; *W.H. Mullins*, Comp. Gen. B-207200, 83-1 CPD ¶ 158; note 81, *supra*, (citing *Webcraft Packaging*, 79-2 CPD ¶ 120).

99 *See, e.g., Reliance Ins. Co. v. Colbert*, 365 F.2d 530, 534 (D.C. Cir. 1966) (cardinal change occurred where obligee revised payment schedule to provide significantly accelerated payments to contractor); *United States v. Reliance Ins. Co.*, 799 F.2d 1382 (9th Cir. 1986) (cardinal change occurred where contract was modified so that bond principal was no longer able to obtain adequate security for the surety's obligation). Changes in the method of payment or financing must be distinguished from overpayments of the principal by the obligee. The former may constitute a cardinal change which fully discharges the surety. The latter is a defense

The availability of the cardinal change defense will depend heavily upon the facts and circumstances of the particular case. However, when a cardinal change in the bonded contract is found to occur, both the contractor and the surety will be discharged from further performance obligations.

4. *Failing to give direction*

The owner also breaches the contract if it fails to act reasonably in carrying out its contract obligations, such as by refusing to instruct the contractor on how to proceed in the face of adverse conditions,[100] or failing to exercise reasonable discretion to stop the work in the face of adverse conditions.[101]

F. Impossibility/Impracticability of Performance

Construction contracts are sometimes simply impossible or impracticable to complete in conformance with their requirements. The doctrines of impossibility and impracticability of performance constitute legal excuses for non-performance. Impossibility excuses contractual non-performance found to be impossible by supervening causes beyond the control and not foreseeable by either party, such as weather[102] or acts of the government. Impracticability, also called "practical impossibility,"

---

which may discharge the surety to the extent of the overpayment. *See* Part VII.C, *infra*.

100 *See Miller v. City of Broken Arrow*, 660 F.2d 450 (10th Cir. 1981).

101 *See Bignold v. King County*, 399 P.2d 611 (Wash. 1965).

102 A classic illustration of impracticability due to weather was presented in *Northern Corporation v. Chugach Electric Ass'n*, 518 P.2d 76 (Alaska 1974), in which the contractor was unable to complete performance of the contract to repair a dam. Although the contract contemplated that the contractor would haul crushed rock to the dam site, the contract was silent about the site access. The mountainous terrain surrounding the lake made rock hauling across winter ice the only practical method for getting access to the site. After the contractor was prevented by ice conditions over two winters from hauling the rock across the ice, the contractor sought to be excused from contract performance because of impracticability. The Alaska Supreme Court agreed with the contractor.

excuses non-performance of contracts made impossible "as a practical matter" because they only can be performed at an excessive or unreasonable cost. "Practical impossibility" thus excuses non-performance of the contracts actually possible but commercially impracticable within the basic contract objectives contemplated by the parties.[103]

G. The Owner's Implied Waiver of Contract Requirements

The owner may impliedly waive requirements of the contract and thereafter may be estopped to compel a contractor to perform in conformance with those requirements. Waiver due to knowledge of and acquiescence in deviations or due to an express course of dealing have long been recognized.[104] Waiver of the contract completion date by taking no action to terminate the contractor's performance and in encouraging the contractor to perform also has long been recognized.[105] The owner also may waive work requirements and specifications through a course of dealing of accepting nonconforming work.[106]

---

103 *See Transatlantic Financing Corp. v. United States*, 363 F.2d 312, 315 (D.C. Cir. 1966):

> The doctrine of [practical impossibility] ultimately represents the ever-shifting line, drawn by courts hopefully responsive to commercial practices and mores, at which the community's interest in having contracts enforced according to their terms is outweighed by the commercial senselessness of requiring performance....

104 *See Allen & O'Hara, Inc. v. Barrett Wrecking, Inc.*, 898 F.2d 512 (7th Cir. 1990); *Transpower Constructors v. Grand River Dam Auth.*, 905 F.2d 1413 (10th Cir. 1990).

105 *See Devito v. United States*, 413 F.2d 1147 (Ct. Cl. 1969).

106 *See Miller Elevator Co. v. United States*, 30 F. Claims 662 (1994); *Hannon Elec. Co. v. United States*, 31 Fed. Cl. 135 (1994). In *Hannon*, the United States Court of Federal Claims expressly adopted the doctrine of constructive waiver of specifications in situations where the government administered an initially unambiguous contract in such a way as to give the contractor the impression that the contract requirements had been waived.

H. The Owner's Insistence Upon Strict Compliance In the Face of Economic Waste

Owners are entitled to require contractors to comply with contract specifications.[107] The owner's right to insist upon strict compliance is not unlimited, however, and is circumscribed sharply by the doctrine of economic waste.[108] An owner is not permitted to require the replacement of nonconforming work where the cost of correction is economically wasteful, and the work is otherwise adequate for its intended purpose.[109]

I. Hypertechnical Inspection

Owner insistence upon contractor conformance to standards more rigorous than those set forth in the plans and specifications is improper. Contractor failure to comply with such excessive standards cannot serve as a basis for termination of the contract for default. The issue of excessive standards frequently arises in situations where the owners' field

---

107 *See Elastomeric Roofing Associates, Inc. v. United States*, 26 Cl. Ct. 1106 (1992); *Farwell Co. v. United States*, 148 F. Supp. 947 (Ct. Cl. 1957).

108 *See Young & Jacobs v. Kent*, 129 N.E. 889 (N.Y. 1921).

109 Illustrative of this point is *Granite Constr. Co. v. United States*, 962 F.2d 998 (Fed. Cir. 1992). In this case, the government insisted that the contractor remove and replace a nonconforming water stop already embedded in the vertical "cold joints" between monolithic concrete slabs poured in place to serve as the walls of a lock and dam on the Mississippi River. The contractor protested that the water stop, although not strictly conforming to the specification, was nevertheless adequate for intended purposes. The government, invoking strict compliance, insisted that the water stop be removed and replaced at a cost to the contractor of more than $3.8 million. At trial, the contractor successfully proved that the water stop exceeded by more than twenty times the project safety margin and could withstand water pressure more than forty times that which would ever exist. Under the circumstances, the United States Court of Appeals for the Federal Circuit ruled that the government's insistence upon strict compliance constituted economic waste and that the contractor was entitled to recover the $3.8 million cost incurred to replace the water stop.

inspectors insist that the work meet new standards or tests not clearly spelled out in the contract.[110]

J. Fraud or Duress

Fraud or duress on the part of the owner that induces the contractor to enter into a contract or waive contract rights is a defense that can be relied upon by the surety.[111]

K. Release or Settlement of Claims

The owner's release or compromise of claims against the contractor will also release the surety. Many construction contracts provide that the owner's final payment will release owner claims except those expressly reserved.[112] During the course of contract performance, disputes also are settled and compromised. The surety should look carefully into the issues of release and settlement.[113] For example, have the owner and

---

110 *See State v. Buckner Constr. Co.*, 704 S.W.2d 837 (Tex. Ct. App. 1985). In this case, the state hypertechnically inspected work under a contract for the painting of structural steel on 27 highway bridges. Although the specifications required that loose paint be removed by sandblasting, the owner's field inspectors insisted upon complete removal of all paint, to the bare steel, and utilized non-specified tests to determine compliance. Such non-specified tests included taping adhesive tape to the bridge steel, pulling the tape off, and then insisting that the contractor keep blasting if any flecks of paint were seen on the underside of the tape. At trial, the jury concluded that the owner's hypertechnical inspection constituted a breach of contract and awarded the contractor a "total cost" recovery exceeding by almost three times the original contract price.

111 *See Taylor & Jennings, Inc. v. Bellino Bros. Constr. Co.*, 393 N.Y.S.2d 203 (N.Y. Sup. Ct. 1977) (holding that a surety for a subcontractor could assert the defense of fraud in the inducement against the contractor's claim on the performance bond).

112 *See, e.g.*, American Institute of Architects Document A201, General Conditions of Contract for Construction ¶ 4.3.5 (1987).

113 *See Nix v. Henry C. Beck Co.*, 572 So. 2d 1214 (Ala. 1990). In *Nix*, the Supreme Court of Alabama upheld the release of an owner's $1.5 million claim against the contractor who installed asbestos fireproofing material during the construction of a shopping mall. The owner's claim was barred

contractor entered into a new agreement during the course of construction as a result of certain conditions encountered. A surety may be released as of a result of a novation.[114] Conversely, duress by the owner can serve as a basis for setting aside a contractor's waiver and release of claim.[115]

L. The Contractor's Dispute Resolution Rights Against the Owner

Contract provisions relating to resolution of disputes may be important defensively to sureties. Most standard construction contracts provide for arbitration or other forms of alternate dispute resolution procedure, such as dispute review boards or mediation, to resolve construction disputes. The almost universal use of nonjudicial forums for resolution of construction disputes is encouraged by the widely-held perception that technically complex matters should not be submitted for decision to local courts or juries. Because the sureties' performance bond invariably references and incorporates the bonded contract, courts routinely allow sureties to arbitrate performance bond disputes with owners and grant sureties stays of judicial proceedings pending arbitration of disputes between contractors and owners under bonded contracts.[116]

---

by a broad general release executed by the owner as part of an earlier $2,000 settlement of certain sprinkler system problems. The court ruled that the broad general release was sufficient to release all claims related to the project.

114 *See, Fidelity Deposit Co. of Maryland v. Olney Assoc., Inc.*, 530 A.2d 1 (Md. Ct. Spec. App. 1987); *Zuni Constr. Co., Inc. v. Great American Ins. Co.*, 468 P.2d 980 (Nev. 1970); *MacKenzie Lab, Inc. v. Lawrence*, 80 F. Supp. 710 (D. Md. 1948).

115 *See Willms Trucking Co., Inc. v. J.W. Constr. Co., Inc.*, 442 S.E.2d 197 (S.C. Ct. App. 1994). In this case, the South Carolina Court of Appeals set aside for duress a contractor's waiver and release of lien because the owner took advantage of the contractor's extreme financial pressure to pay its subcontractors and suppliers by paying the contractor much less than it would have been entitled to for certain extra work.

116 *See Hoffman v. Fidelity & Deposit Co. of Maryland*, 734 F. Supp. 192 (D.N.J. 1990); *Commercial Union Ins. Co. v. Gilbane Bldg. Co.*, 992 F.2d 386 (1st Cir. 1993); *Thomas O'Connor & Co. v. Insurance Co. of North America*, 697 F. Supp. 563 (D. Mass. 1988).

Arbitration of disputes between owner and contractor under the bonded contract is particularly advantageous to the surety where the disputes otherwise would be decided by a local jury likely to be sympathetic to the owner's termination claims.[117]

VII.
Surety Defenses

In addition to its "contractor defenses" the surety is entitled to the protection of its own "surety defenses."

A. Alteration of the Bonded Contract

Historically, sureties were favored by the law and were entitled to have the terms of their bonds strictly enforced. Courts routinely held that any alteration to the bonded contract, whether material or not, served to discharge the surety's obligation.[118] The more recent authorities hold that only material changes to the underlying contract which prejudice the surety will operate to discharge the surety to the extent of the prejudice.[119] This is the result of provisions in most modern performance

---

117 *See Osceola County Rural Water System, Inc. v. Subsurfco, Inc.*, 914 F.2d 1072 (8th Cir. 1990). In this case, a nonprofit owner that operated a rural water system commenced suit against the contractor and its surety in a rural Iowa court seeking $7.2 million to reconstruct a 680-mile rural water distribution system that was losing approximately 40% of the water pumped into the system due to leaks. The owner demanded trial by jury in a county served by the troubled water system. When the contractor demanded arbitration, the court litigation was stayed. In the arbitration, three arbitrators with extensive construction experience concluded that the contractor had installed the pipeline in accordance with the owner's design specifications, and that the leakage was attributable to deficiencies in the specifications. The arbitrators therefore denied the owner's entire claim and awarded the contractor its contract retainage. The surety ultimately closed its file without any loss.

118 *See, e.g., Congregation Ohavei Shalom, Inc. v. Comyns Bros., Inc.*, 507 N.Y.S.2d 28, 29 (N.Y. App. Div. 1986).

119 *See, e.g., United States Fidelity & Guaranty Co. v. United States*, 298 F. 365 (D.C. Cir. 1924) (surety released only to the extent of the cost of the contract modifications); *Equitable Fire & Marine Ins. Co. v. Tiernan Bldg.*

bonds which require the surety to waive its right to object to changes in or extensions of the bonded contract.[120] Even if a particular bond contains the standard waiver language, the surety can argue that it is entitled to be discharged to the extent that its rights are prejudiced by "cardinal" changes in the underlying contract.

In summary, mere alteration of the bonded contract is usually insufficient to discharge the obligations of a compensated corporate surety. If the surety has not waived its right to object to alterations and can prove that the alteration is both material and prejudicial, it may be able to obtain a discharge to the extent it is prejudiced. Only in circumstances where a cardinal change has occurred can the surety successfully argue for complete discharge.[121]

B. Changes in the Obligee or the Principal

Modern corporate sureties have a right to be concerned about a prejudicial increase in risk when the change involves the contracting parties. Unless the bond contains language specifically prohibiting assignment, a change in the obligee by virtue of assignment does not usually discharge the surety.[122] Similarly, a mere change in the form of the bond principal (*i.e.*, from sole proprietorship to partnership or from partnership to corporation) normally will not serve to discharge the surety. Sureties should remain alert to circumstances in which the bond principal

---

Corp., 190 So. 2d 197 (Fla. Dist. Ct. App. 1966) (same); *Zuni Constr. Co. v. Great American Ins. Co.*, 468 P.2d 980 (Nev. 1970) (surety discharged only to the extent that its risk was materially increased).

120 *See, e.g.*, American Institute of Architects Document A311 ("The surety hereby waives notice of any alteration or extension of time made by the owner."). Historically, an extension of time for performance of the bonded contract could operate to discharge the surety. However, sureties now find it extremely difficult to demonstrate prejudice caused by an extension of time. Moreover, since most bonds require sureties to waive their objections to time extensions, this potential defense is no longer significant. *See Kaplan, supra* note 2, at 17-19 (noting that the extension of time defense "appears to be all but extinct").

121 See Part VI.E.3, *supra* (discussing cardinal changes).

122 *Hunters Pointe Partners Ltd. v. United States Fidelity & Guaranty Co.*, 442 N.W.2d 778 (Mich. 1989).

undertakes, with the consent of the obligee, to complete the bonded contract through a joint venture with an unbonded entity. This situation could expose the surety to increased risk of loss, especially if the surety has no knowledge of or confidence in the quality of the work performed by the unbonded entity.

On the other hand, if the obligee allows the principal to substitute another contractor and then releases the principal from further liability, the surety is likewise discharged.[123] Similarly, if the principal attempts to assign its contractual obligations under the bonded contract while remaining secondarily liable as a guarantor, the surety may be entitled to discharge if it can demonstrate that performance by the assignee will materially increase the risk of its bonded obligation.[124]

C. Improper Payment of Contract Funds by the Obligee

Improper payment of contract funds by the obligee is a defense which rarely allows the surety to obtain a full discharge but which often allows the surety to reduce *pro tanto* the cost of its performance obligation.[125] Under most types of bonds, the surety's obligation to perform is conditioned upon the obligee having fully performed its obligations under the bonded contract. One of the obligee's primary obligations is to release payments to the principal in accordance with the terms of the contract.[126]

Most construction contracts provide for progress payments to be made only upon certification by the contractor and the architect that the work

---

123 *See*, Part VI., K., *supra*.

124 *See Leia Hospital & Health Center v. Xonics Medical Systems, Inc.*, 948 F.2d 271 (6th Cir. 1991). *See generally*, Anno. 69 A.L.R.3d 567 (1976).

125 *See, e.g., Nat'l Union Indemnity Co. v. G. E. Bass & Co.*, 369 F.2d 75, 77 (5th Cir. 1966) (stating that the "modern rule" allows a surety to be discharged from its performance bond obligations to the extent that it suffers injury as a result of the obligee's overpayments). *But see Southwood Bldrs., Inc. v. Peerless Ins. Co.*, 366 S.E.2d 104, 107 (Ga. 1988) (holding that surety was entitled to complete discharge as a result of obligee's overpayments).

126 *See, e.g., Southwood Bldrs.*, 366 S.E.2d at 107; *Airtrol Eng. Co. v. United States Fidelity & Guaranty Co.*, 345 So. 2d 1271, 1273 (La. Ct. App. 1977) (the bonding company is entitled to expect that payments will be made in accordance with the contract).

has actually been completed and require the obligee to withhold ten percent of each payment as retainage until all the work is completed. Many contracts also require the contractor to obtain consent of the surety prior to the obligee releasing final payment. The obligee's failure to adhere to these contractual payment requirements, by making progress payments before the work is completed, by paying for work which the obligee knew or should have known was defective, by prematurely releasing the contract retainage, or by making final payment without the required consent of surety will serve to discharge the surety's performance obligation to the extent that the surety is injured as a result.[127]

For the surety to prevail on an overpayment defense, it must demonstrate that it has suffered an injury as a result of the overpayment. Thus, the surety may not be entitled to a partial discharge if the obligee can demonstrate that prematurely-released funds were used to purchase labor or materials which contributed to the completion of the project.[128] One court has gone so far as to require the surety to prove that the prematurely-released funds were not used to benefit the project.[129] Finally, the obligee may be able to defend against a claim of improper payment by claiming that it relied in good faith upon the certification of progress approved by the architect or engineer.[130] In cases where the obligee claims to have relied upon the reasonable, albeit incorrect, certification

---

127 *See, e.g., Ohio Cas. Ins. Co. v. United States.*, 12 Cl. Ct. 590, 596 (1987) (holding that surety was discharged to the extent that government had properly failed to terminate contractor and improperly released contract funds to contractor); *Central Towers Apartments, Inc. v. Martin*, 543 S.E.2d 789, 797 (Tenn. Ct. App. 1969) (holding that surety was discharged to the extent that owner prematurely released contract retainage to contractor); *Merchants Bonding Co. v. Pima County*, 860 P.2d 510 (Ariz. Ct. App. 1993) (holding that surety was entitled to recover as damages the amount of final payment where the obligee had released final payment to the principal without the surety's consent and over the surety's protest).

128 *See Transamerica Ins. Co. v. City of Kennewick*, 785 F.2d 660, 661 (9th Cir. 1986).

129 *See Firemens Fund Ins. Co. v. United States*, 15 Cl. Ct. 225 (1988).

130 *See Argonaut Ins. Co. v. Town of Cloverdale*, 669 F.2d 417, 419-20 (7th Cir. 1983).

of the architect or engineer, the surety may wish to consider pursuing a claim against the architect or engineer for negligence.[131]

In summary, to the extent that the obligee fails to fulfill its contractual obligations by improperly releasing payments to the principal, the surety is entitled to be partially discharged. The extent of the surety's discharge will depend upon the surety's ability to demonstrate an actual injury as a result of the obligee's overpayment.

D. Statutory Defenses

A number of states have enacted suretyship codes which give sureties specific rights vis-a-vis the principal and the obligee. These statutes typically allow the surety to demand that the obligee commence suit against the principal before pursuing the surety[132] or specify circumstances under which the surety will be exonerated from its performance bond obligations.[133] These statutory rights can be extremely valuable

---

131 *See City of Houma v. Municipal & Industrial Pipe Service*, 884 F.2d 886 (5th Cir. 1989) (holding engineering firm liable to surety for negligent certification of progress payments).

132 *See, e.g.*, Mo. Rev. Stat. § 433.010 (1992) ("Any person bound as surety for another in any bond ... may, at any time after an action has accrued thereon, require, in writing, a person having such right of action forthwith to commence suit against the principal debtor and other parties liable"); Okla. Stat. tit. 15, § 379 (1993) ("A surety may require his creditor to proceed against the principal, or to pursue any other remedy in his power which the surety cannot himself pursue, and which would lighten his burden...."); Cal. Civil Code § 2845 (1993) ("A surety may require the creditor, ... to proceed against the principal, or to pursue any other remedy in the creditor's power which the surety cannot pursue, and which would lighten the surety's burden...."); *see also A. J. Kellos Constr. Co. v. Balboa Ins. Co.*, 661 F.2d 402 (5th Cir. 1981) (holding that obligee's failure to comply with a similar Georgia statute, requiring the obligee to initiate legal action against the principal prior to pursuing the surety, entitled surety to be discharged from its performance bond obligations).

133 For example, Okla. Stat. tit. 15, § 377 provides:

> A surety is exonerated:
>
> 1. In like manner with a guarantor;
> 2. To the extent to which he is prejudiced by any act of the creditor which would naturally prove injurious to the reme-

to the surety, particularly in situations where the principal has filed for bankruptcy and may not be easily amenable to suit. Thus, the surety should always be aware of the law applicable to its bonded obligation and should investigate the scope and availability of these statutory rights.[134]

E. Notice

Many private construction bonds contain language requiring the obligee to notify either or both the surety and principal of its claim. The issue of whether the obligee has given adequate notice generally arises in the context of payment bond claims.[135] Nevertheless, a performance bond surety may very well be entitled to a defense based upon untimely or insufficient notice, depending upon the language of the bond or governing statutory or common law.[136] This issue may arise in the context of whether the obligee has met the requirement of declaring the principal in default. Correspondence or other contacts from an obligee expressing dissatisfaction with the principal's performance may not be

---

dies of the surety or inconsistent with his rights, or which lessens his security; or,

3. To the extent which he is prejudiced by an omission of the creditors to do anything, when required by the surety, which it is his duty to do.

134 Determining what law is applicable to the surety's obligation is not always a simple matter and is a topic far too broad for this chapter. Nevertheless, the surety should always look to the language of the bond and the underlying construction contract (which is usually incorporated into the bond) to see if either contains a choice of law provision.

135 *See* PAYMENT BOND MANUAL (Edward G. Gallagher ed., 1991).

136 AIA Document A312 states that the surety's obligation arises only after, among other things:

> The owner has notified the contractor and the surety ... that the owner is considering declaring a contractor default and has requested and attempted to arrange a conference with the contractor and the surety to be held not later than 15 days after receipt of such notice to discuss methods of performing the construction contract....

American Institute of Architects Document A312 at ¶ 3.1.

sufficient to trigger the surety's obligation as no declaration of default has occurred.[137]

If the bond does not contain language specifically providing that the obligee must notify the surety of a default by the principal, the surety may be deemed to take notice of its principal's default.[138] Still, obligees must be concerned about giving the surety adequate notice of their principal's default, even in the absence of specific language requiring notice. Sureties have successfully argued that an implied condition of a performance bond is the obligee's obligation to notify the surety of the principal's defaults and give it the opportunity to remedy them.[139]

F. Contractual and Statutory Limitations

Most performance bonds contain language specifying the period of time within which an obligee must commence suit against the surety. The AIA Document A311 requires suit to be instituted before the expiration of two years from the date on which final payment under the contract falls due. AIA Document A312 requires suit to be instituted within two years after contractor default, or within two years after the contractor ceased working, or within two years after the surety refuses or fails to perform its obligations under the bond, whichever occurs first.

A number of states have enacted statutes which nullify a private party's attempts at shortening contractual limitations.[140] As a consequence, in certain jurisdictions a surety may find that it is unable to rely

---

137 *See L&A Contracting Co. v. Southern Concrete Services, Inc.*, 17 F.3d 106 (5th Cir. 1994) (surety's obligation never arose as obligee never claimed principal to be in default although it requested surety fulfill the contract so as to prevent further delays).

138 *See Continental Bank & Trust Co. v. American Bonding Co.*, 605 F.2d 1049 (8th Cir. 1979); *Insta/Com, Inc. v. Aetna Casualty & Surety Co.*, 589 S.W.2d 494 (Tex. Ct. App. 1979); *United States v. Ohio Casualty Ins. Co.*, 399 F.2d 387 (6th Cir. 1968).

139 *See Blackhawk Heating & Plumbing Co. v. Seaboard Surety Co.*, 534 F. Supp. 309 (N.D. Ill. 1982).

140 *See, e.g.*, Miss. Code Ann. § 15-1-5 (1972); Fla. Stat. Ann. § 95.03 (1982).

upon its contractual limitation provision.[141] In the absence of a statute specifically invalidating a contractual limitation provision, the clause will be upheld if the period of time provided is reasonable.[142] As a practical matter, most case law supports the view that a limitation period of 12 months from the accrual of the cause of action on a bond is reasonable.[143] Even limitations periods as short as six months have been upheld.[144]

Performance bonds issued in connection with a public work are governed by the applicable state's public works statute. Most jurisdictions will incorporate into statutory bonds the terms and conditions mandated for such bonds by the applicable public works act.[145] When the terms of the bond conflict with the requirements of the public works statute, the statutory terms will control if the project is determined to be a public work.[146] An exception to this rule occurs where the terms of the bond provide greater protection than the statute. In these cases, the bond

---

141 *See Sheehan v. Morris Irrigation*, 410 N.W.2d 569 (S.D. 1987) (South Dakota's law was subsequently changed to reflect the fact that subjecting sureties to long statutes of limitations periods was counterproductive as less bonding credit became available for contractors due to the long exposure times).

142 *See, e.g., United Commercial Travelers v. Wolfe*, 331 U.S. 586, 608 (1947).

143 *See, e.g., Camelot Excavating Co. v. St. Paul Ins. Co.*, 301 N.W.2d 275 (Mich. 1981); *1616 Reminic Limited Partnership v. Atchison & Keller Co.*, 14 Bankr. Rep. 484 (1981); *Burlew v. Fidelity & Casualty Co.*, 64 F.2d 976 (6th Cir. 1933), *cert. denied*, 290 U.S. 686 (1933); *Meyer v. Building & Realty Service Co.*, 196 N.E. 250 (Ind. 1935).

144 *Fitger Brewing Co. v. American Bonding Co.*, 149 N.W. 539 (Minn. 1914); *Ilse v. Aetna Indemnity Co.*, 125 P. 780 (Wash. 1912).

145 *See, e.g., Farm Bureau Mutual Ins. Co. v. Wright*, 686 S.W.2d 778 (Ark. 1985); *C.P.S. Distributors, Inc. v. Federal Insurance Co.*, 685 P.2d 783 (Colo. Ct. App. 1984); *American Druggists Ins. v. Thompson Lumber Co.*, 349 N.W.2d 569 (Minn. Ct. App. 1984); *Felix Contracting Corp. v. Federal Insurance Co.*, 468 N.Y.S.2d 39 (N.Y. App. Div. 1983).

146 *See, e.g., Wichita Sheetmetal Supply, Inc. v. Dahlstrom & Ferrell Const. Co.*, 792 P.2d 1043 (Kan. 1990); *Sheldon Pollack Corp. v. Pioneer Concrete of Texas, Inc.*, 765 S.W.2d 843 (Tex. Ct. App. 1989); *Grimes v. Bosque County*, 240 S.W.2d 511 (Tex. Ct. App. 1951).

generally will be interpreted in accordance with the more generous terms.[147] Sometimes it is difficult to determine whether the project in question is private or public.[148] It can be particularly difficult to determine the nature of a project if there is both private and public participation in the undertaking.

If the bond does not contain a contractual limitation provision, or if that provision is deemed unreasonable under state law and the bonded project is not public, then the state's statute of limitations provision applicable to contract actions will most likely apply. The bond's contractual limitation provision/statutory limitation will often have the effect of cutting off any argument that the surety is liable for latent defects or extended warranty obligations.[149]

There may be times when the statute of limitations applicable to the surety is longer than that for its principal. In these cases, the surety quite naturally would seek to be relieved of its obligation on the grounds that its liability is no greater than that of its principal and because its principal cannot be found liable to the obligee nor can the surety.[150] Sureties generally have been able to successfully assert their principal's statute of limitations defenses.[151] Still, sureties have been subject to suit where the statute of limitations has run with respect to their principal in instances

---

147 *See, e.g., Nelson Roofing & Contracting, Inc. v. C.W. Moore Co.*, 245 N.W.2d 866 (Minn. 1976); *American Casualty Co. v. Irvin*, 426 F.2d 647 (5th Cir. 1970); *Reliance Ins. Co. v. Trane Co.*, 184 S.E.2d 817 (Va. 1971); *but see Transamerica Ins. Co. v. Housing Authority*, 669 S.W.2d 818 (Tex. Ct. App. 1984).

148 *See* O'Connor, *Statutory Bonds or Common-Law Bonds: The Public-Private Dilemma*, 29 TORT & INS. L. J., 77 (1993).

149 *See School Board of DeSoto County v. Safety Ins. Co.*, 434 So. 2d 38 (Fla. App. 1983); *Kiva Const. and Engineering, Inc. v. International Fidelity Ins. Co.*, 749 F. Supp. 753 (W.D. La. 1990).

150 *See State v. Bi-States Constr. Co., Inc.*, 269 N.W.2d 455 (Iowa 1978) (statute of limitations ran against the principal, therefore, surety also not liable).

151 *See County of Hudson v. Terminal Constr. Corp.*, 381 A.2d 355 (N.J. 1977); *see also* Thomas & Leo, *Application of Statutes of Limitation Governing Construction Activity to Construction Bond Sureties*, 10 *The Construction Lawyer* (Jan. 1990).

where there is a separate statute of limitations governing suretyship arrangements.[152]

G. Fraud

Fraud or misrepresentation by the obligee which induces the surety to issue the bond will generally result in the surety's obligation being voidable.[153] If the misrepresentation is by someone other than the obligee, the obligee must know or have reason to know of the misrepresentation.[154] For example, if the obligee knows that the principal is in deep financial difficulty or is already in default on other obligations and fails to tell the surety, this failure to disclose can give rise to a discharge of the surety's obligations.[155] If the principal and surety fail to disclose all material facts to the surety, thereby inducing it to issue the bond, the surety is entitled to be relieved of its obligations. For example, if the obligee and principal know that the surety would not issue a bond covering the full contract price due to the principal's limited bond credit and work out an arrangement whereby only a portion of the work is bonded without telling the surety of the true scope of the entire undertaking, the surety is entitled to discharge.[156]

VIII. Performance Options

After carefully considering all the issues and possible defenses described above, the surety ultimately must decide whether or not to

---

152 *See Regents of the University of California v. Hartford Accident & Indemnity Co.*, 147 Cal. Rptr. 486, 581 P.2d 197 (Cal. 1978); *Bellevue School District v. Brazier Constr. Co.*, 691 P.2d 178 (Wash. 1984).

153 *See* RESTATEMENT (SECOND) CONTRACTS § 164 (1981); *Marine Bank, N.A. v. Meat Counter, Inc.*, 826 F.2d 1577 (7th Cir. 1987).

154 *See* RESTATEMENT (SECOND) CONTRACTS § 164 (1981), comment e; RESTATEMENT OF SECURITY § 119 (1941), comment a; *G&S Foods, Inc. v. Vavaroutsos*, 438 F. Supp. 122 (N.D. (Ill. 1977).

155 *See St. Paul Fire & Marine Ins. Co. v. Commodity Credit Corp.*, 646 F.2d 1064 (5th Cir. 1981).

156 *See Employers of Wausau v. Construction Managers of Florida*, 377 S.E.2d 119 (S.C. Ct. App. 1989).

perform. If the surety decides not to perform, it should communicate this decision to the obligee as soon as possible, setting forth all the reasons it believes performance is not required, and should be prepared to defend itself in the litigation which will almost inevitably result. However, if the surety elects to perform, it may have a variety of performance options which it will need to evaluate.[157] In the chapters that follow, the surety's primary performance options, and the advantages and disadvantages of each, are discussed in detail. Following is a brief overview of these options.

A. Financing

One of the surety's performance options is to finance the principal's completion of the project by paying its bills as they accrue. This performance option is most attractive to the surety when (1) the majority of the work on the project has already been completed; (2) the obligee has made no complaints about the quality of the principal's work; and (3) the surety believes that the principal's default was caused primarily by temporary cash flow problems. The main advantage of this performance option is that, when done properly, it allows the surety to fulfill its obligations at very low cost. The major disadvantages of this option are that it exposes the surety to open-ended liability beyond the penal sum of its bond,[158] and exposes the surety to claims (by the principal's creditors or the principal itself) of "domination" of the principal, which can lead to liability for damages beyond the scope of the project itself.[159] Thus, before undertaking to finance the principal, the surety should be convinced of its principal's integrity and competence and should be certain that the project can be easily completed with a limited expenditure of funds.

---

157 Of course, if the surety has entered into a completion bond, a statutory bond, or a specialized manuscript bond, it may have little or no option regarding the manner of performance. *See* Part III, *supra*.

158 *See id.* at 7-7.

159 *See* Gilbert J. Schroeder, *Providing Financial Support to the Contractor*, 5 FORUM 1190, 1195 (1982) (discussing the problem of surety domination in the context of principal financing).

B. Takeover

After the principal's contract has been terminated by the obligee, the surety can enter into a takeover agreement with the obligee in which the surety agrees to complete the project using either a completion contractor or construction manager. This option is most attractive to the surety when the project is nearly complete and completion by the principal is no longer prudent or possible. The primary advantage of this performance option is its potential to minimize the surety's costs. However, like the financing option, once a surety agrees to take over the project, its ultimate liability will no longer be limited by the penal sum of its bond. In negotiating takeover agreements, sureties will often try to get the obligee to agree to a limit to the surety's exposure. However, the obligee is under no obligation to enter into such an agreement. In sum, takeover by the surety has many of the same risks and rewards as financing the bond principal. The surety should consider takeover only when it is confident that the project can be completed with little difficulty.

C. Tender

When a default termination occurs at an early stage of the project, the surety may consider tendering a sum of money to the obligee in full and final settlement of all claims. In the worst case, the amount tendered would be equal to the penal sum of the bond. However, if the obligee is in a situation where it needs an immediate cash infusion, it might be willing to release the surety in exchange for an amount of money less than the full penal sum. The primary advantage of this option is that it ends the surety's obligations quickly and at a fixed cost. The main disadvantages of this option are its expense and the possibility that the bond principal and/or indemnitors will later argue that the surety's tender was premature and excessive, thereby forfeiting the surety's right to seek indemnification. Thus, the surety should carefully evaluate the amount it is willing to tender to the obligee and, when possible, should obtain the principal's consent before tendering.

D. Completion by the Obligee

Finally, the surety can fulfill its performance bond obligations by (1) obtaining bids from other contractors to complete the work; (2) having the low bidder enter into a separate contract with the obligee, providing the obligee with a new performance bond; (3) paying to the obligee a sum of money equal to the difference between the original contract price and the completion contract price, up to the penal sum of the bond; and (4) obtaining a full release from the obligee.

The main advantage of allowing the obligee to complete the contract itself with a new contractor is that it allows the surety to limit its losses and, to a certain extent, shifts the risk of completion from itself to the surety for the completion contractor. The main disadvantages of this option are the up-front expenses which must be incurred by the surety in putting together bid packages and obtaining bids, the fact that the cost of a bonded completion contract usually exceeds the cost of the original contract by a substantial amount, and the fact that the obligee may refuse to accept a completion contractor, particularly when the obligee is a public entity. Since most obligees would prefer to hold the surety liable until the project is actually completed, the obligee may reject this option unless the bond language specifically provides for it. Of course, the surety is always free to negotiate with the obligee in an effort to convince them to accept the completion contractor with its new performance bond.

IX.
Conclusion

The complexities of modern construction, combined with the myriad rights and obligations of the surety, obligee and principal, create conditions conducive to "high stakes" mistakes. Identification of material breaches of contract require careful technical and legal analysis. The decision to terminate, because it involves substantial forfeiture, must be considered even more carefully. Ordinarily, contract termination should be a measure of last resort. Obligees who choose to exercise this "final solution" must do so "by the book." The obligee's motive must be pure, its notice of default clear, its grounds for default specific, its afforded opportunity to "cure" fair and reasonable, and its right to terminate not waived by inconsistent conduct or obviated by prior breach. Upon receipt of an obligee's notice of default and demand for performance, the surety must answer the most demanding and risky of questions: "To perform or not to perform?" The myriad contractor and surety defenses must be considered promptly, giving consideration to the competing positions of both the obligee and the principal. Prompt investigation and careful consideration of the facts in relation to the myriad of defenses, tempered with good faith and fair dealing and leading to correct conclusions, are the surety's constant goals.

CHAPTER 4

FINANCING THE PRINCIPAL

George J. Bachrach

I. Introduction

The goal of any surety handling a claim is to perform the surety's obligations under its bonds in a fair, efficient, and economical manner. When faced with a claim against its performance bond, one of the surety's alternatives is to finance the principal. The surety's objective in financing the principal is to remedy a potential or existing default, and to avoid a

* The author of this chapter wishes to acknowledge that, in addition to my own thoughts, I have liberally stolen material from many prior authors on the subject of surety financing of the principal. These prior authors and their works are listed in the Selected Readings on Surety Financing of the Principal attached to this chapter. Without their leads and prior efforts, this chapter would have been much more difficult to create. With the wealth of talent before me, there was no sense in completely reinventing the wheel.

Where my thefts have been so blatant and egregious that they cannot possibly be covered up, I have given appropriate credit in the footnotes.

termination of the principal's right to proceed under the bonded contracts.[1]

Financing can be defined as the surety providing direct or indirect financial assistance to the principal in the hope that the obligations secured by the performance bond will be completed by the principal. As described below in this chapter, the surety's direct or indirect financial assistance can take several forms.

This chapter concerning the financing of the principal as a means of handling a claim against the surety's performance bond will address a number of issues, including: the information and analysis necessary prior to financing the principal; the methods of financing the principal; the surety's right to finance the principal; the advantages and disadvantages in financing the principal as opposed to other completion options; financing the subcontractor principal; the procedures and mechanics for financing the principal; financing the principal in bankruptcy; the risks to the surety beyond the penal sum of its performance bond; and the subrogation rights of the performance bond surety financing the principal.

---

1 This chapter will not attempt to subjectively analyze the surety's alternative of financing the principal as a means of handling performance bond claims. However, other commentators has been willing to express their views. For example, one set of commentators have described financing the principal as "the most controversial and most maligned of the completion options available to the performance bond surety. This is because financing is not a panacea but a danger-filled mine field which can lead to disaster.... In deciding whether to finance, the surety's natural prejudice should be not to take this step. This prejudice occurs because the arguments in favor of financing are much more persuasive and compelling in theory than they are in practice." Thomas A. Joyce and William F. Haug, *Financing the Contractor*, *in* BOND DEFAULT MANUAL 21 (Richard S. Wisner ed., 1987) (hereinafter referred to as *Joyce and Haug*). Another commentator has stated that "[f]inancing is always a potentially dangerous course of action." Gilbert J. Schroeder, *Procedures and Instruments Utilized to Protect the Surety Who Finances a Contractor*. 14 FORUM 830, 868 (1979) (hereinafter referred to as *Schroeder No. 1*). "Financing is dangerous." Gilbert J. Schroeder, *Providing Financial Support to the Contractor*. 17 FORUM 1190, 1205 (1982) (hereinafter referred to as *Schroeder No. 2*).

II.
Overview—Information And Analysis Necessary Prior To The Surety's Financing The Principal

Chapters 2 and 3 of these materials go into great detail concerning the information that must be gathered during the surety's investigation when there is a performance bond default, and the analysis the surety must perform prior to deciding how to fulfill its performance bond obligations. During the initial underwriting process and prior to executing bonds on behalf of the principal, the surety reviews the three "C's"—the *cash*, *capacity* and *character* of the principal. When faced with the decision on whether to finance the principal, the surety must review and analyze the information collected during the investigation process, and revisit the three "C's" along with a fourth "C"—the *collateral* of the principal and the indemnitors.

A. Cash

1. How Much?

It is obvious when a principal seeks financing from the surety that the principal lacks sufficient cash to continue the performance of the work and to pay all bills of laborers and materialmen on the bonded projects. During the surety's investigation and analysis of the information collected, the surety will learn how much cash the principal has. More importantly, the surety will learn how much more cash the principal needs to pay current bills on the bonded projects, to replace payments from obligees that may be delayed because of disputes with the obligees, real or otherwise, and to fund overhead items required to maintain the principal in business. Furthermore, the analysis must be extended to estimate the principal's cash requirements in the future.[2]

---

2 One question that always arises during the surety's initial investigation, but which rarely can be answered until much later, if at all, is where the cash went. Assuming that the principal's bids on the bonded contracts were within an acceptable range for the surety to write the final performance bonds, in theory there should be sufficient cash to complete the performance of the work and to pay all bills of laborers and materialmen on the bonded projects. Since it is the surety's primary objective to fulfill

2. *Other Sources of Cash*

While an analysis of the contract funds from the bonded contracts is critical, there may be other sources of cash. The principal may have lines of credit on which to draw. The principal may have receivables from nonbonded contracts (i.e., contract balances, retainages, and claims) that may be used to pay certain bills, including overhead items. The principal may have real and personal property (i.e., excess equipment) that may be sold to generate additional cash over time. The indemnitors may have cash or assets that can be converted to cash to fund the principal. Unfortunately, the assets of the indemnitors are frequently less liquid (i.e., real property) and may not be readily converted to cash in the time frame necessary to keep the principal functioning. Finally, depending upon the circumstances, banks or other lenders, with or without the surety's guarantee, may be willing to lend funds to the principal.

B. Capacity of the Principal to Perform the Work.

The principal needs financing when it lacks the cash to meet the costs incurred and to be incurred to perform the work on the bonded projects. The surety can provide that cash to the principal in a number of ways. The surety cannot to any meaningful extent improve the principal's capacity to perform the work. Prior to considering financing the principal, the surety must assure itself that the principal is capable of performing the work in the following three areas:

1. *Technical Ability to Perform the Work*

The surety must be confident that the principal has the manpower, and the field construction and home office expertise to perform the work on the bonded projects. For example:

---

its obligations under the performance bonds, an investigation to answer the question of where the cash went must be left to a later date. Except under rare circumstances, the surety will not incur the costs for such an investigation unless it may lead to substantial salvage recoveries. Even if it is obvious that the cash has disappeared under suspicious circumstances, this may or may not affect the surety's decision on whether to finance the principal.

a. Manpower—The surety must believe that the principal can secure the necessary manpower, both in quality and quantity, to perform the work timely;

b. Technical Ability and Construction Expertise—The surety must believe that the principal's project managers, supervisors, foremen, etc. know what they are doing and have the technical construction expertise to perform and complete the work on the bonded projects; and

c. Home Office Expertise—The surety must believe that the backup services at the principal's home office (i.e., accounting expertise, record keeping, etc.) are sufficient and accurate in order to ensure that the principal's progress in performing the work can be measured and computed. The key factors are whether the work performed by the principal is of sufficient quantity to move the bonded projects forward timely and of sufficient quality that it will be accepted by the obligees.

2. Ability to Manage the Work and Supervise the Subcontractors

Along with the technical ability to perform the work, the surety must believe that the principal has the managerial competence and organization, both in the field and in the home office, to manage the work and supervise the subcontractors. The surety must review the relationships between the principal and the obligees and between the principal and its subcontractors and suppliers. If these relationships are in bad shape, the principal's performance of the work may take more time and be more expensive. If the work being performed is not managed properly in a competent, coherent, and organized manner, financing the principal may not obtain the objectives that the surety wants to reach.

3. Ability to Close Out the Bonded Projects

The biggest drain increasing the surety's loss may well rest on the principal's historic ability to close out the bonded projects. The principal's inability to substantially complete the work and close out the bonded projects will extend the time and cost of financing the principal's overhead and general administrative expenses. Increased time equals an increase in the surety's loss.

C. Character of the Principal and the Indemnitors

The character of the principal and the indemnitors, including their honesty, integrity, trustworthiness, and commitment to completing the work on the bonded projects, is critical. Financing the principal is rarely a short term endeavor, especially when there are multiple bonded projects to complete. Surety financing requires constant contact with the principal, at least on a weekly basis. Numerous issues arise, including disputes with obligees, subcontractors, and suppliers, discussions concerning overhead expenses that the principal maintains must be paid, etc. The surety must believe that the principal and the indemnitors are putting forth their best efforts to complete the work on the bonded projects, providing ready access to their books, records, and other necessary information, and attempting to minimize the surety's loss. This does not mean that the principal and the surety will agree on everything. Rather, it means that the surety must have confidence that the principal is trying its best to provide prompt and accurate information and answers to the surety's questions. This is true whether the principal is determined to stay in business in some fashion or acknowledges a wind down situation ultimately resulting in the cessation of the principal's operations.

If, in the opinion of the surety, the principal and the indemnitors lack the honesty, integrity, character, and trustworthiness that is so necessary for a successful financing arrangement, then the surety should immediately stop its consideration of financing the principal.

D. Collateral—The Big Seducer

There are many times when the surety views financing the principal as a viable option, not necessarily because of the capacity or character of the principal and the indemnitors, but because the principal and/or the indemnitors may have collateral security to reduce or eliminate the surety's loss. The surety should be very careful about the seductive qualities that exist when collateral security appears to be available.

The assets and, therefore, the potential collateral security of the principal and the indemnitors are a factor during the underwriting process. However, the underwriting assumption is that the contract funds coming from the bonded contracts should be sufficient to pay the bills incurred on the bonded contracts as well as providing for the payment of the principal's overhead and profit. The importance of cash, and therefore liquidity in the principal, arises because payments from the bonded contracts normally lag behind the principal's practical obligation of funding the construction process. Assuming that the principal has cash, capacity, and character acceptable to the surety, bonds will be executed for the principal without the surety taking collateral security from either the principal or the indemnitors at the time of the execution of the bonds.[3]

The existence of assets to provide collateral security to the surety raises two issues. The first issue is whether the existence of the collateral security is a factor, in and of itself, in the surety's making the decision to finance the principal. The second issue is how to secure the collateral security in the event that the surety has or will incur a loss.

1. Making the Decision

Assuming that the principal has the capacity to perform the work on the bonded projects and the character to merit the surety's financial support, the existence of sufficient assets to provide collateral security to the surety to reduce or eliminate the surety's potential loss becomes a big factor. By taking the collateral security, the surety may not have to initiate an indemnity or exoneration action against the principal and the indemnitors. This avoids an immediate adversarial situation with the principal and the indemnitors, saving the surety time, costs, and energy, and allowing the surety to focus on resolving its performance bond obligations. Furthermore, if losses are incurred, the surety has a readily available source of salvage for those losses. Finally, because the surety is not required to finance the principal, surety financing should be considered to be new value given to the principal and the indemnitors that

---

3 Many sureties require the principal and the indemnitors to provide collateral security at the time the bonds are first executed. Such a surety may be in a different position when determining whether to finance the principal to reduce its loss. Since the surety already has collateral security, there may be no additional incentive to finance the principal. Furthermore, the surety has a cushion against its loss and may be better able to define its loss through another performance bond option rather than a potentially open-ended financing arrangement with the principal. This chapter will assume that no collateral security has been taken by the surety prior to the time that the principal finds itself in financial difficulties and needs financial assistance from the surety.

will allow the liens on the collateral security to remain in effect in the event that the principal and/or the indemnitors subsequently file bankruptcy proceedings. Providing financing in return for collateral security contemporaneously obtained should not be deemed to be a preference under section 547 of the Bankruptcy Code[4] or a fraudulent conveyance under section 548 of the Bankruptcy Code.[5]

2. *Obtaining the Collateral Security*

Early in its investigation, the surety should obtain information from the principal, the indemnitors and other sources concerning the assets of the principal and the indemnitors, including the present lien status (consensual liens, judgment liens, tax liens, etc.) and the value of the assets to the extent that such information exists. Contemporaneous with the execution of the financing agreement and the initial providing of financing, the liens on the collateral security should be secured by the appropriate mortgages and deeds of trust on real estate, and perfected security interests and filed financing statements on personal property.

Two questions that frequently arise with respect to collateral security taken by the surety are:

---

4 11 U.S.C. § 547. *See* Armen Shahinian and Bogda Clarke, M.D., *Anatomy of a Workout Agreement—Extension of Surety Credit to the Troubled Contractor—Financing Considerations, Strategies and Financing Agreement* (unpublished paper submitted to the Surety Claims Institute, Absecon, N.J., on June 23, 1994) (hereinafter referred to as *Shahinian and Clarke*); Robert J. Berens, *Bankruptcy: Can a Surety be Held Liable for the Prepetition Payments Made by its Principal?* (unpublished paper submitted to A.B.A. Tort and Insurance Practice Section Fidelity & Surety Law Committee annual meeting on August 10, 1993); J. Michael Franks and John J. Rowland, *Surety Strategy in the Chapter 11 Proceeding: Case Study of a Broke Contractor* (unpublished paper submitted to the A.B.A. Tort and Insurance Practice Section Fidelity & Surety Law Committee annual meeting on August 10, 1993); T. Scott Leo, *The Financing Surety and the Chapter 11 Principal,* 26 TORT & INS. L. J. 45 (1990) (hereinafter referred to as *Leo*); T. Scott Leo and Gary A. Wilson, *Suretyship and the Bankruptcy Code*, *in* THE LAW OF SURETYSHIP 9-1 (Edward G. Gallagher ed., 1993).

5 11 U.S.C. § 548.

a. When can or should the collateral security be sold by the principal and the indemnitors, or the surety as a lien or secured creditor, to reduce or eliminate the surety's loss? The simple answer is immediately. If that is not practical or possible, it is important to have an orderly and planned liquidation if sales of collateral security are necessary to reimburse the surety. How and when the sales occur should be discussed with the principal and the indemnitors at the time of the execution of the financing agreement.

b. Where do the proceeds of sale go? Certainly the proceeds of sale of the collateral security, after costs of sale and prior liens are paid, should go to the surety in some fashion. The surety should not release its lien until it has control of the proceeds of sale. Whether the proceeds are "reinvested in the principal" to avoid the surety having to put more of its own money into the principal, or whether the proceeds are used to reduce the loss already incurred by the surety is a decision that must be made under the particular circumstances of each case.

While collateral security given to the surety is an option when assets of sufficient value exist, there are other ways that the surety may benefit from the existence of collateral security without the surety actually taking a lien on the assets. These include:

(a) Guaranteed Bank Loan.[6] The surety may work with the principal's bank to provide the collateral security to the bank in return for a loan from the bank to the principal. With the principal being in financial difficulties, the surety may have to guarantee the bank loan for the principal. However, banks may be more familiar in dealing with issues of collateral security, including foreclosures on real estate and auction sales of personal property. The bank may be more willing than the surety to take the collateral security. A surety guarantee is normally required in the event the collateral security does not bring sale proceeds sufficient for the bank to be repaid in full.[7]

(b) Immediate Sale of Collateral. Rather than taking a lien on the collateral security, the surety may require the principal and the

---

6 *See also* Section III.B. of this chapter.

7 The ideal situation is to have the bank agree to foreclose on part or all of the collateral security before it calls on the surety's guarantee. If the bank does foreclose, it should give notice to the surety. If the surety is required to pay first under its guarantee, the bank should assign its remaining interest in the collateral security to the surety.

indemnitors to immediately liquidate the collateral security and use the proceeds of the liquidation to fund the principal rather than using the surety's money. This method is available if the principal or the indemnitors have marketable securities, cash in bank accounts, or money market funds, certificates of deposit, and/or other more liquid assets. Under most agreements of indemnity, the principal and the indemnitors are required to exonerate the surety prior to the surety spending its own funds. If the collateral security is liquid and can be timely invested in the principal's operations, the surety should require liquidation so that the surety does not have to use its own funds or decide at a later date when and if to liquidate the collateral security it holds. If the collateral security is illiquid, such as stock in a closely held corporation, real estate, or equipment, it may not be feasible to have a sale that will produce proceeds quick enough to invest in the principal to reduce or eliminate the principal's financial difficulties.

The final issue with respect to using real estate as collateral security is the possible existence of hazardous wastes on the real estate "controlled" by the surety, which could potentially expose the surety to liability under various state and federal statutes.[8]

E. Summary

The surety's analysis of the information provided by the principal and the indemnitors during the investigation will probably conclude that the principal lacks sufficient cash to complete the bonded projects. Therefore, the principal's capacity to perform the work and the character of the principal and the indemnitors in their commitment to indemnify and hold harmless the surety become critical. If either of those two factors do not exist to the surety's satisfaction, financing the principal is *not* a viable option in handling the performance bond claims. The existence of collateral security can be a factor, but collateral security only reimburses the surety for its loss. It does not complete the work on the bonded projects. Furthermore, the value of that collateral security can decrease over time, both as a result of market factors and because of the surety's "investments" in the collateral security (mortgage payments, taxes, upkeep, etc.). Generally, for the surety to consider financing the principal

---

8 *See* Section IX.D. of this chapter.

as a performance bond option, the surety must have reached the conclusion that there is nothing wrong with the principal that money cannot cure, and that the other conditions—capacity, character, and collateral—appear favorable.

III.
The Methods Of Financing The Principal

There are a number of methods for the surety to provide financial assistance to the principal. Some of the methods are more direct than others. During any method of financing, the surety must be assured that the contract funds collected from the bonded projects in the future *will* be used by the principal to complete the performance of the work and to pay the bills on the bonded projects. Therefore, the surety should require a joint control trust account for the collection of the contract funds from the bonded projects and joint control over the use of those contract funds in the future. The direct and indirect methods for the surety to provide financial assistance to the principal include the following.

A. Advancing or Lending Money to the Principal

Advancing or lending money directly to the principal is the most obvious method of financing the principal. Initially, the surety may immediately pay the principal's payroll and certain key subcontractors and suppliers for a short period of time to maintain the status quo during the surety's investigation. This "look-see" financing keeps the bonded projects moving, thereby giving the surety time to perform its investigation (to "look") and determine its course of action (to "see" what the surety wants to do).[9] The surety's decision may be the financing of the principal on some or all of the bonded projects. Much of the remainder of this chapter

---

9 The commentators recommend that the principal and the indemnitors be advised both verbally and in writing that such "look-see" financing "is a temporary means to give the surety time to complete its investigation and in no way commits the surety towards financing or any other course of action." *Joyce and Haug*, *supra* note 1 at p. 22. *See* Exhibit 4.2 at p. 471 for a form of a letter covering "look-see" financing (this form was formerly Exhibit 2.1 to *Joyce and Haug* at pp. 39-40). Copies of the letter should be signed by the principal and the indemnitors.

will discuss the right of the surety to advance or loan monies to the principal and the procedures and mechanics for accomplishing the surety's direct financial assistance to the principal.

B. Guaranteed Bank Loan

Rather than directly advancing or lending money to the principal, the surety may guarantee a bank loan or other debt resulting in monies being made available to the principal from third parties.

> Guaranteeing a bank loan will usually be used only when there is a realistic possibility that the contractor will be able to pay it off. It normally doesn't make sense to guarantee a bank loan and incur the interest and financing charges unless you expect these expenses to be borne by the principal.
>
> There are, however, two situations in which it may be wise to accept this burden. One is where the contractor is broke, but he does have some assets, and he does want to complete the work. In a situation such as this, have him pledge his assets to the bank rather than to the surety. The pledging of the assets to the bank in consideration for the bank loan should shelter the assets from attack as a voidable preference under the Bankruptcy Act.
>
> The second situation involves federal contracts. The government does not recognize assignments to sureties. It only recognizes assignments to financial institutions. In addition, it is possible that the Assignments of Claims Act may prevent the United States from offsetting against the contract fund.[10]

When the principal and the indemnitors have assets with which to provide collateral security to the surety, the surety may determine it is best to have the collateral security provided to a bank instead in order for the principal to obtain a bank loan guaranteed by the surety.[11] The surety may never have to pay on the guarantee and incur a resulting loss.

---

10 *Joyce and Haug*, *supra* note 1 at p. 31.

11 *See also* Section II.D.2 of this chapter; *Schroeder No. 1*, *supra*, note 1 at pp. 834-36 and p. 843.

C. "Back Door Financing"

There are many times when a principal requires financial assistance because its cash flow cannot meet the payment of its bills on the bonded projects on a current basis. Every month, the principal scrambles to scrape up enough cash to keep the bonded projects moving, but can never seem to get over the hump. The bonded projects slow down when the subcontractors and suppliers perceive that they will not be paid on a timely basis. While this appears to be a payment bond problem, the principal's slowdown in the performance of the work on the bonded projects may lead to performance bond claims against the surety if the obligees determine that the principal may be in default under the terms of the construction contracts and consider the termination of the principal. The obligees may also attempt to withhold liquidated damages from progress payments, thereby further increasing the principal's cash flow problems.

If the surety pays certain bills on the bonded projects, thereby bringing the subcontractors and suppliers current, the principal benefits in two ways:

1. The subcontractors and suppliers are less likely to drag their feet and slow down the progress of the work on the bonded projects; and

2. By catching up and becoming current with its payments to the subcontractors and suppliers, the principal may use the contract funds from the bonded projects on a monthly basis to complete the performance of the work and to pay the bills of the subcontractors and suppliers as they become due in the future.

This concept of "indirectly" financing the principal is frequently known as "back door financing." The surety's major risk in providing "back door financing" to the principal is that the principal becomes "healthy" on a current basis, and could become less cooperative in the future with respect to providing collateral security to the surety. The surety should make it very clear to the principal and the indemnitors that they are liable to indemnify the surety for the "back door financing,"[12] and should attempt to obtain collateral security immediately for its payments.

---

12 *See* note 9, *supra*. The same type of letter should be sent to and signed by the principal and the indemnitors.

D. Providing Additional Bonds to the Principal

Another method of "indirect financing" is for the surety to provide additional bonding credit to the principal in an effort to rehabilitate the principal. The strategy is that the principal can solve its problems if additional work and additional contract funds become available over time. This may work if the principal has several claims against obligees that have not been resolved, thereby affecting the principal's cash flow and balance sheet. The surety must be extremely selective in this method of financing the principal for the following reasons:

1. Providing additional bonds does not cure the initial problem of a lack of cash to complete the performance of the existing work and to pay current bills on the bonded projects. The lag time from bid to award to payment of the first requisition (after the principal has expended monies for the bonds, mobilization, etc.) will not provide cash on a timely basis. To the extent that the principal and the indemnitors can provide their own cash to the principal, rather than the surety, this lag time might not be of such a great concern;
2. Providing additional bonds that produce immediate new work to the principal may hinder the principal's ability to perform the remaining work on the existing bonded projects in a timely manner. Qualified personnel may be taken from the "problem" projects and put on the new, potentially profitable projects. Furthermore, the additional bonds may also stretch out the principal's work program beyond a comfortable time frame for the surety; and
3. If, in fact, the principal has severe problems that go beyond the temporary shortage of cash, providing additional bonding for projects that may not be profitable may exacerbate the surety's performance bond claim handling problems in the future, increasing the number of bonded projects in default and ultimately increasing the surety's loss.

IV.
The Surety's Right To Finance The Principal

Before the surety makes the decision to directly finance the principal for the completion of the bonded projects, the surety must determine whether it has the right in the first instance to finance the principal. The surety's authority to advance or lend money or otherwise provide financial assistance to the principal is normally found in the agreement of indemnity. The surety's right and ability to finance the principal as an option under the performance bond depends on the language of the performance bond itself and any statutes or regulations governing the performance bond.

A. The Agreement of Indemnity

Most agreements of indemnity taken by sureties contain a provision that allows, but does not require, the surety to guarantee loans or advance or lend money to the principal. For example, a representative agreement of indemnity may state:[13]

> The surety, in its sole discretion, is authorized and empowered to guarantee loans or to advance or lend money to the principal. The surety reserves the absolute right to cancel any such guarantee and to cease advancing or lending money to the principal with or without cause and with or without notice to the principal or the indemnitors. All money lent or advanced to the principal by the surety from time to time, or guaranteed for the principal by the surety, and all related costs and expenses incurred by the surety, shall be conclusively deemed to be a loss to the surety for which the principal and the indemnitors shall be liable under the agreement of indemnity. The surety may make such advances or loans without the necessity of seeing to the application of the proceeds by the principal. The principal and the indemnitors shall be obligated to indemnify and hold harmless the surety in accordance with the terms of the agreement of indemnity for the amount of such advances or loans, notwithstanding that the proceeds or any part thereof have not been utilized by the principal for the purposes for which the money was advanced or loaned by the surety.

If the surety's agreement of indemnity contains a similar provision, the surety may advance or lend money to the principal, with such advances being conclusively deemed to be a loss to the surety for which the principal and the indemnitors are liable to reimburse the surety.

---

13 This provision of the "agreement of indemnity" has been created by the author. Parts or all of the concepts and/or language may be found in actual agreements of indemnity taken by sureties. The author knows of no present agreement of indemnity that contains the exact language "quoted" in this chapter.

B. The Performance Bond

The fact that the agreement of indemnity may authorize the surety to finance the principal does not necessarily mean that the obligee must accept performance of the bonded projects by the principal being financed by the surety. The surety must review the performance bond and any governing statutes and regulations to determine whether financing the principal is a method for the surety to satisfy its performance bond obligations.

1. Miller Act Performance Bond

Under the Miller Act Performance Bond, the surety's obligation is void if the principal "performs and fulfills all the undertakings, covenants, terms, conditions, and agreements of the contract." Nothing is said about how the surety is to fulfill its obligations under the Miller Act Performance Bond if the principal fails to fulfill its obligations under the contract with the federal government.[14]

2. AIA Document A311 Performance Bond (February, 1970 Ed.)

Under the AIA Document A311 Performance Bond, the surety is provided with a number of options:

> Whenever Contractor shall be, and declared by Owner to be in default under the Contract, the Owner having performed Owner's obligations thereunder, the Surety may promptly remedy the default, or shall promptly
>
> 1) Complete the Contract in accordance with its terms and conditions, or

---

14 A review of the cases involving the federal government shows that financing the principal has been used by the surety as a means for performing its obligations under the Miller Act Performance Bond. *Aetna Cas. and Sur. Co. v. United States*, 845 F.2d 971 (Fed. Cir. 1988); *Morrison Assurance Co. v. United States*, 3 Cl. Ct. 626 (1983); *Great American Ins. Co. v. United States*, 481 F.2d 1298, 1300 n. 8 (Ct. Cl. 1973).

> 2) Obtain a bid or bids for completing the Contract....

Certainly, to "obtain a bid" for completing the bonded contract is not surety financing of the principal. However, the surety is authorized to "promptly remedy the default" and to "complete the Contract in accordance with its terms and conditions," both of which may be performed by surety financing of the principal.

3. AIA Document A312 Performance Bond (December, 1984 Ed.)

Under the AIA Document A312 Performance Bond, when the obligee has satisfied its obligations under the Performance Bond, and the surety's obligations under the Performance Bond arise, one of the options of the surety is to promptly, and at the surety's expense:

> 4.1 Arrange for the Contractor, with consent of the Owner, to perform and complete the Construction Contract;....

One of the ways for the surety to arrange for the principal (the "Contractor") to perform and complete the bonded contract is by financing the principal.

One issue that is brought into focus by the AIA Document A312 Performance Bond is whether the obligee must consent to or be a party to any financing agreement between the surety and the principal, or even know of the surety financing of the principal. Certainly under the AIA Document A312 Performance Bond, it is a condition of the performance bond that the obligee's consent be obtained. Where that condition is not required under the particular performance bond, the surety may finance the principal without the knowledge of the obligee. The principal may be on temporary hard times, and believe that if the world at large knows that the surety is financing the principal it will have difficulty staying in business and obtaining new work. The surety may be better off if the world does not know it is financing the principal because knowledge of the financing may generate claims by various persons and entities that are not defined claimants under the payment bond.[15]

As will be described later in this chapter, one of the disadvantages of financing the principal without an agreement or understanding with the

15 *See* Section IX.A. of this chapter on *alter ego* claims against the surety.

obligee is that money advanced to the principal under a financing agreement does not decrease the penal sum of the surety's performance bond.[16] If knowledge of the surety financing of the principal is not a critical factor, the surety may be able to negotiate with the obligee such that the financing of the principal does, in fact, decrease the penal sum of the performance bond by the amount of the surety's money loaned or advanced to the principal.

V.
Advantages And Disadvantages In Financing The Principal

There are a number of apparent advantages and disadvantages to surety financing of the principal as a means of discharging the surety's performance bond obligations. The following is a list of those advantages and disadvantages.

A. Advantages in Financing the Principal

1. Learning Curve

The principal's management, work forces, and subcontractors are familiar with the construction means and methods employed on the project site. A new contractor requires a certain amount of time to organize and become familiar with the work prior to becoming productive and efficient. This learning curve is expensive, and will be reflected in the new contractor's bid and in increased liquidated damages. Assuming that the principal is performing the work efficiently and economically, savings can be realized by eliminating the learning curve experienced by a new contractor.

2. Demobilization and Mobilization/Job Momentum and Continuity

If the project is shut down, manpower, equipment, and supplies will likely be removed from the project site. The cost of such demobilization by the principal and its subcontractors can be significant and may result in claims against the surety's payment bond. After a relet, the new

16 *See* Section V.B.1. of this chapter.

contractor will have to mobilize its own forces, subcontractors, and suppliers, costing time and money that will be built into the new contractor's bid.

By providing financing to the principal to enable the principal to continue with the completion of the work on the bonded project, shutdown of the project is avoided, job disruptions are minimized, subcontractors of the principal remain on the project, and continuity of the work may be maintained. Claims for damages by both the obligee and subcontractors may be minimized. If the bonded work is substantially completed, the delays involved in reletting the work, plus liquidated damages and other claims of obligees and subcontractors, may be so substantial that significant cost savings may be achieved by financing the principal.

3. *New Contractor Mark-Up*

The new contractor estimates the cost to complete the work on the project. The new contractor has to make allowances in its bid price for obtaining bonds, mobilization, correcting possible defective work, and other contingencies that make its price more expensive. The new contractor must also mark-up the bid price for both profit and overhead. Assuming that the principal is performing the work efficiently and economically, the additional allowances and mark-up, overhead, and profit of the new contractor can be saved by financing the principal.

4. *Principal's Image and Presence, and Preservation of Claims*

By keeping the principal out in front and the surety in the background, many of the problems with obligees and the principal's creditors can be minimized. The appearance of business as usual for the principal, whether or not the presence and assistance of the surety is known, can lessen claims and disputes and improve cash flow from the bonded projects. By maintaining the presence of the principal, claims for additional compensation against the obligees and backcharges against subcontractors and suppliers are not lost or heavily discounted as occurs when a new contractor takes over and the surety is forced to litigate claims when the principal is unavailable or uncooperative. The principal's witnesses and documentation necessary to substantiate various claims and backcharges remain available and assessable. Historically, many things that occur on a construction project are "lost" when the principal leaves the project site and is replaced by the new contractor, thereby increasing the surety's loss.

5. *Subcontracts*

If the surety finances the principal and prevents the termination of the principal's right to proceed, subcontractors and suppliers cannot renegotiate their subcontracts and purchase orders. They are bound to the principal at the prices previously agreed upon. This may represent a substantial advantage on projects that are heavily subcontracted.

6. *Salvage Considerations*

Most sureties require the principal and the indemnitors to provide collateral security to the surety as a condition precedent to the surety rendering financial assistance to the principal. Most principals want to complete their work. At the beginning of the financing arrangement, the principal and the indemnitors are more likely to provide their assets as collateral security to the surety for the financing being advanced. Salvage is made easier because:

a. The failure to provide collateral security to the surety, if such collateral exists, will in all likelihood influence the surety *not* to extend financing to the principal;

b. The principal and the indemnitors feel it is in their best interests to continue working on the bonded projects to reduce the surety's ultimate loss, and are willing to provide collateral security to the surety to reduce their potential liability; and

c. By obtaining collateral security at the beginning when financing the principal commences, rather than obtaining collateral security as indemnity once the losses have been incurred, the surety reduces the possibility that its obtaining of collateral security will be deemed to be a preference in the event of a later bankruptcy proceeding filed by the principal and/or the indemnitors.

B. Disadvantages in Financing the Principal

1. No Credit Against the Performance Bond Penalty

Unless agreed to by the obligee, money advanced by the surety to its principal under a financing arrangement does not decrease the penal sum of the surety's performance bond. If the penal sum of the surety's performance bond is in jeopardy because the projected cost to complete the work is close to the penal sum of the performance bond, the surety should refuse to finance the principal. The principal may be reluctant because an agreement with the obligee concerning the surety's advances to the principal and a subsequent credit against the penal sum of the performance bond may defeat the strategy of the surety and the principal to maintain the principal's image and appearance on the project.[17] The obligee may also be reluctant to agree to such a reduction in the penal sum of the performance bond as a result of the surety financing of the principal.

2. Fixing the Loss

The surety is unable to fix the amount of its loss by financing the principal; the surety will not know the final amount of its loss until the last bonded project is completed and the financing ends. The surety takes the same risks as any other contractor, including the risks of bad weather, unreliable subcontractors, late deliveries, wrong deliveries, warranty items, lack of bona fide workers, etc. Reletting the work to third parties at a fixed cost (and obtaining performance and payment bonds) establishes the surety's loss.

When the work has barely commenced on one or more bonded projects, there are many reasons for reletting the work rather than financing the principal, including the following:[18]

---

17 One commentator has argued that obtaining the obligee's agreement to credit all of the surety's advances and loans to the principal against the penal sum of the performance bond may affect the consideration given by the surety financing the principal. *Schroeder No. 2, supra* note 1 at p. 1206. *See also* Section VII.B., note 27, *infra*.

18 Wayne H. Webster, *The Surety's Decision on What to Do.* 17 FORUM 1168, 1176 (1982) (hereinafter referred to as *Webster*).

a. The new contractor does not have to worry about defective work and warranty work, thereby minimizing its price;

b. The surety may generally obtain an agreement from subcontractors to complete their work for the surety or a new contractor for the same price as provided to the principal;

c. Potential new contractors may generally be found among the original bidders whose existing knowledge of the project requirements based upon their recent bid can save time and money; and

d. Payment bond obligations are more easily determined because fewer unpaid bills are likely to exist early in the performance of the work.

3. *Payment of Claims Not Covered by the Performance Bond*

The surety financing the principal must frequently satisfy the principal's debts that are not covered by either the performance bond or the payment bond. Specifically, the surety must generally make a substantial contribution to the principal's overhead.[19] This contribution may be for overhead incurred in the past, and will certainly include overhead costs going forward. While overhead may be reduced, the reductions in overhead rarely decrease as quickly as the revenues generated from the bonded projects.

When the principal has extensive unbonded work, the surety faces a dilemma. Unless the surety takes a security agreement and files financing statements to perfect its security interest in unbonded accounts receivable *and* is perfected ahead of any bank that may have lent money to the principal, the surety *should not finance* the unbonded work. On the other hand, the surety must ensure that a portion of the overhead is collected from the unbonded contract proceeds.

Under any scenario, financing the principal will increase the surety's loss because of necessary expenditures on unbonded obligations. The surety must be certain that financing will decrease its eventual total loss

---

19 In reality, the surety will make a contribution to someone's overhead and general and administrative expenses. If the bonded project is completed by a new contractor, the new contractor will include overhead in its bid price. If the obligee completes the work, it will make a claim for its overhead and general and administrative expenses against the surety's performance bond.

notwithstanding the payment of obligations that would not otherwise be due under the performance or payment bonds.

4. Costs of Monitoring the Work

The costs of monitoring the work of a financed principal can be large depending on the individual situation. Frequently, the surety's representative must spend substantial time in the principal's office and with the principal's project managers to ensure that the work is being performed, requisitions on the bonded projects are being submitted and paid timely, and that the correct bills are being paid. The surety's representative must also deal on a continuous basis with the representatives of the obligees. Frequently, consultants are required to assist the surety's representative in monitoring the work. To the extent that any legal issues arise, the surety will incur additional attorneys' fees. Finally, when there are multiple bonded projects and hundreds of checks involved, an outside accounting firm may be required in order to keep track of the surety's payments and losses and the receipt of bonded contract funds for purposes of reinsurance and indemnity claims against indemnitors.

5. Completing the Work—The 10% Problem[20] and Tail-End Let-Downs[21]

The achievement of substantial completion by the financed principal can be difficult. Many principals have a problem in completing the last 10% of the work under any circumstances. When the principal is going out of business, the principal and its employees may have less interest in completing the projects. At the same time, there may be more incentive to prolong the work in order to obtain a paycheck as opposed to completing the work and ending the financing by the surety. Many problems arise when the work towards substantial completion is reached, and all can cause serious time problems that increase the surety's loss.

---

20 *Joyce and Haug*, *supra* note 1 at p. 26.

21 *Webster*, *supra* note 18 at p. 1176.

6. *Problems of Reinsurance*

Many of the reinsurance treaties require extensive reporting by the surety to the reinsurers, and most require prior approval by the reinsurers before the surety commits to financing the principal.[22] While the existence of reinsurance is not, in and of itself, a disadvantage, the time and requirements in dealing with the reinsurers must be calculated in any financing arrangements with the principal.

7. *Risks to the Surety Beyond the Penal Sum of the Performance Bond*

There are certain risks to the surety in financing the principal that may extend the surety's loss beyond the terms and penal sum of its performance bond. Those risks are more fully discussed below in Section IX.

VI.
Financing The Subcontractor Principal

Many of the issues in determining whether the surety should finance the principal when the principal is a general contractor are similar when the principal is a subcontractor. The same kind of information and analysis is necessary: the surety must determine if it has a right to finance the subcontractor principal, etc. Assuming that the surety has knowledge that the subcontractor principal is in financial difficulty and has the opportunity to make its analysis prior to the subcontractor principal's termination for default, there may be a reduction in the amount of the financing surety's loss when the subcontractor principal faces termination on an ongoing bonded project.

For example, when the principal operating as a general contractor is terminated for default, whether or not the surety has the opportunity or the desire to consider financing, work on the bonded project stops. When a subcontractor principal gets into financial difficulties, and there is a prospect of a termination for default, the overall project keeps going. Depending upon the construction contract involved, and the status of the work of the subcontractor principal, it may be more beneficial to allow

---

22 *Schroeder No. 1*, *supra* note 1 at p. 832, n. 5.

the subcontractor principal to continue to perform the work (electrical, mechanical, etc.) rather than face the claims of the obligee (general contractor) based upon delays and disturbances to the general contractor's work and to the work of other subcontractors.

VII.
Procedures And Mechanics For Financing The Principal

When the surety's decision is made to finance the principal, whether for one bonded project or for many bonded projects, the surety should require a separate agreement with the principal and the indemnitors.[23] Whether the agreement is referred to as a "Joint Control Trust Account Agreement," a "Financing Agreement," or some other name (hereinafter referred to as the "Agreement"), certain provisions concerning the procedures and mechanics governing the financial arrangement between the surety and the principal (and the indemnitors) are necessary. The Agreement should set forth certain recitals; reaffirm the indemnity obligations of the principal and the indemnitors to the surety; provide collateral security to the surety for its agreement to finance the principal; provide for the establishment of a joint control trust checking account or some other bank trust account arrangement for the receipt and collection of bonded contract funds and monies advanced or loaned by the surety to the principal, and for the payment of the bills incurred by the principal on the bonded projects; provide a description of the bills to be paid and the procedures for paying the bills from the trust account; set forth the provisions for terminating the Agreement; provide, where appropriate, for the reimbursement and repayment of the surety for its financing of

---

23 Several commentators have addressed the issue of the extent of the surety financing of the principal and whether it should extend to unbonded work of the principal. *See Joyce and Haug*, *supra* note 1 at p. 28 ("Financing the completion of work that you are contractually obligated to complete is risky enough without taking on additional risks. This can be short-sighted, however. If the unbonded work appears to be profitable, financing it can help to pay for the completion of the bonded work.") Joyce and Haug list a number of factors to maximize the surety's chances for successfully financing unbonded work. *Id.*; *see also Schroeder No. 2*, *supra* note 1 at pp. 1203-05.

the principal;[24] and set forth certain miscellaneous provisions that govern the understandings, relationships, and construction of the Agreement between and among the surety, the principal, and the indemnitors.

Exhibit 4.1 is a sample Joint Control Trust Account Agreement between and among the principal, the indemnitors and the surety. While no one Agreement can necessarily set forth all of the understandings among the principal, the indemnitors and the surety for every case, the attached Agreement provides the framework for any such understandings.[25]

A. Recitals

The recitals are important in any Agreement because they set forth the basic factual understandings between the principal, the indemnitors, and the surety at the beginning of the financing arrangement. The recitals should contain and/or refer to the following:

1. A description of the existing agreement(s) of indemnity, with copies attached;
2. An attached list of the relevant contracts and the bonds executed by the surety on behalf of the principal for those contracts;[26]
3. An acknowledgment that the bonds executed by the surety were induced by and provided in reliance upon the execution of the agreement

---

24 A discussion of any provisions that may be in an agreement for the reimbursement and repayment of the surety for its financing of the principal is beyond the scope of this paper. Frequent provisions found in a repayment agreement include: periodic payments over time, including balloon payments; agreements concerning the sale and liquidation of certain collateral security, and the use of the net proceeds of sale; a description of the surety's rights and remedies in the event that the principal and the indemnitors default under the terms of the repayment agreement; and the return of any collateral not necessary for the full reimbursement of the surety. Each case will have its own facts and require the drafting of specific repayment provisions to comply with the particular circumstances of the case.

25 There are a number of excellent sample forms provided with the works of other authors, which should also be reviewed. *See, e.g.*, Joyce and Haug, *supra* note 4.

26 *See* Exhibit 4.1.2 at p. 456.

of indemnity by the principal and the indemnitors, who should acknowledge and reaffirm their joint and several obligations and liabilities to the surety under the agreement of indemnity; and

4. A statement as follows:

> WHEREAS, the contracts are in various stages of completion, and the principal and the indemnitors hereby acknowledge and admit that: (a) the principal is financially unable to perform or complete the performance of the contracts; (b) certain subcontractors and suppliers of labor and/or materials with respect to the contracts and projects have not been paid; (c) the principal has requested the financial assistance of the surety as a result of (a) and (b) above; and (d) but for the willingness of the surety to enter into the Agreement, the principal is unable to complete the performance of the contracts and pay its subcontractors and suppliers of labor and/or materials with respect to the contracts and projects.

The recitals should also state any specific facts that exist that have induced the surety to enter into the Agreement to finance the principal.

B. Indemnification

The principal and the indemnitors should, within the body of the Agreement, acknowledge and reaffirm their joint and several obligations and liabilities to the surety under the agreement of indemnity. The indemnification section of the Agreement should also contain the following:

1. The granting of a lien and/or security interest in all of the real and personal property (including the bonded contract funds) of the principal and the indemnitors as described in an exhibit to the Agreement.[27] The surety should take all steps necessary to record its liens on real property and perfect its security interest in the personal property by filing the appropriate financing statements. Not only does the agreement of indemnity provide the basis for a demand for collateral security, but the principal and the indemnitors are usually willing to provide to the

---

27 *See* Exhibit 4.1.3 at p. 457. *See* Section IX.D. of this chapter concerning the potential liabilities of the surety for hazardous wastes located on real estate which may be subject to the surety's liens.

surety what collateral security they can in order to obtain surety financing in accordance with the terms of the Agreement.[28]

2. The principal should provide voluntary letters of default and termination for each of the contracts bonded by the surety.[29] The surety should be given the right to use the letters of default, individually as to each of the bonded contracts or as to all of the bonded contracts, at the surety's sole option and discretion.

C. Establishment of the Joint Control Trust Checking Account

The Agreement should provide for the opening of a joint control trust checking account (the "Trust Account"). The Trust Account should be established with a bank in accordance with a separate Trust Account Agreement setting forth those substantive portions of the Agreement relating solely to the Trust Account.[30] Initially, the surety and the principal must decide on the bank to be used for the establishment of the Trust Account. There are three issues that arise in choosing the appropriate bank.

The first issue is whether the bank has the willingness, ability, and capability to establish and maintain the Trust Account. Many banks are unwilling or unable to provide the necessary services in creating and maintaining the Trust Account that provides the surety with the necessary protection. Furthermore, attempting to establish such a Trust Account at a bank unwilling or unable to accept the surety's terms and conditions may cause a delay in the establishment of the Trust Account and the payment of subcontractors and suppliers through the Trust Account, thereby

---

28 Commentators have raised the issue of whether surety financing of the principal is sufficient consideration for obtaining collateral security. There are really two issues. First, is surety financing of the principal anything more than the surety performing its obligations under the performance bond? Second, if the surety does not commit itself to financing the principal, or perhaps providing new bonds in the future for the principal, is there sufficient consideration? These issues have been raised, and the answers are probably that surety financing is sufficient consideration in order to obtain collateral security. *See Schroeder No. 1*, *supra* note 1 at p. 841 and p. 863; *Schroeder No. 2*, *supra* note 1 at pp. 1205-07.

29 *See* Exhibit 4.1.4 at p. 460.

30 *See* Exhibit 4.1.5 at p. 461.

requiring those necessary payments to be made with surety claim drafts. One should *not* assume that opening a Trust Account will be quick or easy.

Second, notwithstanding the trust nature of the Trust Account,[31] certain creditors of the principal may attempt to attach or garnish the funds in the Trust Account. There are few banks that are willing to ignore such an attachment or garnishment at the surety's request, with or without the surety's indemnity. The best the surety can ask for is to receive notice of any such attachment or garnishment in time to go to court to try to have the attachment or garnishment released.

Third, the principal may be a customer of the bank chosen to establish the Trust Account. The Trust Account Agreement provides that none of the contract funds or any monies advanced or loaned by the surety to the principal and deposited in the Trust Account "shall be subject to any right of set-off by the [b]ank as a result of any transactions involving the [b]ank and the [p]rincipal."[32]

When the Trust Account is established, all contract funds from the bonded contracts and all monies loaned or advanced by the surety to the principal should be deposited into the Trust Account. The Agreement provides that letters of direction will be sent by the principal to the obligees of the bonds requesting that the bonded contract funds be made payable jointly to the principal and the surety and sent to the surety for deposit into the Trust Account.[33] The principal should execute an

---

31 For a detailed discussion of the trust fund nature and characteristics of a trust account, *see Schroeder No. 1*, *supra* note 1 at pp. 851-54; *Schroeder No. 2*, *supra* note 1 at pp. 1209-10; *Joyce and Haug*, *supra* note 1 at p. 35.

32 *See* Exhibit 4.1.5, paragraph 11, at p. 463. For a discussion concerning the issue of dealing with the principal's assignee bank, *see Schroeder No. 1*, *supra* note 1 at pp. 854-57.

33 *See* Exhibit 4.1.6 at p. 466. While a letter of direction from the principal to the obligee will assist the surety in collecting the bonded contract funds, it is not enough for a surety to protect its rights in the bonded contract funds from other third-parties. The surety may assert its rights of subrogation, or its secured rights under the UCC if it has either recorded its agreement of indemnity or obtained a security interest under the Agreement and filed financing statements to perfect that security interest. *See Schroeder No. 2*, *supra* note 1 at pp. 1200-01.

assignment and power of attorney authorizing the surety to endorse the checks received from the obligees and to deposit the checks into the Trust Account.[34]

The Agreement should provide that all of the funds in the Trust Account, whether contract funds received from the bonded contracts or monies loaned or advanced by the surety to the principal, are held in the Trust Account as trust funds for the uses and purposes set forth in the Agreement.[35] There are a number of ways to establish the Trust Account with the bank, depending upon the complexity of the case, the proximity of the surety's representative to the principal's office and records, and the number of checks involved on a weekly or monthly basis. Two of these methods include the following:

1. Joint Control Trust Checking Account

The most common method, and the method described in Exhibit 4.1 (and Exhibit 4.1.5, the Trust Account Agreement), is to use one Trust Account. Each check from the Trust Account requires the signature of two people: (a) the surety's representative; and (b) the principal's representative. All bonded contract funds collected and any monies loaned or advanced by the surety are deposited directly to the Trust Account. All withdrawals from the Trust Account for the purposes described in the Agreement are made by a check signed jointly by the surety and the principal. While this method gives the surety control over the trust funds in the Trust Account and is a fairly simple method of paying bills, it can be time consuming and create logistical problems. The surety's representative may be located far away from the principal's office, checks and backup documentation must be sent by overnight mail, and, at times, tens and hundreds of checks requiring the signature of the surety's representative may be necessary on a monthly basis. However, signing checks may provide the surety's representative with a good opportunity

---

34 *See* Exhibit 4.1.7 at p. 468. For a discussion of powers of attorney taken by a surety financing the principal, *see Schroeder No. 2*, *supra* note 1 at pp. 1208-09.

35 *See* note 31, *supra*, for commentaries on the trust fund nature of the Trust Account. The drafter of the Agreement must make sure that the language in the Agreement complies with state law requirements to establish a bona fide express trust.

to visit the principal to see how the bonded projects are progressing and to discuss any other relevant issues.

2. *Two Trust Accounts and an Operating Account*

A second method is to use two trust accounts (Trust Account No. 1 and Trust Account No. 2) and an Operating Account. The Operating Account requires the sole signature of the principal. It is a zero-balance account that draws its funding from Trust Account No. 2. There is *never* any money in the Operating Account. All bonded contract funds and any monies loaned or advanced by the surety to the principal are deposited into Trust Account No. 1. The principal presents the surety with a request for the payment of numerous bills along with checks drawn on the Operating Account that require only the principal's signature. The surety and the principal then agree to the bills to be paid and to the amount of funding from Trust Account No. 1 to Trust Account No. 2 to cover the checks drawn on the Operating Account. Through the use of passwords and facsimile machines, the surety and the principal give approval to the bank to transfer the agreed upon amount of funds from Trust Account No. 1 to Trust Account No. 2. The surety or the principal will then transmit the checks from the Operating Account to the payees. When the checks are returned to the bank on the zero-balance Operating Account, funds are immediately drawn by the bank from Trust Account No. 2 to cover the checks presented on the Operating Account. The surety will know that there is a problem in the arrangement when the bank notifies the surety that Trust Account No. 2 is overdrawn. This can only occur when checks for amounts or in numbers in excess of those approved by the surety to be sent from the Operating Account are presented on the Operating Account, and there are insufficient funds in Trust Account No. 2 to cover those checks.

D. Use of the Contract Funds From the Trust Account

The Agreement should set forth specifically how the trust funds contained in the Trust Account, whether bonded contract funds or monies loaned or advanced by the surety to the principal, must be used. The Agreement provides for the following:

1. *Use of Trust Funds*

The trust funds in the Trust Account should be used solely for the payment of all labor and material costs, including amounts due to subcontractors and suppliers and for rental of equipment incurred by the principal and the principal's subcontractors and suppliers, *which are necessary to complete the work under the bonded projects and for which the surety may become liable under its bonds*. The Agreement should specifically state that the trust funds in the Trust Account should not be used to pay obligations of the principal on contracts not bonded by the surety.

2. *Overhead and General and Administrative Expenses of the Principal*

The provision for the payment of the overhead and general and administrative expenses of the principal is one of the most difficult to negotiate. In any financing arrangement, certain expenses of the principal must be paid that are not attributable to direct bonded contract costs for which the surety would be liable under its bonds. These include home office salaries and expenses, insurance of all types (general liability, automobile, health, life, etc.), rent, telephone, photocopying, postage, legal and accounting services, etc. The principal that wants to stay in business is always concerned about the funding of its overhead to maintain continuity and cohesion. The surety wants to reduce its exposure for the payment of unbonded obligations.

There are a number of ways to approach the payment of the principal's overhead and general and administrative expenses in the Agreement,[36] including the following:

a. The surety may require its review and approval of all payment of overhead expenses. The Agreement attached as Exhibit 4.1 does not obligate the surety to pay the principal's overhead. To the extent that the surety consents to the payment of overhead from the Trust Account, such consent is at the surety's sole option and discretion; or

---

36 For a discussion concerning the payments to be made from the Trust Account, including overhead, *see Schroeder No. 1*, *supra* note 1 at pp. 845-48.

b. The surety may provide a set percentage of the monthly contract funds collected from the bonded contracts to be used to pay for the principal's overhead and general and administrative expenses. This percentage payment from the Trust Account would be the surety's sole contribution to the principal's overhead *unless* the surety, in its sole discretion, authorized additional specific payments requested by the principal. The surety would have no other obligation to fund the overhead expenses beyond the agreed percentage.

No matter what "agreements" are reached or what method is chosen by the surety and the principal to fund the principal's overhead, there will be disagreements and disputes between the surety and the principal because of a basic underlying conflict—the principal wants everything paid while the surety wants to control the payment of expenses and reduce its losses.

3. Payment of the Principal's Bills

The Agreement should set forth with specificity the arrangements between the principal and the surety for the payment of the principal's bills.[37] The Agreement attached as Exhibit 4.1 sets forth these procedures in Section III, Paragraphs 4(a) through 4(h). Generally, the procedures should be as follows:

a. The principal should provide a written request and sufficient backup documentation for each payee for each check drawn on the Trust Account and signed by the principal. There should never be any question that the principal has requested that a particular payment be made (i.e., by the principal's signature on the check) and has acknowledged that the amount of the check is currently due and owing to the payee named on the check. The surety must collect and review all of the backup documentation in order to assure itself that the payments are due on the bonded projects and are in the correct amounts.

b. To the extent that the contract funds in the Trust Account are sufficient to make the payments requested by the principal and approved by the surety, the checks should be signed by the surety and sent by the surety, along with any releases, to the payees. It is important that the

---

37 *See Schroeder No. 1*, *supra* note 1 at pp. 847-48 for the types of bills that might be identified and paid.

surety retain the ability to disapprove any payments requested by the principal. The Agreement attached as Appendix 4.1 provides as follows:

> It is expressly understood by the Principal and the Indemnitors that should the Surety or its representative disapprove any payments requested by the Principal or refuse to countersign any check drawn on the Trust Account, such decision is final as to the Principal and the Indemnitors, and the Principal and the Indemnitors shall have no right or cause of action of any kind or nature against the Surety, its agents, employees, attorneys or representatives as a result of such disapproval.

c. To the extent that the contract funds in the Trust Account are insufficient to make the payments requested by the principal and approved by the surety, the surety may loan or advance monies to the principal or the Trust Account for the payment of those bills. The Agreement provides that any such advances to, loans to or funding of the principal or the Trust Account:

(1) Shall conclusively be presumed to be a loss to the surety; and

(2) Shall constitute and be deemed to be trust funds in the Trust Account.

d. The treatment of the principal's payroll (as opposed to the payment of the principal's subcontractors and suppliers) is handled differently in the Agreement. Frequently, the principal has an automated system for the payment of its payroll, including the net pay for each employee, taxes to be withheld, and all other deductions. Many times it is easier for the surety to fund the principal's existing payroll account directly from the Trust Account rather than prepare checks for each employee on a weekly or bi-weekly basis from the Trust Account. There are three risks in funding the principal's existing payroll account directly from the Trust Account:

(1) The funds transferred to the principal's existing payroll account from the Trust Account are no longer subject to the joint control rights of the surety. While it is unlikely that the principal will divert these funds from its payroll account and use them for other purposes, thereby leaving its employees unpaid (or with checks that bounce), the possibility exists;

(2) The funds transferred from the Trust Account to the principal's existing payroll account at the bank are no longer "trust funds." If the principal is indebted to the bank, the bank may have a right of setoff against the principal's payroll account. If this occurs, the funds will be

gone, the employees will be unpaid, and the surety may have to pay a second time. This "occurrence" can be avoided if the principal does not have any debt obligations to the bank that handles the principal's payroll account, or a separate agreement is reached among the principal, the surety, and the bank that the bank will not exercise any setoff rights it may have against the principal's payroll account; and

(3) The funds transferred to the principal's existing payroll account are at risk to the attachments or garnishments of judgment creditors of the principal, and no longer have any trust fund characteristics.

e. Of critical importance to the surety is the payment of all withholding and payroll taxes and other amounts deducted from employee wages. Under the Miller Act Performance Bond, the surety is liable for certain payroll taxes regardless of whether the surety finances the principal or not. Under the Internal Revenue Service statutes and regulations, the surety may be deemed to be in control of the principal to such extent that the surety may be responsible for the payment of withholding and payroll taxes if the principal fails to make those payments.[38] The Agreement attached as Exhibit 4.1 provides for the direct funding from the Trust Account of all taxes and other deductions from the principal's payroll.

E. Termination

Terminating the Agreement is another difficult drafting area when negotiating a financing arrangement with the principal.[39] The surety wants to retain the ability to terminate the Agreement at its sole option and discretion. The principal and the indemnitors want to terminate the Agreement as soon as possible. Since the surety is looking to the joint control of the contract funds as a means to ensure that they are used to pay bills on the bonded contracts, and also wants to be repaid for its losses and advances to the principal, including interest, the Agreement may last for a long time, including through the liquidation of the collateral security of the principal and the indemnitors.

---

38 *See* Section IX.C. of this chapter concerning tax liabilities.

39 *See Schroeder No. 2*, *supra* note 1 at pp. 1211-13 for certain concerns on termination of the surety financing of the principal.

Exhibit 4.1 does not have a repayment agreement between the principal and the indemnitors and the surety. Frequently, a repayment plan is difficult to negotiate at the beginning of the financing arrangement because the ultimate loss of the surety is unknown and the urgency is for the surety to obtain control of the bonded contract funds and to pay the bills of subcontractors and suppliers to keep the principal's momentum going on the bonded projects. If a repayment agreement exists in the financing arrangement, the termination provision of the Agreement will normally tie in with the repayment agreement.

One right the surety must have at all times is the ability to draw down on the Trust Account to reimburse itself for its loans, advances, losses and expenses as contract funds build up in the Trust Account. Exhibit 4.1 has a provision whereby the surety is permitted to reimburse itself on an ongoing basis from the trust funds in the Trust Account.

F. Miscellaneous Provisions

There are a number of miscellaneous provisions that are recommended:

1. Agreement that the Surety has no Obligation to Provide Financing

It is critical that the principal and the indemnitors acknowledge and agree that the surety has no obligation to fund the Trust Account, provide financial assistance to the principal in any manner or method, or make any payments other than those payments for which the surety has specifically agreed to make pursuant to the terms of the Agreement. Furthermore, the funding of the Trust Account by the surety is in the surety's sole option and discretion and does not bind or commit the surety to any further funding of the Trust Account.[40]

---

40 While there may be an issue of consideration (*see* note 28, *supra*), the author and other commentators would not recommend that a surety commit itself to pay the overhead and general and administrative expenses of the principal or to complete each of the bonded contracts. *See Schroeder No. 2*, *supra* note 1 at p. 1195.

2. *Agreement on the Execution of Future Bonds for the Principal*

Unless otherwise agreed, the surety should require the principal and the indemnitors to acknowledge and agree that their execution of the Agreement has not been induced by or made in reliance upon any oral or written representations by the surety or any of its agents, including a representation that the surety will execute any future bonds on behalf of the principal.

3. *Books and Records and Access to the Bonded Project Sites*

The principal should be required to maintain accurate books, records, and accounts, and make them available for the surety's examination. Furthermore, the principal should specifically authorize the surety and its representatives to visit at any time the bonded project sites, and to obtain whatever project records and information deemed necessary by the surety from any source, including the obligees, subcontractors, suppliers, etc.

4. *Other General Provisions*

Exhibit 4.1 contains other general provisions that should be reviewed and considered for any financing Agreement among the principal, the indemnitors, and the surety.

G. Summary

There is no one set of procedures and mechanics for the surety financing the principal. Exhibit 4.1 and the above discussion deal with the most prevalent issues that arise when the surety finances the principal. Each case requires something different based upon the circumstances involved. The above discussion and Exhibit 4.1 serve as a checklist for the kinds of provisions in such an Agreement that the surety should consider.

VIII.
Financing The Principal In Bankruptcy

Space limitations allow only a brief discussion of surety financing of a principal that has filed a Chapter 11 bankruptcy proceeding. Other commentators have written more extensively on the subject.[41]

The surety faces two financing possibilities when the principal files its Chapter 11 bankruptcy proceeding. First, the surety may already be financing the principal pursuant to an Agreement, receiving the bonded contract funds, depositing them into the Trust Account, and jointly controlling their use. Second, the principal, with or without prior notice to the surety, after filing its Chapter 11 bankruptcy proceeding may request financing from the surety. Substantively and strategically, it may be easier for the surety to approach the Bankruptcy Court requesting the reinstitution of the Agreement and all of its protections in return for surety financing of the principal/debtor during the Chapter 11 bankruptcy proceeding. The surety's argument is that the rights, remedies, mechanics, and procedures have already been established and constitute adequate protection for the surety. However, regardless of whether the bankruptcy court adopts the prior Agreement, or whether some other financing arrangement must be negotiated with the now principal/debtor, the following issues and rights should be encompassed in any financing arrangement between the surety and the principal/debtor, and approved by an appropriate bankruptcy court order after notice and a hearing.

---

41 *See* Leo, *supra* note 4. Mr. Leo's paper was originally presented at the A.B.A. Forum on the Construction Industry Tort and Insurance Practice Section Fidelity & Surety Law Committee joint program in New York, N.Y. on January 26, 1989. Missing from the published article in the Tort and Insurance Law Journal are extensive exhibits and forms which may be found with the unpublished article submitted at the FCI/FSLC Joint Program on January 26, 1989. The exhibits and the forms are valuable, substantive materials to review. *See also* Shahinian and Clarke, *supra* note 4. T. Scott Leo and Gary A. Wilson, *Suretyship and the Bankruptcy Code*, *in* THE LAW OF SURETYSHIP 9-1 (Edward G. Gallagher ed., 1993).

A. Advancing or Lending Money to the Principal/Debtor

Section 364 of the Bankruptcy Code[42] provides that a debtor authorized to operate its business may "obtain unsecured credit and incur unsecured debt in the ordinary course of business ... as an administrative expense."[43] Therefore, the principal/debtor may purchase inventory and materials on an unsecured basis and incur other unsecured debt in the ordinary course of business, and those debts will be paid as administrative expenses on an ongoing current basis ahead of the claims of pre-petition unsecured creditors. However, if the principal/debtor requires the surety's financial assistance, bankruptcy court approval, after notice to all creditors, is required.[44] The surety should not agree to provide financing to the principal/debtor with such advances treated merely as an administrative expense. The Bankruptcy Code provides a number of alternatives for the bankruptcy court to provide protection to the surety beyond an administrative expense, including a super-priority administrative expense, liens on property of the principal/debtor's estate not subject to lien rights, rights secured by a junior lien on property of the estate that is subject to lien, or by priming a prior lien.[45]

The provisions and remedies for the protection of one providing credit or advancing or loaning funds to the principal/debtor are geared toward secured lenders and not the needs of the surety. While the surety would like additional financial protection for the advances and loans made to the principal, the surety has other issues that should be addressed that are not found in the typical lending situation. Therefore, if the surety agrees to finance the principal/debtor during its Chapter 11 bankruptcy proceedings, the surety should also obtain the rights described below in a bankruptcy court order.

B. Additional Rights for the Protection of the Surety

In addition to section 364, other sections of the Bankruptcy Code concern issues that are of significant importance to the surety.

---

42 11 U.S.C. § 364.

43 11 U.S.C. § 364(a).

44 11 U.S.C. § 364(b).

45 11 U.S.C. §§ 364(c) and (d).

1. Section 363 of the Bankruptcy Code [11 U.S.C. § 363]

Section 363 provides that the principal/debtor may not use "cash collateral" as defined in section 363 unless

> (A) each entity that has an interest in such cash collateral consents; or (B) the court, after notice and a hearing, authorizes such use,...in accordance with the provisions of this section.[46]

Furthermore, an entity that has an interest in the cash collateral may request the court to prohibit the use of such cash collateral unless the debtor provides adequate protection for the interest of that entity.[47]

A number of commentators have discussed the rights of the surety to the bonded contract funds as cash collateral.[48] Section 363 of the Bankruptcy Code does not require that the interest in "cash collateral" be a UCC security interest.[49] The surety has several possible types of interests in the bonded contract funds:

---

46 11 U.S.C. § 363(c)(2).

47 11 U.S.C. § 363(e).

48 *See* John V. Burch and Wade H. Purcell, *Cash Collateral Litigation and the Surety* (unpublished paper submitted at the A.B.A. Tort and Insurance Practice Section Fidelity & Surety Law Committee annual meeting on August 10, 1993; Robert L. Lawrence, Robert M. Wright, George J. Bachrach and William M. Dolan, III, *The Agreement of Indemnity—The Surety's Handling of Contract Bond Problems: Enforcement of the Surety's Rights Against the Principal and the Indemnitors Under the Agreement of Indemnity*, *in* THE AGREEMENT OF INDEMNITY: PRACTICAL APPLICATIONS BY THE SURETY, Chapter 2 (1990) (hereinafter referred to as *Lawrence*).

49 The Bankruptcy Code defines "cash collateral" as meaning "cash, ... in which the estate and an entity other than the estate have an interest..." 11 U.S.C. § 363(a). The word "interest" is not defined under the Bankruptcy Code. 11 U.S.C. § 101. The term "security interest" is defined under the Bankruptcy Code and means a "lien created by an agreement." 11 U.S.C. § 101(51). It is clear that the definition of "cash collateral" in the Bankruptcy Code does not limit the surety's "interest" to a "security interest," and the "interest" may include rights other than a "security interest." *See also National Shawmut Bank v. New Amsterdam Cas. Co.*, 411 F.2d 843 (1st Cir. 1969).

a. As a UCC secured party if the surety has previously filed its agreement of indemnity as a financing statement[50], or if the surety has filed financing statements against the bonded contract funds pursuant to an Agreement executed by the principal/debtor prior to the filing of its Chapter 11 bankruptcy proceeding;[51]

b. Pursuant to the trust fund provision of the agreement of indemnity;[52] and/or

c. Pursuant to the surety's subrogation rights to the rights of others.[53]

The surety must take all steps necessary to protect its rights to the bonded contract funds regardless of whether there is a prior existing agreement to finance the principal/debtor. If the surety agrees to finance the principal/debtor during the Chapter 11 bankruptcy proceedings, it *must* obtain all rights to the bonded contract funds under section 363 of the Bankruptcy Code and control over the use of the bonded contract funds pursuant to a financial arrangement with the principal/debtor along the lines of the Agreement,[54] and a bankruptcy court order.

---

50 *Leo*, *supra* note 4 at p. 51; *Shahinian and Clarke*, *supra* note 4 at p. 15.

51 *Leo*, *supra* note 4 at p. 47; J. Michael Franks and John H. Rowland, *Surety Strategy in the Chapter 11 Proceeding: Case Study of a Broke Contractor* at p. 6 (unpublished paper submitted at the A.B.A. Tort and Insurance Practice Section Fidelity & Surety Law Committee annual meeting on August 10, 1993).

52 *Matter of Jenkins*, 110 B.R. 74 (Bankr. M.D. Fla. 1990); *cf.*, *In re Construction Alternatives, Inc.*, 2 F.3d 670 (6th Cir. 1993). *See also Lawrence*, *supra* note 48 at pp. 133-54.

53 George J. Bachrach and John V. Burch, *The Surety's Subrogation Rights*, *in* THE LAW OF SURETYSHIP 26-1, Section V.B.5. (Edward G. Gallagher ed., 1993); *Leo*, *supra* note 4 at p. 59; *Universal Bonding Ins. Co. v. Gittens and Sprinkle Enterprises, Inc.*, 960 F.2d 366 (3rd Cir. 1992).

54 *In re Glover Constr. Co.*, 30 B.R. 873 (Bankr. W.D. Ky. 1983); *In re Ram Constr. Co.*, 32 B.R. 758 (Bankr. W.D. Pa. 1983).

2. *Section 365 of the Bankruptcy Code [11 U.S.C. § 365]*

Section 365 of the Bankruptcy Code authorizes the debtor to assume, assume and assign, or reject any executory contract.[55] A pre-existing financing Agreement between the surety and a principal/debtor may or may not be an executory contract that must be assumed or rejected by the principal/debtor. However, unless substantially completed, the underlying construction contracts for which the surety executed its bonds are most certainly executory contracts subject to assumption or rejection.

Under the Agreement, the surety receives voluntary letters of default and termination and the right to use those letters of default for specific construction contracts or all of the construction contracts bonded by the surety.[56] The surety may be able to reduce its loss significantly if it has control over the ability of the principal/debtor to complete some or all of the principal/debtor's construction contracts. Without this control, the surety should seriously question whether it should finance the principal/debtor during its Chapter 11 bankruptcy proceedings. The surety should argue to the bankruptcy court that its control over the bonded projects will reduce the surety's loss, thereby benefiting all of the pre-petition unsecured creditors of the principal/debtor. Furthermore, the principal/debtor must agree in the bankruptcy court order *not* to assume, assume and assign, or reject any of the bonded contracts without the express written permission of the surety.[57]

3. *Section 362 of the Bankruptcy Code [11 U.S.C. § 362]*

In order to assure the surety that it may exercise its rights under any Agreement, whether the Agreement is executed pre-petition or post-petition pursuant to a bankruptcy court order, the principal/debtor should consent to providing the surety relief from the automatic stay provisions

---

55 Marc I. Fenton, *Executory Contracts and the Role of the Surety* (unpublished paper submitted at the A.B.A. Tort and Insurance Practice Section Fidelity & Surety Law Committee annual meeting on August 10, 1993).

56 *See* Exhibit 4.1, Section I, paragraph 5 at p. 444; and Exhibit 4.1, Exhibit 4.1.4 at p. 460.

57 *Shahinian and Clarke*, *supra* note 4 at p. 28.

of section 362 of the Bankruptcy Code in order for the surety to exercise the following rights:

a. All of the surety's rights against the bonded contract funds as provided in the Agreement, allowing their joint control in a Trust Account of the bonded contract funds, and the use of the bonded contract funds from the Trust Account;

b. Authorize the surety to negotiate and settle all claims of subcontractors and suppliers against the payment bonds without subsequent bankruptcy court approval;

c. Authorize the surety to use the letters of default and termination as it deems necessary;

d. Authorize the surety to begin negotiations and discussions with obligees and other contractors concerning the potential reletting and/or completion of the bonded contracts;[58] and

e. Authorize the surety to exercise any other rights and take any other actions allowed under the Agreement.

C. Summary

The rights described above should be secured by the surety before it agrees to finance the principal/debtor during its Chapter 11 bankruptcy proceedings. The surety's goal is the same in any financing situation, namely taking such steps as are necessary to reduce its ultimate loss. The surety's financing of the principal outside of bankruptcy has been viewed as dangerous.[59] Outside of a bankruptcy proceeding, the surety may take actions that are stayed by the automatic stay of section 362 of the Bankruptcy Code once the principal/debtor files its Chapter 11 bankruptcy proceeding. The rights described above and the providing of relief from the automatic stay will put the surety in the position of financing the principal/debtor under the same circumstances as if the Chapter 11 bankruptcy proceeding had never been filed by the principal/debtor.

---

58 Frequently the surety will obtain a letter of authority from the principal/debtor authorizing the surety to begin negotiations and discussions with any contractors, subcontractors, etc. that the surety deems appropriate for the purpose of reletting or otherwise satisfying the surety's obligations under its performance bond.

59 *Schroeder No. 2*, *supra* note 1 at p. 1205.

IX.
Risks To The Surety Beyond The Penal Sum of The Performance Bond

Absent the consent of the obligee, the primary disadvantage to the surety financing the principal is that the surety receives no credit against the penal sum of its performance bond, thereby risking a loss greater than the penal sum. Cases and commentaries have identified four additional risks to the surety financing the principal that may result in the surety's loss becoming greater than the penal sum of the performance bond.

A. Alter Ego

The surety financing the principal pursuant to a financial arrangement such as the Agreement leads to a certain amount of control by the surety in the receipt of the bonded contract funds and the use of those bonded contract funds. Frequently, there are third-party creditors that are not protected by the surety's performance and payment bonds. These third-party creditors may allege that the surety so controlled the principal's business that the surety is the principal's alter ego and is liable for all of the principal's debts, whether incurred on a bonded project or not. The more control exercised by the surety, the more likely it is that the principal's unpaid third-party creditors will attempt to treat the surety as the alter ego of the principal.

To date, third-party creditors suing the surety on an alter ego theory have been generally unsuccessful.[60] The *McFadden* case is particularly instructive because many of the terms in the financing agreement utilized by the surety in the *McFadden* case[61] are similar to those provided in the Agreement attached as Exhibit 4.1. The court found that the surety did not take absolute and total control of the principal, but rather took steps to minimize its risk of loss as a major creditor of the principal.[62]

---

60 *See James E. McFadden, Inc. v. Baltimore Contractors, Inc.*, 609 F. Supp. 1102 (E.D. Pa. 1985); *John G. Lambros Co. v. Aetna Cas. & Surety Co.*, 468 F. Supp. 624 (S.D.N.Y. 1979); *Irwin & Leighton, Inc. v. W.M. Anderson Co.*, 532 A.2d 983 (Del. 1987). *See also Schroeder No. 2, supra* note 1 at pp. 1193-95.

61 *McFadden*, 609 F. Supp. at 1103-04.

62 *Id*. at 1105.

Therefore, notwithstanding the control exercised by the surety, the third-party creditor not covered by the surety's performance and payment bonds was unable to collect its debt from the surety.

B. Domination

Similar to the alter ego theory, domination by the surety is normally alleged by the principal and the indemnitors either as the result of the failure of the financial arrangement to succeed in allowing the principal to remain in business, or as a result of the surety withdrawing its financial assistance under the Agreement when the surety deems it in its best interest to do so. At that point, the principal and the indemnitors may allege that the surety's control pursuant to the Agreement so dominated the principal's business management and affairs that it inhibited the principal's business from succeeding and forced the principal to go out of business. The major cases discussing domination are the *Lambert* cases, a series of cases where the principal and the indemnitors claimed that the surety so dominated the principal that the surety was liable to the principal and the indemnitors for damages.[63]

It is obvious that the surety financing the principal has an interest in the control of the bonded contract funds and their use under the Agreement in order to ensure that the surety's liabilities under the performance and payment bonds are met and that the surety's loss is minimized. To avoid a claim of domination, the surety must set forth clearly in the financing arrangement and the Agreement all of the surety's rights and the circumstances under which those rights may be exercised. Furthermore, the Agreement must contain a clear understanding that the obligations of the surety to finance the principal (and, if contemplated,

---

63 *Lambert v. Maryland Cas. Co.*, 403 So. 2d 739 (La. App. 1981), *aff'd*, 418 So. 2d 553 (La. 1982). A discussion of the *Lambert* cases, including a chronological order by date of each decision, is contained in *Schroeder No. 2*, *supra* note 1 at pp. 1195-99. Other commentators on the *Lambert* cases include *Joyce and Haug*, *supra* note 1 at p. 34, n. 14, and William R. Sneed and Michael Athay, *Ramifications for the Surety—Domination Revisited* (unpublished paper submitted at the A.B.A. Tort and Insurance Practice Section Fidelity & Surety Law Committee mid-winter meeting in New York, N.Y. on January 29, 1988).

to provide additional future bonds to the principal) are discretionary and the circumstances are clearly spelled out.[64]

C. Tax Liabilities

By financing the principal, the surety will be directly liable for certain taxes of the principal as a result of the surety's payment of the wages of the principal's laborers on the bonded projects. The surety's concern is whether it may become liable for additional unpaid taxes, including taxes not withheld by the principal on bonded or unbonded projects prior to the initiation of the financing arrangements with the principal.[65]

There have been a number of commentators who have discussed the surety's potential tax liabilities in financing the principal.[66] The surety may be liable for withheld taxes under the performance bond itself. For any federal government projects bid after July 15, 1967, the Miller Act

---

64 *See* Exhibit 4.1, Section V, *Miscellaneous Provisions*, paragraph 3 at p. 451 (providing financial assistance to the principal) and paragraph 4 at p. 451 (providing future bonds to the principal).

65 This chapter does not discuss the conflict between the surety and the federal government or any other taxing authority under either of the following scenarios:
(1) The right of the government as obligee to set off against bonded contract funds for obligations such as unpaid taxes owed to the government obligee by the principal; and
(2) The right of the government taxing authority when it is not the obligee (and therefore has no setoff rights) to assert a tax lien against the bonded contract funds.
These issues are more fully discussed in George J. Bachrach and John V. Burch, *The Surety's Subrogation Rights*, *in* THE LAW OF SURETYSHIP 26-1, section V.B.1. (surety v. obligee), and section V.B.6. (surety v. taxing authorities other than the obligee) (Edward G. Gallagher ed., 1993).

66 *Joyce and Haug*, *supra* note 1 at p. 26; *Schroeder No. 1*, *supra* note 1 at pp. 857-59; Donald Mrozek, *The Surety's Responsibility for Withholding Taxes* (unpublished paper submitted at the A.B.A. Section of Insurance, Negligence and Compensation Law Fidelity & Surety Law Committee mid-winter meeting in New York, N.Y. on January 27, 1978).

Performance Bond provides that the surety is liable for withholding taxes.[67] Furthermore, performance bonds executed pursuant to the Little Miller acts of various states or on private contracts may create liability for the surety when the principal is obligated under the contract to pay withholding taxes. Finally, the Internal Revenue Code creates potential new liability for the surety financing its principal in three instances:

1. Section 3401 [26 U.S.C. § 3401]

The surety may be liable for withholding taxes as the "employer" when it has exercised exclusive control over the principal's employees and the payment of wages to those employees.

2. Section 3505 [26 U.S.C. § 3505]

The surety is liable for withholding taxes when it directly pays the wages of its principal's laborers, or, in the alternative, when the surety indirectly funds the payments of those wages knowing that the principal will not withhold and pay over the necessary payroll taxes. In this latter situation, the surety that finances the principal, including the funding of the principal's payroll, and has notice or reasonably believes that the principal does not intend to make timely deposits of withholding taxes, is liable to the United States for taxes and interest totaling up to 25% of the advances made. Section 3505 liability appears to be unavoidable by the financing surety.[68]

3. Section 6672 [26 U.S.C. § 6672]

The surety financing the principal and collecting the bonded contract funds may be deemed to be a "responsible person" for the payment of *all* of the taxes that were to be withheld by the principal, and the surety's

---

67 40 U.S.C. § 270a(d) ["Every performance bond required under this section (the Miller Act) shall specifically provide coverage for taxes imposed by the United States which are collected, deducted, or withheld from wages paid by the contractor in carrying out the contract with respect to which such bond is furnished."]

68 *See Schroeder No. 1*, *supra* note 1 at p. 858; *Joyce and Haug*, *supra* note 1 at p. 26.

"willful" failure to pay the withheld taxes as a "responsible person" may subject the surety to liability beyond the amounts withheld for the principal's laborers on the bonded contracts.[69]

In order to protect the surety from the tax liabilities of section 3505, Exhibit 4.1 contains a specific provision for the payment by the surety and the principal of all withholding and payroll taxes.[70] Furthermore, at the time the tax payments are made by the surety and the principal, the surety must file Form 4219 with the Internal Revenue Service.[71]

D. Environmental Claims

Financing the principal may expose the surety to potential liability for clean up costs for hazardous wastes pursuant to the Comprehensive Environmental Response, Compensation, and Liability Act[72] ("CERCLA") and other state hazardous waste laws. Several recent articles have discussed this potential liability.[73] Two major issues are involved. The first is the surety's potential liability in actually financing the principal. The second is the surety's potential liability in obtaining collateral security containing hazardous wastes.

---

69 *See Anderson v. United States*, 561 F.2d 162 (8th Cir. 1977); *Schroeder No. 2*, *supra* note 1 at pp. 1199-1200.

70 *See* Exhibit 4.1, Section III, paragraph 4(h) at p. 449 ["Payment of all withholding and payroll taxes and other amounts deducted from employee wages from the Contracts bonded by the Surety for the Principal from the date of this Agreement forward shall be made on a priority basis directly from the Trust Account to the appropriate payee(s) for all withholding and payroll taxes and other normal payroll burden expenses."]

71 Form 4219, Statement of Liability of Lender, Surety, or Other Person for Withholding Taxes under Section 3505 of the Internal Revenue Code.

72 42 U.S.C. § 9601.

73 Robert M. Wright and William F. Ryan, Jr., *Hazardous Waste Liability and the Surety Revisited,* 30 TORT & INS. L. J. ________ (forthcoming Spring 1995) (hereinafter referred to as *Wright*); and William F. Ryan, Jr. and Robert M. Wright, *Hazardous Waste Liability and the Surety,* 25 TORT & INS. L. J. 663 (1990).

1. The Surety's "Capacity to Influence" the Principal

Pursuant to the surety's financial arrangements and the Agreement with the principal, the surety may have the "capacity to influence" the principal's decisions on a day-to-day basis, including its decisions on hazardous wastes.[74] The surety's potential liability in financing the principal may be as an "operator" of a "facility" or as an "arranger" for the disposal of hazardous wastes, and may arise in several ways:

a. The surety's control over the collection and use of the bonded contract funds pursuant to the Agreement; and

b. The surety's potential "capacity to influence" through its participation in the principal's management decisions on day-to-day issues (overhead expenses, sale of excess equipment and inventory, access to books and records and the bonded project sites, etc.).[75]

While the *Fleet Factors* case dealt with a secured lending bank, and is applicable to the Eleventh Circuit only, it does raise certain questions concerning the potential liability of the surety financing the principal under CERCLA and other hazardous waste liability laws. There are cases where the surety has not been held liable to third parties when such a financing arrangement exists.[76] However:

> There is little doubt that under the agreements used by the surety in *McFadden* as well as the terms and conditions of most agreements used by sureties who are financing their principal, the surety does have the

---

74 *Wright*, *supra* note 73; *United States v. Fleet Factors Corp.*, 901 F.2d 1550, 1557 (11th Cir. 1990), *cert. denied*, 498 U.S. 1046, 111 S.Ct. 752, 112 L.Ed.2d 772 (1991) ["a secured creditor may incur (Superfund cleanup) liability, without being an operator, by participating in the financial management of a facility to a degree indicating a capacity to influence the (borrower) corporation's treatment of hazardous wastes."]

75 As stated in *Fleet Factors*, "a secured creditor will be liable if its involvement with the management of the facility is sufficiently broad to support the inference that it could affect hazardous waste disposal decisions if it so chose." 901 F.2d at 1557-58. Other circuits require actual participation in the management of a facility before liability will be found. *United States v. McLamb*, 5 F.3d 69 (4th Cir. 1993); *In re Bergsoe Metal Corp.*, 910 F.2d 668 (9th Cir. 1990).

76 *McFadden*, 609 F. Supp. 1102 (E.D. Pa. 1985).

> "capacity to influence" the principal's activities, both by way of its control over the funding of its principal's overhead expenses and field expenses, as well as its control over cash infusion and cash flow from the bonded and perhaps unbonded projects.[77]

While other decisions are more restrictive,[78] and Congress and the Environmental Protection Agency are reviewing ways to minimize the effect of the *Fleet Factors* decision, the potential liability of the surety financing its principal under the theories espoused in *Fleet Factors* remains a risk to the surety.

2. *Collateral Security Containing Hazardous Wastes*

In making the decision to finance the principal, the surety frequently takes collateral security, including mortgages on real property. CERCLA and other hazardous waste laws may have an effect on the collateral security taken by the surety, including:

a. The collateral security forming a part of the basis for the surety's financing of the principal may require hazardous waste clean up that diminishes the value of the collateral security or subjects the collateral security to a superseding governmental lien for the cost of the hazardous waste cleanup;

b. The impact of any hazardous waste cleanup costs funded by the principal may greatly impact on the principal's ability to repay the surety for the loans and advances the surety has made under the financing arrangements; and

c. The surety foreclosing on its collateral security after the principal's and the indemnitor's default may result in the surety becoming an owner/operator/arranger and subject to hazardous waste cleanup costs.

3. *Summary*

The potential risk to the surety for environmental and hazardous waste claims remains a strong factor in determining whether the surety should finance the principal. The surety may face similar risks regardless of what performance bond option the surety chooses (including takeover and

---

77 *Wright*, *supra* note 73.

78 *See* note 75, *supra*.

tender).[79] This is an area of the law that may remain uncertain for a long period of time.

X.
Subrogation Rights Of The Surety Financing The Principal

All of the rights discussed so far in this chapter have been contract rights. The principal enters into a construction contract with the obligee, subcontracts with its subcontractors, and purchase orders with its suppliers. The principal and the surety execute the performance and payment bonds on behalf of the obligee. The principal and the indemnitors execute the agreement of indemnity in favor of the surety. When the surety finances the principal, the principal and the indemnitors execute the Agreement and any liens, security agreements, and financing statements with respect to the collateral security. When disputes arise among the various parties, they are resolved by reference to the existing contracts.

Subrogation is a basic right of the surety arising not by way of a written contract, but by operation of law and equity. The surety's subrogation rights are a creation of the courts, which have ruled that a surety that pays or otherwise performs its obligations under its bonds may step into the shoes of those persons to whom or on whose behalf the surety has performed or made payment. As a result, the surety may enforce the rights of those persons who have received payment or the benefit of the surety's performance against the rights of other parties in order for the surety to obtain reimbursement for its losses. There are many primary and secondary research sources and commentaries on the surety's subrogation rights.[80]

---

79 *Wright*, *supra* note 73.

80 THE SUBROGATION DATABASE: CASES CONCERNING THE SUBROGATION RIGHTS OF THE CONTRACT BOND SURETY (George J. Bachrach ed., 1995); George J. Bachrach and John V. Burch, *The Surety's Subrogation Rights*, *in* THE LAW OF SURETYSHIP 26-7 (Edward G. Gallagher ed., 1993); SUBROGATION RIGHTS OF THE CONTRACT BOND SURETY (1990) (collected papers submitted at the A.B.A. Tort and Insurance Practice Section Fidelity & Surety Law Committee annual meeting on August 7, 1990).

There are four essential elements necessary for a surety to successfully assert its subrogation rights[81]:

1. An obligation of the principal to the obligee;
2. Failure of the principal to perform that obligation;
3. Rights of the obligee arising from the principal's failure to perform; and
4. The performance by the surety, pursuant to the suretyship, of the obligation that the principal failed to perform.

When the above four elements exist, the surety is substituted for the obligee with respect to the rights which the obligee has against the principal as a result of the principal's failure to perform.

Other commentators on the surety financing the principal have briefly discussed the surety's subrogation rights.[82] The law with respect to the subrogation rights of the surety financing the principal is as follows:

1. The surety financing the principal is acting in accordance with its legal obligations under its performance bond and therefore has the rights of a performance bond surety;[83] and
2. The surety financing the principal is not a volunteer lending money to the principal outside of the scope of its performance bond.[84]

In summary, the surety financing the principal is acting as a performance bond surety, and may exercise all of its subrogation rights as a Performance Bond surety to seek reimbursement to reduce its loss.[85]

---

81 Daniel Mungall, Jr., *The Subrogation Rights of the Contract Bond Surety: Some Basics*, *in* SUBROGATION RIGHTS OF THE CONTRACT BOND SURETY (1990).

82 *Joyce and Haug*, *supra* note 1 at pp. 36-37; *Schroeder No. 1*, *supra* note 1 at pp. 861-63.

83 *Aetna Cas. and Sur. Co. v. United States*, 845 F.2d 971 (Fed. Cir. 1988); *Morrison Assur. Co. v. United States*, 3 Cl. Ct. 626 (1983); *Great American Ins. Co. v. United States*, 481 F.2d 1298, 1300 n.8 (Ct. Cl. 1973); *Morganthau v. Fidelity & Deposit Co. of Md.*, 94 F.2d 632 (D.C. Cir. 1937).

84 *Indemnity Ins. Co. of North Am. v. Lane Contracting Corp.*, 227 F. Supp. 143 (D. Neb. 1964).

85 THE SUBROGATION DATABASE: CASES CONCERNING THE SUBROGATION RIGHTS OF THE CONTRACT BOND SURETY (George J. Bachrach ed., 1995). The Subrogation Database contains all of the cases concerning the subrogation rights of the contract bond surety organized in an outline

XI.
Conclusion

Financing the principal may be a dangerous course of action.[86] However, the surety may decide to finance the principal because it believes that financing is the cheapest way to get the bonded projects done. That belief is predicated upon the surety's investigation and its analysis of the information collected. For the surety to consider financing the principal as a performance bond option, the surety must reach the conclusions that there is nothing wrong with the principal that money cannot cure, and that the capacity, character, and collateral of the principal and the indemnitors appear favorable.

The surety should not minimize its substantial financial and management involvement with the principal in an ongoing financing arrangement. From a financial point of view, the surety will frequently pay the principal's debts that are not covered by either the performance or payment bond, including the principal's overhead. From a management point of view, there will be daily and weekly involvement by the surety in the principal's decisions on the bonded projects. To the extent that consultants, attorneys, and accountants are necessary, the surety will incur costs and expenses in this management function.

Finally, it is critical that the financing agreement between and among the surety, the principal, and the indemnitors is clear and unambiguous as to the rights and obligations of the parties. All issues and potential disputes should be discussed and resolved. It is far better to have the negotiations over the financing agreement fall apart at an early stage before the surety commits to financing the principal for any period of time rather than to create and execute a financing agreement that is unclear and ambiguous. The financing agreement should be as detailed as possible,

---

(Matrix) form. The outline (Matrix) lists the significant issues concerning the subrogation rights of the contract bond surety and provides a framework or structure to identify, organize and categorize all cases concerning the surety's subrogation rights. The Subrogation Database contains in excess of 650 cases.

86 *See* note 1, *supra*.

and attempt to resolve anticipated issues as well as those already known and outstanding.[87]

87 "Whether the financing program works depends largely upon tangible factors over which the surety has little control. But whether it works or not, if the financing program was intelligently thought through from the beginning, and the results of that analysis were appropriately documented, the surety will at least find itself in the best available position under the circumstances." *Schroeder No. 2*, *supra* note 1 at p. 1214.

Selected Readings On Surety Financing of The Principal

BOOKS

Thomas A. Joyce and William F. Haug, *Financing the Contractor*, *in* BOND DEFAULT MANUAL Chapter 2 (Richard S. Wisner ed., 1987).

Marilyn Klinger and James P. Diwik, *The Contract Performance Bond*, *in* THE LAW OF SURETYSHIP 7-1 (Edward G. Gallagher ed., 1993).

Stephen J. Trecker and George J. Bachrach, *Contract Surety Claims*, *in* CONTRACT SURETY 12 and 13 (AFSB 152) (The American Institute for Chartered Property Casualty Underwriters and the Insurance Institute of America 1992).

ARTICLES

T. Scott Leo, *The Financing Surety and the Chapter 11 Principal*, 26 TORT & INS. L. J. 45 (1990).

Donald Mrozek, *The Surety's Responsibility for Withholding Taxes* (unpublished paper submitted at the A.B.A. Section of Insurance, Negligence and Compensation Law Fidelity & Surety Law Committee annual meeting on January 27, 1978).

William F. Ryan, Jr. and Robert M. Wright, *Hazardous Waste Liability and the Surety*, 25 TORT & INS. L. J. 663 (1990).

Michael W. Saba, Moderator, *Funds Control—An Underwriting and Claims Mitigation Tool* (unpublished paper submitted at the National Bond Claims Association annual meeting in Pinehurst, N.C., on September 30, 1994).

Gilbert J. Schroeder, *Procedures and Instruments Utilized to Protect the Surety Who Finances a Contractor*, 14 FORUM 830 (1979).

Gilbert J. Schroeder, *Providing Financial Support to the Contractor*, 17 FORUM 1190 (1982).

Armen Shahinian and Bogda Clarke, M.D., *Anatomy of a Workout Agreement—Extension of Surety Credit to the Troubled Contractor—Financing Considerations, Strategies and Financing Agreements* (unpublished paper submitted at the Surety Claims Institute annual meeting in Absecon, N.J. on June 23, 1994).

William R. Sneed and Michael Athay, *Ramifications for the Surety—Domination Revisited* (unpublished paper submitted at the A.B.A. Tort and Insurance Practice Section Fidelity & Surety Law Committee annual meeting on January 29, 1988).

Wayne H. Webster, *The Surety's Decision on What to Do*, 17 FORUM 1168 (1981).

Robert M. Wright and William F. Ryan, Jr., *Hazardous Waste Liability and the Surety Revisited*, 30 TORT & INS. L. J. (1995).

CHAPTER 5

TAKEOVER AND COMPLETION

Richard A. Kowalczyk and Todd C. Kazlow

I. Introduction

This chapter will address the takeover of a project from a defaulted principal and the project's completion by the surety. For the sake of this discussion, we will assume that there has been either a voluntary default by the principal, or that the surety has determined that the obligee has properly terminated the principal's contract. The elements and mechanics of such a termination by the obligee have been covered previously, as has the investigation by the surety. We will therefore deal with the advantages and disadvantages of a takeover and completion by the surety, and the elements of a takeover agreement between the surety and obligee and a completion agreement between the surety and its completing contractor.

II. Disadvantages of Completion By The Surety

The primary disadvantage to the surety of a takeover of the project is that the surety must see the project through to completion despite whatever problems are encountered. Most of the other disadvantages which are attendant to this option flow from this premise. The risk, although quantified somewhat by a good investigation, is unknown. The surety has to consider, at a minimum, the following factors:

1. the difficulty of the work;

2. whether the job is well-organized and run;
3. how onerous the obligee is;
4. the prospect of numerous change orders;
5. how well the specifications are drawn;
6. the quality of the principal's work;
7. how far into the future the job completion extends;
8. the cost of consultants in monitoring the job;
9. the accessibility of the job to both the surety and its consultants; and
10. whether the surety's loss is capped by the bond penalty.

The first two factors can be considered together. If the project involves routine general construction that has been performed over and over, that is one thing. However, if the work involves some novel construction method, the surety, if it undertakes to complete, must have the utmost confidence in its completing contractor. Some of the risk can be passed to the completing contractor and hopefully, its surety, as will be discussed later. However, ultimately any problems the completing contractor encounters are problems for the completing surety. Whether the technical difficulties encountered by the completing contractor can be passed on to another surety or not, the obligee is looking to the original completing surety to get the project completed on a timely basis.

If the novelty of the construction is causing the completing contractor problems, either with quality of construction or maintaining the completion schedule, the surety will have to deal with the obligee about these problems. This obligation adds costs to the surety. The other side of this issue is a job where the problems are caused by the obligee. Whether the terminated principal is a general contractor or a subcontractor, the surety must look carefully at how well the job has been run. A project that has not been well coordinated and scheduled, that has had delays caused by the failure to make timely decisions, that has an owner attempting to save money by cutting corners, or that has been bogged down in a bureaucratic quagmire will cause tremendous headaches, as well as cost money, to the completing surety. Even if the hard cost of such delays are ultimately recoverable from the obligee, the cost to the surety of both administratively dealing with the problems and in paying increased consultant's costs can be significant.

The ease of dealing with the obligee is the next factor to consider. Some general contractors have a reputation, as do some owners, of being very difficult. Even an owner or a general contractor who does not have a reputation for being pugnacious can have a particular project manager or engineer who can make life on that job site particularly difficult. A war of faxes is often waged with such obligees. Constant blame is being assessed, "claims" are being set up, requests for change orders are held up, or routinely denied, pay requisitions are slow in being processed, and in general no one at such an obligee wants to be responsible for a difficult decision. Such obligees are a nightmare at best for contractors, but for sureties are a trip to the nether world. Sureties, as everyone well knows, are not contractors, are not at the job site constantly to verify conditions, and must, on occasion, pay consultants to handle these constant problems. These difficult obligees, in addition to being slow in processing requisitions, are often the same ones who take forever to close out a job and pay the final requisition. The longer a job remains open, the longer a claim file remains open, and the more the cost to the surety increases.

For some of the very same reasons apparent above, the possibility of numerous future change orders is also a significant factor. The surety is not only not a contractor, it is at best an absentee quasi contractor. If the job is fraught with the possibility of change orders, the surety will be caught up in a constant battle in processing them. A surety can attempt to entirely abrogate any review right of such change orders in the completion and takeover agreements, but in doing so loses some control of the completion. In addition, some owners will not agree to be put in a position of dealing directly with the completing contractor. However, even if the completing contractor agrees to accept only such change orders as are approved by the obligee, if there are difficulties with the approvals, the surety then will have to deal with a disgruntled completing contractor who may well try to recoup from the surety one way or another what he feels he should have received from the obligee. Although some of the difficulty and cost can be passed on to the completing contractor in the completion agreement, again the ultimate responsibility lies with the surety. This situation again causes administrative problems and attendant costs, both internally and for consultants.

Directly related to the question of change orders is that of problems attendant to poorly drawn specifications. Such a situation will cause job slow downs, inefficiencies, possibly poor construction which will lead to additional problems somewhere down the line, and at the least, numerous disputes with the obligee, its architect and engineer. Even if the responsibility for the costs which flow from these problems are ultimately found to be the responsibility of the owner's architect or engineer, a surety would have to look closely at such a situation if it had forewarning. These disputes are costly to anyone involved in construction, but perhaps more so to the surety who is not at the scene and has to purchase the engineering expertise necessary to wage these battles.

The quality of the principal's work is the next factor to be considered. It is assumed for the sake of this discussion that any bid obtained to complete the work includes the cost of correcting any patently defective work. If a defect is readily apparent to a bidder walking the job, then he should include the cost of correction of the defect in his bid. If, however, the principal was known to be guilty of poor workmanship as it was getting into financial difficulties, then it can be expected that there will be some latent defective work discovered somewhere during the completion. The completing contractor very seldom will be willing to take on as part of his bid the financial responsibility to correct improper work of the principal which is not readily apparent to him when he walks the job prior to his bid. The reason for this is obvious. As much of such improper work would not be readily apparent, it is extremely difficult, if not impossible, for him to price out this responsibility. Generally, the price the surety would obtain for this would be extremely high and should not be considered. This is not to say that given the proper circumstances, e.g. a job in its early stages of completion, where most of the work performed is readily examinable and apparent, it is not possible to obtain such a price on a satisfactory basis. However, given the fact that most of the time an acceptable price cannot be agreed upon, the completing surety will have to deal with the correction of latent defects in its principal's work on a change order basis. This situation causes problems in the flow of the work, possibly extends the completion date, causes complications in dealing with the completing contractor, and brings into play the attendant internal and external costs mentioned above. Again, because the surety is not a contractor, and is not on the job daily, there will almost necessarily be some delay in this process, no matter how well intentioned the surety may be. This delay will undoubtedly affect the completing contractor who will begin to see the surety as dragging its feet and impacting the efficiency of his performance. This in turn can result in the completing contractor attempting an impact claim back against the completing surety.

The question as to how far into the future the job completion extends relates directly to the cost to the surety, again both in internal and external costs. The number of months left until completion directly relates to the number of job meetings that may have to be attended, the number of requisitions that will have to be verified, and change orders with which the surety must deal. All of this, and the myriad other problems and issues that arise in completing the work, carries a cost to the surety.

The cost of consultants that must be employed by the surety in order to effectively complete the job needs very little amplification here. It has been directly mentioned a number of times above and is a major factor driving any decision by the surety. Because of the size of the project or the technical nature of the work, issues, and monitoring, the surety often must employ consultants. However, in the proper situation, it can be more cost effective to pay a slight premium to tender a new contractor and walk away from a job rather than pay consultants for the next twelve months on the same job, and still have the internal costs and the risks of the job going poorly.

The next factor, the accessibility of the job, is rather obvious and requires little discussion. If the job can be reached quickly from major transportation, the cost for both the surety representative and the consultant to be present on the job may be minimal. As the job gets more inaccessible, not only do the costs rise, but the difficulty becomes a factor, recognized or not, in the decision whether to attend a job meeting. Monitoring of the job could slip in such a situation.

The last factor set out above, whether the surety's liability is capped by the bond penalty, is perhaps the most crucial. The general rule appears to be that once a surety undertakes to complete the work in question, it is liable for all costs of completion. Where the cost to complete exceeds the bond penalty plus the available contract balance at the time of default, the surety's liability may exceed the penal sum of the bond. Although the surety may attempt to limit its exposure to the unknown in completion by passing liability for liquidated damages on to the completing contractor and requiring a bond from the contractor, along with other clauses to be discussed below, nevertheless, in most situations the surety will be looking at liability for latent defects in its principal's work, and perhaps warranty of its principal's work as at least two unknowns as it embarks on completion. The surety should therefore always attempt to have the obligee agree in the takeover agreement, as will be discussed below, to limit the surety's liability to the penal sum of its bond, and further, that any sums the surety disburses in completion of the project are applied towards the reduction of the penal sum of the bond. It has been said that if the takeover agreement is silent on this point, the courts appear to apply an objective test to determine whether the surety stepped into the contractor's shoes and is responsible for all costs of completion, even in excess of the bond penalty.[1] These cases appear to involve the typical indemnity type language in the bond. In such a situation, if the bond is silent as to the surety's options, and the surety undertakes to complete its principal's contract in order to mitigate its loss, then certainly the surety might appear to "step into the contractor's shoes" whether by assignment or subrogation. Query, however, if the situation is different where either the bond itself, on its face, gives the surety the option to complete the work, such as the American Institute of Architects (A312) form,[2] or where the bond requires the surety to complete. To argue in such a situation that by completing the surety waives the protection of its bond penalty would make the bond penalty surplusage and the bond contradictory on its face. A surety on a completion bond should only be obligated to expend the penal sum of its bond in completion.[3] Whatever arguments one might make, however, prudence dictates that the surety cover this point in the takeover agreement. If the obligee refuses to concede this point and limit the surety's liability to the bond penalty, the surety should seriously consider its other options.

III.
Advantages of Completion By The Surety

After a review of the above laundry list of negative factors to be considered in the decision whether to complete, one might wonder why a surety would voluntarily consider completing. The primary advantage for the surety is the control of costs that completion affords the surety. The surety can select a qualified completing contractor at a competitive price. The surety can enter a contract with the completing contractor for

---

1 Luther P. Cochrane, *Obligations of the Principal's Subcontractors and Suppliers at Default or Takeover by the Surety*, 14 FORUM 869 (1979).

2 *See* American Institute of Architects Document A312, December 1984 edition.

3 *See* discussions and cases cited in Bruce C. King, *Takeover and Completion of Bonded Contracts by the Surety* (unpublished paper submitted at the A.B.A. Tort and Insurance Practice Section Fidelity & Surety Law Committee mid-winter meeting in New York, N.Y. on January 27, 1995) at p. 31.

either a lump sum price, or a guaranteed maximum price. The surety may have been able to obtain an agreement by the principal's subcontractors to complete the work for the balance of their subcontracts, enabling the surety to obtain a better price from the completing contractor.

Second, the surety may well gain a measure of good will from the obligee by being willing to complete. An obligee who has just had a contractor terminated is most likely already looking at some delay and confusion in its project completion. If a surety steps in promptly to attempt as smooth a transition as possible with a completing contractor, it may well find an obligee more willing to discuss a waiver, at least partially, of liquidated damages and time extensions for completion. The obligee at this point would have a better idea of the new prospective completion date, and would not be discussing such damages and extensions in a vacuum, leading him to at least consider concessions in return for the surety's swift cooperation.

Third, negotiation of a takeover agreement with the obligee affords an opportunity and vehicle to clearly address the scope of the remaining work, the status of change orders, and the contract balance. As part of this process, the surety may well be able to address effectively any allocation of responsibility for corrective work, flaws in the specifications, and design defects. It is an opportune time to negotiate and settle as many disputes as possible, and determine the surety's liability and exposure. There are motivations on both sides driving this opportunity. The obligee and the surety both want the work to resume as quickly as possible. Both want to know and settle what financial exposure there might be in order to plan and effectively move on with the project.

If the surety's investigation reveals that any negatives associated with completion are either minimal or manageable, completion affords the surety the opportunity early on after termination of its principal to address promptly and effectively the issues that will eventually need to be handled, and to control the costs of completion.

In reality, there are many times when completion by the surety is utilized because no other option appears viable. If financing the principal is out of the question, because of the factors addressed in that chapter, and the obligee will not accept a tender of a new contractor, the surety may be left to decide between either takeover of the work, or allowing the obligee to complete with the surety financing the shortfall. At least control over the costs can be exerted in a takeover, as set out above. It would appear that in many situations, the decision to take over is made because the devil you know is preferred.

IV.
The Takeover Agreement

Once a surety has made a decision to take over and complete the project, the surety should promptly begin negotiations with the obligee on the terms of the takeover agreement. Where completion is compelled by the terms of the bond and is not voluntary on the part of the surety, some obligees fail to see the necessity of a takeover agreement, and refuse to negotiate. Even if it is difficult, if not impossible, to obtain concessions from such an obligee, there are still advantages to setting out the terms of the future working relationship between the parties in writing in order to allow the work to progress smoothly. There may be items in dispute between the parties which can be settled or at least clarified in such an agreement. Certainly in situations where the surety is voluntarily completing, the surety may be able to obtain favorable terms from the obligee to induce the surety to complete. The surety takes on an additional burden, if not risk, in completing. In turn, the obligee obtains a prompt resumption of the work without the burden of obtaining a completion contractor. For the additional burden and risk, the surety should obtain whatever concessions possible in order to reduce its risk and, perhaps, also its loss.

The takeover agreement between the surety and the obligee is generally separate and distinct from the completion between the surety and the completing contractor. It is possible to combine both agreements in a three-party agreement, but this has disadvantages. Many obligees, in fact, will not participate in a three party agreement, firmly believing that it is the surety's place to contract directly with the completing contractor. Some public owners believe that they cannot contract directly with a new contractor without violating the local statutes or regulations. The three party agreement, obviously, places the obligee, surety, and completing contractor in privity with one another in the same agreement.

Sample takeover agreements and completion contracts are set out in the Appendix. See Exhibits 5.1-5.6.[4]

The following items should be addressed, if appropriate, in every takeover agreement:

1. identification of the parties, the contract between the obligee and the principal, the bond, and the termination of the principal;
2. the acceptance of the completing contractor by the obligee;
3. identification of the contract amount, sums paid to the principal, and status of change orders;
4. dedication of the contract balance, including earned but unpaid funds, to the completion of the work;
5. the issue of liquidated damages, whether they are to be waived in whole or part, and the possible establishment of a new completion date;
6. method of payment of requisitions and administration of the work;
7. a recognition by the obligee that any sum advanced by the surety for completion of the work reduces by that amount the penal sum of the bond;
8. a recognition that the surety's maximum loss is limited to the penal sum of the bond; and
9. a specific reservation of rights with respect to those items which cannot be settled in the agreement.

Obviously, both parties are better served by negotiating as many open items as possible. The surety is perhaps never in as strong a negotiating position as it is prior to finalizing a decision to complete and formalizing an agreement with the obligee. It is possible and recommended that the contract funds be identified and agreed upon. This includes identifying as many change orders as possible, and negotiating the dollar values. It is important that the agreement require the owner to first apply the contract balance toward the cost to complete. The completing surety should always have the unpaid contract balance available for completion. In the surety's investigation, it can identify any part the obligee may have played in allowing the work to fall behind schedule. This determination is important in negotiating a reduction or elimination of liquidated

---

4 The authors gratefully acknowledge George J. Bachrach for his contribution of Exhibits 5.2, 5.4 and 5.6.

damages and the establishment of a new completion date for the project. This arrangement makes it cleaner and easier to pass on responsibility for future liquidated damages to the completing contractor. Although the surety may attempt to negotiate a limit to its liability for warranty work and latent defects, generally this is not successful. In general, obligees find it difficult to "let the surety off the hook" for the work of its principal. If the investigation has revealed that there are any other issues that need to be addressed, and if an agreement cannot be reached settling them in the completion agreement, then these items should be identified with particularity, and both parties should reserve their rights to pursue these open items at a later date.

V.
The Completion Agreement

It is obvious that if the surety has decided to take over and complete the project and utilize a completing contractor, then there should be a written agreement with that contractor. The surety should attempt in this contract to set out with as much particularity as possible the details of the agreement. The surety attempts, in this agreement, to pass on to the completing contractor, its insurers, and its surety as much of the liability for the unknown in the completion of the project as it can. The agreement should cover the basics of any contract. It should set out the parties, scope of work, the liabilities of the parties, and the mechanics of the relationship in dealing with such matters as payment and change orders. The following are some of the salient points to be covered in any completion agreement entered into between the surety and its completing contractor:

1. identification of the parties and project;
2. definition of the scope of work—this will generally be the completion of principal's contract and correction of defective work;
3. the new completion date and responsibility for liquidated damages;
4. payment and performance bonds required of the completing contractor;
5. contract price;
6. terms and method of payment;
7. indemnification of surety by completing contractor;
8. insurance requirements;

9. assignment of materials on work site to the completion contractor;
10. contract administration, including processing of change orders and approval of same;
11. warranty responsibilities of completing contractor;
12. responsibility for latent defects; and
13. manner of delivery of required notices under the contract.

There may be special circumstances or issues on a particular job, such as compliance with statutory requirements for minority participation on the job, which should be addressed in the completion agreement. Although it is always preferable that a completion agreement be for a set contract price, there are circumstances where this may not be achievable. However, where this is so, at the least the surety should obtain a guaranteed maximum price. It is just not possible for a surety to efficiently and effectively monitor a contract in which the contractor's payment is determined on a time and material basis.

VI.
Utilization of Principal's Subcontractors

Where the surety's principal was the general contractor, there may be a definite monetary benefit to the surety to have the completing contractor utilize the principal's subcontractors. The advantages are obvious. The subcontractors may have already mobilized, are familiar with the job, and probably have material either available or on order. They should therefore be able to complete the remaining work at a lower price than others, if they agree to hold to the prices in their original agreements with the principal. However, subcontracts are generally considered to be terminated at the time of termination of the general contract. There are several articles which discuss in some detail the possibility of assignment of the subcontract, either by written assignment obtained from the principal, or the terms of the indemnity agreement.[5] There is also a possible argument to be made that the surety is subrogated to the rights

---

5 Cochrane, *supra* note 1, and James W. Smirz, *Takeover Agreement and Maintaining Existing Subcontractors and Suppliers For the Takeover Contract* (unpublished paper submitted at the A.B.A. Tort and Insurance Practice Section Fidelity & Surety Law Committee annual meeting in New York, N.Y. on August 12, 1986).

of its principal in the subcontract. Indeed, there is at least one case that suggests that an assignment of the subcontract does not give the surety anything beyond the traditional subrogation rights. At any rate, whether the surety can or does desire to assume a subcontract from its principal requires a careful analysis both as to the position of the principal and subcontractor prior to the principal's termination, i.e. whether either was in default of the subcontract agreement such as by non-payment or delay, and whether such assumption can enlarge the surety's liability to the subcontractor beyond any payment bond obligation, such as for delay damages.[6] By an assignment, the surety steps into the shoes of its principal and loses the protection of the traditional payment bond limitations.

There is an alternative to the assignment of the subcontract, and that is for the surety to utilize a reaffirmation agreement with the subcontractor. By acting promptly, the surety can hasten the payment of a subcontractor's payment bond claim and in doing so, get the commitment of the subcontractor to complete the balance of his work for the balance of his original subcontract price. The surety must be careful in this situation, however, not to withhold or threaten to withhold the payment in order to extract the reaffirmation agreement. The surety's obligations under the payment bond are separate and distinct and must be fulfilled regardless. A sample reaffirmation agreement is set out in the Appendix. See Exhibit 5.7. In general, such an agreement would set out the subcontract amount, the amount paid, and amount due under the subcontract.

Where the job involves some specialized, unique work, skill, knowledge, or material, the surety may not be able to estimate its loss properly, or evaluate its options without first obtaining some commitment from the subcontractors. This, therefore, may be one of the first steps the surety takes in investigating its options.

There are two final cautions in dealing with the principal's subcontractors. The first is that in reaching any agreement with a subcontractor, it is important not to allow a novation of the contract between the principal and the subcontractor. A novation could arguably result in a cancellation of any warranties or other rights the principal may have had.[7] Lastly, the surety should be careful in tendering a subcontractor to a completing

---

6 Cochrane, *supra* note 1, at 886.
7 Smirz, *supra* note 5, at 26.

contractor to not require that the contractor utilize the particular subcontractor. If the subcontractor in question were to delay the job by its performance or perform defective work, the surety may well be faced with a claim back from the completing contractor who was compelled to use the subcontractor.

VII.
Principal's Claims And Defenses

When a principal who has been declared to be in default under the contract and terminated by the obligee contests the default and maintains that he should not have been terminated, the surety must investigate the situation very carefully. In such a situation, the principal's cooperation in the investigation is essential. Often the conclusion as to whether the principal was wrongfully terminated will turn on a careful reading of the contract documents, and a factual finding as to whether the alleged breach by the principal is substantial or material. A default which would involve the surety requires a material breach or series of breaches which are sufficient to justify termination.[8] It is not always clear when there is a material breach. In such a situation, the surety runs a risk that if it stands firmly behind the principal's position and refuses to act because of the alleged wrongful termination by the obligee, it will be subject to extra contractual damages in any action by the obligee against both the surety and its principal. In addition, such a position will leave completion of the principal's work to the obligee, and there may well be little control over the costs which could escalate sharply and expose the surety to even greater completion costs should the principal be found to have been in default. In such a situation the surety may well attempt to negotiate a takeover agreement with the obligee which acknowledges the principal's position that the termination is contested. Further, as part of such an agreement, the surety should make certain that there is an acknowledgment by the obligee that the principal's position is reserved and not waived, and further that the surety's cost in completing the work, in excess of the contract balance, is an element of the principal's claim for wrongful termination against the obligee.

---

8 *L&A Contracting Company v. Southern Concrete Services, Inc.*, 17 F.3d 106, 110 (5th Cir.1994).

Obviously, an obligee may balk at such a reservation of rights; however, in return the obligee receives the surety's cooperation in completing the work, and the surety's funds are available for excess completion costs. An obligee confident in its position should not hesitate to accept such a reservation. On the other hand, such a reservation allows the surety to navigate a middle position and limit its exposure.

VIII.
Federal Acquisition Regulations

After all of the aforementioned criteria have been considered, the surety must, when dealing with a federal agency, confront the Federal Acquisition Regulations (FAR).[9] The FAR system became effective on April 1, 1984, and was developed pursuant to the Office of Federal Procurement Policy Act of 1974[10] in order to establish a unified government wide procurement system.[11]

It is not the purpose of this section to critically review all of the FAR as they pertain to the surety's responsibility upon a declared default and under a takeover. However, it is appropriate to point out certain provisions of the FAR that affect the fundamental rights of a surety throughout the default, takeover, and completion process.

FAR Section 49.404 applies to fixed price construction contracts terminated for default. When a contractor is declared to be in default and the surety, pursuant to its obligation under the performance bond, attempts to complete the contract, this section calls for the government contracting officer to take action on the basis of the government's interest.[12] The regulations allow the contracting officer to enter into a takeover agreement with the surety and requires that the agreement include both the surety and the defaulting contractor "...in order to eliminate any disagreement

---

9 48 C.F.R., Chapter 1, Subchapter 8-H.

10 Pub. L. No. 93-400 (codified at 41 U.S.C. § 401).

11 D. Crane, *A Critical Examination of the Federal Acquisition Regulations Related to Sureties* (unpublished paper submitted at the A.B.A. Tort and Insurance Practice Section Fidelity & Surety Law Committee annual meeting on August 13, 1991).

12 41 U.S.C. § 49.404(b).

concerning the contractor's residual rights, including assertions to unpaid prior earnings."[13]

Section 49.404(e) is controversial in that it provides that certain conditions be met in the takeover agreement that provides for the surety to complete the work. That section specifies that the government pay the surety the balance of the contract price unpaid at the time of default, but not in excess of the surety's costs and expenses.

The first section appears contrary to established case law and states:

> (1) Any unpaid earnings of the defaulting contractor, including retained percentages and progress estimates for work accomplished before termination, shall be subject to debts due the Government by the contractor, except to the extent that such unpaid earnings may be required to permit payment to the completing surety of its actual costs and expenses incurred in the completion of the work, exclusive of its payments and obligations under the payment bond given in connection with the contract.[14]

This section ignores the ruling in *Pearlman v. The Reliance Insurance Company*[15] which holds in essence that the same equitable rules as to subrogation that apply when a surety completes a contract also apply when a surety pays laborers and materialmen.[16] Unfortunately, the authors of this section gave no weight to precedent as set forth by the Supreme Court of the United States. It is recommended that the surety argue to the contracting officer that the payments made under the payment bond cannot be distinguished from those made under the performance bond for subrogation purposes, and to do so would be in contravention of established precedent. A persuasive argument must be skillfully presented to prevail upon the government on this issue, but success can be achieved. Only a firm grasp of the decisions on this issue will suffice in discussing the surety's equitable right to recover from the government. As with many of the issues involving the FAR, much will depend on the attitude and reasonableness of the government's representative.

---

13 41 U.S.C. § 49.404(d).

14 41 U.S.C. § 49.404(e)(1).

15 371 U.S. 132, 83 S.Ct. 232, 9 L.Ed.2d 190 (1962).

16 *See Henningsen v. USF&G*, 208 U.S. 404, 28 S.Ct. 389, 52 L.Ed. 547 (1908).

The next difficult section is 49.404 (e)(3) which states:

> If the contract proceeds have been assigned to a financing institution, the surety may not be paid from unpaid earnings, unless the assignee consents to the payment in writing.

Again, the government ignores the established law in that this section violates the Assignment of Claims Act.[17] The surety has the burden of prevailing upon the contracting officer to understand this unfair condition and not to impose it upon a party that has no control over the financial institution.

The final provision of the FAR that will be discussed here involves Sec. 49.404 (e)(4) which states:

> A surety should not be paid any amount in excess of its total expenditures necessarily made in completing the work and discharging its liabilities under the payment bond of the defaulting contractor. Furthermore, payments to the surety to reimburse it for discharging its liabilities under the payment bond of the defaulting contractor, shall be only on authority of —
> (i) Mutual agreement between the Government, the defaulting contractor and the surety;
> (ii) Determination of the Comptroller General as to payee and amount; or
> (iii) Order of a Court of competent jurisdiction.

The surety should have to prove only that it performed the obligations of its principal under the performance and payment bonds. Section 49.404(e)(4) is the most objectionable since it strips the surety of a right that is "basic to the law of suretyship."[18]

As a practical matter, the surety must deal with the agencies that are charged with complying with the FAR. The surety may use the assignment provisions of the agreement of indemnity to satisfy the requirements of Section 49.404(e)(4). In many cases this strategy could be successful and convince the government that the "mutual agreement" requirements of the FAR are met.

---

17 31 U.S.C. § 203.

18 *See Crane*, *supra* note 11, at 16.

It is not the intent of this manual to suggest changes in FAR as they apply to the surety. That task has been accomplished by others.[19] Rather, it is hoped that the reader will become aware of the hurdles that are present when dealing with a federal government agency. There are no pat answers to these difficult problems, and the surety claim representative must draw upon his or her experience and the legal precedent available in order to protect the rights that have been rightfully established by the industry.

IX.
Conclusion

A successful decision to complete and a successful completion is determined by a thorough investigation in which the pitfalls of takeover are identified, and by the negotiation and drafting of very specific takeover and completion agreements. The takeover and completion agreements not only identify the risks and issues and assign them to the various parties, but they also set the tenor for the job completion and the mechanism for a smooth completion. Although the completion of any construction project always carries risks and unknowns with it, specifically drafted agreements would minimize the risks, pass most of them on to other parties such as the completing contractor, its surety and insurers, and quantify most of the completing surety's exposure.

---

19 *See Crane*, *supra* note 11, at 17.

CHAPTER 6

TENDER

James H. Baumgartner, Jr.

I. Introduction

Tender is a separate and distinct form of performance and very different from financing the principal [Chapter 4, *supra*] or takeover [Chapter 5, *supra*]. Upon tender, classically the surety pays any deficiency in the existing contract balance up to the price to be paid to the new contractor or the penal limit of the bond, whichever is less. The surety is then released from its bond, the surety's loss fixed, and the file closed as an active claim. Unlike other alternatives that a surety has to consider when confronted with a default, the potential tendering of a new contractor for the performance of the obligation is seldom one to be exercised as a matter of right. Many bond forms contain no provision that would allow the surety, as a matter of right, to tender a new contractor for completion of the bonded obligation. Further, the few bond forms which contemplate a tender not surprisingly require the obligee's concurrence in selecting a new contractor to be tendered.

The unique nature of each and every default precludes any exhaustive analysis of "tender" possibilities. The purpose of this chapter is to raise the question as to the potential appropriateness of a "tender" and provide some basic considerations as a starting point. The forms provided in the

Appendix[1] are intended as "drafts" which need to be tailored for each situation.

II.
The Most Critical Factors

When considering tender in a default situation, there are several critical factors that need to be addressed at the outset:

1. The status of the original contractor;
2. The specific language of the bond, if any, concerning the "tender" option;
3. The willingness of the obligee to accept a "tendered" new contractor;
4. The comparative cost as contrasted to other performance means; and
5. A continuing awareness to avoid exposing more than the penal sum of the bond.

The following analysis of these critical factors raises the reason and rationale for their critical nature, and some matters to be considered, but it is certainly not an exhaustive or preclusive explanation of what may be critical in a given situation.

A. The Status of the Original Contractor

In a tender context, it is imperative that all relationships be clear, and that the original contractor has indeed been placed in default pursuant to the terms and conditions of the bonded contract. If possible, the surety will find it of great assistance to obtain the following types of documents from its defaulted contractor (the attached Appendix contains these forms):

- Principal's Acknowledgment of Default to Surety, see Exhibit 6.1;
- Assignment From Principal to Surety of Contract Rights and Proceeds, see Exhibit 6.2;

---

1 The attached forms were originally prepared and published by James A. Knox and Robert D. Carnaghan, *Tendering of a New Contractor by Surety*, *in* BOND DEFAULT MANUAL, Chapter 2 (Richard S. Wisner ed., 1987). They are reprinted here with the consent of the authors and the ABA.

- Letter of Direction from Principal to Obligee (regarding contract payments), see Exhibit 6.3; and
- Power of Attorney from Principal to Surety (regarding negotiable instruments), see Exhibit 6.4.

Whatever the final decision may be concerning tender, these documents can be of significant value to the surety. Because the new contractor will have a new contract with the obligee, not an assignment of the old, it is essential that the defaulted contractor's position be ascertained, even if his cooperation is not forthcoming. Obviously the less cooperative the original contractor may be, the more formal each step in terminating the contract and the resultant demands upon the surety must be.

B. The Specific Language of the Bond, If Any, Concerning the "Tender" Option

As alluded to previously, many bonds contain no provision whatsoever for a surety to tender a new contractor, and those that do typically require the obligee's consent and concurrence. For example, the American Institute of Architects Document A312 Performance Bond, December 1984 Ed. provides in pertinent part as follows:

> 4. When the Owner has satisfied the conditions of Paragraph 3, the Surety shall promptly and at the Surety's expense take one of the following actions:
>
> * * *
>
> 4.3 Obtain bids or negotiated proposals from qualified contractors acceptable to the Owner for a contract for performance and completion of the Construction Contract, arrange for a contract to be performed for execution by the Owner and the contractor selected with the Owner's concurrence, to be secured with performance and payment bonds executed by a qualified surety equivalent to the bonds issued on the Construction Contract, and pay to the Owner the amount of damages as described in Paragraph 6 in excess of the Balance of the Contract Price incurred by the Owner resulting from the Contractor's default; ...

The presence or absence of such language is not necessarily determinative of the availability of a tender option, but it can materially affect how the surety undertakes to approach the obligee concerning the option. Without regard to the language of the particular bond form, common law or statute, often the practical answer for the surety is a no-nonsense, businesslike approach simply explaining that it may be the quickest and most effective way to cure the default. There is not time to litigate, and even the most hostile obligee is normally willing to consider a legitimate proposal.

C. The Willingness of the Obligee to Accept a "Tendered" New Contractor

Frequently an obligee, whether public or private, will resist the concept of making a totally new contract with a new contractor. Resistance to the concept must be anticipated and a persuasive response planned by the surety. The bond may provide a source for a legal position, but a tailored response demonstrating both practical and legitimate business reasons are often more successful in persuading the owner to consider a new contract directly with a new contractor to be tendered by the surety. Some of those arguments could be:

1. The nature and present status of the construction, i.e., 15% complete, is more conducive to a new contractor relationship (there may be another contractor that the obligee would prefer to work with and the surety will want the obligee's input into the selection of the new contract, etc.);
2. The surety will be out of the picture, and the obligee will have the normal control over the completion of the work without the necessity of resolving on-the-job problems with a noncontractor and its attorneys, i.e., the surety;
3. If the contract funds deficit is to be paid up front by the surety, an early cash payment could have some appeal to the obligee;
4. The obligee's professional representative, architect or engineer, like the obligee, will be in a position to proceed unfettered with knowledgeable construction persons, and not the nonconstruction-oriented surety;
5. The simplicity of the arrangement with a clean slate, determination of liability, and a new start with a new contractor can be argued persuasively; and
6. If the surety has been unable to negotiate a release of its bond, there is a further argument that with the new contractor, the obligee will have a triple layer of security through the financial strength of the new

contractor, the new contractor's surety, plus the balance of the penal sum of the original bond.

If the obligee either remains or becomes inalterably opposed to the tender concept, absent appropriate bond language, the surety should probably concentrate its efforts on some other type of performance. In the final analysis, it will be necessary for the obligee to at least be willing to consider the proposal if there is to be any success.

D. The Comparative Cost of Tender as Contrasted to Other Performance Means

The surety's investigation [Chapter 2, *supra*] in a potential tender situation is often more detailed and needs to be more exhaustive than one in which other potential performance options are the surety's probable method of performance. Particular emphasis needs to be directed toward job materials on site, in the original contractor's yard, in a bonded warehouse, in the possession of the supplier, en route to the job, and/or in the process of being specially fabricated for the job. The better the identification of these materials, which have either been paid for or are typically the subject of payment bond claims when combined with other estimated job completion costs, provides the surety with an informed basis to consider the potential of reletting the work and analyzing any bids received for completion by the new contractor.

When considering tender as an option, the surety is by definition attempting to balance the cost of tender versus other estimated costs of performance. Almost by definition, the new contractor will be critically interested in providing an ample cushion for any "unknown" or "hidden" costs that are not apparent based upon the new contractor's review of the contract requirements and the status of performance to date. By having an accurate up-to-date materials list, the potential for the unknowns is less, and hopefully the amount of the cushion reduced when the new contractor undertakes to bid the job. The closer the inventoried materials can be identified, the better the surety's estimate to complete ought to be, with the result being that the surety is then in a position to more accurately assess the cost of the tender option as distinguished from other performance options. Almost without exception the estimated cost to complete is less than the effects of the probable bid by a potential new contractor for tender. However, the surety's internal costs, combined with its attorneys' fees, consultants' costs, and other intangible costs can justify the tender as a preferred means of resolution. It is the necessity to undertake this balancing analysis which renders the comparative cost analysis of a tender option so critical in the surety's assessment.

E. A Continuing Awareness to Avoid Exposing More Than the Penal Sum of the Bond

The tender option can and should encompass numerous agreements and understandings among the obligee, the surety, and the new contractor before any work on the project resumes. While agreeable to the tender, the obligee often will not agree to release the original surety from its bond, and as alluded to previously, this possibility could very well be a potential selling point in trying to convince an obligee to accept tender as a viable option. Due to typical time constraints and heat of the moment demands, it is essential that the surety continually keep the penal limit of the bond in the forefront of all of its considerations. In many states, the bond may be a single penalty bond for both payment and performance obligations. The apportioning of those obligations is an integral part of any tender consideration; the potential of residual liability if the surety is not released must be addressed and specifically agreed upon; and definite contractual agreements must be reached concerning the effects of claimed latent and patent defects in the work previously undertaken by the original contractor. In the pressure cooker that typically arises when confronted with a default and the tender option, the surety must continually reassess its position concerning its obligations and commitments remaining within and limited to the penal sum of its bond at all times. Otherwise, it is very easy for a surety to expose itself, unnecessarily, beyond the penal limit of its bond.

Even before the surety gets to the issue of potentially obtaining bids from new contractors, the surety needs to reach an underlying written agreement of understanding with the obligee, if only in letter form, which should contain at least the following points of unquestioned agreement:

1. Confirmation that the original contractor was placed in default by the obligee or has voluntarily acknowledged its default, as the case may be.

2. Subject to acceptability, the obligee has agreed to execute a contract with another contractor for the performance of the work including approved change orders and modifications.

3. With the owner's cooperation, the surety has agreed to undertake to obtain bids from other contractors for the performance of the bonded work including the approved change orders and modifications.

4. The exact amount of the remaining contract balance is specifically identified including any change orders or modifications, any earned but unpaid amounts, and the retainage, if any.

5. The obligee has rededicated the entire remaining contract balance to pay for the performance by the new contractor, or if the unpaid funds exceed the cost of completion, a commitment to pay such funds to the surety to the extent of its legal and equitable rights and remedies as a surety. The resolution of any potential liquidated damage claim should be encompassed in this rededication if at all possible, and an agreement reached on the extension of time necessary to complete the work estimated, but subject to revision based upon the new contractor's bid.

6. An affirmation that all work performed to date by the original contractor was in accordance with and met contract requirements, except as noted in an attached schedule, or as noted in the anticipated bid invitation. This allows the new contractor to include in its bid the cost to correct all defective work, whether visible or not on reasonable inspection. If some type of agreement cannot be reached as to the responsibility for latent defects, those issues may have to be excepted from the new contract.

7. A resolution of which party will bear the burden of warranties. In certain instances it may be possible to have the new contractor accept all those responsibilities within its bid, or as a separate line item cost to the surety, but if not, the surety may rather hold the risk and address it at a later point in time. Obviously, it is to the surety's advantage to address this issue up front, and if feasible cost-wise, to pass that responsibility on to the new contractor and its surety.

8. The extent to which the surety will receive a release of its bond upon the execution of a new contract by the obligee with the new contractor. If possible, the surety should attempt to either have its bond returned, or be released from all liability based upon the security of the new contractor being bonded by a reputable surety. If the release is not obtained, the remaining balance of the penal sum of its bond not otherwise paid in connection with the tender needs to be subordinated to the commitment of the new contractor and his surety. This subordination agreement ought to be executed between the surety and obligee simultaneously with the execution of the contract between the new contractor and

his surety. Depending upon the claims of the original contractor as against the obligee, the surety should not purport to release those claims or the claims that it may have against the obligee for caused delays, changed conditions, etc. However, experience has shown that if claims are reserved for the benefit of the original contractor or the surety, the likelihood of obtaining any type of release from the obligee is virtually nonexistent.

9. An express provision that under no circumstance shall the surety be exposed to more than the penal sum of its bond.

10. The timing and method by which the surety will pay the difference between the new contract with the new contractor and the remaining contract balance in the obligee's hands. Conceptually, this could be in either a lump sum payment, typically preferred by the obligee, or some type of pro rata payment as pay estimates are approved.

Having reached a written agreement with the obligee containing at least the foregoing understandings, the surety is now for the first time in a position to proceed with the bidding process and the obtaining of a new contractor. The attached Appendix contains the following forms:

- Invitation to Bid, Fixed or Cost Plus Fee, see Exhibit 6.5;
- Invitation to Bid, Unit Price, see Exhibit 6.6;
- Bid Proposal, see Exhibit 6.7;
- Schedule of Prices (per unit price work), see Exhibit 6.8; and
- Bidder's Affidavit (required in some jurisdictions), see Exhibit 6.9.

III.
Advantages/Disadvantages of Tender

A. The Advantages of Tender

Too often by the time a surety is called in on a potential default, an acrimonious relationship has existed between the obligee and the original contractor for months, and the well intended surety is immediately immersed in those hostilities which can and often do continue throughout the performance and completion of the bonded obligation. Tender allows the surety and the obligee to extricate themselves from an otherwise acrimonious relationship, establish a clean break, and from the obligee's point of view start anew. By virtue of the tender, the surety can ascertain its loss at a much earlier date; relieve its claim staff of the burden of following the contract through completion; and insulate itself from continually being exposed to unforeseen claims and events which can substantially increase the risk of financial loss. The surety relieves itself of the potential horrors of continued warranty claims and latent defect assertions, and the surety eliminates its exposure to claims that it has undertaken financial responsibility for obligations not typically encountered under either its performance bond or its payment bond.

In dealing with its indemnitors, the surety is more likely to be in a position to act quickly and more successfully, while the realities of the default are clearer to the indemnitors, and the bidding process virtually precludes the possibility of the indemnitors claiming excessive costs incurred by the surety as to its actual performance, use of consultants, use of attorneys, etc., as well as the myriad of other claims of mismanagement in the performance process, which indemnitors frequently assert. The advantages of the tender option are probably most apparent in projects that have just commenced or are less than 25% complete, for a variety of reasons:

1. The acrimonious relationship previously mentioned has not developed to the point that it permeates the entire job and every issue that may arise;

2. Other than possibly foundation problems, the work that typically gives rise to latent defect claims has not commenced, the new contractor is much less concerned about such defects, and the surety will not be confronted with an insurmountable cost premium for the new contractor's assumption of potential liabilities;

3. Assuming the project was originally one that was let for bid, the familiarity of the other bidders on the project will significantly improve their responsiveness to a request for bid and the likelihood of their availability to mobilize is greater; and

4. Most importantly the opportunity for significant cost savings to the surety, both internal claims costs, and external fees and costs for attorneys, consultants, and the like is greater in the early stages of any project.

As a project progresses toward completion, the obligee's receptiveness to a tender generally decreases, and the new contractor's "cost premium" for the assumption of potential liabilities for work in place and warranty claims increase dramatically. The impact of percentage of completion cannot be understated when considering tender as an option.

B. Disadvantages of Tender

Time and potential costs pose the two greatest disadvantages to the tender option. When confronted with a default, the obligee's position, virtually without exception, is one of a demand that the default be cured immediately, and that work on the project commence immediately. When confronted with the prospect of tender, the obligee is immediately wary of the potential time required to obtain the new contractor, execute a new contract, and proceed with the project. Similarly, depending upon the completion condition of the project, the surety's investigation and analysis in the tender context must be one of greater detail as referred to above, and the resultant time necessary to complete consideration of the option, may preclude the surety from successfully completing its default analysis and subsequent tender of a new contractor. If the obligee believes the surety's investigation is taking too long, the obligee may commence to complete the project on the basis that the surety has refused to act in a timely manner. The obligee may also argue that the surety has breached its bond by failing to perform. The inherent time constraints and the surety's continuing relationship with the obligee must be carefully dealt with in an ultimately successful manner.

Except for those projects in the very early stages of completion, the surety could very well be confronted with spending significantly greater sums to effectuate the tender option than any one of the other three traditional options. The surety's investigative costs are typically higher, the bidding process adds additional costs, negotiation with the bidders and successful bidder increases the expenses, and by definition the surety is going to pay some premium for having a new contractor assume the liabilities of the old. The cost in negotiating with the obligee and new contractor concerning the tender option can often be cost prohibitive and again the potential difficulties concerning the prospects of latent defects and warranty claims can render the option untenable. The payment bond obligations can increase dramatically, particularly in those states where dual penalty bonds are used as opposed to single penalty, and the potential loss of nonretained subcontractors then increases the cost to the new contractor when it relets the work to a new subcontractor. Most often potential claims against the subcontractor are lost due to a lack of specific information concerning the suitability of their separate work, which in turn then increases the overall cost of the tender option.

An additional disadvantage in the tender option is the reality that the obligee may be unwilling to totally release the surety from its bond obligations, and the resulting potential of yet additional cost remains. The successful tender can save the surety significant long-term dollars, but the amount and extent of those dollars are typically unknown, and not subject to ready quantification.

IV. Negotiations with the Obligee

A. Obligee's Concerns

The obligee's concerns can generally be described as why, when, who and how? The "why" issue will most certainly be raised by the obligee as it will be looking to the surety to "perform" as stated in the bond in the event of a default. Whether based upon legal propositions, such as the option as specifically spelled out in the bond itself; the surety is not licensed to perform the work; or a more pragmatic approach based upon the premise that a tender would be the best way to cure the default, the surety must be in a position to provide a well reasoned response to the obligee's inquiry as to "why."

"When" is largely a function of how far the project has progressed, and how quickly a new contractor can be presented to the obligee. Particularly in the early stages of a project, this may be the easiest solution to the obligee's concerns. However, the surety must be prepared to address this issue when it presents its tender proposition to the obligee. The obligee's primary concern will be to get the project moving and to the extent that the surety can provide some comfort or assurance that the tender of a new contractor would be the most expeditious means of handling the default, the more receptive an obligee will be to the concept.

The "who" of the obligee's concern is typically not the identity of the new contractor, but rather which entity is going to be responsible for what? The obligee has a bond, is looking to the surety to perform, and the surety in satisfaction of its performance is proposing to tender a new contractor, and a new surety. The more specific and direct the surety's response to this concern, the more likely that a tender is a viable option. This aspect really assists the surety because the ideal presentation here would contemplate a response which in essence says you just look to the new contractor and his surety for everything. Yet, if there is a significant amount of technical completion of the work contemplated by the project, the premium to be paid for this type of comfort could make the tender an untenable or a less viable option.

The "how" of the obligee's concern deals specifically with the surety's funding of a deficit necessary to complete the performance of the bonded obligation. Under no circumstance does the obligee want to become involved in a situation where it is not absolutely certain that the funds committed by the surety will be instantly available for payment of the work undertaken by the new contractor. If the performing surety is in a position to immediately fund the obligee with the entire deficit amount as of the date the new contractor's contract is executed, this concern evaporates. However, in many instances the performing surety is proposing to pay the obligee on some type of percentage of completion basis which heightens the obligee's concerns and in essence raises a red flag concerning the tender option. The obligee may be satisfied with the payment of interest on the funds to be drawn from the date of the default, and/or may insist upon a letter of credit from a bank that the obligee is familiar with. This issue can normally be dealt with successfully, but in presenting the obligee with the tender option, this aspect of the obligee's eventual concern must be addressed at the outset and a common understanding reached.

B. Surety's Concerns

The surety is primarily concerned with the timely performance of its obligation and the cost of that performance as it relates to the penal sum of its bonded obligation. Unfortunately, an obligee often views a performance bond as a "completion bond" which is an obligation the surety has not assumed under the normal terms of its performance bond. The surety's risk analysis from both a "timely performance" point of view and a "cost of performance" point of view will vary drastically depending upon the nature of the project at issue and the sophistication required of the new contractor to undertake any performance obligation. For example, if you assume two projects, both of them being approximately 60% complete, and involving a two-story structure, but one is a high dollar condominium project, while the other is a community hospital, the timeliness of performance and the cost of risk will be by definition vastly different. None of these matters can be viewed in a vacuum, and in the latter example of the community hospital, notwithstanding the fact that the surety might have to pay a significant premium to a new contractor before the new contractor would be willing to assume the risk and obligations with regard to latent defect claims and warranty items, from the surety's standpoint the tender option could readily be the most favored as a result of the opportunity to shift the potential of latent defect and warranty claims to third parties.

The prospect of the surety not obtaining a release of its bond in the final analysis is additionally of great concern. To have proceeded on a proposed tender option basis which in the final analysis results in the remaining amount of the penal sum of the surety's bond still being at risk, even under a proper subordination agreement, can materially affect the surety's decision whether to proceed with the tender option. This "glitch" most often arises when in response to the bidding documents, the bidding contractors exclude responsibility for certain portions of the work in place and yet provide a viable bid for the performance of the work at issue. In the form of the bid, the surety can try to eliminate or deter this possibility, but a limiting exclusion is very common in the bidder's response. See Exhibit 6.5.

V.
Negotiations with the Tendered Contractor

Inasmuch as the tendered contractor's primary points of concern are virtually mirror images of the surety's concerns in the negotiation process, rather than separately addressing those concerns, they are dealt with jointly. The typical topics of negotiation concerns are nature of the contract, flat fixed fee, or cost plus fee with an upset price; the assumption of responsibility for all work in place versus limited assumption and when and how lines of responsibility are drawn; the timing of paying nonretained subcontractors earned retainage to date; the potential effects of not retaining a supplier of specially fabricated materials; and, of course, line item negotiations as to the proposed cost of virtually anything that may appear out of line or heavily cushioned.

In this aspect of "tender" the new contractor is operating virtually within its normal business, while the surety is typically involved in areas about which it has little experience, and in turn must rely upon an analysis by its outside experts, in the form of consultants, accountants, and attorneys.

The original bids received by the obligee for the work, and the bids received by the surety in response to its invitation to bid can be of incalculable value to the surety in this process. Fortunately, the ultimate "risk analysis" is one that the surety is uniquely situated to undertake which does tend to somewhat level the field insofar as bid acceptability is concerned. The following types of agreements are necessary in this process, and are contained in the attached Appendix as follows:

- Surety's Notice of Its Legal and Equitable Rights, combined with Surety's Waiver of Right to Complete, and Proposal to Tender New Contractor, see Exhibit 6.10;
- An Agreement of Release (with suggested alternates), see Exhibit 6.11;
- Agreement for Contract Between Owner and New Contractor, see Exhibit 6.12;
- Contract Between Owner and New Contractor, see Exhibit 6.13; and
- Surety-Subcontractor Agreement, see Exhibit 6.14.

VI. Special Problems and Issues

A. Public Contracts and Statutory Bidding Requirements

Generally speaking most public contracts are required by statute to be bid, and neither contracting officer, if a federal project, nor the awarding authority's representative, if a state project, are even remotely familiar with the concept of "tender" as a means of a surety's performance in the event of a default. If confronted with such a concept, the public entity often responds on the premise that such a proposal would be unacceptable because it would be necessary to go through the entire public bidding process again, which from a time standpoint would be unacceptable. However, if the situation otherwise warrants a "tender situation," the initial response is not necessarily determinative. In the federal context, tender is not disallowed, and FAR § 49.405[2] specifically grants the contracting officer discretion in the method of completing the project if a surety declines to execute a takeover agreement. Similarly,

---

2 48 C.F.R. Ch. 1 § 49.405 (10-1-03 Edition).

you may find opinions from an attorney general's office[3] that relieves the awarding authority from the requirement to go with a new public bidding process where that process has already been undertaken and a subsequent default has occurred.

Absent such "authority" various commentators[4] have observed that due to the fact that the requirement for public bidding contemplates the use of public funds, and in the tender context no additional public funds are necessary or will be involved in the reletting, logically the public bidding process ought to be irrelevant. Persuasiveness of the surety in presenting the tender option to public entities will typically be determinative of the acceptance of the option rather than the initial justifications for its impossibility from public entities.

B. Subcontractor Issues

Unique issues arise when dealing with subcontractors in a potential tender situation. As to the subcontractors generally, the surety should not attempt to burden the potential new contractor with designated subcontractors of the original contractor. In order to negotiate the best new contract agreement possible, the new contractor must be free to choose those subcontractors that it desires to use and not be encumbered or otherwise saddled with the surety's request to use existing subcontractors. Virtually any participation by the surety in the new contractor selection process concerning subcontractors could very well result in subsequent claims of damage from both the new contractor and the old subcontractor, which is precisely the types of claims that the surety is attempting to dispose of by exercising the tender option. Subcontractor hold agreements similar to the attached Exhibit 6.14 can provide significant cost savings to both the surety and the new contractor, but the new contractor needs to be allowed to pick and choose which subcontractors to use and not be required or otherwise forced by the surety to continue an existing subcontract. An exception to this general rule can arise when dealing with specially fabricated materials that may be in process and potentially either

---

3 Legality of Acceptance of Informal Bids for Completion of Work Under Defaulted Contract, Texas A.G. Opinion No. 0-3361 (1941).

4 Patricia H. Thompson, *Completion Options Available to a Performance Bond Surety Other Than Financing Its Principal*, 17 FORUM 1215, 1221-22 (1982).

impossible to obtain in a timely manner, or the damage caused is prohibitively expensive if termination at partial completion were tantamount to substantial completion cost.

In those circumstances where the surety's principal is a subcontractor, additional problems are immediately encountered. General contractors normally have the capability of obtaining performance and unfortunately are too often more than willing to assume that burden on the premise that the surety will ultimately be responsible for any additional costs. As a result, the surety is given too little time to make an adequate investigation and decision concerning the possibility of a tender option and due to the general contractor's knowledge of subcontractors, they tend to move much quicker and are more resistive to the tender concept. The surety's best protection in these circumstances is the straightforward business approach, with the surety's demand for adequate time to investigate the default being in writing and formally served on the general contractor. The surety's timely responsiveness in this circumstance is just as critical. If the surety fails to act in a timely manner, the entire job can be delayed, and the general contractor can become liable for potential liquidated damages or other damages that are not within its control. Thus in a defaulted subcontractor situation, it is imperative that the surety move quickly and decisively to undertake its investigation, analyze the problem, and make a decision as quickly as possible under the circumstances.

C. Claims of the Defaulted Principal

The claims of wrongdoing by a defaulted principal against the surety's obligee, who is now making demand upon the surety to perform the bonded contract can under no circumstance be disregarded or taken lightly by the surety. The surety should not do anything that might alienate its defaulted principal's rights, and it should not by definition agree to hold the obligee harmless from the principal's claims. From a purely pragmatic approach, whether the principal asserts claims or doesn't assert claims should be irrelevant, because it was the obligee that declared the contractor in default, and it is the obligee that is making the demand on the surety. Assuming the obligee is correct, there should not be a problem; however, while the obligee is adamant as to the justness of its position, it is seldom certain. This lack of certainty can adversely impact the potential of the obligee's willingness to accept a tendered new contractor, as well as its other negotiations with the surety. Typically, a surety must nevertheless proceed if it is to mitigate its own damage and in doing so it must proceed cautiously.

VII.
Conclusion

The tender option raises complex and difficult issues for all parties. It requires quick and thorough analysis of the situation by the surety and often involves complicated and extended negotiations. But, when used following careful analysis and planning, it can help meet the objectives and goals of all parties to a project.

This article discusses many of the issues that arise when a surety considers tendering a contractor. Many other resource materials are available that address these issues as well as issues that may be unique to any given project. The practitioner is well advised to consult all available resource material to ensure that all applicable issues are considered and addressed.

CHAPTER 7

COMPLETION BY THE BOND OBLIGEE

Deborah S. Griffin[1]

I.
Introduction

The purpose of a performance bond is to guarantee to the owner/obligee the financial responsibility of the contractor to perform its obligations under the construction contract. The performance bond assures that the owner will have a completed project upon agreed terms. How a surety may and should respond to a demand under a performance bond is the subject of much analysis.[2]

Authorities discussing a surety's options in responding to a claim on a performance bond traditionally have included a "do nothing" option. One circumstance in which the surety will "do nothing" is when the surety's investigation indicates that the obligee's declaration of default on the part of the principal is unjustified or wrongful, or when the surety has

---

1 This Chapter is a revision of portions of Chapter 5 of the BOND DEFAULT MANUAL (Richard S. Wisner ed., 1987), entitled *Completion of Contract by the Owner*, written by Patrick E. Hartigan and Andrew J. Ruck. Much of their work has been preserved in this revision. The author gratefully acknowledges the invaluable assistance of John P. Connelly and Thomas C. Farrell, both of Peabody & Arnold, in preparation of this revision.

2 P. Thompson, *Completion Options Available to a Performance Bond Surety Other Than Financing Its Principal*, 17 FORUM 1215, 1223 (1982).

some other defense which discharges the surety, voids the bond or otherwise excuses performance by the surety.[3] In such circumstances, the surety denies liability under the bond and, literally, does nothing to advance the completion of the work.

There are also instances when the surety will be justified in electing to neither complete the work nor to pay damages to the owner immediately, even when the surety acknowledges, or is not prepared to deny, liability under the bond. In other words, in some instances, the surety may refrain from taking any affirmative action at the time of the default and require the owner to complete or otherwise liquidate its damages prior to the surety taking affirmative action. The circumstances in which a surety has this option, and the practical considerations influencing a surety's decision to elect it, will be examined in this article. As with any of the surety's options, no decision should be made until after an investigation of the facts and circumstances leading up to the declaration of default and demand on the bond.

II.
Legal Limitations on the Surety's Right to Require Completion by the Obligee

Whether the surety has the right to demand that the owner complete depends on the specific bond language and statutes confronting the surety.

A. Terms of the Performance Bond Regarding Responsibility of Owner/Surety to Complete

Although there are numerous performance bond forms in use today, the most widely used performance bond forms have been the federal government's Standard Form 25 Performance Bond,[4] AIA Document

---

3 For a comprehensive discussion of defenses which may relieve the surety of the duty to respond under the bond at all, see Chapter 3, *supra*.

4 Standard Form 25, Performance Bond, January 1990 Edition, General Services Administration, 48 C.F.R. § 53.301-25 (1993). *See* Appendix, Exhibit 1.2.

A311 Performance Bond[5] and AIA Document A312 Performance Bond.[6] While acknowledging that countless variations of these bond forms exist, this article will focus on the federal and AIA bond forms.

1. Miller Act Performance Bond

The Miller Act[7] requires performance bonds for any federal government construction contract exceeding $100,000, unless waived by the contracting officer. The Federal Acquisition Regulations (FAR) require that the Government's Standard Form 25 Performance Bond be used on all such projects.[8]

Standard Form 25 does not list any specific options for the surety's response to a demand under the bond. The bond form only states that:

> ... the Principal and Surety(ies), are firmly bound to the United States of America ... in the above penal sum ....
>
> ...
>
> The above obligation is void if the Principal
>
> (a)(1) Performs and fulfills all the undertakings, covenants, terms, conditions, and agreements of the contract ....
>
> (b) Pays to the Government the full amount of the taxes imposed by the Government ....

This language provides no explicit guidance to the surety as to the circumstances under which the surety may respond to a demand under the bond by telling the obligee to complete the principal's contract and present the surety with a claim for damages after they have been liquidated. However, this form of bond is similar to the forms of bond most commonly in use before the development of the AIA forms discussed below. The case law interpreting such bond forms makes it clear that the surety's only duty is to respond in money damages resulting from the

---

5 American Institute of Architects Document A311, Performance Bond and Labor and Material Payment Bond, February 1970. *See* Appendix, Exhibit 1.3.

6 American Institute of Architects Document A312, Performance Bond and Payment Bond, December 1984 Edition. *See* Appendix, Exhibit 1.4.

7 40 U.S.C. §§ 270a, *et seq.*

8 48 C.F.R. § 28.106-1 (1985); Standard Form 25, *supra* note 4.

principal's default, up to the penal sum of the bond.[9] The surety is not obligated to complete the work, but rather must indemnify the obligee for damages suffered in the event of termination of the principal for default. The surety normally will be permitted to complete construction unless the government exercises its contract right to complete the work itself.[10]

The government's right to complete a terminated contract arises out of the standard "default" clause in the General Provisions of the construction contract.[11] The "default" clause reads:

> In this event [of termination for default], *the Government may take over the work and complete it by contract or otherwise*, and may take possession of and use any materials, appliances, and plant on the work site necessary for completing the work. *The Contractor and its sureties shall be liable for any damage to the Government resulting from the Contractor's refusal or failure to complete the work* within the specified time, whether or not the Contractor's right to proceed with the work is terminated. *This liability includes any increased costs incurred by the Government in completing the work.* (emphasis added)

In the event of a termination for default, the FAR provide that inquiry should be made with the surety to determine if the surety desires to arrange for completion of the work.[12] Although the FAR further provide that the contracting officer shall carefully consider proposals concerning completion of the work,[13] the contracting officer retains the discretion to determine the manner in which the work is to be completed.[14] The language of the FAR does not require the surety to present a completion

---

9 The surety's obligation under such a bond may be satisfied either by completing the contract in exchange for receiving the contract balance, or by paying any contract damages over the contract balance which the owner will incur as a result of the default. *Trinity Universal Ins. Co. v. U.S.*, 382 F.2d 317, 321 (5th Cir. 1967).

10 48 C.F.R. § 49.404(c).

11 Default (Fixed-Price Construction) (April 1984) 48 C.F.R. § 52.249-10(a) (1985). *Compare* Art. 14.2, American Institute of Architects Document A201, *General Conditions of the Contract for Construction*, 1987 Edition.

12 48 C.F.R. § 49.402-3(h).

13 48 C.F.R. § 49.404(b).

14 48 C.F.R. § 49.402-3(i).

proposal, thereby implicitly permitting the surety to utilize the cash settlement approach.

2. *AIA Performance Bonds*

The AIA has been publishing contract forms for the construction industry since 1888[15] and since 1958 it has been publishing the A311 Performance Bond.[16] There is a wide body of case law based on the A311 Bond form and interpreting the surety's rights and obligations thereunder.[17]

In 1984, the AIA introduced AIA Document A312 Performance Bond.[18] At the same time, the Engineers' Joint Contract Documents Committee (EJCDC) published the identical document, EJCDC No. 1910-28-A.[19] The A312 Performance Bond was not a replacement of the earlier A311 Performance Bond, but rather another form option, that was designed mainly for use on private sector projects, which expanded and clarified provisions in the A311 Bond. The AIA continues to publish the older form A311, which has incorporated some of the Miller Act[20] and "Little Miller Act" requirements, as well as the A312 and the A311/CM, the construction management edition of the A311 bond.[21]

---

15 Form of Contract, Joint Committee of the American Institute of Architects, the Western Association of Architects and the National Association of Builders, August 1988.

16 American Institute of Architects Document A311, Performance Bond and Labor And Material Payment Bond, 1958 Edition; J. McNamara, *New Forms of Surety Bonds*, 26 INS. COUNS. J. 370 (1959).

17 *AIA Building Construction Legal Citator*, Vol. I, American Institute of Architects, 1984 Supplement, 47-48.

18 American Institute of Architects Document A312, *supra* note 6.

19 EJCDC Document No. 1910-28-A, Construction Performance Bond, Engineers' Joint Contract Documents committee, 1984.

20 40 U.S.C. §§ 270a-270f (Supp. 1986).

21 American Institute of Architects Document A311/CM, Performance Bond and Labor Material Payment Bond—Construction Management Edition, June 1980.

a. A311 and A311/CM Performance Bonds

The current edition of the A311 and A311/CM Bonds provides that, upon default of the principal/contractor, the surety has two options: 1) complete the contract itself; or 2) obtain bids for completion from contractors and finance the project to completion, if necessary, over and above the remaining contract balance.

b. A312 Performance Bond

The A312 Performance Bond provides the surety with *five* options once the owner has duly declared the principal to be in default.[22] Those are:

1. *Financing the Principal* — The surety enables the defaulted original contractor to complete its contract;
2. *Surety Completing* — The surety undertakes completion of the contract itself through agents or independent contractors;
3. *Tendering New Contractor and Cash* — The surety obtains bids or negotiates a proposal with a new contractor acceptable to the owner. The new contractor enters into a new contract with the owner. The surety is obligated to pay "damages," as defined in the bond,[23] resulting from the principal's default, in excess of the contract balance, subject to the limits of the penal sum of the bond;
4. *Tendering Cash Only* — The surety waives all of the above rights to effect completion of the contract, investigates, determines the amount for which the surety may be liable, and tenders payment in that amount to the owner. If the obligee rejects the cash tender, it may sue the surety for whatever remedies it may have; or
5. *Denying Liability* — The surety denies liability in whole or in part and notifies the owner of the reason therefor.

Option 4 gives express recognition to the surety's traditional right to respond with a payment of money damages alone. However, it also (a) conditions the right to respond in this fashion upon the surety first investigating reasonably promptly and (b) imposes upon the surety the express obligation to tender payment "as soon as practicable after the

---

22 Art. 4, American Institute of Architects Document A312, *supra* note 6.
23 Art. 6, American Institute of Architects Document A312, *supra* note 6.

amount [of the surety's probable liability] is determined."[24] These terms represent a change from the rules applicable under the federal form and under traditional short form bonds.[25]

B. Statutes and Regulations Regarding Surety's Right Not to Complete

In certain states a surety has the right by statute or regulation to deny liability after giving proper notice to the obligee.[26] Such statutes and regulations should be checked in each instance.

III.
Under What Circumstances Should the Surety Leave Completion of the Project to the Obligee?

As with any demand on a performance bond, a surety contemplating the "do nothing" option must first conduct a thorough investigation into the circumstances surrounding the principal's alleged default. Such an investigation is evidence of good faith on the surety's part and will enable the surety to make an informed decision whether to accept or deny liability and, if it accepts liability, which option it should elect in responding to the demand.

The AIA A312 Bond expressly requires an investigation by the surety prior to an election not to participate in the completion of the work, whether by cash settlement or by denial of liability. The surety's investigation is a standard practice in the industry, even when not required by the express terms of the bond. It has been the subject of several articles and will not be addressed further herein.[27]

---

24 Art. 4.4.1, American Institute of Architects Document A312, *supra* note 6.

25 Standard Form 25, *supra* note 4; American Institute of Architects Document A311/CM, *supra* note 21; *Continental Realty Corp. v. Andrew J. Crevolin Co.*, 380 F. Supp. 246, 251 (S.D.W.V. 1974); *Bill Curphy Co. v. Elliott*, 207 F.2d 103, 107 (5th Cir. 1953).

26 California Code of Regulations, Title 10 § 2695.10(b).

27 R. Britt, *The Surety's Investigation*, 17 FORUM 1151 (1982); W. Jensen & D. Purcell, *Handling Fidelity and Surety Claims*, *in* THE SURETY'S INVESTIGATION § 6.16 (R. Cushman & C. Stamm eds., 1984).

However, in order to ensure that the investigation will yield the information necessary, one must understand what factors will be most influential in prompting a surety to elect to respond with payment of money damages rather than participating in completion.

A. Simplicity

A cash settlement with the owner is the simplest alternative available to the performance bond surety. The act of paying money is unquestionably a simpler act than the complex process of obtaining bids from completing contractors, monitoring the progress of the work, requesting multiple payments of funds from the obligee if the work extends over several months or years, and making multiple payments to the completing contractor.

Sureties are not in business to be general contractors and usually should not be anxious to jump into the role of contractor on a construction project. There are enough risks and liabilities in the surety industry without assuming the risks of a general contractor and the accompanying liability to workmen, subcontractors, suppliers, the public and the owner.

Rarely will the surety be familiar with local construction practices and regulations. Such expertise has to be hired as needed for each project.

B. Ability to Limit Liability to the Penal Sum of the Bond

When the surety's post-default investigation shows that its exposure is likely to exceed the amount of the bond, "buying back the bond" with a cash settlement is the preferred option. If the surety undertakes completion of the project, whether by becoming the completing contractor,[28] financing the principal[29] or otherwise, and part way through the process realizes that its costs may exceed the remaining contract balance

---

28 For a discussion of the surety's ability to limit its liability to the penal sum of the bond when entering into a take-over agreement and becoming the completing contractor, see Chapter 5 *supra*; Wisner, Jensen and Leo, *Completion By The Surety: Assessing Risk & Limiting Loss*, *in* BOND DEFAULT MANUAL (Richard S. Wisner ed., 1987).

29 For a discussion of the surety's ability to limit its liability to the penal sum of the bond when financing completion by the principal, see Chapter 4 *supra*; Wisner, Jensen and Leo, *supra* note 28.

plus the penal sum, it will be difficult, as a practical matter if not as a legal matter, and costly, to extricate itself from the completion process in order to cut off its liability when the penal sum is exhausted.

As a general rule, the surety's liability will be limited to the penal sum of the bond. For example, in *Bill Curphy Co. v. Elliott*,[30] the performance bond gave the surety the same options as in the AIA A311 Bond discussed above, that is, to complete the contract according to its terms (either by principal or by surety) or complete the project using a new contractor after obtaining bids. The surety refused to take action under either option, forcing the owner to complete construction on its own. The owner sued for the total cost of completion which exceeded the bond penalty. The trial court found that the surety had breached its obligations, but limited the surety's damages to the amount of the bond. The Appellate Court affirmed, stating,

> If appellant's contention that the surety's liability may exceed the sum stated on the face of the bond is correct, and it is not, it would be futile to state any amount of liability on the bond. This contention completely overlooks the well-established rule ... that the sole object of stating the penalty in a bond is to fix the limit of the liability of the signers, and no *recovery can be had on such bond against the principal or surety beyond the penalty named in the bond.*[31]

Similarly, in *Miracle Mile Shopping Center v. National Union Indemnity Co.*,[32] the surety declined to perform upon default of the principal. The court found the surety in breach of its bond obligations, making it liable for special and consequential damages in excess of the cost to complete. However, the court stopped short of awarding damages over the bond amount.

Until 1974, the general rule discussed above went unquestioned: with the exception of interest and costs,[33] the surety's liability for damages

---

30 207 F.2d 103 (5th Cir. 1953).

31 *Id.* at 106 (emphasis added).

32 *Miracle Mile Shopping Center v. National Union Indem. Co.*, 299 F.2d 780 (7th Cir. 1962).

33 *Insurance Co. of N. America v. United States*, 951 F.2d 1244, 1246 (Fed. Cir. 1991) (prejudgment interest may increase surety's liability beyond penal sum); 72 C.J.S. *Principal and Surety* §§ 93, 113-115 (1951).

under a performance bond was limited to the bond penalty. The decision of a United States District Court in *Continental Realty Corp. v. Andrew J. Crevolin Co.*[34] shattered that belief. That court's decision is the most troubling consideration for a surety contemplating an option under which it does not participate in the completion of the work.

In *Crevolin*, the contractor was declared to be in default by the architect following abandonment of the project and numerous construction problems. The owner made demand on the surety to complete the project under the terms of the performance bond. The bond in question provided the surety with only two options:

1. Within fifteen days after determination of default, take over and assume completion of the contract; or
2. Pay the owner the reasonable cost of completion less the balance of the contract price including the retained percentage.

The surety chose to deny liability, rather than exercise either of the bond options, arguing that the owner's material breaches of the construction contract resulted in a complete discharge of the surety. The court found that the surety was wrong in its determination and held that the owner was not in breach of the contract, nor did the owner do anything to the detriment of the surety. The court proceeded to award damages, not only up to the amount of the bond, but *in excess* of the penal sum. The court ruled that the surety

> chose not to exercise its right under the bond and its failure, by whatever designation, negligence, bad faith, error in judgment, mistake of law, etc., constituted a breach of its obligation to [the Owner], *the liability for which is limited only by the amount of damages sustained as a result thereof.*[35]

The court felt that the bond imported "an unconditional obligation" on the surety which it chose not to fulfill.

There is ample authority supporting the premise in *Crevolin* that a surety which wrongfully chooses the "do nothing" option is in breach of

---

34 380 F. Supp. 246 (S.D.W. Va. 1974). For an in-depth discussion of the *Crevolin* case, see Richard S. Wisner, *Liability In Excess of the Contract Bond Penalty*, 43 INS. COUNS. J. 105 (1976).

35 380 F. Supp. at 252 (emphasis added).

its performance bond obligations.[36] Sureties have been held liable for attorney's fees, special damages and consequential damages in excess of the cost of completion up to, but not exceeding, the penal sum of the bond.[37]

Although *Crevolin* appears to have been confined to the specific facts of the case, subsequent caselaw suggests that the "do nothing" approach may subject the surety to claims for tort damages.[38] Moreover, there is a growing trend nationwide to subject sureties to unfair trade or settlement practice claims, which may include claims for punitive damages.

The risk of unfair practice and/or tort claims reduces the advisability of electing the "do nothing" option for the cautious surety. Further, where, as a result of the surety's post-default investigation, the surety is prepared to accept liability, the surety may wish to notify the obligee unambiguously and in writing of the surety's intention to pay money damages.

C. Cost

A principal focus of the post-default investigation, in addition to the propriety of the declaration of default and any potential defenses to the

---

36 On federal projects, the surety is not exposed to the risk of the *Crevolin* decision. A Miller Act bond is an indemnification bond and there is no affirmative duty upon the surety to undertake any type of completion program. The surety is only liable to the federal government for its completion costs in excess of the contract balance.

37 *Housing Auth. of City of Clinton v. Baumann*, 512 S.W.2d 436, 440 (Mo. App. 1974). *See generally, Allowance of Attorney's Fees Over and Above Penal Sum Stated in Private Contractor's Bond*, 59 A.L.R.2d 469 (1958); *Surety's Liability for Obligee's Attorney's Fees Under Provisions of Performance Bond of Public Contractor or Subcontractor*, 69 A.L.R.2d 1046 (1960); *See also, Miracle Mile, supra* note 32.

38 *Dodge v. Fidelity & Deposit Co. of Md.*, 161 Ariz. 344, 778 P.2d 1240 (1989) (performance bond surety has obligation to act in good faith when responding to obligee's claim that its principal was defaulted and a breach of the duty will subject surety to tort damages). Another case suggests that a surety may have no right of indemnification against its principal for damages based on the surety's independent tortious conduct. *Szarkowski v. Reliance Ins. Co.*, 404 N.W.2d 502 (N.D. 1987).

surety's liability, will always be an assessment of the cost of completing the work and consequential damages stemming from the default.

The cost of completion can vary greatly, depending upon whether completion is arranged by the surety or by the obligee. The biggest disadvantage in electing not to complete is that the surety loses all control over the project's completion, including control over the project cost and, ultimately, control over the amount of damages suffered by the obligee. This basic disadvantage to the surety in loss of control over the project costs should be weighed against the advantages in having the obligee complete, which, in a large measure, will be dictated by the facts and circumstances of each project.

The surety will need to consider whether, in the market from which completing bids will be drawn, the fact that bids are solicited by a surety will induce bidders to bid higher than if bids are solicited by the obligee.

The surety will also need to consider whether it or the obligee is in a better position to foster efficiency, speed and integrity in the completion process. When the principal is a subcontractor and the obligee is a general contractor, the obligee is likely to be better situated to accomplish these goals than the surety. However, if the obligee is a public entity, often the surety can achieve a quicker completion than the obligee because it faces less red tape in soliciting bids for the completion work.

If the default occurs after substantial completion and a monetized punch list is available or imminent, the surety is usually better off tendering cash in the amount of the punch list, plus whatever consequential damages have been established.

When the obligee completes, the surety avoids the cost of in-house administration, and the financial, consulting and legal costs inherent in undertaking to complete a project itself. The surety will need to assess, prior to making its election, whether under the terms of the bond or applicable law, the obligee will be entitled to recover its cost of in-house administration, and the financial, consulting and legal costs inherent in completion.[39] If the surety is unlikely to have liability for those costs, and can avoid incurring them itself, this difference may weigh heavily in favor of letting the obligee complete. If the surety is likely to be liable for such costs if the obligee incurs them, the surety will have to estimate

---

39 *See* Kevin L. Lybeck, *Scope of the Performance Bond Surety's Obligation*, *in* THE LAW OF SURETYSHIP 10-1 (Edward G. Gallagher ed., 1993).

whether the costs for such items is likely to be more or less if the obligee completes than if the surety does so.

If the surety denies liability or makes a cash tender which is not accepted by the obligee, the chances that the surety's liability will be litigated are high. The obligee retains the discretion to accept or refuse a cash settlement offer, and, if the obligee refuses, can bring suit. The AIA A312 Bond expressly provides:

> If the surety proceeds as provided [above], and the Owner refuses the payment tendered or the Surety has denied liability, in whole or in part, without further notice the Owner shall be entitled to enforce any remedy available to the Owner.[40]

The administrative and legal costs involved in defending a suit by the owner, and in appealing an adverse judgment, often outweigh the burden of paying the cost to complete. This becomes a business decision rather than a legal one, even where sufficient defenses appear to exist. As with any litigation, there is risk and uncertainty no matter how clear the basis for the surety's position appears to be at the time the decision is made to deny liability or tender a cash settlement.

D. Cash Flow

In many instances, when the obligee completes the work, the surety can avoid financing the project to completion, thus avoiding an ongoing cash drain during construction. This advantage may not be applicable when the AIA bond forms A311 or A312 are in use. Those forms expressly require, in the case of the form A311, that payment be made "as the work progresses," and, in the case of form A312, that the surety:

> After investigation, determine the amount which [the Surety] may be liable to the Owner and, *as soon as practicable after the amount is determined*, tender payment therefor to the Owner.[41]

---

40 Art. 5, American Institute of Architects Document A312, *supra* note 6.

41 Art. 4.4.1, American Institute of Architects Document A312, *supra* note 6 (emphasis added).

Under the federal form and standard short forms, there is no requirement that payment be made until after the obligee completes construction, liquidates its damages and presents a demand for payment to the surety.[42]

E. Additional Time to Investigate

While the obligee completes, the surety gains time for additional investigation of the project. Such investigation may focus on the obligee's consequential damages (other than increased completion costs) for which the surety might ultimately be liable. If the surety has denied liability, or reserved its rights to do so, such additional investigation may reveal defenses to performance bond liability not apparent upon the initial post-default investigation, or additional support for those defenses upon which a denial of liability was based.

If bond liability or the measure of damages is disputed, the obligee might contend that the fact the surety's investigation continued after a denial of liability proves that the surety's initial post-default investigation was inadequate and the denial or the cash tender was a breach of the bond or done in bad faith. Such a contention is most likely to be advanced when the AIA A312 Bond is in place, because of the requirement of paragraph 4.4 that, if a surety is going to deny liability, it must promptly give a statement to the owner of the fact of and reason for denial of liability.[43] However, the standard to which a surety should be held in conducting an initial post-default investigation should not require an investigation as exhaustive as that which one would conduct for litigation. So long as the initial post-default investigation was reasonable in scope, the surety should not be penalized for conducting a more in-depth investigation later.

Nor should the specification of one or more reasons for denying liability preclude the assertion of additional defenses discovered later.

F. Reservation of Defenses

The surety which elects not to complete construction, and can do so without having to admit liability, avoids unwittingly waiving any known

---

42 48 C.F.R. 49.406 (October, 1993).

43 Art. 4, American Institute of Architects Document 312, *supra* note 6.

or unknown defenses that it may have to either performance bond liability or its right to indemnity.

G. Dedication of Contract Funds to Completion

Leaving completion to the obligee gives the obligee possession and absolute control over the contract funds, in order to use them toward completion of the work without the danger of creditors of the principal or the completing contractor tying up these funds by attachment, garnishment or otherwise.

H. Closure

If the surety tenders a cash settlement to resolve its liability under the bond, and the obligee accepts the tender, the surety's liability is fixed and certain, and the surety's involvement with the project comes to an end. If, however, the tender is rejected, or if the surety denies liability or otherwise declines to complete while reserving its defenses, the surety's ultimate liability will be left unresolved for an indeterminate time.

Resolution of the surety's liability usually will be deferred at least until after the obligee completes the work, which could be a matter of months or years. Thereafter, the time period within which the obligee must make demand upon the surety for payment is generally set forth in the bond.[44]

If the obligee makes demand after liquidating its damages and the surety refuses payment, the determination of the surety's liability will await the commencement and ultimate resolution of arbitration or litigation. As with any claim on a contract, such arbitration or litigation must be commenced within the applicable limitation period. The AIA A312 Bond requires suits under the Bond to be brought:

> ... within two years after contractor Default or within two years after the Contractor ceased working or within two years after the surety refuses or fails to perform its obligations under this bond, whichever occurs first.[45]

---

44 Art. 9, American Institute of Architects Document A312, *supra* note 6.
45 *Id.*

The terms of the underlying contract should also be reviewed for any applicable time limits for commencement of arbitration.

In the absence of such a contractual limitation period, the statute of limitations will govern when suit must be brought. Most bonds are executed under seal and, in some jurisdictions, the statute of limitations for contracts under seal is as long as twenty (20) years.[46]

If the lack of closure following a refusal to complete or a refusal of the tender of a cash settlement is troubling to a surety, the surety can take the initiative to bring the issue to a head by filing a declaratory judgment action.

I. Business Concerns

If the surety denies liability or makes a cash tender which is not accepted by the obligee, and litigation ensues, along with the burden of fighting a lawsuit, the surety risks damage to its reputation and marketing ability. In rare instances sureties have been "blacklisted" by owners and architects/engineers as unacceptable for future work because of a perception that the sureties did not honor their bond obligations.

Additionally, the completing surety occasionally may find some salvage in the job as a result of undertaking completion itself. If the same surety issued a payment bond on the job and is faced with claims from subcontractors and suppliers for labor or materials provided prior to the principal's default, job funds in excess of the cost of completion may be used to defray payment bond obligations. Note, however, that on federal projects there is an exception to the surety's right to use excess funds in this manner.[47]

J. Effect on Indemnification Rights

Occasionally, the principal and/or indemnitors will argue that the default was improper and that the surety's payment was premature and in error, which results in voiding the surety's entitlement to indemnifi-

---

46 *See, e.g.*, Mass. G.L. c. 260, § 1.

47 48 C.F.R. 49.404 (October, 1993).

cation. Close consultation with the principal during the decision-making process may reduce the risk of such claims.[48]

IV.
Conclusion

The process of responding to a demand upon a performance bond must begin with an analysis of the bond language and applicable statutes to determine what options the surety has. The surety must conduct a post-default investigation, which is reasonable in scope and with reasonable promptness. The investigation should focus on all the facts and circumstances which will enable the surety to make an informed decision as to which of its response options is most appropriate to the situation: the simplicity of a cash tender, the surety's ability to protect the limitation of the penal sum, cost of completion and consequential damages, cash flow, potential for additional investigation, preservation of defenses, dedication of the contract funds to the cost of completion, closure, protection of indemnification rights and other business concerns. The process of weighing all these factors is the essence of responding to a performance bond claim. Given the uniqueness of each project and each default, this process will continue to present an endless variety of challenges to bond claims staff and counsel.

---

48 See cases cited, *supra* note 38.

CHAPTER 8

PUBLIC WORKS PROJECTS

Donald G. Gavin
Hugh N. Anderson
Gavin P. Craig

The federal government and nearly all state and local governments require that contractors on major construction projects provide performance and payment bonds. Public works bonding ("statutory bonds") constitutes a substantial portion of total construction bonding, and many key surety bond cases have arisen from a public works context. This chapter discusses some of the special factors with respect to contractor default on publicly funded projects.

I.
The Surety's Options When The Principal Defaults On A Public Works Project

As discussed in detail elsewhere in this manual, a surety may typically choose from several options depending on the statutory bonding requirements and the terms of the bond when the principal (the contractor) under a performance bond is in default. The surety may:

1. finance the contractor;
2. tender a new contractor to the owner;
3. take over and complete the work of the contractor;
4. make a monetary settlement with the owner and arrange to have the owner complete the project (tender up to the penal sum); or

5. take no action and await litigation from the owner seeking damages under the performance bond.

As a general matter, neither the statutes requiring performance bonds (*e.g.*, the Miller Act[1] and the various Little Miller Acts) nor the performance bond forms typically used on public works (*e.g.*, the Standard Form 25 required by 48 C.F.R. § 53.301-25) preclude the surety from choosing any of the traditional options. However, the Federal Acquisition Regulations (FAR) do affect the manner in which certain options may be executed, and factors such as the requirement of competitive bidding for any new contract entered into directly by the governmental obligee may eliminate other options, as a practical matter.

The FAR applies to federal projects and provides that certain specific courses of action, "among others," are available to the Government in lieu of termination for default, including: (a) permitting "the contractor, the surety, or the guarantor, to continue performance of the contract under a revised delivery schedule" and (b) permitting the contractor to continue performance of the contract by means of a subcontract or "other business arrangement with an acceptable third party."[2] This provision provides flexibility at a critical point in the default process and opens the door for some options, such as financing the contractor.

If the Government chooses not to pursue the procedures (other options) in lieu of termination for default, but instead terminates the contractor, then the surety, owing to its "liability for damages resulting from the contractor's default," is advised by the FAR to present a proposal concerning completion of the work.[3] If the surety does offer to complete the work, the regulations instruct the Government to permit the surety to do so, unless there is reason to believe that the replacement contractor proposed by the surety to complete the work is not competent, such that the interests of the Government would be substantially prejudiced.

The Federal Acquisition Regulations dictate some of the features of the takeover agreement between the surety and the Government. Several areas are of significant concern to sureties:

---

1 40 U.S.C. § 270a *et seq.*

2 Federal Acquisition Regulation Systems ("FAR"), 48 C.F.R. § 49.402-4 (1984).

3 *Id.* at § 49.404.

1. The FAR suggests that the defaulting contractor be made a party to the takeover agreement. Although this may reduce disagreements concerning the contractor's residual rights, it may also make the process of negotiating the agreement very difficult, and it may give the defaulted contractor leverage against the surety that it would not otherwise have.
2. The takeover agreement requires the surety to complete the work of the contract and allows the surety to be paid the balance of the contract price that was unpaid at the time of the default. The FAR limits payment to the surety's actual costs and expenses.
3. The Government is allowed to take any unpaid earnings of the defaulting contractor, including retainage, and apply it to other governmental debts (such as taxes) unless the unpaid earnings are needed to compensate the completing surety for its actual costs and expenses; the surety's payments to subcontractors and suppliers under the payment bond are not regarded as "actual costs and expenses" for this purpose.
4. If the defaulting contractor has assigned the contract proceeds to a financial institution, the institution has priority over the surety as to entitlement to unpaid earnings.
5. Reimbursement to the surety for payment bond disbursements can only be made if: (1) the Government, the defaulting contractor and the surety mutually agree, or (2) the U.S. Comptroller General validates the payment and amount, or (3) the surety obtains a court order.

The Federal Acquisition Regulations provide that if the surety does not arrange for completion of the contract, the Government will arrange for completion of the work by awarding a new contract, and after using retainage and other unpaid earnings shall "take steps to recover the additional sum from the contractor and the surety."[4]

One of the problems created by the FAR provisions noted above is that the surety is compelled to surrender some of its rights under the law as the price of entering into the takeover agreement. A surety with payment bond losses, for example, is asked to agree that an assignee bank has priority over the surety when the law is clearly to the contrary. The surety is compelled to go to the expense of a court proceeding or General

4 *Id.* at § 49.406.

Accounting Office ruling to vindicate its subrogation rights as to payment bond losses unless the defaulting contractor agrees.

The case law, however, is very clear that the payment bond surety's subrogation claim is superior to any claim of the defaulting contractor.[5] At least since the *Henningsen*[6] case in 1908, the courts have held that a subrogated payment bond surety prevails over a rival claim by an assignee of the contractor.[7]

Even worse is the requirement that the defaulting principal has to consent to use of the contract funds to reimburse the payment bond surety. *Pearlman v. Reliance Insurance Co.*[8] surely put to rest the argument that the contractor could fail to pay its subcontractors and suppliers and still be entitled to the contract funds. The Supreme Court concluded:

> We therefore hold in accord with the established legal principles stated above that the Government had a right to use the retained fund to pay laborers and materialmen; that the laborers and materialmen had a right to be paid out of the fund; that the contractor, had he completed his job and paid his laborers and materialmen, would have become entitled to the fund; and that the surety, having paid the laborers and materialmen, is entitled to the benefit of all these rights to the extent necessary to reimburse it.

A surety faced with an obdurate government official who insists on provisions which would surrender the surety's rights should consider an ultimatum to the government stating:

---

5 An exhaustive discussion of the surety's subrogation rights is beyond the scope of this paper. The cases are collected in THE SUBROGATION DATABASE: CASES CONCERNING THE SUBROGATION RIGHTS OF THE CONTRACT BOND SURETY, (George Bachrach ed., 1995); a scholarly exposition of subrogation theory can be found in Daniel Mungall, Jr., *The Buffeting of the Subrogation Rights of the Construction Bond Surety By United States v. Munsey Trust Co.*, 46 INS. COUNS. J. 607 (1979).

6 *Henningsen v. United States Fidelity and Guarantee Co.*, 208 U.S. 404 (1908).

7 Among the many such cases are: *Great American Ins. Co. v. United States,* 492 F.2d 821 (1974); *Central National Ins. Co. v. Tri-County State Bank*, 823 F. Supp. 652 (D. Minn. 1993); and *Transamerica Ins. Co. v. Barnett Bank of Marion County,* 540 So.2d 113 (Fla. 1989).

8 *Pearlman v. Reliance Ins. Co.*, 371 U.S. 132 (1962).

1. the surety has a completion contractor ready, willing and able to complete the work and post new bonds to guarantee its performance;
2. the Surety has arranged to pay the completion contractor any costs in excess of the contract funds;
3. the Surety will not sign a takeover agreement which waives its legal rights to contract funds;
4. if the Government insists on such provisions, it can re-procure the work itself, but the surety will be responsible for only the difference between the contract balance and the completion contractor's price; and
5. any costs in excess of that difference are due to the Government's failure to mitigate its damages.

In 1988, and again in 1989, the Public Contract Law Section of the American Bar Association exercised its standing authority to comment on Federal Acquisition Regulations by recommending to the Federal Acquisition Regulation Council revisions in the FAR language dealing with takeover agreements. Despite these recommendations, no changes have yet to be acted upon. A copy of the recommendation and the report of the Public Contract Law Section of the American Bar Association are attached as Exhibit 8.1. For the assistance of practitioners who negotiate takeover agreements under the existing regulations, a sample takeover agreement is provided which attempts in some respects to deal with the deficiencies of the FAR language.[9] Also enclosed are forms utilized by a surety in tendering a contractor to the federal government.[10] Practitioners may also wish to review some of the excellent materials published by the ABA's Fidelity & Surety Law Committee of the Tort and Insurance Practice Section.[11]

---

9 Exhibit 8.2.

10 Exhibit 8.3.

11 *See e.g.*, Crane, *A Critical Examination of the Federal Acquisition Regulations Related to Sureties* (unpublished paper submitted at the A.B.A. Tort and Insurance Practice Section Fidelity & Surety Law Committee annual meeting in Atlanta, Ga., on August 13, 1991).

II.
Requirements Relative To Surety Bonds Imposed On Recipients Of Federal Assistance

The federal government imposes bonding requirements on state and local recipients of federal funding for construction projects. The basic questions in each program are, what surety bonds are required, and what approvals are necessary from the federal government, for state and local construction projects which are wholly or partially funded by federal grants.

OMB Circular A-102 previously covered federal grants and cooperative agreements with state and local governments. The 1977 edition of A-102 required no bonds for contracts up to $100,000, and for contracts over $100,000 the federal government could accept the grantee's policies and requirements, provided that the federal government made a determination that the federal interest was adequately protected. In the absence of such a determination, performance bonds and payment bonds were required for 100% of the contract price.

Bonds had to be obtained from companies holding certificates of authority from the U.S. Treasury as acceptable sureties.[12] However, in 1988, the former A-201 requirements were dropped in favor of the requirements now found in the Uniform Administrative Requirements for Grants and Cooperative Agreements to State and Local Governments.[13] The present uniform policy of the federal Government is to allow states and local governments to utilize their own bonding requirements[14] when contracting for construction using federal funds, unless the individual grantor agency seeks to impose more stringent requirements.

Those recipients of federal assistance from the U.S. Environmental Protection Agency that are subject to the procurement requirements of 40 C.F.R. Part 33 will be subject to more definite requirements.[15] The award official may accept the recipient's bonding policy or may impose requirements which are similar to the old 1977 A-201 provisions.

The current Uniform Administrative Requirements do not address the issue of what local procedures apply. However, the awarding agency,

---

12 31 C.F.R. § 223 (1975).

13 45 C.F.R. § 1234 (1988).

14 45 C.F.R. § 1234.36(h) (1988).

15 40 C.F.R. § 33.265 (1983).

when it is a local or state government, should have a procedure based on applicable state law or regulation. For state and local projects, the "Little Miller Acts" will establish the requirements for statutory bonding. While most contracts and "Little Miller Acts" are vague or silent about the specific obligations of the surety in connection with project completion, in some cases the bond form itself, approved of by the public agency, may impose particular obligations. There may be obligations of the grantee included in the grant agreement. If the grantor agency requires notice of a default to the federal government, the grantee must comply in accordance with the grant documents. If the grant document is incorporated into the contract, the contractor must comply with the requirements set forth.

The surety is not a party to the grant, nor to the contract between the grantee and the contractor. However, the underlying construction contract frequently is incorporated into the obligations of the performance bond. For additional discussion of procurement under Federal Assistance there are a number of publications.[16]

III.
Public Entities' Exercise of Special Leverage and Powers Against Sureties

Public entities, especially those that do a high volume of construction business, such as state governments and the federal government, have substantial advantages in disputes and other dealings with sureties. As project owners, these entities are in a broad sense the ultimate "clients" or customers of the sureties' services and are the ultimate source of a substantial portion of the sureties' revenues. Government entities typically have access to quality legal services at minimum incremental cost and have the resources to sustain and protract disputes if it suits their purposes. In addition, governmental entities may be able to threaten debarment or other constraints to a surety's ability to do business in the event the surety does not capitulate to the government's position.

---

16 *See* Donald G. Gavin and Steven T. Halverson, *Contracts Under Federal Assistance, Federal Grant Law*, 161 A.B.A.J. (1982); J. Kent Holland, *EPA Construction Grants Disputes: Surviving the Audit*, 42 (1990); Paul G. Dembling and Malcom S. Mason, *Essentials of Grant Law Practice*, A.L.I./A.B.A. (1991).

To do business on federal projects, a surety must be listed on the United States Department of the Treasury's List of Acceptable Sureties. This list, commonly known as "the Treasury List," or T.D. Circular 570, is also relied upon by many state and local governments as a prerequisite for acceptability. Sureties that fail to promptly pay claims on federal projects can be threatened with removal from the list of acceptable sureties. The regulations require sureties to promptly honor their "bonds naming the United States or one of its agencies or instrumentalities as obligee."[17]

Under the regulation, if the governmental agency makes a demand on a bond that is not settled to the agency's satisfaction, and the agency takes the position that the bonding company's refusal to pay is not based on adequate grounds, the agency may report the surety to the Treasury Department.[18] The Treasury Department then investigates, and it gives the surety an opportunity to state its case and obtain a hearing if it makes a request within 20 days of receipt of the notification letter.[19] If the Treasury Department agrees that the surety wrongfully has failed to make payment, then the Treasury will remove the company from the Treasury List for a period of one year.[20] The vital importance of remaining on the list provides strong incentive to sureties not to dispute without cause the government's position with respect to claims and demands associated with the default of the surety's principal. Even a surety that is convinced that its position is correct, and that the Treasury would ultimately sustain the surety's position, would be reluctant to allow itself to become embroiled in the delisting process.

Contractors and sureties may be suspended or debarred from government contracting based on "adequate evidence" of misconduct. Such misconduct might be in the nature of civil procurement fraud or unsatisfactory performance. Although the Treasury Department regulations do not state that debarred or suspended sureties are ineligible for listing on T.D. Circular 570, a finding of ineligibility is certainly a likely result under such circumstances. Even if the surety was not removed from the Treasury List, if it was debarred or suspended it is likely that either the

---

17 31 C.F.R. § 223.18(a).

18 *Id.*

19 31 C.F.R. § 223.19(a).

20 31 C.F.R. § 223.20 (1977).

procuring agency or a second low bidder would successfully challenge its ability to continue securing a contractor's performance.

The enormous pressure that government entities may place on a surety is illustrated in a reported decision involving the performance bond surety for a bridge construction project.[21] The owner, a state highway department, discovered defects in the bridge after it was completed and made a claim against the contractor. The contractor denied liability and refused to make repairs. The highway department declared the contractor in default and then made a claim against the surety under the performance bond. When the surety did not promptly concede liability, the highway department disqualified the surety from bonding any further state contracts. This blacklisting motivated the surety to settle with the highway department. Later, the contractor resisted the surety's indemnification claim by asserting that the surety had acted in bad faith by settling with the highway department, because its motivation was to avoid being blacklisted. The appellate court ultimately held that merely because the surety was concerned about being blacklisted did not mean that its decision to settle was improper.[22]

In *Bristol Steel* the surety did a very smart thing. It included in its agreement with the obligee a provision which required the obligee to refund the surety's payment, with interest, if the contractor prevailed in the arbitration proceeding contesting its default termination. The agreement between the surety and the obligee also specifically reserved the contractor's rights. When the surety later sued its principal and indemnitors, the court found that "the Sureties acted with utmost good faith toward their principal and sought in making their payment to protect fully the interests of the Contractor."[23] Sureties entering into takeover agreements would be well advised to consider the lesson of *Bristol Steel* and include such provisions to protect themselves and their principals.

As discussed elsewhere in this chapter and manual, it is common in cases of contractor default for the surety to take over the project and complete performance. When it does so, it becomes "directly subject to the vast array of civil and criminal laws governing financial dealings with

---

21 *Fidelity & Deposit Co. of Md. v. Bristol Steel & Iron Works, Inc.*, 722 F. 2d 1160 (4th Cir. 1983).

22 *Id.*

23 *Id.* at 1165.

the government."[24] Each time the surety submits a pay request or a claim, it is subjecting itself to the potential of an audit, a government investigation, and liability. Legislation ranging from the Truth in Negotiations Act to the False Claims Act[25] may come into play.

IV.
Procedures For Sureties To Communicate, Negotiate With And Litigate With The Federal Government

The surety's position in regard to the federal government prior to the declaration of a default and/or termination of the principal's construction contract is very similar to that when dealing with a private obligee. The surety has the duty to investigate, while being mindful of its principal's rights prior to the obligee finding a default and terminating the contract with the principal. However, once a default and termination has been formally declared, the surety's options, as discussed in Section I of this chapter, include financing, tendering a new contractor to the public owner, taking over and completing the work of the contractor, making a monetary settlement with a public owner, and arranging to have the public owner complete the project, or taking no action and awaiting litigation from the public owner seeking damages under the performance bond.

If the surety enters into a takeover agreement, it normally will wish to reserve its right to recover the cost of completion and the associated expenses in order to be made whole, provided that the termination for default of its principal is converted to a termination for the convenience of the Government. If the principal's termination for default is found to have been wrongful under a contract with the federal government, that wrongful termination for default automatically will be converted to a termination for the convenience of the Government under the default

---

24 Donald G. Gavin and Michael A. Gatje, *Surety Exposure to Federal Procurement Fraud Liability for Bad Faith, Shaping the Future of Public Construction and Suretyship* (unpublished paper submitted at the A.B.A. Tort and Insurance Practice Section and Public Contract Law Section joint program in Arlington, Va. on October 29-30, 1992).

25 10 U.S.C. § 2306(a) (1994); 31 U.S.C. § 3729 *et seq.* (1986).

termination article.[26] A convenience termination provides the principal with a contractual measure of recovery.[27]

Under a takeover agreement, a surety would have contractual privity with the U.S. government and could, upon the principal's conversion of the termination for default to one for convenience, have the right to proceed against the federal government under the Contract Disputes Act of 1978 ("CDA").[28] A surety may wish to pursue a claim for an equitable adjustment which it believes its principal is due under the original contract with the Government. Unless the takeover agreement is drafted broadly and the surety is afforded the same rights as its principal to bring disputes under the terminated contract to include challenging the wrongful termination of the principal, the surety may have a right to proceed under the CDA only as to claims which are reserved in the takeover agreement.[29] Of course, the surety which has entered into a takeover agreement can pursue in its own name a dispute over a breach of that agreement. Also, the surety may appeal, in a representative capacity, in the name of the defaulted contractor, with the defaulted contractor's written permission.[30]

However, even without a takeover agreement directly with the federal government, the surety still has its right of equitable subrogation. The Court of Federal Claims has concluded that a surety may recover costs of completion even though a surety has not undertaken responsibility for supervising contract completion.[31] The Court has determined that under the right of equitable subrogation, the surety that incurs costs in providing

---

26 FAR, 48 C.F.R. § 52.249-10 (Apr. 1984).

27 FAR, 48 C.F.R. § 52.249-2 (Apr. 1984).

28 Contract Disputes Act ("CDA"), 41 U.S.C. § 601 *et seq.*

29 *Universal Surety Co. v. United States*, 10 Cl. Ct. 794 (1986); *Transamerica Ins. Co. v. United States*, 6 Cl. Ct. 367 (1984); and *Morrison Assurance Co. v. United States*, 3 Cl. Ct. 626 (1983). However, lacking an actual takeover agreement, there may not be a right of appeal under the CDA. *Rogers Construction, Inc.* and *Federal Insurance Company*, IBCA Nos. 2777 *et seq.*, 92-1 BCA ¶ 24,503.

30 *United States Fidelity and Guarantee Company,* 71-1 B.C.A. (CCH) ¶ 8815 (Armed Serv. B.C.A. 1971); and *Golden Gate Building Maintenance Company,* 68-1 B.C.A. (CCH) ¶ 6739 (Armed Serv. B.C.A. 1968).

31 *Transamerica Ins. Co. v. United States*, 31 Fed. Cl. 532 (1994).

a completion contractor would be subrogated against the federal government at least as to the contract balance. The surety may challenge the government's management of the contract balance.[32] However, in order to have a right of equitable subrogation, it has been held that a surety must actually have expended funds and not merely have incurred a contingent liability. Without having entered into a takeover agreement, the surety cannot challenge the termination of its principal as wrongful under the CDA.[33] The requirements of the Contract Disputes Act, including the obligation to certify claims, do not arise under the theory of equitable subrogation.[34] Under limited circumstances a surety may recover damages against the government by virtue of being a third party beneficiary of a clause in the contract between the government and the principal. Where the retainage clause left the government without discretion to release retainage until it approved an arrow diagram, the government is bound by this contractual limitation.[35]

The right of equitable subrogation is sufficiently broad that the United States Court of Appeals for the Federal Circuit has held that a surety, after giving proper notice to a contracting officer on contracts other than the defaulted contract in which the surety incurs completion or payment bond costs, can reach the contract balances on such separate contracts that would otherwise be paid to the surety's principal.[36] The Government would still have the right to utilize such contract balances for the completion of such unrelated contracts, but the surety would have a preference over its own principal to receive the final contract balance.

Should the surety find it necessary to proceed under the Contract Disputes Act against the federal government, it will need to be cognizant of the complex procedures applicable to disputes resolution under this statute and its many amendments. The surety must assert a claim in a sum certain.[37] It is not sufficient to state that the surety simply is requesting

---

32 *Id.*

33 *Fidelity and Deposit Co. of Maryland v. United States*, 31 Fed. Cl. 540 (1994).

34 *Transamerica Ins. Co. v. United States*, 31 Fed. Cl. 602 (1994).

35 *Nat'l Sur. Corp. v. United States*, 31 Fed. Cl. 565, 573-74 (1994).

36 *Transamerica v. United States*, 989 F.2d 1188, rehearing denied, 998 F.2d 972 (Fed.Cir. 1993).

37 *Harnischfeger Corporation*, 80-2 B.C.A. (CCH) ¶ 14,541 (Armed Serv. B.C.A. 1980).

to be reimbursed in an amount equal to all sums which it may expend in the completion of the contract to be determined at the time that the work is actually completed. The surety will have to have either expended an actual sum and state an exact amount, or estimate its completion costs and thereafter amend its claim should such estimate prove to require revisions.

The law had been that in order for a claim to proceed under the CDA it must be certified correctly.[38] The problem of what constituted a proper certification plagued the federal boards and courts for several years until resolved in two separate legislative enactments. First, the Federal Courts Administration Act of 1992[39] amended the Contract Disputes Act so that the certification required may be executed by any person duly authorized to bind the contractor or surety with respect to the claim. This means that under state corporate law any individual properly authorized by the corporation can certify a claim. Usually a resolution of the Board of Directors will authorize a category of individuals, *i.e.* Vice President for Surety Claims and surety claims counsel. Finally, the Federal Acquisition Streamlining Act of 1994 ("FASA")[40] raised the amount of a claim that requires certification from $50,000 to $100,000.

Likewise, FASA unifies the certification requirements of the Department of Defense and the civilian agencies by repealing the special rules applicable only to the Department of Defense. Prior to FASA, DOD regulations had added several additional requirements that tended to have a "chilling effect" on those who would wish to certify claims.[41] Under the new FASA provisions, this inconsistency has been eliminated and the added certification requirements found in the DFARs for claims being certified to the Department of Defense will no longer be required.

---

38 *Ball, Ball & Brosamer, Inc. v. United States*, 878 F.2d 1426 (Fed.Cir. 1989); *United States v. Grumman Aerospace Corp.*, 927 F.2d 575 (Fed.Cir. 1991), *cert. denied*, 60 U.S.L.W. 3293.

39 Federal Courts Administration Act, Public Law No. 102-572 (1992).

40 Federal Acquisition Streamlining Act ("FASA"), Public Law No. 103-255, 108 Stat. 3243 (1994).

41 *See* the DOD certification requirements in DFAR § 252.233-7000. Section 8813(a) of the Defense Authorization Act of 1993 had added § 2410(e) to the Title 10 of the United States Code. It repealed the old 10 U.S.C. § 2410 when the new regulations for certification applicable to the Defense Department were issued.

However, in order for a claim to proceed under the CDA it must clearly be in dispute. The decision in *Dawco Constr. v. United States*[42] held that a contractor could not submit a claim to the contracting officer until it was actually "in dispute." As a practical matter *Dawco* requires that negotiations must be at a "impasse." Cases decided after *Dawco*, however, have articulated a different standard. For example, the court in *Transamerica Ins. Corp. v. United States*[43] found a dispute, despite the fact that the parties were still in negotiations. Adopting an analysis described as "common sense," the court stated that:

> [t]here is no necessary inconsistency between the existence of a valid CDA claim and an expressed desire to continue to mutually work towards a claim resolution.

Obviously, these cases have led to confusion as to what constitutes a sufficient "dispute." The recent legislation in FASA does not address this issue, and the confusion is likely to continue unless resolved by the courts.

On December 5, 1994, the Federal Circuit withdrew the prior panel decision and granted *en banc* review in *Reflectone, Inc. v. Kelso*, which withdrew the prior decision in *Reflectone, Inc. v. Dalton.*[44] There is some reason to believe that the full court will limit the holding in *Dawco*.

Another question which arises in the context of a surety pursuing its rights is whether or not the principal must appeal the default termination decision of the government or it may await a decision on the amount of excess reprocurement costs before taking an appeal. The rule for many years had been that only the decision on excess reprocurement costs need be appealed and the decision to hold a contractor in default and terminate its contract need not be appealed.[45] If an appeal was filed from the original default termination, a later assessment of excess costs could be contested under the original appeal without the filing of a notice of appeal to the excess cost of reprocurement assessment.[46]

---

42 *Dawco Constr. v. United States,* 930 F.2d 872 (Fed. Cir. 1991).

43 *Transamerica Ins. Corp. v. United States*, 973 F.2d 1572 (Fed. Cir. 1992).

44 *Reflectone, Inc. v. Dalton,* 34 F.3d 1031 (Fed. Cir. 1994).

45 *Fulfort Manufacturing Co.*, ASBCA No. 2143 (1955); *Universal Lumber Co.*, 66-1 B.C.A. (CCH) ¶ 5421 (Armed Serv. B.C.A. 1966).

46 *El-Tronics, Inc.*, 61-1 B.C.A. (CCH) ¶ 2961 (Armed Serv. B.C.A. 1961).

However, this rule, usually referred to as the "Fulfort Doctrine," was called into question by the decision in *Overall Roofing and Construction, Inc. v. United States*.[47] The decision in *Overall Roofing* has now been overturned by the Federal Courts Administration Act of 1992,[48] expanding the jurisdiction of the United States Court of Federal Claims.

Now it is once again clear that under the Fulfort Doctrine, the principal has a choice of appealing the default termination decision or awaiting the decision on assessment of excess costs of reprocurement. A surety which has obtained the rights of its principal under a takeover agreement or is proceeding in the name of the principal would have a similar option.

FASA imposes a six year statute of limitations on claims asserted by contractors, their sureties, and the federal government, except for government claims alleging fraud.[49] However, FASA does not bar the government from raising "latent defect" claims beyond six years. Nevertheless, the continuing vitality of the ambiguity as to what constitutes a claim in dispute under the decision in *Dawco* may mean that the limitation period in FASA is effectively meaningless. The new statute of limitations in FASA begins to run only when the contractor's claim has "accrued." Under *Dawco*, however, a contractor's claim does not accrue until it is "in dispute." A principal should be able to preserve its rights by giving

---

47 929 F.2d 687 (Fed. Cir. 1991). The U.S. Court of Appeals for the Federal Circuit reviewed an appeal from a contractor whose complaint was dismissed in the Claims Court after seeking review of a termination for default. The court dismissed the complaint without prejudice, holding that it had no jurisdiction to consider the propriety of the default termination until one of the parties made a specific claim for monetary relief.

48 § 907(b)(1). The jurisdiction of the United States Court of Federal Claims now includes:

> [a] dispute concerning termination of a contract, rights in tangible or intangible property, compliance with Cost Accounting Standards, and other non-monetary disputes on which a decision of the contracting officer has been issued under Section 6 of that Act.

49 FASA § 2351, Public Law No. 103-255, 108 Stat. 3243 (1994).

adequate notice of its position and reserving its right to pursue an equitable adjustment when it receives final payment.

The CDA provides[50] that for claims involving $50,000 or less, the contracting officer has sixty days within which to issue a decision from the time he or she receives a "written request from the contractor that a decision be rendered within that period." Nevertheless, this requirement usually is observed in the breach. The CDA also requires for claims of more than $50,000, that the contracting officer has sixty days from "receipt of a submitted certified claim" either to issue a decision or to "notify the contractor of the time within which a decision will be issued."[51] Likewise, this requirement frequently is ignored.

However, the failure of a contracting officer to issue a final decision may be appealed to a Board of Contract Appeals for the respective agency, and now under FASA the language permits the "tribunal concerned" to direct a contracting officer to issue a final decision.[52] This recent legislative change permits a contractor or its surety under a takeover agreement to appeal the lack of a final decision to the United States Court of Federal Claims.

Upon issuance of a contracting officer's final decision which is disputed there are two different choices as to where to appeal. Under the CDA, an appeal can be taken to the appropriate Board of Contract Appeals for the particular agency within 90 days[53] or within 12 months of the issuance of the contracting officer's final decision an appeal can be taken to the United States Court of Federal Claims.[54]

FASA increases from $50,000 to $100,000 the maximum amount in dispute for utilization of an accelerated claims procedure at the Boards of Contract Appeals.[55] Under these accelerated procedures, time limits and litigation expenses are substantially less than traditional litigation before both the United States Court of Federal Claims and the Boards of Contract Appeals. A board renders a decision on the merits of the dispute within 180 calendar days after receiving the contractor's or surety's election to use the procedures. Frequently pleadings are simplified and

---

50 CDA § 6(c)(2), 41 U.S.C. § 601.
51 CDA § 6(c)(3).
52 FASA § 2351.
53 CDA § 7.
54 CDA § 10(a)(3).
55 FASA § 2351 (amending 41 U.S.C. § 607(f)).

discovery is eliminated or limited. The Act also increased from $10,000 to $50,000 the maximum amount in dispute for the small claims procedure.[56]

Each Board of Contract Appeals has its own published rules and provides for discovery, pre-trial submittals and a hearing before a single board member. The board decisions normally are reviewed by a three judge panel and issued only after completion of an assessment for correctness and uniformity with other board decisions. Decisions by the United States Federal Claims Court likewise are issued by a single judge hearing the case without jury and normally are not reviewed by other members of the court. It is not uncommon for the decisions of the United States Court of Federal Claims to conflict with other decisions issued by different judges of the court.

A notice of appeal to a Board of Contract Appeals is merely a letter directed to the clerk of the particular board identifying the final decision from which an appeal is taken, the name of the contracting officer and the subject contract and the amount in dispute. Such a letter normally is copied to the contracting officer. An appeal to the United States Court of Federal Claims is a much more formal endeavor requiring a complaint meeting the requirements of the rules of the court.

Both the Boards of Contract Appeals and the United States Court of Federal Claims have nationwide subpoena power and will hear cases outside of Washington, D.C. Judicial review from both the decisions of the Boards of Contract Appeals and the United States Court of Federal Claims is to the United States Court of Appeals for the Federal Circuit.[57] Under the CDA,[58] the government may only appeal an adverse decision from a board of contract appeals if the appeal is filed within 120 days and if the determination to take an appeal is made by (a) the head of the agency; (b) with prior approval of the Attorney General. The standard of review before the United States Court of Appeals for the Federal Circuit is whether or not a decision of a Board of Contract Appeals is supported by "substantial evidence," while the standard of review from a decision of the United States Federal Claims Court is whether or not the holding is "clearly erroneous."

---

56 FASA § 2351 (amending 41 U.S.C. § 607(g)).

57 Federal Courts Improvement Act of 1982 ("FCIA"), § 127(a), Public Law No. 97-164 (1982).

58 CDA § 8(g).

The federal government has statutory authority to use alternative means of dispute resolution ("ADR") to resolve disputes. FASA extends the government's authority to use ADR procedures until October 1, 1999.[59] Most Boards of Contract Appeals and the United States Court of Federal Claims have in their rules procedures for implementing the utilization of ADR even after disputes are appealed.

V.
Disputes With State And Local Governments

As with the federal government, several states have created specialized courts of claims in order to hear disputes against their state governments, *i.e.*, Pennsylvania[60] and Ohio,[61] while at least one state has created a board of contract appeals, *i.e.*, Maryland.[62] In California, a statute imposes on all local public agencies a duty to include administrative claims procedures in their public works contracts and to elect to submit claims either to the state construction arbitration process or to a judicial process which incorporates mandatory mediation and judicial arbitration. The law applies to all claims of $375,000 or less.[63] In other states, proceedings must be brought in particular courts of general jurisdiction, such as in Virginia, where contract actions against the Commonwealth may be brought in the appropriate circuit court only.[64]

In seeking legal redress from a state or local governments it is a necessity first to ascertain what requirements have to be satisfied as a condition precedent which usually requires review of the state procurement code, local implementing ordinances and judicial decisions, as well as the contract provisions. In some instances, contractual arrangements will

---

59 FASA § 2352 (amending 41 U.S.C. §§ 605(d) & (e)).

60 Commonwealth of Pennsylvania Board of Arbitration of Claims, 72 P.S. § 4651.

61 Ohio Rev. Code, Ch 2743.

62 Md. Code Ann., § 15-219 (1988).

63 Cal. Pub. Cont. Code § 20104 *et seq.* (1990).

64 Va. Code Ann. § 11-69 and 11-70 (1994); *Wiecking v. Allied Medical Supply Corp.*, 391 S.E.2d 258 (Va. 1990).

provide for administrative prerequisites prior to initiating judicial review.[65]

---

65 *See* Paul F. Dauer, STATE AND LOCAL GOVERNMENT CONTRACTING (1993); John A. Jenkins, OHIO PUBLIC CONTRACTING LAW (1989); and FIFTY STATE CONSTRUCTION LIEN AND BOND LAW.

CHAPTER 9

BANKRUPTCY CONSIDERATIONS AND BOND DEFAULTS

T. Scott Leo

A contractor's financial condition is the number one reason for an event of default. The contractor may fail to pay subcontractors and vendors that furnished labor and materials. The contractor may be unable to adequately man the project, or the work will slow down because of the contractor's inability to pay key suppliers. Sureties invariably discover the root of most defaults is a contractor whose financial condition is worse than when the bonds were underwritten.

Given the competitive nature of construction bidding and the uncertainties of the construction process, even a seemingly healthy contractor lurks only one or two projects away from financial doom. Construction companies are, for the most part, closely held and highly leveraged. They possess very few unencumbered assets. They rely on their good will in attracting and keeping solid relationships with their vendors, subcontractors and laborers.

Just as the inevitability of death adds significance to every phase and age of one's life, the prospect of a contractor's future bankruptcy adds significance to the actions and expectations of the surety claims representative and underwriter. All contractors do not go bankrupt. In the surety business, however, bankruptcy is a common denouement to the story that begins with a contractor with minor cash flow problems and some small technical problems on a couple of projects. The cash flow problems and technical glitches are the small coughs that are symptoms of the cancer that ultimately kills the patient.

There is an adage among bankruptcy practitioners who have experience with construction bankruptcies to the effect that "a construction company cannot be reorganized." There are a number of reasons for this gloomy outlook. Construction companies, because they are highly leveraged, closely held, possess very few unencumbered assets, rely upon their reputation, and require an additional source of credit in the form of surety bonding, are not suitable subjects for reorganization. The Bankruptcy Code[1] and Rules are not equipped to deal with construction contracts and the practical constraints of the construction business. Debtors' attorneys are not familiar with construction law and the practical requirements of the construction business, and consequently tend to focus on the debtor's rights while losing the debtor's business. Construction companies do not tend to file a petition seeking relief after extensive pre-petition negotiations. It is rare that there has been substantial pre-filing planning.

Continuity of performance and the time frame for completion of performance are critical to the successful completion of construction work. Projecting the cost to complete with some accuracy is essential to profitably completing the work. For contractors who seek relief in the hope of reorganizing their companies, the effect of the bankruptcy proceeding on the cost of doing business, the disruption to the ordinary operations as the company must administratively deal with the demands of the bankruptcy proceeding, and the impact of the filing on the continuity of construction work, often thwart the reorganization efforts at the very start of the case. Most construction companies, however, file for relief without any pre-filing planning and under the apparent misconception that the bankruptcy proceeding will be something the contractor will control that will provide relief from creditors and an opportunity to decide what to do and how to reorganize its debts.

Bankruptcy practitioners often refer to the debtor's "breathing space"—a time to decide what contracts to assume and reject. In construction, any breathing space taken by a contractor in the middle of a project only increases the cost to complete, reduces the contractor's incentive and ability to complete the contracts profitably, and increases

---

1 The Bankruptcy Code will be referred to throughout this chapter as the "Code." The Code shall mean 11 U.S.C. § 101, et. seq (1994) including the Bankruptcy Reform Act of 1994.

the loss to the parties affected by the contractor's likely inability to perform the contract. A contract remains in limbo while the debtor decides whether or not it wants to assume the obligations of the contract. Naturally, the owner, subcontractors and vendors on a project are paralyzed by the uncertainty of the debtor's performance. If this paralysis lasts for an extended period of time it results in the certainty that the debtor cannot perform leading to the ultimate rejection of the contract.

Lack of planning on the part of putative debtors and the time allowances of the Code are the elements that doom most, if not virtually all, reorganization efforts by contractors. Despite this pre-disposition for failure, a very large percentage of petitions filed by construction companies start out as Chapter 11 reorganizations.

Certain provisions of the Code may impact a surety's efforts to cure defaults while the debtor attempts to fulfill the pipedream of reorganizing its company. Any contract that has not been terminated prior to the filing of the petition by the debtor is a contract in which the debtor's estate possesses a property interest.[2] Consequently, contracts that have not been terminated as of the date of the petition are property of the estate. Termination of the contract can only then be effected after the debtor's rejection of the contract or after the lifting of the automatic stay.[3]

The procedure for lifting the stay and obtaining rejection of the contracts takes time. During that time an obstinate debtor can increase the exposure for the surety. A takeover agreement cannot be entered into

---

2 The automatic stay must be lifted to terminate a contract that may be property of the estate. 11 U.S.C. §§ 362 and 541(a). Unless the debtor's right to proceed under the contract terminated before the filing of the petition, the debtor can attempt to assume the contract. 11 U.S.C. § 365(a). *See In re Computer Communications, Inc.*, 824 F.2d 725 (9th Cir. 1987); *Moody v. Amoco Oil Co.*, 734 F.2d 1200 (7th Cir. 1984), *cert. denied*, 469 U.S. 982 (1984) (contract executory where debtor filed bankruptcy with one day remaining in cure period); *In re Horton*, 15 Bankr. 403 (Bankr. E.D. 1981). *See generally* McDonald and Mintz, *Section 365: Executory Contracts, Lending Transactions and the Bankruptcy Code,* 1983 (Rosenberg, ed.), Practicing Law Institute (1983).

3 There is some divergence of opinion over whether a rejection of a contract would automatically permit the contract's termination without lifting the automatic stay.

until there is a termination. Whether such a termination takes place depends upon the ability of the debtor to assume the contract.

The bankruptcy of the principal is usually preceded by some warning signs to the surety. Claims activity increases; the principal might be slow in responding to requests for financial information. In a minority of cases, the surety is surprised by its principal seeking relief under the Code. The greater likelihood today is that the surety and the principal will have engaged in active claims workout efforts, perhaps even financing, prior to the filing of the petition by the principal.

Bankruptcy will affect the options of the surety in addressing defaults and the manner in which the surety exercises those options. A surety engaging in financing of its principal under circumstances suggesting the principal will likely seek relief will want to structure the financing arrangements in contemplation of the prospect of bankruptcy, securing whatever protection might be available. After the petition is filed the surety will need to assess its options under the Code and assert those provisions of the Code that protect its rights.

In theory, liens and other rights of ownership survive bankruptcy. Presumably, the Code should not affect the surety's right to look to the remaining contract consideration as security for performance of the contract and payment of contract obligations. In other words, the surety's subrogation rights ought to be protected by the Code. Most theories, however, fall short of full realization in practice. And in some instances what are regarded as purely procedural steps, inhibit the ability of the creditor to exercise its rights to such a degree that those rights are useless.

The Code was not drafted with a creditor like a surety in mind. A surety's status as a joint and several obligor with the debtor and the surety's equitable rights in contract funds create practical problems that the Code does not directly address.[4] The operating provisions of the Code were not prepared in anticipation of the operational needs of a business like a construction contractor.

This chapter looks at the provisions of the Code that impact the surety's traditional options for curing defaults, steps sureties might take in anticipation of a principal's future filing of a bankruptcy petition, how the provisions of the Code might impact a surety's ability to exercise its

---

4 Leo and Wilson, *Suretyship and the Bankruptcy Code*, *in* THE LAW OF SURETYSHIP 9-1 (Edward G. Gallagher ed., 1993).

rights and how the surety should use the Code to protect its rights. How the Code affects the surety's ability to recover salvage, through the prosecution of claims, will also be addressed, since the prospect of salvage is a factor in deciding which option the surety elects to pursue in curing the principal's default. The focus will be on those provisions of the Code that immediately impact the surety's ability to take action in curing defaults—the automatic stay imposed by § 362, adequate protection and cash collateral orders under §§ 361 and 363, the extent of the debtor's property rights under § 541, and the assumption of executory contracts under § 365. There will be very little discussion of the pure Bankruptcy Code issues that might affect a surety as an unsecured creditor generally but will have little impact on the surety's actions in responding to the declaration of a default.

I.
Some Basics Concerning Chapter 7 And Chapter 11

Contractor bankruptcies will either be Chapter 7 liquidations or Chapter 11 reorganization proceedings. Although an individual indemnitor might opt to file a proceeding under Chapter 13 to work out repayment of his or her individual debts, this option is not available to construction companies except for sole proprietors who otherwise qualify for Chapter 13 relief.[5] The contractor can be placed in a Chapter 7 or Chapter 11 proceeding voluntarily or involuntarily. Often a party placed in an involuntary Chapter 7 will seek either dismissal of the bankruptcy proceeding or conversion of that proceeding to Chapter 11.

There are some differences between Chapters 7 and 11 that could affect sureties. A trustee is appointed in a Chapter 7, and the purpose of the proceeding is to liquidate the corporation's assets for the benefit of its creditors. A corporation in a Chapter 7 proceeding does not receive a discharge of its debts.[6] The fact the debt has not been discharged does not enhance recovery by the creditors from the estate, but the continued existence of the debt allows the creditors to pursue recovery from others

---

5 11 U.S.C. § 1304.

6 11 U.S.C. § 727(a)(1).

who may be obligated for that debt.[7] Most importantly for a surety, a Chapter 7 trustee will have no real interest in operating the company and performing contracts that might yield a marginal profit. In a Chapter 7, contracts not expressly assumed by the trustee within 60 days of the date of the petition are deemed rejected.[8] A trustee does not want to remain in the construction business. A surety is far less likely to have disputes over the assumption or rejection of executory contracts in dealing with a Chapter 7 trustee.

In a Chapter 11, the debtor remains in possession of the company, and the goal is typically a reorganization of the company and composition of its debts through a plan of reorganization. It is not uncommon that companies are liquidated through plans. The company's debts can be discharged through the terms of a plan.[9] Confirmation of a plan, unlike a Chapter 7 liquidation, results in a discharge of the corporation's debts.

Although a Chapter 11 company has a number of reporting and administrative requirements under the Code, it remains under the control of the management in place prior to the filing of the petition. Nevertheless, management changes often occur after the filing of the petition. In most cases involving construction companies that are closely held, however, the owners remain in control. These owners are typically indemnitors of the surety or sureties that furnished bonds to the company pre-petition. They are personally liable to the surety for losses on contracts.

With management in control that is personally liable for the obligations on the contracts that are bonded, a debtor-in-possession is prone to attempt to assume marginally profitable and even marginally unprofitable contracts. Historically, one of the reasons for corporate existence was to shield individuals from obligations of a business enterprise. In a Chapter 11, one can expect that management will tend to use the company to

---

7 For a general discussion of the effect of discharge on a surety's rights see, M. Gamell, *Objections and Exemptions to Discharge: Surety and Fidelity Considerations* (unpublished paper submitted at the annual meeting of the A.B.A. Tort and Insurance Practice Section Fidelity & Surety Law Committee on August 10, 1993).

8 11 U.S.C. § 365(d)(1).

9 A corporation can only receive a discharge upon the confirmation of a plan of reorganization that does not amount to a Chapter 7 liquidation in disguise. 11 U.S.C. § 1141(d)(1)(A) and § 1141(d)(3).

reduce personal obligations. In a Chapter 11, a debtor is more apt to attempt to assume a contract that it might not be able to profitably perform. In Chapter 11, a debtor will fight with the surety for control of contracts to the extent the contracts will provide cash flow or profit and to the extent management perceives the debtor's performance will reduce management's personal obligations to the surety.

In a Chapter 11 proceeding the debtor can assume or reject executory contracts, contracts that still require performance, any time up until the confirmation of a plan of reorganization.[10] Many reorganizations take years. The absence of a tight time limit provides an opportunity for some debtors to wallow. In some cases, debtors continue performance of the work without assuming the contracts. If no one requires the debtor to assume the contract as a condition for payment, the debtor can perform without assuming and continue to receive payment. Ultimately the debtor might attempt to reject the contract should a problem arise on the project or should it appear the warranty obligations might be too burdensome.

Sureties face the most difficult problems in Chapter 11. The debtor often attempts to secure the benefits of the contracts without assuming the burdens. The management will attempt to use the company to shield personal obligations. Abusive tactics occur in cases in which there is no sincere reorganization strategy. Sureties face the most difficult procedural quandaries in addressing claims related to principals in Chapter 11.

II.
Pre-Petition Arrangements and Actions

A surety may learn of problems with its principal's performance and its financial condition prior to the filing of the petition. The surety, as a result of such notice, may undertake arrangements to conclude the principal's work on certain contracts. The surety may enter into a comprehensive workout agreement with the principal contemplating financing of certain obligations and the recovery of salvage over a specified period of time. The principal's filing of a petition can unravel the efforts to arrange for a workout or negate the terms or consideration pledged to the surety under a workout agreement.

---

10 11 U.S.C. § 365(d)(2).

A. Termination of Contracts and The Automatic Stay

The automatic stay provision of § 362 of the Code acts to stay all action against the debtor or the debtor's property upon the filing of a petition.[11] The correct procedure for a party to take action with respect to property in which the debtor has no equity is to move the bankruptcy court to lift the stay as provided in § 362(d)(1) and (2).

The extent of the debtor's property interest as of the date of the petition is set forth in § 541, and would include the debtor's interest in a contract. If a contract has been terminated in accordance with its terms prior to the filing of the petition, then the debtor has no rights in the contract and the automatic stay would not affect the ability of the owner and the surety to make arrangements for completion, such as a takeover agreement or tender.

A contract that has not been terminated pre-petition in accordance with its terms on the date the petition is filed is a contract in which the debtor still has rights. The contract cannot be terminated without the party to the contract lifting the automatic stay. Even if the obligee issued a notice of default, a contract has not been terminated if the period for curing defaults has yet to expire.[12] The mere declaration of a default does not complete the termination process. It is not uncommon for contractors to file a petition before the expiration of a cure period after the default notice has issued to prevent the termination of the contract at the end of the cure period. If the contract represents a substantial portion of the contractor's work in process, the default notice could precipitate the principal's filing.

The debtor principal may halt tender or takeover arrangements by filing a petition before the contract is formally terminated. The time required for lifting the stay and fighting the attempted assumption of the contract by the debtor may cause the completion contractor to lose interest as the cost of the project escalates with the passage of time, increasing the difficulty in profitably completing the work.

---

11 11 U.S.C. § 362(a)(1)-(8) stays, among other things, the commencement of any legal action against property of the estate, including taking possession of the property of the estate, any act to create or perfect liens in property of the estate and the setoff of debts.

12 *Moody v. Amoco Oil Co.*, 734 F.2d 1200 (7th Cir. 1984), *cert. denied*, 469 U.S. 982 (1984) (contract executory where debtor filed bankruptcy with one day remaining in cure period).

Other creditors could place the principal into an involuntary bankruptcy while completion arrangements are being negotiated or the terms finalized.[13] Once it is determined that the surety will obtain a replacement contractor to cure a declared default, there should be no delay in making sure the contract is formally terminated. Otherwise work on the contract might be delayed pending the lifting of the automatic stay or after litigating the debtor's motion to assume the contract.

As noted above, the proper procedure for lifting the stay is by motion. (A sample motion to lift the stay is in Exhibit 9.1). A surety is not technically a party to the underlying contract and may not have standing to lift the stay to terminate the contract—the action needed to terminate must be undertaken by the obligee. The surety can seek to lift the stay to recover contract funds where the surety has sustained a loss on the contract and where the debtor has no equity in the contract funds because of the surety's equitable right to recoup its losses from the contract funds.[14] If the termination of the contract is necessary to conclude completion arrangements between the surety and obligee, the surety should seek the obligee's assistance in moving to lift the stay.

---

13 11 U.S.C. § 303. A drastic remedy for the surety is the filing of a petition to place the principal into an involuntary bankruptcy proceeding. This option becomes necessary under circumstances where the surety has information revealing that the principal cannot be trusted to continue in operation without the scrutiny of the bankruptcy court. Preferential transfers of the principal's assets to the principal's insiders and fraudulent conveyances can be avoided in a bankruptcy proceeding. In one reported decision involving a surety that filed an involuntary petition, the surety's petition was initially dismissed, the court finding the solicitation of other parties that the surety had an obligation to pay as co-petitioners for the involuntary petition amounted to a bad faith filing of the petition. The bankruptcy court was later reversed, the district court finding the surety's action in filing the petition was not bad faith given the evidence of assets transferred from the principal company pre-petition. *In re Vincent J. Fasano, Inc.*, 55 Bankr. 409 (Bankr. N.D.N.Y. 1985), *rev'd*, *U.S. Fidelity & Guar. Co. v. DJF Realty & Suppliers, Inc.*, 58 Bankr. 1008 (N.D.N.Y 1986).

14 The grounds for lifting the stay include the debtor's lack of equity in the property coupled with the property not being necessary for an effective reorganization. 11 U.S.C. § 362(d)(2).

In the absence of a proper termination of the contract, an uncooperative debtor can interfere with the surety's efforts to effect a takeover or tender for completion of the contract. The contract remains subject to the automatic stay and the debtor presumably has a right to assume the contract. The surety may be compelled to fight with the debtor over the assumption or rejection of the contract, as discussed below.

B. Pre-petition Financing By the Surety

A surety may consider financing and workout arrangements with the debtor prior to the filing of the petition. Such financing could contemplate advancing funds to the principal for the performance of work. Arrangements for the surety to recover amounts financed may be part of a workout agreement.

After the filing of the petition, the financing surety will want to make sure that it preserves the right to recover amounts financed from any contract funds available, that any funds advanced but not expended before the filing of the petition cannot be claimed by the principal's bankruptcy estate, that the surety has the election to discontinue financing and that any salvage that has been recovered by the surety pre-petition will not be recovered or claimed by the principal's bankruptcy estate. A surety cannot bullet-proof itself from every risk. The terms of a pre-petition agreement cannot avoid a debtor's substantive rights under the Code to recover preferences, fraudulent conveyances and to marshall assets. A surety, however, can take steps to guard against unpleasant surprises.

One risk for any surety that has recovered salvage from the principal before the bankruptcy filing is a claim to recover "preferential" payments. Section 547 of the Code enables the trustee or debtor-in-possession to avoid transfers: 1) to or for the benefit of a creditor; 2) for or on account of an antecedent debt; 3) made while the debtor was insolvent[15]; 4) made on or within 90 days of the date of the filing of the bankruptcy petition; and 5) that enables the creditor to recover more than it would have received in a Chapter 7 liquidation. For transfers earlier than 90 days of the date of the filing of the petition, but within one year of the petition date, the party receiving the transfer could face preference liability if it

---

15 Any transfer within 90 days of the date of the filing of the petition is presumed to be at a time the debtor was insolvent. 11 U.S.C. § 547(f).

is an insider of the debtor company. An "insider" is usually deemed to be someone who controls the debtor's operations before the filing of the petition.[16]

To protect salvage recovered through financing and workout arrangements, parties contrive fairly baroque strategies for masking preferences. A surety might, for example, want to take a secured interest in some of the principal's property to guarantee repayment of funds advanced to the principal for its overhead and operations. Had the surety advanced the funds without the secured interest in the property or had the surety merely paid claims after the default of the principal, the surety might never have recovered the amount represented by the value of the secured interest in the property. If the contracts result in a net loss and cannot be assumed by the estate, the surety received a preference to the extent the secured interest reduces that loss.

One contrivance to avoid a preference claim is to structure financing through a bank guarantee, by having a bank take the secured interest in the property in exchange for guaranteeing the advance made to the principal by the surety.[17] Conversely, the surety could guarantee a loan to the principal by a bank. This is, in fact, an indirect preference and still subject to avoidance.[18] The surety receives a guarantee that it might not

---

16 11 U.S.C. § 547(b)(4)(B). Section 101 (30) provides the definition of "insider." For a corporate debtor, insiders include directors, officers and control persons. Section 101 (30)(B). Economic leverage may result in a party being deemed an insider and subject to the one year preference period. The key is whether the transferee had operational control of the debtor before the filing of the petition. *In re Octagon Roofing*, 124 Bankr. 522 (Bankr. N.D. Ill. 1991). Under most circumstances, the pre-petition workout arrangements between a surety and principal will not result in the surety asserting operational control of the principal.

17 See discussion in Chapter 4, *supra* and Joyce and Haug, *Financing the Contractor*, *in* BOND DEFAULT MANUAL (Richard S. Wisner ed., 1987) at 31.

18 *Aulick v. Largent*, 295 F.2d 41 (4th Cir. 1961); *Virginia Nat'l Bank v. Woodson*, 329 F.2d 836 (4th Cir. 1964) (transfer to bank found to be preferential to the extent of the collateral given by debtor to third party to pay debtor's bank debt); *In re Compton Corp.*, 831 F. 2d 586 (5th Cir. 1987) (payment through letter of credit found to be a preference).

Some have argued the surety receives an indirect preference through the payment by the principal of parties furnishing labor and materials on

otherwise receive by having the principal pledge property to the bank. The secured interest given to the bank is for the benefit of the surety. From the perspective of the debtor, the bank becomes a secured creditor by guaranteeing what would otherwise be the unsecured claim of the surety.[19] If the surety guaranteed a bank loan, any preference can be undone by compelling the bank to recover on the guarantee from the surety instead of the property pledged by the principal.[20]

If a transfer is truly a preference under the Code, any contrivance to mask the nature of that transfer can fall victim to the avoidance power of § 547. The terms of an agreement cannot protect the parties from the later exercise of substantive rights that cannot be waived.

The potential insider liability of sureties for preference claims became a common topic in the secondary literature after the *Deprizio*[21] decision, but did not appear as a topic in any reported decisions. The dearth of reported authority does not mean that sureties did not face *Deprizio* claims, only that those claims did not find their way into the reported decisions.

---

bonded contracts within the 90 days before the filing of the petition. In one such case this theory was characterized as follows:

> [The principal's] theory is based on a bankruptcy maxim that the estate may proceed directly against a surety, instead of circuitously recouping the preference from the creditor, forcing the creditor to proceed against the surety and then waiting for the surety to assert a claim against the estate for reimbursement.

In re Newbery Corp., 106 Bankr. 186, 187 (D. Ariz. 1989). For a discussion of this issue see R. Berens, *Bankruptcy: Can A Surety Be Held Liable For The Prepetition Payments Made By Its Principal?* (unpublished paper submitted at the A.B.A. Tort and Insurance Practice Section Fidelity & Surety Law Committee annual meeting on August 10, 1993).

19 See the discussion regarding bank guarantee arrangements in T. Leo, *The Financing Surety and the Chapter 11 Principal*, 26 TORT & INS. PRACTICE J. 1 (1990) at 51.

20 The bankruptcy court can compel the bank to recover on the guarantee before resorting to property pledged by the principal. *In re Tampa Chain Co.*, 53 Bankr. 772 (S.D.N.Y. 1985).

21 *Levit v. Ingersoll Rand Fin. Corp.* (*In re V.N. DePrizio Construction Co.*), 874 F. 2d 1186 (7th Cir. 1989).

Deprizio created such a furor within the banking industry that it was a key concern addressed in the Bankruptcy Amendments of 1994.[22] The *Deprizio* case held that a transfer to a non-insider that benefits an insider made within one year of the date of the filing of the petition could qualify as a preferential transfer, even if the payment to the non-insider, such as a regular loan payment, was not itself a preference. A surety, for example, that is not an insider and that recovers salvage from the principal within one year of the date of the petition may be obligated to repay the salvage to the estate, even if the surety received the salvage outside of the ordinary 90 day preference period, because of the benefit the insider indemnitor of the surety received through the principal's payment. The insider indemnitor receives a preference because the payment serves to reduce his or her personal obligation to the surety under the indemnity agreement.

Deprizio was effectively overturned by Congress in 1994 by an amendment to Section 550 of the Code to provide that a preference can only be recovered from an initial transferee if all of the elements of a preference are met with respect to that initial transferee.[23] This eliminates

---

22 103 P.L. 394, Section 202.

23 The amendment to § 550 is as follows:

> Section 202. Limitation On Liability Of Non-Insider Transferee For Avoided Transfer.
>
> > Section 550 of title 11, United States Code, is amended—
> >
> > (1) by referencing subsections (c), (d), and (e) as subsections (d), (e), and (f), respectively, and
> >
> > (2) by inserting after subsection (b) the following:
> >
> > > "(c) If a transfer made between 90 days and one year before the filing of the petition—
> > >
> > > > (1) is avoided under section 547(b) of this title; and

the *Deprizio* problem for banks and other transferees, like sureties who recover salvage, because the mere benefit to a guarantor or indemnitor can no longer give rise to preference liability on the part of the initial transferee.

With respect to concerns other than preferences, a financing surety can seek terms in the financing agreement that will protect its rights. A surety wants to assure that it retains the right to look to the contract funds to reimburse it for losses paid. By financing after a default of the principal, a surety does not waive its equitable right to recover the amount financed from the remaining contract consideration.[24] The fact that the payments are made to cure defaults ought to be documented in the agreement. The surety should make sure that the funds advanced are applied towards bonded contract obligations. Funds advanced and held for a time in any fashion ought to be subject to trust fund terms to insure that these funds can only be used for contract obligations and would not be property of the principal's bankruptcy estate.[25]

> > (2) was made for the benefit of a creditor that at the time of such transfer was an insider;
>
> the trustee may not recover under subsection (a) from a transferee that is not an insider."

103 P.L. 394, Section 202. The provision is intended to overrule *Deprizio* by clarifying that non-insider transferees should not be subject to preference liability beyond the 90 day period. 103 H.Rpt. 835 (103rd Congress, 2nd Session), October 4, 1994, Commentary on Section.

24 For a discussion of the surety's subrogation rights when financing, see discussion in Chapter 13, *infra* and T. Joyce and W. Haug, *Financing the Contractor*, *in* BOND DEFAULT MANUAL (Richard S. Wisner ed. 1987) at 37. As a general rule, the financing surety's payments to the principal will not be regarded as voluntary and the amounts financed can be recovered from the contract funds.

25 Funds held by the debtor in trust are not regarded as property of the estate. 11 U.S.C. § 541(d); *In re Kennedy & Cohen, Inc.*, 612 F.2d 963 (5th Cir. 1980), *cert. denied*, *Wisconsin v. Reese*, 449 U.S. 833 (1980); *In re Dunwell Heating & Air Conditioning Contractors Corp.*, 78 Bankr. 667 (Bankr. E.D.N.Y. 1987); *See also*, *In re Foam Systems Co.*, 92 Bankr.

If the financing fails to save the principal, the surety will want the flexibility to remove the principal immediately from the job and terminate the contract. The very purpose of the agreement may be to permit the principal to perform without bankruptcy. At least one commentator suggests that the surety might consider a provision in a pre-petition workout agreement that authorizes the surety to lift the stay subject to the principal acknowledging that it has no equity in the contract or remaining contract funds.[26] A limited number of decisions have enforced pre-petition agreements to lift the automatic stay in bank forbearance agreements. These cases offer some authority for the enforceability of these provisions in surety workout agreements.

The key drafting considerations in entering into a financing, forbearance or workout agreement with the principal, include the following:

---

406 (Bankr. 9th Cir. 1988) (stating the general proposition that property held in trust is not property of the estate but finding no express trust created in favor of surety in bank account under California law).

26 See discussion in J. Franks and J. Rowland, *Surety Strategy In The Chapter 11 Proceeding: Case Study Of A Broke Contractor* (unpublished paper submitted at the A.B.A. Tort and Insurance Practice Section Fidelity & Surety Law Committee annual meeting on August 10, 1993) at 6. A couple of recent decisions have enforced agreements to lift the automatic stay inserted in pre-petition forbearance agreements with lenders. *In re Club Tower L.P.*, 138 Bankr. 307 (Bankr. N.D.Ga. 1991); *In re Hudson Manor Partners, Ltd.*, 28 Collier Bankr. Cas. 2d (MB) 221 (Bankr. N.D. Ga. 1991). The limited number of decisions dealing with these provisions involve single asset limited partnerships. *In re Citadel Properties, Inc.*, 86 Bankr. 275 (Bankr. M.D. Fla. 1988); *In re Orange Park South Partnership*, 79 Bankr. 79 (Bankr. M.D. Fla. 1987). Although the single asset partnership is often filed to avoid foreclosure of the property, suggesting a valid reason for enforcing these waiver provisions, the policy of creating an environment in which lenders and sureties will attempt workouts would apply in the case of construction contractors. The likelihood that the future debtor/principal would have equity left in a contract after a failed workout arrangement with the surety is remote. An unpublished paper first addressing the possible use of these provisions in prepetition surety workout arrangements is J. Burch, *Pre-Bankruptcy Agreement to Abandon an Executory Construction Contract—A New Tool For the Surety* (unpublished paper submitted at the Third Annual Southern Surety and Fidelity Claims Conference on May 7, 1992).

1. acknowledgement of default by the principal;
2. acknowledgement of the sureties' rights by the principal;
3. advance of funds for bonded obligations only—the safest financing is to pay payables that would otherwise be payment claims against the bond;
4. with respect to property of the principal pledged as salvage, where possible, obtain subordination agreements from any other parties claiming an interest in the pledged property;
5. funds advanced should be held in trust for the express purpose of paying bond obligations on bonded contracts; and
6. remedy provisions, such as an agreement to lift the automatic stay, in the event of a bankruptcy filing ought to be inserted in the agreement to enable the surety to act promptly in the event of a bankruptcy filing.

(A sample pre-petition agreement is Exhibit 9.2 of this Chapter).

Although the surety cannot draft around a substantive preference problem in the terms of an agreement, the surety must keep in mind that in order to be avoided as preferential, the transfer must have all the elements of a preferential transfer under § 547, discussed previously, and not be subject to any of the statutory exceptions.[27] To the extent the surety would be able to recover contract funds through its equitable lien, any transfer that benefits the surety and serves to release that lien does not permit the surety to recover more than it would in a Chapter 7 liquidation and is therefore not preferential.[28] Moreover, the release of a surety's equitable lien qualifies as a contemporaneous exchange for value, an exception to preference liability under § 547.[29]

Another exception to preference liability is for payments made in the "ordinary course of business."[30] In some instances, sureties have faced

---

27 11 U.S.C. § 547(c).

28 *In re E.R. Fegert, Inc.*, 88 Bankr. 258 (Bankr. 9th Cir. 1988), *aff'd*, 887 F.2d 955 (9th Cir. 1989). See also *Newbery Corp. v. Fireman's Fund Ins. Co.*, 106 Bankr. 186 (D. Ariz. 1989) (recognizing the release of a surety's equitable lien is a contemporaneous exchange for value but finding payment to a subcontractor exceeding the amount of the contract proceeds subject to the surety's equitable lien was not an exchange for "new value" and thus subject to avoidance as a preference).

29 *In re E.R. Fegert, Inc.*, 88 Bankr. 258 (Bankr. 9th Cir. 1988).

30 11 U.S.C. § 547(c)(2)(B).

the argument that the payments to claimants by the principal within the 90 day preference period are preferential.[31] One reason such transfers should not be considered preferences is because a contractor pays such payables in the "ordinary course" of its business. Determining the course of dealing that qualifies as ordinary course may be difficult.[32] In some cases finding an ordinary course of business for making the payment or payments may be as simple as pointing out to the court that such payments were required of the principal by statute or regulation, for example, the federal Prompt Payment Act.[33]

An event that often precipitates a bankruptcy is the action of other creditors who perceive the principal is granting preferential treatment to the claims of other creditors. Any pledge of an asset by a financially disabled contractor to a specific creditor affects all of the other creditors by eliminating an asset that the other creditors might secure to reduce their claims. A surety may need to approach workout and financing efforts globally, to prevent the principal from pledging assets to other creditors, such as a financing bank, and to avoid precipitous actions by other creditors, primarily the financing bank.

---

31 For a paper entirely devoted to the topic of the surety's liability for preferences by reason of the principal's pre-petition payments see, R. Berens, *Bankruptcy: Can A Surety Be Held Liable For The Prepetition Payments Made By Its Principal?* (unpublished paper submitted at the A.B.A. Tort and Insurance Practice Section Fidelity & Surety Law Committee annual meeting on August 10, 1993). This paper highlights the defenses a surety can raise to such a claim.

32 The test for determining whether a payment is in the ordinary course of business is either an industry standard or based on the dealings between the debtor and the party allegedly receiving the preference. At the very least, there must be some objective facts which demonstrate that the payment was made in ordinary course of business. *See In re Loretto Winery Ltd.*, 107 Bankr. 707 (Bankr. 9th Cir. 1989). Where the dealings between the debtor and transferee are so haphazard that no reasonable basis for describing the payments as ordinary can be ascertained, the ordinary course exception will not apply. *Id.* at 710. For cases examining whether the course of dealing with the debtor was also consistent with industry practice *see In re Classic Drywall, Inc.*, 121 Bankr. 69 (D. Kan. 1990); *In re Unimet Corp.*, 85 Bankr. 450 (Bankr. N.D. Ohio 1988).

33 31 U.S.C. § 3905 and the applicable FAR provision relating to certification 48 C.F.R. 52.232-5(c).

C. Pre-petition Workout and Composition Agreements

Sureties are far more likely today than they were during the decade immediately following the enactment of the Bankruptcy Code in 1978 to engage in pre-petition negotiations with the principal's other creditors in an effort to develop an out of court workout or composition arrangement. The reasons for this were outlined at the beginning of this chapter. Construction companies are very dubious candidates for Chapter 11 reorganization. The expense of a Chapter 11 proceeding when considered in light of the probable result is unbearable. During a recent program, one commentator summarized the effectiveness of Chapter 11 proceedings for construction contractors by saying that the proceedings are "phenomenally expensive and marginally effective."[34]

Practitioners, contractors and surety representatives are increasingly aware of the marginal effectiveness of Chapter 11 proceedings when they involve construction businesses. In recognizing this problem and in looking for alternatives, these parties discover that anything that can be achieved through a bankruptcy proceeding can be worked out by the creditors and the principal without a bankruptcy proceeding. The worldly wise and sophisticated contractor finding itself in financial trouble will contact its creditors to attempt an out of court composition before filing for relief under the Code.

Financing and salvage arrangements are often part of a composition worked out with the principal and its creditors, typically the financing bank. Some of the elements of the composition agreements between sureties and financing banks may be subordination agreements with respect to specific pledged assets, sharing arrangements for litigation risk and costs, as well as allocation of litigation recoveries. (Exhibit 9.3 is a sample subordination agreement between a financing bank and a surety). The purpose of such agreements is to effect the collection and liquidation of assets for the creditors without the administrative expense and delay of a bankruptcy proceeding.

The type of pre-petition negotiations leading to an out of court composition of the principal's debts could also provide the basis for

---

34 Comments of J. Michael Franks during the A.B.A. Tort and Insurance Practice Section Fidelity & Surety Law Committee annual meeting on August 10, 1993.

negotiating a pre-packaged Chapter 11. The principal and its creditors can develop a plan by determining which contracts can be assumed and will benefit the creditors by the principal's performance. If financing is needed for the principal to complete an ultimately profitable contract, the contract can be assumed in the Chapter 11 proceeding and the party advancing financing needed to complete the project could be granted a super priority under the Code in consideration of the advance of additional financing.[35] These procedural devices work well if planned and promptly implemented. As noted in the introductory comments to this Chapter, the lack of sufficient pre-petition planning dooms many of these strategies to failure.

D. Filing of The Indemnity Agreement to Perfect Secured Interest in Assigned Property and Joint Control Arrangements

A perennial debate in the surety literature is the effect or benefit of filing the General Agreement of Indemnity as a financing statement to perfect the assignment of the principal's property contained in most of these agreements.[36] In most situations involving principal/contractors on the verge of bankruptcy, the perfecting of the assignment will be of no help to the surety.[37] The principal's financing bank will probably have a perfected first secured interest in most of the hard assets of the principal. If the surety does not perfect this interest in the ordinary course of business, and upon learning of the principal's imminent financial demise files the agreement to perfect its rights, the perfected security interest, if filed within 90 days of the petition date, could be avoided as a preference. The collateral descriptions in many of the typical indemnity agreements may not adequately describe the assigned collateral.[38]

---

35 11 U.S.C. § 364(c) and (d).

36 R. Smith and V. Covalt, *Should the Surety Stand on Its Equitable Subrogation Rights or File Its Indemnity Agreement Under the Uniform Commercial Code*, 69 Neb. L. Rev. 664 (1990).

37 E. Cushman, *Surety's Right of Equitable Priority*, 39 TEMPLE L.Q. 239, 251 (1966).

38 Many indemnity agreements assign equipment on contracts bonded by the surety. A third party would be unable to determine whether a specific item of equipment is subject to the surety's assignment. *In re Softalk Pub. Co.*, 856 F.2d 1328 (9th Cir. 1988) (ordinary test for adequacy of description is whether financing statement indicates the existence of prior incumbrance

There are circumstances in which the surety should consider filing the indemnity agreement. If the principal borrowed on an unsecured basis or the bank did not obtain a blanket perfected first secured interest in all of the hard assets, the surety's perfection of the assigned rights might result in some later recovery. The principal's primary bank could be over secured. The surety may file the indemnity agreement as a blanket filing and then work out the relative allocation of the principal's assets through subordination and other agreements with the principal's financing bank. The perfecting of the surety's rights would be less subject to avoidance as a preference if the surety has financed the principal by advancing new cash for operations.

Where special financing is undertaken as part of a workout with the consent of the financing bank, it is best to prepare new documentation for any perfected interests taken in conjunction with the workout. Sureties might be reluctant to file their original indemnity agreements and the description of collateral might be inadequate to notify third parties of the property in which the surety has a perfected interest, and thus, be unenforceable.

The legal effect of filing the indemnity agreement has been debated. Some feared that the exercise of this right by the surety might cause the courts to refuse to enforce the surety's equitable rights.[39] There are some

---

to a third party).

39 The idea that a surety elects remedies by inserting contractual assignment provisions in the indemnity agreement has caused some courts to hold that the surety must perfect to secure its rights in contract funds:

> In effect, the remedy of equitable subrogation merely implies in law reimbursement, agreement or assignment of rights in favor of one (the plaintiff) whose property was used to discharge the obligation of another. However, this just does not seem to describe the situation of the modern day payment or performance bond surety who regularly and in the course of business for profit undertakes the calculated risk of guaranteeing to an owner payment and performance by a contractor. Once such a surety performs under its bond it is merely fulfilling its own undertaking. Such a surety has ample opportunity to make any contractual subrogation agreement it desires, not only with the contractor, but also with the owner for whose protection the surety bonds are issued. The original purposes of equitable subrogation do not

cases holding the filing of the agreement is not an election of legal rights over equitable rights by the surety.[40]

> appear to exist where surety has, as appellant surety company has in this case, intentionally and contractually, for a consideration, obligated itself to perform a contractor's contractual duties and the surety is not seeking to enforce the original obligee's (owner's) rights against the original obligor (the contractor) or vice versa.

Transamerica Ins. Co. V. Barnett Bank of Marion County N.A., 524 So. 2d 439, 445-446 (Fla. Dist. Ct. App. 1988), *rev'd*, 540 So. 2d 113 (Fla. 1989). Some bankruptcy decisions have followed this type of reasoning. *In re Universal Builders, Inc.*, 53 Bankr. 183 (Bankr. M.D. Tenn. 1985); *In re Kuhn Constr. Co.*, 11 Bankr. 746 (Bankr. S.D. W.Va. 1981).

40 *American Oil Company v. L.A. Davidson, Inc.*, 290 N.W.2d 144 (Mich App. 1980) (filing a financing statement is not a waiver of other rights). When the Florida Supreme Court reversed the ruling of the appellate court in the *Transamerica Ins. Co.* decision *supra*, it clearly stated the historical reasons for recognizing that the surety's equitable rights in contract funds should not require perfection under the U.C.C.:

> Nonsurety assignees of a contractor in default have no enforceable claim on funds withheld by the owner/obligee because of contractor default. The interests of all concerned parties, whether they be contractors in default, nonsurety assignees, owners, or other obligees, are best served by prompt performance by the surety. Under these circumstances, it is appropriate to give priority to the claims of the surety, up to the limits of its performance....
>
> As Chief Judge Sharp pointed out in her dissent below, the overwhelming and essentially unanimous post-U.C.C. decisions in this country, federal as well as state courts, have held that (1) the surety's equitable right of subrogation is not a consensual security interest, (2) no U.C.C. filing is necessary to perfect the surety's interest, and (3) the surety's interest continues to be, as it was under pre-Code law, superior to the claim of a contract assignee, such as a bank.

Id. at 117 (citations omitted).

A couple of recent cases addressing the relative priorities of the surety and IRS in contract funds suggest in *dicta* the surety can protect itself from losing to the IRS only by perfecting its rights.[41] Although these cases do not represent the majority view, a surety might want to perfect by filing the indemnity agreement to avoid the risk an IRS lien might later prime the surety's equitable lien or interest in contract funds.

A surety may consider joint control arrangements with the principal at the time the surety issues bonds. In those states that do not have trust fund statutes, the sureties can assert there is an identifiable trust *res* that is held in furtherance of the duties imposed on the principal under the trust fund provision of the indemnity agreement.[42] Property a debtor holds

---

41 The Sixth Circuit in *In re Construction Alternatives*, 2 F.3d 670 (6th Cir. 1993), and the Seventh Circuit in *Capitol Indemnity Corp. v. Mount Vernon School District*, 41 F.3d 320 (7th Cir. 1994), both held that an IRS lien that arose prior to the default on the project primed the surety's claim to contract funds. Both cases suggest that the surety could only protect itself from the IRS lien by having a prior perfected secured interest in the contract receivables. Neither case recognized that the surety's equitable lien could qualify as a prior interest to the IRS lien under § 6323 of the Internal Revenue Code. The same bankruptcy court that rendered the initial ruling against the surety in the *Construction Alternatives* case, extended that holding by finding that the bankruptcy estate of a contractor could recover contract funds even though subcontractors and materialmen remained unpaid, finding no valid lien against the funds that primed the claim by the estate. *In re William Cargile Contractor, Inc.*, 151 Bankr. 854 (Bankr. S.D. Ohio 1993).

These cases fail to recognize that the surety's rights derive from the owner's rights under the contract, and the case of *Capitol Indemnity Corp.*, fails to find that the owner can waive these rights. These cases, however, suggest that the surety addressing contractor defaults in Ohio and Illinois should consider imposing joint control arrangements over the disbursement of contract funds and actually encourage claimants to assert lien rights that can be assigned to the surety upon payment of the claim.

42 In both the *Construction Alternatives* and *Capitol Indemnity Co.* cases *supra*, the courts found that there was no trust as the surety failed to prove all of the elements of a trust, including an identifiable *res*, under state law. These cases can be distinguished from a Third Circuit case, *Universal Bonding v. Gittens & Sprinkle Enter.*, 960 F. 2d 366 (3rd Cir. 1992), which found a trust in favor of the subcontractors of the debtor. The court

in trust is not property of the estate. Sureties who have tried to argue the principal/debtor has no equity in contract funds because those funds are held in trust under the terms of the indemnity agreement have often been unsuccessful, the courts finding the trust arguments fail because the sureties cannot identify a segregated trust *res*. Courts tend to find a trust only if the surety can show all of the elements of a *de facto* trust under state law.[43]

Filing the indemnity agreement is advisable if the principal has unencumbered assets, has defaulted and the surety has no other means of obtaining a consensual financing statement from the principal other than the indemnity agreement. The surety may face a later preference action. The surety may be lucky—the principal might survive outside of bankruptcy longer than ninety days after the filing of the indemnity agreement as a financing statement.

In deciding whether joint control arrangements are undertaken, a surety must balance the administrative burden against the relative risks. Where substantial payments are anticipated on the principal's contracts and other creditors are poised to actively undertake collection efforts, the surety should strongly consider exercising the rights it might have under the indemnity agreement to assert control of the contract funds, especially if the surety is supplying new cash to help finance the principal's operations for completing the bonded work. In states that have no trust fund statutes, the actual segregation of contract funds may help the surety convince a bankruptcy court later that there was a *de facto* trust.

III.
The Post Petition Principal And The Surety's Default Options

After the filing of the petition by the principal, the contracts that were not terminated pre-petition are property of the estate and can be assumed by the debtor. Before the surety can act to replace the debtor, the contract must be rejected, the automatic stay lifted and the contract terminated.

---

in *Gittens* found the state trust fund statute evidenced the existence of a trust.

43 *In re Foam Sys. Co.*, 92 Bankr. 406 (Bankr. 9th Cir. 1988) (absent elements of a *de facto* trust, indemnity agreement did not create an enforceable trust in favor of a surety).

The status of the contracts remains uncertain during the period from the filing of the petition and the ultimate assumption or rejection of the contract. Indecision in assuming contracts will usually prevent the debtor from assuming the contracts and increase the loss related to the performance of the contract to the surety. Most filings are not well planned. The debtor will want time to decide what to do with the contracts, often continuing to perform just enough work on the project to keep the obligee from exercising the drastic remedy of terminating the contract for whatever delay has occurred.

Right after filing the petition, the principal/debtor will naturally demand payment for the work performed to date. The debtor often makes these demands before any attempt to assume contracts. The debtor wants the benefits of its contracts while it decides whether to assume the burden by performing the balance of the work post petition and formally assuming the contracts under the Bankruptcy Code.

The primary goals of the surety after the filing of the petition are to make sure that any unpaid contract consideration is used towards performance and payment of bonded obligations and to avoid loss due to delay. Whether the principal is inside or outside of bankruptcy, control over contract funds and prompt action to cure defaults remain constant goals.

A. Cash Collateral Orders and Adequate Protection

A threshold question at the beginning of virtually every Chapter 11 proceeding is the ability of the debtor to use cash collateral.[44] Every business enterprise requires cash and cash equivalent property to operate. In the case of a Chapter 11 debtor-in-possession, its secured lender may have a perfected secured interest in accounts and contract receivables. The Code prohibits the debtor from using cash collateral unless each creditor with a security interest in the cash collateral consents, or the bankruptcy court, after notice and hearing authorizes the use of the cash collateral.[45] The bankruptcy court should not permit the debtor to use property that

---

44 *See generally*, J. Burch, *Cash Collateral Litigation And The Surety* (unpublished paper submitted at the A.B.A. Tort and Insurance Practice Section Fidelity & Surety Law Committee annual meeting on August 10, 1993).

45 11 U.S.C. § 363.

results in the diminution of the value of another party's interest in that property.[46]

On contracts that have not been assumed by the debtor, the use of contract funds will increase the loss to the surety if the contract or contracts from which funds are used are later rejected. The fact that the principal filed a petition for bankruptcy relief cannot be deemed an act of default.[47] In most cases, the principal commits some act of default before filing. A surety has an equitable interest in the remaining contract consideration and must look to the remaining contract consideration as security for performance and payment of contract obligations should the debtor fail to perform.[48] Although some decisions suggest the surety's

---

46 11 U.S.C. §§ 361 and 363(e). The concept of adequate protection arises out of the Constitution's Fifth Amendment protection over property interests. *Wright v. Union Central*, 311 U.S. 273 (1940). Adequate protection serves to protect a creditor's interest in property, and prevent a decrease in the value of the property interest during the bankruptcy as a consequence of the automatic stay. 2 Collier on Bankruptcy, § 361.01 at 361-67 (15th ed. 1984). For this reason, one of the remedies for a creditor whose property interest is not afforded adequate protection is to move the court to lift the automatic stay to take possession of the property or take whatever other action is required to protect the creditor's property rights.

A condition precedent for a debtor obtaining turnover of property that a creditor has an interest in is providing adequate protection. Title 11 U.S.C. § 542(a) authorizes turnover of "property that the trustee may use, sell, or lease under § 363 of this title." However, the debtor's authority to compel turnover under Section 542 is dependent upon a favorable balance of equities between the debtor and the holder of the property. *In re Alpha Corp.*, 11 Bankr. 281 (Bankr. D. Utah 1981). The Supreme Court in *United States v. Whiting Pools, Inc.*, 462 U.S. 198 (1983) affirmed the debtor's right to turnover of property subject to a federal tax lien, contingent upon the debtor's ability to provide adequate protection of the secured creditor's interest. *Accord In re World Communications, Inc.*, 72 Bankr. 498 (D. Utah 1987); *In re Taco Ed's, Inc.*, 63 Bankr. 913 (Bankr. N.D. Ohio 1986).

47 A clause terminating a contract because of the insolvency or bankruptcy of a party is invalidated by operation of 11 U.S.C. § 365(e)(1).

48 *National Shawmut Bank of Boston v. New Amsterdam Casualty Co.*, 411 F.2d 843 (1st Cir. 1969).

equitable rights do not arise until an actual default by the principal, under the Code any loss to the surety from the later rejection of an executory contract would be treated as a pre-petition unsecured claim, the rejection of the contract being treated as a breach or default as of the date of the filing of the petition. On contracts later rejected, if the surety's rights are deemed to arise upon default, the surety would still have a superior right to the use of the contract funds as of the date of the petition by virtue of the default arising out of the later rejection of the contract. If the debtor uses contract funds from a contract it later rejects, there will be less contract funds available for the surety to perform the obligations of the contract.

The Code offers several methods for providing adequate protection. The surety's interest in the contract funds could be adequately protected by giving the surety a lien or priority in property to cover the value of the contract funds used by the debtor in the event of default or rejection.[49] The surety's interest might also be protected by making sure that the value of the work performed on the project by the debtor had the same value as the amount of the contract funds used by the debtor.[50]

Bankruptcy is often the setting for disputes over the surety's equitable subrogation rights. It is not an accident that *Pearlman v. Reliance Ins. Co.*[51] involved a fight for contract funds between a bankruptcy trustee and a surety. If a Chapter 11 debtor is permitted to continue to use contract funds and then reject contracts, the surety's equitable rights are rendered meaningless. There is limited authority addressing the treatment of the surety's equitable lien in Chapter 11 cases on contracts that a debtor proposes or has assumed. That authority suggests a surety's interest in contract funds is entitled to adequate protection before the debtor is entitled to use of the contract funds.[52]

---

49 11 U.S.C. § 361(2) authorizes the court to grant replacement liens.

50 Performance by the principal might be the indubitable equivalent of the surety's rights. 11 U.S.C. § 361(3).

51 371 U.S. 132 (1962).

52 See T. Leo, *The Financing Surety and the Chapter 11 Principal*, 26 TORT & INS. PRACTICE J. 1 (1990), for the discussion in the section entitled "Is the Surety's Equitable Right to Earned but Unpaid Contract Funds Entitled to Adequate Protection Under Section 361?" at 59-63. Sureties have difficulty in convincing courts that the equitable interest should be afforded adequate protection. The surety's rights cannot be treated like a garden

Adequate protection is a term contained in § 361 of the Code. As noted, cash collateral orders typically involve providing adequate protection to the secured claim of the principal financing bank. The legislative history of § 361 reveals adequate protection should protect property interests other than secured interests; there is no reason the concept of adequate protection cannot apply to protect the surety's equitable interest in contract funds on bonded contracts.

Another way of looking at the rights of the surety in the context of a cash collateral order is as a subrogee of the obligee's rights. With respect to earned but unpaid contract funds, the obligee has a secured interest in these funds by virtue of possession and can claim these funds under the contract or through setoff or recoupment. Sureties are subrogated to the obligee's contract and setoff rights. Moreover, a condition precedent for the debtor obtaining turnover of the funds is to provide adequate protection to the party compelled to turnover the funds. In the case of a construction contract, providing such adequate protection is impossible absent the assumption of the contract by the debtor.[53]

---

variety secured interest in property of the debtor. Section 361 was intended to extend to equitable interests as well as perfected secured interests. H.R. Rep. No. 95-595, 95th Congress, 1st Session 338-40 (1977).

53 The court found the debtor's proposed use of contract funds without assumption of the contract did not provide adequate protection to the owner and prohibited the debtor's use of contract proceeds in *In re FLR Co.*, 58 Bankr. 632 (Bankr. W.D. Pa. 1985). Assumption of contracts under § 365 and the providing of adequate protection under § 361 are ordinarily unrelated concepts. A party to a contract protects itself by moving to compel the assumption or rejection of the contract under § 365(d)(2); a secured party protects itself by conditioning the use of secured property under the terms of a cash collateral order that provides adequate protection. A party holding a security interest can be adequately protected through the grant of a replacement lien or a priority that will result in the realization of the indubitable equivalent of the secured party's interest in property. See, for example, *In re Delbridge*, 61 Bankr. 484 (Bankr. E.D. Mich. 1986).

A surety agrees to extend credit and possesses an equitable interest in the contract funds. Contract funds together with the performance of the principal secure the surety from loss. *National Shawmut Bank of Boston v. New Amsterdam Casualty Co.*, 411 F.2d 843, 845 (1st Cir. 1969). A mechanism that assures the surety the principal will use the contract funds

In obtaining control of the funds, a surety can and should notify the obligees of the bankruptcy of the principal and advise the obligees on the contracts that they should take appropriate steps to protect their rights and the surety's rights to the contract funds. The surety might warn the obligees that the failure to take action to protect these rights might discharge the surety. The surety should also advise the obligees to seek the prompt assumption or rejection of the contract so that there is no delay and to make certain the rights of the parties to the use of contract funds are determined by the court. To the extent a bankruptcy court will not recognize the surety's right itself to request adequate protection and condition the use of cash collateral, the surety might obtain such relief by making demand upon the obligee. (A copy of a form notice to the obligee is Exhibit 9.4 to this Chapter).

An aggressive debtor might claim the notice violates the automatic stay. There is at least one bankruptcy court decision that held this type of notice by a surety does not violate the automatic stay.[54] The notice should thus be artfully worded. Instead of telling the obligee to withhold payment, the notice should tell the obligee that it should seek adequate protection through the assumption of the contract and notify the obligee that the surety will regard the failure to take reasonable steps to assert such rights as an impairment of the surety's rights to the contract funds and a defense to any later performance claim. Such a notice does not interfere with the debtor's rights but merely asserts the surety's rights against the obligee.

The first threshold for a Chapter 11 proceeding is the cash collateral order. Because such orders often involve the granting of replacement liens

---

for the performance of the work and payment of bond obligations can be a means of affording the surety adequate protection. Such a means of providing adequate protection to the surety to permit the debtor the use of the contract receivables was approved in the *Glover* cases. *In re Glover Constr. Co.*, 35 Bankr. 233 (Bankr. W.D. Ky. 1983) and *In re Glover Constr. Co.*, 30 Bankr. 873 (Bankr. W.D. Ky. 1983). The *Glover* decisions found adequate protection through the debtor continuing the work, the segregation of the funds and application of these funds first to pay bonded obligations.

54 *In re Hughes-Bechtol, Inc.*, 117 Bankr. 890 (Bankr. S.D. Ohio 1990) (non-repetitive single mailing by surety to obligee that was largely informational did not violate stay).

or other adequate protection liens to secured parties, and require an assessment of the debtor's total assets, these orders will either reflect the ultimate reorganization plan for a debtor who has undertaken some planning, or will determine the limits of the reorganization prospects for the debtor who has done little or no planning. Attendance at the cash collateral hearing is a must for any significant creditor. Even if the debtor is not proposing the assumption of any bonded contracts, a surety having a substantial unsecured claim ought to attend the cash collateral hearing to protect its interests and to learn about the debtor's financial condition. A surety that fails to attend a cash collateral hearing might later learn a financing party was granted a super priority or replacement lien priming the surety's equitable rights to contract funds.[55] If the purpose of the hearing is to provide other parties with adequate protection, the surety should appear to make sure the vehicle for providing adequate protection to others does not affect or impair the surety's rights.

The use of cash collateral is brought to the court's attention either through a motion by the debtor seeking use of cash collateral or the motion of a creditor requesting the court sequester or prohibit the use of cash collateral.[56] A cash collateral order is often presented by stipulation after intense negotiations between the creditors and the debtor during the first week or two of the Chapter 11 proceeding.

A debtor should only use cash collateral with the consent of the creditor having an interest in the cash collateral or by furnishing adequate protection.[57] A surety should seek to establish its interest in cash

---

55 In the *Hughes Bechtol* case *supra*, the surety also claimed contract funds that the financing bank claimed it was entitled to by virtue of the super priority lien granted the bank at the cash collateral hearing. The bank provided new cash for debtor's operations and was granted the priority. The surety, having been notified of the hearing, was bound by the order granting the bank a priority over the surety's equitable rights. *Id.*

56 A surety that questions the integrity of the principal or its ability to continue to operate should consider requesting the appointing of an examiner either in conjunction with a cash collateral order or in a separate motion. The grounds for seeking appointing of an examiner are set forth in § 1104 and include fraud and gross mismanagement.

57 The burden is on the debtor to establish that a creditor is adequately protected. Without adequate protection, use of cash collateral should be prohibited. *In re Martin*, 761 F. 2d 472 (8th Cir. 1985).

collateral (receivables) from bonded contracts early in the case. If the principal/debtor has not approached the surety regarding the disposition of the bonded contracts and the surety learns of demands made by the debtor to obligees for payment, the surety should bring a motion to sequester or prohibit use of cash collateral. (A sample form for such a motion is Exhibit 9.5). The ultimate outcome of such a motion might be a hearing at which the debtor and other creditors challenge the surety's right to seek adequate protection. The court might enter an order that the debtor can only use contract funds on those contracts it assumes, or establish other conditions for affording the surety adequate protection.

The goal in seeking adequate protection is to make certain contract funds are only used to reduce the surety's potential exposure or loss. A debtor who is able to assume the contract, perform the work and pay all of the obligations without loss to the surety is able to provide adequate protection. The order should protect the surety until that work is completed by segregating contract funds and requiring that they be applied first to pay obligations that might otherwise be obligations on the bonds. A debtor who is able to obtain another surety for the obligation may also be able to furnish adequate protection.

A comprehensive cash collateral order ought to include provisions that address the following[58]:

---

58 A comprehensive agreement regarding the use of contract receivables can be a very extensive document. A copy of such an agreement does not accompany this Chapter. (Many of the terms a surety will want post petition are the same as those contained in the pre-petition agreement that is Exhibit 9.2). A comprehensive post petition cash collateral agreement between a debtor and surety can be found as Exhibit D to T. Scott Leo, *The Financing Surety and Chapter 11 Principal* (unpublished paper submitted at the A.B.A. Forum on the Construction Industry/Tort and Insurance Practice Section Fidelity & Surety Law Committee joint meeting in New York, N.Y. in January 1989).

A comprehensive agreement should seek protection of the surety's rights under the following Code provisions:

1) under §§ 361 and 363, acknowledge that contract funds are property of the surety and the agreement is to provide adequate protection, provide for segregation of the funds and establish first priority of payment of obligations that would otherwise be surety obligations under the bonds;

2) waive any claim by the debtor under § 506(c) or any other Code provision to seek recovery of any funds that are subject to the surety's

1. assumption of the contracts from which the debtor wants to use cash;
2. disbursement from contract receivables to pay obligations that might be bond claims first;
3. some remedy for the surety in the event of a post-petition default or the inability of the debtor to assume the contract (this might be achieved by granting the surety a replacement lien or super priority lien in certain assets or allowing an administrative expense claim to the extent of losses from rejected or defaulted bonded contracts);
4. an acknowledgement of the surety's right to contract funds in the event of the rejection or post petition default and a waiver of any claim by the debtor to recover or use contract funds other than as consideration for the successful performance of contract obligations;
5. the lifting of the automatic stay to enable the surety to exercise remedies upon default or rejection of the contract(s); and
6. if the surety is agreeing to keep the bonds in effect post petition, language in the agreement that recognizes that the surety is providing post petition financing and that any priority acknowledged by the debtor, if not a valid priority under the law, is a super

---

equitable rights;

3) provide for the lifting of the automatic stay imposed by § 362(a) pursuant to §§ 362(d)(1) and (2) for the surety to seek any relief against the debtor post petition allowed by virtue of its rights at law and under the indemnity agreement;

4) state that § 552 will not void any interest the surety possesses in contract funds post petition;

5) provide a super priority or the highest administrative claim the surety can negotiate under § 364 or § 503 to secure the surety from losses post petition;

6) require the assumption and performance of the contracts under § 365 and provide for the automatic lifting of the stay so the surety can seek relief in the event of nonperformance; and

7) for any priority allowed provide for "safe harbor" language in § 364(e) to prevent reversal of protection offered in exchange for financing on appeal; characterize the entire agreement by which the surety permits the use of cash collateral as a financing agreement.

priority allowed under § 364(c) or (d) in exchange for the post petition extension of credit on behalf of the principal.

This list is by no means exhaustive but sets forth the main points that are key to the surety's ability to obtain protection in a Chapter 11 proceeding. If the principal is to undertake the completion of the contracts and the surety intends to keep its bonds in effect, the surety must protect its rights through a cash collateral arrangement. Any such arrangement must also enable the surety to act promptly to cure defaults in the event of a later rejection of the contract or a post petition default.

B. Assumption and Rejection of Executory Contracts

In order for the obligations and benefits of a contract to be brought into the Chapter 11 estate, it must be assumed under § 365 of the Code. As noted above, the surety should push for a prompt decision from the debtor on assumption and rejection of contracts. Delay in assuming a contract often assures that the contract cannot be assumed and increases the loss for the surety that must perform.

A Chapter 7 trustee must assume a contract within 60 days of the date of the petition or conversion of the case; after 60 days the contract is deemed rejected.[59] One does not normally anticipate a Chapter 7 trustee will assume any construction contract. The administrative and overhead requirements of construction work do not make these contracts suitable enterprises for a trustee concerned with liquidating the company.

In a Chapter 11 there is no outer time limit for the assumption or rejection of executory contracts, except that contracts must be assumed or rejected upon the confirmation of a plan of reorganization.[60] Many plans of reorganization contemplate this by including boiler-plate language to the effect that all contracts not previously assumed will be deemed rejected upon entry of a confirmation order, or vice versa.

Section 365 requires the debtor to cure pre-existing defaults and provide adequate assurance of future performance in order to assume an executory contract.[61] These requirements present many difficulties in attempting to assume construction contracts. Curing defaults should

---

59 11 U.S.C. § 365(d)(3).

60 11 U.S.C. § 365(d)(2).

61 11 U.S.C. § 365(b).

require the debtor to cure all payment and performance defaults upon assumption. A debtor may be able to show that it can perform the work to complete the contract but cannot prove it will survive for the entire warranty period contained in the contract. The warranty provision may involve repair and replace obligations to be performed over a substantial period of time.[62] The type of work covered in a warranty provision, e.g., extended clean up obligations for environmental work, might condemn any assumption attempts to failure.

Construction contingencies make it difficult to precisely determine the benefit of assuming the contract. A debtor might be entitled to forced extras on a contract that without the extra compensation would be unprofitable. Litigation and claims disputes that are contingent, although part of the ordinary construction business, represent risk to the estate.

The standard for permitting the assumption of a contract may vary from court to court.[63] Some judges allow the debtor to assume contracts based on the debtor's business judgment. Others, despite the debtor's request to assume a contract, will want to determine there is a tangible benefit or profit to the estate to be made from the assumption of the contract.[64] In light of the difficulties inherent in construction work, the

---

62 A debtor might propose assuming a contract and assure performance of the warranty by covering the warranty obligations with an escrow—a portion of the contract funds the obligee can hold to cover future warranty problems. The amount of the escrow might be based on the principal's historical warranty exposure.

63 A general discussion of the standards applied by the courts in deciding whether to permit the assumption of contracts by the debtor can be found in Mann and Schexnayder, *An Overview of Surety and Bankruptcy Law* (Defense Research Institute 1990) at pp. 35-37.

64 See M. Fenton, *Executory Contracts And The Role of the Surety* (unpublished paper submitted at the A.B.A. Tort and Insurance Practice Section Fidelity & Surety Law Committee annual meeting on August 10, 1993) at 12. The court must decide whether the contract is advantageous to the estate and whether the debtor will perform. *In re Joshua Slocum, Ltd.*, 103 Bankr. 601 (Bankr. E.D. Pa. 1989). In construction, the principal focus is on the ability of the contractor to profitably conclude the work. *In re C.M. Systems, Inc.*, 64 Bankr. 363 (Bankr. M.D. Fla. 1986).

profit test appears to be commonly adopted in determining whether construction contracts should be assumed.[65]

The assumption of an unprofitable contract will affect the other creditors. Upon assumption of the contract the burdens of the contract become burdens of the debtor's estate. Losses on assumed contracts increase the ordinary administrative expenses of the estate, reducing assets available to other creditors. Had the unprofitable contracts been rejected, any losses would be unsecured pre-petition claims, rejection of the contracts resulting in their being breached as of the date of the filing of the petition.[66]

There may be some limited circumstances in which a debtor asks the court to allow assumption of an unprofitable contract. Several contracts may be performed in phases, the last of which was bid as the most profitable. A debtor might assert business reasons for assuming the first phase contract. The debtor may have two contracts with the same obligee, one profitable and the other a loser. If the obligee is entitled to setoff the funds due on the profitable contract to cover the losses on the unprofitable contract, the debtor might propose the assumption of both contracts if there will be a net profit to the estate from the performance of both contracts. Continuity of performance and good will are other factors that could cause a debtor to attempt the assumption of an unprofitable contract. Whatever other factors cause a debtor to propose the assumption of a specific contract that appears unprofitable, the debtor will likely be required to show these other factors will produce a net benefit or profit to the estate from other contracts.

The effect of the rejection of a contract has been the subject of some debate in the secondary literature.[67] For construction contracts, the debate is academic. A debtor rejecting a contract will not perform and will be

---

65 The court in the *C.M. Systems* decision refused to permit assumption of the contract by the debtor based solely on the debtor's business judgment. The court examined cash flow and profitability of the contract as well as the prospect of the surety completing the contract and reducing the overall losses to everyone concerned. *Id.* at 365.

66 *In re Drexel Burnham Lambert Group, Inc.*, 138 Bankr. 687 (Bankr. S.D.N.Y. 1992).

67 See J. Westbrook, *A Functional Analysis of Executory Contracts*, 74 MINN. L. REV. 227 (1989) and M. Andrew, *Executory Contracts in Bankruptcy: Understanding "Rejection,"* 59 COLO. L. REV. 845 (1988).

terminated for default, terminating the debtor's rights under the contract. Moreover, consistent with the practical consequence of a debtor's non-performance upon rejection of a contract, most courts find that the rejection of a contract is an actual breach of that contract as of the date of the filing of the petition.[68]

A debtor or its attorneys may claim receivables from obligees on contracts that are rejected. Upon rejection of contract, the debtor has no right to the contract receivables. Most contracts contain provisions forfeiting any right to recover under the contract in the event of a termination for default. Contracts governed by the Federal Acquisition Regulations bar any claim for contract receivables by the contractor on a terminated contract and provide that all unliquidated contract payments should be applied to liquidate the liability of the contractor and its surety to the government.[69]

A miracle could occur and a contract might be completed profitably after its rejection. If the contract terms or regulations governing the contract provide the principal waives all right of recovery from the contract in the event of a termination for default, the debtor may have no right to recover any excess funds remaining after all of the contract obligations are completed. Otherwise, if the contract and the law governing its terms allows, the most a debtor might claim from a contract that it rejected and on which it was consequently terminated for default might be some form of *quantum meruit* recovery. For example, if a contractor pre-petition enters into a contract for $1,000, performs $200 in work, is paid nothing on the date of the petition, and the obligee performs the work for $700 after the rejection of the contract, the contractor, now the debtor, might assert a $200 *quantum meruit* claim. The contractor could not assert a claim for the full $300 in net excess funds because the right to collect the full amount terminated with the

---

68 *In re Public Service Company of New Hampshire*, 884 F. 2d 11 (1st Cir. 1989). Section 365(g) of the Code provides the rejection of a contract is deemed a breach immediately prior to the filing of the petition.

69 The viability of a debtor's claim for *quantum meruit* recovery on federal contracts is questionable. The United States is not subject to suit for *quantum meruit* or under implied-in-law contract theories. *Haberman v. United States*, 18 Cl. Ct. 302 (1989); *Mega Constr. Co. v. United States*, 29 Fed. Cl. 396 (1993).

contract.[70] Any *quantum meruit* claim would be subject to any setoffs the obligee might assert against the debtor. So that if the same obligee in the example above incurred a $300 loss on another rejected contract with the contractor/debtor, the excess funds could be setoff to cover that loss and the debtor's *quantum meruit* claim disallowed.[71]

Assumption or rejection determines the debtor's rights and obligations under contracts.[72] One source of conflict for sureties is the attempt by some debtors to secure the benefits of the contracts without assuming the burdens. An order addressing the assumption and rejection of executory contracts ought to expressly provide that the automatic stay is lifted with respect to any rejected contract to permit their termination and to enable the surety to take the necessary steps to cure defaults and arrange for completion.

The time taken to assume contracts often prevents the debtor from meeting the requirements for assuming the contracts and increases the loss to the surety.[73] There are some procedural devices that might enable the surety to push the debtor to a prompt decision regarding assumption and rejection. Section 365(d)(2) permits a party to a contract to request a specific time frame for the assumption or rejection of an executory contract with the debtor. Debtors have argued that because a surety is not a party to the underlying contract they cannot use this provision to shorten

---

70 There is one construction contract case that allowed a debtor subcontractor to recover from the general contractor on a rejected contract. *In re Howdeshell, Inc.*, 56 Bankr. 122 (Bankr. M.D. Fla. 1985). This case held that the prepetition breach of the payment conditions entitled the debtor to recovery.

71 One of the elements of *quantum meruit* is the unjustifiable retention of a benefit conferred by one party to another. A holder of a valid setoff claim, however, possesses a valid reason for claiming the benefit. Retaining a benefit to cover a valid debt due on another contract is not inequitable.

72 Losses and other obligations on an assumed contract are expenses of the estate and entitled to treatment as ordinary administrative expense claims under § 503.

73 The policy followed by the bankruptcy courts in giving the debtor "breathing space" to decide whether to assume or reject executory contracts can wreak havoc upon construction workouts. *See In re Whitcomb & Keller Mortgage Co.*, 715 F. 2d 375, 378 (7th Cir. 1983) (debtor must be afforded breathing space).

the time frame for the debtor to assume the contract.[74] The surety might bring a motion under § 105 of the Code seeking a date certain for the assumption or rejection of executory contracts.[75] Section 105 is the general provision that authorizes the bankruptcy court to issue injunctions for the protection of the estate and its creditors.

In the Bankruptcy Amendments of 1994, section 105 was amended to provide that "any party in interest" could move for a status hearing at which the acceptance or rejection of contracts could be addressed. A surety should also consider moving for such a status hearing if it is unable to reach an agreement with the debtor about the rejection and assumption of certain contracts.

If the surety presents evidence to the court demonstrating the situation that typically results from delay in construction—increased cost to complete—then the court should grant relief once it recognizes that the increase in cost to complete may prevent the assumption of a once profitable contract and increase the unsecured debt by increasing the loss to the surety. The surety seeking a specific date by which a contract or contracts must be assumed or rejected should be ready to present evidence demonstrating the delay in assuming the contract(s) will destroy the debtor's ability to assume and increase the surety's losses. (Sample motions seeking a "drop dead" date by which the debtor must assume a contract and asking for a status conference are contained in Exhibit 9.6).

---

74 Section 365(d)(2) provides the court can set a time for assumption or rejection upon "the request of any party to such contract."

75 Section 105 of the Code is a catch-all provision that provides the court with the power to issue injunctions and other orders in the bankruptcy proceeding. Even if the surety has no standing as a party to the contract under § 365(d)(2), it can ask the court to exercise its injunctive powers to prevent loss to the estate as a result of the debtor's delay in acting to assume or reject a contract. Section 105 was amended in 1994 and now more exhaustively describes the powers of the court. Among the provisions of the recently amended § 105 is a section authorizing the court to hold status conferences to discuss scheduling and other substantive concerns affecting the estate and the proceeding, including the question of the assumption and rejection of executory contracts. § 105(d).

C. The Bond As a Financial Accommodation

It is commonly believed that if the debtor can assume the contracts, the surety must remain on the hook as the surety for post petition performance—the debtor can assume the bond with the underlying contract. As a practical matter, if the principal can meet all the elements of § 365 by proving it can cure defaults and provide adequate assurance of future performance, there is no reason why a surety should not go along with the principal's attempt to perform.

A surety may face an uncooperative principal, potentially dishonest, that receives favorable treatment from a debtor oriented court, and that attempts to assume contracts it is either incapable of performing or cannot perform profitably. The motive for such efforts may be to protect the principal's insider indemnitors from claims by the surety or others. The principal could be plain wrong in its evaluation of the contracts.

In attempting to assume a contract, contrary to common belief, the debtor cannot assume the surety bonds securing the performance of the contract obligations. A suretyship obligation is an extension of credit, an agreement to stand for the debt of another.[76] Under the Code, a suretyship obligation is a financial accommodation and in accordance with § 365(c) cannot be assumed.[77] The Code cannot compel a party extending credit to the debtor pre-petition to continue to extend that credit post petition.

In countering this argument, a debtor seeking to assume a contract over the objection of the surety will argue the bond is more in the nature of an insurance policy in which the debtor has an interest and can assume.[78] A fairly small but consistent line of cases holds that surety

---

76 RESTATEMENT OF SECURITY § 82 (1941).

77 *In re Sun Runner Marine, Inc.*, 945 F.2d 1089 (9th Cir. 1991); *In re Matter of Edward's Mobile Home Sales, Inc.*, 119 Bankr. 857 (Bankr. N.D. Fla. 1990); *In re Adana Mortgage Bankers, Inc.*, 12 Bankr. 977 (Bankr. N.D. Ga. 1980); *In re Wegner Farms*, 49 Bankr. 440 (Bankr. N.D. Iowa 1985).

78 *Louisiana World Exposition, Inc. v. Federal Insurance Co.*, 832 F.2d 1391, 1400-01 (5th Cir. 1987) describes five factors for determining whether an instrument is a policy of insurance in which the debtor has a property interest. A surety bond written *on behalf of* the debtor as principal has none of the elements.

bonds are financial accommodations. There are no reported cases holding that contractor's performance and payment bonds are financial accommodations.[79] The reasoning of the cases that hold license and other miscellaneous bonds are financial accommodations support similar treatment for performance bonds. None of the factors noted in bankruptcy decisions for finding an insurance policy is property of the debtor's estate apply to performance and payment bonds.[80]

---

79 The author is aware of at least one unreported order holding that a performance bond is a financial accommodation. *In re Johnson Constr. Co.*, Bankruptcy No. 89-05397 (D.N.D. unpublished Order June 19, 1989).

80 The *Louisiana World Exposition* decision, *supra* n. 78, described five factors for deciding whether a "policy" was property of the estate.

First Factor—Who is the beneficiary of the "policy"?

Where performance and payment bonds are issued for the principal's performance and payment for claimants, the beneficiaries are the obligee (usually the owner) and any parties who furnish material and labor to the principal to fulfill the contract between the principal and the obligee. *The principal/debtor is not a beneficiary of the bond but is a co-obligor with the surety on the bond.*

Second Factor—To whom are the "policy" proceeds payable?

Proceeds are payable to the owner or materialmen and subcontractors having valid claims and *not the principal/debtor*.

Third Factor—Whether the "policy" covers liability exposure of the corporation.

The principal/debtor always remains liable. If the surety makes a payment it will have a claim against the debtor's estate. (For rejected contracts, the surety can assert as an unsecured claim the amount of payment claims and completion costs incurred by it to finish the principal's work).

Fourth Factor—Whether the object of the proceeding before the court is to enlarge the estate.

The question has no bearing to a surety—the surety's liability is as a rule the liability of the principal to other non-bankrupt parties, and the payments by the surety merely shifts the obligation of the principal from the third parties to the surety. Payments by the surety are not for the purpose of holding the principal harmless.

Fifth Factor—Whether the debtor would have owned the proceeds if it were solvent.

The surety desiring to cancel the bonds can either move to lift the stay to cancel the bonds as financial accommodations or issue a notice advising the obligees the surety will not consent to continuing financial accommodations on behalf of the debtor post petition. The procedure may depend on the circuit. In the Ninth Circuit, there is authority to the effect that to end a financial accommodation there is no need to lift the stay. The Code simply provides a financial accommodation cannot be assumed. In other jurisdictions, however, some cases hold the automatic stay must be lifted before a financial accommodation can be canceled.[81] One of the reasons for requiring the lifting of the stay to cancel an instrument that the debtor clearly cannot assume under the Code is to give the debtor an opportunity to obtain financial accommodations from someone else. (Exhibit 9.7 is a sample motion to lift the automatic stay to cancel surety bonds).

By canceling the bonds, the surety does not eliminate its obligation to the obligee and the third party payment claimants. The surety remains obligated to perform or pay in the event the principal fails to perform or pay. What the surety tells the parties in interest and the principal by canceling the bonds is that the surety will not agree to bond the post petition performance of the contracts by the principal. When the principal attempts to assume the contracts, if a bond is required by the terms of the contract, the principal will need to obtain a new surety bond to secure its post petition performance. Otherwise, the principal will not be able to meet the bonding requirements of the contract and will fail to prove adequate assurance of future performance within the meaning of § 365.

If the contract is deemed rejected, the original surety despite the cancellation is obligated to cure the pre-petition breach that occurs upon rejection. If the contract is assumed, the principal will have cured pre-existing defaults by paying all parties. If the original surety cancels the bonds and the principal obtains new bonds in assuming the contracts, in acquiescing to the assumption of the contract by the principal/debtor and accepting new bonds, the obligee might be deemed to have waived its rights against the original surety. The assumption of the contract by the

---

A *non sequitur* when applied to the surety. The principal has no standing as a claimant on the bond, and therefore, no right to its proceeds.

81 *In re Wegner Farms* 49 Bankr. 440 (Bankr. N.D. Iowa 1985) (bond cannot be assumed but surety must lift stay to cancel).

debtor and the posting of new bonds might be deemed a novation that serves to discharge the original surety. Whether the original surety is discharged with respect to the obligee is likely irrelevant, the principal will have cured pre-existing defaults (by paying all parties supplying labor and materials and curing performance defaults) and obtained a substitute surety that must be regarded as the principal surety for post petition defaults.[82]

A surety compelled to seek cancellation of surety bonds over the objection of the debtor is obviously embroiled in a very hostile bankruptcy proceeding. The attempt to cancel bonds on contracts the debtor hopes to assume is the nuclear war maneuver of the surety in the principal's bankruptcy. Because effective measures in bankruptcy are for the most part consensual, use of this procedure is not generally recommended. This step should only be taken where consensus is impossible and the court is compelling the surety to remain at risk on behalf of a principal that is incompetent or dishonest. This desperate option should only be taken when desperation is appropriate.

D. Post Petition Financing

The debtor might request additional surety credit or the advance of funds by the surety to enable it to complete bonded work. Any extension of credit the debtor is otherwise unable to obtain in the ordinary course of business can be secured by the grant of a super priority administrative expense claim or lien. Section 364 provides the debtor can request a super priority in exchange for such financing.[83] A super priority granted under this section can prime all other administrative claims and secured interests in the property in which such a lien is granted. The court can grant a

---

82 In the absence of an express agreement between the sureties, or in the order assuming the contract, where the prior surety is refusing to undertake the post-petition risk, the subsequent post-petition surety would have the principal obligation to perform or pay. RESTATEMENT OF SURETYSHIP § 47 Distinguishing Subsuretyship from Co-Suretyship, Tent. Draft No. 3 (April 1994).

83 Section 364 authorizes the grant of a super priority lien in specified property under § 364(c) and an administrative priority under § 364(d) only if the trustee is unable to obtain unsecured credit that would be allowable as an ordinary administrative expense claim under § 503(b)(1).

super priority lien in specific property or an administrative expense priority claim against the estate generally.

A surety might extend post petition credit to the debtor by providing new surety credit, continuing existing surety credit, advance funds for certain job costs or advancing funds for certain overhead items, such as payroll. To obtain a priority under § 364, the debtor must make the request. Obtaining this priority is therefore the product of negotiations with the debtor. (A sample application requesting a priority lien in exchange for the issuance of new bonds by the surety is Exhibit 9.8).

An application for a priority administrative expense claim may face challenge from other creditors, especially secured parties looking to the debtor's total assets as a source of adequate protection. A priority for certain types of financing, even with the debtor's agreement to the priority, will face serious challenge. A debtor proposing to assume a contract that requires extraordinary financing for the debtor to complete may be challenged by creditors who will contend that the grant of a priority administrative claim diminishes the value of assuming the contract for the estate.

If these requests are made on a piecemeal basis without creditor consensus over the direction of the debtor's reorganization efforts in general, the greater the likelihood these requests will be continuously disputed. Creditors vie for the limited assets of the estate while the debtor offers priority interests in its assets to obtain cash for its operations. A debtor making a number of applications for administrative priorities on a piecemeal basis without the consent of the primary creditors to the proposed financing and the priorities offered for this financing will not continue in operation very long.

Some unusual financing options exist for the surety. A principal might be essential for the work but the contract funds insufficient for the principal to prove a profit and assume the contract. The contract itself could involve a unique process or construction technique that necessitates the principal's participation for completion of the work. The need for the principal's participation may be a greater concern for the surety than obtaining the absolute lowest price for the completion work. Because financing in exchange for a super priority could draw creditor objections resulting in the ultimate rejection of the contract and a substantial loss to the surety because the principal cannot perform the work, the surety can arrange for back door financing by paying the obligee funds that can be added to the contract balance to make the contract profitable for the principal to assume. Although the amount financed in this manner does not qualify for treatment as an administrative expense claim and would at best be treated as part of the surety's unsecured claim, the real value received by the surety is the principal's performance. The surety should obtain the obligee's concession that the penal amount of the bond can be reduced by the amount "financed" by the surety. (A sample agreement for this type of financing appears as Exhibit 9.9).

Extending additional credit to the principal in bankruptcy is regarded as among the most foolish actions a surety can take. Actions, however, can only be judged by the circumstances—when a building is on fire it suddenly makes sense to jump from a high ledge. Some protection can be obtained by demanding the debtor request an administrative priority to the extent of any new credit offered. Under the appropriate circumstances, the best alternative for the surety may be to advance new credit to the Chapter 11 principal.

IV.
Other Bankruptcy Considerations

The status of the contracts, control of the contract funds and protection of the surety's equitable rights are among the chief concerns affecting the surety's approach to defaults in bankruptcy. The scope of this chapter, dealing with bankruptcy issues that influence the surety's options upon default, precludes discussion of bankruptcy procedure, case administration and Chapter 11 plans. A few other issues should be addressed.

A. Setoff In Bankruptcy

The United States Court of Federal Claims recently held a surety was subrogated to the obligee's right of setoff and could assert a claim against the government for releasing excess funds on one project to a contractor that the government could have setoff to cover losses incurred by the surety on another contract between the contractor and the government.[84] In so holding, the court noted the only "competing interest" to the excess funds was the contractor.

---

84 *Transamerica Ins. Co. v. United States*, 989 F. 2d 1188 (Fed. Cir. 1993).

The question naturally arises whether this principle could operate when the contractor is in bankruptcy. Section 553 of the Code preserves all rights of setoff arising pre-petition.[85] Inasmuch as the trustee's or estate's claim is no better than the claim of the contractor pre-petition, there is no reason why such a setoff right should not exist on contracts that are rejected and deemed breached pre-petition.

Bankruptcy courts tend to disfavor such setoff claims, which are perceived as obstacles to a debtor's reorganization of its debts. One means of limiting setoff rights is to find that the debts are not mutual as required under § 553.[86] Contract revenue earned on a contract with one agency of the government, for example, cannot be setoff to cover the deficiency on a SBA loan, as the debts are not mutual.[87]

---

85 Section 553 provides that the Code does not affect any right of setoff that arose before the commencement of the case. 11 U.S.C. § 553(a). To exercise the right of setoff, however, the party claiming setoff must lift the automatic stay. Procedurally, either the surety as subrogee or the obligee must move the court to lift the stay to permit setoff for the benefit of the surety.

86 Courts have limited setoff by finding that different agencies of the government are different entities in determining setoff rights. There is a split of authority regarding the treatment of the government departments for setoff purposes. Some cases permit setoff between departments and agencies, broadly interpreting the government's right to assert setoff. *Cherry Cotton Hills, Inc. v. United States*, 327 U.S. 536 (1946); *In re Thomas*, 84 Bankr. 438 (Bankr. N.D. Tex. 1988). Other courts strictly and narrowly interpret the mutuality requirement of § 553 and hold the government should not be allowed to assert setoff between different agencies. *In re Lakeside Community Hosp, Inc.*, 151 Bankr. 887 (Bankr. N.D. Ill. 1993); *In re Ionosphere Clubs*, 164 Bankr. 839 (Bankr. S.D.N.Y. 1994).

87 In addition to some of the cases cited in note 86, there are other cases that narrowly construe mutuality for setoff purposes and hold that the government can only be deemed the same entity in the same capacity of § 553 setoff purposes where the debts arise between the debtor and the same government agency. An important consideration in finding one governmental agency the same entity as another governmental agency for setoff purposes is the source of the appropriations for the agencies. The same source of funding indicates the agencies should be treated as the same entity for setoff purposes. *In re Lessig Construction, Inc.*, 67 Bankr. 436

The language of the cases upholding setoff refer to "competing interests" limiting the surety's right to claim setoff as subrogee and may also cast doubt on setoff claims in bankruptcy. Obvious valid competing interests include perfected assignments under the Assignment of Claims Act and the government's own competing right of setoff for some other debt.[88] Bankruptcy courts are not inclined to uphold setoff claims that could inhibit a debtor's reorganization. If the government's setoff rights are recognized, a contractor that exclusively performs government contracts could not reorganize by assuming profitable contracts and rejecting unprofitable contracts. Only if the contracts proved profitable in the aggregate would reorganization be possible. Bankruptcy courts might be inclined to find other creditors' interests, such as ordinary perfected assignments, qualify as competing interests and thus disallow setoff.

Bankruptcy courts might also tend to treat subrogation rights as arising on a contract-by-contract basis. This would permit a debtor, as part of a reorganization strategy, to reject the one contract causing the debtor's entire loss without worrying about anyone claiming the revenue received from the other contracts should be setoff. A number of subrogation cases in the bankruptcy context discuss how the surety's rights exist on a contract-by-contract basis. These cases are distinguishable from the cases allowing sureties to assert setoff rights as a subrogee of the obligee. The cases standing for the proposition that subrogation arises on a contract-by-contract basis deal with the rights of payment bond sureties.[89] On the

---

(Bankr. E.D. Pa. 1986); *In re Pyramid Indus., Inc.*, 170 Bankr. 974 (Bankr. N.D. Ill. 1994) (United States as the SBA could not claim setoff for amount due on loan from construction contract with United States for construction at naval base).

88 31 U.S.C. § 3727 (1988), 41 U.S.C. § 15 (1988). The Assignment of Claims Act provides a specific means for a financing bank to protect itself from setoff claims when financing federal work.

89 In *Security Ins. Co. of Hartford v. United States*, 428 F.2d 838 (Ct. Cl. 1970), the court addresses when the Government can setoff contract funds for unrelated obligations, and held that the Government can setoff to the detriment of a payment bond surety but not a performing surety. In *Dependable Ins. Co. v. United States*, 846 F.2d 65 (Fed. Cir 1988), the court held the surety could not improve its position as a payment bond surety by invoking its status as a performance bond surety on other

other hand, those cases permitting a surety to assert the obligee's right of setoff involve performing sureties.[90] The distinction courts recognize

---

contracts. There is no decision directly holding that a performance surety suffering a loss cannot assert by subrogation the rights of the obligee to setoff against the principal. *Ram Constr. Co. v. American States Ins. Co.*, 749 F.2d 1049 (3rd Cir. 1984) and *Western Casualty & Surety Co. v. Brooks*, 362 F. 2d 486 (4th Cir. 1966) both involved rights of sureties that paid payment bond losses.

90 *Transamerica Ins. Co. v. United States*, 989 F.2d 1188 (Fed. Cir. 1993); *District of Columbia v. Aetna Ins. Co.*, 462 A.2d 428 (D.C. 1983).

There are some non-surety cases supporting the assertion of setoff claims in bankruptcy. In *Tatelbaum v. United States*, 10 Cl. Ct. 207 (Cl. Ct. 1986), the court recognized the right of the Government Printing Office to setoff funds due on contracts claimed by an assignee for the benefit of creditors to cover reprocurement costs on other defaulted contracts. In recognizing this right, the court in *Tatelbaum* addressed the impact of bankruptcy and insolvency law on the Government's right to setoff. In that case, Tatelbaum, the assignee, conceded the Government could recoup reprocurement costs on each defaulted contract from the amounts due on those contracts, but argued it was improper to extend setoff to complete contracts that were not in default. *Id.* at 208.

Tatelbaum argued four points in the case: 1) state law and bankruptcy law precluded setoff; 2) reprocurement costs were not sufficiently liquidated at the time of the assignment for the benefit of creditors; 3) there was no mutuality; and 4) equitable considerations restricted or eliminated setoff. *Id.* at 210.

With respect to the limits imposed by bankruptcy law upon setoff, the *Tatelbaum* court noted:

> Under federal bankruptcy law, the United States' broad rights of setoff are not limited by insolvency. When a debtor is adjudged a bankrupt and a trustee is appointed to administer his estate, the estate assets pass to the trustee subject to the equitable right of setoff then existing. A debtor of the bankrupt may set off debts of the insolvent company rather than pay off what he owes and attempt to collect from the estate as a general creditor.

Id. The Government's right to setoff is prior and superior to a secured party's claim to a receivable. *In re Defense Services, Inc.*, 104 Bankr. 481 (Bankr. S.D. Fla. 1989).

between performance bond and payment bond subrogation rights has been harshly criticized.[91] A failure to pay is as much a default as a failure to perform.[92] The distinction between the rights of payment bond and performance bond sureties, however, again appears in the cases addressing setoff rights.

The validity of setoff will influence the debtor's and surety's actions at the beginning of the case. There is nothing in the Code prohibiting the performing surety from claiming the obligee's rights of setoff. The surety must recognize, however, bankruptcy courts will be reluctant to accept the assertion of these rights. A contractor that has a number of contracts with the same obligee might not be able to assume the very profitable contracts without addressing the potential setoff problem. The contractor might opt to assume all of the contracts if in the aggregate performance of every contract would yield a net profit. The principal/contractor might not challenge the obligee's setoff rights and reach an agreement regarding the assumption of a profitable contract or contracts. Such an agreement could provide that the obligee share in some of the profit received by the principal in performing the contract(s) in exchange for the obligee's (and by subrogation the surety's) compromise of setoff claims. The negotiation of setoff rights could be a factor in determining the surety's position at the very beginning of the bankruptcy case, and could be a factor for the debtor in deciding its reorganization strategy.

B. Assumption of Government Contracts

The FAR prohibit assignment of government contracts.[93] At one time, a majority of cases held that this prohibition of assignment precluded the assumption of government contracts without the consent of the

---

91 Mungall, *The Buffetting of the Subrogation Rights of the Construction Contract Bond Surety by U.S. v. Munsey Trust Co.*, 46 INS. COUNS. J. 607 (1979). The Restatement of Suretyship rejects the distinction between the rights of a payment bond surety and a performance bond surety. RESTATEMENT OF SURETYSHIP § 27, Tent. Draft No. 2 (1993). A failure to pay is a default and there is no reason why a surety should not be able to assert the obligee's rights through subrogation.

92 *Martin v. National Surety Co.*, 300 U.S. 588 (1937).

93 41 U.S.C § 15.

government.[94] The more recent decisions have retreated from this view, holding that the anti-assignment provisions were intended to prevent the government from finding itself in a contract with parties with whom it did not consent to enter into a contract.[95] A Chapter 11 debtor that remains *essentially the same* as the pre-petition contractor is not regarded as a different party. Some decisions hold the anti-assignment provision does not prohibit the assumption of contracts by a Chapter 11 contractor. The cases offer the curious qualification that the Chapter 11 contractor remains essentially the same as the pre-petition contractor, suggesting a Chapter 11 debtor that is not essentially the same as the pre-petition entity, such as a liquidating debtor, could not assume a government contract containing an anti-assignment provision.

C. Vesting Provisions in Government and Other Contracts

Equipment and materials required for the prosecution of bonded work usually secure the principal's line of credit.[96] The surety often attempts

---

94 *In re West Electronics, Inc.*, 852 F.2d 79 (3rd Cir. 1988).

95 *In re American Ship Bldg. Co.*, 164 Bankr. 358 (Bankr. M.D. Fla. 1994); *In re Hartec Enterprises, Inc.*, 117 Bankr. 865 (Bankr. W.D. Tex. 1990) *vacated*, *U.S. v. Hartec Enterprises, Inc.*, 130 Bankr. 929 (Bankr. W.D. Tex. 1991). These cases apply the "actual test" for determining whether the assignment is prohibited under the Anti-Assignment Act and § 365 of the Code, requiring proof that the contract obligations are to be assigned to a third party that is not the debtor.

96 48 C.F.R. § 52.232-16 vests in the government title to all materials chargeable to the contract. Subparagraph (d)(1) and (2) provide in part:

> (d) *Title.* (1) Title to the property described in this paragraph (d) shall vest in the Government. Vestiture shall be immediate upon the date of the contract, for property acquired or produced before that date. Otherwise vestiture shall occur when the property is or should have been allocable or properly chargeable to this contract.
>
> (2) *Property,* as used in this clause, includes all of the below-described items acquired or produced by the Contractor that are or should be allocable or properly chargeable to this contract under sound and generally accepted accounting principles and practices.
>
> (i) Parts, materials, inventories, and work in process; ...

to gain use of equipment and materials on bonded projects to complete the work. The principal's bank may attempt to liquidate the equipment and materials which serve as collateral for the loan to the principal.

Sureties have unsuccessfully asserted the provision in the typical indemnity agreement assigning equipment on bonded projects to the surety permits the surety to use the equipment and liquidate it to cover losses.[97] Absent a perfected assignment, the surety loses out to a trustee or any prior assignee holding a perfected interest in the equipment.

The vesting provisions in contracts and under the Federal Acquisition Regulations provide that title to certain equipment and materials purchased for the project vests in the government or obligee.[98] A minority of cases

---

Subparagraph (d)(6) of § 52.232-16 provides:

> (6) When the Contractor completes all of the obligations under this contract, including liquidation of all progress payments, title shall vest in the Contractor for property (or proceeds thereof) not—
>
> (i) Delivered to, and accepted by, the Government under this contract; or
>
> (ii) Incorporated in supplies delivered to, and accepted by, the Government under this contract and to which title is vested in the Government under this clause.

97 *United States Fidelity & Guaranty Co. v. United Penn Bank*, 524 A.2d 958 (Pa. Super. Ct. 1987) held a bank holding a perfected assignment possessed superior title to the proceeds from the sale of materials even though the surety paid claims for the delivery of the materials. The materials in that case were not incorporated into the project. *In re Merts Equipment Co.*, 438 F. Supp. 295 (M.D. Ga. 1977) (surety could not claim equitable assignment in equipment).

98 *United States v. Ansonia Brass and Copper Co.*, 218 U.S. 452 (1910); *In re American Pouch Foods*, 769 F. 2d 1190 (7th Cir. 1985) *cert. denied*, *American Pouch Food Co. v. United States*, 475 U.S. 1082 (1986); *In re Double H Products Corp.*, 462 F.2d 52 (3rd Cir. 1972); *In re Wincom Corp.*, 76 Bankr. 1 (Bankr. D. Mass. 1987); *In re Reynolds Mfg. Co.*, 68 Bankr. 219 (Bankr. W.D. Pa. 1986); *In re Economy Cab & Tool Co.*, 47 Bankr. 708 (Bankr. D. Minn. 1985).

find these provisions give rise to a lien in the equipment and materials.[99] The majority of cases hold that these provisions are effective in transferring title to the equipment and materials specified to the government obligee. Under a takeover agreement or tender agreement, the surety would be entitled to the use of the property belonging to the government under the vesting provision of the contract or regulation.

Bankruptcies often begin after a scramble for assets, and later entail motions to lift the automatic stay by secured parties seeking to liquidate collateral. The surety should make sure that equipment and materials that are subject to vesting provisions are preserved for the performance of contract work.

D. Jurisdiction of The Bankruptcy Court Over Contract Disputes

One of the murkier areas of bankruptcy law and practice is the jurisdictional limits of the bankruptcy court over disputes among third parties. Another question is the extent to which bankruptcy courts must defer issues to other courts set up to address the subject matter of certain disputes, for example, the United States Court of Federal Claims.

Third parties might be subjected to bankruptcy court jurisdiction in a number of ways. They could be enjoined from pursuing actions against insiders of the debtor company or their actions could be subject to the automatic stay.[100] And finally, a dispute between non-debtors might be

---

99 Some cases do not find absolute vestiture of title in the government but find the government possesses a lien in the property. *Marine Midland Bank v. United States*, 687 F. 2d 395 (Ct. Cl. 1982) *cert. denied*, 460 U.S. 1037 (1982).

100 *In re Otero Mills, Inc.*, 25 Bankr. 1018 (D.N.M. 1982) (affirming bankruptcy court's issuance of § 105 injunction upon execution of state court judgment against debtor's president), *A.H. Robins Co. v. Piccinin*, 788 F.2d 994 (4th Cir. 1986), *cert. denied*, 479 U.S. 876 (1986) (citing § 362(a)(3) and § 105 as authority regarding the debtor's ability to administer the bankruptcy estate). *See also In re McDonald Assoc., Inc.*, 54 Bankr. 865 (Bankr. D. R.I. 1985). Under some circumstances a stay may be imposed on a proceeding against the surety of a bankrupt principal. *See United States Use of Central Bldg. Supply, Inc. v. William F. Wilke, Inc.*, 685 F. Supp. 936 (D. Md. 1988).

heard by the bankruptcy court because of its effect on the debtor or the debtor's estate.[101]

The Bankruptcy Code as originally drafted in 1978 was held to be unconstitutional in granting the power to hear cases and controversies to bankruptcy judges who were not appointed under Article III of the Constitution.[102] This problem was resolved in the Bankruptcy Amendments and Federal Judgeship Act of 1984 ("BAFJA") which placed bankruptcy matters within the jurisdiction of the District Court subject to referral to the bankruptcy court.

Bankruptcy court jurisdiction is described as either "core" jurisdiction or "related to" jurisdiction.[103] Core matters are those which involve rights created by federal bankruptcy law or which would only arise in bankruptcy.[104] Core matters include allowance or disallowance of claims, discharge of debts, procedural matters, such as, conversion of the case to Chapter 7 or dismissal.[105] Related matters subject to the jurisdiction of the bankruptcy court could include a large variety of disputes that have an impact on the estate and its administration.[106] There is some disagreement over the scope of the bankruptcy courts' subject matter jurisdiction that is reflected in the case decisions.

If an issue is a non-bankruptcy issue and uniquely one of federal law, a party can move for the district court to withdraw the reference of the case to the bankruptcy court and have that matter heard in the district

---

101 See generally, Buschman and Madden, *The Power and Propriety of Bankruptcy Court Intervention in Actions Between Nondebtors*, 47 Bus. Law. 3 (May 1992).

102 *Northern Pipeline Constr. Co. v. Marathon Pipe Line Co.*, 458 U.S. 50 (1982).

103 28 U.S.C. § 157.

104 *In re Wood*, 825 F.2d 90, 97 (5th Cir. 1987).

105 11 U.S.C. § 157(b)(2).

106 11 U.S.C. § 157(c)(1) permits a bankruptcy judge to hear matters related to the proceeding and submit proposed finding of fact and conclusions of law to the district court. Section 157(c)(2) enables the parties to consent to the bankruptcy court hearing a related to matter. Section 157(d) sets forth the procedure for withdrawing the reference to the district court and directs the district court to withdraw a the reference upon timely motion for matters involving issues of federal law.

court.[107] There are other procedural options for related actions. Bankruptcy proceedings can be stayed until a court of competent jurisdiction rules on issues that might have an impact on the bankruptcy court proceeding.[108] A state ruling might determine the propriety of a claim. A United States Court of Federal Claims action might determine the rights or priorities of litigants in the bankruptcy court. Even if a matter is within the bankruptcy court's subject matter jurisdiction as a "related to" proceeding, it might be appropriate for that matter to be heard in another court.[109]

The 1994 Amendments added some new provisions that could influence how the courts will view bankruptcy jurisdiction in the future. Certainly, these amendments suggest the bankruptcy court has expansive jurisdiction to resolve a wide range of disputes. The 1994 Amendments provide for waiver of sovereign immunity by the United States Government and also expands the power of the bankruptcy court under § 105 to issue supplementary injunctions.[110] Although the waiver of immunity

---

107 11 U.S.C. § 157(d).

108 A number of cases compel the bankruptcy court to transfer matters that are subject to the jurisdiction of a court specifically established for those matters, such as the United States Court of Federal Claims. *In re Gary Aircraft Corp.*, 698 F.2d 775 (5th Cir. 1983), *cert. denied, Gary Aircraft Corp. v. United States*, 464 U.S. 820 (1983). See generally, S. Ransick, *Adverse Impact of the Federal Bankruptcy Law on the Government's Rights in Relation to the Contractor in Default*, 124 Mil.L.Rev. 65 (Spring 1989). *But see, Quality Tooling, Inc. v. United States*, ____ F.3d _____, 1995 U.S. App. LEXIS 1852 (Fed. Cir. 1995) (holding that the matter of deferral is within the sound discretion of the district court which is reviewable on an abuse of discretion standard).

109 Whether the bankruptcy court opts to exercise jurisdiction over a related non-core matter is within the court's discretion and depends upon the extent to which the case has an impact on the administration of the bankruptcy proceeding. *In re Watson Mahaney*, 70 Bankr. 578 (Bankr. N.D. Ill. 1987) (court declined to find indemnity action that would only affect surety's unsecured claim required litigation in bankruptcy court).

110 103 P.L. 394; 108 Stat. 4106, Section 112 amends § 105 of the Bankruptcy Code and significantly specifies the powers of the court to enter supplemental injunctions. § 106 of the Code as amended, provides for waiver of sovereign immunity. Reading the amended provisions together, Congress has provided the bankruptcy courts with a mechanism for hearing

was aimed at some unique problems for debtors pursuing IRS claims and supplementary injunctions were added to permit bankruptcy courts to enter orders that will assist in reorganizing debtors facing numerous claims in mass tort cases, these provisions could be viewed as empowering the court to hear a wide range of cases, including contract disputes that might otherwise be heard by the United States Court of Federal Claims.

Jurisdictional concerns are sometimes the motive for the debtor's filing. Sureties encounter attempts by debtors to stay payment bond and other claims against the sureties, in an effort to have those matters heard in conjunction with the bankruptcy proceeding. In some cases, the procedural consolidation that results from a bankruptcy filing might help sureties. A number of disputes with various obligees can be resolved in a single forum. Claims related to a contract or project might be resolved through the principal's efforts to assume that contract.

In most cases, however, debtors use bankruptcy procedure to delay or skirt obligations that the surety also has. Although some cases permit enjoining actions against certain parties related to the debtor, the general rule is that claims and suits against co-obligors with the debtor, like sureties, are not subject to the automatic stay.[111] A surety might be tempted to hide behind the principal's bankruptcy proceeding. Such a tactic is only beneficial for the surety if pursued to aid a principal that seriously proposes undertaking performance of contracts.

Bankruptcy courts should defer matters to those courts set up to hear specific types of issues, such as, tax and federal claims.[112] The bank-

---

a number of disputes and fashioning relief in areas in which the bankruptcy courts previously questioned their authority and jurisdiction to address.

111 *Pitts v. Unarco*, 712 F.2d 276 (7th Cir.), *cert. denied*, *Pitts v. GAF Corp.*, 464 U.S. 1003 (1983); *Lynch v. Johns-Manville Sales Corp.*, 710 F.2d 1194 (6th Cir. 1983).

112 A recent case from the United States Court of Appeals for the Federal Circuit held that the bankruptcy courts and the United States Court of Federal Claims have concurrent jurisdiction to hear claims by a *debtor against the Government* under the Contract Disputes Act and the Tucker Act. *Quality Tooling, Inc. v. United States*, _____ F.3d _____ 1995 U.S. App. LEXIS 1852 (Fed. Cir. 1995) (interpreting amended § 106). The *Quality Tooling* opinion outlined five criteria for determining whether to defer the matter to the United States Court of Federal Claims. The criteria, derived from the 10th Circuit case of *United States v. Bagley*, 990 F.2d

ruptcy court may have jurisdiction over the issue but should defer to the court charged with specific jurisdiction over the type of question. On matters of federal law subject to the jurisdiction of other courts, the surety can move to withdraw the reference of the case or stay the bankruptcy proceeding until there is an adjudication of these matters. A bankruptcy judge may not be familiar with the subject matter which ought to be heard in other courts set up to address such issues.

The surety must know the jurisdictional limits of the court and options of bankruptcy practice to avoid delay in matters that should not be delayed by a bankruptcy, and to avoid adjudication of issues in bankruptcy court that are more capably and fairly adjudicated in other courts. If related disputes become mired in the bankruptcy court, the surety will face delay in the resolution of claims and performance demands that ought to be immediately resolved as well as delay in salvage efforts.

---

567 (10th Cir. 1993), are the following: 1) resolution of the claims by the specialized tribunal would not impair the requirement that satisfaction of all claims against the bankrupt's estate should proceed in a central forum; 2) technical or esoteric issues related to government contracting law are present; 3) the specialized forum designed specifically to resolve government contract disputes may fulfill the needs for expertise, speed, and uniformity in resolving government contract disputes; 4) the bankruptcy court may not have authority to grant affirmative relief in excess of the amounts of the claim filed by the Government, and the contract dispute may consequently have to be tried twice; and 5) Congress has endorsed the transfer of particular disputes to specialized tribunals.

The *Quality Tooling* case is significant in addressing the concurrent jurisdiction of contract disputes under the amended § 106 waiver of sovereign immunity provision. The decision reflects a balancing approach between the extremes of past cases that either found the bankruptcy court was compelled to transfer government contract disputes, *In re Gary Aircraft*, 698 F.2d 775 (5th Cir. 1983) *cert. denied*, *Gary Aircraft Corp. v. United States*, 464 U.S. 820 (1983), or favored the adjudication of all related matters in the bankruptcy courts. *In re Macleod Co.*, 935 F.2d 270, 1991 U.S. App. LEXIS 12510 (6th Cir. 1991) (unpublished disposition).

The scope of the waiver of sovereign immunity in amended § 106 is probably limited by the Eleventh Amendment to the Constitution which bars suits against states in federal court. See, for example, *In re Guerra Const. Co.*, 142 Bankr. 826 (N.D. Ill. 1992).

V.
Conclusion

Several issues will arise that impact the handling of surety defaults after the principal seeks relief under the Code. These predominately arise in Chapter 11 proceedings, and less frequently in Chapter 7 proceedings. The following is a summary checklist of bankruptcy issues a surety might face and the procedures for addressing these issues.

A. The obligee and surety want to arrange for completion of a contract in default without the participation of the principal through takeover, tender or obligee completion.

1. If the contract was terminated pre-petition, the surety and obligee should be free to complete the contract by replacing the principal. Their actions should not be subject to the automatic stay.
2. If the contract was never terminated pre-petition, terminating the contract will require a motion to lift the automatic stay. See, *Exhibit 9.1*.
3. The debtor can attempt to assume the contract under § 365. The surety may need to move to compel a prompt decision by the debtor. See, *Exhibit 9.6*.
4. At the outset of the case, the surety should move as promptly as possible to prohibit use of cash collateral to prevent contract funds from being used for obligations other than contract obligations. See, *Exhibit 9.5*.
5. The surety should make sure that there is an order clearly providing that the stay is lifted for all rejected contracts. See, *Exhibits 9.1 and 9.2*.
6. A surety dealing with an antagonistic principal that cannot be trusted to complete the work should consider refusing to extend credit to secure the principal's attempt to perform the contracts post petition by canceling the bonds. See, *Exhibit 9.7*.

B. The surety and principal cooperate in completing all or some of the bonded contracts post petition.

1. The surety and principal should arrive at a stipulated time for making a decision regarding assumption and rejection of bonded contracts. See, *Exhibit 9.2*.
2. There should be an agreement and an order determining the terms and restrictions for the use of cash collateral (contract receivables). See, *Exhibit 9.2*.

3. There should be an effort to reach a consensus with other key creditors on the goals for the debtor's continued operations.

4. If the surety provides new value to the debtor, the surety should try to obtain the highest administrative priority possible in exchange for additional credit. At the very least, the order reflecting that a contract is assumed and the bond remains in effect post petition ought to recognize the surety is entitled to an ordinary administrative expense claim. See, *Exhibit 9.8.*

5. In exchange for keeping the bonds in effect post petition, the agreement and order ought to reflect the post petition debtor has assumed the same duties and obligations to the surety as did the pre-petition contractor under the indemnity agreement. See, *Exhibits 9.2 and 9.8.*

6. Whatever agreement or order is entered for the principal's continuation of bonded work ought to afford remedies to the surety to enable it to exercise its rights and promptly cure post petition defaults or defaults that arise out of the later rejection of contracts—terms that authorize the lifting of the automatic stay and permit the surety immediate use of the contract funds. See, *Exhibit 9.2.*

The principal's bankruptcy should not prevent the surety from exercising its options after a default. Sureties have traditionally encountered problems in contractor bankruptcies for two fundamental reasons: 1) the attempt by debtors and others to claim contract funds subject to the surety's equitable rights, and 2) the time and delay caused by bankruptcy procedure. The foregoing is offered as a guide to help sureties reduce delay and to promptly assert their substantive rights in the context of the principal's bankruptcy. This should also help others understand the surety's concerns in the event of a default and the surety's rights in relation to the rights of the key parties in a contractor bankruptcy.

Bankruptcy is essentially a consensual process. Reaching a fair consensus can only be achieved by advocacy of the surety's position. To achieve effective advocacy in bankruptcy, the surety lawyer or representative must know the surety's rights and how those rights can be asserted in the context of the principal's bankruptcy proceeding.

CHAPTER 10

EXTRA-CONTRACTUAL DAMAGES CONSIDERATIONS

Gary Rouse

I.
A Changing Trend

During the 1980's, bad faith allegations were included in almost every suit against insurers; and juries, in cases where actual damages were negligible, could and did award huge punitive damages to plaintiffs. Gradually, bad faith allegations also began to appear in actions against construction bond sureties—with similar results.

Recently, however, the United States Supreme Court decided the cases of *Haslip*[1] and *TXO*[2]. In them, the justices clearly recognized that the purpose of punitive damages is to punish the wrongdoer and deter others in the future from acting similarly. But they also recognized that, in fairness, the alleged wrongdoer must be given some of the protection afforded accused criminals, and not have his punishment left to the unlimited discretion or "feelings" of the jury.

Although no brightline rules were set forth in those case, the Supreme Court's influence is inspiring state supreme courts to change their punitive damages law.

---

1 *Pacific Mut. Life Ins. Co. v. Haslip*, 499 U.S. 1 (1991).
2 *TXO Prod. Corp. v. Alliance Resources Corp.*, 113 S.Ct. 2711 (1993).

In *Gamble v. Stevenson*[3] the South Carolina Supreme Court found that South Carolina's trial procedures conformed to *Haslip's* concerns, but changed the review procedure as follows:

> Hereafter, to ensure that a punitive damage award is proper, the trial court shall conduct a post-trial review and may consider the following: [Listing 8 factors].
>
> Upon completing its review, dedicated to the postulate that no award be grossly disproportionate to the severity of the offense, the trial court shall set forth its findings on the record.

In 1992, the Tennessee Supreme Court reviewed that state's rules for awarding damages, found them vague and overbroad, and changed the entire law of Tennessee.[4] Punitive damages can now be awarded only if the court finds defendant has acted intentionally, fraudulently, maliciously or recklessly—all four terms being specifically defined. Plaintiffs must prove a defendant's conduct falls within the four requirements by clear and convincing evidence, and the trial must be bifurcated. The trial's first phase determines liability, the amount of compensatory damages and liability for punitive damages. No evidence of defendant's financial condition is admissible in the first phase of the trial. The second phase is a separate proceeding to determine the amount of any punitive damage award.

In 1994, the Texas Supreme Court, citing *Haslip* and *TXO*, completely rewrote that state's law of punitive damages in the case of *Transportation Ins. Co. v. Moriel*.[5] To show bad faith, a claimant must prove that the insurer had no reasonable basis for denying or delaying payment of the claim *and* that insurer knew or should have known that fact. If there is a bona fide dispute about the insurer's liability or if the insurer is merely wrong about the factual basis for its denial or in its interpretation of the policy, no bad faith can be found.

Punitive damages are proper only in the most exceptional cases, i.e., only if gross negligence, intentional injury, fraud or malice accompany the bad faith tort. To show gross negligence both of the following elements must be proved:

---

3 406 S.E.2d 350, 354 (S.C. 1991).

4 *Hodges v. S.C. Toof & Co.*, 833 S.W.2d 896 (Tenn. 1992).

5 879 S.W.2d 10 (Tex. 1994).

> (1) viewed objectively from the standpoint of the actor, the act or omission must involve an extreme degree of risk, considering the probability and magnitude of the potential harm to others, and (2) the actor must have actual, subjective awareness of the risk involved, but nevertheless proceed in conscious indifference to the rights, safety, or welfare of others.[6]

"Potential harm," as used above, means one of great magnitude "such as death, grievous physical injury, or financial ruin"—not the lesser harms "ordinarily associated with breach of contract or bad faith denial of a claim."[7]

Two changes were also made in Texas procedure. First, bifurcation of the trial similar to that outlined for Tennessee above is now required. (California, Georgia, Kansas, Missouri, Montana, Nevada, Ohio, Utah and Wyoming have similar procedures. Minnesota, New Jersey and North Dakota require bifurcation of both liability and amount of punitive damages).

Secondly, a Texas appellate court affirming punitive damages awards must now follow the same procedure used when reversing, i.e., it must "detail the relevant evidence in its opinion, explaining why that evidence either supports or does not support the punitive damages award in light of the *Kraus* factors."[8]

The ever-widening ripples from the *Haslip* and *TXO* pebbles may or may not continue. But the present changes in punitive damages law applicable to insurers are certainly encouraging to construction bond sureties who have all too often been mistakenly confused with insurers.

II.
Construction Surety Bonds Are Not Insurance Policies

A. Definitions

Insurance is a two-party contract which has been defined as:

---

6 *Id.* at 23.
7 *Id.* at 24.
8 *Id.* at 31.

> A contract whereby, for a stipulated consideration, one party undertakes to compensate the other for loss on a specified subject by specified perils. The party agreeing to make the compensation is usually called the 'insurer' or 'underwriter'; the other, the "insured" of 'assured'; the agreed consideration, the 'premium'; the written contract, a 'policy'; the events insured against, 'risks' or 'perils'; and the subject, right, or interest to be protected, 'the insurable interest.' A contract whereby one undertakes to indemnify another against loss, damage, or liability arising from an unknown or contingent event and is applicable only to some contingency or act to occur in future. An agreement by which one party for a consideration promises to pay money or its equivalent or to do an act valuable to other party upon destruction, loss, or injury of something in which other party has an interest.[9]

A contract of suretyship is a three-party contract which has been defined as:

> Contract whereby one party engages to be answerable for debt, default, or miscarriage of another and arises when one is liable to pay debt or discharge obligation, and party is entitled to indemnity from person who should have made the payment in the first instance before surety was so compelled.... An accessory promise by which a person binds himself for another already bound, and agrees with the creditor to satisfy the obligation, if the debtor does not. A lending of credit to aid a principal having insufficient credit of his own; the one expected to pay, having the primary obligation, being the 'principal,' and the one bound to pay if the principal does not, being the 'surety.'[10]

In addition to legal differences, there is a significant historical difference between the two. Suretyship was in use and well understood 4,500 years ago, while insurance was first developed in the 12th century by the maritime states of Venice, Florence and Genoa in Italy.

Even construction surety bonds pre-dated insurance. Records show that a performance bond was required to guarantee a gateway construction project in Rome in 106 B.C.[11]

---

9 BLACK'S LAW DICTIONARY (5th Ed. 1979).

10 *Id.*

11 *See* J. Harry Cross, *Suretyship Is Not Insurance*, 30 INS. COUNS. J. 235 (1963).

The apportionment of liability also distinguishes an insurance policy from a surety bond. Under the contractor's liability policy, all of his liability is assumed by the insurer in accordance with the policy terms. In contrast, under a contractor's construction surety bond, his liability to complete the work is never shifted to the surety. Even after a default and completion and/or payment by the surety, the primary liability remains with the contractor—the difference being he is now liable to the surety instead of the owner. "The ultimate liability as between a principal and a surety rests upon the principal."[12]

Some cases talk of the "premium" paid by the contractor to the surety as an additional indication that the construction bond should be treated as an insurance policy. However, the amount paid for a surety bond is in no way comparable to an insurance premium.

Insurance operates on the law of large numbers. There are millions of people, millions of cars, and millions of homes; a statistical evaluation of the probabilities of death, accident, fire and sickness is possible and valid. From such statistics, actuaries can calculate the premium charges necessary to cover these risks. Thus, although an insurance company may lose money on any individual risk, it makes an overall profit.

This law of large numbers is not available to the construction bond surety. Actuarial science is of no help. There are, relatively speaking, too few contractors and too few construction projects. Therefore, as stated by Senior Circuit Judge Kilkenny, the truth is:

> [A surety's] survival in its line of endeavor depends, almost entirely, upon good faith performance by the contractors and the subcontractors.[13]

A recognized authority analyzes the difference between a surety bond fee and an insurance premium as follows:

> [T]he Surety should theoretically suffer no loss since the risk is within the control of the Principal, whereas the Insurer expects losses, due to fortuitous events over which it has no control, in accord with a table of averages or experience ... [T]he premium paid for a surety obligation

---

12 74 AM. JUR. 2d, Suretyship § 3, p. 13 (1974).

13 *Gerstner Electric, Inc. v. American Ins. Co.*, 520 F.2d 790, 794 (8th Cir. 1975).

> or bond is comparable to a service charge or fee ... whereas the insurance premium even for a fidelity bond is actuarily computed upon the assumption that certain losses will occur in accordance with the table of averages or experience.[14]

As stated by another authority, "Surety bonds issued by compensated sureties, are meant to function as credit accommodations in which the surety anticipates no loss."[15]

Finally, there are great differences in the duties of the parties and in their intent and expectations. Construction bonds are not obtained or intended to protect the contractor.[16] The well-established duties of a liability insurer to its insured arise from the legal fact that the insurer has taken on all of the insured's liability covered by the policy. Those duties include: (a) a duty to defend the insured against third party claims, (b) a duty to make reasonable efforts to settle claims within the policy limits, and (c) a duty to consider the insured's interest at least equally with its own. In contrast, the construction bond surety, having assumed none of the contractor's liabilities, does not owe the contractor/principal any of the duties listed above.

Chapter 4 of the Restatement of Security[17] discusses the duties between surety and principal. It is significant that nearly all twenty-one pages of that chapter discuss various duties of the principal to the surety. The only duty of the surety to the principal mentioned is to account for any profit made over and above the costs and expenses of completing the work after the contractor's default, and to return the contractor's machinery and any unused materials.

The intentions and expectations of the parties are clear. Liability insurance is intended to protect the insured contractor; losses are expected and the premium is calculated to provide an overall profit to the insurer. A construction surety bond is intended to protect the owner/obligee; losses are not expected by the surety and the premium is a service charge or fee

---

14 RICHARDS ON INSURANCE (5th ed.), § 35, pp. 114-15.

15 Armen Shahinian, *The General Agreement of Indemnity*, *in* THE LAW OF SURETYSHIP 27-1 (Edward G. Gallagher ed., 1993).

16 *Warrior Constructors, Inc. v. Harders, Inc.*, 387 F.2d 727, 729 (5th Cir. 1967).

17 RESTATEMENT OF SECURITY (1941).

which will not provide a profit to the surety unless the contractor performs as agreed.

III.
The General Indemnity Agreement Is Not Part Of The Construction Bond

Once a project goes into default, legal confusion is confounded. Quite often a plaintiff contractor will not only treat the bond as a liability insurance policy with himself as the insured; he will also treat the general indemnity agreement as an insurance policy with himself and all other indemnitors as insureds and the surety as the insurer.

Precisely because the surety is *not* an insurer and so will suffer a loss unless the construction contract is timely performed in accordance with the plans and specifications, a general indemnity agreement is necessary. Under such an agreement, the contractor and others financially interested in his success agree to reimburse the surety for any losses it suffers by reason of issuing the performance and/or payment bond on the project. The intent of all the parties is to protect the surety.

The legal effect of this document has been described by the Fifth Circuit Court of Appeals as follows:

> The contract of indemnity forms the law between the parties and must be interpreted according to its terms and conditions ... [I]n an indemnity contract, the principal and indemnitors can be bound to the surety in any manner they elect in consideration of the surety issuing the bond covering the principal obligation.[18]

Typically, a GIA gives the surety, among other rights, the right to determine in good faith whether any claim on the bond shall be paid. Sometimes, the indemnitors will allege that the surety's payment of claims was in bad faith and so they should be released from their obligation to reimburse the surety.

In one such case, the court had no difficulty in finding for the surety. Pointing out that an essential element of bad faith is improper motive, the court said:

---

18 *Abbott v. Equity Group, Inc.*, 2 F.3d 613, 627 (5th Cir. 1993).

> The Court is unable to find a bad motive in the plaintiff's [surety's] payment of these claims, particularly in light of the fact that the plaintiff expended its own money in circumstances in which the financial conditions of its indemnitors made recovery of the money spent less than completely certain.[19]

Montana is the only jurisdiction in the United States which had allowed the bad faith tort to be asserted in *any* type of contract. Commenting that "the 'tort tail' has begun to wag the 'contract dog,'" in 1990 the Montana Supreme Court reviewed the concept of good faith and fair dealing from its first appearance in classical Roman law to date.

In early twentieth century America, courts first implied this concept in commercial contracts. The imprecise business environment of those days often required that some contract term be left to the discretion of one party. Thus, the implied covenant prevented such a party from using that discretion to deprive the other of the benefit of the contract. Later, courts also used the implied covenant to interpret contract situations not anticipated in the writing. Finally, its use became so common that it was codified into the Uniform Commercial Code.

After reassessing this implied covenant, the Montana Supreme Court decided that the UCC now provides a more workable model for contracts not specifically covered by statutes. Hence, in Montana, tort-type damages can no longer be recovered for breach of an ordinary contract's implied covenant of good faith and fair dealing except when the following conditions are involved:

1. fraud, fraudulent inducement, or tortious interference, or
2. special relationships.

Such a special relationship must contain the following elements:

a. the parties are in inherently unequal bargaining positions;

b. the inferior party's motivation in entering the contract must be to secure peace of mind, security, future protection, i.e., a non-profit motivation;

c. ordinary damages do not make the inferior party whole nor require the superior party to account for its action;

d. the inferior party is vulnerable because of the type of harm he may suffer, and necessarily trusts the superior party to perform; and

---

19 *Safeco Ins. Co. v. Criterion Inv. Corp.*, 732 F. Supp. 834, 841 (E.D. Tenn. 1989).

e. the superior party is aware of this vulnerability.[20]

IV.
Suggested Procedures for Avoiding And/Or Winning Bad Faith Issues

A. Communication

1. Surety's Communication With Indemnitors

The surety's primary tool for avoiding bad faith exposure is good communication with all parties involved—both before and after default occurs and claims are made. This good communication should start with the general indemnity agreement which the principal and individuals interested in his success are required to sign. Even though this contract is for the protection of the surety, overloading it with legalese in favor of the surety can be counterproductive.

As the Iowa Supreme Court noted in voiding an insurance policy clause for unconscionability, "[One] may defeat his own ends by the use of complex printed forms devised with the intent to get the most and give the least."[21]

A general indemnity agreement which is short, well-organized and written in layman-readable language is quite possible—without abandoning any essential protection of the surety, and without abandoning legal terms of art which have been jurisprudentially established.

Accompanying that agreement when presented for signature could be a letter from the surety to the indemnitors emphasizing the seriousness of the indemnitor's commitment, and urging them read the agreement carefully and consult legal counsel about anything not understood.[22]

Such a letter would preclude later claims by an indemnitor in a bad faith action that he or she did not read or understand the agreement.

---

20 *Story v. Bozeman*, 791 P.2d 767, 775 (Mont. 1990).

21 *C & J Fertilizer, Inc. v. Allied Mut. Ins. Co.*, 227 N.W.2d 169, 180 (Iowa 1975).

22 *See generally* H. Koch, *Armorplating the Indemnity Agreement Against Modern Day Legal Weaponry*, § IV (unpublished paper submitted at the A.B.A. Tort and Insurance Practice Section Fidelity & Surety Law Committee annual meeting in San Francisco, CA, 1982).

After a default, the surety, although not required to do so, is well-advised to notify all indemnitors in advance of any contemplated settlements which would substantially affect their liability, and invite them to submit written objections within a ten day period. Any such objections could provide the surety with valuable input, and failure to object may defuse subsequent complaints.

2. *Surety's Internal Communication*

A surety's internal communication includes policy manuals, letters, telephone calls, and formal and informal memoranda among officers, employees and agents of the surety. The rule is simple: Assume everything that you say or write about a construction bond case will be presented to a judge and jury in a bad faith action against the surety.

3. *Surety's External Communication*

Letters, telephone calls, etc. from claimants, principal, obligee, and others should be immediately acknowledged, even though additional time may be required to provide answers or other specifics requested in these communications. All matters covered in telephone conversations should be promptly memorialized by letter to the caller.

4. *Surety-Attorney Communication*

The usual precautions should be taken of labelling as privileged attorney opinion letters to the surety client. When the attorney also conducts the factual investigation of the case, there is the possibility of having him called as a witness, and of having him disqualified to act as the surety's attorney.

B. Actions

1. *Objective Investigation*

The most important action that the surety can take after receiving notice of default or claims is to initiate a prompt and unbiased investigation. It needs to know all of the pertinent facts, not just those favorable to itself.

2. *Payment or Completion*

Once the surety determines that a default by the principal has occurred, it should move with all possible speed to complete the work or have it completed. If valid claims for unpaid work or supplies are involved, it should pay those. When there are disputes among the parties, a declaratory judgment action might be filed accompanied by payment into court of any amount that is clearly due. Showing a willingness to pay whatever is due is one of the best ways to douse bad faith fires.[23]

V.
Conclusion

Avoiding and/or winning bad faith issues hinges upon facilitating good communication and understanding between surety, principal and obligee from the onset of the surety/principal relationship, as well as initiating a prompt and unbiased investigation as soon as there is a slightest indication of problems, without depending upon a formal notice of default or claim to act as the catalyst. Through good communication and prompt investigation the surety can place itself in a position to quickly resolve those issues which are clear and correctly determine the most effective strategy for reconciling those which are not.

---

23 For additional details on the above, and other suggestions for avoiding bad faith allegations, *see* Nelson, Wielinski, Maness, *Bad Faith Claims As Applied to Contract Bond Sureties* (unpublished paper submitted at the Surety Claims Institute annual meeting on June 18, 1993), at pp. 18-23.

CHAPTER 11

CONSIDERATIONS WITH RESPECT TO INSURANCE COVERAGE

Martha Crandall Coleman

I.
Introduction

When confronted with a bond default a surety must evaluate the insurance coverage on the project. Insurance coverage may provide an alternative source of recovery to the obligee, the principal and the surety. The lack of insurance coverage may increase the severity of the default or, in some instances, may serve to cut off the surety's liability.

Many problems that at first appear to be contract defaults, and thus the principal's responsibility, may be compensable by insurance. For example, if the general contractor does faulty work that fails during the course of construction, the cost of repairing the faulty work will not be covered by insurance. The cost to repair the resulting damage, however, may be covered. Similarly, if a roof fails months after construction is completed, and a subcontractor performed the original roof work, the cost to repair the roof itself *and* the resulting damage will be covered by the principal's CGL policy.

To analyze the insurance situation, the practitioner must be aware of the types of insurance products on the market, the applicable contractual provisions regarding insurance and the insurance policies actually procured. The practitioner must also be sensitive to the type of losses that may be covered by insurance so as to be able to assert the appropriate claims in a timely manner. In addition to the claims that can be asserted by or on behalf of the principal, the practitioner should also be aware of the claims available to all other parties. That way, *all* interested parties and their insurers can be engaged in discussions regarding the repair of the project and/or the resolution of the subsequent claims.

The first step in the proper analysis of a default that potentially involves insurance coverage is to request, receive and review all available construction contracts, all available insurance policies and all correspondence with the various insurers. Without this information, it is impossible to evaluate the potential claims that can be made and the potential recoveries available. The following discussion describes some of the typical coverages available on a construction project, the importance of certain contractual provisions and the pitfalls that may be encountered if the proper coverage was not obtained or maintained.[1]

II.
Builders Risk Coverage

Property damage insurance is usually purchased in the form of a fire or homeowner's policy. These types of policies are not typically available for new construction, however, due to the increased risks during construction, and the difficulty of valuing ever-progressing construction. Instead, a "builders risk" or "all risk" policy insures against property damage during construction. Coverage typically runs to the benefit of the property owner, or other parties with an insurable interest in the property, for accidental loss, damage or destruction of the insured property, regardless of fault.

---

1 For more information on construction insurance, *see generally* OWEN SHEAN and DOUGLAS PATIN, CONSTRUCTION INSURANCE: COVERAGE AND DISPUTES (1994); SCOTT C. TURNER, INSURANCE COVERAGE OF CONSTRUCTION DISPUTES (1992); CONSTRUCTION INDUSTRY INSURANCE HANDBOOK (1991).

A. Coverage

1. Insurable interests

Work in progress at the site is obviously the major item parties seek to insure. But other important insurable property may also be present at the site. For example, construction equipment, tools, materials and fixtures to be incorporated into the improvements may be on site. If the work is a renovation effort, existing property will be on the site. These items can all be insured under a builders risk policy *if* the proper policy is purchased. All parties with an insurable interest on a project site must confirm that coverage in the proper amount has been obtained and is being maintained and that the policy covers all insurable interests.

2. Risks covered

The risks covered by a particular builders risk policy depend on the form used and the endorsements purchased. Typically, two types of policies are available – "named peril" and "all risk" (or "open peril"). In a named peril policy, the covered causes of loss are specifically enumerated; they typically include fire, lightning, explosion and vandalism, among others. Endorsements are available for named peril policies to expand the types of covered losses. An "all risk" (or "open peril") policy insures against "risks of direct physical loss," except those specifically excluded. Typical exclusions are for losses resulting from violations of building ordinances, earth movement and governmental action. Again, endorsements are available to modify the coverage conferred by these policies.

There is no "standard" builders risk policy in the marketplace. The prospective insured should, therefore, carefully read the policy under consideration to confirm that all appropriate perils are included. A builders risk policy is not intended to cover non-performance of contractual obligations that result in defective or deficient work.[2] Faulty, inadequate or defective design, workmanship and construction, and the costs to correct

---

2 *Trinity Industries, Inc. v. Insurance Co. of North America*, 916 F.2d 267 (5th Cir. 1990).

these conditions, typically are excluded.[3] If, however, the defective work causes a covered loss, then typically the loss will be covered.[4]

3. Premium calculation

There are generally two methods by which insurers calculate the premium of a builders risk policy. One method is based on the value of the property when completed. The other is based on the changing value of the property as reported periodically throughout the project. The reported value method can be somewhat problematic for insureds (and for their sureties) because coverage can be affected by the failure to report the property's value or the failure to *accurately* report the property's value.

4. Procurement of coverage

The owner or the contractor may obtain builders risk coverage. The contract between the owner and the contractor should specify who will procure the coverage, and the type and amount of coverage that will be procured. The contract should specifically state whose interests are protected by the policy. The contract should also specify how long the coverage will be maintained and set forth certain notification provisions in case the coverage is not maintained.

If the owner is contractually required to provide insurance and fails to do so, or fails to provide enough insurance, the owner becomes liable to the contractor for damages to the extent the insurer would have been liable had the owner obtained the insurance required by the contract.[5] If the contractor is contractually required to provide insurance and fails to do so, the contractor will be liable for damages caused by that failure.

Obtaining coverage is of particular importance to the surety. The principal's failure to obtain or maintain a builders risk policy is a breach

---

3 *Allianz Ins. Co. v. Impero*, 654 F. Supp. 16 (E.D. Wash. 1986).

4 *See Fu-Kong Tzung v. State Farm Fire and Casualty Co.*, 873 F.2d 1338, 1341 (9th Cir. 1989); *Southern California Edison Co. v. Harbor Insurance Co.*, 148 Cal. Rptr. 106 (Cal. Ct. App. 1978).

5 *Temple Eastex, Inc. v. Old Orchard Creek Partners, Ltd.*, 848 S.W.2d 724, 731 (Tex. App.—Dallas 1992, writ denied).

for which the surety is answerable.[6] A defense for the surety arises where the procurement of a builders risk policy is a condition precedent to the contract. In this case, the surety may be excused from performance. However, if the contract does not make procurement of a builders risk policy a condition precedent, the failure to procure the policy will not release the surety from its obligations under the performance bond.[7]

5. *Insureds*

It is important for all parties to a construction project, including the surety, to be aware of the identity of all insureds on the builders risk policy. That information will determine what losses are covered and who may make a claim for any resulting damage. If an entity is not "mentioned by name or otherwise" it cannot make a claim against the insurer.[8] Even if the owner is contractually required to provide builders risk coverage to benefit the contractor and the subcontractor, that contractual requirement will not be binding on the insurer.

Determining the insureds under a builders risk policy usually involves a straightforward analysis of a policy's named insureds. The more difficult analysis involves the identification of entities that, although not specifically named, are described specifically enough in the policy to constitute insureds.[9]

---

6 *Hartford Fire Ins. Co. v. Riefolo Constr. Co.*, 410 A.2d 658 (N.J. 1980); *Carroll-Boone Water Dist. v. M. & P. Equipment Co.*, 661 S.W.2d 345 (Ark. 1983).

7 *Facilities Dev. Corp. v. Nautilus Constr. Corp.*, 550 N.Y.S.2d 127 (N.Y. App. Div. 1989).

8 *Metric Constructors, Inc. v. Industrial Risk Insurers*, 401 S.E.2d 126, 128 (N.C. Ct. App. 1991), *aff'd*, 410 S.E.2d 392 (N.C. 1991); *Le Master Steel Erectors, Inc. v. Reliance Ins. Co.*, 546 N.E.2d 313 (Ind. Ct. App. 1989); *McBroome-Bennett Plumbing v. Villa France, Inc.*, 515 S.W.2d 32 (Tex. Civ. App.—Dallas 1974, writ ref'd n.r.e.).

9 *See J.F. Shea Co. v. Hynds Plumbing & Heating Co.*, 619 P.2d 1207 (Nev. 1980).

6. *Termination of coverage*

Builders risk policies typically cover loss or destruction to the construction improvements only during construction; after the improvements are completed, coverage will terminate. Questions may arise as to when construction is complete for purposes of coverage termination. The language of the applicable policy should be examined for the definition of completion. Alternatively, industry standards as to completion may apply. It is important for all parties protected by the policy to ensure that the builders risk policy does not terminate prior to commencement of other applicable insurance.

B. Subrogation

1. *Subrogation generally available*

Subrogation is the right of an insurer to be put in the position of its insured so that the insurer may pursue recovery from any third parties who are legally responsible for the loss.[10] Subrogation is generally available to an insurer that pays a claim. If a subrogated insurer has a claim against a principal, it can assert that same claim against the principal's surety. The rights of a subrogated insurer can rise no higher than the rights of its insured.[11] If the insured has no claim the subrogated insurer likewise has no such claim.

2. *Subrogation not available against an insured*

a. Named insured

An insurer is not entitled to subrogation, however, against one whose interests are insured by the policy, even if the insured's protection is

---

10 16 COUCH ON INSURANCE § 61:1 at 75. (Rev. 2d ed. 1983).

11 *Travelers Ins. Co. v. Impastato*, 607 So.2d 722 (La. Ct. App. 1992); *Hockelberg v. Farm Bureau Ins. Co.*, 407 N.E.2d 1160 (Ind. Ct. App. 1980).

indirect.[12] Therefore, the practitioner must carefully review the applicable builders risk policies to determine who are named insureds.

b. Unnamed insured

A practitioner must also carefully review the applicable builders risk policies to determine what parties, if any, can claim to be insureds under the policy provisions. If a party involved in the construction project can show that its interests were insured by the builders risk policy, even though it was not named in the policy, it can avoid a subrogation action.[13] If a party is not a named insured and its interests are not described in the policy, it is not an insured, and a subrogation action can stand against it and its surety.[14]

---

12 *South Tippecanoe School Bldg. Corp. v. Shambaugh & Son, Inc.*, 395 N.E.2d 320 (Ind. Ct. App. 1979); *Richmond Steel, Inc. v. Legal & Gen. Assurance Soc'y, Ltd.*, 821 F. Supp. 793, 798 (D. Puerto Rico 1993); *E.C. Long, Inc. v. Brennan's of Atlanta, Inc.*, 252 S.E.2d 642 (Ga. Ct. App. 1979); *J.F. Shea Co.*, 619 P.2d at 1207.

13 *Louisiana Fire Ins. Co. v. Royal Indem. Co*, 38 So. 2d 807 (La. Ct. App. 1949) (subcontractor was an insured when the builder's risk policy included coverage for "builder's tools" and did not expressly limit coverage to tools owned by the named insured); *see also United States Fire Ins. Co. v. Beach*, 275 So.2d 473 (La. Ct. App. 1973) (same result even when the subcontractor did not suffer a loss); *J.F.Shea Co.*, 619 P.2d at 1207. *But see, McBroome-Bennett Plumbing v. Villa France, Inc.*, 515 S.W.2d 32 (Tex. Civ. App.—Dallas 1974, writ ref'd n.r.e.); *Turner Constr. Co. v. John B. Kelly Co.*, 442 F. Supp 551 (E.D. Pa. 1976); and *Paul Tishman Co. v. Carney and Del Guidice, Inc.*, 320 N.Y.S.2d 396 (N.Y. App. Div. 1971).

14 *Le Master Steel Erectors, Inc. v. Reliance Ins. Co.*, 546 N.E.2d at 313 (Ind. Ct. App. 1989).

3. *Waiver of subrogation clauses*

a. Between parties to the contract

Many construction contracts contain waiver of subrogation clauses whereby the parties waive rights against each other for damages caused by fire or other peril. The purpose of a "waiver of subrogation" clause is to avoid disruptions and disputes between the parties working on a project.[15]

Generally, when a construction contract contains a waiver of subrogation between the parties, this clause precludes an insurer of one of the parties from bringing a subrogation action against the other party to the contract.[16] It also prevents the party obtaining the policy from pursuing the other parties. The waiver of subrogation language shows the parties' intent to allocate the property loss to the insurer and to limit the recourse of the party obtaining the policy to the insurance proceeds.[17]

b. Between entities that are not parties to the contract

Subcontractors can benefit from waiver of subrogation clauses in general contracts if the clauses specifically include the subcontractors. If the subcontractor is specifically included in a waiver of subrogation clause, the subcontractor is a third party beneficiary to the contract and is entitled to rely on and enforce its provisions.[18] Since the owner waived its subrogation rights against the subcontractor and the owner's insurer has no more rights than its insured, the insurer is not entitled to maintain a subrogation claim against the subcontractor.[19]

---

15 *See Tokio Marine & Fire Ins. Co. v. Employers Ins. of Wausau*, 786 F.2d 101 (2nd Cir. 1986).

16 *Richmond Steel*, 821 F. Supp. at 793, 800; *Len Immke Buick, Inc. v. Architectural Alliance*, 611 N.E.2d 399 (Ohio Ct. App. 1992).

17 *Rosemont v. Lentin Lumber Co.*, 494 N.E.2d 592, 598 (Ill. App. Ct. 1986).

18 *Temple Eastex, Inc. v. Old Orchard Creek Partners, Ltd.*, 848 S.W.2d 724 (Tex. App.—Dallas 1992, writ denied).

19 *United States Fidelity & Guar. Co. v. Farrar's Plumbing & Heating Co.*, 762 P.2d 641, 642 (Ariz. Ct. App. 1988); *Fire Ins. Exch. v. Thunderbird Masonry*, 868 P.2d 948 (Ariz. Ct. App. 1993); *State v. United States*

Conversely, if the waiver of subrogation clause in the general contract does not specifically include subcontractors, a subcontractor can not use that clause to bar liability.[20]

c. Scope of waiver of subrogation clauses

AIA A-201 ¶ 11.3.1 provides that the "Owner shall purchase and maintain property insurance upon the entire Work at the site ..." ¶ 11.3.6 provides that the owner and contractor waive rights "for damages ... to the extent covered by property insurance obtained pursuant to this Paragraph 11.3 or other property insurance applicable to the Work ..." Courts are divided about how to handle damage to property that is not part of "the Work." Some courts have held that if the damage is covered under the policy obtained by the owner in compliance with Paragraph 11.3.1, the parties waived all subrogation rights.[21] These courts have so held even when the applicable property insurance was more extensive than that required by contract. These courts find that the parties intended there to be no subrogation rights if the injured party was reimbursed by insurance.

Other courts have held that by limiting the waiver of subrogation language to "the Work," the contract allocates responsibility among the parties; the owner/builders risk carrier is responsible for the project itself and the contractor's liability carrier is responsible for damage to any other property.[22] These cases permit a subrogation suit by the builders risk carrier against the contractor for injury to property outside the scope of the Work.

Fidelity & Guar. Co., 577 So.2d 1037 (La. Ct. App. 1991, *cert. denied*, 581 So.2d 684 (La. 1991); *Richmond Steel*, 821 F. Supp. at 793.

20 *Touchet Valley Grain Growers, Inc. v. Opp. & Seibold General Constr., Inc.*, 831 P.2d 724 (Wash. 1992).

21 *Lloyd's Underwriters v. Craig & Rush, Inc.*, 32 Cal. Rptr. 2d 144 (Cal. Ct. App. 1994); *Haemonetics Corp. v. Brophy & Phillips Co.*, 501 N.E.2d 524 (Mass. App. Ct. 1986).

22 *Public Employees Mut. Ins. Co. v. Sellen Constr. Co.*, 740 P.2d 913 (Wash. Ct. App. 1987); *S.S.D.W. Co. v. Brisk Waterproofing Co.*, 544 N.Y.S.2d 139 (A.D. 1989); *Travelers Ins. Co. v. Dickey*, 799 P.2d 625 (Okla. 1990).

C. Importance to the Surety

The insurance policies procured and the terms of the applicable construction contracts will greatly affect a surety's liability when confronted with a claim that is potentially covered under a builders risk policy. A surety is subrogated to the rights of its principal. This includes any rights which the principal has against an insurer.[23] Any claim a principal has against an insurer can be asserted by the surety. If an accident occurs, damaging the principal's work at the site, the surety can expect a claim to be made against it by the owner. Depending on the policies procured, the surety may be able to assert a claim against the builders risk carrier to recover some, if not all, of the costs to repair the damage.

Similarly, the surety can assert the same defenses as its principal. If the owner failed to obtain the proper insurance, the surety can assert that failure as a defense to a subsequent claim by the owner. If the contractual waiver provisions provide a defense to the principal in a subrogation action, that same defense is available to the surety. By the same token, the surety's liability may be increased by its principal's actions. If the principal failed to obtain the proper insurance, that breach may be answerable by the surety. If the principal failed to include proper waiver language in the contract, the surety may have to answer to a subrogation claim. Accordingly, the insurance and subrogation provisions applicable to a project are very important to a surety confronted with a bond default.

III. Commercial General Liability

A. Coverage

The CGL policy covers "bodily injury" or "property damage" caused by an "occurrence" in the "coverage territory" and occurring during the policy period.[24]

---

23 *American Ins. v. Ohio Bur. of Workers' Comp.*, 577 N.E.2d 756 (Ohio Ct. App. 1991); *Western World Ins. Co. v. Travelers Indem. Co.*, 358 So.2d 602 (Fla. Dist. Ct. App. 1978).

24 Insurance Services Office, Inc. Form CG 00 01 11 88 (1988) (hereinafter, the "Policy"), Section I, ¶ 1a and ¶ 1b, 1988.

1. Bodily injury

The CGL policy defines "bodily injury" as "bodily injury, sickness or disease sustained by a person, including death resulting from any of these at anytime."[25]

2. Property damage

The CGL policy defines "property damage" to include two different forms of property damage:

> a. Physical injury to tangible property, including all resulting loss of use of that property. All such loss of use shall be deemed to occur at the time of the physical injury that caused it; or
> b. Loss of use of tangible property that is not physically injured. All such loss shall be deemed to occur at the time of the "occurrence" that caused it.[26]

Physical injury to tangible property may occur from an identifiable event at a specific date and time, or it may result from a gradual event such as water seepage or soil settlement. The time of the occurrence is generally recognized to be the time the property damage resulted and not the time of the wrongful conduct.[27] Loss of use of property due to physical injury is defined in the policy as occurring at the time of the physical injury that resulted in the loss of use, even if the loss of the use is later, in a different policy period. In the second part of the definition of "property damage" pertaining to loss of use of tangible property *not* physically injured, the loss of use is deemed to occur at the time of the "occurrence" or event causing the loss of use, even if the loss of use is experienced later, outside the policy period.

---

25 Policy, Section V, ¶ 3.

26 Policy, Section V, ¶ 12.

27 *Michigan Chemical Corp. v. American Home Assurance Co.*, 728 F.2d 374, 381 (6th Cir. 1984); *American Motorists Ins. Co. v. Trane Co.*, 544 F. Supp. 669, 681 (W.D. Wis. 1982), *aff'd*, 718 F.2d 842 (7th Cir. 1983); *Transport Ins. Co. v. Lee Way Motor Freight, Inc.*, 487 F. Supp. 1325, 1331 (N.D.Tex. 1980).

a. Consequential damages

Under the first part of the definition of "property damage," if consequential damage such as damage to business, loss of productivity, lost profits, etc., result from underlying property damage, they will generally be covered.[28] Under the second part of the definition, "loss of use of tangible property that is not physically injured," consequential damages will generally be covered when they result from the loss of use of the property.[29] In general, however, consequential damages *alone* do not constitute "property damage" and are not covered.[30]

b. Diminution in value

Several courts have considered whether diminution in value *alone* constitutes property damage. Some jurisdictions have held that diminution in value, by itself, constitutes property damage.[31] Others have held that property damage does not result unless it occurs with physical injury to tangible property or loss of use.[32]

c. Poor workmanship

Generally, courts have found that although poor workmanship itself is not "property damage,"[33] damage resulting from physical injury to

---

28 *See, e.g., American Home Assurance Co. v. Libbey-Owens-Ford Co.*, 786 F.2d 22 (1st Cir. 1986); *but see, Liberty Mut. Ins. Co. v. Consolidated Milk Producers Ass'n.*, 354 F. Supp. 879 (D.N.H. 1973).

29 *Turner, supra* note 1, at 129-130.

30 *Diamond State Ins. Co. v. Chester-Jenson Co.*, 611 N.E.2d 1083 (Ill. App. Ct. 1993); *Lazzara Oil Co. v. Columbia Casualty Co.*, 683 F. Supp. 777 (M.D.Fla. 1988), *aff'd* 868 F.2d 1274 (11th Cir. 1989); *Turner, supra* note 1, at 99.

31 *W.E. O'Neil Constr. Co. v. National Union Fire Ins. Co.*, 721 F. Supp. 984 (N.D. Ill. 1989); *Aetna Casualty & Sur. Co. v. PPG Industries, Inc.*, 554 F. Supp. 290 (D. Ariz. 1983).

32 *See, e.g., Federated Mutual Ins. v. Concrete Units*, 363 N.W.2d 751, 756 (Minn. 1985).

33 *Hamilton Die Cast, Inc. v. United States Fidelity & Guaranty Co.*, 508 F.2d 417 (7th Cir. 1975); *St. Paul Fire & Marine Ins. Co. v. Coss*, 80 Cal. App. 3d 888, 145 Cal. Rptr. 836 (Cal. Ct. App. 1978).

or loss of use of tangible property caused by defective workmanship is covered.[34]

3. Occurrence

Early CGL policies define an "occurrence" as "an accident, including continued or repeated exposure to conditions which result in bodily injury or property damage neither expected nor intended from the standpoint of the insured." In the 1988 CGL policy, "occurrence" is defined as "an accident, including continuous or repeated exposure to substantially the same general harmful conditions."[35] (The "expected or intended" language from the earlier policies has been incorporated into exclusion (a).)

Contract defaults and faulty construction do not constitute an "occurrence."[36] The CGL policy does not provide coverage for economic loss because the work product was defectively produced.[37]

B. Exclusions

If coverage exists under the Insuring Agreement in Coverage A, it nonetheless may be excluded by one of the CGL policy's many exclusions.

1. Exclusion (a)—Expected or Intended

Exclusion (a) states:

> This insurance does not apply to:
> (a) "Bodily injury" or "property damage" expected or intended from the standpoint of the insured.[38]

---

34 *W. E. O'Neil Constr. Co.*, 721 F. Supp. at 984; *Maryland Casualty Co. v. Reeder*, 270 Cal. Rptr. 719 (Cal. Ct. App. 1990).

35 Policy, Section V, ¶ 9.

36 *Swarts v. Woodlawn, Inc.*, 610 So.2d 888 (La. Ct. App. 1992).

37 *George A. Fuller Co. v. United States Fidelity & Guar. Co.*, 613 N.Y. S.2d 152 (N.Y. App. Div. 1994).

38 Policy, Section I, ¶ 2(a).

In earlier CGL policies, exclusion (a) was incorporated in the definition of "occurrence." Though the current policy severs the "expected or intended" language from the definition of "occurrence," courts interpret the language in the same way.

Courts hold that when a contractor intentionally breaches or fails to perform its contract, the resulting damage is "expected or intended" by the insured and excluded from coverage.[39] However, much less than an intentional breach can also result in an exclusion from coverage. Some courts apply an objective standard to the insured's conduct, questioning whether a reasonable person in the position of the insured would have expected or intended the damage to occur:[40]

> [T]he word "expected" denotes that the actor knew or should have known that there was a *substantial probability* that certain consequences will result from his actions.... The results cease to be expected ... as the probability that the consequences will follow decreases and becomes less than a substantial probability.[41]

---

39 *Johnson v. AID Ins. Co.*, 287 N.W.2d 663, 665 (Minn. 1980). (Damage resulted from an insured contractor's willful and knowing violations of contract specifications and expected standards of workmanship.)

40 *See, e.g., Carter Lake v. Aetna Casualty & Sur. Co.*, 604 F.2d 1052, 1058-59 (8th Cir. 1979); *see also Continental Western Ins. Co. v. Toal*, 244 N.W. 2d 121, 125 n. 3 (Minn. 1976); *Sylvester Bros. Dev. Co. v. Great Cent. Ins. Co.*, 480 N.W.2d 368, 372 (Minn. Ct. App. 1992), *appeal after remand,* 503 N.W.2d 793 (Minn. Ct. App. 1993).

41 *Auto-Owners Ins. Co. v. Jensen*, 667 F.2d 714, 720 (8th Cir. 1981), quoting *Carter Lake*, 604 F.2d at 1058-59 (emphasis added); *see also, United States Fire Ins. Co. v. CNA Ins. Co.*, 572 N.E.2d 1124, 1128-29 (La. Ct. App. 1991) ("An insured need not know to a virtual certainty that a result will follow its acts or omissions for the result to be expected ... the word 'expected' denotes that the actor knew or should have known that there was a substantial probability that certain consequences will result from his actions."); *Bituminous Casualty Corp. v. Tonka Corp.*, 9 F.3d 51, 53 (8th Cir. 1993), *cert. denied,* ____ U.S.____, 114 S.Ct. 1834 (1994); *United States Fidelity & Guar. Co. v. Morrison Grain Co.*, 734 F. Supp. 437, 445 (D. Kan. 1990), *aff'd,* 999 F.2d 489 (10th Cir. 1993) (distinguishing an intentional injury and an unintended injury resulting from an intentional act to hold insured "had the desire to cause the consequences of his acts or he believed the consequences were substantially certain to

Other courts interpret the exclusion more narrowly, excluding from coverage only those losses that were subjectively intended by the insured.[42]

2. *Exclusion (b)—Assumption of Liability*

Exclusion (b) states:

> This insurance does not apply to:
> (b) "Bodily injury" or "property damage" for which the insured is obligated to pay damages by reason of the assumption of liability in a contract or agreement. This exclusion does not apply to liability for damages:
> (1) Assumed in a contract or agreement that is "an insured contract," ...; or
> (2) That the insured would have in the absence of the contract or agreement.[43]

In the construction context, exclusion (b) is important because most construction contracts include indemnity provisions. This exclusion is intended to limit insurers' liability to that which the law imposes on all insureds alike, thus making overall exposure more certain.[44]

---

result," in environmental damage case.); *Alert Centre, Inc. v. Alarm Protection Services, Inc.*, 967 F.2d 161, 164 (5th Cir. 1992) (holding that exclusion (a) excludes an injury "which the insured intended, not one which the insured caused, however intentional the injury-producing act."); *American Casualty Co. v. Timmons*, 352 F.2d 563, 566 (6th Cir. 1965); *Green Constr. Co. v. National Union Fire Ins. Co.*, 771 F. Supp. 1000, 1002-1003 (W.D. Mo. 1991); *Ohio Casualty Ins. Co. v. Terrace Enterprises*, 260 N.W.2d 450, 452 (Minn. 1977); *American Mutual Liability Insurance Co. v. Neville Chemical Co.*, 650 F. Supp. 929 (W.D. Pa. 1987).

42 For example, *Johnstown v. Bankers Standard Ins. Co.*, 877 F.2d 1146, 1150 (2d Cir. 1989) ("recovery will be barred only if ... the insured knew that the damages would flow directly and immediately from its intentional act").

43 Policy, Section I, ¶ 2(b).

44 *Merchants Mut. Ins. Co. v. Transformer Serv.*, 298 A.2d 112, 114 (N.H. 1972).

There are two exceptions to exclusion (b). The first is that the exclusion will not apply to damages assumed by the insured in an "insured contract." "Insured contract" is defined in the policy's definition section, subdivision (f), in pertinent part, as:

> That part of any other contract or agreement pertaining to your business (including an indemnification of a municipality in connection with your work performed for a municipality) under which you assume the tort liability of another party to pay for "bodily injury" or "property damage" to a third person or organization. Tort liability means a liability that would be imposed by law in the absence of any contract or agreement.[45]
>
> An "insured contract" does not include that part of any contract or agreement ... that indemnifies an architect, engineer or surveyor for injury or damage arising out of
>
> > (1) Preparing, approving or failing to prepare or approve maps, drawings, opinions, reports, surveys, change orders, designs, or specifications; or
> >
> > (2) Giving directions or instructions or failing to give them, if that is the primary cause of the injury or damage. An "insured contract" must be a contract pertaining to the insured's business. If the incident out of which the damage arose is found not to pertain to the insured's business, any results will not be covered.[46]

An "insured contract" must be a contract pertaining to the insured's business. If the incident out of which the damage arose is found not to

---

45 Policy, Section V, ¶ 6(f). This portion of the definition was added to the new form of the policy to avoid previous holdings that the exception was ambiguous. *See* H. James Wulfsberg and Timothy A. Colvig, *The 1986 Commercial General Liability Insurance Program,* 308 PLI/Real 395, 421 (1988).

46 Policy, Section V, ¶ 6(f)(b).

pertain to the insured's business, any resulting damage will not be covered.[47]

Note that this first exception does not provide coverage for breaches of contract. Instead, the exception "only afford[s] coverage for liability assumed by a contractual provision, not liability arising out of a breach of a contractual provision."[48]

The second exception to exclusion (b) relates to liability the insured would have had in the absence of any contract or agreement. Under this exception, the policy covers any of the insured's liabilities, even if expressly assumed under a construction contract, if such liabilities are imposed upon the insured by operation of law. This exclusion clause will therefore not preclude coverage if the insured would have been liable regardless of this contractual undertaking.[49]

Two Louisiana cases dealing with this exclusion are of particular interest to a surety.[50] In both cases, the courts held that the principal's liability carrier was liable for the surety's defense costs incurred by the surety in defending a claim against it. In both cases, the courts construed the predecessor to exclusion (b), which provided coverage for liability assumed under "an incidental contract" which was defined to mean any contract relating to the insured's business. The courts found that the general agreement of indemnity was an "incidental contract," and so the surety's defense costs were not excluded by exclusion (b). The surety's defense costs were, therefore, covered by the policy.

---

47 *See, e.g., Holland Corp. Inc. v. Maryland Casualty Co.*, 775 S.W.2d 531 (Mo. Ct. App. 1989).

48 *Aetna Cas. & Sur. v. Spancrete of Illinois, Inc.*, 726 F. Supp. 204, 207 (N.D. Ill. 1989); *see also First Wyo. Bank v. Continental Ins. Co.*, 860 P.2d 1064 (Wyo. 1993); *Musgrove v. Southland Corp.*, 898 F.2d 1041 (5th Cir. 1990).

49 *Reliance Ins. Co. v. Armstrong World Indus., Inc.*, 614 A.2d 642 (N.J. Super. 1992), opinion modified, 625 A.2d 601 (N.J. Super. 1993).

50 *Merrick Constr. Co. v. Hartford Fire Ins. Co.*, 449 So.2d 85 (La. Ct. App. 1984); *Natchitoches Parish Sch. Bd. v. Shaw*, 620 So.2d 412 (La. Ct. App. 1993).

3. *Exclusion (f)—Pollutants*

Exclusion (f) is a very broad exclusion for:

(1) "Bodily injury" or "property damage" arising out of the actual, alleged or threatened discharge, dispersal, seepage, migration, release or escape of pollutants:

(a) At or from any premises, site or location which is or was at any time owned or occupied by, or rented or loaned to, any insured;

(b) At or from any premises, site or location which is or was at any time used by or for any insured or others for the handling, storage, disposal, processing or treatment of waste;

(c) Which are or were at any time transported, handled, stored, treated, disposed of, or processed as waste by or for any insured or any person or organization for whom you may be legally responsible; or

(d) At or from any premises, site or location on which any insured or any contractors or subcontractors working directly or indirectly on any insured's behalf are performing operations:

(i) if the pollutants are brought on or to the premises, site or location in connection with such operations by such insured, contractor or subcontractor; or

(ii) if the operations are to test for, monitor, clean up, remove, contain, treat, detoxify or neutralize, or in any way respond to, or assess the effects of pollutants.[51]

...

Exclusion (f) also excludes losses arising out of demands to respond to the effects of pollutants or suits under state or federal statutes to require payment of costs relating to cleanup. Pollutants are defined as:

any solid, liquid, gaseous or thermal irritant or contaminant, including smoke, vapor, soot, fumes, acids, alkalis, chemicals and waste. Waste includes materials to be recycled, reconditioned or reclaimed.[52]

---

51 Policy, Section I, ¶ 2(f).

52 *Id.*

The predecessor to exclusion (f) excepted releases that were sudden and accidental. These predecessor policies were frequently construed in a strained or tortured fashion, distorting the terminology and frustrating the intent of the insurance industry.[53] In addition, claims experience demonstrated enormous expense and exposure resulting from the explosion of environmental litigation. As a result, the 1986 ISO CGL policy deleted this exception and substituted the "absolute pollution exclusion."[54]

Another change in the new CGL policy has sparked debate. The old form excluded coverage for releases into "land, atmosphere, or watercourse." As courts held that "land, atmosphere, and watercourse" pollution implied industrial pollution,[55] the quoted text was replaced[56] by pollution from premises "owned or occupied by, or rented or loaned to" in order to broadly exclude from coverage all kinds of pollution, including any pollution that might not be industrial pollution.[57] Confronted with the absolute pollution exclusion, the only issue that many courts view as preserved relates to whether a particular substance constitutes a contaminant, pollutant or irritant.[58]

There are two exceptions to the absolute pollution exclusion. The first is the hostile fire exception, found in (f)(1)(d)(ii).[59] The other exception

---

53 *Vantage Dev. Corp. v. American Environment Technologies*, 598 A.2d 948, 953 (N.J. Super. 1991).

54 *Bureau of Engraving v. Federal Ins. Co.*, 793 F. Supp. 209, 211 (D. Minn. 1992), *aff'd,* 5 F.3d 1175 (8th Cir. 1993).

55 *See Minerva Enter., Inc. v. Bituminous Casualty Corp.*, 851 S.W.2d 403 (Ark. 1993) (interpreting an old form of the policy excluding occurrences "into or upon land, the atmosphere or any watercourse or body of water").

56 Policy, Section I, ¶ 2(f)(1)(a).

57 *But see Atlantic Mut. Ins. Co. v. McFadden*, 595 N.E.2d 762, 764 (Mass. Sup. 1992) (holding that no language in the policy suggests that lead in paint, putty or plaster is a "pollutant" within the meaning of the provision in interpreting an absolute pollution exclusion to a policy).

58 *Westchester Fire Ins. Co. v. Pittsburg*, 768 F. Supp. 1463, 1470 (D. Kan. 1991), *aff'd,* 987 F.2d 1516 (10th Cir. 1993); *Regent Ins. Co. v. Holmes*, 835 F. Supp. 579 (D. Kan. 1993). (Both Kansas cases apparently involve absolute pollution exclusions, but the references to the applicable policies are unclear.)

59 *American Star Ins. Co. v. Grice*, 854 P.2d 622 (Wash. 1993), *opinion supplemented*, 865 P.2d 507 (Wash. 1994).

to the exclusion involves the "products-completed operations hazard" ("PCOH") exception. PCOH is defined by the Policy as including all:

> "bodily injury" and "property damage" occurring away from premises you own or rent and arising out of "your product" or "your work" except:
>
> (1) Products that are still in your physical possession; or
> (2) Work that has not yet been completed or abandoned.[60]

Exclusion (f) contains four limitations on the application of the PCOH exception.[61]

"Your product" is defined as:

> (a) Any goods or products other than real property, manufactured, sold, handled, distributed or disposed of by
> (1) You;
> (2) Others trading under your name; or

---

60 Policy, Section V, ¶ 11(a).

61 The limitations read:

> provided that:
> (1) the emission, discharge, dispersal, seepage, release or escape of "pollutants"; (a) does not occur at or from any site or location used by or for you or others for the handling, storage, disposal, processing or treatment of "waste"; or (b) does not arise out of the transportation, handling, storage, treatment, disposal or processing of "waste" at any time, by or for you or any person or organization for whom you may be legally responsible; (2) "Your work" does not or did not involve any "clean-up" of "pollutants"; (3) The "pollutants" were not brought on or to any site or location in connection with operations performed by you or any contractors or subcontractors working directly or indirectly on your behalf; (4) Any loss, cost or expense incurred as a result of any "clean-up" of "pollutants" is not the result of a governmental directive or request, and would otherwise be covered by this insurance.

(3) A person or organization whose business or assets you have acquired ...[62]

"Your work" is defined as:

(a) Work or operations performed by you or on your behalf; and
(b) Materials, parts or equipment furnished in connection with such work or operations ....[63]

Whether an insured's emissions are covered by the CGL policy exception depends on the interpretation of "your product" and "your work" in the policy's definitions.[64]

Coverage for "bodily injury" and "property damage" based on the PCOH exception generally applies to insureds who place the products they make into the stream of commerce or who construct to completion buildings or similar types of physical work.[65] Under this exception, there will be coverage when the damage occurs away from the insured's premises, arises out of its work, and its work is completed before the damage occurs.

4. *Exclusion (j)—Property Damage*

The portions of exclusion (j) relevant to construction projects state:

This insurance does not apply to:

(j) "Property damage" to:

...

(5) That particular part of real property on which you or any contractors or subcontractors working directly or indirectly on your behalf are performing operations, if the "property damage" arises out of those operations; or
(6) That particular part of any property that must be restored, repaired or replaced because "your work" was incorrectly performed on it.

---

62 Policy, Section V, ¶ 14(a).

63 Policy, Section V, ¶ 15(a) and (b).

64 *Hydro Sys., Inc. v. Continental Ins. Co.*, 929 F.2d 472, 472 (9th Cir. 1991).

65 *Gregory v. Tennessee Gas Pipeline Co.*, 948 F.2d 208 (5th Cir. 1991).

> Paragraph 6 of this exclusion does not apply to "property damage" included in the "products-completed operations hazard."[66]
>
> ...

For exclusion (j)(5) to apply several requirements must be met. First, the use of the term "particular part" in the exclusion limits the exclusion's application to exclude only the damages to the smallest portion of the property on which the insured is working. Second, the damage must be damage to real property. Third, the property damage must arise out of the work of the insured, its contractors or its subcontractors while they are "performing operations."[67] Finally, exclusion (j)(5) applies only to property damage resulting from ongoing work and not after completion.

The requirement that the property damage occur to that "particular part of real property" has been a significant limitation on coverage, with some courts reading the provision very narrowly[68] and others being more expansive.[69] Any damage to other property, including the insured's

---

66 Policy, Section I, ¶ 2(j).

67 *National Union Fire Ins. Co. v. Structural Systems Technology*, 756 F. Supp. 1232 (E.D. Mo. 1991), *aff'd as amended*, 964 F.2d 759 (8th Cir. 1992).

68 *See Travelers Ins. Co. v. Volentine*, 578 S.W.2d 501 (Tex. Civ. App.—Texarkana 1979, no writ), which held that when a contractor was hired to replace valves on an engine, ultimately causing the entire engine to explode, the damage to the engine itself was not excluded since the contractor had been hired only to perform operations on the valves and not the entire engine. *See also Blackfield v. Underwriters at Lloyd's, London*, 53 Cal. Rptr. 838 (Cal. Ct. App. 1966) in which the builders of a tract of homes were sued by buyers who discovered the homes had faulty foundations. The court interpreted an exclusion similar to (j)(5) to exclude only the damages to those parts of the house which were defective. The insurer argued that the whole house was "that particular part," since the insureds were responsible for overseeing all of the construction. The court held the insurer's interpretation of the policy exclusion to be unreasonable, requiring the insurer to cover all damages, except the damages to the foundation itself.

69 In *Utility Maintenance Contractors v. West Am. Ins. Co.*, 866 P.2d 1093 (Kan. Ct. App. 1994), the court held that the entire 115 feet of sewer line between a manhole access and the site of a clog should be held to be that

nonfaulty work, is not excluded by this provision.[70] Exclusion (j)(5) is limited to damages *to* the work performed, rather than *due to* the work performed.

> A liability policy containing such an exclusion does not insure the policyholder against liability to repair or replace his own defective work or product, but it does provide coverage for the insured's liability for damages to other property resulting from the defective condition of the work, even though injury to the work product itself is excluded.[71]

Exclusion (j)(6) pertains to property damage sustained to "that particular part" of *any* property requiring repair due to "your work." "Your work" means "work or operations performed by you or on your behalf," and "materials, parts or equipment furnished in connection with such work or operations."[72] Therefore, exclusion (j)(6) requires the same "particular part" test as (j)(5),[73] but excludes coverage for damages arising out of the work the insured contracted to perform which must be restored, repaired or replaced. Exclusion (j)(6) requires the damages to be due to the insured's own work in order for the exclusion to apply.[74]

Exclusion (j)(6) only pertains to repair or replacement of defective work while construction is ongoing; the policy excepts from the exclusion

---

"particular part of real property" subject to the exclusion. Since the sewer line served as an access, the insured was "performing its operations" all along that part of the sewer line; *See also Jet Line Services, Inc. v. American Employers Ins. Co.*, 537 N.E.2d 107 (Mass. 1989).

70 *See Gardner v. Lakvold*, 521 So.2d 818 (La. Ct. App. 1988).

71 *Volentine*, 578 S.W.2d at 503-04.

72 Policy, Section V, ¶ 15.

73 *See supra* text accompanying notes 69 and 70.

74 *LISN, Inc. v. Commercial Union Ins. Cos.*, 615 N.E.2d 650, 653 (Ohio Ct. App. 1992). The insured was in the business of removing nonfunctional and abandoned telephone switching cable and salvaging valuable elements contained within the removed cable. The insured was hired by New York Telephone Company to remove obsolete cable, and in doing so severed part of the functioning cable. The court held that the insured incorrectly performed its work in failing to protect the functioning cable, causing the property to need repair. Thus, the damage done to the functioning cable was excluded under the plain and unambiguous provisions of (j)(6).

property damage included in the products-completed operations hazard.[75] By virtue of that exception, exclusion (j)(6) does not apply to property damage included in the "products-completed operations hazard." The "products-completed operations hazard" is defined as

> damage ... arising out of "your product" or "your work" except:
> (1) Products that are still in your physical possession; or
> (2) Work that has not yet been completed or abandoned.

Work is completed when, "that part of the work done at the jobsite has been put to its intended use by any persons or organizations other than another contractor or subcontractor working on the same project." Furthermore, "work that may need service, maintenance, correction, repair or replacement but which is otherwise complete will be treated as completed."[76]

Exclusions (j)(5) and (j)(6) exclude claims relating to the insured's failure to carry out its contractual responsibilities:

> [T]he insurers clearly do not intend to provide coverage for claims against their insured for breach of express or implied warranties of workmanship when the damages claimed were the cost of correcting the work itself. The risk that the insurers clearly intended to cover was the possibility that the work product of the insured, once completed, would cause bodily injury or damage to property other than to the product or completed work itself, and for which the insured might be found liable.[77]

5. *Exclusion (k)—Property Damage to "Your Product"*

Exclusion (k) states:

> This insurance does not apply to:

---

75 Wulfsberg and Colvig, *supra* note 45 at 426.

76 *J.Z.G. Resources v. King*, 987 F.2d 98 (2nd Cir. 1993), *cert. denied*, ____ U.S.____, 114 S.Ct. 553 (1993).

77 *George A. Fuller Co. v. United States Fidelity & Guar. Co.*, 613 N.Y.S.2d 152, 156 (N.Y. App. Div. 1994).

(k) "Property damage" to "your product" arising out of it or any part of it.[78]

Be reminded that the policy defines "your product" as:

(a) Any goods or products, other than real property, manufactured, sold, handled, distributed or disposed of by:
  (1) You;
  (2) Others trading under your name; or
  (3) A person or organization whose business or assets you have acquired; and
(b) Containers (other than vehicles), materials, parts or equipment furnished in connection with such goods or products.

"Your product" includes:

(a) Warranties or representations made at any time with respect to the fitness, quality, durability, performance or use of "your product;" and
(b) The providing of or failure to provide warnings or instructions.[79]

In the construction context, this exclusion would deny coverage for damages arising out of items manufactured or fabricated by the insured contractor.

A question often arises whether a building constitutes a general contractor's "product." Although some jurisdictions consider a building constructed by the insured to be a "product" of the insured,[80] others do not.[81] Furthermore, "real property" has been deleted from the definition of "product" in the new policy, seemingly clarifying that work on homes,

---

78 Policy, Section I, ¶ 2(k).

79 Policy, Section V, ¶ 14.

80 *See, e.g.*, *Swarts v. Woodlawn, Inc.*, 610 So.2d 888 (La. Ct. App. 1992); *Federated Service Ins. Co. v. R.E.W., Inc.*, 770 P.2d 654, 656 (Wash. Ct. App. 1989); *Indiana Ins. Co. v. De Zutti*, 408 N.E.2d 1275, 1280 (Ind. 1980).

81 *Mid-United Contractors, Inc. v. Providence Lloyd's Ins. Co.*, 754 S.W.2d 824, 826 (Tex. App.—Fort Worth 1988, writ denied); *Maryland Casualty Co. v. Reeder*, 270 Cal. Rptr. 719 (Cal. Ct. App. 1990).

buildings, or other structures is not considered to be the insured's product.[82]

As stated, exclusion (k) only applies to damage to the insured's product. Property damage caused *by* the insured's product to other parts of the construction project would therefore not be affected by this exclusion.[83] This rule is consistent with the general goal of CGL policies, which is to protect the insured from the claims of injury or damage to others, but not to insure against economic loss sustained by the insured due to repairing or replacing its own defective work or products.

6. Exclusion (l)—Property Damage to "Your Work" Included In the "Products-Completed Operations Hazard"

Exclusion (l) states:

> This insurance does not apply to:
>
> (l) "Property damage" to "your work" arising out of it or any part of it and included in the "products-completed operations hazard."
>
> This exclusion does not apply if the damaged work or the work out of which the damage arises was performed on your behalf by a subcontractor.[84]

Exclusion (l) excludes coverage for damage to "your work" arising out of it or any part of it and included in the "products-completed

---

82 Wulfsberg and Colvig, *supra* note 45 at 427-28; *National Union Fire Ins. Co. v. Structural Systems Technology*, 756 F. Supp. 1232 (E.D. Mo. 1991), *aff'd as amended*, 964 F.2d 759 (8th Cir. 1992). *See also, Spring Vegetable Co. v. Hartford Casualty Ins. Co.*, 801 F. Supp. 385, 393-94 (D. Or. 1992) (holding that potatoes are the "product" of a distributor who "handled" them).

83 *See Pittsburgh Plate Glass Co. v. Fidelity & Casualty Co.*, 281 F.2d 538, 541 (3rd Cir. 1960); *Aetna Casualty & Sur. Co. v. Monsanto Co.*, 487 So.2d 398, 400 (Fla. Dist. Ct. App. 1986); *Superior Steel, Inc. v. Bituminous Casualty Corp.*, 415 So.2d 354, 358 (La. Ct. App. 1982); *Elco Industries, Inc. v. Liberty Mut. Ins. Co.*, 414 N.E.2d 41, 46 (Ill. App. Ct. 1980).

84 Policy, Section I, ¶ 2(l).

operations hazard." Since "your work" is defined to include work by subcontractors, this exclusion without more would exclude all coverage for damage occurring after construction is complete caused by the work of the general contractor or any of its subcontractors. However, the exclusion contains an additional paragraph, quoted above, providing that the exclusion does *not* apply, "if the damaged work or the work out of which the damage arises was performed on your behalf by a subcontractor."

In prior CGL policies, exclusion (o), if modified by the addition of a Broad Form Endorsement, was similar to the current exclusion (l). Exclusion (o) excluded from coverage "property damage to work performed *by or on behalf of* the named insured." Through the addition of the Broad Form Endorsement, exclusion (o) could be modified to exclude only "work performed *by* the named insured." Because current exclusion (l) corresponds with the intent and effect of prior policies' exclusion (o), as modified by the Broad Form Endorsement, the analysis in cases interpreting such exclusion, modified by the Broad Form Endorsement, is generally equally applicable to exclusion (l).

Courts have consistently contrasted the provision in earlier policies applicable to work in progress, which excluded property damage to "real property on which you or any other contractors or subcontractors" *are* working, with this provision covering only completed operations, which excludes only property damage to work already performed by the named insured.[85] In the better reasoned opinions, the courts conclude that the industry intended to expand coverage to include the work of subcontractors in completed operations.

> If a general contractor's liability policy insures against risks outside his or her control, such a risk surely can arise from a subcontractor's work. Having selected subcontractors, a general contractor may have little or no effective control over the manner in which subcontractors perform work.... From this perspective, we find unpersuasive the argument that

---

85 *Fireguard Sprinkler Systems, Inc. v. Scottsdale Ins. Co.*, 864 F.2d 648, 652 (9th Cir. 1988); *Maryland Casualty Co. v. Reeder*, 270 Cal. Rptr. 719, 725 (Cal. Ct. App. 1990); *Mid-United Contractors*, 754 S.W.2d at 824; *Southwest Louisiana Grain, Inc. v. Howard A. Duncan, Inc.*, 438 So.2d 215, 221-22 (La. Ct. App. 1983), *cert. denied*, 441 So.2d 1224 (La. 1983).

> because the prime contractor's control makes the work of a subcontractor a contractual business risk, the prime contractor should not be able to obtain insurance against that risk.[86]

In addition to the case law cited, the F. C. & S. Bulletins provide helpful illustrations:

> [A]ssume the named insured, a general contractor, constructs a building that is accepted by its owner. Sometime later the building is damaged by fire as the result of a faulty heating system installed by the insured. The insured is *not* covered for the damage to the completed work—the heating system and any other work performed by the insured—but *is covered* for damage to work performed by subcontractors. Or, suppose the cause of damage—faulty heating system—was the work of a subcontractor. Any subsequent damage to the building—whether the work of the insured (general contractor) or of subcontractors—*is* covered.[87]

Much construction litigation involves suits by owners against general contractors for defects in construction. Potential coverage under the contractor's CGL policy is overlooked because it is assumed that no coverage exists for correction of defects in the insured's own work. However, when the defects complained of are in work performed by a subcontractor to the insured, coverage may exist based upon the language of exclusion (l) in the current policy, and under older policies if the insured procured a broad form endorsement to the policy. When the defective work of a subcontractor causes "property damage" to the construction project, coverage may exist for repair or correction of that

---

86 *Fireguard*, 864 F.2d at 653.

87 F. C. & S. Bulletins, Epb-8 (1982). *See also*, *Southwest Louisiana Grain, Inc.*, 438 So.2d at 215, wherein the Court stated "... there is no completed operations coverage for work performed by [the named insured] itself ... Contrariwise, the damage to all portions of the work on the structure performed by subcontractors will be covered." *But see*, *Knutson Constr. Co. v. St. Paul Fire & Marine Ins. Co.*, 396 N.W.2d 229 (Minn. 1986); *Bor-Son Bldg. Corp. v. Employers Commercial Union Ins. Co.*, 323 N.W.2d 58 (Minn. 1982); *Vari Builders, Inc. v. United States Fidelity & Guar. Co.*, 523 A.2d 549 (Del.Super.Ct. 1986). In each of these cases, the completed operations exclusion was arguably misapplied.

"property damage," including arguably the cost of repairing the subcontractor's own defective work.

These exclusions are complicated enough in a vacuum, and get even more difficult when "real life" facts are applied. Accordingly, it is useful to keep the general rules in mind when analyzing coverage questions. First, in general, there is no coverage to repair faulty work done by the insured. Second, in general, there is no coverage for damage to that particular part of the project being worked on, unless the damage results from another part of the work. Third, there is no coverage for defective workmanship done by the insured that does not damage other property. And, fourth, there is broader coverage for damage caused by a subcontractor once the project has been completed.

C. Importance to the Surety

Since the surety will be subrogated to its principal's claims and will be able to pursue those claims in the principal's name, it is important for the surety to realize what potential claims the contractor has against its CGL insurer.[88] It is equally important to know what notice and cooperation clauses apply to avoid waiving any rights under the CGL policy.

In addition, the surety must understand the interlocking relationship between the parties working on the project and the policies that potentially exist. Without this understanding, it is impossible to be certain that all potential parties have been brought to the negotiating table and that all potential claims have been made.

---

88 *See* discussion and cases cited *supra* at note 23.

CHAPTER 12

THE ETHICAL CONSIDERATIONS OF REPRESENTING A PRINCIPAL AND A SURETY

F. Malcolm Cunningham, Jr.[1]

I. Introduction

This chapter will address conflicts of interest that an attorney may encounter during his joint representation of both a principal and a surety. A surety is "[o]ne who undertakes to pay money or to do any other act in the event that his principal fails therein."[2] In essence, a surety guarantees the performance of the principal if the principal fails to perform his obligations.[3]

Given that the principal and surety are both liable under the same agreement, the defenses that both have arising out of that agreement will typically be the same; the surety, however, may also have its own, unique surety defenses not available to the principal. As in all types of law practice, conflicts arise between two people who are equally liable on an instrument or on a contract or are equally responsible for a crime. For example, in the area of criminal law, two people may have allegedly participated in the same criminal act and would both share identical

---

1 The author wishes to acknowledge Daryl M. Kennedy, B.A. Yale University (1990), J.D. Duke University School of Law (1993), for his assistance in the preparation of this chapter.

2 BLACK'S LAW DICTIONARY, 1611 (4th Ed. 1968).

3 *Id.*

defenses, but information acquired from one client during the course of his representation may be detrimental to the other. When this happens, the potential for a conflict of interest arises and the attorney must then decide whether he can adequately represent the interests of both defendants.

Another situation which demonstrates the potential for a conflict of interest involves partners in a business. There may be situations in which an entire partnership has become liable for the failure to perform a specific act. One attorney would normally be sufficient to represent their interests. However, if the partners are in a state of discord and lawsuits between the partners seem likely, the attorney will face a potential conflict of interest in representing each of the partners, and must make a judgment as to whether he can represent all of their interests (especially if there is a question in the case as to whether a partner was engaged in personal or "partnership" business when the obligation being sued upon was incurred).

The problems that the attorney representing both principal and surety has are problems that have plagued lawyers for decades in this country and around the world. In the end, lawyers should use a certain amount of common sense and closely examine other situations in which lawyers have been accused of representing interests that were not common. The lawyer should heed these important words from Hesiod as written by Aristotle.

> Far best is he who knows all things himself; good he that harkens when men counsel rights; but he who neither knows nor lays to heart another's wisdom is a useless.[4]

II.
The Model Rules and Case Law

The ABA Model Rules of Professional Conduct, the ABA Model Code of Professional Responsibility, and state professional responsibility codes or statutes deal directly with the problems and the issues that attorneys

---

4 ARISTOTLE, THE BASIC WORKS OF ARISTOTLE, 938 (Richard McKeon, trans., 1941).

representing both principals and sureties encounter.[5] One of the most important rules of professional conduct that directly applies to the representation of both principal and surety is the duty of loyalty. Simply stated, a lawyer must be loyal to his client. Indeed, the comment to Rule 1.7 of the ABA Model Rules states that "[l]oyalty is an essential element in the lawyer's relationship to a client."[6] Generally, a lawyer's duty of loyalty prohibits the lawyer from representing a client if the representation of that client will be directly adverse to the interests of another client.[7] Rule 1.4 of the ABA Model Rules must also be considered in an attorney's simultaneous representation of a principal and a surety. The rule provides that "[a] lawyer shall keep a client reasonably informed about the status of a matter and promptly comply with reasonable requests for information."[8] This rule obligates a lawyer to furnish his client with all relevant information in order that the client can make intelligent decisions regarding the conduct of the case.[9]

Another rule that is often implicated in the relationship between an attorney and his principal and surety clients is ABA Model Rule 1.6. This rule provides that "[a] lawyer shall not reveal information relating to representation of a client ... [except in limited circumstances set forth in the rule,] unless the client consents after disclosure to the client."[10] The comment to Rule 1.6 states that the rule of confidentiality applies not only to matters communicated in confidence by the client but to all information relating to the representation, whatever its source.[11]

Oftentimes, Rule 1.6, obligating the attorney to maintain his client's confidences, is at odds with Rule 1.4, obligating the lawyer to keep his client informed, thereby placing the attorney representing the principal and surety in an ethical dilemma. This dilemma might find expression in a situation where the attorney learns from one client, information that if the other client knew, would cause the other client to exercise rights which would affect the initial client adversely. For example, the attorney

---

5 *See* MODEL RULES OF PROFESSIONAL CONDUCT RULES 1.4, 1.6-1.10 (reproduced in the Appendix, Exhibit 12.1).

6 MODEL RULES OF PROFESSIONAL CONDUCT RULE 1.7 cmt (1994).

7 MODEL RULES OF PROFESSIONAL CONDUCT RULE 1.7 (1994).

8 MODEL RULES OF PROFESSIONAL CONDUCT RULE 1.4 (1994).

9 MODEL RULES OF PROFESSIONAL CONDUCT RULE 1.4 (1994).

10 MODEL RULES OF PROFESSIONAL CONDUCT RULE 1.6 (1994).

11 MODEL RULES OF PROFESSIONAL CONDUCT RULE 1.6 cmt (1994).

representing both principal and surety may learn that the principal (general contractor) is insolvent or likely will become insolvent. The insolvency of the principal would directly affect the surety's right to indemnity against the contractor under the surety's general agreement of indemnity. The lawyer in this particular situation would be in danger of violating numerous rules of professional conduct. If the lawyer failed to disclose the contractor's insolvency to the surety, the lawyer would be in violation of the duty to keep his clients informed. Conversely, if the lawyer disclosed the contractor's insolvency to the surety without the principal's consent, the lawyer would also potentially be at risk of violating his duty of confidentiality to his contractor client.[12] Needless to say, an attorney who finds himself in this Catch 22 position would have impaired loyalty and should seriously consider withdrawing from the representation of both principal and surety.

Another problem that the attorney representing the principal and surety may encounter is a conflict of interests between a present and former client.[13] Under Model Rule 1.9:

> [a] lawyer who has formerly represented a client in a matter shall not thereafter ... represent another person in the same or a substantially related matter in which that person's interests are materially adverse to the interests of the former client unless the former client consents after consultation.[14]

This rule also demonstrates the type of conflict of interest possible for the attorney with dual representation of principal and surety. The reason is that the attorney representing the contractor and surety has a previously established relationship with one of the parties which the attorney seeks to continue after the dual representation has concluded. To the extent litigation ensues after the dual representation has concluded, the lawyer, believing his loyalty to rest with his original client, may seek to represent his original client in subsequent litigation, and in some

---

12 MODEL RULES OF PROFESSIONAL CONDUCT RULE 1.6 (1994). *But cf.* CAL. EVID. CODE § 962 (West 1994), and FLA. EVID. CODE § 90.502 (West 1994) (Providing that no attorney client privilege exists between joint clients).

13 MODEL RULES OF PROFESSIONAL CONDUCT RULE 1.9 (1994).

14 MODEL RULES OF PROFESSIONAL CONDUCT RULE 1.9 (1994).

instances against his former client. Indeed, in some instances, the lawyer may have anticipated this result and may have obtained the former client's written consent to participate in the litigation. For example, an attorney representing a principal and a surety may have agreed with both that if the surety later claims against, or sues, the principal for indemnification, the attorney will then represent the principal.[15]

In the Oregon State Bar Legal Ethics Committee, criteria are set down as to when it is appropriate for a lawyer to represent both surety and principal. The committee states that it is permissible for one lawyer to represent both surety and principal against third parties where there is a definite unity of interests but that it is never appropriate for a lawyer to represent two clients with conflicting interests even if those two clients have consented to that type of representation.[16] In essence, the Oregon State Bar Legal Ethics Committee has created an absolute limit on the right of consenting parties to contract, stating that some agreements between the surety and the principal as to joint representation will not bar a later lawsuit against the attorney for damages that were caused by the conflict of interest.[17]

Rule 1.7 of the Model Rules of Professional Conduct provides a method for a lawyer to determine whether the representation of one client will be in conflict with the interest of another client.[18] This rule provides that a lawyer must not represent a client if the representation of that client would adversely affect another client unless both clients agree to the representation in advance.[19]

While this particular part of Rule 1.7 has been in existence for some time, it is clear that this section may be at odds with the Oregon State Bar Legal Ethics Committee. The Model Rules seem to indicate that as long as both parties understand the nature of the representation and understand the problems that might result from one lawyer representing two clients

---

15 *See* Oregon State Bar Legal Ethics Committee, Op. 49894, 1984. *See also Insurance Company of North America v. Westergren*, 794 S.W.2d 812, 815 (Tex. App.—Corpus Christi 1990, orig. proceeding) (Attorney who simultaneously defended contractor and surety disqualified from representing contractor against surety in subsequent bad faith action).

16 Oregon State Bar Legal Ethics Committee, Op. 49894, 1984.

17 *Id.*

18 MODEL RULES OF PROFESSIONAL CONDUCT RULE 1.7(a) (1994).

19 *Id.*

with potentially different interests, the representation that follows is acceptable. Of course, under the ABA Model Code of Professional Responsibility, Disciplinary Rule 5-105, a lawyer must never knowingly represent clients whose interests would clearly be adverse to each other.[20] However, the standard under Disciplinary Rule 5-105 still appears to have some measure of subjectivity. Therefore, it can be argued that the clients would know better than the attorney whether their interests were going to be adversely affected by being represented by the same lawyer.[21]

III.
Defining Conflicts Between the Principal and Surety

Very little case law discusses when a conflict of interest exists between the contractor and its surety such that an attorney should refuse the dual representation. Most determinations as to whether a conflict exists are done by analogy to other cases and rules. Cases which may be consulted to determine whether a conflict exists are those addressing when the surety is entitled to recover its defense costs from the contractor under an indemnity agreement where the surety retains separate defense counsel to defend suits by bond claimants. The leading case addressing this issue is *Central Towers Apartments, Inc. v. Martin*.[22]

In *Central Towers*, the court considered the issue of when and under what circumstances a surety could incur attorney's fees and litigation expenses at the cost of the contractor, when the indemnity agreement provided for the reimbursement of such costs in the event the surety incurred the fees and expenses in good faith. McGuire, a general contractor, entered into an agreement with the owner, Central Towers Apartments, Inc. for the construction of an apartment building. Royal Indemnity Company had executed a performance bond on behalf of the general contractor. Retainage in the amount of 10% was deducted from payments throughout the project. Several months after completion of the project, extensive leaks developed in the heating and air conditioning units in the apartment building. Despite knowledge of these problems, the

---

20 MODEL CODE OF PROFESSIONAL RESPONSIBILITY DR 5-105 (1969).

21 *See* Rules Regulating Florida Bar 4-1.6, 4-1.9 (1994); MODEL RULES OF PROFESSIONAL CONDUCT RULES 1.9(c), 1.6 (1994); MODEL CODE OF PROFESSIONAL RESPONSIBILITY EC 4-6 (1969).

22 453 S.W.2d 789 (Tenn. Ct. App. 1969).

owner made final payment to the general contractor including the retainage. The owner then filed suit against the contractor and the surety. The surety requested the contractor to employ attorneys to protect the interests of the surety. Complying with the surety's demand, the contractor employed, as found by the court, "competent attorneys" to represent the contractor and the surety, and notified the surety of the fact of this representation. However, the surety decided that a conflict of interest existed between it and the contractor, since its subrogation rights to the amount of the final payment were prejudiced by the owner's final payment after the owner had notice of substantial problems with the work.[23] Therefore, the surety hired separate counsel even though the contractor was solvent and financially able to pay any judgment which might have been obtained.[24]

The Tennessee Appeals Court held that no conflict existed between the surety and the contractor which made an expenditure of attorney's fees and litigation expenses by the surety reimbursable under the indemnity agreement.[25] According to the court, the owner's premature final payment and the payment of the retainage released the surety from liability to the owner to the extent of the final payment.[26] Furthermore, this fact in and of itself did not result in a conflict of interest as between the contractor and the surety.[27] To the contrary, the court observed that the contractor and the surety remained interested in defeating the claims of the owner.[28]

The court was similarly unpersuaded that a cross-claim for indemnity by the surety against the contractor resulted in a conflict of interest.[29] According to the court, the contractor was liable to indemnify the surety for any amount awarded against the surety.[30] Therefore, the cross claim asked the court to order what the contractor was obligated to pay anyway, and could not be interpreted to create a conflict of interest.[31]

---

23 *Id.* at 794.
24 *Id.*
25 *Id.* at 797.
26 *Id.*
27 *Id.*
28 *Id.*
29 *Id.*
30 *Id.*
31 *Id.*

Finding that there was no particular test to determine when a surety would be entitled to recover its fees and litigation expenses, necessitated by the hiring of separate counsel, the court observed that the following factors would bear upon the necessity of a surety hiring separate counsel, thereby allowing recovery of the expenses associated with the hiring of separate counsel:

1. the amount of risk to which the surety was exposed;
2. whether the principal was solvent;
3. whether the surety has called on the principal to deposit with it funds to cover the potential liability;
4. whether the principal, on demand by the surety to deposit with it the amount of the claim, has refused to do so;
5. whether the principal was notified of the action and given opportunity to defend for itself and the surety;
6. whether the principal hired the attorney for both himself and the surety;
7. whether the principal notified the surety of the hiring of the attorney;
8. the competency of the attorney hired by the principal;
9. the diligence displayed by the principal and his attorney in the defense;
10. whether there is a conflict of interest between the parties;
11. the attitude and cooperativeness of the surety; and
12. the amount charged and diligence of the attorney hired by the surety.[32]

The case of *Central Towers* is followed in a number of other jurisdictions in determining when a surety is entitled to reimbursement for fees and expenses incurred in retaining separate counsel. The Fifth Circuit in *Jackson v. Hollowell*[33] adopted the holding in *Central Towers* and found that an award of separate counsel fees was justified where at least one unique surety defense existed to be pursued by the surety. Similarly, the Tenth Circuit, in *United Riggers & Erectors v. Marathon Steel Co.*,[34] found that the surety's retention of separate counsel was justified because the surety's defense of discharge due to material

---

32 *Id.* at 799-800.

33 714 F.2d 1372 (5th Cir. 1983).

34 725 F.2d 87, 90-91 (10th Cir. 1984).

alteration was adverse to the contractor's interest, and the contractor's financial ability to satisfy the ultimate judgment was questionable as was the principal's ability to remain solvent through the completion of the litigation.

The factors used to determine whether a surety can in good faith incur expenses for litigation and separate attorney's fees, should also serve to indicate whether the same counsel can properly represent both the principal and surety. Yet, courts applying the factors set forth in *Central Towers* have reached inconsistent results. As acknowledged in *Central Towers*, some of the factors are more important than others in determining whether a surety is entitled to retain separate counsel and thereby recover its counsel fees and litigation expenses. Clearly, under *Central Towers*, if the principal had not been solvent, the court would have reached a different result. The contractor's solvency, of course, ultimately determines whether the contractor could pay any judgment rendered against it and the surety, and whether the contractor could provide a defense that would adequately protect the surety. Almost as important would be whether the principal was able to make the deposit of funds that the surety called upon it to make in order to cover any potential liability.

Also important in determining whether counsel can represent both the principal and the surety is the extent to which there is commonality in the defenses of the principal and the surety. Generally, a surety's liability under its bond is co-extensive with that of its principal.[35] On the basis of that legal maxim, some courts have held that sureties are responsible for all consequences caused by their principals.[36] In the jurisdictions where courts have followed the legal maxim that a surety's liability is co-extensive with that of its principal, the defenses of the surety are generally consistent with the defenses of the principal. There is a growing minority of jurisdictions, however, that focus on the bond to determine the surety's liabilities to the obligee.[37] These courts hold that the surety's

---

35 *Paisner v. Renaud*, 149 A.2d 867, 869 (N.H. 1959); *See* 72 C.J.S., *Principal and Surety*, § 92 (1987).

36 *E.g.*, *Aluma Glass v. Bratton Corp.*, 8 F.3d 756, 759 (11th Cir. 1993); *Phoenix Assurance Co. v. Appleton City*, 296 F.2d 787, 796 (8th Cir. 1961); *General Builders Supply Co., Inc. v. McArthur*, 179 A.2d 868, 871-872 (Md. App. 1962).

37 For example, *American Home Assurance Co. v. Larkin General Hospital Ltd.*, 593 So.2d 195, 198 (Fla. 1992).

liability is defined by the bond itself rather than by the bonded contract between the principal and the obligee. Under this approach, courts have held that the surety is not liable for anything beyond the precise terms and obligations of the bond.[38] Therefore, under this view of the surety's liability, there would be fewer situations in which commonality between the principal's and the surety's defenses would exist. As a result, the incidents of conflict of interest between the surety and the principal would occur more frequently and a single attorney retained by the principal would be less likely to adequately represent both the principal and the surety. In these circumstances, as well as in jurisdictions where courts generally observe that a surety's liability is co-extensive with that of its principal, joint counsel should carefully investigate the facts to determine what defenses the surety has as compared to the principal, and then determine whether there are defenses of one or the other, but not both, which would preclude counsel from adequately representing both the interests of principal and surety. In conducting an investigation of the surety's defenses, counsel should be aware of defenses which are unique to the surety.[39]

The principal and surety do not always share identical defenses. Surety defenses that may not be available to the principal contractor include, among others, defenses relating to the language of the bond, discharge of the surety, and actions by the obligee.

A. Language of the Bond

Generally speaking, the statute of limitations for suits against the surety may be different from that applicable to suits against the principal

---

38 *Id.*

39 For an excellent discussion of the ethical considerations of the dual representation of a principal and surety, *see* M. Kelly Allbritton and Charles W. Langfitt, *Legal & Practical Problems With Joint Representation of the Principal & Surety* (unpublished paper submitted at the A.B.A. Tort and Insurance Practice Section Fidelity & Surety Law Committee annual meeting in Atlanta, Ga., on August 13, 1991), and Linda A. Klein, *Ethical & Other Pitfalls of Dual Representation in Surety Bond Litigation* (unpublished paper submitted at the A.B.A. Tort and Insurance Practice Section Fidelity & Surety Law Committee annual mid-winter meeting in New York, N.Y. on January 25, 1991).

because the bond may provide for a shorter period of limitations, or state law applicable to the bond may provide for a shorter period of limitations. For example, in Florida, the period of limitations applicable to a statutory bond is one year from substantial completion,[40] whereas the period of limitations applicable to claims against the contractor arising out of the construction project is four years.[41] Additionally, the bond may contain language limiting the extent of the surety's liability. For example, in jurisdictions where courts focus on the language of the bond to determine the extent of the surety's liability, the bond may be interpreted as merely guarantying the completion of the construction contract and nothing more. As such, claims for delays and other consequential damages may not be recoverable against the surety whereas such claims may be maintained against the principal.[42] Under either a limitations defense or a defense arising out of the limiting language of the bond, the differences between the principal's defenses and the surety's defenses should alert joint counsel to proceed with extreme caution.

B. Discharge of Surety

Affirmative acts taken by the principal may, in some instances, discharge the surety from liability under the performance bond. For example, a material alteration resulting in an increase in the scope of the surety's obligation under the original contract agreed to between the principal and the obligee, without the knowledge or consent of the surety, may result in the discharge of the surety under the bond.[43] Similarly, a change in the time for performance and a departure from the contract

---

40 FLA. STAT. ch. 255.05(2) (1965); *Florida Board of Regents v. Fidelity & Deposit Co. of Maryland*, 416 So.2d 30, 31 (Fla. 5th DCA 1982) ("When the architect certifies the building is substantially completed, and the owner accepts the building, then the contractor is deemed to have fully performed and *any* lawsuit which could be brought against the surety under the bond must be brought within one year, according to the statute.").

41 FLA. STAT. ch. 95.11(3)(c) (1965).

42 *See e.g. American Home Assurance Company v. Larkin General Hospital*, 593 So.2d 195, 198 (Fla. 1992).

43 *See* Allbritton and Langfitt, *supra* note 39, at pp. 12-14 and cases cited therein.

provisions governing payment could result in a discharge of the surety, as well.[44]

The surety's success in advancing these defenses depends upon proof that the surety can adduce showing the principal's actions in this regard. To the extent the surety is successful in advancing these arguments, the surety reduces its liability and therefore exposes the principal. It would be difficult to imagine the circumstances in which joint counsel for principal and surety could adequately represent the surety in pressing these defenses.

C. Actions By Obligee

Additional unique surety defenses may arise from actions by the obligee which may be difficult for joint counsel to effectively advance due to the principal's potential involvement in such actions. Such defenses include the obligee's failure to give notice or timely notice of the principal's default to the surety,[45] and impairment or misappropriation by the obligee of contract balances or other security[46]. The obligee's acceptance or acquiescence of the acts or omissions giving rise to a default[47] and actions or representations by the obligee to induce the surety to forego steps to protect itself will also cause a discharge of the surety's liability under the bond.[48] Additionally, if the surety elects to settle with the obligee in order to reduce its exposure, without the consent of the principal, a conflict of interest would clearly exist such that joint counsel could no longer represent the principal and the surety.

IV.
Pre-suit Investigations and Bad Faith

Another area fertile with conflicts, casting doubt on whether a single attorney can serve the principal as well as the surety, is in the pre-suit

---

44 *Id.*

45 *Dockendorf v. Orner*, 293 N.W.2d 395, 397-398 (Neb. 1980).

46 *St. Paul Fire Marine Ins. Co. v. Commodity Credit Corp.*, 646 F.2d 1064, 1073 (5th Cir. 1981).

47 *Scott v. Gaulding*, 2 S.E.2d 69-71, 72 (Ga. 1939).

48 *Franklin Savings & Loan Co. v. Branan*, 188 S.E. 67, 70 (Ga. App. 1936).

investigation of bond claims.[49] Under the Model Unfair Claim Settlement Practice Act, enacted with various modifications in every state, sureties[50] are required to undertake an investigation of the claim.[51] In addition, under the law of most states, a surety has a duty of good faith toward its obligee therefore prohibiting the surety from denying or failing to process or pay a claim without a reasonable basis for such action.[52] This duty of good faith may in some jurisdictions extend as well to bond claimants that the bond seeks to protect.[53]

In times past, the surety may have investigated claims by referring the claims to its principal. Generally, the principal would undertake an investigation, often through joint counsel, and report back to the surety with information supporting the principal's position including relevant documents. Relying on the information supplied by joint counsel, the surety would make an independent judgment as to the validity of the claim.

Recently, claimants have called into question whether the surety's reliance on the principal's investigation discharges the surety's duty of good faith and its duty to investigate claims under the Model Act. In *Loyal Order of Moose, Lodge 1392 v. International Fidelity Insurance Co.*,[54] the Supreme Court of Alaska held that a surety failed to adequately

---

49 For a more thorough discussion of the surety's exposure to extra-contractual claims arising out of the surety's investigation of a bond claim, *see* Chapter 10, *supra*.

50 Many courts follow the syllogism that sureties are insurance companies, the Model Act applies to insurance companies and therefore, the Model Act applies to sureties. M. Michael Egan, *Dispute Resolution* (unpublished paper submitted at the A.B.A. Tort and Insurance Practice Section Fidelity & Surety Law Committee mid-winter meeting in New York, N.Y. on January 27, 1995).

51 For example, section 626.9541(1)(i)(3)(d) of the Florida Statutes defines as an unfair claim settlement practice "[d]enying claims without conducting reasonable investigations based upon available information ...."

52 *See, e.g., Noble v. National Am. Life Ins. Co.*, 624 P.2d 866, 868 (Ariz. 1981).

53 *Szarkowski v. Reliance Insurance Co.*, 404 N.W.2d 502, 505 (N.D. 1987) (subcontractor, as third party beneficiary or intended claimant under the bond, was owed a duty of good faith and fair dealing by the surety in the handling of its claim).

54 797 P.2d 622, 628 (Alaska 1990).

investigate the obligee's claims. Although the record is unclear as to how the surety had investigated the claim, the court observed that the surety's "abortive inquiries, and professed reliance without question upon its principal's ... position created enough of an issue of fact to preclude the grant of summary judgment."[55]

In *Dodge v. Fidelity & Deposit Co. of Maryland*,[56] the plaintiff sought to maintain a bad faith action against the surety on the ground that the surety had failed to investigate the obligee's claim against the bond. The surety defended on the ground that its duty of good faith only ran toward the principal and at best, it was a middleman between the principal and the obligee owing no duty to the obligee. The Supreme Court of Arizona rejected this defense and held that the surety owed a duty of good faith to the obligee and that the tort of bad faith arises when the surety intentionally denies, or fails to process or pay a claim without a reasonable basis for such action.[57] Finding the middleman position unpersuasive in avoiding a duty of good faith regarding the obligee, the court observed that:

> [T]he surety often finds it difficult to decide whether to accede to the demands of the claimant [obligee] or abide by the position desired by the principal. Notwithstanding this difficulty, the surety is in a position of having accepted a premium in exchange for its promise to pay or perform in case of specified events .... Additionally, it makes its promise with full knowledge that at times it will possibly be called upon to perform when it can do so only at some risk of losing its recovery rights against or inviting suits from its [principal]. Given the nature of a corporate surety's business, and its knowledge of the inherent risk it entails, it can have no real confidence that a "middleman" plea on its part ... will find a favorable reception with the court.[58]

Under the Model Act, a surety has an independent obligation to investigate the claims of obligees and intended beneficiaries under the bond. In so doing, the surety owes a duty of good faith to the bond

---

55 *Id.*

56 778 P.2d 1240 (Ariz. 1989).

57 *Id.* at 1243 (quoting *Noble*, 624 P.2d at 868).

58 *Id.* at 1243-44 (quoting Brumley, *Duty Of A Shielded Surety To Investigate*, 17 FORUM 266, 280 (1981)).

claimant as well as to its principal. If the principal looks to its counsel to perform the surety's investigation, questions arise as to whether counsel for the principal can properly perform that investigation, in light of the duty of loyalty assumed by the principal's counsel toward the principal. An interesting question is presented by the situation in which principal's counsel discovers information adverse to the principal's position during the claim investigation. Is the principal's counsel prohibited from disclosing that information to the surety in light of Model Rule 1.6 which prohibits a lawyer from revealing confidential information to third parties without the consent of the client? Suffice it to say that joint counsel's discharge of the surety's independent duty to investigate claims is fraught with potential conflicts and both joint counsel and the surety should proceed with extreme caution in this situation.

V.
Proposals for Attorneys Representing Sureties and Contractors

1. Attorneys should recognize that conflict of interest rules applicable to dual representation of surety/principal differ very little from conflict of interest rules applicable to other areas of law. If anything, the conflict of interest rules are more stringent for attorneys representing a surety and a principal because of the inherent potential for conflict that exists by virtue of the surety's indemnity rights against the principal.

2. For malpractice purposes, it is probably better to be safe than sorry and for attorneys to follow the mandates of the Oregon State Bar Legal Ethics Committee and never represent clients that have adverse interests regardless of whether there is a written agreement giving the attorney the authority to do so.

3. The existence of a conflict of interest or other factors suggesting the impropriety of a single lawyer designated by the principal to represent both the principal and the surety will not become apparent unless the joint counsel and the surety conduct a thorough investigation of the claim. The surety should initiate the investigation and determine whether a conflict exists with respect to the surety's defenses, by immediately requesting from the bond claimant any information that the bond claimant has in support of its claim. Upon receipt of the claim letter or the summons and complaint, the surety should send a letter to the bond claimant requesting that the bond claimant voluntarily furnish the surety any information that

the bond claimant deems to be supportive of its claim. An example of such a letter is included as Exhibit 12.2.

4. The surety's investigation should not stop with its request of information from the bond claimant. After the surety receives the claim from the bond claimant, the surety should tender the defense of the claim to the principal. In so doing, the surety should take the opportunity in its tender of defense letter to request information of the principal supportive of the principal's defenses to the claim. The surety's request for information to the principal should include a request for the contract documents, any correspondence relating to the claim generated by the parties during the course of the job and any settlement offers that have been made by either party. Included as Exhibit 12.3 is a sample letter that the surety can use to tender the defense as well as to request information that would facilitate the surety's investigation into the nature and extent of the surety's defenses and the defenses of the principal.

5. Assuming the principal accepts the tender of the defense, and retains counsel to represent the principal and the surety, it is essential that the surety communicate with the counsel provided by the principal in an effort to establish ground rules for the representation. The surety must establish as a ground rule that the joint counsel provide the surety with all pleadings filed in the case, and that joint counsel obtain the surety's approval before filing pleadings on behalf of the surety. Included as Exhibit 12.4 is a sample letter which the surety can use to establish ground rules that permit the surety to receive information that would alert the surety to defenses that are being interposed on the surety's behalf, as well as alert the surety to defenses the surety may have independently of the principal. Indeed, the surety should consider a case management plan to be prepared by joint counsel and the surety in an effort to track the nature, extent and timing of pleadings filed by joint counsel on behalf of the surety.

6. If the surety receives a claim, joint counsel and the surety must be mindful of the surety's independent duty to investigate the claim. To the extent the surety relies on its principal to investigate the claim, the surety should seek and obtain from the principal, source data which the surety can evaluate independently of the principal's interpretations. Contract documents and project correspondence represent good sources of information. Where circumstances dictate that the surety use its own sources to conduct its investigation, the surety should consider interviewing project personnel in addition to reviewing source data. Of

utmost importance, whether the surety relies on the principal to initiate the investigation or conducts the investigation itself, is that the surety document what it has done in conducting the investigation.

7. Lastly, it is important for the surety to know whether the principal is financially able to fund the defense of the surety, as well as to pay any judgment that might be entered against the principal and surety. As indicated in *Central Towers*,[59] the solvency of the principal is the best indicator as to whether the surety needs separate counsel. As a part of the surety's investigation, the surety should consider requesting current financial statements from the principal as a first step in determining whether the principal is capable of adequately defending the surety.

VI.
Conclusion

Conflicts of interests can occur in the joint representation of a principal and surety. Since there is very little case law governing when a surety should retain independent counsel, joint counsel and the surety must in part rely on cases addressing when the surety is entitled to reimbursement for retaining independent counsel, as guidance for when a conflict exists such that counsel should not jointly represent the principal and surety. Whether joint counsel or independent counsel is retained, the parties must remain cognizant of the potential for conflicts and must continuously monitor the case to discern and resolve them.

---

59 453 S.W.2d 789 (Tenn. Ct. App. 1969).

CHAPTER 13

SALVAGE/SUBROGATION CONSIDERATIONS

Lawrence Lerner and Keith Witten

I.
Introduction

A contract bond surety possesses a number of substantial rights to recover what it has already paid out under its payment or performance bonds or what it may have to pay out in the future to the obligee or other claimants under the bonds. A surety's prompt and informed exercise of those rights can reduce and sometimes even eliminate any surety exposure for losses and expenses. These rights to recover losses and expenses are addressed in this chapter under the general topic of salvage/subrogation.

In every construction dispute that arises, where some of the contracting parties may be at fault—the obligee and its architects and engineers, or the claimant and its subcontractors and suppliers, or some combination of these—the surety is immediately placed into the middle of a squeeze between competing interests.

The surety could begin its investigation immediately in order to:

1. discover the financial condition of the principal and the indemnitors;
2. determine the surety's liabilities on its bonds;
3. ascertain how best to discharge those obligations; and

4. determine how best to obtain exoneration and indemnification from the principal and the indemnitors.[1]

At the time of an alleged default under a performance bond, we know that one of the important decisions that a surety may be faced with is whether or not to complete the project. This decision primarily depends upon the outcome of an expedited engineering/technical evaluation by the surety of what happened to cause the default, usually conducted in the midst of principal and obligee claims and counterclaims.

The obligee may claim the work is defective or not progressing satisfactorily. A subcontractor may claim that it has not been paid. Upon receipt of a notice of claim under one of its bonds, a surety could immediately commence an evaluation of its rights of salvage at the same time it begins an investigation of the facts surrounding the alleged claims. The two could proceed hand in hand, as the nature and extent of available salvage rights may also suggest cost-effective ways of discharging a surety's duties, if any, under either its payment or performance bond.

If the surety, through its investigation of the claims, determines that it is the obligee's (or the obligee's architect's/engineer's) failure to perform their respective contractual obligations, then the surety's task is to convey its decision and the basis for its decision to the owner; and most importantly to gather further documents and facts in support of its position and those which allegedly may be raised against its position.

A surety claim operation should not ignore the potential political or networking contacts available to agents. These contacts, used properly and with integrity, can be exceedingly useful in legitimately cutting through bureaucracies or bringing important items to the attention of important people.[2]

This chapter does not in an exhaustive fashion discuss a surety's salvage and subrogation rights and obligations, but instead attempts to provide helpful practical applications of many of the important procedures, issues, principles and considerations with which a surety could concern itself when assessing its salvage/subrogation rights and duties. A surety may use these to review its options when confronting a default under the

---

1 *See* Britt, *The Surety's Investigation*, 17 FORUM 1151, 1152-53 (1982); *see also*, Chapters 2 and 3 *supra*.

2 Jack Curtain, *Ethical Considerations and the Effect of the Agent's Involvement in Claims* (unpublished paper submitted at the Surety Claims Institute annual meeting on June 25, 1992).

bonds and general agreement of indemnity in order to help preserve, protect and defend the surety's rights of salvage/subrogation.

II.
Sources of Salvage/Subrogation Rights

A. In General

A surety's salvage rights arise from a variety of sources: statutory, common law, and contractual. *Statutory salvage rights* vary from jurisdiction to jurisdiction, but may include the right to require the claimant to proceed first against the obligee and the right to enforce statutory trust provisions which make contract proceeds a trust in favor of those who could make claims against the bond, i.e.—laborers, material and equipment suppliers, subcontractors, sub-subcontractors and suppliers to subcontractors. The surety's *common law salvage rights* include subrogation, indemnity (also called reimbursement), exoneration and contribution. Those rights based upon common law principles generally exist independent of any statutory or contractual provisions. And, a surety's *contractual salvage rights*, which may vary depending on the precise terms of the particular indemnity agreement, include indemnity, exoneration, assignment, and trust fund provisions.

B. Choice of Law

In determining the nature and extent of the surety's salvage rights, particularly those which arise out of the common law, a surety must consider which state's law applies. In some states, the law of the state with the most significant contacts will be applied in construing a contract.[3]

Ordinarily, the law of the place of contracting will constitute the most significant contact and, consequently, will govern the contractual

---

3 The contacts to be considered generally include: (a) the place of contracting; (b) the place of negotiation of the contract; (c) the place of performance: (d) the location of the subject matter of the contract; and (e) the domicile, residence, nationality, place of incorporation, and place of business of the parties. Courts evaluate all of these factors in accordance with their relative importance with respect to the particular issue involved. RESTATEMENT (SECOND) OF CONFLICT OF LAWS § 188 (1971).

construction of performance and payment bonds and the exercise of the surety's rights of salvage.[4]

C. Statutes

A surety should carefully review all potentially applicable statutes to ascertain whether any of them may provide additional rights and remedies, with additional bases for existing rights, or may limit or condition the exercise of its traditional salvage rights. In that connection, the surety should carefully consider which state's law will apply. Since a surety bond merely constitutes a type of contract, the choice of law rules applicable to contracts mentioned in the preceding section of this chapter will govern what law applies in construing a bond.

In addition, some states have enacted "trust fund" statutes which make any funds a contractor receives from the owner subject to a trust in favor of those who have supplied labor or materials used in or incorporated in the completion of the job. Those provisions may insulate those funds from a claim by the principal's trustee in bankruptcy that they comprise property of the estate.[5] Moreover, if a surety pays obligations to beneficiaries of a statutory trust, it is subrogated to their rights to pursue the trust funds.[6]

Finally, even if the statutory trust does not come into existence, a surety may argue that the principal has a fiduciary relationship with laborers and materialmen or the surety (particularly where the principal has executed an indemnity agreement containing a trust) may urge that equity should impose a constructive trust on the funds.[7] A surety should remember that, even though it may not be one of the beneficiaries of a statutory trust, to the extent that contract proceeds are used to pay those who could make claims against the surety, the surety benefits.

---

4 *See, e.g., Audrain County ex rel. First Nat'l Bank v. Walker*, 155 S.W.2d 251 (Mo. Ct. App. 1941).

5 *Selby v. Ford Motor Co.*, 590 F.2d 642 (6th Cir. 1979).

6 *Universal Bonding Ins. Co. v. Gittens & Sprinkle Enters., Inc.*, 960 F.2d 366 (3d Cir. 1992).

7 *In re Western Urethanes, Inc.*, 61 B.R. 243, 246-47 (Bankr. D. Colo. 1986).

III.
Common Law And Contractual Rights

A surety's common law and contractual salvage rights tend to overlap since most indemnity agreements, at least in part, attempt to restate and amplify upon common law principles. However, a surety should carefully examine the precise terms of any indemnity agreement in its favor because these terms often provide more favorable relief to the surety than would have been available under the common law.

A. Indemnity

Common law indemnity (also called reimbursement) refers to the principal's duty to repay any loss sustained by a surety when it has performed an act which the principal had the primary duty to perform. A surety's right to indemnity or reimbursement does not depend upon the existence of a contract, but if there is a contractual right to indemnity or reimbursement, it may expand or otherwise change that right.[8]

Usually, as a condition of executing a contract bond, a surety requires its principal, and frequently other parties associated with the principal who may have the financial wherewithal, such as the owners of the principal and their spouses, to enter into a written indemnity agreement in favor of the surety. Typically, an indemnity agreement requires the indemnitors to indemnify the surety from all loss, costs, expenses, attorneys' fees and other expenses which the surety may incur in connection with the execution of the bonds, such as the expenses of conducting an independent investigation, adjusting claims against the bonds, and pursuing its rights of indemnity against the principal and indemnitors.

B. Exoneration

Exoneration gives a surety the right to demand that the principal pay or perform an obligation which has matured and which, if performed by the surety, would give it the right to reimbursement from the principal.[9] Exoneration recognizes that as between the principal and the surety, the

---

8 RESTATEMENT OF SECURITY § 111 (1941).

9 *Id.* at § 112.

principal has the primary duty of performance and, accordingly, should be required to discharge its duties before the surety is forced to perform.[10]

Upon the principal's default and before the surety makes any payment to payment bond claimants or to the obligee, the surety has the right to obtain the equitable remedy of exoneration. It does so by compelling its principal either to pay the claimants and obligee, to perform its obligations under the bonds, or typically if any indemnity agreement so provides, to furnish collateral to the surety.[11]

A surety may seek exoneration and indemnity under a written indemnity agreement in its favor even before its obligation to the obligee has matured, by a *quia timet* action, which is an action in equity by one who fears some future injury to his property, if it can show it has justification under the terms of the indemnity agreement in its favor.[12]

C. Assignment

Indemnity agreements generally contain provisions assigning to a surety all of the principal's rights in its tools, equipment, materials, and accounts receivable from bonded jobs. They typically also contain a provision making the indemnity agreement a security agreement and a financing statement under the Uniform Commercial Code. The latter provision will allow a surety to perfect its security interest by filing it in the office designated by the UCC if it so desires.[13]

---

10 The surety's right to be exonerated was declared early by Judge Learned Hand in *Admiral Oriental Line v. United States*, 86 F.2d 201 (2nd Cir. 1936). "...[B]efore paying the debt a surety may call upon the principal to exonerate him by discharging it; he is not obliged to make inroads into his own resources when the loss must in the end fall upon the principal." *Id.* at 204 (citations omitted).

11 *Riddle v. Dean Machinery Co.*, 564 S.W.2d 238, 260 (Mo. Ct. App. 1978).

12 *See* section VI.A., *infra*; *see also*, *Morley Constr. Co. v. Maryland Casualty Co.*, 90 F.2d 976, 977 (8th Cir. 1937), *cert. denied*, 302 U.S. 748 (1937).

13 *See* section IV.D., *infra*.

In addition, to effectuate a surety's rights of assignment, the indemnity agreement usually gives the surety the right to examine the books and records of its principal.

D. Trust Fund Provisions

Many indemnity agreements include a provision in which the principal agrees that all contract proceeds from bonded contracts constitute a trust for the benefit of suppliers, laborers and others who could make claim against a payment bond. Such a provision may effectively protect contract proceeds from other potential claimants such as the principal's bankruptcy trustee, judgment creditors and others.

IV.
Rights Under Indemnity Agreements

A. Indemnity

An indemnity agreement in favor of a surety usually confirms and expands the surety's common law rights by requiring the indemnitors to indemnify the surety from any liability, loss, cost, expense, damages, attorneys' fees, or other expenses which the surety may sustain or incur as a result of having executed the bond for the principal, whether or not it was actually liable for such amounts. Such provisions, while perhaps onerous, have been held to be valid and binding.[14] The only exception arises when a surety makes payment through fraud or lack of good faith.[15]

Under a typical indemnity agreement, a surety does not have the burden of determining whether the owner or the contractor first breached the contract. Rather, once an owner or subcontractor makes demand on a surety under the bonds, the surety may make good faith disbursements if it believes it is liable, or if it believes disbursement is necessary or expedient, whether or not such liability, necessity or expediency actually

---

14 *Fidelity & Deposit Co. v. Bristol Steel & Iron Works, Inc.*, 722 F.2d 1160, 1163 (4th Cir. 1983).

15 *See*, section VIII.A., *infra*; *see also*, *Engbrock v. Federal Ins. Co.*, 370 F.2d 784, 786 (5th Cir. 1967).

exists.[16] Typically, such an indemnity agreement will give the indemnitors a means to prevent such payments by providing that the surety's right to settle claims terminates if the indemnitors (1) request the surety to litigate the claims, and (2) at the time of the request, deposit appropriate collateral with the surety to satisfy any potential judgments and expenses.

B. Advisability of Perfecting Security Interest

Generally, sureties do not take the necessary steps to perfect their rights under the UCC until after there is a default. Usually the defaulted contractor's lender has a perfected security interest in receivables which may prevail over the surety's unperfected security interest, at least as to amounts paid out by the obligee prior to default. The surety could file its general agreement of indemnity with the appropriate office as a UCC-1 financing statement as soon as default under the indemnity agreement occurs, at least. However, the advisability of doing so at that point will depend upon a number of factors, including whether the principal has unencumbered assets against which the surety can assert a security interest, whether doing so offers a real possibility of increasing the assets from which the surety might recover its loss, whether the principal has other on-going jobs which the surety's assertion of its security interest might adversely affect, and the likelihood that the principal's bankruptcy might allow the avoidance of the surety's security interest.

Despite the protection afforded by perfecting a security interest in the contractor's assets, sureties traditionally have been reluctant to file indemnity agreements until after a default occurs, choosing instead to remain unsecured. This reluctance can be explained by several reasons. First, there is the belief that an encumbrance of a contractor's assets with a perfected security interest will impair the contractor's credit and weaken its ability to raise capital necessary for it to perform its construction contract. Such an impairment of collateral may raise the cost of a contractor's financing or may prevent it from obtaining financing at a reasonable rate of interest. Since a weakening of a contractor's credit in

---

16 *Fidelity & Deposit Co. v. Fleischer*, 772 S.W. 2d 809, 815-16 (Mo. Ct. App. 1989).

this manner could cause the contractor to default on its contract, the surety risks causing the contractor's demise by perfecting a security interest.[17]

There are several reasons why a surety should not rely entirely on equitable subrogation when underwriting a surety bond. One reason is that the equitable subrogation remedy is limited in scope. A surety can rely on the doctrine to obtain contract balances. However, the surety's equitable subrogation rights do not cover the contractor's materials or equipment. Equitable subrogation rights also do not extend to contract balances due to the principal from the owner on other construction contracts, sometimes referred to a "cross-collateralization." Although the surety's indemnity agreement may grant the surety an assignment of these assets, the assignment is an unperfected security interest. The surety thus stands as an unsecured creditor with regard to these assets, and it will lose in any contest it has with a creditor possessing a perfected blanket lien over the contractor's assets.[18]

A second reason is that reliance on the doctrine of equitable subrogation encourages litigation. The doctrine of equitable subrogation has never satisfactorily settled the competing rights of sureties and lending banks as to unpaid contract balances.[19] Whenever a contractor defaults, the lending bank looks to every possible asset that it can reach to enable it to cover its losses. Because of the uncomfortable relationship between the doctrine of equitable subrogation and Article 9 of the UCC, the bank is encouraged to test its perfected security interest against the surety's claims through litigation.[20] If the surety were to perfect a superior security interest, however, it would avoid this potential litigation because

---

17 *See* Smith & Covalt, III, *Should the Surety Stand on Its Equitable Subrogation Rights or File Its Indemnity Agreement Under the Uniform Commercial Code?*, 69 NEB. L. REV. 664, 692 (1990); *see also*, Reimer, Jankowski, Dybrkopp, *Whether Sureties Should Perfect Security Interests In Contractors Assets* (unpublished paper submitted at the Surety Claims Institute annual meeting on June 25-26, 1992).

18 *Id*.

19 *See* Gillmore, SECURITY INTERESTS IN PERSONAL PROPERTY 973-82 (1965); Dunne, *The Quarrel That Will Not Die—Financing Bank v. Construction Surety*, 106 BANKING LAW J. 115 (1989).

20 *See* Friedberg, *Construction Sureties: Don't Put All Your Eggs in the Equitable Subrogation Basket*, 41 CASE WESTERN RESERVE L. REV. 305, 321 (1990).

the rights of all parties would clearly be established according to the priorities of the UCC.

A surety will lose equipment and materials to a holder of a perfected security interest.[21] the surety were to be the first to perfect a security interest in such materials and equipment assets, it would receive priority over competing claims. This can be especially important where the contractor possesses special equipment that is necessary to perform the contract. A limitation of this priority will occur where a bank lends money to the contractor that is used to purchase new equipment and materials. If the bank takes out a security interest in these assets, it will have a "purchase money security interest," which grants the bank priority as to those assets.[22] Consequently, although perfecting a security interest will provide a surety with a better chance of getting a contractor's equipment and materials, the surety will not get these assets where the bank executes a subsequent purchase money security interest or where the bank has an earlier perfected security interest.

C. Subrogation

The doctrine of equitable subrogation arises from the surety's payment under a performance or payment bond. Under performance bond, when a contractor defaults in its performance and the surety cures the default, the surety becomes subrogated to the rights of the owner, who holds the unpaid contract balances, to apply those balances to pay the cost of curing the default. Under a payment bond, when a contractor fails to pay for equipment or materials and the surety cures the default by paying off the materialmen and laborers, the surety becomes subrogated to the rights of materialmen and laborers to assert a lien against the property, thereby entitling it to the unpaid balances held by the owner.[23]

---

21 *See* Smith & Covalt, III, *supra* note 17 at 683-84, 687-89; Friedberg, *Construction Sureties: Don't Put All Your Eggs in the Equitable Subrogation Basket*, 41 CASE WESTERN RESERVE L. REV. 305, 321 (1990).

22 U.C.C. § 9-312(4) (1972).

23 *See Pearlman v. Reliance Ins. Co.*, 371 U.S. 132, 137-42 (1962); Hart & Kane, *What Every Real Estate Lawyer Should Know About Payment and Performance Bonds*, 17 REAL PROPERTY PROBATE & TRUST J. 674, 685-86 (1985); Hollabaugh, *Surety's Right to Equitable Subrogation:*

Subrogation places a surety in the shoes of the obligee or lienholder, meaning that the surety can assert the rights of the obligee or lienholder.

Where a surety either completes performance of a contract for a defaulted contractor or pays laborers or materialmen, it is subrogated to the rights of both the owner and laborers and materialmen to the extent of its loss, and the contractor, accordingly, has no property interest in those contract funds.[24]

Overture For An Arrow, 51 INS. COUNS. J. 547 (1984).

24 Any discussion of a surety's subrogation rights must begin with a trilogy of United States Supreme Court decisions. In *Prairie State Nat'l Bank v. United States*, 164 U.S. 227 (1896), a surety who completed performance of a federal construction contract upon default by the principal sought to recover the retainage held by the government. The Court held that the surety was entitled to resort to the securities of the government, among which was the right to appropriate the retainage in order to complete the contract under the doctrine of subrogation. The Court considered the surety's subrogation right to be superior to the rights of a bank which held a power of attorney from the contractor giving it the right to receive final payment on the contract. Similarly, in *Henningsen v. United States Fidelity & Guaranty Co.*, 208 U.S. 404 (1908), a surety which paid claims of laborers and materialmen upon a contractor's default was held to have an equity in amounts due under the contract superior to that of a bank which received an assignment of contract proceeds to secure a loan to the contractor.

More recently, in *Pearlman v. Reliance Ins. Co.*, 371 U.S. 132 (1962), the Supreme Court followed the "firmly established rule" that a surety which completes performance of a contract is subrogated to the rights of the owner in contract funds and that a surety which pays laborers and materialmen is, likewise, subrogated to their rights in contract funds. Consequently, it held that those funds did not become vested in the trustee in bankruptcy of a defaulted contractor because:

> "property interest in a fund not owned by a bankrupt at the time of adjudication, whether complete or equitable, mortgages, liens or simple priority rights, are of course not a part of the bankrupt's property and do not vest in the trustee."

Id. at 135.

So long as the contractor has actually failed to perform its obligations, a formal declaration of default is not needed to trigger the surety's subrogation rights.[25] Indeed, the failure of the principal to pay laborers and materialmen (even though it has otherwise completed the work satisfactorily) constitutes a default under the payment bond, which is read into the indemnity agreement so that the surety's subrogation rights spring into existence at that point.[26] Consequently, if the owner, after notice from the surety, disburses monies to someone other than the surety, it may be required to pay a second time.[27] Furthermore, a surety's rights relate back to the date of execution of the bond and take priority over an assignee of the contractor for money due under the underlying contract.[28]

However, since a surety's right of subrogation only covers the amount necessary to reimburse it, a surety may only recover the entire amount held by the owner if the surety has paid out more than the amount of that retained fund.[29] Also, a surety's subrogation right only applies to contract proceeds which remain undisbursed and in the hands of the owner at the time of the principal's default.[30]

Frequently, other creditors of the principal also assert rights against the contract proceeds. The following sections of this chapter explore briefly the relative priorities of a surety and other creditors to those funds.

D. Surety's Subrogation Rights Vs. Creditor With Security Interest In Principal's Accounts Receivable

A surety's rights arise by operation of law, independent of any contract, and include the right to earned but unpaid funds in the hands

---

25 *Great American Ins. Co. v. United States*, 481 F.2d 1298 (Ct. Cl. 1973).

26 *Fireman's Fund Ins. Co. v. United States*, 421 F.2d 706, 708 (Ct. Cl. 1970).

27 *Home Indem. Co. v. United States*, 376 F.2d 890 (Ct. Cl. 1967).

28 *United States Fidelity & Guaranty Co. v. First State Bank*, 208 Kan. 738, 494 P.2d 1149 (1972).

29 *First State Bank v. Reorganized School Dist. R-3*, 495 S.W.2d 471, 482 (Mo. Ct. App. 1973).

30 *See, e.g.*, *American Casualty Co. v. Line Materials Indus.*, 332 F.2d 393, 395 (10th Cir. 1964), *cert. denied*, 379 U.S. 960 (1965).

of the owner, as well as retainage.[31] Consequently, a surety's rights to earned but unpaid funds are superior to those of a bank which perfected its security interest in the principal's accounts receivable after execution of the bond.[32]

E. Surety's Subrogation Rights In Bankruptcy

The rights of a payment or performance bond surety to contract balances when the principal has declared bankruptcy have become less clear than once seemed to be the case. A surety which has paid laborers and materialmen has an equitable right to contract retainage by subrogation to (a) the rights of the government to use retained funds to pay laborers and materialmen, (b) the contractor's right to receive those funds had it completed the job and paid its laborers and materialmen, and (c) the laborer's and materialmen's right to be paid from the funds.[33]

Courts have also ruled that the right of subrogation extends not only to retainage, but also to progress payments, provided the principal is in default under its contract with the owner of the project.[34]

Some courts have interpreted a surety's rights under the Bankruptcy Code (enacted in 1978) less expansively, holding that ongoing progress payments of a Chapter 11 debtor constituted property of the estate subject to the control of the debtor in possession.[35]

---

31 *First State Bank v. Reorganized School Dist. R-3*, 495 S.W.2d 471, 480-83 (Mo. Ct. App. 1973).

32 *National Shawmut Bank v. New Amsterdam Casualty Co.*, 411 F.2d 843 (1st Cir. 1969).

33 *Pearlman v. Reliance Ins. Co.*, 371 U.S. 132, 138 (1962). The Court, therefore, ruled that the retainage never became part of the bankruptcy estate and the trustee in bankruptcy, accordingly, had no rights in those funds. *Id.* at 141-142.

34 *Ram Constr. Co. v. American States Ins. Co.*, 749 F.2d 1049 (3d Cir. 1984).

35 *In re Glover Constr. Co., Inc.*, 30 B.R. 873 (Bankr. W.D. Ky. 1983). However, even though it considered that those funds remained part of the bankruptcy estate, it required them to be used first to pay bona fide claims against the jobs for which the surety might become liable under its bonds. *Glover* in effect recognized a surety's right of subrogation even though it ruled that the funds were part of the estate. *Id.* at 882.

Courts have gone further by refusing to grant an injunction in favor of a surety prohibiting the debtor in possession from using the contract balances other than to pay laborers and materialmen.[36] The courts have yet to resolve fully any inconsistencies between these decisions. Moreover, some courts have now held that a surety in the bankruptcy context must have a UCC filed general agreement of indemnity.[37]

For a more detailed discussion of a surety's subrogation rights in the context of the principal's bankruptcy, see Chapter 9.

F. Surety's Subrogation Rights Vs. Federal Tax Liens

A surety's equitable right on a non-federal contract to undisbursed contract funds is superior to the rights of the government under a federal tax levy against the contractor served on the owners, where the contractor is in default and has not paid claims of subcontractors, laborers and materialmen. Since the contractor has no right to the funds by virtue of its default, the government cannot foreclose on its levy.[38]

Separate federal principles govern a surety's rights vis-a-vis the federal government's claim of set-off on a federal job. The government can set-off

---

36 *In re Universal Builders, Inc.*, 53 B.R. 183 (Bankr. M.D. Tenn. 1985).

37 *United States v. G.P. Fleetwood and Co.*, 165 F. Supp. 723 (W.D. Pa. 1958) held that the surety could not assert any priority over the bankruptcy trustee where it failed to file its performance bond application containing the assignment of collateral as a financing statement. The court held:

> Since it is not disputed that the instrument involved was not filed of record as provided by Pennsylvania law, I am compelled to conclude that the assignment contained therein gives the assignee no right as a lien holder against the Trustee in Bankruptcy, having failed to comply with the provisions of the Pennsylvania Uniform Commercial Code.

Id. at 725.

38 *City of Kansas City v. Tri-City Constr. Co.*, 666 F. Supp. 170, 172 (W.D. Mo. 1987).

retainages on one job against excess costs incurred to complete a second job.[39]

On the other hand, where a surety, in accordance with its *performance* bond obligations, completes a federal contract upon its principal's default, it gains a right to retainage and remaining payments not subject to set-off in favor of the government's tax claim.[40] Moreover, payments by a surety which has issued both performance and payment bonds and which completes performance after its principal's default are considered to have been made under the performance bond even though paid to laborers and materialmen, thus defeating the government's claim of set-off.[41]

G. Surety's Subrogation Rights Vs. Creditor Holding Judgment Against Principal

When a judgment creditor of the principal seeks to garnish contract funds in the hands of the owner, a surety generally should prevail because a judgment by itself does not automatically create a lien upon personal property until levy upon that property occurs.[42] Furthermore, a garnishment only reaches the property, assets and credits of the debtor, and cannot extend to that which the debtor formerly owned, or which he lawfully assigned to a third party.[43]

---

39 In *United States v. Munsey Trust Co.*, 332 U.S. 234 (1947), a surety paid laborers and materialmen, as required by its *payment* bond, on a job which its principal had completed satisfactorily. When the same contractor failed to enter into a contract on another federal project for which the government had accepted its bid, the government asserted the right to set off retainage from the first job against its excess costs incurred in completing the second job. The Supreme Court held that the government could do so since it possesses the same right as any other creditor to apply unappropriated monies of its debtor in its hands, in extinguishment of the debts due to it. *Id.* at 239.

40 *Trinity Universal Ins. Co. v. United States*, 382 F.2d 317, 320 (5th Cir. 1967), *cert. denied*, 390 U.S. 906 (1968).

41 *Aetna Casualty & Surety Co. v. United States*, 435 F.2d 1082 (5th Cir. 1970).

42 *In re Rodriquez*, 140 B.R. 562, 564 (Bankr. D. Kan. 1992).

43 *Nelson v. Boula*, 207 Kan. 771, 773, 486 P.2d 1340, 1342 (1971).

The subrogation rights of a surety are superior to the rights of a creditor garnishing the contract proceeds in the hands of the owner.[44]

H. Surety's Rights As To Obligee

1. Payments by Obligee After Surety Issues "Stop Pay" Notice

Upon learning of its principal's default, a surety's first concern is to preserve the remaining contract funds so that it may use them to complete the project, if necessary. Under those circumstances a surety commonly serves a notice on the owner demanding that it not disburse additional contract proceeds to the principal.[45]

Where an obligee makes payments to the principal despite a payment and performance bond surety's request that it not do so because the principal has defaulted by failing to pay bills on the project, a surety may recover those payments from the obligee, at least under some circumstances.[46] If, however, the contractor's default mainly lies in failing to carry out its work under the bonded contract, courts generally give the owner broad discretion to continue paying the contractor as long as there has been no formal default and the contractor at least arguably is still performing.[47]

---

44 In *Trinity Universal Ins. Co. v. Bellmead State Bank*, 396 S.W.2d 163 (Tex. Civ. App.—Dallas 1965, writ ref'd n.r.e.), the Court reasoned that (a) the contractor had no rights to the funds since the owner had the express right under the contract to withhold payment of the amount of any claim by a third party against the contractor based upon an alleged failure to perform, (b) since the contractor had no rights to the funds, neither did a garnishing creditor, (c) the surety which paid to complete the project and to discharge bills incurred in the construction was subrogated to the rights of the owner, and (d) consequently, the surety had a better right to the contract proceeds through principles of subrogation than a garnishing creditor.

45 *See* Exhibit 13.7 *infra*, Notice of Principal's Default to Obligee and Direction Not to Pay.

46 *Home Indem. Co. v. United States*, 313 F. Supp. 212, 216 (W.D. Mo. 1970).

47 *United States Fidelity & Guaranty Co. v. United States*, 676 F.2d 622, 630-32 (Ct. Cl. 1982).

Furthermore, if the obligee does not have the right to withhold funds from the contractor upon completion of the contract, its payment to the principal will not discharge the surety even if the obligee knows of the existence of unpaid labor and material bills.[48] In any event, a surety's making of a request to an obligee that it make no further payments to the principal does not constitute tortious interference with the principal's contract because of the surety's obvious and substantial interest in the matter.[49]

I. Surety's Rights Against Third Parties

1. Design Professionals

A surety may have the right to pursue architects or engineers for negligent misrepresentation or negligent supervision of construction which results in loss to the surety.[50]

---

48 *J.R. Meade & Co. v. Barrett & Co.*, 453 S.W.2d 632, 635 (Mo. Ct. App. 1970).

49 *Gerstner Electric, Inc. v. American Ins. Co.*, 520 F.2d 790, 794-95 (8th Cir. 1975).

50 In *United States ex rel. Los Angeles Testing Lab. v. Rogers & Rogers*, 161 F. Supp. 132 (S.D. Cal. 1958), the court held that a prime contractor could bring suit for negligent supervision and negligent misrepresentation against an architect for breach of its duty to supervise the project with due care. Similarly, in *Westerhold v. Carroll*, 419 S.W.2d 73 (Mo. 1967), the court upheld the right of an indemnitor of a surety to sue an architect for negligently certifying the amount of work completed and materials furnished for the project. In *Aetna Ins. Co. v. Hellmuth, Obata & Kassabaum, Inc.*, 392 F.2d 472 (8th Cir. 1968), the court allowed a surety which provided financial assistance to its principal to complete a bonded project to recover directly against the architect for negligent supervision of the construction. Frank D. Wagner, Annotation, *Tort Liability of Project Architect for Economic Damages Suffered by Contractor*, 65 A.L.R.3d 249 (1975), contains a helpful discussion of the considerations involved in this area, including various sources of liability, defenses, and strategy.

2. *Accountants*

A surety may also have the right to sue an accountant who fraudulently or negligently prepared financial statements which the underwriters of the surety reviewed before making the decision to issue bonds.[51] It seems likely that a surety might make such a claim against an accountant except in those states which require that a party suing an accountant have been in privity with the accountant.[52]

3. *Banks*

The underwriters may have received inaccurate or incomplete information from third parties such as lending institutions or others who may have fraudulently induced the surety to issue construction bonds which later resulted in substantial losses to the surety.[53]

Also, contractors, subcontractors and their sureties have been successful in pursuing equitable claims against undisbursed loan proceeds where the circumstances make it unjust to allow the construction lender to retain both the improved property and any remaining loan proceeds which are not disbursed due to some default by the owner borrower.[54]

---

51 In *Travelers Indem. Co. v. A.M. Pullen & Co.*, 289 S.E.2d 792 (Ga. Ct. App. 1982), a surety sued an accounting firm retained by the principal, claiming it had negligently or fraudulently prepared financial statements concerning the principal's condition. The surety also alleged that it had relied on those financial statements in issuing bonds upon which it subsequently incurred losses. The court rejected the accountant's argument that the surety could not maintain the action because it lacked privity with the accountant.

52 *Aluma Kraft Mfg. Co. v. Elmer Fox & Co.*, 493 S.W.2d 378, 383 (Mo. Ct. App. 1973).

53 *See*, Seidl, Knoll, Joyce, *A Surety's Guide for Claims Against Providers of Inaccurate Underwriting Information* (unpublished paper submitted at the A.B.A. Tort and Insurance Practice Section Fidelity & Surety Law Committee mid-winter meeting on January 28, 1994).

54 *See*, Gary, *Remedies for Collection: Alternatives to Mechanic's Liens and Bond Claims, A Guide for Sureties and Contractor's to Owner's Financing of Construction Projects* (unpublished paper submitted at the A.B.A. Forum on the Construction Industry/Tort and Insurance Practice Section Fidelity & Surety Law Committee joint program in New York, N.Y. on January

The remedies obtained are typically referred to as "equitable lien" or "constructive trust."[55]

4. *Equitable Liens Against Third Parties*

Where a third party is aware of the surety's interest in an indemnitor's assets and obtains the assets for himself, the circumstances should be carefully reviewed to see whether an equitable lien could be imposed in favor of the surety.[56]

5. *Fraudulent Conveyances to Third Parties*

Where transfers of assets occur without sufficient consideration, at a time when the principal or indemnitors had existing or contemplated indebtedness, and where the transfer had the effect of making less property

---

28, 1993).

55 Reitz, *Construction Lender's Liability to Contractors, Subcontractors, and Materialmen*, 130 U. PA. L. REV. 416 (1981).

56 In *General Ins. Co. of Am. v. Lowry*, 412 F. Supp. 12 (S.D. Ohio 1976), *aff'd*, 570 F.2d 120 (6th Cir. 1978), the court stated that an equitable lien could be imposed in favor of the surety "in narrowly-circumscribed situations." *Id.* at 14. In that case, the contractor's attorney was aware of the surety's attached, but unperfected interest in stock. After loaning the contractor additional money and giving legal advice, the attorney took possession of the stock, thereby perfecting his own interest in the collateral after having executed and signed a "memorandum of agreement" in which he and his client agreed not to impair the surety's security. The court found:

> CONCLUSIONS OF LAW
>
> B. Where defendant Edward F. Lowry as first party for consideration agrees to secure a bond issued by plaintiff General Insurance Company of America as second party with collateral security and agrees further not to impair such security, he creates an equitable lien on such collateral in favor of such second party.
> C. The Uniform Commercial Code does not preclude the imposition of an equitable lien under appropriate circumstances.

Id. at 15.

available to creditors the surety should consider whether a fraudulent conveyance has occurred. Most states have adopted the Uniform Fraudulent Transfer Act in one form or another.[57] Some states require proof of actual intent to defraud by clear and convincing evidence, whereas some simply require a transfer resulting in the debtor failing to retain sufficient property to pay the indebtedness.[58]

---

57 For example in Illinois, the definition of a fraudulent conveyance is found at 740 ILCS 160/5 (1993), which provides, in pertinent part:

160/5 Transfer or obligation fraudulent as to creditor—Claim arising before or after transfer

§ 5. (a) A transfer made or obligation incurred by a debtor is fraudulent as to a creditor, whether the creditor's claim arose before or after the transfer was made or the obligation was incurred, if the debtor made the transfer or incurred the obligation:

(1) with actual intent to hinder, delay, or defraud any creditor of the debtor; or

(2) without receiving a reasonably equivalent value in exchange for the transfer or obligation, and the debtor:

(A) was engaged or was about to engage in a business or a transaction for which the remaining assets of the debtor were unreasonably small in relation to the business or transaction; or

(B) intended to incur, or believed or reasonably should have believed that he would incur, debts beyond his ability to pay as they became due.

58 The Illinois statute provides factors that a court may consider in determining whether there is actual intent to hinder under ¶ (a) (1). However, "fraud is presumed and the transferor's actual intent is irrelevant" for a claim under (a) (2), "fraud in law." *Regan v. Ivanelli*, 617 N.E.2d 808, 814 (Ill. App. Ct. 1993).

A very succinct statement of Illinois law on fraudulent conveyances is found in *re Martin*, 145 B.R. 933 (Bankr. N.D. Ill. 1992). There, the court stated:

> 2. Under Illinois fraudulent conveyance law, Ill. Rev. Stat. 1987 ch. 59, ¶ 4, there are two kinds of fraudulent conveyances. One involves actual fraud or "fraud-in-fact." *Indiana National Bank v.Gamble*, 612 F. Supp. 1272, 1276 (N.D. Ill. 1984). Actual fraud occurs when the debtor transfers property with the intent to hinder, delay, or defraud his creditors. Ill. Rev. Stat. 1987 ch. 59, ¶ 4 [new statute 1991, ch. 59, ¶ 105(a)(1)]; *In re Aluminum Mills Corp.*, 132 B.R. 869, 885 (Bankr. N.D. Ill.

6. *CGL Insurance Policies*

In every default involving alleged defective work or materials and especially in those contracts where the owner or obligee has purchased materials directly for use by the principal, the surety should examine all of the principal's and obligee's insurance policies.[59]

J. Surety's Right To Settle Claims of The Principal

Most indemnity agreements grant to the surety the right to pay or compromise claims, demands, suits, judgments or expenses relating to or arising out of the bonds issued. The general agreements of indemnity usually include provisions of assignment by which the principal assigns, transfers and conveys to the surety monies due or to become due under contracts covered by the bond. This usually is considered to include progress payments, deferred payments, retainages, extra work, additional work, change orders and damage claims. The indemnity agreement will also have an assignment of right and title to supplies, tools, plants and equipment and materials, as well as subcontracts entered into by the principal. This assignment usually is stated to be effective as of the date

---

1991), *citing Tcherepnin v. Franz*, 457 F. Supp. 832, 836 (N.D. Ill. 1978). The other involves constructive fraud or "fraud-in-law." Constructive fraud occurs when (1) a voluntary gift is made, (2) there is an existing or contemplated indebtedness against the debtor, and (3) the debtor has failed to retain sufficient property to pay the indebtedness. Ill. Rev. Stat. 1987 ch. 59, ¶ 4 [new statute 1991, ch 59, ¶ 105(a)(2) or 106]; *Aluminum Mills*, 132 B.R. at 888; *Gendron v. Chicago & North Western Transportation Co.*, 139 Ill.2d 422, 437, 151 Ill. Dec. 545, 552, 564 N.E.2d 1207, 1214 (1990).

Id. at 946.

59 In *Natchitoches Parish School Bd. v. Shaw*, 620 So.2d 412 (La. Ct. App. 3d Cir.), *writ. denied*, 629 So.2d 414 (La. 1993), the issue was whether a comprehensive general liability insurance policy issued to a general contract or provided coverage for the contractor's obligation to indemnify his performance and payment surety for legal and investigative costs. The court concluded that the costs were covered by the contractual liability provisions of the CGL policy. *See also*, Chapter 11 *supra*.

of the execution and delivery of the general agreement of indemnity with regard to previously bonded contracts and effective as of the date of the issuance of the bond.[60]

The surety, in exercising its rights to claims of its principal as provided in the general agreement of indemnity and/or under its right of subrogation, exposes itself to a multitude of claims by the principal and indemnitors. The most prevalent claims involve allegations that the surety has failed to fulfill its duty to properly investigate claims the contractor had against owners, subcontractors, materialmen or others for extras, change orders, breaches of contract, and impairment of performance. Further, principals and indemnitors may allege that the surety has failed to properly analyze defenses and counterclaims to be utilized in mitigating damages to or obtaining recoveries or offsets from owners, subcontractors or suppliers. Such claims of misuse of the surety's right to contractors claims can impair the duty of indemnity owed by principals and indemnitors or expose the surety to damages. The surety must act in a manner so as not to appear to have failed to mitigate its losses, as well as those of the principals and the indemnitors. It must act in a reasonable manner in attempting to obtain salvage and mitigation through use of its rights to the principal's claims.

The surety will fulfill its duty to its principal and thereby properly exercise its rights to the principal's claims if it could perform a comprehensive claim evaluation, which should encompass a thorough investigation of the principal's documents. The surety should be able to show that it has taken under consideration the known available counterclaims or offensive claims of its principal.[61]

When exercising the surety's rights to settle the principal's claims, some courts construe the compensated surety and related indemnity agreements as an insurance contract and hold that the surety owes "a duty of fair treatment" to the "insured."[62]

---

60 *See*, Marks, *The Rights of a Surety to Settle or Compromise Claims or Chosen in Action of the Principal* (unpublished paper submitted at the Surety Claims Institute annual meeting on June 23-24, 1994).

61 *Horton v. United States Fidelity & Guaranty Co.*, 392 S.E.2d 25 (Ga. Ct. App. 1990).

62 *Windowmaster Corp. v. Morse/Diesel, Inc.*, 722 F. Supp. 1532, (N.D. Ill. 1988).

Some courts have held, under the assignment of rights granted to the surety by the indemnity agreement, that the surety is required to compromise claims "so that the reasonable expectations of the parties would be effectuated." This expectation included the belief that the surety should conduct a reasonable investigation not only of claims by the owner, but also the "viability" of counterclaims and defenses.[63] The surety, when acting under a general agreement of indemnity and related collateral security agreements, should urge any and all reasonable defenses and claims or other forms of action that its principal may have in order to offset claims of the obligee and others and to mitigate damages.

It would appear that the general and more well-reasoned course of decision concerning the exercise of a surety's rights to settle or compromise claims assigned to it by the principal under a written indemnification agreement or obtained by the route of subrogation is to determine whether or not settlement was reasonable under the available circumstances and facts at the time of decision and whether or not there is substantive evidence of fraud or collusion. The surety may also be expected to have settled, compromised or disposed of a claim only after a reasonable investigation of claims, counterclaims and possible defenses and, in order to maintain its position, to have notified the principal and indemnitors of the final settlement.[64]

V.
Contribution

Sometimes, more than one surety executes a bond. Contribution allows a surety which has discharged more than its proportionate share of the principal's obligations to recover the amount in excess of its proportionate share from a co-surety.[65] In the event of a loss under such a bond, the surety which makes payment ordinarily may seek contribution from a co-surety under the bond of a proportionate share of its payment.[66]

---

63 *City of Portland v. Ward*, 750 P.2d 171 (Or. Ct. App. 1988).

64 *United States v. D Bar D Enters., Inc.*, 772 F. Supp. 1167, 1170 (D. Nev. 1991); *United States Fidelity & Guaranty Co. v. Lipsmeyer Constr. Co.*, 754 F. Supp. 81 (M.D. La. 1990); *United States for use of IBEW v. United Pac. Ins. Co.*, 697 F. Supp. 378 (D. Idaho 1988).

65 RESTATEMENT OF SECURITY § 149 (1941).

66 *Phelps v. Scott*, 30 S.W.2d 71, 76 (Mo. 1930).

VI.
Surety's Remedies

A. Quia Timet

Where a surety seeks relief under an indemnity agreement and a claim has been made against the surety or suit is pending, the indemnitors have failed to apply the claim or perform under the indemnity agreement, and the surety may be required to make good the default, a surety ordinarily has the right to indemnification and exoneration from liability and to specific performance of the indemnity agreement as well as other equitable relief. Where the surety fears that the principal will not properly apply the bonded contract proceeds to pay for bonded contract obligations, this is the classic situation justifying the remedy in equity known as *quia timet*.[67]

The remedies afforded by a writ of *quia timet* include the rights of exoneration and indemnity and attendant equitable remedies, both preliminary (i.e.—temporary restraining order and preliminary injunction) and permanent (i.e.—permanent injunction), to insure the effectiveness of such rights.[68] A surety's right of exoneration from the principal and the principal's assets, in the event of fraud, insolvency or absconding of the principal, may require further protection, including injunctions, receiverships, recovery of property from third parties, equitable garnishments and tracing of funds.[69]

---

67 A surety traditionally has the right after the maturity of the debt or accrual of the liability for which it stands as surety, but before making any payment, to compel the principal to exonerate it from liability or to secure it against loss, particularly where the principal has agreed to indemnify the surety and place it in funds before payment is required. *Northwestern Nat'l Ins. Co. v. Alberts*, 741 F. Supp. 424, 430 (S.D.N.Y. 1990). Such an agreement is universally recognized to be legally valid and enforceable. *Tennant v. United States Fidelity & Guaranty Co.*, 17 F.2d 38 (3d Cir. 1927).

68 *Glades County v. Detroit Fidelity & Surety Co.*, 57 F.2d 449 (5th Cir. 1932).

69 *Republic Nat' Bank & Trust Co. v. Massachusetts Bonding & Ins. Co.*, 68 F.2d 445 (5th Cir. 1934).

The remedy of *quia timet* seeks to prevent wrongs or anticipated mischief by seeking the aid of a court of equity because the surety plaintiff fears (*quia timet)* some probable future injury to its rights or interests, rather than because an injury has already occurred which requires relief. The relief granted depends upon the circumstances, but may include the appointment of a receiver, an order to pay an amount into the registry of the court, an order directing that security be given or money paid over, or even the issuance of temporary restraining orders, preliminary or final injunctions or other remedial process.[70]

B. Constructive Trusts

A constructive trust is not a trust at all, but instead a judicial device to prevent fraud by making the person who has wrongfully acquired property, or who has acquired property under circumstances that make it inequitable for him to retain it, a "trustee" for the person defrauded or injured by the fraudulent conduct.[71] A surety may benefit from the imposition of a constructive trust in many situations.

For example, where a bank has a perfected security interest in the principal's accounts receivable, a surety may require that a check payable jointly to the principal and one of its suppliers be applied to payment of the supplier (a beneficiary of the surety's payment bond) using a constructive trust theory.[72] The question whether a constructive trust will attach to general funds held by the principal's trustee in bankruptcy is a matter of federal law which requires the tracing of funds from a particular bonded project to an identifiable trust in the hands of the trustee.[73] Where a surety can identify specific trust assets, the bankruptcy court should recognize state-law created constructive trusts, and those assets will not become part of the bankrupt estate.[74]

---

70 *Morley Constr. Co. v. Maryland Casualty Co.*, 90 F.2d 976 (8th Cir. 1937), *cert. denied*, 302 U.S. 748 (1937).

71 *Reliance Ins. Co. v. Brown*, 40 B.R. 214, 217 (W.D. Mo. 1984).

72 *Mid-Atlantic Supply, Inc. v. Three Rivers Aluminum Co.*, 790 F.2d 1121 (4th Cir. 1986).

73 *Reliance Ins. Co. v. Brown*, 40 B.R. 214, 218 (W.D. Mo. 1984).

74 *In re Kennedy & Cohen, Inc.*, 612 F.2d 963, 966 (5th Cir. 1980), *cert. denied sub nom.*, *Wisconsin v. Reese*, 449 U.S. 833 (1980).

VII.
Surety's Exercise of Its Rights

A. Necessity of Default

As soon as the surety has received a notice of claim from alleged unpaid subcontractors or suppliers under the payment bond or a notice of default from the obligee under the performance bond, the surety should examine the specific definition of what constitutes "default" under the general indemnity agreement. It is prudent to obtain early documents and letters from creditors, owners, engineers, construction managers, subcontractors, suppliers, equipment suppliers, etc., that clearly establish that there is a default under the general agreement of indemnity.[75]

---

75 Under the agreement of indemnity of one surety, "EVENT OF DEFAULT" means any one or more of the following:

(A) Any notice of default by an obligee on any BOND due to abandonment, forfeiture, breach of, or failure, refusal or inability to perform any CONTRACT or obligation contained in a BOND, whether actual or alleged;

(B) Any failure, delay, refusal or inability of PRINCIPAL to pay claims, bills or other indebtedness incurred in, or in connection with the performance of any CONTRACT;

(C) The failure to perform, or comply with the terms, covenants or obligations in this Agreement;

(D) The failure to pay or discharge, when due, all indebtedness of PRINCIPAL to SURETY;

(E) An assignment by PRINCIPAL for the benefit of creditors, or the appointment or an application by PRINCIPAL for the appointment of a receiver or trustee for PRINCIPAL or its property, solvent or not, or if proceedings for the appointment of a receiver or trustee for liquidation, reorganization or arrangement of PRINCIPAL shall be initiated by other persons;

(F) If PRINCIPAL or INDEMNITOR is an individual, PRINCIPAL's or INDEMNITOR's dying, absconding, disappearing, becoming incompetent, being convicted of a felony or imprisoned, or, if PRINCIPAL or INDEMNITOR is any other type of entity, any change or treat of change in the character, identify, control, arrangement, beneficial ownership or existence of PRINCIPAL or INDEMNITOR;

Equity generally implies a right to indemnification in favor of a surety when the surety pays off a debt for which its principal is liable. However, a surety need not resort to implied principles of indemnity when it can rely upon the provisions of an express indemnity contract, for it is entitled to stand on the letter of its contract.[76] Where the indemnity contract so provides, a surety may be entitled to reimbursement for any payment made by it in good faith under the belief that it was necessary or expedient to make that payment, whether or not it was actually liable or the necessity or expediency existed.

B. Right To Specific Performance

Most courts agree that the provisions of an indemnity agreement are subject to specific performance. The remedy of specific performance

---

(G) Any proceeding or the exercise of any rights by any individual or entity which deprives or impairs PRINCIPAL's use of its plant, machinery, equipment, plans, drawings, tools, supplies or materials.

And, under another surety's general indemnity agreement "DEFAULT" is defined:

DEFAULT—Principal shall be in Default with respect to a Contract and hereunder if any of the following occur:

(A) Principal breaches, abandons or repudiates any Contract.
(B) Any Obligee declares Principal to be in Default.
(C) Principal fails to pay for any labor or materials when such payment is due.
(D) Principal diverts any Contract funds from one Contract to another, prior to the complete discharge of Surety.
(E) Principal, or any of the Undersigned, breaches any provision of his Agreement.
(F) Principal, or any one of the Undersigned, becomes the subject of any Agreement or proceedings of composition, insolvency, bankruptcy, receivership, trusteeship, or assignment for credits.
(G) Principal, or any one of the undersigned, becomes actually insolvent
(H) Principal (if an individual) dies, is adjudged mentally incompetent, convicted of a felony, becomes a fugitive.

76 *Commercial Ins. Co. v. Pacific-Peru Constr. Corp.*, 558 F.2d 948, 953 (9th Cir. 1977).

generally includes the requirements that: (1) no adequate remedy at law exists; (2) the performance sought from the defendant is substantially identical to the performance promised by the defendant; (3) the terms of the contract are definite as to what performance is agreed to by the parties; (4) the contract is fair and reasonable; and (5) both parties are entitled to specific performance.[77]

The surety seeking specific performance must convince the court that it should exercise its judgment in favor of the relief requested, since specific performance is a discretionary remedy.[78] A surety's right to specific performance of the agreement of indemnity may include requiring the deposit of collateral.[79]

The four most important factors in determining whether a preliminary injunction should issue on behalf of a surety against the principal in federal court are:

(1) the threat of irreparable harm to the surety;
(2) the state of the balance between this harm and the injury that granting the injunction would inflict on the principal or indemnitors;
(3) the probability that the surety will succeed on the merits; and
(4) the public interest.[80]

---

77 Compare *Tamarind Lithography Workshop, Inc. v. Sanders*, 142 Cal. App. 3d 552 (Cal. Ct. App. 1983) (stating requirements for specific performance), with *Niagara Mohawk Power Corp. v. Graver Tank and Mfg. Co.*, 470 Supp. 1308, 1324 (N.D.N.Y. 1979) (stating New York requirements for specific performance as: a valid contract; substantial performance by plaintiff; defendant's ability to perform; and, no adequate remedy at law).

78 *See generally*, 71 AM. JUR. 2d, *Specific Performance* §§ 4-92 (1973); C. Meeker, *Surety's Right to Specific Performance of Indemnity Agreements*, THE CONSTRUCTION LAWYER, Vol. 3, No. 2 Spring 1982, at 1 (providing an annotated discussion of each requirement).

79 *See, e.g.*, *Milwaukee Constr. Co. v. Glens Falls Ins. Co.*, 367 F.2d 964 (9th Cir. 1966); *United Bonding Ins. Co. v. Stein*, 273 F. Supp. 929 (E.D. Pa. 1967); *Doster v. Continental Casualty Co.*, 105 So.2d 83 (Ala. 1958); *Flaherty v. Bookhultz*, 207 Or. 462, 291 P.2d 221 (1955); and *Standard Surety Co. v. Caravel Indus. Corp.*, 128 N.J.Eq. 104 (N.J. Super. Ct. App. Div. 1940).

80 11 Charles A. Wright & Arthur R. Miller, FEDERAL PRACTICE AND PROCEDURE § 2948 (1973).

Ordinarily, a surety will be able to meet these tests because the validity of its indemnity agreement generally cannot be seriously challenged, which helps to demonstrate that the threat of an irreparable injury exists when a default under the agreement occurs.[81]

A surety can make a strong argument that little if any harm would be inflicted on the indemnitors, since the preliminary injunction merely seeks to preserve the status quo. The validity of the indemnity agreement, a written document about which there can be no dispute, also demonstrates the probability that plaintiff will succeed on the merits. Finally, the public interest will be served by enforcement of the indemnity agreement.[82]

However, a minority view holds that a surety cannot demonstrate irreparable injury merely by showing breach of the indemnity agreement and accordingly, is not entitled to specific performance, at least in the absence of a showing by the surety that it would be unable to recover fully from the indemnitors after a trial of the indemnity action on the merits.[83]

C. Bankruptcy Considerations

For a more detailed discussion of a surety's subrogation rights in the context of the principal's bankruptcy, see Chapter 9. However, the following lists those bankruptcy issues which have particular significance in the context of salvage and subrogation.

1. Automatic Stay

Section 362 (a) of the Bankruptcy Code prohibits certain acts which may have an adverse effect on the debtor, including any act to obtain possession or to exercise control over property of the estate,[84] or any act to create, perfect, or enforce any lien against property of the estate[85] any act to create, perfect, or enforce any lien against property of the estate to the extent that such lien secures a claim that arose before the commencement of the case[86] and any act to collect, assess, or recover

---

81 *N.I.S. Corp. v. Swindle*, 724 F.2d 707 (8th Cir. 1984).

82 *Id.*

83 *Firemen's Ins. Co. v. Keating*, 753 F. Supp. 1146 (S.D.N.Y. 1990).

84 11 U.S.C. § 362(a)(3) (1993).

85 11 U.S.C. § 362(a)(3) (1993).

86 11 U.S.C. § 362(a)(3) (1993).

a claim against the debtor that arose before the commencement of the case.[87]

In order to assert and protect its subrogation rights to contract proceeds on bonded jobs, a surety generally will wish to inform the obligee promptly of its rights to those funds. Similarly, a surety in an appropriate case might wish to assert its contractual right to use the debtor's tools and equipment to complete bonded projects. However, particularly in a Chapter 11 case, one could argue that giving such a notice would, in view of the extreme breadth of the definition of property of the estate in the Bankruptcy Code, violate the automatic stay, especially a notice which demands that the obligee pay the funds over to the surety. On the other hand, a surety's failure to notify the obligee of its interest in those funds and the trustee or debtor in possession of its right to use equipment may result in the squandering of those funds or equipment or at least their use or expenditure on non-bonded obligations.

In view of the penalties for violation of the automatic stay,[88] perhaps the best course of action for a surety lies in refraining from demanding payment of the contract funds and possession of equipment, but instead, merely advising the obligee and principal that the surety claims an interest in those funds and equipment and suggesting that the obligee consider holding the funds and that the principal not transfer the equipment pending a bankruptcy court determination of the parties' rights to the funds and equipment. Generally, upon receiving notice of the principal's bankruptcy, the obligee's first instinct will be not to make any further disbursements anyway.

2. *Seeking Relief from the Automatic Stay*

The Bankruptcy Code allows any party in interest to request relief from the automatic stay, after notice and a hearing, based on cause, including the lack of adequate protection of an interest in property of the party in interest or if the debtor does not have an interest in the property and the property is not necessary to an effective reorganization.[89] When a surety has begun completion or intends to complete a project for a

---

87 11 U.S.C. § 362(a)(3) (1993).

88 § 362(h) provides sanctions including the debtor's actual damages, court costs, attorneys' fees and even punitive damages.

89 11 U.S.C. § 362(d)(1) and (2) (1993).

principal in Chapter 11 proceedings, it will generally want to seek such an order as soon as possible so as to allow it to receive construction draws from the obligee and to enforce its right to use tools and equipment in accordance with its rights under an indemnity agreement. The Bankruptcy Code provides that if the bankruptcy court does not order that the stay continue within thirty days of the request for relief, the stay automatically lifts.[90]

3. *Cash Collateral*

If the contract proceeds are considered property of the estate, they constitute "cash collateral.[91] The Bankruptcy Code prohibits a debtor in possession or trustee from using cash collateral unless each entity that has an interest in it consents or the court allows its use, after notice and a hearing. It also requires a debtor in possession or trustee to segregate and account for any cash collateral.

The surety should not rely on the good faith of the trustee or debtor in possession, but should promptly: (a) notify the principal or trustee in writing that the surety does not consent to the use of cash collateral from projects it bonded and (b) file a motion to prohibit or condition use of the cash collateral.[92] As an alternative to an outright prohibition on the use of cash collateral, the court may award "adequate protection." Adequate protection might include a requirement that the debtor segregate contract proceeds, account for them daily, and use them only for expenses incurred on bonded projects.

4. *Preferences*

Certain pre-petition transfers of an interest in a debtor's property face scrutiny in the event of a bankruptcy filing.[93]

---

90 11 U.S.C. § 362(d) (1993).

91 11 U.S.C. § 363(a) (1993).

92 11 U.S.C. § 363(e) (1993).

93 A debtor in possession or trustee may avoid such a preferential transfer if the transfer was:
(1) to or for the benefit of a creditor;
(2) for or on account of an antecedent debt owed by the debtor before such transfer was made;

The practical negative effect of these provisions upon the surety is that the bankruptcy estate may recover from the surety payments and transfers made to it within ninety days of the filing of bankruptcy. Accordingly, a surety should always keep in mind when considering how best to deal with a principal in default that any payments or transfers it receives from the principal or an indemnitor may be divested, or at least challenged, if the principal or indemnitor goes into bankruptcy within ninety days. If that happens, what a surety believes it has collected in salvage may turn out to have been illusory.

On the other hand, two exceptions to the avoidance powers may allow a surety to hang on to payments and transfers if can fit itself within their provisions. The trustee or debtor in possession may not avoid a payment or transfer if:

(1) the transfer was intended by the debtor and the creditor to or for whose benefit the transfer was made to be a contemporaneous exchange for new value to the debtor and was actually a substantially contemporaneous exchange; or[94]

(2) the transfer was in payment of a debt incurred by the debtor in the ordinary course of business or financial affairs of the debtor and the transferee, and the transfer was made in the ordinary course of business of the debtor and the transferee, and made according to ordinary business terms.

A surety may be able to structure its dealings with a principal in certain instances by carefully structuring its actions so as to give new value or by seeing to it that the debtor makes payments in the ordinary course of business which also happen to comprise bonded obligations.[95]

---

(3) made whole the debtor was insolvent;

(4) made either within ninety days of the date of filing the petition or, within one year of the date of filing the petition if the creditor at the time of the transfer was an insider; and

(5) that enables the creditor to receive more than it would have received if the case was a Chapter 7 case, the transfer had not been made and the creditor received payment of the debt under the provisions of the Bankruptcy Code.

94 11 U.S.C. § 547(c)(1) (1993).

95 *See, e.g.*, *In re E.R. Fegert, Inc.*, 88 B.R. 258 (Bankr. 9th Cir. 1988) (trustee not entitled to recover otherwise preferential payments to subcontractors of debtor made in exchange for their release of debtor and

A recent change in the Bankruptcy Code has eliminated a vexing potential problem for sureties. Under the so-called *DePrizio* decision,[96] if an individual who was an insider of the principal entered into an indemnity agreement in favor of the surety and the principal made payments to the surety within one year of its filing of bankruptcy, even though the surety was not an insider of the principal, since the indemnitor most probably would have been an insider, the payment to the surety might be deemed to have been avoidable. However, the new Bankruptcy Reform Act of 1994 amended § 550 of the Code to allow the recovery of payments made more than ninety days before the filing of the petition only from insiders, thus effectively abrogating *DePrizio*.

5. *Objecting to Discharge of Principal*

When an individual principal or indemnitor declares bankruptcy, a surety may still have recourse against him or her. The Bankruptcy Code provides that a debt for fraud or defalcation while acting in a fiduciary capacity is non-dischargeable.[97]

For example, where the principal receives bonded contract proceeds, and fails to pay laborers and materialmen, but instead pays the indemnitor (debtor); under a general indemnity agreement that requires the principal to hold monies in trust for the benefit of the surety and to discharge bonded obligations, then a court may deem the debtor to be a fiduciary and his use of the funds non-dischargeable in bankruptcy.[98]

---

its surety since payments avoided surety's imposition of equitable lien on future payments under construction contract).

96 *Levit v. Ingersoll Rand Fin. Corp.*, 874 F.2d 1186 (7th Cir. 1989).

97 U.S.C. § 523(a)(4) (1993).

98 *In re Jenkins*, 110 B.R. 74 (Bankr. M.D. Fla. 1990), the debtor who was the sole shareholder of a construction company, failed to pay numerous subcontract laborers and materialmen, although he had received draws from owners sufficient to have done so. At the same time, however, the corporation paid him substantial funds as loan repayments or advances, a substantial part of which he then transferred to another construction company of which he was also the sole shareholder.

The debtor had executed an indemnity agreement in favor of the corporation's payment and performance bond surety which provided that the principal would hold monies from bonded contracts in trust for the

D. Practical Steps To Assert A Surety's Rights

1. Notification of Receipt of Claim

When a surety receives notice of a claim against its bond, it could provide to its principal and each of the indemnitors prompt written notice of the receipt of the claim. The notice could cite generally to the agreement of indemnity, include a copy of the indemnity agreement, advise that the surety has begun an investigation of the matter, invite their participation in resolving those claims at the least possible expense, itemize any payments which it has already made and demand that the principal and indemnitors comply with the indemnity agreement by indemnifying the surety. Since claims from subcontractors and suppliers may not have all been resolved at the time of this initial notice, simply inform the indemnitors of their joint and personally individual obligations to reimburse the surety. *See* Notice of Claims to Indemnitors, Exhibit 13.1.

At the time of receipt of any claim from any payment bond claimant, or the obligee, the surety should provide notice to the principal requesting verification (1) that the amounts claimed are properly due and owing, (2) that the principal and/or indemnitors agree with the amounts due, and (3) that there are no backcharges, offsets, damages or other defenses to the alleged claim. See Notice of Claims to Principal, Exhibit 13.2.

Also, after receipt of a claim from the obligee or payment bond claimant the surety could provide an acknowledgment of receipt of the claim, typically enclosing a proof of loss form and specifically requesting copies of all relevant documents, i.e., contracts, purchase orders, or other evidence of any agreements, and invoices, signed delivery receipts, summaries, letters to/from the principal, engineer or others, and back up documentation. It is usually easiest to obtain this kind of information near the time of receipt of any claim. This will allow the surety to determine the basis for and the validity of the claim and whether another party actually caused the situation giving rise to the claim, and the surety to

---

benefit of the surety and use them for no purpose other than discharging bonded obligations until it completely exonerated the surety. The court found that the trust provision made the debtor a fiduciary and that his use of the funds constituted a non-dischargeable defalcation. *See also*, *In re Specialized Installers, Inc.*, 12 B.R. 546 (Bankr. Colo. 1981).

raise any defenses and open the path towards settlement. It is important that the surety, at each step, specifically reserve its rights and defenses so that the principal, indemnitor or claimant cannot allege that the surety's actions or inactions waived or modified any of the surety's rights or defenses under the indemnity agreement, contracts or bonds. See Acknowledgment of Receipt of Claim to Claimant, Exhibit 13.3.

At the same time, the surety should seek a copy of all financial data. The surety should obtain a copy of the underwriting file from the home office and field office, as well as the files of the producing agent. The surety should seek out accountant reports, balance sheets, and other financial documentation at least for the last three (3) years. In particular, the surety should look for unusual transfers of assets.

The surety may also deem it appropriate at the time of receipt of claim to demand that the principal and/or indemnitors immediately pay the claim or post adequate collateral. The Demand for Collateral Security to Indemnitors is a similar form of letter as the Notice of Claims contact letter, however, at this stage more finite information as to claim amounts and contract balance usually has been obtained or determined for each bonded job and known claim (there may be various approaches to convey this information simply as shown on the attached form). The indemnitors and principal have either provided cooperation or not, and the surety has incurred technical engineering consulting fees, legal expenses, and has set reserves (usually an element necessary under the general agreement of indemnity). Again, it is most important to reserve all rights and defenses. See Demand for Collateral Security to Indemnitor, Exhibit 13.4.

Upon failure of the indemnitors to respond to a demand for collateral, the indemnitors nevertheless may be very willing to begin to discuss how they can settle up their indemnity obligations to the surety. Indemnitors usually are eager to get the default behind them and move on to other, more profitable endeavors. It is at this time that the surety could request to receive copies of at least the last three (3) years of federal, state and local tax returns with all supporting schedules and documents for the principal and each indemnitor and a complete list of all assets and liabilities for each as a beginning to the discussions.

In some jurisdictions, it is necessary for payment bond claimants to file notices of claim with the obligee in order for the surety to become subrogated to the rights of the unpaid claimants to any unpaid retainages. The surety could simply direct the claimants to provide such notices, obtain copies and confirm in writing to the obligee that such claims have been filed.[99]

It is a wonderful opportunity at the time of receipt of claims to begin to develop a rapport with the claimants and obligee so as to obtain information, data, and documents in support of what the obligee, principal, their respective engineers/architects, suppliers or subcontractors allegedly did or did not do. It is a wonderful opportunity for the engineering construction picture to come out along with, of course, its associated construction/contract surety legal issues.

2. *Seeking Voluntary Acknowledgment of Default*

Upon receiving notice of a default from an obligee or otherwise, a surety could immediately contact its principal to ascertain its position on that issue. If the principal does not contest the existence of a default, the surety could urge it (and the indemnitors) to acknowledge in writing the existence of the default.

The surety could draft the form of acknowledgment. It could include the principal and indemnitor's acknowledgment of the execution of the general indemnity agreement in favor of the surety, and their agreement that they will cooperate in notifying the obligee of the default, make the principal's books and records available to the surety for examination, allow the surety to contact all laborers, subcontractors and material suppliers and not contend that the surety made any promises of financing or other inducements for their execution of the acknowledgement. The surety should also obtain proper corporate resolutions acknowledging the above if the principal or any of the indemnitors operate in the form of a corporate entity. As most of us have experienced, however, this may *not* always be possible especially where the principal or indemnitors choose not to cooperate. See sample Acknowledgment of Default by Principal and Indemnitor, Exhibit 13.5, and Certified Copy of Resolutions of Special Meeting of Board of Directors, Exhibit 13.6.

---

99 *See Leatherby Ins. Co. v. City of Tustin*, 76 Cal. App. 3d 678 (Cal. Ct. App. 1977) (concerning materials, supplier's and subcontractor's stop notices).

3. Notification to Obligee of Surety's Rights

After an incident of default has occurred under the general indemnity agreement, in order to assert and protect its subrogation rights to contract proceeds on bonded jobs, a surety generally will wish to inform the obligee of its rights to those funds and demand that the obligee make no further disbursements. Once again, if the principal does not contest the existence of a default, the surety could urge the principal to sign a written form (most often prepared by the surety) giving notice to the obligee of the surety's rights, directing the obligee not to disburse further contract funds except to the surety, and stating that such direction shall be irrevocable without the written advance consent of the surety. See Notice of Principal's Default to Obligee and Direction Not to Pay, Exhibit 13.7, and Principal's Voluntary Default and Direction to Obligee to Pay Contract Funds to Surety, Exhibit 13.8.

4. Using Principal's Tools and Equipment to Complete Job

Another provision typically found in general indemnity agreements gives a surety the right to use the principal's tools and equipment to complete the bonded project. If a surety has not perfected its security interest by filing the general indemnity agreement as a financing statement in accordance with the requirements of the Uniform Commercial Code, it will probably not be able to rely on its contractual right to use equipment if another creditor such as the defaulting contractor's bank holds a prior perfected security interest in that equipment.

VIII.
Tort Liability For Bad Faith And Similar Claims

Recently, principals and indemnitors have adopted novel means of attempting to resist enforcement of their indemnity obligations. Principals and indemnitors have attempted to impose liability upon the surety and avoid their agreed upon indemnity obligations by alleging that the surety acted in bad faith when the surety attempted to enforce its rights under the general indemnity agreement.

For every allegation of bad faith, the plaintiff must show that the surety's conduct was *unreasonable*. For punitive damages, plaintiffs generally must show that the surety *in bad faith*, while consciously aware of the wrongfulness and harmfulness of its conduct, continued to act with such outrageous, oppressive, or intolerable conduct as to create a tremendous risk of harm to others.

The common bases of defense throughout all of the bad faith cases is that the surety must show that it acted reasonably and had a proper contractual basis for its actions.[100] Sureties should be very reluctant to allow the threat of tort claims to deter them from seeking to enforce their salvage rights since tort claims in the indemnity context have met with very little success.

A. Bad Faith

The basis for "bad faith" claims generally lies in the principle that every contract imposes upon each party a duty of good faith and fair dealing.[101] Originally, principals and indemnitors limited the remedies requested for a surety's alleged breach of that duty solely to relief from their indemnity obligation. They typically asserted two defenses to a demand for indemnity:

1. the surety failed to perform or failed to settle a claim against its bond in "good faith," i.e., the surety paid when it should not have paid,[102] or
2. the surety failed to act in a reasonable or prudent manner, i.e., the surety paid too much.[103]

---

100 *See*, BAD FAITH CLAIMS (Lawrence Lerner ed., 1993).

101 RESTATEMENT (SECOND) OF CONTRACTS § 205 (1981).

102 In *City of Portland v. George D. Ward & Assocs., Inc.*, 750 P.2d 171 (Or. Ct. App. 1988), the Oregon court held that the surety was bound by an implied covenant of good faith to exercise its discretion in compromising a claim so that the reasonable expectations of all the parties to the indemnity agreement would be effectuated. The court went on to hold that there was sufficient evidence in the record to indicate a lack of good faith on the part of the surety in settling the claim, largely because "it failed to make a reasonable investigation."

103 *See, e.g.*, *Seaboard Sur. Co. v. Dale*, 230 F.2d 625, 630 (1st Cir. 1956) (principal asserted counterclaim against surety for damages for maliciously and wrongfully causing a breach of principal's contract by taking over principal's contract upon obligee's demand); *National Sur. Corp. v. Peoples Milling Co.*, 57 F. Supp. 281 (W.D. Ky. 1944) (plaintiff defended

In some jurisdictions, the surety may allege *comparative bad faith* as a defense to the bad faith claim.[104] Any delays, lack of notice, noncooperation or bad faith conduct on the part of the obligee or claimant may give rise to a comparative bad faith defense. However, recovery for the surety may bc limited to only contract damages in any action for breach of the covenant of good faith and fair dealing.[105]

B. Inapplicability of Insurance Principles To Sureties

Insurance has been defined as a contract whereby one undertakes to indemnify another against loss, damages, or liability arising from an unknown or contingent event; whereas the contract of suretyship is one to answer for the debt, default, or miscarriage of another.[106]

In an insurance contract, the undertaking is to indemnify the *insured* and the insurance contract's purpose is that the *insured* may have its valid claims paid by the insurer. The insurance premium constitutes the insured's proportionate share of the risk of the entire class of *insureds*. When a claim is paid, the insured is not expected to indemnify the insurer.[107]

---

surety's claim for indemnity for claims payments alleging invalidity of claims; court allowed claim of indemnity where surety paid in "good faith"); *United States Fidelity & Guaranty Co. v. Jones*, 87 F.2d 346 (5th Cir. 1937) (court denied indemnitor's defense of invalidity of claim where surety sued under indemnity agreement and principal made no showing of bad faith, collusion or fraud); *New Amsterdam Casualty Co. v. Lundquist*, 198 N.W.2d 543 (Minn. 1972) (indemnitor discharged from its indemnity obligation due to surety's failure to exercise good faith in disposing of principal's equipment).

104 *See*, *California Casualty Gen. Ins. Co. v. Superior Court*, 173 Cal. App. 3d 274, 218 Cal. Rptr. 17 (Cal. Ct. App. 1985), which points out that the duty of good faith is a two-way street. *See also*, Patrick J. Wielinski, *Bad Faith Claims Handling As Applied to Sureties* (unpublished paper submitted to the Dallas Bar Association Construction Law Section in April, 1989).

105 *See*, *California Fair Plan Ass'n. v. Politi*, 220 Cal. App. 3d 1612, 270 Cal. Rptr. 243 (1990).

106 *Meyer v. Building & Realty Serv. Co.*, 196 N.E. 250 (Ind. 1935).

107 *See*, BAD FAITH CLAIMS, *supra* note 100, at 10.

The distinctions between the surety/principal/obligee relationship and the liability insurer/insured relationship have often been discussed and recognized.[108] In summary, these distinctions include:

1. suretyship creates a tripartite relationship in which the surety and principal are liable to the obligee; but
2. between surety and principal, the principal is primarily liable and the surety is secondarily liable;
3. the surety's obligation to the obligee is primarily the extension of standby credit;
4. the charges imposed by the surety are not based upon an actuarial computation of loss, but instead are fees for the extension of credit;
5. the principal, and not the obligee, makes the application for the surety bond and generally is obligated for the cost of the bond, as opposed to the obligee;
6. there is generally no issue of unequal bargaining power between the obligee and the surety, and indeed, the surety has little, if anything, to say about the drafting of the underlying contract;
7. the bond is generally not an adhesion agreement, but is generally prepared by the obligee and execution of the required form of bond is made a condition of the principal's performance;
8. courts generally do not impose fiduciary responsibilities upon the surety toward the obligee, but limit the surety's obligation to those of the principal, including the right of the surety to assert any defenses that the principal might assert against the obligee; and
9. the surety has a divided obligation of good faith not only to the obligee, but also to the principal and indemnitors, resulting in a dilemma of potential liability to one party or the other.[109]

No reported decision has held a surety liable to its principal or indemnitors on the basis of the special relationship that has been found in insurance cases. The probable reason for this absence of authority lies

---

108 *National Shawmut Bank of Boston v. New Amsterdam Casualty Co.*, 411 F. 2d 843 (1st Cir. 1969); *Hadison County Farmers Ass'n v. American Employers' Ins. Co.*, 209 F.2d 581 (8th Cir. 1954); *Meyer v. Building & Realty Serv. Co.*, 196 N.E. 250 (Ind. 1935); *Pearlman v. Reliance Ins. Co.*, 371 U.S. 132, 140 (1962) ("suretyship is not insurance").

109 *United States ex rel. Ehmcke Sheet Metal Works v. Wausau Ins. Cos.*, 755 F. Supp. 906 (E.D. Cal. 1991).

in the fact that none of the tests used to justify imposing a special relationship in insurance cases applies to sureties.

The factors distinguishing the relationship between a surety and principal/indemnitor from the special relationship between an insurer and insured that has supported the liability of an insurer to its insured may be listed as follows:

1. unlike an insurance obligation, the surety has no such obligation to the principal and the indemnitors. The reverse holds true since many cases have analogized the principal's/indemnitor's duty to the surety to the surety's obligation to the obligee. Indeed, the obligation works the other way since the principal is primarily liable and the surety is entitled to receive indemnity from the principal and the indemnitors for any loss, liability, cost, damages or expense incurred by reason of the execution of the concerned bonds;

2. the principal does not seek protection against calamity from the surety, but instead seeks the commercial advantage of obtaining a contract with the obligee, which requires, as a condition, that the principal provide a performance or payment bond;

3. the principal does not repose trust or confidence in the surety, but instead tenders the surety to the obligee as an assurance of the principal's performance;

4. the surety does not undertake a fiduciary responsibility to the principal or the indemnitors; and

5. the relationship between the principal and the surety does not involve the degree of public interest that is generally found in the insured/insurer relationship (as evidenced by the lack of governmental regulation of the rights and liabilities between surety and principal);[110] and

6. there does not appear to be the consideration of unequal bargaining power or an adhesion contract that is often cited as a factor in finding

---

110 In the few cases that have discussed this point, it has been held that the Unfair Claims Practice Acts do not apply to the surety/principal relationship since the principal does not meet the definition of an "insured." The Model Unfair Claims Practices Act specifically provides that suretyship contracts are not covered by the Act; however, some state legislatures have deleted this language, leaving it for courts to determine applicability of the Act to the sureties. *See, e.g.*, *Tufts v. Madesco Inv. Corp.*, 524 F. Supp. 484 (E.D. Mo. 1981); *but see, K-W Indus. v. National Sur. Corp.*, 231 Mont. 461, 754 P.2d 502 (1988).

liability as between an insurer and insured. Many principals, as contractors, may exercise as strong or stronger economic power and position in the industry as the sureties whom they tender to the obligees in performance of their contract conditions. Also, the indemnity agreement is not consistently uniform and the liability of the principal and indemnitors may well be tailored to the particular contract or bond line by the underwriter.

Consequently, courts have rejected claims that a surety was liable to its principal where it undertook to finance the principal on uncompleted contracts, but later withdrew financing, claimed the unpaid contract balances on its bonded obligations and attempted to enforce its rights under its indemnity agreement.[111]

C. Tortious Interference

Similarly, courts have rejected claims that a surety was liable under a theory of tortious interference with contract when the surety attempted to enforce its rights under its general indemnity agreement.[112] Also, a contractor's attempt to recover against a surety under a theory of interference with business relations when the surety allegedly prevented it from procuring new bonding and for abuse of process in attaching contract funds on another project to apply those against the surety's damages also proved unsuccessful.[113]

D. Lender Liability Type Theories

While sureties have generally defeated claims of interference with contractual or business relationships and abuse of process claims, another claim approach alleges liability analogous to that in lender liability cases.

No reported appellate cases have established liability of the surety to the principal analogous to the liability of a lender to a borrower under the

---

111 In *Lambert v. Maryland Casualty Co.*, 403 So.2d 739 (La. Ct. App. 1981), *aff'd*, 418 So.2d 553 (La. 1982), the court ruled that the surety had a legal right to take those actions under the indemnity agreement and that they did not constitute bad faith or a violation of any fiduciary duty.

112 *Gerstner Electric, Inc. v. American Ins. Co.*, 520 F.2d 790 (8th Cir. 1975).

113 *Wilcon, Inc. v. Travelers Indem. Co.*, 654 F.2d 976 (5th Cir. 1981).

lender liability cases; however, a number of writers have theorized as to the potential exposure of the surety for a liability analogous to that imposed in the lender liability cases.[114] Possible analogies between the types of actions or claims brought by borrowers against lenders, and those which might be brought against sureties include:

1. failure of the lender to honor a loan commitment (analogized to the surety's failure to execute a performance bond after having issued the bid bond);[115]
2. failure to advance funds under the lending agreement (analogized to a surety's refusal to finance or withdrawal from financing);[116]
3. unfair acceleration of note obligations (analogized to premature declaration of default);[117]
4. seizure of collateral in accordance with loan documents, but without notice and where a contrary course of conduct had been followed between bender and borrower (analogized to a seizure of contract funds).[118]

Sureties can continue to expect the courts not only to recognize a surety's implied obligation of good faith in enforcing its indemnity rights, but also the principal's and indemnitors' contractual duties. A surety's efforts to document the reasons for its actions in attempting to obtain salvage, notification to the principal and indemnitors of intended action

---

114 *See* William Snead and Michael Athay, *Ramifications for the Surety—Domination Revisited* (unpublished paper submitted at the A.B.A. Tort and Insurance Practice Section Fidelity & Surety Law Committee mid-winter meeting in New York, N.Y. on January 29, 1988); Luther S. Ott, et al., *Lender Liability: Surety Beware* (unpublished paper submitted at the Surety Claims Institute annual meeting on June 22, 1989); Luther S. Ott, et al., *Lender Liability and Construction Loans—And How to Avoid It*, 57 DEF. COUNS. J. 323 (July 1990).

115 *Commercial Ins. Co. v. Hartwell Excavating Co.*, 407 P.2d 213 (Idaho 1965); *L.F. Pace & Sons, Inc. v. Travelers Indem. Co.*, 514 A.2d 766 (Conn. App. Ct. 1986), *cert. denied*, 516 A.2d 886 (Conn. 1986).

116 *K.M.C. Co., Inc. v. Irving Trust Co.*, 757 F.2d 752 (6th Cir. 1985).

117 *Brown v. AVEMCO Inv. Corp.*, 603 F.2d 1367 (9th Cir. 1979).

118 *Alaska State Bank v. Fairco*, 674 P.2d 288 (Alaska 1983); *See also*, *Centerre Bank of Kansas City N.A. v Distributors, Inc.*, 705 S.W.2d 42 (Mo. Ct. App. 1985).

and reliance on well-drafted indemnity agreements should minimize the potential for the imposition of tort liability.

E. Equal Credit Opportunity Act

In the past, several attempts have been made to apply provisions of the Equal Credit Opportunity Act[119] (ECOA) to surety transactions. To date there have been no reported decisions on the applicability of the ECOA to surety bonds.[120]

The ECOA makes it unlawful for any "creditor" to discriminate against any "applicant" with respect to a "credit transaction.[121] Suretyship, however, may not constitute a credit transaction as defined by the ECOA. The term credit transaction is defined in both the statute and promulgated regulations as "the right granted by a creditor to a debtor to *defer* payment of debt or to incur debts and *defer* its payment or to purchase property or services and *defer* payment therefor."[122]

Some indemnitors have argued that a general agreement of indemnity constitutes a guarantee of the extension of suretyship to a principal, and is, therefore, a covered extension of credit. Thus the question is whether "suretyship" is the same as "credit" as defined under the Act. Applying the above definitions of credit, it seems obvious that no "right to *defer* payment of an obligation is granted." Instead, suretyship creates a liability of the surety if the principal fails to perform under the contract. A general indemnity agreement usually requires the principal and indemnitors to pay any obligation incurred by reason of the surety's execution of bonds *before* the surety is forced to make payment. The principal does not incur debt until the surety makes payment under the bond and does not have any right to defer any payment. Since suretyship is not "credit,"[123] it thus

---

119 15 U.S.C. § 1691, *et seq.*

120 *See*, Balkin, Witten, Holbrook, *Legal Aspects of the Underwriting Process* (unpublished paper submitted at the A.B.A. Tort and Insurance Practice Section Fidelity & Surety Law Committee mid-winter meeting on January 28, 1994).

121 15 U.S.C. § 1691a. (1976).

122 15 U.S.C. § 1691a.(d) (1976); TREAS. REG. B., 12 C.F.R. Ch.II (1-1-93 edition), § 202.2(j).

123 *See*, Balkin, Uitten, Holbrook, *Legal Aspects of the Underwriting Process*, *supra* note 120.

appears that neither a general agreement of indemnity, guaranteeing an extension of suretyship, nor the issuance of bonds, is an extension, renewal or continuation of "credit" under the ECOA.[124]

The requirement of a spousal signature on a credit document, where the applicant individually qualified for a loan, is not a violation of the ECOA.[125] The general agreement of indemnity does not constitute such a covered credit document, since it is not given with regard to a "credit transaction" and, moreover, may be executed in such a form as to constitute a security instrument suitable for filing under the Uniform Commercial Code.[126]

Lastly, a violation of the ECOA does provide for both legal and equitable relief to an aggrieved applicant, as well as the recovery of attorney's fees, where there has been a successful action brought.[127] However, such a violation may not render the credit document unenforceable as to any of the signatories.[128]

---

124 15 U.S.C. § 1691a.(d) (1976).

125 *Anderson v. United Fin. Co.*, 666 F.2d 1274, 1277 (9th Cir. 1982); *Evans v. Centralfed Mortgage Co.*, 815 F.2d 348 (5th Cir. 1987); *see also*, *Poe v. First Nat'l Bank*, 597 F.2d 895 (5th Cir. 1979) where the court held that the Act exempts from its scope extensions of credit for business or commercial purposes 15 U.S.C. § 1603(l); 12 C.F.R. § 226.3(a) "As to consumer credit transactions, the Act provides that the adjective 'consumer' is specifically intended to characterize the transaction as one in which the party to whom credit is extended is a natural person and the money is primarily for personal, family, household, or agricultural purposes. 15 U.S.C.A. § 1602(h) (1982)." *Id.* at 896.

126 Certain exemptions are provided in the ECOA: If the applicant requests secured credit, the signature of another person may be required on "any instrument necessary, or reasonably believed by the creditor to be necessary, under applicable state law to make the property being offered as security available to satisfy the debt in the event of default." 12 C.F.R. § 202.7(d)(4) (1994).

127 15 U.S.C. § 1691e.; *Anderson v. United Fin. Co.*, *supra*.

128 *Diamond v. Union Bank & Trust*, 776 F. Supp. 542 (N.D. Okla. 1991).

F. Fair Debt Collection Practices Act

The Fair Debt Collection Practices Act[129] was enacted in 1977 and was intended to eliminate abusive, deceptive, and unfair debt collection practices. The creditor surety and the surety's officers and employees, collecting in the name of the surety are specifically excluded from the definition of "debt collector" under the Act. As originally enacted attorneys were excluded from coverage; however in 1986 the Act was amended to eliminate the exclusion of attorneys. Attorneys may be deemed to be "debt collectors" under the Act.[130]

Indemnitors may argue that the Fair Debt Collection Practices Act applies to the surety's recovery efforts. However, the term "debt" is defined under the Act as arising out of a transaction in which the money which was the subject of the transaction was primarily for "personal, family or household purposes." Since the indemnitor's indemnity obligations arise out of the general agreement of indemnity under which construction bonds have been provided for business purposes, the Act arguably may not apply to such transactions.

IX.
Collateral Deposited At The Inception of The Suretyship Relationship

Further, a number of sureties now take collateral, such as certificates of deposit and irrevocable letters of credit, as security at the inception of the surety/principal/indemnitor relationship. The surety's determinations with respect to the disposition of such collateral should simply be governed by the same concepts of default, fairness and reasonableness as in the surety's enforcement of its rights under the general agreement of indemnity.

---

129 15 U.S.C. § 1692, *et seq.*

130 The term "debt collector" means any person who uses any instrumentality of interstate commerce or the mails in any business the principal purpose of which is the collection of any debts, or who regularly collects or attempts to collect, directly or indirectly, debts owed or due or asserted to be owed or due another. 15 U.S.C. § 1692a(6) (1982).

X.
Conclusion

Upon notice or receipt of a claim from either payment bond claimants or the obligee under the performance bond, a surety should immediately begin to evaluate all available sources of funds and the surety's salvage and subrogation rights. Prompt action at the outset may materially assist the surety in analyzing and remedying its principal's default, if any, and in recovering its losses and expenses incurred in connection with its bonded obligations. A surety should immediately review the definition of "default" under the general agreement of indemnity. A surety should review each of the rights it possesses to determine which best apply to the particular circumstances at hand. It should consider whether a bankruptcy of the principal appears imminent and, indeed, whether bankruptcy may or may not work to its advantage (by the immediate imposition of judicial authority over the principal's affairs). Although, a surety's first concern should be the availability of contract proceeds, the surety should by no means limit its focus to those funds since other sources of recovery (including from: the principal, indemnitors, obligee, architects, engineers, subcontractors, suppliers, vendors, co-prime contractors, comprehensive general liability carriers, other sureties, IRS, banks, other creditors, or others) may prove equally useful under the particular circumstances.

APPENDIX

CONTENTS

Contents (continued)

Contents (continued)

Contents (continued)

Contents (continued)

Exhibit 1.1

Standard/Short Form Performance Bond

Bond No. ________

KNOW ALL MEN BY THESE PRESENTS: That we,

as Principal, and the as Surety, are held and firmly bound unto

as Obligee, in the sum of

($) DOLLARS, for which sum, we bind ourselves, our heirs, executors, administrators, successors and assigns, jointly and severally, by these presents.

WHEREAS, on the day of , 19 , the Principal entered into a contract with the Obligee for

which contract is by reference made a part hereof and is hereafter referred to as the Contract;

NOW, THEREFORE, THE CONDITION OF THIS OBLIGATION IS SUCH, That, if the Principal shall faithfully perform said contract according to its terms, covenants, and conditions, then this obligation shall be void; otherwise it shall remain in full force and effect.

Dated this day of , 19

____

____

____

PRINCIPAL

By: ____________________________

ATTORNEY-IN-FACT

Exhibit 1.2

Miller Act Performance Bond

PERFORMANCE BOND (See instructions on reverse)	DATE BOND EXECUTED (Must be same or later than date of contract)	FORM APPROVED OMB NO. **9000-0045**

Public reporting burden for this collection of information is estimated to average 25 minutes per response, including the time for reviewing instructions, searching existing data sources, gathering and maintaining the data needed, and completing and reviewing the collection of information. Send comments regarding this burden estimate or any other aspect of this collection of information, including suggestions for reducing this burden, to the FAR Secretariat (VRS), Office of Federal Acquisition Policy, GSA, Washington, D.C. 20405; and to the Office of Management and Budget. Paperwork Reduction Project (9000-0045), Washington, D.C. 20503.

PRINCIPAL (Legal name and business address)	TYPE OF ORGANIZATION ("X" one) ☐ INDIVIDUAL ☐ PARTNERSHIP ☐ JOINT VENTURE ☐ CORPORATION STATE OF INCORPORATION
SURETY(IES) (Name(s) and business address(es))	**PENAL SUM OF BOND** MILLION(S) | THOUSAND(S) | HUNDRED(S) | CENTS CONTRACT DATE | CONTRACT NO.

OBLIGATION:

We, the Principal and Surety(ies), are firmly bound to the United States of America (hereinafter called the Government) in the above penal sum. For payment of the penal sum, we bind ourselves, our heirs, executors, administrators, and successors, jointly and severally. However, where the Sureties are corporations acting as co-sureties, we, the Sureties, bind ourselves in such sum "jointly and severally" as well as "severally" only for the purpose of allowing a joint action or actions against any or all of us. For all other purposes, each Surety binds itself, jointly and severally with the Principal, for the payment of the sum shown opposite the name of the Surety. If no limit of liability is indicated, the limit of liability is the full amount of the penal sum.

CONDITIONS:

The principal has entered into the contract identified above.

THEREFORE:

The above obligation is void if the Principal —

(a)(1) Performs and fulfills all the undertakings, covenants, terms, conditions, and agreements of the contract during the original term of the contract and any extensions thereof that are granted by the Government, with or without notice to the Surety(ies), and during the life of any guaranty required under the contract, and (2) performs and fulfills all the undertakings, covenants, terms conditions, and agreements of any and all duly authorized modifications of the contract that hereafter are made. Notice of those modifications to the Surety(ies) are waived.

(b) Pays to the Government the full amount of the taxes imposed by the Government, if the said contract is subject to the Miller Act, (40 U.S.C. 270a-270e), which are collected, deducted, or withheld from wages paid by the Principal in carrying out the construction contract with respect to which this bond is furnished.

WITNESS:

The Principal and Surety(ies) executed this performance bond and affixed their seals on the above date.

PRINCIPAL

SIGNATURE(S)	1. (Seal)	2. (Seal)	3. (Seal)	Corporate Seal
NAMES(S) & TITLE(S) (Typed)	1.	2.	3.	

INDIVIDUAL SURETY(IES)

SIGNATURE(S)	1. (Seal)	2. (Seal)
NAME(S) (Typed)	1.	2.

CORPORATE SURETY(IES)

	NAME & ADDRESS		STATE OF INC.	LIABILITY LIMIT $	Corporate Seal
SURETY A	SIGNATURE(S)	1.	2.		
	NAME(S) & TITLE(S) (Typed)	1.	2.		

NSN 7540-01-152-8060 EXPIRATION DATE 12-31-92 25-107
Previous edition not usable

STANDARD FORM 25 (REV. 1-90)
Prescribed by GSA-FAR (48 CFR) 53.228(b)

Exhibit 1.2 (continued)

CORPORATE SURETY(IES) (Continued)

SURETY B	NAME & ADDRESS			STATE OF INC.	LIABILITY LIMIT $	Corporate Seal
	SIGNATURE(S)	1.	2.			
	NAME(S) & TITLE(S) (Typed)	1.	2.			
SURETY C	NAME & ADDRESS			STATE OF INC.	LIABILITY LIMIT $	Corporate Seal
	SIGNATURE(S)	1.	2.			
	NAME(S) & TITLE(S) (Typed)	1.	2.			
SURETY D	NAME & ADDRESS			STATE OF INC.	LIABILITY LIMIT $	Corporate Seal
	SIGNATURE(S)	1.	2.			
	NAME(S) & TITLE(S) (Typed)	1.	2.			
SURETY E	NAME & ADDRESS			STATE OF INC.	LIABILITY LIMIT $	Corporate Seal
	SIGNATURE(S)	1.	2.			
	NAME(S) & TITLE(S) (Typed)	1.	2.			
SURETY F	NAME & ADDRESS			STATE OF INC.	LIABILITY LIMIT $	Corporate Seal
	SIGNATURE(S)	1.	2.			
	NAME(S) & TITLE(S) (Typed)	1.	2.			
SURETY G	NAME & ADDRESS			STATE OF INC.	LIABILITY LIMIT $	Corporate Seal
	SIGNATURE(S)	1.	2.			
	NAME(S) & TITLE(S) (Typed)	1.	2.			

BOND PREMIUM ▶	RATE PER THOUSAND	TOTAL
	$	$

INSTRUCTIONS

1. This form is authorized for use in connection with Government contracts. Any deviation from this form will require the written approval of the Administrator of General Services.

2. Insert the full legal name and business address of the Principal in the space designated "Principal" on the face of the form. An authorized person shall sign the bond. Any person signing in a representative capacity (e.g., an attorney-in-fact) must furnish evidence of authority if that representative is not a member of the firm, partnership, or joint venture, or an officer of the corporation involved.

3. (a) Corporations executing the bond as sureties must appear on the Department of the Treasury's list of the approved sureties and must act within the limitation listed therein. Where more than one corporate surety is involved their names and addresses shall appear in the spaces (Surety A, Surety B, etc.) headed "CORPORATE SURETY(IES)." In the space designated "SURETY(IES)" on the face of the form insert only the letter identification of the sureties.

(b) Where individual sureties are involved, a completed Affidavit of Individual Surety (Standard Form 28), for each individual surety, shall accompany the bond. The Government may require the surety to furnish additional substantiating information concerning its financial capability.

4. Corporations executing the bond shall affix their corporate seals. Individuals shall execute the bond opposite the word "Corporate Seal," and shall affix an adhesive seal if executed in Maine, New Hampshire, or any other jurisdiction requiring adhesive seals.

5. Type the name and title of each person signing this bond in the space provided.

STANDARD FORM 25 (REV. 1-90) BACK

Exhibit 1.3

The American Institute of Architects AIA Document A311 Performance Bond

KNOW ALL MEN BY THESE PRESENTS: that

(Here insert full name and address or legal title of Contractor)

as Principal, hereinafter called Contractor, and,

(Here insert full name and address or legal title of Surety)

as Surety, hereinafter called Surety, are held and firmly bound unto

(Here insert full name and address or legal title of Owner)

as Obligee, hereinafter called Owner, in the amount of

Dollars ($),

for the payment whereof Contractor and Surety bind themselves, their heirs, executors, administrators, successors and assigns, jointly and severally, firmly by these presents.

WHEREAS, Contractor has by written agreement dated __________________, 19___, entered into a contract with Owner for

(Here insert full name, address and description of project)

in accordance with Drawings and Specifications prepared by

(Here insert full name and address or legal title of Architect)

which contract is by reference made a part hereof, and is hereinafter referred to as the Contract.

NOW, THEREFORE, THE CONDITION OF THIS OBLIGATION is such that, if Contractor shall promptly and faithfully perform said Contract, then this obligation shall be null and void; otherwise it shall remain in full force and effect.

The Surety hereby waives notice of any alteration or extension of time made by the Owner.

Whenever Contract shall be, and declared by Owner to be in default under the Contract, the Owner having performed Owner's obligations thereunder, the Surety may promptly remedy the default, or shall promptly

1) Complete the Contract in accordance with its terms and conditions, or

2) Obtain a bid or bids for completing the Contract in accordance with its terms and conditions, and upon determination by Surety of the lowest responsible bidder, or, if the Owner elects, upon determination by the Owner and the Surety jointly of the lowest responsible bidder, arrange for a contract between such bidder and Owner, and make available as Work progresses (even though there should be a default or a succession of defaults under the contract or contracts of completion arranged under this paragraph) sufficient funds to pay the cost of completion less the balance of the contract price; but not exceeding, including other costs and damages for which the Surety may be liable hereunder, the amount set forth in the first paragraph hereof. The term

Exhibit 1.3 (continued)

"balance of the contract price," as used in this paragraph, shall mean the total amount payable by Owner to Contractor under the Contract and any amendments thereto, less the amount properly paid by Owner to Contractor.

Any suit under this bond must be instituted before the expiration of two (2) years from the date on which final payment under the Contract falls due.

No right of action shall accrue on this bond to or for the use of any person or corporation other than the Owner named herein or the heirs, executors, administrators or successors of the Owner.

Signed and sealed this ________ day of ________________________________, 19____.

	______________________________	
	(Principal)	*(Seal)*
______________________________ *(Witness)*		
	______________________________	
	(Title)	

	______________________________	
	(Surety)	*(Seal)*
______________________________ *(Witness)*		
	______________________________	
	(Title)	

Exhibit 1.4

The American Institute of Architects
AIA Document A312 Performance Bond

Any singular reference to Contractor, Surety, Owner or other party shall be considered plural where applicable.

CONTRACTOR (Name and address):

SURETY (Name and Principal Place of Business):

OWNER (Name and Address):

CONSTRUCTION CONTRACT
Date:
Amount:
Description (Name and Location):

BOND
Date (Not earlier than Construction Contract Date):
Amount:
Modifications to this Bond: □ None □ See Page 3

CONTRACTOR AS PRINCIPAL
Company: (Corporate Seal)

Signature: ______________________
Name and Title:

SURETY
Company: (Corporate Seal)

Signature: ______________________
Name and Title:

(Any additional signatures appear on page 3)

(FOR INFORMATION ONLY—Name, Address and Telephone)

AGENT or BROKER:

OWNER'S REPRESENTATIVE
(Architect, Engineer or other party):

1 The Contractor and the Surety, jointly and severally, bind themselves, their heirs, executors, administrators, successors and assigns to the Owner for the performance of the Construction Contract, which is incorporated herein by reference.

2 If the Contractor performs the Construction Contract, the Surety and the Contractor shall have no obligation under this Bond, except to participate in conferences as provided in Subparagraph 3.1.

3 If there is no Owner Default, the Surety's obligation under this Bond shall arise after:

3.1 The Owner has notified the Contractor and the Surety at its address described in Paragraph 10 below that the Owner is considering declaring a Contractor Default and has requested and attempted to arrange a conference with the Contractor and the Surety to be held not later than fifteen days after receipt of such notice to discuss methods of performing the Construction Contract. If the Owner, the Contractor and the Surety agree, the Contractor shall be allowed, a reasonable time to perform the Construction Contract, but such an agreement shall not waive the Owner's right, if any, subsequently to declare a Contractor Default; and

3.2 The Owner has declared a Contractor Default and formally terminated the Con-

Exhibit 1.4 (continued)

tractor's right to complete the contract. Such Contractor Default shall not be declared earlier than twenty days after the Contractor and the Surety have received notice as provided in Subparagraph 3.1; and

3.3 The Owner has agreed to pay the Balance of the Contract Price to the Surety in accordance with the terms of the Construction Contract or to a contractor selected to perform the Construction Contract in accordance with the terms of the contract with the Owner.

4 When the Owner has satisfied the conditions of Paragraph 3, the Surety shall promptly and at the Surety's expense take one of the following actions:

4.1 Arrange for the Contractor, with consent of the Owner, to perform and complete the Construction Contract; or

4.2 Undertake to perform and complete the Construction Contract itself, through its agents or through independent contractors; or

4.3 Obtain bids or negotiated proposals from qualified contractors acceptable to the Owner for a contract for performance and completion of the Construction Contract, arrange for a contract to be prepared for execution by the Owner and the contractor selected with the Owner's concurrence, to be secured with performance and payment bonds executed by a qualified surety equivalent to the bonds issued on the Construction Contract, and pay to the Owner the amount of damages as described in Paragraph 6 in excess of the Balance of the Contract Price incurred by the Owner resulting from the Contractor's default; or

4.4 Waive its right to perform and complete, arrange for completion, or obtain a new contractor and with reasonable promptness under the circumstances:

.1 After investigation, determine the amount for which it may be liable to Owner and, as soon as practicable after the amount is determined, tender payment therefor to the Owner; or

.2 Deny liability in whole or in part and notify the Owner citing reasons therefor.

5 If the Surety does not proceed as provided in Paragraph 4 with reasonable promptness, the Surety shall be deemed to be in default on this Bond fifteen days after receipt of an additional written notice from the Owner to the Surety demanding that the Surety perform its obligations under this Bond, and the Owner shall be entitled to enforce any remedy available to the Owner. If the Surety proceeds as provided in Subparagraph 4.4, and the Owner refuses the payment tendered or the Surety has denied liability, in whole or in part, without further notice the Owner shall be entitled to enforce any remedy available to the Owner.

6 After the Owner has terminated the Contractor's right to complete the Construction Contract, and if the Surety elects to act under Subparagraph 4.1, 4.2, or 4.3 above, then the responsibilities of the Surety to the Owner shall not be greater than those of the Contractor under the Construction Contract, and the responsibilities of the Owner to the Surety shall not be greater than those of the Owner under the Construction Contract. To the limit of the amount of this Bond, but subject to commitment by the Owner of the Balance of the Contract Price to mitigation of costs and damages on the Construction Contract, the Surety is obligated without duplication for:

6.1 The responsibilities of the Contractor for correction of defective work and completion of the Construction Contract;

6.2 Additional legal, design professional and delay costs resulting from the Contractor's Default, and resulting from the actions or failure to act of the Surety under Paragraph 4; and

6.3 Liquidated damages, or if no liquidated damages are specified in the Construction Contract, actual damages caused by delayed performance or non-performance of the Contractor.

7 The Surety shall not be liable to the Owner or others for obligations of the Contractor that are unrelated to the Construction Contract, and the Balance of the Contract Price shall not be reduced or set off on account of any such unrelated obligations. No right of action shall accrue on this Bond to any person or entity other than the Owner or its heirs, executors, administrators or successors.

8 The Surety hereby waives notice of any change, including changes of time, to the Construction Contract or to related subcontracts, purchase orders and other obligations.

9 Any proceeding, legal or equitable, under this Bond may be instituted in any court of competent jurisdiction in the location in which the work or part of the work is located and shall be instituted within two years after Contractor Default or within two years after the Contractor ceased working or within two years after the Surety refuses or fails to perform its obligations under this Bond, whichever occurs first. If the provisions of this Paragraph are void or prohibited by law, the minimum period of limitation available to sureties as a defense in the jurisdiction of the suit shall be applicable.

Exhibit 1.4 (continued)

10 Notice to the Surety, the Owner or the Contractor shall be mailed or delivered to the addres shown on the signature page.

11 When this Bond has been furnished to comply with a statutory or other legal requirement in the location where the construction was to be performed, any provision in this Bond conflicting with said statutory or legal requirement shall be deemed incorporated herein. The intent is that this Bond shall be construed as a statutory bond and not as a common law bond.

12 DEFINITIONS

12.1 Balance of the Contract Price: The total amount payable by the Owner to the Contractor under the Construction Contract after all proper adjustments have been made, including allowance to the Contractor of any amounts received or to be received by the Owner in settlement of insurance or other claims for damages to which the Contractor is entitled, reduced by all valid and proper payments made to or on behalf of the Contractor under the Construction Contract.

12.2 Construction Contract: The agreement between the Owner and the Contractor identified on the signature page, including all Contract Documents and changes thereto.

12.3 Contractor Default: Failure of the Contractor, which has neither been remedied nor waived, to perform or otherwise to comply with the terms of the Construction Contract.

12.4 Owner Default: Failure of the Owner, which has neither been remedied nor waived, to pay the Contractor as required by the Construction Contract or to perform and complete or comply with the other terms thereof.

MODIFICATIONS TO THIS BOND ARE AS FOLLOWS:

(Space is provided below for additional signatures of added parties, other than those appearing on the cover page.)

CONTRACTOR AS PRINCIPAL
Company: (Corporate Seal)

Signature: ______________________________
Name and Title:
Address:

SURETY
Company: (Corporate Seal)

Signature: ______________________________
Name and Title:
Address:

Exhibit 2.1

Typical Acknowledgement Letter by Agent to Obligee Regarding Potential Default

(Owner's Name and Address)

Re: Principal:
Surety:
Obligee:
Project:

Dear (*Obligee*):

The undersigned is an agent for (*surety company*) which is the payment and performance bond surety for (*principal*) with regard to the above-referenced construction project. This is to acknowledge receipt of your correspondence indicating a problem with respect to (*principal's*) performance of its contract. We have directed your letter to the principal with a request that it respond appropriately in writing directly to you with a copy to us.

Kindly contact this office if the principal has satisfactorily responded to your concerns or you have any other concerns that should be brought to the attention of surety. If the principal has not satisfactorily responded or you intend to pursue a claim on the bond, please notify surety promptly and in accordance with the terms of the bond and the contract.

This letter is written for acknowledgement purposes only. Surety reserves all rights and defenses under the bond, the contract and the law.

Very truly yours,

(*Surety's Agent*)

Exhibit 2.2

Typical Letter to Principal by Agent Concerning Potential Performance Bond Problem

(Principal's Name and Address)

Re: Principal:
Surety:
Obligee:
Project:

Dear (*Principal*):

As agent for (*surety*), which issued the above referenced payment and performance bond, we were notified of a problem on this project by (*obligee*). A copy of the notice is attached for your convenience.

Please respond in writing directly to (*obligee*) with your intentions for resolving the problem or your reasons for disputing any part or all of the obligee's contentions. Please be as specific as possible in your response. Please forward a copy of this response to my attention.

If a copy of this response is not received by (*date*), surety may continue its investigation into the matter which may result in additional costs to you.

Please note that (*principal*) has an obligation and a liability under the terms of the bond, and the General Agreement of Indemnity which it and the personal indemnitors executed, to see that this matter is resolved and to hold surety harmless for any costs, including attorneys' fees, it may incur in undertaking the resolution of this matter.

Your prompt attention and cooperation is requested.

Very truly yours,

(*Surety's Agent*)

cc: (*Surety*)

Exhibit 2.3

Typical Form of Notice to the Obligee Acknowledging Receipt of Claim

(*Owner Name & Address*)

Re: Principal:
Surety:
Obligee:
Project:

Dear (*Owner*):

The undersigned represents (*surety company*) which is the payment and performance bond surety for (principal) with regard to the above-referenced construction project. On behalf of surety, we acknowledge receipt on (*date*) of your correspondence asserting a claim. It is our understanding that (*identify facts of actual or impending default, e.g.*:

(a) numerous claims for payment have been asserted against our client's payment bond by subcontractors and suppliers or principal; or
(b) a notice of default has been received from you concerning the principal; or
(c) the principal has indicated that it is financially unable to proceed with its contract for the project or pay the outstanding claims for payment of its subcontractors and suppliers; or
(d) Surety has been required to make payment upon certain claims for payment of sub-contractors and/or suppliers of principal under surety's payment bond furnished for the project; or
(e) the principal is clearly in default under its contract with you due to its failure to make payment to its subcontractors and suppliers and its lack of progress under such contract.)

We are attempting to communicate with the appropriate representative of (*principal*) to investigate the facts concerning this matter. As of this time, however, we hereby demand, on behalf of (*surety*) that no further funds be released under the above-reference contract without the written consent and direction of (*surety*). This request is being made on the basis of and to protect the surety's rights of subrogation and to enable the surety to protect its interests under its bond furnished for this project. (*Optional*: Please note that any failure

Exhibit 2.3 (continued)

or refusal to observe the foregoing demand (may or will) be prejudicial to the surety, and result in serious legal consequences.)

(*Optional*): To further our investigation of this matter, we request that you supplement your correspondence with additional information and documentation. This should include (e.g.):

1. A current accounting of the contract fund setting forth the following:
   a. Original contract price
   b. Net change orders
   c. Adjusted contract price
   d. Amount paid to date
   e. Contract balance
   f. Earned but unpaid progress payments
   g. Retainage
   h. Unearned contract balance

2. Contract documents, including the plans and specifications;
3. Change orders and back charges;
4. Job minutes, progress reports, punchlists, and inspection reports;
5. Pay applications including schedules of value certifications for payment and copies of canceled checks;
6. Job schedules (both original and revised) and notice to proceed;
7. Notices of nonpayment from subcontractors and suppliers of the principal;
8. A list of all original bidders with the amounts of their bids; and
9. Correspondence with the principal.

If you have any other information of which you feel surety should be made aware, please supply it. We reserve the right to request additional information as our investigation proceeds.

Please note that this letter is sent to you for investigatory purposes only. It should not be construed by you or your company as an admission of liability or a promise to perform or pay your company's claim in whole or in part. Our activities are undertaken with a full reservation of surety's rights and defenses under the terms of its bond, the contract and the law. This reservation of rights shall remain in full force and effect unless expressly revoked by surety in writing.

Exhibit 2.3 (continued)

Should you have any questions with regard to this demand, kindly contact the undersigned as soon as possible.

Very truly yours,

(*Surety's Claim Representative*)
(*Title*)

Exhibit 2.4

Typical Form of Notice to the Indemnitor

(DATE)

(*ADDRESS TO PRINCIPAL AND INDEMNITORS*)	CERTIFIED MAIL NO. ___________ RETURN RECEIPT REQUESTED
	CERTIFIED MAIL NO. ___________ RETURN RECEIPT REQUESTED

RE: PRINCIPAL:
SURETY:
OBLIGEE:
BOND NO./PROJECT:
INDEMNITORS:

Dear ____________________:

As you are aware, (*name of surety company*) is the payment and performance bond surety for (name of principal) with regard to the above-referenced project. (*Surety*) has recently been notified by (*owner*) that (*name of principal*) is in default upon its contract with such obligee, and demand is being made upon (surety), as the performance bond surety, to arrange for the completion of such contract or cure a default. In addition, (*surety*) has received notices of claims for payment from several subcontractors and suppliers of (*principal*) on such projects for which recovery is being sought for monies claimed to be due to them for work performed at or materials delivered to such project. As a result of these matters, (*surety*) is being exposed to the possibility of substantial losses under its bonds furnished for this project and has commenced an investigation.

On or about (*date*) you executed and furnished to (*surety*) your Agreement of Indemnity, a copy of which is enclosed herewith for your review. Pursuant to such Agreement, you agreed, among other things, to exonerate, indemnify and hold (*surety*) harmless from any and all liability for losses, costs, damages, attorneys fees and expenses of whatever kind which (*surety*) may sustain or incur by reason of having executed any and all bonds for or at the request of (*principal*). Due to the occurrence of the above-mentioned demands which have been made upon the bonds issued by (*surety*), we hereby request that you take all action that is necessary to exonerate and indemnify (surety) from and against

Exhibit 2.4 (continued)

any and all liabilities and losses which it may be exposed to as a result of the default of (*principal*).

Surety may retain the services of legal counsel for its own legal representation during the investigation and handling of the claim. You may not rely upon surety or its legal counsel for legal representation or legal advice. If you believe you require the services of any attorney, you should take the necessary steps to obtain representation.

Please contact the undersigned upon your receipt of this letter so that arrangements can be made for the honoring of your indemnity obligations. Your cooperation with regard to this matter will be appreciated.

Very truly yours,

(*Company Representative & Title*)

Exhibit 2.5

Construction Contract Claim Analysis Sheet

Claim Number ______________ Date ______________
Bond Number ______________

____
Principal (Name, Address and Telephone Number)

____
Company (Name, Address and Telephone Number)

____
Architect or Engineer (Name, Address and Telephone Number)

Amount of Contract $__________ Yes No Date
Per Bond Amount $__________ Job Completed
Payment Bond Amount $__________ Job Accepted
Combination Bond $__________ If Incomplete % Completed ______%
(attach copy of last estimate)
Last day principal was on job: ______ Scheduled Completion Date ______ Liquidated Damages ______

Contract Price $__________
Net Change Orders (+ or -)
(itemize on page 2) $__________
Adjusted Contract Price $__________
Amount Paid Contractor (-) $__________
CONTRACT BALANCE $__________
Retainage ______% $__________
Unearned Contract Bal. $__________

ESTIMATED COST TO COMPLETE
(Performance Bond)

Time needed to Complete ______ weeks ______ months
Direct Costs:
Labor cost for ______ weeks ______ months
(gross payroll) $__________
Fringe Benefits $__________
Insurance & Taxes etc. $__________
Balance due on Subcontracts $__________
(itemize on page 2)
Estimated Material Needed $__________
Equipment rental not included in
unpaid bills $__________
Equipment operating costs and
maintenance $__________
Total Direct Costs: $__________
Indirect Costs:
Office and shop salaries
for ______ weeks $__________
(gross payroll) $__________
General Overhead costs $__________
Fringe Benefits $__________
Insurance & Taxes, etc. $__________
Total Indirect Costs $__________
Contingency Allowance $__________
Total Cost to Complete $__________
Contract Balance $__________ $__________
Less Liquidated Damages, If any (-) $__________
Estimated (Deficit) Surplus of Cost to Complete $__________

Exhibit 2.5 (continued)

Claim Number ____________
Date ____________

ANALYSIS OF CHANGE ORDERS

Contract Price $____________

Change Orders $____________
Change Orders $____________
Change Orders $____________
Change Orders $____________
Total Change Orders $____________

Adjusted Contract Price $____________

EXPLANATION OF BENEFITS

SALVAGE

Name of Indemnitor	Address	Date of Notice

ANALYSIS OF SUBCONTRACTS

Subcontractor	Amt. of Subcontract	Change Order	Adjusted Contract	Paid to Date	Cont. Bal.

Exhibit 2.5 (continued)

ANALYSIS OF UNPAID MATERIAL ACCOUNTS

Name of Supplier	Type of Material	Last Delivery Date	Date Claim Received	Amount Due on Invoice

Exhibit 2.6

Surety Company Engagement Policy

PREAMBLE

The relationship between Surety and its outside counsel is a partnership managed and controlled by Surety that strives for the most effective and efficient resolution of legal matters that arise in the claims handling process. The goal of this Engagement Policy is to establish guidelines and improve communication between Surety and outside counsel regarding Surety's engagement of counsel for specific matters. The guidelines are intended to apply to situations that normally arise in litigation and claim matters, but Surety recognizes that in unusual or emergency situations, application of the guidelines may be impractical and exceptions may be necessary. The policy clarifies Surety's expectation that counsel provide Surety with advance notice of any unusual items that will appear on bills for legal services. We understand that many of the expectations included in the Engagement Policy are currently being met by outside counsel. However, Surety retains many outside legal professionals and we believe that a uniform policy will facilitate the communication process between attorney and client.

BUDGET AND PLAN OF ACTION

1. If it appears likely that legal fees for a matter will exceed $20,000.00, or that Surety faces a potential claim liability of $100,000.00 or more, your firm shall submit an initial budget estimating fees and costs along with a plan of action.
2. Your firm is to prepare its budget and plan of action as soon as practicable after Surety has assigned the matter to you.
3. The plan of action is to be as detailed as possible as to each function your firm will perform in order to accomplish its assignment. As much as feasible, the plan of action should also identify which individual within your firm will perform what function. If consultation between attorneys is necessary, the plan should set forth what consultation will be necessary, why such consultation is necessary and how it will benefit the Surety. Any exceptions to the Engagement Policy should be set forth in the plan.
4. In preparing the budget and plan of action for a matter in litigation, counsel will presume that the case will be tried. However, Surety recognizes that the overwhelming majority of the lawsuits in which it participates are settled or otherwise disposed of before trial. Accordingly, budgets and plans of action should focus on positioning a case for settlement or other disposition, including the use of motions for summary judgment and alternative dispute resolution. Plans

Exhibit 2.6 (continued)

of action should also state types and methods of discovery, including the identification of important witnesses and documents, which will be necessary to position the case for final resolution as soon as practicable.

5. Once Surety accepts your original proposed budget, your firm is not to incur charges in excess of the budget without first consulting us.

6. The budget and plan of action are to be updated whenever any major changes occur, but in any event, not less than once every six months. Surety expects your firm to provide these updates without reminder from us.

7. In considering your budget and plan of action, as well as throughout the course of your representation, Surety anticipates that you will weigh the respective values of settlement, alternative methods of dispute resolution, and litigation.

EXPENSES

1. Surety will reimburse your firm's expenses at your cost, except for the following certain disbursements that we will not pay unless agreed to by us in advance:

   a. secretarial or word processing services (normal, temporary, or overtime);
   b. photocopy expenses at more than 25 cents per page;
   c. any other staff charges, such as meals, "in-house" filing, etc. regardless of when incurred;

2. Photocopy costs in excess of $1,000.00 for a single job are to be authorized in advance by Surety. Large photocopying jobs are to be performed by a professional photocopy service if it will be more cost effective. Surety will pay the photocopy service's bills.

3. In deciding whether to transmit documents by regular mail, express mail, or facsimile, Surety expects your firm to consider the urgency of the transmittal along with the cost-effectiveness of each method of transmittal.

4. For facsimiles, the maximum Surety will reimburse your firm will be for its long distance telephone charges plus any actual costs charged to the firm by a third party. It is not necessary to follow every facsimile transmittal to Surety with an original sent through the mail. Surety expects your firm to use its judgment in deciding whether such a follow-up is needed.

5. Surety will pay no more than the local market rate for messenger delivery service.

6. Surety will not reimburse disbursements for local telephone expenses or office supplies.

7. Surety expects that travel expenses such as lodging, meals, and transportation shall be at reasonable rates and that your firm will exercise prudence in

Exhibit 2.6 (continued)

incurring such expenses. Surety will not reimburse the costs of first-class travel and expects that travel arrangements will take advantage of any cost-effective discounts or special rates.

8. Your firm must obtain written approval from Surety before retaining any consultant or expert in support of litigation on our behalf.

STAFFING

1. While Surety recognizes that staffing changes may be necessary from time to time, we will not pay for the learning time that may result from such a staffing change.
2. Surety expects your firm to consult with us before you undertake any extensive legal research, especially computer-based research such as Lexis or Westlaw. Research undertaken on Surety's behalf should be made available to Surety.
3. Surety requires consultation and approval before you change your billing rate or the personnel utilized in any matter on our behalf.
4. Surety expects that under most circumstances only one attorney from your firm will attend meetings, depositions, hearings and other proceedings other than trials.
5. Under most circumstances, Surety will pay only for the time of the lead attorney for intra-firm conferences, and for telephone conference calls with Surety.
6. Regarding air and rail travel, Surety recognizes that such may involve unproductive periods of time for an attorney. However, Surety also recognizes that in some cases, an attorney may be productive during such travel. Accordingly, Surety expects your firm to contact Surety, prior to undertaking such travel, to discuss and agree upon a reasonable method of compensation for unproductive travel time which is not within the attorney's control. Surety expects your firm to consult with us if you believe such travel by more than one attorney is necessary.
7. Under most circumstances the maximum number of hours Surety will pay per day for any individual, except during trial, is twelve (12).
8. Surety will not pay for the summarization of depositions unless your firm provides prior notification that such a charge will appear on the bill.

BILLING

1. Surety does not pay charges for time spent preparing bills.

Exhibit 2.6 (continued)

2. Surety recognizes the fact that the members of your firm have to meet certain deadlines for submitting items to be included on your bills. Within those constraints, Surety expects each of your bills to accurately reflect the fees and disbursements incurred during the bill's time period.

3. Surety requests that we receive your firm's bills at least quarterly. Upon review of the budget, Surety may determine that monthly billing is more appropriate.

4. Surety expects your firm to bill for its time in tenths of an hour.

5. Surety expects your firm's bills to include the following:

   a. an itemization of all disbursements and costs;
   b. a description of all legal research performed;
   c. daily entries stating the identity of the professional performing the task, his or her hourly rate, a description of the task performed, and the total amount of time he or she spent on the task;
   d. a summary of the total number of hours contributed by each professional.

6. Surety expects that, with respect to intra firm conferences and telephone calls, your firm's bill will identify the persons involved and describe the content of the conversation.

7. Surety reserves the right to review or audit your firm's receipts and other documentation of charges.

Exhibit 2.7

Consultant's Budget

PROJECT	*NAME ENGINEER PROJECT MANAGER CONSTRUCTION MANAGER	FEE/HR.
I.	**INITIAL EVALUATION**	*
	Site Visit	(HRS.)
	Book and Record Review	* (HRS.)
	Project Budget, Analysis & Planning	* (HRS.)
	Total Initial Evaluation	$__________
II.	**REPORT PREPARATION**	
	Cost to Complete Estimates	* (HRS.)
	Verify Contract Balances	* (HRS.)
	Preparation of Bid Package	* (HRS.)
	Miscellaneous/Other Describe:	* (HRS.)
	Total Report Preparation	$__________
III.	**OTHER BUDGET ITEMS TO BE BUDGETED AS NEEDED**	
	Latent Defects	* (HRS.)
	Expert Testimony	* (HRS.)

Exhibit 2.7 (continued)

Assist in Claim Against Obligee	* (HRS.)	
Review Payment Bond Claims (if authorized)	* (HRS.)	
Evaluate Suits Against Other Professionals	* (HRS.)	
Periodic Site Visits	* (HRS.)	
Total other items	$________	

IV. **MISCELLANEOUS**

Costs/Additional Charges		$
Copies Per Page	$________	$
Local Messenger Rate	$________	$
Contingencies		$
Travel		$
Expert Help		$
Total Miscellaneous		$________

BUDGET SUMMARY

Initial Evaluation	$________
Report Preparation	$________
Other Budget Items	$________
Miscellaneous	$________

Exhibit 4.1

Joint Control Trust Account Agreement

This Joint Control Trust Account Agreement ("Agreement") is made and entered into this ___ day of _________, 19___, by and among _________ ______________________________ (hereinafter referred to as the "Principal"), and ____ (hereinafter referred to collectively as the "Indemnitors"), and ____________________________ (hereinafter referred to as the "Surety").

RECITALS

WHEREAS, on or about _______________________, the Principal and the Indemnitors executed an Agreement of Indemnity with the Surety (the "Agreement of Indemnity"), a copy of which is attached hereto as **Exhibit 1**;

WHEREAS, the Principal has entered into various construction contracts (the "Contracts") with various entities (the "Obligees") for the construction of various projects (the "Projects") as more fully set forth in a List of the Contracts and Bonds attached hereto as **Exhibit 2;**

WHEREAS, as required by the Contracts, and induced by and in reliance upon the execution of the Agreement of Indemnity by the Principal and the Indemnitors, the Surety executed certain Performance Bonds and Labor and Material Payment Bonds (the "Bonds") as more fully set forth in Exhibit 2;

WHEREAS, the Principal and the Indemnitors hereby acknowledge their execution of the Agreement of Indemnity and reaffirm their joint and several obligations and liabilities to the Surety thereunder;

WHEREAS, the Contracts are in various stages of completion, and the Principal and the Indemnitors hereby acknowledge and admit that: (a) the Principal is financially unable to perform or complete the performance of the Contracts; (b) certain subcontractors and suppliers of labor and/or materials with respect to the Contracts and Projects have not been paid; (c) the Principal has requested the financial assistance of the Surety as a result of (a) and (b) above; and (d) but for the willingness of the Surety to enter into this Agreement, the Principal is unable to complete the performance of the Contracts and pay its subcontractors and suppliers of labor and/or materials with respect to the Contracts and Projects; and

WHEREAS, in order to specifically perform their obligations and duties to the Surety under the Agreement of Indemnity and the Bonds, the Principal and the Indemnitors are willing to execute this Agreement.

Exhibit 4.1 (continued)

AGREEMENT

NOW, THEREFORE, for and in consideration of these premises and other good and valuable considerations, the receipt and sufficiency of which is hereby acknowledged, it is hereby mutually understood and agreed by and among the Principal, the Indemnitors and the Surety as follows:

I. Indemnification

1. The Principal and the Indemnitors hereby acknowledge their execution of the Agreement of Indemnity and reaffirm their joint and several obligations and liabilities to the Surety thereunder.

2. Nothing contained in this Agreement and done pursuant hereto shall in any way impair, alter or modify any and/or all of the rights and remedies of the Surety against the Principal and/or the Indemnitors under or in connection with the Agreement of Indemnity.

3. In the event that the Surety makes any payments under the Bonds, or in accordance with the terms of this Agreement or the Agreement of Indemnity, interest shall run at the rate of 10% per annum on the amounts paid by the Surety, compounded monthly from the date of each payment by the Surety. Any reimbursements made by the Principal or the Indemnitors to the Surety shall be first applied to any and all expenses incurred by the Surety as provided in the Agreement of Indemnity, then to interest which has accrued on the payments made or losses incurred by the Surety, and then to the principal amounts of the payments or losses.

4. To secure the obligations of the Principal and the Indemnitors to the Surety pursuant to the terms of the Agreement of Indemnity and this Agreement, the Principal and the Indemnitors hereby grant to the Surety a security interest and lien in all of the real and personal property more fully described in the List of Collateral (the "Collateral") attached hereto as **Exhibit 3,** including but not limited to any and all monies loaned or advanced by the Surety to the Principal or otherwise as provided in accordance with the provisions of this Agreement. The Principal and the Indemnitors shall execute a sufficient number of financing statements under the Uniform Commercial Code (UCC Form 1) in order for the Surety to perfect its security interests and liens in the Collateral. Furthermore, the Principal and the Indemnitors agree to execute such other and further instruments or documents reasonably required or deemed necessary by the Surety to confirm, perfect or otherwise establish the liens, security interests and rights granted in the Collateral to the Surety under this Agreement.

Exhibit 4.1 (continued)

5. As part of this Agreement, and with the consent and approval of the Indemnitors, the Principal shall execute voluntary letters of default and termination (the "Letters of Default") addressed to the Obligees for each of the Contracts and Projects shown on the List of the Contracts and Bonds attached as Exhibit 2, a sample copy of which is attached hereto as **Exhibit 4.** In accordance with the terms of the Agreement of Indemnity and this Agreement, the Surety may use the Letters of Default on each Contract and Project, individually as to each separate Contract or as to all of the Contracts, in the sole option and discretion of the Surety, whether or not there is a default under any of the Contracts, the Agreement of Indemnity or this Agreement, or whether or not this Agreement has been terminated by the Surety.

II. Establishment of Joint Control Trust Checking Account

1. The Principal and the Surety shall open and establish a joint control trust checking account (the "Trust Account") in ______________________________ (the "Bank") in the name of "____(the Principal)____ Trust Account for ____(the Surety)____" in accordance with a Trust Account Agreement, a copy of which is attached hereto as **Exhibit 5**. The Principal authorizes the Bank to establish the Trust Account. The Principal shall not open any other trust account(s) without the express knowledge and consent of the Surety.

2. For the purposes of this Agreement, "Contract Funds" shall mean any and all monies payable to or received by the Principal under or in connection with the Contracts, including but not limited to monies earned and to be earned, payment of retained percentages and final payments due or to become due to the Principal of every kind or nature under the Contracts, including payments for all extras, claims, bonuses and/or of any other kind or nature which may be received by the Principal from the Contracts.

3. The Principal, with the agreement of the Surety and the Indemnitors, shall execute Letters of Direction addressed to the Obligees, a sample copy of which is attached hereto as **Exhibit 6**, directing that all Contract Funds from the Contracts be made payable jointly to the Principal and the Surety, and mailed to the Surety at ____

____

attention: ____.

4. The Principal, the Indemnitors and the Surety agree to deposit or cause to be deposited in the Trust Account all Contract Funds from the Contracts collected by the Principal or the Surety, and all monies which the Surety may, in its sole discretion and/or in accordance with the terms and conditions of this Agreement or the Agreement of Indemnity, advance or loan to the Principal. The

Exhibit 4.1 (continued)

Principal and the Indemnitors acknowledge and agree that all funds on deposit in the Trust Account are the sole property of the Surety. The Contract Funds shall not be deposited in any other account of the Principal.

5. Pursuant to the Assignment and the Power of Attorney attached hereto and incorporated herein by reference as **Exhibit 7**, the Surety, through its authorized representatives, is authorized and empowered to endorse in the name of the Principal any and all checks received by the Surety or its representatives constituting Contract Funds from the Contracts, and to deposit said checks solely and only into the Trust Account. The Principal hereby agrees that the Surety may name one or more substitutes for the attorneys named in the Power of Attorney, with notice to the Principal. Furthermore, the Principal hereby ratifies and confirms all acts that any attorney or his substitute or substitutes may lawfully do or cause to be done by virtue of the Power of Attorney contained in Exhibit 7.

6. The Contract Funds are hereby irrevocably segregated, earmarked and set aside solely and only for the purposes set forth in this Agreement. The Contract Funds and all other monies deposited in the Trust Account shall be considered and constituted as trust funds for the purposes set forth in this Agreement. The Principal shall hold all Contract Funds in the Trust Account in trust for the Surety separate and apart from all other funds and property of the Principal. The Principal hereby covenants and agrees that it will not knowingly permit any funds in the Trust Account, whether represented by checks, vouchers, orders or otherwise, to be used for any purpose other than as more particularly set forth in this Agreement.

7. Except as provided in Section IV, paragraph 2, all checks and charges against the Trust Account shall be required to have two signatures, one signature being that of an authorized representative of the Principal and the other by an authorized representative of the Surety. The Principal and the Surety mutually agree that they will work in conjunction with the Bank to establish such other means and methods of transferring funds from the Trust Account so long as such means or methods require the consent of both the Principal and the Surety for any withdrawal or transfer of funds from the Trust Account. The Principal is restricted from making any wire transfers, use of counter-checks or other non-check transfers from the Trust Account without the express written approval of the Surety.

8. The persons now designated to countersign checks or approve transfers on the Trust Account on behalf of the Surety are any one of the following: ____.

It is understood and agreed that the Surety may, in its sole discretion, substitute or add another representative or representatives for the persons originally named, without the prior consent of, but upon notice to the Principal and the Bank.

Exhibit 4.1 (continued)

9. The persons now designated to countersign checks or approve transfers on the Trust Account on behalf of the Principal are: ____________________

____.

It is understood and agreed that the Principal may substitute or add another representative or representatives for the persons originally named, but only with the approval in writing of the Surety and the Indemnitors, and upon notice to the Bank.

10. The Principal hereby agrees that any Contract Funds it may receive contrary to the Letters of Direction sent to the Obligees (see sample attached as Exhibit 6) or because of the Principal's failure to promptly issue such Letters of Direction or for any other reason shall be held as trust funds by the Principal and shall be immediately presented to a representative of the Surety for deposit in the Trust Account.

11. The Principal shall maintain possession of the checkbook for the Trust Account. However, the Surety shall receive directly from the Bank all bank statements and the originals of all deposit slips, canceled checks, debit memos, service charges, etc. from the Trust Account. The Principal hereby authorizes the Bank to furnish to the Surety such information as the Surety may desire concerning deposits to and withdrawals from the Trust Account. The Principal also authorizes the Obligees to furnish to the Surety complete information concerning payments made to the Principal of Contract Funds from the Contracts and to furnish any other information concerning the Contracts which the Surety may require. Upon request from the Principal, the Surety shall furnish to the Principal copies of all bank statements and checks which have been returned.

12. None of the Contract Funds deposited in the Trust Account shall be subject to any right of set-off by the Bank as a result of any transactions involving the Bank, the Principal and/or the Indemnitors, nor be assigned or diverted from the uses or purposes set forth in this Agreement. The Surety may require of the Bank a written acknowledgment of this paragraph as a condition to the establishment or continuance of the Trust Account at the Bank.

III. Use of the Contract Funds from the Trust Account

1. The Contract Funds contained in the Trust Account shall be used solely for the payment of all labor and material costs, including amounts due to subcontractors and suppliers and for rental of equipment from others which is actually used in the prosecution of the work under the Contracts, incurred by the Principal, and the Principal's subcontractors and suppliers, which are necessary to complete the work under the Contracts and for which the Surety may become liable under the Bonds. The Principal agrees that it will not use or rent any of

Exhibit 4.1 (continued)

its equipment or machinery in any manner which will interfere with or delay the prompt completion of the Contracts. It is specifically understood and agreed by the Principal, the Indemnitors and the Surety that the Contract Funds contained in the Trust Account shall not be used to pay the obligations of the Principal on contracts not bonded by the Surety.

2. The Surety is not obligated to pay or cause to be paid any of the overhead and general and administrative expenses of the Principal. The Surety, at its option and sole discretion, may consent to the use of funds from the Trust Account to pay all or a portion of the Principal's overhead and general and administrative expenses. The Principal acknowledges, agrees and consents that the Surety reserves the right to reject the payment of any bill(s) requested by the Principal pursuant to the procedures described below if the Surety deems, in its sole discretion, that the requested payment or payments are for the overhead and general and administrative expenses of the Principal.

3. On a monthly basis, the Principal shall provide to the Surety a budget of its anticipated revenues from the Contracts and estimated expenses for labor, materials, subcontractor payments and any other payments, including the overhead and general and administrative expenses described in Section III, paragraph 2 above, that the Principal anticipates will be requested from the Trust Account.

4. Absent other mutually agreeable arrangements which must be reduced to a written document between and among the Principal, the Indemnitors and the Surety, the procedure for the payment of the Principal's bills on the Contracts, including its direct payroll, shall be as follows:

(a) On a weekly basis or as otherwise required, the Principal shall provide to the representative of the Surety the following information:

(i) A summary sheet listing all of the invoices to be paid, broken down by Contract, showing the person to be paid, the amount to be paid, the date of the check, the check number and the total payments to all payees. The Principal shall designate on the summary sheet those invoices it believes should receive priority for payment in the event that the Contract Funds in the Trust Account are insufficient to pay all of the invoices submitted for payment. The Principal shall sign off its approval of the summary sheet and the payments described therein;

(ii) A copy of each invoice to be paid, showing the Contract for which the invoice was incurred, along with a copy of all necessary supporting documentation for the invoice;

(iii) A check drawn on the Trust Account, said check clearly indicating the specific invoices being paid and the Contracts for which the invoices are being paid, and signed by an authorized signator of checks for the Principal drawn on the Trust Account;

Exhibit 4.1 (continued)

(iv) If requested by the Surety, a partial waiver and release in a form acceptable to the Surety in the amount of the check, which must be signed by the payee and returned to the Surety; and

(v) A stamped envelope addressed to the payee of the check drawn to pay the invoice.

(b) The Principal represents and warrants that all invoices shown on the summary sheet and all checks from the Trust Account presented to the Surety's representative are for the purposes authorized by Section III., paragraph 1 of this Agreement, and that the amount of any such invoice and/or check is currently due and owing to the payee named therein.

(c) The representative of the Surety shall review all of the invoices and back-up information provided above and sign off his or her approval on the summary sheet for all of the invoices that the Surety agrees are to be paid from the Trust Account. The representative of the Surety shall not be obligated to pay or approve the payment of invoices according to the priorities designated by the Principal on the summary sheet. The representative of the Surety shall receive from the Principal for the Surety's records an originally signed copy of the summary sheet along with a copy of the invoice and the backup information, said records to be kept and maintained by the representative of the Surety.

(d) In the event that there are Contract Funds sufficient in the Trust Account to cover those payments which have been approved, the representative of the Surety shall sign the checks drawn on the Trust Account on behalf of the Surety, and mail the checks, and the partial waiver and release forms if required, to the named payees in the above described stamped and addressed envelopes. Any check from the Trust Account not approved by the Surety for payment shall be voided by the Surety's representative.

(e) It is expressly understood by the Principal and the Indemnitors that should the Surety or its representative disapprove any payments requested by the Principal or refuse to countersign any check drawn on the Trust Account, such decision is final as to the Principal and the Indemnitors, and the Principal and the Indemnitors shall have no right or cause of action of any kind or nature against the Surety, its agents, employees, attorneys or representatives as a result of such disapproval.

(f) In the event that the Contract Funds in the Trust Account are insufficient to cover those payments which have been requested by the Principal and approved by the representative of the Surety, the Surety reserves the right, in its sole option and discretion, to advance monies, loan monies or otherwise fund the Principal or the Trust Account. Any such advances to, loans to or funding of the Principal or the Trust Account by the Surety shall be at the written request of the Principal, and signed by a representative of the Principal. In the event that the Surety

Exhibit 4.1 (continued)

advances to, loans to or otherwise funds the Principal or the Trust Account at the request of the Principal:

(i) Any such advances to, loans to or funding of the Principal or the Trust Account by the Surety shall be conclusively presumed to be a loss to the Surety, notwithstanding the use or misuse of such advances or loans by the Principal, for which the Principal and the Indemnitors obligated to indemnify the Surety in accordance with the terms of the Agreement of Indemnity and this Agreement;

(ii) All monies advanced to, loaned to or otherwise used to fund the Principal or the Trust Account by the Surety shall constitute and be deemed trust funds in accordance with the terms of this Agreement; and

(iii) Any such advances to, loans to or funding of the Principal or the Trust Account by the Surety shall also be deemed to be a payment by the Surety under its Bonds for which interest shall run in accordance with the provisions of Section I, paragraph 3 of this Agreement.

In the event that the Surety refuses to advance monies, loan monies or otherwise fund the Principal or the Trust Account, the Surety may, in its sole discretion, send only such checks drawn on the Trust Account to the payees as the Surety deems necessary and expedient under the circumstances.

(g) On a weekly basis, the Principal shall provide to the representative of the Surety for approval the payroll for the Contracts bonded by the Surety for the Principal (the "Payroll"), broken down by Contract, including the net pay for each employee, taxes to be withheld, and all other deductions. In the event that there are sufficient Contract Funds in the Trust Account, upon the approval by the Surety of the Payroll of the Principal, the Principal and the Surety shall take all steps necessary to fund the presently existing payroll account of the Principal from the Trust Account. It shall be the responsibility of the Principal to present the net Payroll checks to its employees directly rather than through the representative of the Surety.

(h) Payment of all withholding and payroll taxes and other amounts deducted from employee wages from the Contracts bonded by the Surety for the Principal from the date of this Agreement forward shall be made on a priority basis directly from the Trust Account to the appropriate payee(s) for all withholding and payroll taxes and other normal payroll burden expenses. It shall be the responsibility of the Principal, within the time limits of all appropriate statutes and regulations, to prepare and present to the representative of the Surety the necessary information to pay all such taxes and other deductions from the Payroll, including the appropriate check(s) from the Trust Account and an envelope addressed to the appropriate payee(s) or with an appropriate deposit slip to the correct account to receive the appropriate check(s). Upon receipt of the above documentation,

Exhibit 4.1 (continued)

and to the extent there are sufficient Contract Funds in the Trust Account, the Surety shall promptly release the check(s) from the Trust Account for payment of such Payroll taxes and deductions.

5. The Surety and the representative(s) of the Surety shall incur no liability to the Principal or to any other person in connection with the due discharge of their duties under this Agreement.

IV. Termination

1. The Surety shall have the right, at any time in its sole option and discretion, to terminate this Agreement, whether or not the Principal is in default under the terms of any of the Contracts, the Agreement of Indemnity or this Agreement.

2. Whether or not this Agreement is terminated by the Surety, the Principal and the Indemnitors hereby authorize any two of the signators of the Surety on the Trust Account to countersign one or more checks from the Trust Account and to withdraw all or a portion of the trust funds from the Trust Account. Furthermore, at the time of the execution of this Agreement, ten (10) checks drawn on the Trust Account, blank with respect to date and amount, made payable to the Surety and signed by the representative of the Principal, shall be placed in the hands of the authorized representative of the Surety. The Surety, at its sole option and discretion, whether or not this Agreement is terminated, is authorized by the Principal and the Indemnitors to: (a) insert the date and amount on such check for the whole or any part of the trust funds on deposit in the Trust Account; (b) countersign said check and receive the proceeds thereof; and (c) use said checks at the sole option and discretion of the Surety at anytime it deems it in the best interest of the Surety alone to do so, without notice to the other parties to this Agreement, which rights shall be unquestioned, final and conclusive. The Principal and the Indemnitors hereby expressly waive any and all legal or equitable rights, and any claim for damages, as a result of the Surety exercising its rights under this paragraph.

V. Miscellaneous Provisions

1. This Agreement shall be construed and governed by the laws of the State of _____________, exclusive of the __________ conflict of law rules, and shall bind the heirs, personal representatives, assignees and successors in interests of the parties hereto.

2. The Principal, the Indemnitors and the Surety hereby represent, covenant and warrant that they have full right, power and authority, uninhibited by contract

Exhibit 4.1 (continued)

or otherwise, to execute and perform this Agreement, that the Principal and the Surety have been duly authorized by all proper and necessary corporate action, and that all consents and approvals of stockholders or of any public authority or regulatory body required as a condition to the validity or enforceability of this Agreement against the Principal and the Surety have been obtained. Furthermore, the Principal, the Indemnitors and the Surety hereby represent, covenant and warrant that the execution of this Agreement and the full performance of this Agreement will not result in the breach of or default under any agreement to which they may be a party.

3. THE PRINCIPAL AND THE INDEMNITORS HEREBY ACKNOWLEDGE AND AGREE THAT THE SURETY HAS NO OBLIGATION TO FUND THE TRUST ACCOUNT, PROVIDE FINANCIAL ASSISTANCE TO THE PRINCIPAL IN ANY MANNER OR METHOD, OR MAKE ANY PAYMENTS OTHER THAN THOSE PAYMENTS FOR WHICH THE SURETY HAS SPECIFICALLY AGREED TO MAKE PURSUANT TO THE TERMS OF THIS AGREEMENT. THE PRINCIPAL AND THE INDEMNITORS SPECIFICALLY ACKNOWLEDGE AND AGREE THAT THEIR EXECUTION OF THIS AGREEMENT HAS NOT BEEN INDUCED BY OR MADE IN RELIANCE UPON ANY ORAL OR WRITTEN REPRESENTATIONS BY THE SURETY OR ITS AGENTS, EMPLOYEES, ATTORNEYS OR CONSULTANTS THAT THE SURETY WILL FUND THE TRUST ACCOUNT OR PROVIDE ANY FINANCIAL ASSISTANCE TO THE PRINCIPAL. IN THE EVENT THAT THE SURETY AGREES TO FUND THE TRUST ACCOUNT, PROVIDE FINANCIAL ASSISTANCE TO THE PRINCIPAL IN ANY MANNER OR METHOD, OR MAKE ANY PAYMENTS OTHER THAN THOSE PAYMENTS FOR WHICH THE SURETY HAS SPECIFICALLY AGREED TO MAKE PURSUANT TO THE TERMS OF THIS AGREEMENT, SAID ACTION SHALL BE IN THE SOLE JUDGMENT, OPTION AND DISCRETION OF THE SURETY AND IN THE BEST INTERESTS OF THE SURETY AND NOT THE PRINCIPAL OR THE INDEMNITORS. FURTHERMORE, THE SURETY's AGREEMENT TO TAKE ANY SUCH ACTION DOES NOT BIND AND COMMIT THE SURETY TO ANY OTHER FUNDING OF THE TRUST ACCOUNT, PROVIDING OF FINANCIAL ASSISTANCE, OR MAKING OF ANY PAYMENTS OTHER THAN THOSE PAYMENTS FOR WHICH THE SURETY HAS SPECIFICALLY AGREED TO MAKE PURSUANT TO THE TERMS OF THIS AGREEMENT.

4. THE EXECUTION OF THIS AGREEMENT BY THE SURETY IN NO MANNER BINDS THE SURETY TO EXECUTE ANY FUTURE BOND OR BONDS ON BEHALF OF THE PRINCIPAL. THE PRINCIPAL AND THE

Exhibit 4.1 (continued)

INDEMNITORS SPECIFICALLY ACKNOWLEDGE AND AGREE THAT THEIR EXECUTION OF THIS AGREEMENT HAS NOT BEEN INDUCED BY OR MADE IN RELIANCE UPON ANY ORAL OR WRITTEN REPRESENTATIONS BY THE SURETY OR ITS AGENTS, EMPLOYEES, ATTORNEYS OR CONSULTANTS THAT THE SURETY WILL EXECUTE ANY FUTURE BOND OR BONDS ON BEHALF OF THE PRINCIPAL. IN THE EVENT THAT THE SURETY EXECUTES ANY FUTURE BOND OR BONDS ON BEHALF OF THE PRINCIPAL, ANY SUCH BOND SHALL BE DEEMED INCLUDED IN THE LIST OF CONTRACTS AND BONDS ATTACHED HERETO AS EXHIBIT 2 AND SHALL BE SUBJECT TO THE TERMS AND PROVISIONS OF THIS AGREEMENT. THE EXECUTION OF BONDS BY THE SURETY FOR THE PRINCIPAL WHILE THIS AGREEMENT IS IN EFFECT SHALL BE IN THE SOLE JUDGMENT, OPTION AND DISCRETION OF THE SURETY, PURSUANT TO ITS UNDERWRITING POLICIES AND PROCEDURES, AND SHALL BE IN THE BEST INTERESTS OF THE SURETY AND NOT THE PRINCIPAL. THE AGREEMENT BY THE SURETY TO EXECUTE ANY ONE BOND IN ACCORDANCE WITH THIS PARAGRAPH DOES NOT BIND AND COMMIT THE SURETY TO EXECUTE ANY OTHER BOND OR BONDS AT THE REQUEST OF THE PRINCIPAL.

5. The Principal shall maintain accurate books, records and accounts showing clearly, among other things, the itemized receipts and disbursements allocable to the Contracts. The books, records and accounts shall be available for examination by the Surety and its representatives at the Principal's principal office at all times during regular business hours. The Surety is entitled to receive copies of all bank account records of any and all accounts of the Principal, including but not limited to the Trust Account, of any kind or nature, including canceled checks, bank statements, deposit slips, debit memos, etc.

6. The Principal hereby authorizes the Surety and its representative(s), including attorneys, accountants, consultants or employees, to visit at any time the job site of the Contracts, to obtain at any time access to all job records and personnel of the Principal to determine the status of the progress on the Contracts, and to obtain at any time any and all other information and documentation with respect to the Contracts deemed necessary in the sole discretion of the Surety and/or its representative(s).

7. The Principal agrees to use its best efforts to complete the Contracts on a timely basis.

8. It is further agreed that this Agreement is solely for the benefit of the parties hereto and shall not create any rights in any person not a party hereto, or in any way increase the rights of third persons, or increase the obligations of

Exhibit 4.1 (continued)

any party hereto to any third person, or increase the liability or obligations of the Surety under its Bonds.

9. The terms and provisions of the Agreement of Indemnity shall remain in full force and effect. Nothing contained in this Agreement shall in any way prejudice or waive the legal and equitable rights of subrogation of the Surety. The rights of the Surety under this Agreement are in addition to, and not in lieu of, any of the rights which the Surety may have against the Principal or any other parties, including the Indemnitors, at law, in equity or by the terms of any other agreement, including the Agreement of Indemnity. All rights of the Surety pursuant to the Agreement of Indemnity and this Agreement shall inure to the benefit of the Surety, its co-sureties, if any, and its and their reinsurers.

10. The Principal agrees to provide its full and complete cooperation to the Surety in any and all future litigation involving the Contracts and the Bonds.

11. It is agreed and understood by the Principal, the Indemnitors and the Surety that there have been no oral or other agreements of any kind whatsoever as a condition precedent or to induce the execution and delivery of this Agreement by any party hereto. It is further agreed that no change, addition or amendment shall be made herein or to any of the terms, covenants or conditions hereto except by writing, signed by the parties to this Agreement.

12. In the event that one or more provisions of this Agreement shall be declared to be invalid, illegal or unenforceable in any respect, unless such invalidity, illegality or unenforceability shall be tantamount to a failure of consideration, the validity, legality and enforceability of the remaining provisions contained in this Agreement shall not in any way be affected or impaired thereby.

13. Except as otherwise specifically provided herein, or as specifically and subsequently agreed to by the parties in writing, all notices, requests or other communications required or permitted to be given hereunder shall be deemed duly given if mailed by the United States mail, postage prepaid and addressed as follows:

To the Principal and the Indemnitors:

____

____

____

____

Exhibit 4.1 (continued)

With a copy to:

____
____
____
____

To the Surety:

____
____
____
____

With a copy to:

____
____
____
____

14. It is further understood and agreed by the Principal and the Indemnitors that this Agreement shall be construed without any regard to any presumption or other rule requiring construction against the party causing this Agreement, or any Exhibits attached to this Agreement, to be drafted.

15. This Agreement may be executed in one or more counterparts, each of which shall be deemed to be an original.

IN WITNESS WHEREOF, the parties have executed this Agreement on the date indicated above, and each of the undersigned personally represent and warrant that they have the full right, power and authority to execute this Agreement on behalf of the respective parties.

ATTEST	PRINCIPAL
__________________________	__________________________
	By: __________________, President

Exhibit 4.1 (continued)

INDEMNITORS

________________________ ________________________

________________________ ________________________

SURETY

________________________ ________________________

By: ____________________

Exhibit 4.1.2

LIST OF THE CONTRACTS AND BONDS

Exhibit 2

Attached hereto and incorporated herein by reference as Attachment A is a list of all or substantially all of the Performance Bonds and Labor and Material Payment Bonds executed by the Surety on behalf of the Principal.

The fact that any bond or bonds executed by the Surety on behalf of the Principal have been left off of or inadvertently omitted from the list attached as Attachment A does not absolve the signers of the Agreement from any liability for any losses paid by the Surety as described in the Agreement for any such bonds, and the signers of the Agreement agree to be bound to the Surety for each such bond or bonds as if it or they had been included in the list attached as Attachment A. It is the intent of Exhibit 2 and Attachment A to include all of the bonds executed by the Surety on behalf of the Principal.

Furthermore, in the event that the Surety should, now or in the future, execute any bond or bonds on behalf of the Principal for any reason whatsoever, it is the intention of the parties to the Agreement that such future bond or bonds shall be deemed to be included in Attachment A to Exhibit 2, whether listed or not, as if said bond or bonds had, in fact, been listed in Attachment A to Exhibit 2, and said future bond or bonds shall be included within the terms of the Agreement between the parties.

Exhibit 4.1.3

LIST OF COLLATERAL

Exhibit 3

As Collateral for this Agreement and the Agreement of Indemnity executed by the Principal and the Indemnitors, the Principal and the Indemnitors grant, convey and assign to the Surety a lien on the real property and a security interest in all of the personal property more fully described below and in the Attachments to this List of Collateral.

1. All of the Principal's right, title and interest in and to all accounts, accounts receivable, contract rights and other similar rights in all contracts of the Principal, whether bonded by the Surety, bonded by a surety other than the Surety, or unbonded. The security interest granted by the Principal to the Surety shall attach to all existing contracts of the Principal, whether bonded by the Surety, bonded by a surety other than the Surety, or unbonded, including but not limited to those contracts listed in Attachment A to Exhibit 3, along with all after executed and acquired contracts of the Principal, whether bonded by the Surety, bonded by a surety other than the Surety, or unbonded, including the proceeds and products thereof.

2. All of the Principal's right, title and interest in and to all machinery, equipment, plant, tools, inventory and materials which are now or may hereafter be utilized in connection with any of the Contracts or Projects regardless of whether located at the Project site(s), in transit, in storage or elsewhere, including the proceeds and products thereof.

3. All of the Principal's right, title and interest in and to all subcontracts and purchase orders let or to be let in connection with any of the Contracts or Projects, and in and to all surety bonds supporting such subcontracts and purchase orders, including the proceeds and products thereof.

4. All of the Principal's right, title and interest in and to any actions, causes of action, claims or demands whatsoever which the Principal may have or acquire against any party to the Contracts, or any actions, causes of action, claims or demands whatsoever arising out of or in connection with any of the Contracts or Projects, including but not limited to those against obligees, design professionals, subcontractors, laborers or materialmen, and against any of their sureties, including the proceeds and products thereof.

5. All of the Principal's right, title and interest in and to any monies due or to become due under any policy of insurance relating to any claims arising out of the performance of any of the Contracts or Projects, including but not limited to claims under builder's risk, fire, employee dishonesty or worker's

Exhibit 4.1.3 (continued)

compensation insurance policies, including premium refunds, and including the proceeds and products thereof.

6. All proceeds of any claim, suit, settlement or judgment against ____ or any related entity, wherever instituted, prosecuted or obtained, all as reflected in an Assignment of Judgment to be executed by the Principal in favor of the Surety, a copy of which is attached hereto as Attachment B to Exhibit 3, including the proceeds and products thereof.

7. All fixtures or property to be affixed as a fixture to the real property commonly known as ________________________________, whether now existing or hereinafter arising, including the proceeds and products thereof.

8. A Mortgage from the Principal on certain real property located at ____, a copy of which is attached hereto as Attachment C to Exhibit 3.

9. A Mortgage from the Indemnitors on certain real property located at ________________________, a copy of which is attached hereto as Attachment D to Exhibit 3.

The Surety shall have all of the rights and remedies of a secured party under the Uniform Commercial Code in effect in the state in which the personal property is located.

The Collateral shall be properly insured by the Principal and the Indemnitors until the Surety's security interest and lien rights are terminated. Such policies shall be payable to both the Surety and the Principal and/or the Indemnitors as their interests may appear. The Principal and the Indemnitors shall furnish the Surety with certificates or other evidence satisfactory to the Surety in compliance with the foregoing insurance provisions.

The Principal and the Indemnitors shall execute alone or with the Surety any financing statement required by the Uniform Commercial Code and necessary to perfect the security interest in any of the Collateral described herein.

The Surety may, at any reasonable time, enter upon the premises of the Principal and/or the Indemnitors to inspect the Collateral and the books and records of the Principal and the Indemnitors pertaining to the Collateral or its proceeds, and the Principal and the Indemnitors shall assist the Surety in making such an inspection.

The rights of the Surety against the Collateral shall be governed by the terms of the Agreement to which this Exhibit 3 is attached. The Surety may delay or refrain from exercising any past, present or future right or remedy hereunder without waiving any such right or remedy, and no waiver by the Surety of any

Exhibit 4.1.3 (continued)

default shall operate as a waiver of any other default or the same default on a future occasion.

All of the rights of the Surety hereunder shall inure to the benefit of its successors and assigns.

PRINCIPAL

____________________ ____________________
Witness By: ________________

INDEMNITORS

____________________ ____________________
Witness

____________________ ____________________
Witness

SURETY

____________________ ____________________
Witness By: ________________

Exhibit 4.1.4

VOLUNTARY LETTER OF DEFAULT AND TERMINATION

Exhibit 4

[Principal's Letterhead]

[Date]

To: Obligee

____

____

____

RE: Principal: __________________________
Obligee: ___________________________
Contract and Project: _______________
Bond No.: _________________________
Surety: ____________________________

Dear Sir:

This is to advise you that the Principal, ______________________________, the contractor on the above-referenced construction Project, is financially unable to perform or complete the performance of the work or comply with its contractual obligations on the above Project, and is in default under the above Contract for the Project. Therefore, the Principal hereby irrevocably and voluntarily abandons and terminates the above construction Contract effective upon your receipt of this letter. The Surety for the Principal, _______________, will be in contact with you within a short period of time to discuss this matter.

Very truly yours,

PRINCIPAL

By: ____________________________, President

c.c. Surety

Exhibit 4.1.5

TRUST ACCOUNT AGREEMENT

Exhibit 5

THIS TRUST ACCOUNT AGREEMENT (the "Agreement") is made and entered into this _____ day of ____________________, 19____, by and among ____ (the "Principal"), and ____ (the "Surety"), and ______________________________________ (the "Bank").

RECITALS

WHEREAS, the Principal has entered into various construction contracts (the "Contracts") with various entities (the "Obligees") for the construction of various projects (the "Projects") as more fully set forth in a List of the Contracts and Bonds attached hereto as **Exhibit 1;**

WHEREAS, as required by the Contracts, and induced by and in reliance upon the execution of a General Agreement of Indemnity, the Surety executed certain Performance Bonds and Labor and Material Payment Bonds (the "Bonds") as more fully set forth in Exhibit 1; and

WHEREAS, the Surety has agreed to furnish certain assistance to the Principal, including financial assistance, upon the establishment of a joint control trust checking account with the Bank.

NOW, THEREFORE, in consideration of the premises, the undersigned have agreed and do agree as follows:

1. The Principal and the Surety shall open and establish a joint control trust checking account (the "Trust Account") in the Bank in the name of "_____(the Principal)_____ Trust Account for _____(the Surety)_____." The Principal authorizes the Bank to establish the Trust Account.

2. For the purposes of this Agreement, "Contract Funds" shall mean any and all monies payable to or received by the Principal under or in connection with the Contracts, including but not limited to monies earned and to be earned, payment of retained percentages and final payments due or to become due to the Principal of every kind or nature under the Contracts, including payments for all extras, claims, bonuses and/or any other kind or nature which may be received by the Principal from the Contracts.

3. The Principal and the Surety agree to deposit or cause to be deposited in the Trust Account all Contract Funds from the Contracts, whether held in hand by the Principal as of the date of this Agreement or subsequent thereto

Exhibit 4.1.5 (continued)

representing Contract Funds collected by the Principal, and all monies which the Surety may, in its sole discretion and/or in accordance with the terms and conditions of any agreements with the Principal, advance or loan to the Principal. The Bank and the Principal acknowledge and agree that all funds on deposit in the Trust Account are the sole property of the Surety. The Contract Funds shall not be deposited in any other account of the Principal.

4. The Surety, through its authorized representatives, is authorized and empowered to endorse in the name of the Principal any and all checks received by the Surety or its representatives constituting Contract Funds from the Contracts, and to deposit said checks solely and only into the Trust Account. The Principal hereby agrees that the Surety may name one or more substitutes for the attorneys named in the Power of Attorney, with notice to the Principal. Furthermore, the Principal hereby ratifies and confirms all acts that any attorney or his substitute or substitutes may lawfully do or cause to be done.

5. The Contract Funds and all other monies deposited in the Trust Account shall be considered and constituted as trust funds to be used exclusively for the payment of all labor and material costs, including amounts due to subcontractors and suppliers, necessary to complete the work under the Contracts for which the Surety may become liable under the Bonds, for such other payments the Principal and the Surety deem appropriate, including the payment of general overhead expenses, and to reimburse the Surety for any losses and expenses incurred by the Surety under the Bonds. The Principal shall hold all Contract Funds in the Trust Account in trust for the Surety separate and apart from all other funds and property of the Principal. The Principal hereby covenants and agrees that it will not knowingly permit any funds in the Trust Account, whether represented by checks, vouchers, orders or otherwise, to be used for any purpose other than as more particularly set forth above. The Bank assumes no responsibility if the above covenant and agreement by the Principal is breached.

6. Except as provided in paragraphs 12 and 13 below, all checks and charges against the Trust Account shall be required to have two signatures, one signature being that of an authorized representative of the Principal and the other by an authorized representative of the Surety. The Principal and the Surety mutually agree that they will work in conjunction with the Bank to establish such other means and methods of transferring funds from the Trust Account in accordance with the provisions of this Agreement so long as such means or methods require the consent of both the Principal and the Surety for any withdrawal or transfer of funds from the Trust Account. Except as otherwise set forth in this Agreement, the Principal is restricted from making any wire transfers, the use of counter-checks or other non-check transfers from the Trust Account without the express written approval of the Surety.

Exhibit 4.1.5 (continued)

7. The persons now designated to countersign checks or approve transfers on the Trust Account on behalf of the Surety are any one of the following: ______________________________.
It is understood and agreed that the Surety may, in its sole discretion, substitute or add another representative or representatives for the persons originally named, without the prior consent of, but upon notice to the Principal and the Bank and by completing such signature cards and other documentation required by the Bank.

8. The persons now designated to countersign checks or approve transfers on the Trust Account on behalf of the Principal are any one of the following: ______________________________.
It is understood and agreed that the Principal may substitute or add another representative or representatives for the persons originally named, but only with the approval in writing of the Surety, and upon notice to the Bank and by completing such signature cards and other documentation required by the Bank.

9. The Bank is hereby irrevocably authorized and directed by the Principal and the Surety to honor, in the ordinary course of business and to the extent of the collected balance of the Trust Account, each and every check drawn against or other transfer from the Trust Account when signed or authorized as herein set forth in this Agreement.

10. The Principal shall maintain possession of the checkbook for the Trust Account. However, the Surety shall receive directly from the Bank all bank statements and the originals of all deposit slips, canceled checks, debit memos, service charges, etc. from the Trust Account. The Principal hereby authorizes the Bank to furnish to the Surety such information as the Surety may desire concerning deposits to and withdrawals from the Trust Account. The Surety shall furnish upon request to the Principal copies of all bank statements and checks which have been returned from the Trust Account.

11. In the event that an attachment, garnishment or other legal proceeding with respect to the Principal or the Trust Account is served on the Bank, the Bank shall promptly notify the Surety of such service in writing and shall provide to the Surety copies of any relevant documents and pleadings. None of the Contract Funds or any advances or loans which may be made by the Surety to the Principal and deposited in the Trust Account shall be subject to any right of set-off by the Bank as a result of any transactions involving the Bank and the Principal. The Bank agrees that its execution of this Agreement is a written acknowledgment of this paragraph and is a condition precedent to the establishment or continuance of the Trust Account at the Bank.

12. The Principal hereby authorizes and empowers any two of the signators of the Surety on the Trust Account to countersign one or more checks from the

Exhibit 4.1.5 (continued)

Trust Account, and, at the sole option and discretion of the Surety, to withdraw all or a portion of the trust funds from the Trust Account. It is expressly understood by and between the Principal and the Surety that the Bank shall have no duty to make inquiry as to the purpose of any transfer or check from the Trust Account, whether made or done pursuant to this paragraph or any other provision of this Agreement.

13. At its sole option and discretion, the Surety may notify the Bank in writing, by wire or orally (wire or oral notice shall be confirmed in writing as soon as practicable) to stop payment on and not to honor any checks drawn against the Trust Account after the receipt of such notice unless said check or checks are made payable to the Surety and signed by any two of the signators of the Surety on the Trust Account as provided in paragraph 12 above. The Principal hereby acknowledges to the Bank that the Principal may <u>not</u> issue a stop-payment request on any check drawn on the Trust Account without the express written approval of the Surety presented to the Bank.

14. Any notice required to be given under this Agreement by any party to another shall be given in writing by prepaid United States certified or registered mail directed as follows:

As to the Principal:

____

____

____

____

As to Bank:

____

____

____

____

As to the Surety:

____

____

____

____

Exhibit 4.1.5 (continued)

With a copy to:

____
____
____
____

15. All fees assessed by the Bank with respect to the Trust Account shall be the joint and several obligation of the Principal and the Surety.

IN WITNESS WHEREOF, the parties hereto have caused this Agreement to be executed by their duly authorized representatives.

PRINCIPAL

______________________________ By: ____________________________
Witness Title: __________________________

SURETY

______________________________ By: ____________________________
Witness Title: __________________________

BANK

______________________________ By: ____________________________
Witness Title: __________________________

Exhibit 4.1.6

LETTER OF DIRECTION

Exhibit 6

[Principal's Letterhead]

[Date]

To: Obligee

____
____
____

RE: Principal: ________________________
Obligee: _________________________
Contract and Project: _______________
Bond No.: ________________________
Surety: __________________________

Dear Sir:

This is to advise you that the Principal, _____________________________, hereby irrevocably requests that any and all payments due or to become due of any kind or nature on account of the above described Contract and Project be made payable jointly to the Principal and _____________________________, which is the Surety on the Performance Bond and the Labor and Material Payment Bond for the above Project. All such joint check payments should be forwarded directly to:

Surety ______________________
Attention: ____________________ ____________________________________
(address

Please be advised that the Surety agrees to this arrangement. Furthermore, there will be no modification or change in these instructions without the written authorization and express consent of the Surety.

Exhibit 4.1.6 (continued)

Very truly yours,

PRINCIPAL

By: __________________________, President

c.c. Surety

Exhibit 4.1.7

ASSIGNMENT

Exhibit 7

KNOW ALL MEN BY THESE PRESENTS THAT, ________________ ____ (hereinafter referred to as the "Principal"), hereby intending to be legally bound, and in consideration of One Dollar ($1.00), and other good, valuable and sufficient considerations, the receipt and adequacy whereof being hereby acknowledged by the Principal and for the Principal's successors and assigns, does hereby assign, transfer, and set over to ____ (the "Surety"), its successors, assigns and affiliates, all of the Principal's right, title and interest in and to any and all payments on account of estimates, change orders, including the final estimate, final payment and retainage, and any other money now due or hereafter to become due, arising out of the Contracts described and identified in the annexed Exhibit A, together with all rights of action accrued or which may accrue thereunder; and the Principal does hereby constitute and appoint said Surety as the Principal's true and lawful attorney-in-fact, irrevocably in the premises, to do and perform all acts, matters, and things touching upon the premises, in like manner, and to all intents and purposes as the Principal could do if personally present.

IN WITNESS WHEREOF, the Principal has caused these presents to be executed and sealed this ____ day of ______________, 19___.

WITNESS/ATTEST PRINCIPAL

________________________________ By: ____________________ (SEAL)

____________________, President

Exhibit 4.1.7 (continued)

POWER OF ATTORNEY

KNOW ALL MEN BY THESE PRESENTS THAT, _______________ (hereinafter referred to as the "Principal") does constitute and appoint ______ ____ (the "Surety"), and its representatives, ________________________________, and their successors and assigns, its true and lawful attorney-in-fact, for it and in its name to receive, endorse and collect any and all checks and drafts or other forms of remittance payable to the Principal, and issued in payment of money earned or to be earned, or to become due and payable under the Contracts described in the list attached hereto as Exhibit A, including all retained percentages, estimates, final payments, any other monies now due or which may become due in payment for work performed and materials furnished under the Contracts described in Exhibit A, and all other Contract Funds as defined in a Joint Control Trust Account Agreement between the Principal, the Surety and others dated _________ (the "Agreement"), which may require endorsement for deposit and collection. This Power of Attorney shall give the Surety the right to endorse any such checks or drafts on behalf of the Principal solely and only for the purpose of depositing said checks or drafts in the Trust Account more fully described in the Agreement.

The Principal does hereby authorize and empower its said attorney-in-fact, or any of them, to give full discharge and acquittance for the same and hereby ratifies and confirms all that lawfully may be done by virtue of this Power of Attorney. This Power of Attorney is coupled with an interest and is irrevocable. The Principal hereby revokes any and all previous Powers of Attorney executed in reference to the disposition of the proceeds of the Contracts described in Exhibit A.

IN WITNESS WHEREOF, the Principal has caused this instrument to be executed and sealed by its duly authorized officers this _________ day of __________, 19___.

WITNESS/ATTEST: PRINCIPAL

______________________________ By: ____________________ (SEAL)

____________________, President

Exhibit 4.1.7 (continued)

STATE OF ___________________, COUNTY OF _________________, to wit:

I HEREBY CERTIFY that on this _____ day of ____________, 19___, before me, the subscriber, a Notary Public of the State of _________________, personally appeared ___________________, the President of __________________________, who is personally known to me; who, being duly sworn, did depose and say that he is the President of ______________________________________, the corporation described in and which executed this Power of Attorney; and that he has been duly authorized by all proper and necessary corporate actions to execute this Power of Attorney.

AS WITNESS, my hand and Notarial Seal.

____
Notary Public

Exhibit 4.2

Letter to Cover Financing

December 21, 1983

Mr. John J. Jones
Construction & Son, Inc.
111 North Center Street
Midtown, U.S.A.

Re: Projects bonded by Surety

Dear Mr. Jones:

You have requested financial assistance from Surety for the purpose of completing projects bonded by Surety and paying obligations to various subcontractors and suppliers of labor, material and services used in the performance of the work on such projects incurred by Construction & Son, Inc.

Before Surety can respond to your request, an investigation must be conducted by its representatives. You must not construe any statement or action of Surety's representatives during such investigation to be an agreement or promise to render financial assistance to Construction or to engage in any course of conduct for the benefit of Construction.

Construction & Son, Inc. represents that it has no other source of funding its financial needs available to it and that it is unable to perform the obligation secured by the bonds without financial and/or other assistance from Surety.

Construction gives permission to Surety and its representatives to conduct such investigation as Surety's representatives deem necessary including, but not limited to: a review of Construction's books, records and files; interviews with all officers and employees of Construction; interviews with Construction's attorneys, accountants and other professionals retained by Construction; interviews with Construction's banker and other creditors and interviews with the owner's representatives with regard to the aforesaid bonded projects.

You, your wife and Construction executed a Master Surety Agreement in favor of Surety. You and Construction, upon acceptance of this letter, affirm the obligations undertaken by you, your wife and Construction pursuant to such agreement and agree to execute all documents necessary to secure Surety for all loss and expense it may incur in behalf of Construction. You also agree to execute any other documents necessary for you or Construction to perform and implement the obligations undertaken under the Master Surety Agreement. This Agreement

Exhibit 4.2 (continued)

is not to be construed as consideration to Surety in exchange for Surety's agreeing to render financial or other assistance to Construction.

Be advised that: the decision with respect to giving financial or other assistance to Construction will be made by the executives of Surety in its Home Office and that no other representative of Surety, including its attorney, has the authority to make such a decision; Surety's obligations under its bonds are to the obligees named therein or the beneficiaries thereof; and, Surety has not undertaken any obligation to Construction or its indemnitors under the bonds, the Master Surety Agreement or this letter.

Yours very truly,

cc: Mr. & Mrs. John J. Jones

ACCEPTED:
CONSTRUCTION & SON, INC.

By: ______________________________
John J. Jones, President

____
John J. Jones

____
Mable L. Jones

Exhibit 5.1

Takeover Agreement (Alternate No. 1)

THIS AGREEMENT made this ______ day of ________________, by and between the ____________________________ (hereinafter called "Owner"), and _________________________ (hereinafter referred to as "Surety").

RECITALS:

1. On or about _______________, Owner entered into a contract with _____________________________ (hereinafter called "Principal") for the reconstruction of ____ (hereinafter referred to as "Contract"); and

2. Surety as Surety for Principal executed a Performance and Payment Bond in favor of Owner, each in the penal sum of ______________________ (said sum hereinafter referred to as the "Bond Penalty"); and

3. On ___________________, Owner issued a Notice of Termination of Default of the Contract, and on _______________ made demand upon Surety that Surety complete the Contract pursuant to the Performance Bond; and

4. Principal has appealed to Owner's Termination for Default and contends that Owner improperly terminated the Contract; and

5. Principal has submitted numerous claims for extra work and time extension which as of this date have not yet been resolved. Attached as exhibit A is a list of the claims and requests for the time extensions submitted by Principal; and

6. By letter dated _________________, a copy of which is attached as Exhibit B, Surety requested the Owner to make no further payments to Principal. However, the Owner claims there is no present record of Owner's receipt of the original of the letter dated _________________. A copy of the letter dated _____________ was received by Owner on ________________________.

7. On or about the _________________, Owner paid to Principal the sum of ________________________________ ($___________) representing the proceeds of Estimate No. _____ on the Contract; and

8. On or about _____________, Owner and ______________ entered into an agreement which is attached hereto as Exhibit C. Pursuant to said Agreement, (subcontractor) performed the work described in Exhibit C and has submitted an invoice which is attached hereto as Exhibit D. The back-charge against the Contract Balance, pursuant to Exhibits C and D, is ___________________. ____________________ has accepted the work described in Exhibit C, and for the work described in Item #5, the Contract will be adjusted to reflect completion

Exhibit 5.1 (continued)

of those quantities, and Contract earnings will also be adjusted commensurate with the increased quantities.

9. Surety is willing to undertake the Completion of the Contract, provided the entire unpaid Contract balance (subject to adjustment for variations of the estimated quantities), including retainage, and work heretofore done by Principal for which payment has not been made by Owner, is paid to F&D, and certain other agreements hereinafter set out are made with Owner; and

10. In consideration of Surety agreeing to complete the work required by said Contract and for other good and valuable consideration, the receipt of which is hereby acknowledged, Surety and the Owner hereby agree as follows:

AGREEMENTS:

1. Owner will pay Surety the entire unpaid Contract balance of the Contract price as determined by final measurements, plus or minus any additional amounts of money on account of modifications requested and authorized by Owner as the work progresses, less proper deductions. The amount to be paid includes the balance of all monies that would be due or become due to Principal arising out of or incidental to the performance of the Contract including, but not limited to, monies heretofore earned but unpaid to Principal, including retained percentages and extras, less proper deductions. The payment of said monies to Surety under this paragraph, with the exception of the sum of ____________________ earned by Principal for the period ending __________ shall be made in accordance with the terms of the contract as to time, amounts and methods of payment. The amount of ____________ earned by Principal for the period ending __________ shall be paid to Surety within thirty (30) days of the date of the execution of this Agreement.

2. Insofar as Owner has any right, title or interest therein, Owner agrees that Surety, or a contractor completing for it, will have a right to use, without charge, any of the equipment, materials, and appurtenances furnished or supplied to Principal which may be stored on or about the premises of the Project or on which it may have been fabricated for use in connection with the Project, whether or not presently upon the project.

3. Surety as surety for Principal shall perform or cause to be performed all the work required by said Contract and Surety shall complete or cause to be completed said Contract in accordance with the terms and conditions of said Contract.

4. The Completing Contract shall be ______________ and Surety will give to ______________ a Notice to Proceed to start construction of the remaining

Exhibit 5.1 (continued)

work no later than ___________. __________ will use its best efforts to obtain substantial completion, as defined in the Contract, no later than __________. Owner agrees to waive twenty (20) working days of liquidated damages in recognition of Surety's best efforts to achieve substantial completion on or before ______________. However, in the event the ________________ date is not achieved, Surety's and Owner agree that the twenty (20) days of liquidated damages waived under this Agreement may be reinstated.

5. Surety's hereby agree to indemnify the Owner against loss, claim or suit, including attorneys fees and costs, by Principal or any person, firm, corporation or governmental body, exclusive of any claim by the Comptroller of the Treasury of the State of _____________ on account of payment by the Owner to F&D on the Contract funds as set forth in this Agreement, the conditions of the foregoing indemnity being:

(a) The amount of indemnity shall be limited to the total compensation paid by the Owner under this Agreement; and
(b) The Owner shall promptly notify Surety of any such claim or suits; and
(c) Surety shall have the right, but not the obligation, to resolve all such claims and to control and defend all such suits through counsel of Surety's election, in full cooperation with the Attorney General of the State of ____________________.

6. It is recognized that Surety, in completing the Contract, may incur obligations and make payments which may exceed in the aggregate the Bond Penalty and that Surety has undertaken to complete in reliance upon this Agreement. In consideration thereof, owner agrees that in the event (a) aggregate payments and obligations accrued by Surety in completing the Contract for labor and materials furnished to or by Surety and any completing contractor or subcontractor(s) engaged by it in completing the Contract shall exceed (b) the aggregate of all sums then and theretofore paid or accrued to Surety under paragraph 1 hereof plus the Bond Penalty, Owner shall pay to F&D or to those holding such accruing obligations, such amounts as shall exactly eliminate such excess. In the amplification of the purpose of the foregoing, it is the intention of the parties that the differences between the amounts in (a) and (b) in the preceding sentence (Surety's ultimate loss) shall not, upon completion, exceed the amount of the Bond Penalty.

7. Surety contends that the payment made to Principal described in Paragraph 6 of the Recitals of this Agreement was improperly made to Principal and should have been paid to Surety. The Owner contends that the payment was properly made to Principal and it has no liability to Surety for such payment. By execution of this Agreement, Surety does not waive its right to contest the propriety of the payment to Principal and Surety specifically reserves its rights

Exhibit 5.1 (continued)

to contest the propriety of that payment. The Owner, by execution of this Agreement, does not admit that the payment was improperly made, and reserves all rights it has to contest Surety's position.

8. Owner contends that the Contract is substantially past the time for completion and liquidated damages may be assessable at the conclusion of this Project. By execution of this Agreement, Surety does not waive any rights either it or its Principal may have to contest the propriety of the assessment of liquidated damages and specifically reserves its rights to contest the accessibility of any liquidated damages. Owner, by execution of this Agreement, does not waive any rights, except as provided in Paragraph 4 above, it may have to assess liquidated damages against the Contract balance.

9. By execution of this Agreement, Surety does not waive principal's rights, if any, to contest the validity of the default or any other rights principal may have. Owner likewise reserves all rights it may have against principal.

10. This Agreement shall inure to the benefit of and be binding upon the parties hereto, their successors and assigns.

11. This Agreement may not be amended or altered in any way except in writing executed by both the parties hereto.

12. This Agreement shall be governed and controlled by the laws of the State of _______________.

IN WITNESS WHEREOF, the parties hereto have duly executed this Agreement on the date first written above.

WITNESS:

______________________________ By: ___________________________

APPROVED AS TO FORM AND
LEGAL SUFFICIENCY:

____
Assistant Attorney General

Exhibit 5.2

Takeover Agreement (Alternate No. 2)

This Takeover Agreement (the "Agreement") is made and entered into this _____ day of ______________, 19___, by and between ________________ (the "Surety") and ________________________________ (the "Owner").

RECITALS:

WHEREAS, ________________________ (the "Former Contractor") and the Owner entered into a contract (the "Original Contract") for the Former Contractor to furnish all labor and material and perform all work for ____ (the "Project") in accordance with the terms and provisions of the Original Contract, including all contract documents forming a part of the Original Contract;

WHEREAS, as required by law and under the terms of the Original Contract, for Former Contractor and the Surety made, executed and delivered to the Owner a Performance Bond, Bond No. _____________, and a Payment Bond, Bond No. ________________ (collectively, the "Bonds"), both in the penal sum of $___________;

WHEREAS, the Former Contractor has voluntarily terminated its performance of the Original Contract, and the Owner has called upon the Surety to fulfill its obligations as surety under the terms of the Performance Bond; and

WHEREAS, the Surety is willing to undertake the completion of the Original Contract in accordance with the terms of the Performance Bond and this Agreement provided that in doing so it will receive the entire Contract Balance hereinafter defined as set forth below.

NOW, THEREFORE, in consideration of the agreements and undertakings hereinafter set forth, and for other good and valuable consideration, the receipt and adequacy therefor being hereby acknowledged, the Owner and the Surety agree as follows:

AGREEMENTS:

1. The Surety hereby undertakes to cause the performance of each and every one of the terms, covenants and conditions of the Original Contract, including all modifications thereto, and agrees to be bound by the Original Contract. The Owner acknowledges that the Surety, by its execution of this Agreement, is acting in its capacity as the surety for the Former Contractor in making arrangements for the performance and completion of the Original

Exhibit 5.2 (continued)

Contract, and not as a completing contractor, and that the Surety is not assuming any obligations or liabilities beyond those set forth in the Bonds. As to the completion of the Original Contract, except as otherwise provided in this Agreement, the Surety is entitled to all rights, title and interest of the Former Contractor in and to the Original Contract in all respects as if the Surety were the original party to the Original Contract. The term "Contractor" is used in the Original Contract shall be deemed, after the effective date of this Agreement, to refer to the Surety rather than to the Former Contractor.

2. The Owner acknowledges that the Surety will subcontract the performance of the work under the Original Contract to a completion contractor (the "Completion Contractor"). The Surety may satisfy the required insurance obligations under the Original Contract by providing evidence of the required insurance coverage carried by the Completion Contractor, with the Surety being named as an additional insured under the policy or policies.

3. The Owner and the Surety agree that as of the date of this Agreement:

(a) The authorized amount of the Original Contract, including all approved change orders, is the sum of $________;

(b) The Former Contractor and/or the Surety have been paid the sum of $________;

(c) The Owner is holding the sum of $________ as retainage pursuant to the terms of the Original Contract;

(d) The "Contract Balance" shall be hereinafter defined as the sum of $______ [subsection] (a) minus subsection (b)]. The Contract Balance shall be increased or decreased, as appropriate, as a result of certain pending change orders to the Original contracts submitted by the Former Contractor and/or the Owner, and as a result of any change orders for extra work (work that is different from, in excess of, or beyond the scope of the work required by the Original Contract) requested or required by the Owner after the date of the execution of this Agreement; and

(e) As of the date of the execution of this Agreement, the Owner represents and warrants that, according to the records available to it, the Contract Balance as defined herein is accurate. The Surety reserves the right to verify the accuracy of the Contract Balance. The Surety's sole remedy against the Owner for breach of this representation and warranty is reformation of the Contract Balance to the proper amount.

4. The Owner agrees that the Contract Balance is dedicated to and will be applied to the completion of the Original Contract pursuant to this Agreement. The Owner shall pay directly to the Surety the Contract Balance, plus or minus any additional amounts of money on account of any modifications requested and

Exhibit 5.2 (continued)

authorized by the Owner, as the work progresses. The payment of the Contract Balance to thc Surety shall be made in accordance with the terms of the Original Contract as to the time, amount and method of payment, and not payment shall be delayed by reason of any slow down or cessation of work in connection with the takeover of the Original Contract by the Surety. The Surety agrees to spend its own funds as may be necessary from time to time to pay for the performance of the Original Contract by the Completion Contractor in the event that the Contract Balance is insufficient, with any such payments being credited against the penal sum of the Performance Bond. The Owner agrees that it shall not assess any liquidated damages against progress payments due to the Surety under this Agreement. The assessment of any liquidated damages, if applicable, shall be made against the retainages only.

5. The Surety shall complete the work required under the Original Contract pursuant to this Agreement on or before ______________ (the "Completion Date"). The Surety is hereby granted a non-compensatory time extension from the original completion date in the Original Contract until the Completion Date. As consideration for the non-compensatory time extension, the Surety, for itself and on behalf of the Former Contractor, hereby waives any right to any claim for any additional time extensions and/or damages as a result of any delays which may have been caused by the Owner up to and including the date of this Agreement. The assessment of any liquidated damages under the Original Contract and this Agreement may begin on the day after the Completion Date; provided, however, that any such assessment of liquidated damages shall *not* include any alleged delays of the Former Contractor which occurred at anytime during the Former Contractor's performance of the work under the Original Contract, and that the calculation and assessment of any such liquidated damages shall include the recognition of any excusable delays by the Surety in the performance of the Original Contract and this Agreement.

6. Insofar as the Owner has any right, title or interest therein, the Owner agrees that the Surety and its Completion Contractor shall have the right to use, without charge, any of the equipment, materials and appurtenances furnished or supplied by the Former Contractor which may be stored on or about the premises of the Project site or materials which may have been fabricated for use in connection with the Original Contract, whether or not presently upon the Project site.

7. The Surety shall be represented at the Project by the Completion Contractor. Prior to the issuance of the Notice to Proceed, the Surety shall specifically authorize in writing an individual with the Completion Contractor to be its representative (the "Authorized Individual") solely for the purposes set forth in this paragraph. The Authorized Individual will represent the Surety in dealing with the Owner on day to day construction issues with respect to the Project. The

Exhibit 5.2 (continued)

Surety hereby designates the Authorized Individual to prepare and process pay requisitions on the Original Contract. However, the Surety will sign all pay requisitions submitted to the Owner. Payments from the Owner shall be made payable to the Surety and transmitted to the Surety at the following address, unless and until the Owner is notified in writing of any different addresses:

____

____

____

____

The Authorized Individual shall have, on behalf of the Surety, the authority to negotiate and sign change orders for extra work (work that is different from, in excess of, or beyond the scope of the work required by the Original Contract) requested or required by the Owner (hereinafter "Change Order") without the Surety's prior written approval, provided the Change Order does not exceed $__________ and the Completion Contractor is given additional time to perform the Change Order. If the Change Order does exceed $__________, or no additional time is given to the Completion Contractor to perform the Change Order, then the Surety's prior written approval is required to negotiate the Change Order and the final Change Order must be signed by the Surety and not the Authorized Individual. If the total of all of the approved Change Orders exceeds the sum of $__________, then the Surety, not the Authorized Individual, must approve in writing all additional or subsequent Change Orders regardless of the amount of each such Change Order. The Authorized Individual has no authority to negotiate deductive Change Orders, credits, backcharges or net deductions from the Original Contract or the Contract Balance of any nature whatsoever without the Surety's prior written approval. Any agreements with respect to the warranty work of the Former Contractor or corrective work as a result of latent defect in the work performed by the Former Contractor shall require the written approval of the Surety.

8. The total liability of the Surety under this Agreement and the Performance Bond for the performance of the work, after the expenditure of the Contract Balance, is limited to and shall not exceed the penal sum of the Performance Bond in the amount of $_________. All payments properly made by the Surety for the performance of the Original Contract shall be credited against the penal sum of the Performance Bond. Nothing in this Agreement constitutes a waiver of such penal sum or an increase in the liability of the Surety under the Performance Bond.

Exhibit 5.2 (continued)

9. In no event shall the Owner withhold any of the Contract Balance from the Surety because of or on account of any claims, liens, suits or demands by any persons or entities furnishing or alleging to have furnished labor and/or materials to the Project. The Payment Bond shall remain in full force and effect in accordance with its terms and provisions. The total liability of the Surety under the Payment Bond is limited to and shall not exceed the penal sum of the Payment Bond in the amount of $__________. All Payment Bond payments properly made by the Surety shall be credited against the penal sum of the Payment Bond. Nothing in this Agreement constitutes a waiver of such penal sum or an increase in the liability of the Surety under the Payment Bond.

10. This Agreement is solely for the benefit of the Owner and the Surety. The Owner and the Surety do not intend by any provision of this Agreement to create any rights in or increase the rights of any third-party beneficiaries, nor to confer any benefit upon or enforceable rights under this Agreement or otherwise upon anyone other than the Owner and the Surety. Specifically, the Owner and the Surety acknowledge that nothing in this Agreement shall extend or increase the rights of any third-party claimants or the liabilities or obligations of the Surety under the Bonds.

11. This Agreement constitutes the whole of the understanding, discussions, and agreements by and between the Owner and the Surety. The terms and provisions of this Agreement are contractual and not mere recitals. The Owner and the Surety acknowledge that there have been no oral, written or other agreements of any kind as a condition precedent to or to induce the execution and delivery of this Agreement. Any written or oral discussions conducted prior to the effective date of this Agreement shall not in any way vary or alter the terms of this Agreement.

12. This Agreement shall not be changed, amended or altered in any way except in writing and executed by both the Owner and Surety.

13. This Agreement may be executed in one or more counterparts, each of which shall be deemed to be an original.

14. This Agreement shall be governed by and controlled by the laws of the State of ______________.

15. Any notices which are required to be given by the terms of this Agreement or the Bonds shall be made as follows:

Exhibit 5.2 (continued)

As to the Owner:
Via certified mail, return receipt requested, postage prepaid to:

____

____

____

With a copy to:

____

____

____

As to the Surety:
Via certified mail, return receipt requested, postage prepaid to:

____

____

____

With a copy to:

____

____

____

16. This Agreement is effective as of the date first written above.

17. This Agreement shall be binding upon the parties and their respective successors and assigns.

18. In the event that one or more provisions of this Agreement shall be declared to be invalid, illegal or unenforceable in any respect, unless such invalidity, illegal or unenforceable in any respect, unless such invalidity, illegality or unenforceability shall be tantamount to a failure of consideration, the validity, legality and enforceability of the remaining provisions contained in this Agreement shall not in any way be affected or impaired thereby.

19. It is understood and agreed by the owner and the Surety that this Agreement shall be construed without regard to any presumption or other rule requiring construction against the party causing this Agreement to be drafted.

IN WITNESS WHEREOF, the parties have executed this Agreement on the date indicated above, and each of the undersigned personally represent and warrant that they have the full right, power and authority to execute this Agreement on behalf of the respective parties.

Exhibit 5.2 (continued)

OWNER

By: ______________________________
Title: ____________________________

SURETY

By: ______________________________
Title: ____________________________

Exhibit 5.3

Takeover Agreement (Alternate No. 3)

THIS AGREEMENT, made and entered into this _____ day of ________, 19___, by and between the Owner and Surety.

WITNESSETH:

WHEREAS on or about ___________, Owner entered into a Contract with Contractor for all work under Project (herewith called the "Contract"), and

WHEREAS Surety, executed the required Performance and Payment Bonds (Bond No. ___________) each in the penal sum of $__________, and

WHEREAS Owner declared contractor in default in performance of the Contract and on ______________ Owner terminated contractor right to proceed thereunder prior to the full completion of the work required, and Owner has made demand on Surety, under the provisions and conditions of said Performance Bond, to take over and complete all required work that remains to be performed, and

WHEREAS Surety is willing to undertake the completion of the Contract in the manner hereinafter related provided the entire unpaid balance of the contract price, including retainage together with any additional amount of money added to the contract price on account of extra work or changes, is paid to Surety or in accordance with its directions in writing, and

WHEREAS, as of Requisition #________ dated and signed ___________, the adjusted contract price, after Change Orders ________ through _______ is $_________ and there remains a balance including retainage still held and unpaid by Owner, in the amount of $_______________.

NOW, THEREFORE, in consideration of Surety agreeing to complete the work required by Contract and for other valuable considerations, the receipt of which is hereby acknowledged, the parties to this agreement do covenant and agree as follows:

1. Owner will pay the entire unpaid Contract balance, which as of Requisition ________ dated and signed __________________, is approximately $___________, together with any additional amount of money added to Contract price on account of extra work or changes as the work progresses. The amount to be paid includes all monies due or to become due contractor arising out of or incidental to the performance of the Contract, including, but not limited to, unpaid Contract balances including unpaid monies relating to approved change orders, retained percentages, and monies relating to pending or subsequently submitted change orders approved by the owner (collectively hereinafter called "Contract Balances"). Owner will not withhold any amounts for any alleged damages caused

Exhibit 5.3 (continued)

by contractor alleged failure to substantially complete on time. The only exception acknowledged by the parties shall be back charges effective as of __________ for Architect ________________ in accordance with the charges enumerated in Exhibit "A" and attached hereto. Any such damages shall be settled with Owner in accordance with paragraph 9 below. The Owner will pay the Contract Balances to Surety or in accordance with Surety's written directions (1) in accordance with the terms of this Agreement; (2) in accordance with the terms of the Contract as to time, amounts and methods of payment. Where there is a conflict in such terms, this Agreement shall control. The monies shall be paid to Surety or such other persons, firms or corporations as Surety may direct in writing at any time or times hereafter.

Owner further agrees, notwithstanding any provision to the contrary in the contract, to make such payments, regardless of whether or not any lien or other claims to said funds have been made, provided Surety (1) agrees to take over the owner's defense of such claims or any claim or lien filed or presented after such payment, at the expense of Surety and (2) agrees to indemnify Owner and its members, agents and employees, to the extent of the amounts so released, against liability for making such payments notwithstanding the pendency of such lien or other claim or lien or claim filed or presented after such payments.

2. Insofar as Owner has any right, title or interest therein. Owner agrees that Surety or its subcontractors will have the right to use, without charge, any of the materials, supplies, equipment or personal property furnished or supplied to or by Morello which may be stored on the premiss of the project or which may have been fabricated for use in connection with the project, whether or not presently upon the project.

3. Surety shall perform with reasonable speed all of the remaining work required by the contractors Contract, including warranties and guarantees therein contained, in accordance with the terms and conditions of said Contract except as to the time of completions. Owner agrees that in no event shall Surety be liable for any and all sums, amounts, claims, liquidated or unliquidated damages, compensations, actual or punitive damages, penalties, assessments, fees, fines whether claimed or imposed for any reason by any person, comptroller, entity, or Federal, State, County or Municipal governmental agency or political subdivision thereof for any sum in excess of the penal amount of the Performance Bond, $____________. Surety may cause further work to complete the Contract to cease on its behalf if it has expended the full bond penalty. Nothing in this agreement shall be construed in any way to release any other liability of Surety to the Owner under the aforesaid Bond.

4. Owner and Surety agree that any and all agreements, judgmental decisions, and any other matters pertaining to the day-to-day coordination of the work

Exhibit 5.3 (continued)

to be performed under the Contract will be made between Surety's designated representative, and the Owner's engineer/architect in charge or a designated representative of the Owner as provided in the contract. Surety may designate a procedure contractor and/or a third-party to represent its interests and owner agrees to cooperate with Surety's designated representative(s) in providing any information concerning the performance of the Contract. Surety may provide a representative on the job site but in the event Surety has not designated a representative to receive oral or written communications, all communications from Owner to Surety are to be made to ________________________________. It is agreed that in the event Surety exercises their right to procure a new contractor, that the parties shall engage in mutual cooperation in order to insure a smooth transition of work.

5. Surety will be entitled to time extensions (a) in accordance with the terms and conditions of the Contract allowing same and (b) with respect to any latent defects as of the date of this Agreement adversely affecting the scheduled completion date.

6. Surety will, with all reasonable dispatch, investigate and discharge its liability under the Payment Bond as to all demands upon it by subcontractors and suppliers to Contractor of labor and material in connection with the Contract.

7. Regardless of any claim or contentions which Contractor has made or may make against the Owner or which the Owner has made or may make against Contractor, the Owner will fully perform all of the obligations undertaken by it in the Contract and among other things, will make payment to Surety of all amounts due or to become due in relation to the Contract as if Surety were the original "contractor" under the Contract.

8. Neither this Agreement nor any provision hereof shall be deemed or construed to be an admission or concession of liability of any kind or nature by Contractor, Surety or the Owner or a waiver of (i) any of the rights or claims of Contractor or Surety in relation to the Contract including, but not limited to, the claim that Owner prejudiced Surety by reducing the Contract retainage from _____% to _____%, contrary to the terms of the Contract, the claim that the Owner prejudiced Surety by not mitigating Surety's damages, claims for pending change orders and extensions of time; or (ii) of any rights or claims of the Owner in the Contract, including, but not limited to, the Owner's claim for liquidated damages and back charges, all of which rights and claims Contractor, Surety and the Owner specifically reserve, it being the understanding and intention of the parties that any claims or contentions which may have been made or which may be made in relation to the Contract including alleged breaches thereof by Contractor on the one hand, and the Owner on the other, are in no way affected by this Agreement, and that in entering into this Agreement the parties recognize

Exhibit 5.3 (continued)

that any and all rights or claims which Contractor or Surety may believe themselves to have against the Owner or the Owner may believe itself to have against Contractor or Surety in relation to the Contract are in no way impaired or reduced by this Agreement and are fully reserved.

____

Owner's Representative

____

Surety's Representative

Exhibit 5.4

Completion Agreement (for FAR Compliance)

Contract No. _________

THIS AGREEMENT is entered into this ____ day of _______________, 19_____, by and between the UNITED STATES OF AMERICA (hereinafter called "the Government") represented by the Contracting Officer executing this agreement, the ________________________________ Insurance Company, a ____________ corporation, with its principal place of business in _______ ________________________________ (hereinafter called, "the "Surety"); and _____________ Contracting, Inc., a ____________ corporation with its principal place of business in ________________________________ (hereinafter called "the Principal").

WITNESSETH:

WHEREAS, on ______________, 19___, the Government and the Principal entered into Contract No. ________________, which was for ____________ ____ as set forth in the specifications made a part of thereof, and which is attached hereto as Exhibit A (hereinafter called "the Contract"); and

WHEREAS on _______________, 19___, and in conjunction with the Principal's performance of the Contract, the Surety executed a performance bond and a payment bond, Number _________, copies of which are attached hereto as Exhibits B and C, respectively, obligating itself to the Government in the amount of $________ and $__________, respectively, except as modified by change orders consented to by the Surety increasing or decreasing said amounts, in the event that the Principal did not well and truly perform all the conditions of the Contract (hereinafter called "the Performance Bond" and "the Payment Bond," respectively; and

WHEREAS, on ________________, 19___, the Government terminated the right of the Principal to proceed under the Contract, due to the following:

A. By letter dated _________________, 19___, attached hereto as Exhibit D, the Principal notified the Government that it could no longer proceed under the Contract; and

B. [Recite the other pertinent facts and correspondence.]; and

WHEREAS, the Government desires to effect the completion of the work covered by the Contract in order to expedite completion and to avoid the delay and inconvenience of reletting; and

Exhibit 5.4 (continued)

WHEREAS, the Surety is willing and desires to complete or procure the completion of the Contract in accordance with the terms of this Agreement, as a measure of cooperation with the Government, and as a measure to minimize costs; and

WHEREAS, under the Performance Bond, the Surety is willing to cause the contract to be completed in accordance with the provisions of this Agreement, provided that in so doing it will receive the contract balances as hereinafter set forth;

NOW, THEREFORE, in consideration of the agreements and undertakings hereinafter set forth, the Government, the Principal, and the Surety agree as follows:

1. The Surety hereby undertakes to cause the performance of each and every one of the terms, covenants, and conditions of the Contract, including all modifications thereto, to be completed, and agrees to be bound by the Contract. All obligations and liabilities to the Government by the Principal under the Contract, and under the bonds of the Principal and Surety, shall remain unimpaired by this Agreement, and the Principal shall not be released therefrom.

2. The Government hereby recognizes the ______________________ Insurance Company as the completing Surety under the Contract. As to completion of the Contract, except as otherwise provided in this Agreement, the Surety is entitled to all rights, title and interest of the Principal in and to the Contract in all respects as if the Surety were the original party to the Contract. The term "Contractor" as used in the Contract shall be deemed, after the effective date of this Agreement, to refer to the ______________________ Insurance Company, rather than to ______________________ Contracting, Inc.

3. The Government will pay to the Surety the unpaid balance under the Contract, plus or minus any approved change order additions or deletions, to which the Surety may become entitled pursuant to the terms of the Contract; subject, however, to the following conditions and limitations:

a. Any unpaid earnings of the Principal, including retained percentages and progress estimates for work accomplished before termination, shall be subject to claims by the Government against the Principal, except to the extent that such unpaid earnings may be required to permit payment to the Surety of its actual costs and expenses incurred in the completion of the work, exclusive of its payments and obligations under the Payment Bond.

b. Nothing in this Agreement shall be construed as a waiver of any rights of the Government against the Principal. All rights the Government now has or may hereafter acquire against the Principal or the Surety, or against the Principal and Surety together, including the right to liquidated damages for delays

Exhibit 5.4 (continued)

in completion of the work, except to the extent that such delays may be excused under the provisions of the Contract, are hereby reserved.

c. Nothing in this Agreement shall be construed as a waiver of any rights, remedies, claims or defenses by the Principal against the Government. All rights, remedies, claims or defenses the Principal now has or may hereinafter acquire against the Government are hereby reserved.

d. By entering into this Agreement, the Surety does not thereby waive, prejudice, or in any way adversely affect any claim that it, as Surety, or the Principal might have against the Government, except as to the Government's mitigation of damages in accepting completion of the Contract by the Surety.

e. On the effective date of this Agreement, liquidated damages against the Principal had been assessed by the Government in the amount of $________, Except to the extent liquidated damages are excusable under the Contract, the Government reserves its rights to assess liquidated damages from the effective date of this Agreement until the date the work remaining under the contract is substantially complete and accepted by the Government. Such assessment will be made if, in fact, it is determined that the assessment of liquidated damages is proper.

f. In no event shall the Surety be entitled to be paid any amount in excess of its total expenditures necessarily made in completing the work and discharging its obligations under the Payment Bond. Furthermore, payments to the Surety to reimburse it for discharging it's liabilities under the Payment Bond shall be only on authority of (I) mutual agreement between the Government, the Principal, and the Surety, or (II) determination of the Comptroller General as to payee and amount, or (III) order of a court of competent jurisdiction.

g. If the Contract proceeds have been assigned to a financing institution, the Surety may not be paid form unpaid earnings, unless the assignee consents to the payment in writing.

4. The Surety shall have present on the jobsite throughout Contract performance, a full-time representative experienced in construction contract management who is solely the representative of the Surety.

5. The Surety shall maintain separate records and accounts covering all costs incurred and expenditures made by it in completing the work under the Contract. The Surety shall make such records and accounts and supporting vouchers available for inspection and verification by the Contracting Officer, the Comptroller General, or other authorized representatives of the Government, until the expiration of three (3) years from the date of final payment under the Contract.

6. This Agreement constitutes the whole of the understanding, discussions, and agreements by and between the parties hereto. Any written or oral discussions

Exhibit 5.4 (continued)

conducted prior to the effective date hereof shall not in any way vary or alter the terms of this Agreement.

7. This Agreement is effective as of the date first written above.

IN WITNESS WHEREOF, all parties hereunder have caused to set their hands and seals.

THE UNITED STATES OF AMERICA

By: ______________________________

____

Contracting Officer

ATTEST:

____

[Insurance Company]

______________________________ By: ______________________________

ATTEST:

______________ CONTRACTING, INC.

______________________________ By: ______________________________

Exhibit 5.5

Completion Contract (Alternate No. 1)

THIS AGREEMENT, made this ______ day of ____________________, 19___, by and between ________________________________ ("Surety"), whose address is ____, and ____ ("Contractor"), whose address is ____.

WITNESSETH:

Section 1. **Contract Documents**. The Contractor agrees to furnish all supervision, labor, tools, equipment, materials and supplies necessary to perform, and to perform all work set forth in Section 2 hereof in connection with the construction of ____

____

at ____

in accordance with the terms and provisions of all the Plans, Specifications and other documents forming or by reference made a part of this Contract. These governing Plans and Specifications and other documents shall be those that originally were as agreed to by ________________________________

____.

These documents are available for your use at ________________________

____.

Section 2. **Scope of Work**. The Contractor agrees to perform the following described work:

The Contractor shall commence the performance of the work called by the Contract (hereinafter called the "Work") within ten (10) work days after written notice by the Surety to the Contractor that the Contractor commence therewith and shall thereafter diligently complete the performance of the Work.

The Contractor shall furnish a 100% Performance and 100% Payment Bond each in an amount equal to the full Contract price. Such bonds shall be on forms and with a bonding company satisfactory to the Surety.

Section 3. **Payment**. The Surety agrees to pay to the Contractor for the work and materials to be furnished under this Contract the sum of _______ ______________ dollars. No interim payments will be made. Full payment will be made within _______ days after acceptance by the ____________________ or its authorized agent. The above payment will be made to the Contractor simultaneously upon the receipt of satisfactory evidence by affidavit or otherwise that (i) all of the Contractor's indebtedness by reason of this Contract has been

Exhibit 5.5 (continued)

fully paid and, (ii) complete releases of all liens for work, labor and materials furnished or claim to be furnished by the Contractor and any Sub-Contractor employed by the Contractor in connection with the work under this Contract. The Surety may withhold payment to the Contractor for failure by the Contractor to comply fully with the provisions of this Section "3" or any other provisions of this Contract. The amount withheld shall not be paid until the cause or causes for withholding them has or have been removed by the Contractor and satisfactory evidence to that effect is furnished to the Surety.

In the event of any breach by the Contractor of any provision or obligation of this Contract, or in the event of the assertion by other parties of any claim or lien against the Surety or Owner or the premises arising out of the Contractor's performance of this Contract, the Surety shall have the right to retain out of the monies due or to become due to the Contractor an amount sufficient to completely protect the Surety from any and all loss, damage or expense therefrom, until the situation has been satisfactorily remedied or adjusted by the Contractor.

Section 4. **Prosecution of the Work**. The Contractor shall furnish all labor, supervision, tools, equipment, materials and supplies necessary for the performance of this Contract in a proper, efficient and workmanlike manner. Any materials that are to be furnished by the Contractor hereunder shall be furnished in sufficient time to enable the Contractor to perform and complete his work within the time or times provided for herein.

In the event the Contractor fails to comply or become disabled from complying with the provisions herein as to character or time of performance, and the failure is not commenced within five days and diligently prosecuted after written request by the Surety to the Contractor, the Surety, by Contract or otherwise, may without prejudice to any other right or remedy, take over and complete the performance of this Contract at the expense of the Contractor, or without taking over the work, may furnish the necessary materials and/or employ the workmen necessary to remedy the situation at the expense of the Contractor. If the Surety takes over the work pursuant to this paragraph it is specifically agreed that the Surety may take possession of the premises and of all materials, tools and equipment of the Contractor at the site for the purpose of completing the work covered by this Contract.

It is agreed that the Contractor shall be considered as disabled from so complying whenever a petition in Bankruptcy or for the appointment of a receiver is filed against him.

The Contractor's bonding company shall receive a copy of the written request to commence within five days after failing to comply or within five days after becoming disabled and if the Contractor fails to satisfactorily remedy the situation, the Surety has the option to declare the Contractor in default thence

Exhibit 5.5 (continued)

calling upon the Contractor's bonding company to pay and/or perform under the terms of the bond(s).

Section 5. **Labor**. The Contractor shall, in the performance of the Work, employ a competent foreman, and if necessary, assistants, all satisfactory to the Surety, and always a sufficient number of skilled workmen and laborers to perform the Work properly and diligently. The Contractor shall discontinue employment of any of its employees who may be unsatisfactory to the Surety. If, by reason of strikes, or disputes of any nature between the Contractor and any individuals, group or organization, this Contractor should be persistently, repeatedly, or for a period of ten (10) consecutive days, unable to supply enough properly skilled workmen or proper materials to execute the work defined in this Contract, then the Surety may terminate the Contract for default and proceed in accordance with Section (?) hereof.

Section 6. **Insurance**. The Contractor shall provide and maintain such types and amounts of coverages as required by all local, state and federal laws and as specifically designated by the documents of Section 1 hereof. Written proof satisfactory to the Surety of compliance with this section shall be furnished to the Surety *before* any work is performed under this Contract. Such proof of insurance shall provide for ten (10) days written notice to the Surety prior to the cancellation or modification of any insurance referred to therein.

Section 7. **Indemnification**. The Contractor further specifically obligates himself to the Surety in the following respects, to-wit: (a) To indemnify the Surety against and save him harmless from any and all claims, suits, liability, expense or damage for any alleged or actual infringement or violation of any patent or patent right, arising in connection with this Contract and anything done hereunder; (b) To indemnify the Surety against and save him harmless from any and all claims, suits or liability on account of any act or omission of the Contractor, or any of his officers, agents, employees or servants; (c) To pay for all materials furnished and work and labor performed under this Contract, and to satisfy the Surety thereupon whenever demand is made, and to indemnify the Surety against and save them and the premises harmless from any and all claims, suits or liens therefore by others than the Contractor; (d) To obtain and pay for all permits, licenses, and official inspections made necessary by his work, and to comply with all laws, ordinances and regulations bearing on his work and the conduct thereof; (e) The Contractor warrants and guarantees the work and materials covered by this Contract and agrees to make good, at his own expense, any defect in materials or workmanship which may occur or develop prior to the Surety's release from responsibility to the Contractor.

And the Contractor shall indemnify the Surety against, and save them harmless from, any and all liability, loss, damage, costs, expenses and attorneys' fees

Exhibit 5.5 (continued)

suffered or incurred on account of any breach of the aforesaid obligations and covenants, and any other provision of covenant of this Contract.

If at any time there shall be filed any lien or claim for work, labor or materials furnished or claimed to be furnished in the performance of the Work or the supplying of materials under the Contract, the Contractor shall within five (5) days after the filing thereof cause the same to be fully discharged at its own cost and expense. The Surety shall have the right to retain out of any payment then due or thereafter to become due under the terms of the Contract an amount sufficient to indemnify it completely against any such lien or claim, including the costs of its discharge and of defending against it. Should there prove to be any such lien or claim after all payments have been made to the Contractor hereunder the Contractor shall refund to the Surety all moneys which the Surety may be compelled to pay in discharging such lien or satisfying such claim and all costs in connection therewith.

Section 8. **Independent Contractor**. The Contractor specifically agrees that he is, or prior to the start of work hereunder will become, an independent contractor and an employing unit subject as an employer to all applicable Unemployment Compensation statutes so as to relieve the Surety of any responsibility or liability for treating Contractor's employees as employees of the Surety for the purpose of keeping records, making reports and payment of Unemployment Compensation taxes or contributions; and the Contractor agrees to indemnify and hold the Surety harmless and reimburse it for any expense or liability incurred under said statutes in connection with employees of the Contractor, including a sum equal to benefits paid to those who were Contractor's employees, where such benefit payments are charged to the Surety pursuant to any state unemployment compensation statute.

Section 9. **Compliance with Law**. The Contractor further agrees as regards (a) the production, purchase and sale, furnishing and delivering, pricing and use or consumption of materials, supplies and equipment: (b) the hire, tenure or conditions of employment of employees and their hours of work and rates of and the payment of their wages, and (c) the keeping of records, making of reports, and the payment, collection, and/or deduction of Federal, State and local taxes and contributions, that the Contractor will keep and have available all necessary records and make all payments, reports, collections and deductions, and otherwise do any and all things so as to fully comply with all Federal, State and local laws, ordinances and regulations in regard to any and all said matters insofar as they affect or involve the Contractor's performance of this Contract, all so as to fully relieve the Surety from and protect it against any and all responsibility or liability therefore or in regard thereto.

Exhibit 5.5 (continued)

Section 10. **Safety**. In the performance of this Contract, the Contractor shall, at no additional cost to the Surety, comply with current OSHA, local, state and any other applicable safety rules and regulations.

Section 11. **Protection of Work**. The Contractor specifically agrees that he is responsible for the protection of his work until final completion and acceptance thereof by the Surety and Owner and that he will make good or replace, at no expense to the Surety, any damage to this work which occurs prior to said final acceptance.

Section 12. **Assignment**. The Contractor shall not assign or sublet the Contract or any right or interest therein nor shall the Contractor assign any moneys due or to become due hereunder. Any such assignment of the Contract or assignment of any moneys due or to become due or subletting of the Contract shall be null and void and of no force and effect and the Surety shall not be required to recognize any such assignment or subletting. The Contractor shall not sub-contract the Contract or any part thereof without the prior written consent of the Surety. If the Contractor shall sub-contract the Contract or any part thereof with the prior written consent of the Surety, the Contractor shall cause to be inserted in every Sub-contract the provisions of the Insurance requirements of Section 9 hereof.

Section 13. **Prior Understanding or Representation**. The Surety assumes no responsibility for any understanding or representations made by any of its officers or agents prior to the execution of this Contract, unless such understanding or representations by the Surety are expressly stated in the Contract.

Section 14. **Captions**. The captions at the beginning of each Section of this Contract are for convenience only and are to be given no weight in construing the provisions of this Contract.

The Contract shall be binding upon the parties hereto, their respective heirs, executors, administrators, successor an assigns. It contains the entire agreement of the parties and cannot be changed orally.

IN WITNESS WHEREOF, the parties hereto have executed this Contract by their proper officers or duly authorized agents.

______________________________	______________________________
By: ___________________________	By: ___________________________
Contractor	Surety

Exhibit 5.6

Completion Contract (Alternate No. 2—Lump Sum)

THIS COMPLETION CONTRACT (the "Contract") is entered into this _______ day of ___________, 19___ by and between ____________________ (the "Surety") and ____ (the "Completion Contractor").

RECITALS:

WHEREAS, (the "Former Contractor") and (the "Owner") entered into a contract (the "Original Contract") for the Former Contractor to furnish all labor and material and perform all work for ______________________________ (the "Project") in accordance with the terms and provisions of the Original Contract, including all contract documents forming a part of the Original Contract.

WHEREAS, as required by law and under the terms of the Original Contract, the Former Contractor and the Surety made, executed and delivered to the Owner a Performance Bond, Bond No. ________, and a Payment Bond, Bond No. __________ (collectively, the "Bonds"), both in the penal sum of $__________.

WHEREAS, the Former Contractor has voluntarily terminated its performance of the Original Contract, and the Owner has called upon the Surety to fulfill its obligations as surety under the terms of the Performance Bond;

WHEREAS, the Completion Contractor has submitted a Bid Form dated _____________ to the Surety to complete the Original Contract, said Bid Form being attached hereto and incorporated herein by reference as Exhibit 1; and

WHEREAS, the Surety and the Completion Contractor desire to enter into this Contract under the terms and conditions hereinafter set forth.

NOW, THEREFORE, the Surety and the Completion Contractor, for and in consideration of the mutual obligations and promises hereinafter set forth, do contract and agree as follows:

AGREEMENTS:

1. **Conditional Effect of this Contract.** Notwithstanding the date of the execution of this Contract, this Contract shall be conditioned upon and shall be not be effective or in force. until the execution of a takeover agreement by the Owner and the Surety. If this Contract is executed by the Surety and the Completion Contractor prior to the execution of a takeover agreement by the Owner and the Surety, the effective date of this Contract shall be the same as the takeover

Exhibit 5.6 (continued)

agreement. The failure of the Owner and the Surety to execute a takeover agreement shall, at the option of the Surety, render this Contract null and void and of no effect.

2. **Contract Documents.** This Contract consists of the terms and provisions contained herein, including the Instructions to Bidders and all of the Bid Documents described in the Instructions to Bidders; the Completion Contractor's Bid Form dated ________________ attached hereto as Exhibit 1; all documents or specific portions of documents which may be referred to herein or in any Exhibits attached hereto and incorporated herein by reference, thereby making them a part hereof; and the Original Contract, including all General, Supplementary and Special Conditions, drawings, specifications, forms, addenda and documents forming a part of the Original Contract, and any modifications to the Original Contract, all of which are incorporated herein by reference and which are hereinafter referred to collectively as the "Contract Documents."

3. **Strict Compliance.** The Completion Contractor shall be bound to the Surety by all of the terms and provisions of the Contract Documents, including administrative as well as technical provisions, and shall strictly comply therewith in all respects. Furthermore, the Completion Contractor shall be bound in the same manner and to the same extent that the Surety and the Completion Contractor or either of them would be bound to the Owner under the Original Contract, including but not limited to the conditions or determinations by the Owner. with respect to all work done thereunder. The Completion Contractor shall have no responsibility or liability for indebtedness incurred by the Former Contractor.

4. **Full Investigation.** The Completion Contractor agrees that it has fully investigated and is fully informed as to the status and conditions affecting the work to be done and that no representations in reference thereto have been made to it by the Surety or any of its representatives. The Surety makes no warranties or representations, express or implied, to the Completion Contractor with respect to the Contract Documents.

5. **Work to be Performed.** The Completion Contractor shall furnish and pay for all labor, materials, services and equipment and shall do everything else necessary to perform and satisfactorily complete the Original Contract as required by the Contract Documents to the satisfaction of the Surety and the Owner in such manner as to fully protect and save the Surety harmless as to its liability to the Owner for the completion of the Original Contract.

6. **Time for the Performance of the Work.** The Completion Contractor shall commence work within five (5) days after receipt of a written Notice to Proceed issued by the Surety and shall complete all work in accordance with the terms and conditions of the Contract Documents on or before ____________.

Exhibit 5.6 (continued)

Time is of the essence. Subject to allowable time extensions as provided under the terms of the Original Contract, if the Completion Contractor fails to complete the work under the Contract in the time allowed by this paragraph, the Completion Contractor is liable to the Surety for all liquidated damages assessed by the Owner against the Surety under the Original Contract *after* the date of completion set forth herein. The Surety may withhold from the Completion Contractor payments which otherwise may be due to the Completion Contractor in an amount equal to the liquidated damages assessed by the Owner. Any time extensions granted by the Owner to the Former Contractor or the Surety for issues that occurred prior to the date of the Notice to Proceed to the Completion Contractor shall not change the time for completion of the work by the Completion Contractor in this paragraph.

7. **Price.** The Surety shall pay to the Completion Contractor and the Completion Contractor agrees to receive and accept ____________________ (the "Price") as full compensation for the performance and completion of the work as described in the Contract Documents. The cost of all corrective work performed by the Completion Contractor for patently defective work previously performed by the Former Contractor is included in the Price.

8. **Performance and Payment Bonds.** The Completion Contractor shall provide the Surety with Performance and Payment Bonds each in the penal sum of ________________ in the form attached hereto and incorporated herein as Exhibit 2 prior to the Completion Contractor commencing work. The surety must be a commercial surety company currently listed with the U.S. Department of the Treasury, acceptable to the Surety, and licensed to conduct business in the State of__________. At the option of the Surety, the Performance Bond and the Payment Bond may name either the Surety or the Owner as obligee, or both as obligees.

9. **Indemnification Insurance.** The Completion Contractor shall indemnify the Surety and the Owner against any and all loss, liability, costs, expenses and attorney's fees on account of any injury or claimed injury to persons or property arising out of or claimed to arise out of any act or omission by the Completion Contractor, its agents, servants, employees or subcontractors. In this connection, the Completion Contractor shall provide the insurance in the amounts and types as required by the terms of the Original Contract, naming the Surety and the Owner as the named insureds under the policy or policies. The Completion Contractor shall also provide the Surety with an Indemnification and Hold Harmless Agreement and a Notice of Cancellation [providing that the insurance may not be canceled except upon thirty (30) days written notice from the insurer to the Surety and the Owner] in the form attached hereto as Exhibit 3. All

Exhibit 5.6 (continued)

insurance and certificates evidencing said insurance shall be provided to the Surety prior to the Completion Contractor commencing work.

10. **Payment.** As specified in the Original Contract, the Completion Contractor shall prepare, sign and submit to the Surety for the Surety's signature and transmittal to the Owner a request for payment (the "Surety/Owner Requisition") showing the value of the work completed and the materials stored to date in accordance with the terms of the Original Contract. The Surety/Owner Requisition shall be based on the Original Contract price of the Former Contractor. The amount of the Surety/Owner Requisition as approved by the Owner and the Surety shall be due and payable to the Completion Contractor within fifteen (15) days after the Surety receives payment from the Owner.

If the Owner refuses to pay the Surety for any reason related to the Completion Contractor's performance, nonperformance, or in any way related to the Completion Contractor's actions, the Surety shall have no obligation to pay the Completion Contractor until the Owner pays the Surety. In this event, the Surety shall only be obligated to pay the Completion Contractor whatever amounts are received by the Surety within fifteen (15) days of the Surety's receipt of payment from the Owner. The Completion Contractor expressly agrees to accept the risk that it will not be paid for work performed by the Completion Contractor in the event that the Surety is not paid by the Owner for the reasons previously set forth.

In the same time frame as specified in the Original Contract, the Completion Contractor shall prepare and submit to the Surety a request for payment (the "Surety/Completion Contractor Requisition") based upon the amount of the Completion Contractor's price to the Surety. The Surety/Completion Contractor Requisition shall be based on the same percentages of completion (the value of the work completed and the materials stored to date) as the Surety/Owner Requisition. The Completion Contractor shall credit against any such Surety/Completion Contractor Requisition any amounts paid by the Former Contractor or the Surety for equipment and/or materials used by the Completion Contractor in the performance of the work on the Project. The Surety shall pay the Completion Contractor for the Surety/Completion Contractor Requisition as specified in the immediately preceding paragraph.

Each Surety/Completion Contractor Requisition submitted by the Completion Contractor to the Surety shall contain the following certification:

> The Completion Contractor hereby certifies to the Surety that the Completion Contractor has paid or will pay from each Surety/Completion Contractor Requisition all bills and invoices of all subcontractors, materialmen and suppliers on the Project for which the Completion

Exhibit 5.6 (continued)

> Contractor has submitted or is currently submitting a Surety/Completion Contractor Requisition, and that the materials, supplies and equipment placed on the Project by the Completion Contractor for which the Completion Contractor has submitted or is currently submitting a Surety/Completion Contractor Requisition are in accordance with the plans and specifications of the Original Contract.

The Completion Contractor represents and warrants to the Surety that it will use any payments received from the Surety under this section to pay the claims of all laborers, subcontractors and suppliers of equipment and materials on or to the Project. If requested by the Surety or the Owner, it shall become a further condition precedent to payment that the Completion Contractor furnish to the Surety proper waivers of liens, releases, affidavits, sworn statements listing all contracts let and to be let and obligations due or to become due for equipment (and rentals thereof), materials, labor and services under subcontracts entered into by the Completion Contractor, and other evidence establishing that all accounts for services, labor, materials, equipment (and rentals thereof) furnished by or for the Completion Contractor in the performance of this Contract and the prosecution of the work have been fully paid.

Final payment shall be made to the Completion Contractor within thirty (30) days after final completion of the Original Contract, the Owner's acceptance of the Project, and receipt of final payment by the Surety from the Owner, provided that (1) the Completion Contractor shall have furnished evidence satisfactory to the Surety that there are no claims, obligations or liens outstanding or unsatisfied for labor, services, materials, equipment, taxes or other items performed, furnished or incurred for or in connection with the work, and (2) the Completion Contractor shall have fully performed its obligations under this Contract, including but not limited to all obligations required pursuant to the terms of the Original Contract for final payment. Should there be any such claim, obligation or lien after final payment is made, the Completion Contractor shall (1) have the first option to defend any such claim, obligation or lien at the sole cost and expense, including attorney's fees, of the Completion Contractor; (2) indemnity and hold harmless the Surety from any such claim, obligation or lien; and (3) pay to the Surety all monies that the Surety and the Owner shall pay in satisfying, discharging or defending against any such claim, obligation or lien or any action brought or judgment recovered thereon and all costs and expenses, including attorney's fees, disbursements and court costs incurred in connection therewith. Any payments to the Completion Contractor at variance with the provisions of this Contract shall not prejudice or impair the Surety's rights and remedies under the Contract Documents.

Exhibit 5.6 (continued)

11. **Subcontractors.** The Completion Contractor hereby covenants and agrees that it shall pay all of its subcontractors and suppliers. In the event that the Completion Contractor does not pay its subcontractors and suppliers any amounts *not* disputed by the Completion Contractor, the Surety shall have the right to pay such unpaid subcontractors or suppliers directly and deduct said amounts paid from any payment otherwise due to the Completion Contractor.

12. **Maintenance of Records and Accounts.** The Completion Contractor shall maintain separate records and accounts covering all costs incurred and expenditures made by it in completing the work under the Contract. The Completion Contractor shall also maintain separate cost records and accounts reflecting the cost of work identified by the Surety, the Owner, or the Completion Contractor as beyond the scope of the work required under the Original Contract sufficient to allow the Surety to charge the Owner for these costs. The Completion Contractor shall make such records and accounts and supporting vouchers available for inspection and verification by the Surety and/or any authorized representatives of the Owner until the expiration of three (3) years from the date of final payment under the Contract.

13. **Latent Defects and Warranty Work Applicable to the Work of the Former Contractor.** The Completion Contractor shall correct all latent defective work performed by the Former Contractor and perform all warranty work applicable to the work of the Former Contractor. The Completion Contractor shall notify the Owner and the Surety in the event that any latent defects of any type in the workmanship and/or materials provided by the Former Contractor or a subcontractor of the Former Contractor become evident during the performance of the Completion Contract. The Completion Contractor shall obtain the approval of the Owner and the Surety in writing before proceeding to correct such defects if the corrective work is to be the basis for any claim for additional compensation under this Contract. The Completion Contractor shall be paid by the Surety for such warranty work and the correction of all latent defective work in accordance with the provisions of Exhibit 4 which is attached hereto and incorporated herein by reference.

14. **Defects In Work.** The Completion Contractor shall be responsible for any and all defects in the work which is performed by the Completion Contractor or any of the Completion Contractor's subcontractors or materialmen.

15. **Independent Contractor.** Except as otherwise provided in this Contract and the Original Contract, the Completion Contractor will be permitted to exercise the full prerogatives of a prime contractor in prosecuting the work, including but not limited to the selection and classification of supervisors and workers, scheduling, determination of equipment and material requirements, and the establishment of work hours and work week, including overtime. It is further

Exhibit 5.6 (continued)

understood and agreed that the Completion Contractor is an independent contractor in connection with all work to be performed by it pursuant to the Contract Documents.

16. **Changes.** Any and all provisions relating to changes contained in the Original Contract are specifically incorporated herein by reference and shall be binding between the Completion Contractor and the Surety.

17. **The Completion Contractor as the Surety's Representative on the Project.** The Surety shall be represented at the Project by the Completion Contractor. Prior to the issuance of the Notice to Proceed, the Completion Contractor shall name, and the Surety shall specifically authorize in writing an individual with the Completion Contractor to be its representative (the "Authorized Individual") solely for the purposes set forth in this paragraph. The Authorized Individual will represent the Surety in dealing with the Owner on day to day construction issues with respect to the Project. The Surety hereby designates the Authorized Individual to prepare and process pay requisitions on the Contract. However, the Surety will sign all pay requisitions submitted to the Owner. Payments from the Owner shall be made payable to the Surety and transmitted to the Surety at the following address, unless and until the Owner is notified in writing of any different address:

____

____

____

____

The Authorized Individual shall have, on behalf of the Surety, the authority to negotiate and sign change orders for extra work requested or required by the Owner (hereinafter "Change Order") without the Surety's prior written approval, provided the Change Order does not exceed $___________ and the Completion Contractor requests and is given additional time to perform the Change Order. If the Change Order does exceed $_____________, or if the Completion Contractor requests additional time but no additional time is given to the Completion Contractor to perform the Change Order, then the Surety's prior written approval is required to negotiate the Change Order and the final Change Order must be-signed by the Surety and not the Authorized Individual. If the total of all of the approved Change Orders exceeds the sum of $_________, then the Surety, and not the Authorized Individual, must approve in writing all additional or subsequent Change Orders regardless of the amount of each such Change Orders. The Authorized Individual has no authority to negotiate deductive Change Orders, credits, backcharges or net deductions from the Original Contract of any

Exhibit 5.6 (continued)

nature whatsoever without the Surety's prior written approval. The Authorized Individual has no authority to negotiate on behalf of the Surety with the Completion Contractor with respect to any issues or disputes arising between the Surety and the Completion Contractor.

18. **Disputes.** The contractual remedial procedure described in the General Provisions of the Original Contract is specifically incorporated herein by reference and made a part of this Contract.

The Completion Contractor shall first pursue and fully exhaust said procedure before commencing any other action against the Surety for any claims it may have arising out of its performance of the work herein. The Completion Contractor shall have the first option to prosecute and settle claims against the Owner prior to the Surety incurring costs and expenses, including attorney's fees, for which the Surety would seek reimbursement from the Completion Contractor. However, upon the Completion Contractor's written request, the Surety agrees to prosecute all claims submitted by the Completion Contractor under the contractual remedial procedure of the Original Contract on behalf of and to the extent required by the Completion Contractor. The Completion Contractor agrees to be responsible for preparation and active prosecution of the claims to the extent permitted and shall reimburse the Surety all expenses and costs, including attorney's fees, incurred by the Surety on behalf of the Completion Contractor. The Surety agrees not to settle any of the Completion Contractor's claims with the Owner without the Completion Contractor's written consent, which consent shall not be unreasonably withheld, and to pay the Completion Contractor whatever amounts it receives from the Owner for the Completion Contractor's claim(s), less the Surety's actual costs, including but not limited to attorney's fees, consulting engineer fees and accounting fees. The Surety's receipt of said costs from the Completion Contractor shall be in addition to any recovery the Surety shall receive for itself from the Owner, which may be incurred by the Surety during prosecution of the completion contractor's claims. To the extent that the Surety shall receive, along with the completion Contractor, any recovery from the owner under this paragraph, the Surety and the completion Contractor shall share in the cost of the claim process on a pro rata basis calculated on the amounts received by the Surety and the completion Contractor, or on any other basis mutually agreed to by the Surety and the Completion Contractor. The Completion Contractor agrees that the Surety's liability herein is strictly limited to the amount(s) the Surety actually receives from the Owner, less the above noted costs. Final determination of the Completion Contractor's claim(s) by the appropriate Board or Court shall be final and binding on the Completion Contractor.

Upon receiving the written consent of the Surety, the Completion Contractor may pursue any claims it may have against the Owner in the name of the Surety

Exhibit 5.6 (continued)

if the claims arise out of the Completion Contractor's performance of the work herein and are not encompassed by the contractual remedial procedure in the Original Contract and this Contract. The Completion Contractor agrees to be totally responsible for the preparation and prosecution of any such claims and shall reimburse the Surety for all expenses and costs, including attorney's fees incurred by the Surety in this regard. Final determination of the Completion Contractor's claims by the appropriate forum shall be final and binding on the Completion Contractor, and the Surety shall have no liability, responsibility or obligation to the Completion Contractor except as may be otherwise provided in this Contract.

Any disputes between the Surety and the Completion Contractor *not* involving the Owner in any way shall be determined as follows. At the sole option and election of the Surety, claims disputes or other matters in question between the parties to this Contract arising out of or relating to this Contract or breach thereof shall, at the option of the Surety, be subject to and decided by arbitration in accordance with the Construction Industry Arbitration Rules of the American Arbitration Association in effect as of the date of this Contract; provided, however, the parties agree to allow the arbitrators to, in their discretion, grant discovery to the parties as would otherwise be available in a court of competent jurisdiction under the ________ Rules of Civil Procedure. In the absence of the Surety exercising its right to arbitrate, all disputes shall be resolved in the __________ Court for ________________ and the parties hereby consent to and agree to the jurisdiction of that Court; provided, however, in the event the presence of third parties is required for the complete resolution of the dispute over whom the __________ Court for ____________ does not have jurisdiction, then the Surety, at its sole option, may elect to have the dispute resolved in any court of appropriate jurisdiction.

Additional persons or entities may be joined in any arbitration instituted under this Contract in any circumstances where such joinder would be authorized by the law of the State of _______ in a court of competent jurisdiction.

19. **Termination of Agreement.**

(a) *Termination for Convenience*. This Contract may be terminated in whole or in part by the Surety at any time for the Surety's convenience, provided the Completion Contractor is given not less that ten (10) calendar days written notice of intent to terminate and an opportunity for consultation with the Surety prior to termination. Upon receipt of the termination notice, the Completion Contractor shall promptly discontinue all services (unless the notice directs otherwise) and delivers or otherwise make available to the Surety all data, drawings, specifications, reports, estimates, summaries, and such other information and materials that may have been accumulated by the Completion Contractor

Exhibit 5.6 (continued)

in performing this Contract. Subject to the provisions of this paragraph, the Completion Contractor shall be entitled to payment of all costs and profit which it would be entitled to recover under the terms of the Original Contract as if the Owner had terminated this Contract for convenience. The termination of this Contract for any reason, whether for convenience or for cause as described in paragraph 19(b) below, shall not relieve the Completion Contractor of its responsibilities under this Contract and the Original Contract for the work performed and materials supplied, nor shall it relieve the surety for the Completion Contractor of its obligations under the Completion Contractor's Performance Bond and Payment Bond for any claims arising out of the work performed and the materials supplied by the Completion Contractor.

(b) *Termination for Cause.* Should the Completion Contractor, at anytime, in the judgment of either the Owner or the Surety, refuse or fail to supply a sufficient number of properly skilled workmen or materials, tools, equipment, facilities, or supplies of a proper quality; or fail in any respect to prosecute the work with promptness and diligence; or interfere with unduly or impede the work of others on the Project; or fail in the performance of any of its obligations under this Contract or under the Original Contract, and should the Completion Contractor fail within three (3) days after receipt of written notice from either the Owner or the Surety to remedy such default; or if a Petition of Bankruptcy should be filed by or against the Completion Contractor; or if the Completion Contractor shall become insolvent or fail to make prompt payment to all the subcontractors and/or materialmen or laborers; or shall disregard any applicable state, federal, local or municipal law, ordinance, rules and regulations pertaining to the work; or disregard the instructions of the Owner or the Surety; or for any other cause whatsoever shall not carry on the work in an acceptable manner, the Surety may, in any such event, either terminate this Contract or may exclude the Completion Contractor and its employees and agents from the work without terminating this Contract. In any case, the Surety may take possession of all materials, equipment and tools, and complete, itself or through others, the Completion Contractor's work, charging such completion costs incurred as a result of default against the unpaid balance. If such costs or expenses shall exceed the unpaid balance, the Completion Contractor agrees to pay the deficit to the Surety. The Surety's costs for correcting defective work done by the Completion Contractor shall be reimbursed in full by the Completion Contractor. In the event of any default under this paragraph, the Completion Contractor shall not be entitled to any further payments under this Contract until the Completion Contractor's work shall be entirely finished and accepted by the Owner, and payment therefore made to the Surety. The remedies afforded to the Surety in the above circumstances are cumulative to any remedies available under the

Exhibit 5.6 (continued)

Original Contract, which remedies specifically are also declared to be available to the Surety as against the Completion Contractor.

If the Completion Contractor is terminated for cause in accordance with this paragraph, and it is later determined that the Completion Contractor did not fail to fulfill its contractual obligations, then any such termination by the Surety shall be deemed to have been a termination for convenience, and in such event, adjustment of the contract price provided for in this Contract for termination for convenience shall be made as provided herein.

Under any and all circumstances, the Surety shall not be responsible to the Completion Contractor for damages for wrongful termination in excess of the payments herein set forth, whether or not such damages are defined as direct or consequential and whether or not determined to be in tort, contract, negligence, strict liability, warranty, expressed or implied, or otherwise.

20. **Force Majeure.** In the event the construction of the Project is interrupted or prevented by acts of God, acts of war or rebellion, labor disturbances (other than those caused by the Completion Contractor), acts of Government or governmental officers or any cause beyond the control of the Surety, the Surety shall be absolved of any responsibility therefore. The Surety's responsibility shall be limited to the presentation of the Completion Contractor's claim to the Owner. Any expense incident thereto shall be borne by the Completion Contractor. The Completion Contractor further agrees that, with respect to such claim, it shall have no greater rights against the Surety than the Surety has against the Owner under the terms of the Original Contract, and the Completion Contractor will abide by whatever final decision is made under the Original Contract regarding these claims. In the event of an interruption of the work caused by the Acts described above, the Completion Contractor shall return to its performance at the earliest possible date.

21. **Whole Agreement.** This Contract contains the entire understandings and agreements of the parties hereto. All oral or written agreements prior to the effective date of this Contract and which relate to this Contract and the matters set forth herein are declared null and void. Any modification of this Contract must be made in writing and executed by the parties hereto.

22. **Interpretation.** In the event that there is any provision of this Contract which is inconsistent or conflicting with any other documents forming a part of this Contract, including but not limited to the Original Contract referred to herein, the terms and conditions of this Contract shall govern and control.

23. **Governing Law.** This Contract is executed pursuant to and governed by the laws of the State of ___________.

Exhibit 5.6 (continued)

24. **Notice.** Any notice required to be made under the terms of this Contract shall be deemed made if either party mails such notice by first class mail, postage prepaid, as follows:

As to the Completion Contractor:

As to the Completion Contractor:

____

____

____

Attention: ________________________________

As to the Surety:

____

____

____

Attention: ________________________________

25. **Construction of Contract.** It is understood and agreed by the Surety and the Completion Contractor that this Contract shall be construed without any regard to any presumption or other rule requiring construction against the party causing this Contract, or any Exhibits attached to this Contract, to be drafted.

26. **Execution in Counterparts.** This Contract may be executed in one or more counterparts, each of which shall be deemed to be an original.

IN WITNESS WHEREOF, the parties hereto have affixed their hands and seals to this Contract the day and year first set forth above, and the individuals who execute this Contract personally represent and warrant that they have full authority to execute this Contract on behalf of the respective parties.

WITNESS:	COMPLETION CONTRACTOR
________________________	By: ________________ (SEAL)
WITNESS:	SURETY
________________________	By: ________________ (SEAL)

Exhibit 5.7

Agreement With Subcontractor

Date ____________

To: SURETY
Re: CONTRACT BETWEEN ________________________________
____
____

I (We) am (are) a Subcontractor of ____________________________ on the above named contract for the work described as follows: __________ ________________________________, per plans and specifications, including Addenda Nos. ______________________________

1. Amount of original subcontract . . . . ____________
2. Approved changes in subcontract amount . . . . ____________
3. Total or adjusted present subcontract amount . . . . . . ____________
4. Value of work performed and/or approved material stored on work-site through ____________ . . . . ____________
5. Value to be performed after ____________ . . . . ____________
6. Retainage on No. 4 above . . . . ____________
7. Value of No. 4 above less retainage (No. 6) . . . . ____________
8. Total payments received from ____________ . . . . ____________
9. Net amount due through ______________ per affidavit of Claim being filed with you . . . . ____________

In consideration of my (our) being paid within ten days from above date by ______________________________, Surety for (PRINCIPAL), the net amount of $____________ now due (No. 9 above), and its agreement to pay me (us) our retainage of $____________ (No. 6 above) upon acceptance of the project by the Owner, I (we) hereby agree to perform the balance of my (our) work, amounting to $____________ (No. 5 above) for whoever completes the project.

Exhibit 5.7 (continued)

____
Subcontractor

Date: ________________

SURETY hereby agrees to the above and to pay you $___________ on or before ten days above date and $___________ or acceptance of the project by the Owner.

SURETY

____
Authorized Representative

Exhibit 6.1

Principal's Acknowledgment of Default to Surety

Owner/General Contractor
Address

Re: *(Description of Contract)*

Gentlemen:

We regret to advise you that we are unable to complete the captioned contract. We, accordingly, hereby irrevocably acknowledge that we are in default on said contract and waive any notice required under the contract documents.

We request that you discuss with our surety the matter of completing this contract.

Very truly yours,

Exhibit 6.2

Assignment from Principal to Surety of Contract Rights and Proceeds

KNOW ALL MEN BY THESE PRESENTS:

THAT, we (*Principal's name and address*), hereby intending to be legally bound, and in consideration of One and 00/100 ($1.00) Dollar, and other good and valuable considerations, receipt whereof is hereby acknowledged, for ourselves and our successors and assigns, do hereby assign, transfer and set over unto ____________________, its successors and assigns, all of our right, title and interest in and to any and all payments on account of estimates, change orders, including the final estimate, final payment and retainage, and any other money now due or hereafter to become due, arising out of our contract described and identified as follows:

(Describe contract)

together with all rights of action accrued or which may accrue thereunder; and we do hereby constitute and appoint said ______________________ our true and lawful attorney-in-fact, irrevocably in the premises, to do and perform all acts, matters and things touching upon the premises, in like manner, and to all intents and purposes as we could if personally present.

IN WITNESS WHEREOF, we have caused these presents to be executed by (Our duly authorized officers) this _____ day of __________, 19___.

PRINCIPAL

By: ______________________________

(CORPORATE SEAL)

(ATTEST OR WITNESS)

____

Secretary

Exhibit 6.3

Letter of Direction from Principal to Obligee

Owner
Address

Re: *(Description of Contract)*

Gentlemen:

We hereby irrevocably request that all payments due or to become due on account of the contract dated (*Date*) between (*Obligee*) and (*Principal*) for (*Describe work*) be forwarded to the undersigned in care of (*Surety*), (*Address of field claim office*), which company is surety on Performance and labor and Material Payment bonds given in connection with the aforesaid contract.

There will be no modification or change in these instructions without the written authorization and consent of (*Surety*).

PRINCIPAL

By: ______________________________

Exhibit 6.4

Power of Attorney from Principal to Surety

KNOW ALL MEN BY THESE PRESENTS:

THAT (*Principal's name and address*) does constitute and appoint (*Surety and Field Office Address*), its Claims Attorney, of the same address, and either of them and their successors and assigns, its true and lawful Attorney-in-fact, for it, and in its name, to receive, endorse, and collect any and all checks and drafts or other forms of remittance payable to (*Principal*) and issued in payment of money earned or to be earned, or to become due and payable upon the contract hereinafter described or identified, and including all retained percentages, estimates, final payments, and any other moneys now due or which may become due, drawn by (*Obligee*) in payment for work performed and materials furnished and representing the proceeds of a certain contract dated (*Date*) between (*Obligee*) and (*Principal*) for (*Description of Work*) and which may require endorsement for deposit, cashing, collection or payment and does authorize and empower its said Attorney-in-Fact, or either of them, to give full discharge and acquittance for the same and hereby ratifies and confirms all that lawfully may be done by virtue hereof. This Power of Attorney being coupled with an interest is irrevocable; and (*Principal*) hereby revokes any and all previous Powers of Attorney executed in reference to the disposition of the proceeds of the above-described contracts.

IN WITNESS WHEREOF, (*Principal*) has caused this instrument to be executed by (*its duly authorized officers*) this day of ________________, 19___.

PRINCIPAL

By: ______________________________

(CORPORATE SEAL IF APPROPRIATE)

(ATTEST OR WITNESS)

____

____

Exhibit 6.5

Invitation to Bid (Fixed or Cost-Plus Fee)

TO: Invited Bidders

RE: Project	—	(Description of Project)
FORMER CONTRACTOR	—	(Name, Address, and Telephone Number of Former Contractor)
SURETY FOR FORMER CONTRACTOR	—	(Name, Address, and Telephone Number of Surety)

On ______________, 19_____, the City of ________________ terminated its contract with the former contractor in connection with the captioned job.

The Surety (*Name of Surety*) is interested in obtaining proposals for the completion of all uncompleted work in accordance with the original documents, including plans, ________________ City Department of Works' Standard Specifications, modifications and any addenda thereto.

Time is of the essence in completing this project. Bidders should state the length of time in consecutive calendar days that will be required to complete the work. Stipulation of completion time shall be considered as an element of importance in determining the contract award.

At this time it is not known if the successful bidder will enter into a contract with the Surety or directly with the owner.

Award of the contract will be made to the bidder who, in the judgment of the Surety and owner, submits the best responsible bid, however, the right is reserved to reject any and all bids, and waive any informalities.

No bid bond or bid security is required, however, the successful bidder will be required at the time of execution of the contract to furnish contract bonds at his own expense. If the contract is entered into directly with the owner, then the bonds shall comply with the bond form set forth in the contract book. If the contract is executed with the Surety, Performance and Payment Bonds each in the penal sum equal to the amount of his bid will be required, and will run in

Exhibit 6.5 (continued)

favor of the Surety. In any event, such bonds are to be executed by a corporate surety authorized to do business in the State of ____________ and acceptable to the owner and/or (*Surety*).

The successful bidder will be required to furnish, at his own expenses, the necessary workers' compensation and public liability insurance, or other insurance as may be required in the original contract between the owner and the former contractor.

The proposal shall include the cost of furnishing all equipment, tools, labor, materials, and appurtenances as may be required and necessary to complete the project.

Surety has been informed by the owner that subsequent to the award of this contract to the former contractor, there has been an increase in the minimum hourly wage rates. However, notwithstanding the subsequent increase, the owner has advised that the wage rates scheduled in the contract will be accepted. It is recommended that you verify this by contacting Mr. ____________________, Department of ____________, Phone (____) __________.

Questions concerning the nature and extent of any part of the work may be presented to Mr. ________________ or Mr. ____________, owner's representative.

Submission of a bid will be deemed a representation without reservation that the bidder has fully examined the drawings and all the bid documents (including all addenda); and,

That it has verified all information given in the contract documents and specifications or shown on drawings and has availed himself of the opportunity to obtain such further information regarding the drawings, the specifications, and other bid documents as he may require; and,

That it knows, understands, and will comply with all laws, codes, ordinances, rules and regulations of the City of __________ and the State of __________, and,

That it has examined the various locations of repairs and the adjoining premises and has made his own estimate of the facilities and difficulties attending the execution of this work and that he has based his bid upon his own investigations

Exhibit 6.5 (continued)

and has allowed sufficient sums in his bid to provide for or against any and all contingencies.

No extra compensation or allowance shall subsequently be made to the contractor for omissions, errors, misunderstandings, misinterpretations or ignorance on his part of any requirement of the drawings and specifications or of any conditions or requirements of the contract documents or any of their terms or provisions.

As to any warranties in the contract documents, including those as to defective workmanship and materials, the successful bidder assumes responsibility for his own work, including any visibly defective work done by the former contractor, however, the successful bidder assumes no responsibility as to such warranties as regards any unknown present, latent and invisible defective work performed by the former contractor.

The successful bidder will not be liable for unpaid accounts or indebtedness incurred by the former contractor.

All costs and expenses attendant to estimating, preparing and submitting the bids herein invited are to be borne in their entirety by the bidder whether or not such bid is accepted.

Subcontracts for portions of the work were entered into by Former Contractor. It is anticipated that these subcontractors will be willing to enter into new subcontract agreements directly with the successful bidder and for amounts equivalent to the value of their uncompleted work to be performed after ______________, 19_____.

A list of such subcontractors is attached and marked Exhibit A. HOWEVER, it will be incumbent upon the successful bidder to directly enter into any subcontract agreements for such portions of the work which he may desire to subcontract; and directly enter into any purchase orders for additional materials; all of which must be assumed by such bidder as a part of his costs in completing the project. Final choice in the selection of subcontractors or vendors is with the bidder subject to owner's approval.

Attached is a listing of materials which each bidder should verify as to quantity, quality, availability and usefulness. These materials have been or will be paid for by the surety where proper bond claims have been or will be made, and to the extent that these materials can be used by the successful bidder, there will

Exhibit 6.5 (continued)

be no costs to said bidder. The surety makes no representations or warranties as to these materials.

The project shall be bid (1) as a lump sum, and (2) as a cost plus, not to exceed a guaranteed maximum.

Sealed bids addressed to (*Surety*), attention the undersigned, will be received at (*address*), (*city*), (*state*), (*zip*), on or before p.m. on the ____________ day of ____________, 19___.

SURETY

By: ______________________________

Exhibit 6.6

Invitation to Bid (Unit Price)

TO: Invited Bidders

RE: (DESCRIPTION OF PROJECT)

OWNER: (NAME AND ADDRESS)

FORMER CONTRACTOR — (NAME, ADDRESS, AND TELEPHONE NUMBER OF FORMER CONTRACTOR)

SURETY FOR FORMER CONTRACTOR — (NAME, ADDRESS, AND TELEPHONE NUMBER OF SURETY)

The contract between the Owner and the Former Contractor was terminated on or about _____________, 19___. The contract was partially performed at that time. Copy of last estimate showing work completed as of _______________, 19_____ is available to you at the District office of the State Road Commission of ___________________ at _________________. There is attached to this invitation a proposal form which schedules approximate remaining quantities.

There is now, or will be within the immediate future, a cross-sectioning being done of the bottoms of the cuts to determine with perhaps greater accuracy than reflected by the last estimate the remaining quantities in that phase of the work and a further estimate will be made as a result of the cross-sectioning; however, your bid should be based upon the approximate remaining unit quantities as shown by the attached Schedule of Prices. Of course, it will be necessary that you make your own inspection of the job and your bid should be based on that inspection.

Surety desires to obtain bids in the form of a gross lump-sum proposal for completion of all visibly uncompleted work in strict accordance with the contract documents, including plans and specifications thereof, including correction of any patent or visibly defective work, if any, done by, or under, the Former Contractor, and to provide all necessary machinery, tools and apparatus and furnish all labor and materials and things necessary in the completion of said project. The lump-sum proposal referred to herein will be based on your estimate of the uncompleted quantities shown on your proposal form and final payment will be based upon actual work done at the unit prices shown as measured by State Road Commission of _______________.

Exhibit 6.6 (continued)

Your proposal should include a completion date. Time is of the essence in the completion of this project and liquidated damages may be assessed at the rate fixed in the original defaulted contract of the Former Contractor for any delay beyond the stated completion date in your proposal.

A contract for completion will be entered into with the successful bidder. In the event the successful bidder's unit prices exceed those of the Former Contractor for the remaining work in the original contract, it will be provided in the completion contract that such excess amounts will be paid to the completing contractor by Surety in the same manner and at the same times as the State Road Commission of ________________ will pay on future estimates for the completion of the remaining work at the original contract unit prices.

Bidders may obtain a copy of the original proposal and plans and specifications and change orders from the District Office of the State Road Commission of _________ in __________, ________. Mr. _____________ of that office will be of assistance to you.

Award of a contract will be to the bidder who, in the judgment of Surety and the Owner, submits the most acceptable bid, with the right reserved to reject any and all bids.

No bid bond is required; however, successful bidder will be required at the time of execution of a contract for completion of the work to furnish, at his own expense, to Owner and to Surety a performance and payment bond in form similar to that provided by the Former Contractor, in a penal sum equal to the amount of his bid, such bond to be executed by a corporate surety authorized to do business in the State of West Virginia and acceptable to the Owner and to Surety.

The successful bidder will be required to furnish at his own expense, the necessary compensation, public liability, builders risk or other insurance as required in the contract documents and to provide Surety and the Owner with certificates of such insurance providing for a notice of at least ten days to be given.

The lump-sum proposal shall also include cost of furnishing all equipment, tools, labor, materials, and appurtenances as may be required and necessary to complete the project.

There are four approved subcontractors on this project. These subcontractors and the nature of their work are as follows:

_____________ Clearing Contractors — Clearing and grubbing.

_____________ Drilling Company — Drill, blast, and break up rock, unclassified excavation.

Exhibit 6.6 (continued)

______________ Service, Inc. — Limestone, fertilizer, seeding and mulching.

______________ Corporation — Right-of-Way fence.

______________________ Clearing Contractors has completed its work, and ____________ Drilling Company has performed part of its subcontract though the amount earned is presently in question. ____________ Corporation has notified us that they would want to renegotiate their subcontract. __________ Drilling Company is located at ________________, ________________; ____________ Service, Inc. is located at _____________, _____________; and ____________ Corporation is located at ______________, __________, telephone (____) _________). It will be the sole responsibility of the successful bidder to arrange and enter into agreements with subcontractors or vendors for the required materials of their choice.

Claims and indebtedness against Former Contractor by all subcontractors and material furnishers for labor performed or material furnished will not be the responsibility of the successful bidder. This company as Surety for the Former Contractor will make payment in due course and manner of all such proper and valid claims.

The successful bidder assumes full responsibility for his own work done by any subcontractor working under him, including any patent or visibly defective work done by the Former Contractor and subcontractors working under the Former Contractor. All bids shall be sealed in an envelope identified on the outside as to the project and name of the bidder and shall be delivered by mail or otherwise the office of ________________, Attorneys, ________________ Building, ________________, ________________ by _____ o'clock p.m. on the _____ day of ________________, 19___, at which time they will be opened in the presence of any invited bidders who are present.

The successful bidder shall furnish the Owner an acceptable progress schedule. Any tools or equipment found on the job site and not required or intended by corporation into the project as materials are not in the control or possession of either Surety or Owner and so far as either is aware are not available for use by the successful bidder.

Rental of the trailer being used by the State Road Commission on the project is now being paid by Surety. It is suggested that the successful bidder may wish to continue the leasing of this field office trailer with ________________ ________________ Company, ________________ Avenue, ______________,

Exhibit 6.6 (continued)

_______________ (Telephone (____) __________). The rental period runs from month to month beginning with the second of each month. Surety will pay the rental up to the second day of the month following the date that the successful bidder enters into a contract for the completion of the remaining work on this project.

Attached is a listing of materials which each bidder should verify as to quantity, quality, availability, and usefulness. These materials have been or will be paid for by the Surety but the Surety makes no representations or warranties as to these materials. To the extent these materials can be used by the successful bidder there will be no costs to said bidder.

Surety has arranged with ____________ Gas Company of ___________, ____________ for the supplying of fuel to the trailer-office being used by the State Road Commission. The successful bidder may wish to continue this arrangement.

All cost and expense incurred in estimating, preparing and submitting the bids herein invited are to be assumed entirely by the prospective bidder, or bidder whether or not his bid is accepted.

Should any information be required from Surety, please contact ________ _______________ (Telephone (____) _________). For any information desired from the Owner you may contact _______________________ at the District office (Telephone (____) __________).

SURETY

By: ______________________________

Exhibit 6.7

Bid Proposal

Contract No.: ____________
F. A. Project: ____________

Proposal of ______________________________________ *(Name)*, ______________________________________ *(Address)*, to furnish and deliver all materials and to do and perform all work, in accordance with the Specifications and Contract, appropriate edition, of the State Highway Administration of ____________, except as specifically stated otherwise in the "Special Provisions" relating to this contract for the ________________ County, State of ________________ on which proposals will be received until ________ on the _____ day of ___________, 19____, this work being situated as follows:

SPECIAL PROVISIONS
See attached sheets

To the *(Name and Address of Surety)*

Gentlemen:

In accordance with the Invitation for Bids of *(Surety)* for the work hereinbefore named and in conformity with the plans and specifications now on file in the office of the State Highway Administration, I/we hereby certify and I/we am/are the only person, or persons, interested in this proposal as principal(s), that it is made without collusion with any person, firm or corporation, that an examination has been made of the Specifications and Contract forms, including the "Special Provisions" contained herein, also of the plans, and of the site of the work, and hereby propose to furnish all necessary machinery, equipment, tools, labor and other means of construction, and furnish all materials specified, in the manner and at the time prescribed, and understand that the quantities of work as shown herein are approximate only and are subject to increase or decrease, and further understand that all quantities or work, whether increased or decreased, are to be performed at the following unit prices:

Exhibit 6.7 (continued)

Date: ________________ ______________________________
(Name of Affiant)

Sworn to and subscribed before me this ____ day of ________________, 19___.

____
Notary Public

My Commission Expires:

____

Exhibit 6.8

Schedule of Prices

ITEM NO.	APPROXIMATE ORIGINAL QUANTITIES	ITEM	APPROXIMATE REMAINING QUANTITIES	UNIT PRICE BID IN WRITING	UNIT PRICE BID IN FIGURES	TOTAL AMOUNT
1	73 Acres	Clearing and Grubbing	1 Acre			
2	1,546,950 CY	Unclassified Excavation	475,000 CY			
15	167 CY	Traffic Bound Base Course Material	167 CY			
42-3 (18")	1,412 LF	Full Bituminous Coated and Paved Invert Corrugated Metal Pipe, Type 2	1,195 LF			
42-3 (24")	470 LF	Full Bituminous Coated and Paved Invert Corrugated Metal Pipe, Type 2	397 LF			
42-3 (30")	1,584 LF	Full Bituminous Coated and Paved Invert Corrugated Metal Pipe, Type 2	1,272 LF			
42-3 (36")	138 LF	Full Bituminous Coated and Paved Invert Corrugated Metal Pipe, Type 2	138 LF			
42-3 (36")	308 LF	Full Bituminous Coated and Paved Invert Corrugated Metal Pipe, Type 2, 10 Gauge	-0-			
42-3 (42")	38 LF	Full Bituminous Coated and Paved Invert Corrugated Metal Pipe, Type 2	38 LF			
42-3 (42")	438 LF	Full Bituminous Coated and Paved Invert Corrugated Metal Pipe, Type 2, 8 Gauge	-0-			
42-3 (48")	464 LF	Full Bituminous Coated and Paved Invert Corrugated Metal Pipe, Type 2, 10 Gauge	-0-			
42-3 (54")	442 LF	Full Bituminous Coated and Paved Invert Corrugated Metal Pipe, Type 2, 8 Gauge	-0-			

Exhibit 6.8

Schedule of Prices (continued)

ITEM NO.	APPROXIMATE ORIGINAL QUANTITIES	ITEM	APPROXIMATE REMAINING QUANTITIES	UNIT PRICE BID IN WRITING	UNIT PRICE BID IN FIGURES	TOTAL AMOUNT
126	500 M. Gal.	Water for Dust Palliative	500 M. Gal.			
129-1	1 Ea.	Project Markers	1 ea.			
129-2	4 Ea.	Right-of-Way Markers	4 ea.			
131-1	29,385 LF	Right-of-Way Fence	29,385 LF			
133-1	71.1 Ton	Ground Agricultural Limestone	71.1 Ton			
133-2	19.8 Ton	Fertilizer	19.8 Ton			
133-3	49.36 Acre	Seeding	49.36 Acre			
133-4	49.36 Acre	Mulching	49.36 Acre			
136-1	L.S.	Standard Field Office and Storage Building	L.S.			
136-3	L.S.	Building Equipment	L.S.			
138	L.S.	Construction Layout Stakes	L.S.			
48-1(IYI) 42	148 LF	Reinforced Concrete Culvert, Storm Drain and Sewer Pipe	148 LF			

Exhibit 6.9

Bidder's Affidavit

CONTRACT NO. ________

FAP NO. ______________ EFFECTIVE ____________________

PROJECT: ____

I HEREBY CERTIFY that I am the ______________ (title) and duly authorized representative of the firm of ______________________ whose address is ____________________________ and that neither I, nor, to the best of my knowledge, information and belief, the above firm, nor any officer, director or partner of the above firm, nor any employee of the above firm directly involved in obtaining contracts with the State, or any county or other subdivision of the State, has been convicted of bribery, attempted bribery, or conspiracy to bribe under the laws of any state or federal government, except as here expressly stated (if any):____

____

____.

I acknowledge that this Affidavit is furnished to the Secretary of the ______________ Department of Transportation and may be distributed to boards, commissions administrations, departments and agencies of the State of ___________, counties, or other subdivisions of the State of ___________, other states and the federal government. I further acknowledge that this Affidavit is subject to applicable State laws, both criminal and civil, and that any misrepresentation herein made may disqualify the above firm with respect to the work sought.

I DO SOLEMNLY DECLARE AND AFFIRM UNDER THE PENALTIES OF PERJURY THAT THE CONTENTS OF THE FOREGOING DOCUMENT ARE TRUE AND CORRECT.

Exhibit 6.9 (continued)

Date: ________________ ______________________________

(Name of Affiant)

Sworn to and subscribed before me this ____ day of ________________, 19___.

____

Notary Public

My Commission Expires:

____

Exhibit 6.10

Surety's Notice of Its Legal and Equitable Rights, Surety's Waiver of Right to Complete, and Proposal to Tender New Contractor

Owner/Obligee
Address

RE: (*Description of Contract*)

Gentlemen:

Receipt is hereby acknowledged of your letter dated ________________ advising that (*Principal*) has defaulted on its contract as identified in the caption.

The (*Surety*), as surety for (*Principal*), hereby waives any right it may have to take over and complete this contract. However, it will promptly undertake, with your assistance, to obtain bids from other contractors and submit to you, at the earliest date practicable, the lowest responsible and responsive bidder so that a new contract can be made between (*Obligee*) and such bidder to undertake completion of the work in accordance with the plans and specifications.

We propose that the successful bidder will provide surety bond(s) in the same form as provided by this company and its principal, (*Principal*). The amount(s) of this (these) bond(s) will be determined by the amount of the bid submitted by the successful bidder in the same manner as was (were) the original bond(s).

Simultaneously, with the execution of the new contract this company will make payment to (*Obligee*) in an amount sufficient to pay for any costs to complete beyond any remaining unpaid amount under the terms of the original contract.

NOTE: In the event that the contract is unit priced, the above paragraph will have to be modified. The following language is proposed:

> To the extent that the unit prices bid by the new contractor are higher than unit prices chargeable under the original contract on work performed and approved for payment, we propose to promptly fund such difference by payment to the new contractor or to (*Obligee*).

It is our view that the interest of all concerned is best served by the use of this proposal in that (*Obligee*) will have direct control over the new contractor

Exhibit 6.10 (continued)

in the same manner as before, and that arrangements for completion can most expeditiously be completed. Additionally, and most significantly, (*Obligee*) will receive fully the benefits of the surety bond.

The surety has received formal notice of claims for outstanding unpaid bills incurred by the contractor in connection with this work, including claims of subcontractors and claims for labor and materials furnished. The total amount is unknown but presently available information indicates the surety will sustain losses under the payment obligation of the surety bond given in this matter. Subject to your right to expend the unpaid portion of contract funds for completion of the work, the surety hereby makes claim to such funds. This claim includes the right of the surety to be paid any and all estimates for work performed by the contractor prior to its default, but which at that time were unpaid, retained percentage which occurred prior to such default, as well as any and all of the unexpended balances of the contract funds after completion, including, but not limited to, all retained percentage, and also including any and all amounts that may have been or may hereafter be determined to be due the contractor for extra work performed.

The surety's claim to all of the unexpended part of the contract funds as aforesaid is based upon its legal and equitable rights as surety to receive, to the extent of losses sustained by it as surety as aforesaid, all such funds to the exclusion of all other persons, firms or corporations claiming under assignment given by the contractor, or otherwise.

Attached hereto is a copy of an assignment dated ________________ from (*Principal*) to this company. Rights under this assignment shall be considered to be in addition to, and not to the exclusion of, other legal and equitable rights available to this company.

Very truly yours,

SURETY

By: ______________________________

Exhibit 6.11

An Agreement of Release (with alternates)

THIS AGREEMENT, by and between ________________ (hereinafter referred to as "Surety") and ______________________ (hereinafter referred to as "Obligee").

WITNESSETH:

WHEREAS, on or about (*Date*), (*Principal*) (hereinafter referred to as "Principal") entered into a construction contract with Obligee, pursuant to which it agreed to perform all of the work necessary to construct the (*Name of Project*) (hereinafter referred to as the "Project"), in connection with which contract Principal and Surety executed and delivered to Obligee their payment and performance bonds conditioned as required under (*Statute or Act, if applicable*), which bonds were in the full amount of said contract; and

WHEREAS, by letter dated ________________, Obligee formally declared such contract to be in default and called upon the surety to complete the construction contemplated by said contract; and

WHEREAS, Surety thereafter tendered to Obligee a completing contractor, the same being (*Name of New Contractor*) (hereinafter referred to as "Completing Contractor"), and arranged for Obligee to enter into a new contractual agreement (hereinafter referred to as the "Completion Contract"), under which Completing Contractor will complete all of the work to be performed under the above-described contract, will warrant all of the work previously performed and to be performed to complete said contract, and will furnish to Obligee its payment and performance bonds guaranteeing said performance; and

WHEREAS, Surety has agreed to make payment to Obligee in the amount of $__________ as a cash settlement of Obligee's previous claims asserted against the performance bond furnished by Principal and Surety which amount shall be paid to Obligee upon the execution of this Release Agreement; and

WHEREAS, the tender proposal and cash settlement offer is acceptable to Obligee, and the parties desire to document the terms of such agreement as set forth hereinbelow:

NOW, THEREFORE, KNOW ALL MEN BY THESE PRESENTS:

THAT for and in consideration of the sum of $_______________, to it in hand paid by (*Surety*), and the other good and valuable consideration described hereinabove, the receipt and sufficiency is hereby acknowledged and confessed, (*Obligee*) does hereby expressly RELEASE, ACQUIT and FOREVER DISCHARGE (*Surety*) and its successors and assigns of and from any and all

Exhibit 6.11 (continued)

claims, rights, demands and/or causes of action of whatsoever kind or nature which (*Obligee*) has or may ever claim to have, now or in the future, against (*Surety*) under and/or by reason of its performance bond previously furnished to (*Obligee*) [Insert applicable option from the following]; and

Option No. 1—and said Obligee hereby agrees to return the original and said performance bond to Surety upon the execution of this Agreement.

Option No. 2—provided however, that it is expressly understood and agreed by and between Obligee and Surety that the foregoing complete Release is qualified and limited by the following exception thereto: Obligee hereby expressly agrees (1) to accept the performance bond being furnished by Completing Contractor as the primary performance bond pertaining to the Project following the execution of this Agreement, and (2) to reduce, and Obligee does hereby reduce the present penal amount of the performance bond previously furnished by the Surety from its stated penal limit of $________ to the reduced amount of $________, the same representing the original amount of said bond less the amount being paid by Surety pursuant to the cash settlement portion of this Agreement; and Obligee further expressly agrees (1) that it will at no time call upon or attempt to call upon the Surety with regard to said performance bond, as reduced in its penal amount, except in the event that (a) Completing Contractor should default upon its Completion Contract and fail to cure any such default, causing the Completion Contract to be terminated, and (b) as a result of such default, Obligee calls upon the performance bond surety of Completing Contractor and the entire penal limits of the performance bond of Completing Contractor and its surety should be exhausted, and (2) that Surety shall only have continuing potential exposure upon its performance bond, as reduced in its penal amount, for any excess liability, if any, resulting from the aforementioned events; and Obligee further agrees that in the event that any such default of Completing Contractor should occur, Obligee will provide written notice of such event to Surety.

Option No. 3—provided however, that it is expressly understood and agreed by and between Obligee and Surety that the foregoing complete Release is qualified and limited by the following exception thereto: Obligee hereby expressly agrees (1) to accept the performance bond being furnished by Completing Contractor as the primary performance bond pertaining to the Project following the execution of this Agreement, and (2) to reduce, and Obligee does hereby reduce the present penal amount of the performance bond previously furnished by the Surety from its stated penal limit of $________ to the reduced amount of $________, the same representing the difference between the original amount of the Principal's contract and the amount for which Completing Contractor has agreed to complete the work remaining to be performed; and Obligee further

Exhibit 6.11 (continued)

expressly agrees (1) that it will at no time call upon or attempt to call upon the Surety with regard to said performance bond, as reduced in its penal amount, except in the event that (a) Completing Contractor should default upon its Completion Contract and fail to cure any such default, causing the Completion Contract to be terminated, and (b) as a result of such default, Obligee calls upon the performance bond surety of Completing Contractor and the entire penal limits of the performance bond of Completing Contractor and its surety should be exhausted, and (2) that Surety shall only have continuing potential exposure upon its performance bond, as reduced in its penal amount, for any excess liability, if any, resulting from the aforementioned events; and Obligee further agrees that in the event that any such default of Completing Contractor should occur, Obligee will provide written notice of such event to Surety.

THAT for the aforementioned consideration, (*Obligee*) by these presents does hereby assign unto (*Surety*), its successors and assigns any and all rights, demands, claims and/or causes of action which (*Obligee*) has as against (*Principal*) arising out of, as a result of and/or on the basis of the default and breach by (*Principal*) of the original contract for the Project, and (*Obligee*) gives (*Surety*), its successors and assigns full power and authority for its own use and benefit, but at its own cost, to ask, demand, collect, receive, compound and/or release, and in its name or otherwise, to prosecute and withdraw any claims, suits or proceedings at law or in equity as against Principal in its efforts to obtain recovery upon its rights under said assignment; and

THAT for and in consideration of the foregoing Release (or alternatively, subordination agreement as set forth in Options No. 2 and 3), (*Surety*) does hereby agree to make and hereby delivers payment to (*Obligee*) in the amount of $_____________, simultaneously with the execution of this Agreement, as a cash settlement of any and all claim(s) previously asserted and which could have been asserted by said Obligee (optional, if using subordination options: as of this date) against said performance bond in full and complete settlement of said claim(s), (alternatively, if using subordination options: provided, however, that said performance bond shall remain in force and effect pursuant and subject to the foregoing subordination terms); and

THAT Surety acknowledges and agrees that its payment bond previously furnished for said Project shall continue to remain in full force and effect in accordance with its original tenor, except that it is expressly agreed by and between Surety and Obligee that the scope and coverage of said payment bond shall be limited to and shall only apply to statutory claims for payment of subcontractors and suppliers of Principal for work performed and/or materials delivered prior to the date hereof, and that said payment bond shall not apply to

Exhibit 6.11 (continued)

or cover the Completing Contractor or any of its subcontractors and suppliers for any work performed and/or materials delivered after the date hereof; and

This Release Agreement shall extend to and be binding upon the parties hereto and their respective successors, assigns and privies.

EXECUTED on this the ________ day of _____________, 19___.

(NAME)

By: ________________________________
Its: ________________________________

By: ________________________________
Its: ________________________________

STATE OF ____________ §
§
COUNTY OF _________ §

BEFORE ME, the undersigned authority, on this date personally appeared ______________________, known to me to be the person and agent subscribing hereinabove on behalf of ________________, who upon oath acknowledged to me that he is duly authorized to execute the above and foregoing Release Agreement on behalf of __________________, that he has read the foregoing Release Agreement, and that he has executed the same on behalf of _________ ____________________ for the purposes and consideration therein expressed.

GIVEN UNDER MY HAND AND SEAL OF OFFICE on this the _____ day of _____________, 19___.

____
NOTARY PUBLIC,
In and For the State of ________________

My Commission Expires:

____

Exhibit 6.11 (continued)

STATE OF ____________ §
§
COUNTY OF _________ §

BEFORE ME, the undersigned authority, on this date personally appeared ______________________, known to me to be the person and agent subscribing hereinabove on behalf of ________________, who upon oath acknowledged to me that he is duly authorized to execute the above and foregoing Release Agreement on behalf of ________________, that he has read the foregoing Release Agreement, and that he has executed the same on behalf of _________ for the purposes and consideration therein expressed.

GIVEN UNDER MY HAND AND SEAL OF OFFICE on this the _____ day of _________________, 19___.

____
NOTARY PUBLIC,
In and For the State of _________________

My Commission Expires:

____

Exhibit 6.12

Agreement for Contract Between Owner and New Contractor

THIS Agreement entered into this _____ day of ____________, 19_____, by and between the CITY OF _______________ ("Owner") and _________ __________________ COMPANY ("Surety").

WHEREAS, the Owner entered into a written contract dated the _____ day of _____________, 19_____ with ____________________ COMPANY, INC. ("Contractor") for work described as _________________________________ ("Project"), and

WHEREAS, Surety, on or about the _____ day of _______________, 19___ provided its statutory Performance Bond in favor of the Owner to secure the performance obligation of Contractor pursuant to the contract referred to above, and

WHEREAS, on _____________, 19____, Contractor advised Surety that it was financially unable to complete the contract work, and

WHEREAS, by letter received ______________, 19____, the Owner called upon Surety to complete work on the Project in accordance with the contract bonded by Surety, and

WHEREAS, on _____________, 19____, Surety invited bids for completion of the work remaining and in due course received bids from several contractors, the most advantageous bid being that of ______________________________ Company of ________________ ("Bidder"), and

WHEREAS, there remains the sum of $____________ under the terms of the original contract between Contractor and Owner for completion of the work remaining.

NOW, THEREFORE, in consideration of the mutual promises set forth herein, the Owner and Surety do hereby covenant and agree to the following:

1. Surety agrees to pay to the order of the Owner the sum of $________ in full settlement of the claim of the Owner under the Performance Bond referred to above, said sum representing the difference between the contract balance remaining under the original contract with Contractor and the amount bid by Bidder on the _____ day of __________, 19___.
2. The Owner agrees to enter into a contract with Bidder for the work remaining on the Project and in due course to obtain the required statutory Performance and Payment Bonds from _____________________, Surety for Bidder.
3. The Owner hereby releases and forever discharges Surety from any and all claims, demands, causes of action, damages, and/or expenses arising out of or in any way related to the contract entered into between the Owner and

Exhibit 6.12 (continued)

Contractor and the Surety's statutory Performance Bond, and its bond is hereby returned.

4. The Owner hereby assigns, sells, and transfers and subrogates to Surety all of its right, title and interest in and to all its rights and causes of action against Contractor.

5. Surety agrees to investigate and discharge its liability under the statutory Payment Bond issued by it as to all demands upon it by subcontractors and furnishers to Contractor for labor and material used, consumed and expended in connection with Contractor's contract prior to its abandonment of the work.

THE parties hereby confirm that this Agreement constitutes the entire terms of their agreement and further acknowledge that they have read and understand this Agreement constitutes a full, complete and final settlement and release.

OWNER

By: ______________________________

SURETY

By: ______________________________

Exhibit 6.13

Contract Between Owner and New Contractor

THIS AGREEMENT made this ____ day of ____________, 19____ by and between the State of ___________________, hereinafter called "Owner" and _____________________________________ Construction, Inc., hereinafter called "New Contractor."

WITNESSETH:

WHEREAS, Owner did enter into a contract with ___________________ Construction Co., Inc., hereinafter called "Original Contractor" dated _____________, 19____, copy of which is attached hereto and made a part hereof, wherein Original Contractor agreed to complete the construction of the ______________ in accordance with plans and specifications therefor prepared by ________________, Architect, hereinafter called "the project," for the sum of __________; and

WHEREAS, Owner thereafter issued Change Orders 1 through _____ on the project which were accepted by Original Contractor resulting in a revised contract amount of $_____________; and

WHEREAS, the Owner and New Contractor are desirous of entering into a contract whereby New Contractor will complete the project in accordance with the terms of said contract (with change orders) and any other modifications which may be made, between Original Contractor and the Owner on the terms and conditions hereinafter set forth.

NOW THEREFORE, in consideration of the covenants and conditions hereinafter set forth the parties hereto do hereby agree:

1. **Covenants of Contractor**

(a) The Contractor represents that it has received copies of the plans and specifications for the project including addendum #1, Change Orders 1 through _____ and the original contract between Original Contractor and the Owner, that it is fully familiar with the contents thereof, and with the job site and the condition thereof, the materials available upon the job site or elsewhere, as made known to it, but not yet incorporated in the project; the nature and status of the work previously performed on the project by Original Contractor and others and is aware of the work to be performed in order to complete the project, including conditions resulting from deterioration during the present period of cessation or work on the project, if any, and conditions resulting from omissions, oversights and errors by Original Contractor, if any, concerning such matters as strength of materials, adequacy of soil compaction, etc., and precise adherence

Exhibit 6.13 (continued)

to plans and specifications, except such conditions as are ordinarily not discoverable by routine examinations at this stage of construction and have not been made known to or discovered by New Contractor, which, other than the exceptions stated, shall be the responsibility of New Contractor under the terms hereof.

(b) New Contractor will promptly, upon the execution of this contract, commence work on the project and perform and complete the project in accordance with the terms contained in the contract between Original Contractor and the Owner, except:

1. The contract sum for the completion of the project shall be $________.
2. Time of commencement shall be as soon as practicable after the execution of this contract; and time for completion shall be 250 days from the date hereof.

(c) New Contractor will provide, with the execution of this Contract surety bonds and insurance policies in such forms as is required by the contract between Owner and Original Contractor.

2. **Covenants of the Owner**

(a) The Owner shall pay to New Contractor the sum of $________ for the completion of the project in the same manner and upon the same terms as set forth in the contract between Original Contractor and the Owner.

(b) The Owner accepts New Contractor for the completion of the project.

(c) As of _____________, 19____, all work performed on and materials incorporated in the project by Original Contractor was in accordance with the contract terms and acceptable to the Owner except:

> Conditions resulting from determination during the present period of cessation of work on the project, if any, and conditions resulting from omissions, oversights and errors by Original Contractor, if any, concerning such matters as strength of materials, adequacy of soil compaction and precise adherence to plans and specifications, which conditions ordinarily would not be discoverable by routine examinations at this stage of construction and have not been discovered by or made known to New Contractor.

Exhibit 6.13 (continued)

IN WITNESS WHEREOF, we have hereunto set our hands and seals the day and year first above written.

Signed, sealed and delivered in the presence of:

OWNER

____

By: ______________________________

____

NEW CONTRACTOR

____

By: ______________________________

STATE OF ____________ §
§
COUNTY OF __________ §

BEFORE ME, the undersigned authority, personally appeared __________, who acknowledged himself to be the ________________________ of the State of ______________, and that he as such __________________ being authorized so to do, executed the foregoing instrument for the purposes therein contained, by signing the name of the State of ______________ by himself as _____________.

____
NOTARY PUBLIC
In and For the State of __________

STATE OF ____________ §
§
COUNTY OF __________ §

BEFORE ME, the undersigned authority, personally appeared __________, who acknowledged himself to be the ________________________ of the State of ______________, and that he as such __________________ being authorized so to do, executed the foregoing instrument for the purposes therein contained, by signing the name of the State of ______________ by himself as _____________.

____
NOTARY PUBLIC
In and For the State of __________

Exhibit 6.14

Surety-Subcontractor Agreement

Date: ________

To: (*Surety*)

Re: CONTRACT BETWEEN ______________________________________

____

____

I (We) am (are) a Subcontractor of ______________________________
on the above named contract for the work described as follows:
______________________________, per plans and specifications,
including Addenda Nos. ____________________________________

1. Amount of original subcontract ___________________________
2. Approved changes in subcontract amount ____________________
3. Total or adjusted present subcontract amount ________________
4. Value of work performed and/or approved material stored on work-site through ____

   ____
5. Value to be performed after ______________________________
6. Retainage on No. 4 above ________________________________
7. Value of No. 4 above less retainage (No. 6) __________________
8. Total payments received from ______________________________
9. Net amount due through ______________ per affidavit of claim being filed with you.

In consideration of my (our) being paid within ten days from above date by (*Surety*), Surety for ______________________________________, the net amount of $________ now due (No. 9 above), and its agreement to pay me (us) our retainage of $________ (No. 6 above) upon acceptance of the project by the Owner, I (we) hereby agree to perform the balance of my (our) work, amounting to $________ (No. 5 above) for whoever completes the project.

____
Subcontractor

Date: ____________________

Exhibit 6.14 (continued)

(*Surety*) hereby agrees to the above and to pay you $____________ on or before ten days from above date and $________ on acceptance of the project by the Owner.

SURETY

By: ______________________________
Authorized Representative

Exhibit 8.1

Section of Public Contract Law Comments to FAR Secretariat

AMERICAN BAR ASSOCIATION **Section of Public Contract Law**
Writer's Address and Telephone

8230 Boone Boulevard
Suite 400
Vienna, Virginia 22182
(703) 790-8750

October 19, 1989

General Services Administration
FAR Secretariat (VRS)
18th and F Sts. N.W.
Washington, D.C. 20405

Attn: Ms. Margaret A. Willis

Re: FAR 49.404 "Surety Takeover Agreements"

Dear Ms. Willis:

This letter is written on behalf of the Section of Public Contract Law of the American Bar Association pursuant to special authority extended by the Association's Board of Governors for comments by the Section on Acquisition regulations. The views expressed are those of the Section and have not been considered or adopted by the Association's Board of Governors or its House of Delegates.

The subject of this letter is a frequently occurring problem encountered by sureties in negotiating takeover agreements with the United States Government. The problem involves specific mandatory language contained in the Federal Acquisition Regulations that is contrary to established case law and negates a surety's right to contract balances remaining in the hands of the Government after a contractor is default terminated.

The following report has been approved by the Council of the Public Contract Law Section of the American Bar Association, which has standing authority to comment on Federal Acquisition Regulations to the Federal Government. The report is forwarded with the recommendation that this FAR provision be made consistent with existing legal authority as discussed in the report.

We believe that the report has been previously submitted, but are submitting this report again because we have not received any response to our previous

Exhibit 8.1 (continued)

submission. Additionally, Under-Secretary of Defense for Acquisitions John Betti has requested that we provide assistance with identifying and eliminating conflicts in the FAR.

We respectfully request that these comments be considered by the FAR Secretariat in evaluating the existing language.

Very truly yours,

Donald G. Gavin
Chairman
Section of Public Contract Law

cc: Kurt Fraizer, Esquire
Allan H. Goodman, Esquire
William T. Avila, Esquire
David R. Trachtenberg
John S. Pachter, Esquire
Norman L. Roberts, Esquire
Ms. Marilyn Neforas

Exhibit 8.1 (continued)

REPORT OF THE BONDS AND SURETIES COMMITTEE OF THE PUBLIC CONTRACT LAW SECTION OF THE AMERICAN BAR ASSOCIATION

I. INTRODUCTION

This report was originally approved by the Council of the Public Contract Law Section during the 1988 Annual Meeting and submitted to the Federal Acquisition Regulation Council, the Defense Acquisition Council, and the Office of Federal Procurement Policy in the Office of Management and Budget. Since that time, additional case law from the United States Claims Court has given further support for the position taken in this paper. Accordingly, the paper has been updated to include this information.

Sureties for defaulted contractors negotiating takeover agreements with the Government continue to encounter difficulty because of the inclusion of mandatory language required by the Federal Acquisition Regulations. The language in question is contrary to law and yet is required by FAR 49.404 "Surety—Takeover Agreements." [The complete language in FAR 49.404 is attached].

The particular language which is the subject of this memorandum is the following:

> (e) The agreement shall provide for the surety to complete the work according to all the terms and conditions of the contract and for the Government to pay the surety the balance of the contract price unpaid at the time of default, but not in excess of the surety's costs and expenses, in the manner provided by the contract subject to the following conditions:
>
> (3) ... *if the contract proceeds have been assigned to a financing institution, the surety may not be paid from unpaid earnings unless the assignee consents to the payment in writing*. (Emphasis added.)
>
> (4) The surety shall not be paid any amount in excess of its total expenditures necessarily made in completing the work and discharging its liabilities under the payment bond of the defaulting contractor. Furthermore, payments to the surety to reimburse it for discharging its liabilities under the payment bond of the defaulting contractor shall be only on authority of —

Exhibit 8.1 (continued)

(i) Mutual agreement between the Government, the defaulting contractor, and the surety;
(ii) Determination of the Comptroller General as to payee and amount; or
(iii) Order of a court of competent jurisdiction.

First, the emphasized language gives an assignee financing institution rights that may effectively negate the otherwise superior position of the surety company. This result is directly in conflict with the legal rights of the surety company as determined by the United States Supreme Court and applied by the United States Claims Court and United States Court of Appeals for the Federal Circuit.

Secondly, the additional language following greatly weakens the surety's entitlement to be subrogated to the contract balance in favor of unreasonable certainty being afforded to the Government. This latter position is not substantiated by the relevant case law; to the contrary, the surety that pays labor and materialmen has a superior right to funds held by the Government.

II. THE UNITED STATES SUPREME COURT HAS HELD THAT A COMPLETING SURETY ON A PAYMENT BOND HAS SUPERIOR RIGHTS OVER A FINANCING INSTITUTION AND IS ENTITLED TO CONTRACT MONIES TO SATISFY PAYMENT BOND OBLIGATIONS

In the case of *Prairie State National Bank of Chicago v. United States*, 164 US 227 (1896), the United States Supreme Court held that a completing surety on a defaulted contract had a right to funds held by the Government superior to the claims of a financing institution which had lent money to the contractor. The surety was entitled to assert the equitable doctrine of subrogation, as the surety expended its own funds to complete the project and discharged an obligation of the contractor for the performance of which the surety was bound under its obligation of suretyship.

The bank, on the other hand, by lending money to the contractor, did not discharge an obligation of the contractor, but acted as a "mere volunteer." The Court also found that the stipulation in a building contract for the retention until the completion of the work of a certain portion of the consideration, is as much for the indemnity of the surety, as for the owner.

The rights of a surety on a payment bond to the contract balance were determined by the Supreme Court in *Henninasen v. United States Fidelity & Guaranty Company*, 208 US 404 (1908). In that case, the surety did not complete the contract upon default, but paid claims of laborers and materialmen. The Court held that the surety that pays claims of labors and materialmen has a superior

Exhibit 8.1 (continued)

right to funds held by the Government, and this right is superior to that of an assignee bank. The Court used the same reasoning as that in *Prairie State National Bank*, *supra*, which held that whatever rights the bank had arose solely by reason of the loans it made directly to the contractor. However, the rights of the surety arose upon its paying an obligation incurred by the contractor, and was therefore entitled to assert the equitable doctrine of subrogation. The bank on the other hand, was a "mere volunteer" and under no legal obligation to loan its money to the contractor.

The rights of both a completing surety on a performance bond and one that makes payments to unpaid subcontractors, suppliers and materialmen pursuant to a payment bond were confirmed again by the Supreme Court in *Pearlman v. Reliance Insurance Company*, 371 US 138 (1962). In *Pearlman*, the completing surety was held to have priority over the claims of the contractor's trustee in bankruptcy. In so holding, the Court reviewed the previous decisions in *Prairie State* and *Henningsen*, and reaffirmed the logic of those decisions.

III. THE FEDERAL CIRCUIT COURT OF APPEALS HAS AFFIRMED THE SURETY'S RIGHT OVER AN ASSIGNEE'S RIGHTS

This topic has recently been discussed in great detail by the United States Court of Appeals for the Federal Circuit in its decision in the appeal of *Balboa Insurance Company v. United States*, 775 F.2d 1158 (Fed. Cir. 1985). The Court, citing *Pearlman*, *supra*, stated that a completing surety is subrogated to the contractor's property right in the contract balance. This right is superior to the right of a bank which has loaned funds to the contractor before the surety began to complete the work. Upon subrogation, a surety's rights date back to the execution of the performance bond, and prevail over an assignee's rights. *Fidelity and Deposit Insurance Company v. United States*, 393 F.2d 834 (Ct. Cl. 1968).

A case cited by the Federal Circuit in the *Balboa* decision is directly on point on this issue. *Great American Insurance Company*, 492 F.2d 821 (Ct. Cl. 1974), held that upon notification of the Government by the surety of claims of materialmen and assertion of a claim to the contract balance, the Government holds the funds as a stakeholder, and must hold such funds for the benefit of the surety, even if an assignee has received an assignment under the Assignment of Claims Act. In this case, the Government, after receiving notice from the surety that the contractor was in default, disbursed funds to a bank that held an assignment under the Assignment of Claims Act. The Court held that such a disbursement was improper, and that the Government must pay the surety for the funds improperly disbursed to the bank.

Exhibit 8.1 (continued)

IV. OTHER ISSUES

There are several other issues raised by the language in FAR 49.404(e). One such issue is that the Government has drafted language which protects its own position by insisting on complete agreement of all concerned, or the Comptroller General, or a Court order before contract moneys can be utilized by a surety to reimburse for costs incurred in discharging payment bond obligations. See FAR 49.4O4(e)(4). This language attempts to limit those rights given to a surety as a matter of law. Obviously improvement in this language should be made to facilitate prompt reimbursement to a surety as required by the case decisions. There does not appear to be a clear rationale as to the requirement for the defaulted contractor to agree to allow the Government to reimburse the surety for funds disbursed for discharging payment bond obligations. Generally, a contractor and surety enter into an indemnity agreement as a condition for issuing a bond, in which the contractor consents to the surety's settling claims under the payment bond and remains liable to the surety to indemnify it for all sums spent. Additionally, under the common law right of subrogation, a surety would be entitled to the contract funds remaining. To require the surety to acquire additional consent from the contractor after default is redundant and often difficult, as defaulted contractors are sometimes not cooperative. Finally the language in FAR 49.404 fails to recognize that a surety will want to insist on limiting its obligations under any takeover agreement to the penal sum under the bonds.

V. CONCLUSION AND SUGGESTED REVISED FAR LANGUAGE

From the point of view of the Government Contracting Officer, FAR 49.404 does not provide workable guidance upon which a takeover agreement can be negotiated.

The mandatory language in FAR 49.404(e)(3) which allows the Government to withhold payment to a completing surety unless the assignee financing institution consents is contrary to established case law and violates the surety's right to the unpaid earnings. It stands as an impediment to the surety's willingness to complete the project, as it forces the surety to complete without the benefit of the funds to which the surety is legally entitled. The Public Contract Law Section of the American Bar Association is in a position to recommend changes which will bring FAR 49.404(e)(3) into conformance with the case law.

The surety's superior right to the funds which remain in the hands of the Government should not be abrogated by regulatory language contrary to law.

Exhibit 8.1 (continued)

We suggest the following revision to FAR 49.404. The language in brackets is language which currently appears in FAR and is to be *deleted*. The italicized language is proposed *additional* language:

(a) The procedures in this section apply primarily, but not solely, to fixed-price construction contracts termination for default.

(b) Because of the surety's liability for damages resulting from the contractor's default, the surety has certain rights and interests in the completion of the contract work and application of any undisbursed funds. Accordingly, the contracting officer shall carefully consider proposals by the surety concerning completion of the work. The contracting officer shall take action on the basis of the Government's interest, including the possible effect of the action upon the Government's rights against the surety. *The Contracting Officer in order to obtain a Takeover Agreement, must understand that the surety will normally have to limit its obligation to the original penal sum of the bond and will additionally insist on a reservation of rights. The Contracting Officer should be willing to recognize the position of the surety in order to effectuate a Takeover Agreement which is in the mutual best interest of the parties.*

***

(e) The agreement shall provide for the surety to complete the work according to all the terms and conditions of the contract and for the Government to pay the surety the balance of the contract price unpaid at the time of default, but not in excess of the surety's costs and expenses, in the manner provided by the contract subject to the following conditions:

(1) Any unpaid earnings of the defaulting contractor, including retained percentages and progress estimates for work accomplished before termination, shall be subject to debts due the Government by the contractor, except to the extent that such unpaid earnings may be required to permit payment to the completing surety of its actual costs and expenses incurred in the completion of the work, exclusive of its payments and obligations under the payment bond given in connection with the contract. *However, nothing in this Agreement shall prevent payment of claims consented to be paid for in (3) below.*

Exhibit 8.1 (continued)

***

[(3) ... if the contract proceeds have been assigned to a financing institution, the surety may not be paid from unpaid earnings unless the assignee consents to the payment in writing. (Emphasis added.)]

((4)] (3) The surety shall not be paid any amount in excess of its total expenditures necessarily made in completing the work and discharging its liabilities under the payment bond of the defaulting contractor. [Furthermore,] (P)ayments to the surety to reimburse it for discharging its liabilities under the payment bond of the defaulting contractor shall be [only on authority of —] *made upon submission by the Surety of proof that amounts have been paid to discharge the surety's obligation under the payment bond.*

[(i) Mutual agreement between the Government, the defaulting contractor, and the surety;]
[(ii) Determination of the Comptroller General as to payee and amount; or
[(iii) Order of a court of competent jurisdiction.]

VI. ADDITIONAL CASE LAW

Since this report was originally prepared, the United States Claims Court has rendered a decision which further supports the surety's rights against an assignee. In *Reliance Insurance Company v. United States*, 15 Cl. Ct. 62 (1988), the court explained the relative rights of sureties and assignees. Citing *Prairie State Bank, supra*, the court emphasized that a surety's rights attach from the date of the contract, while an assignee's rights will only attach, at the earliest, as of the date it files its notice of assignment under the Assignment of Claims Act.

In this case, the equity interest of the surety arose before that of the assignee, and the court held that the assignee therefore took its assignment subject to the equity interest of the surety. The court emphasized:

> The contract proceeds *must* be paid to the claimant with the superior right. As between the plaintiff-surety and the third-party plaintiff assignee, on the facts of this case, the plaintiff surety has the *superior right*. (emphasis added)

Exhibit 8.1 (continued)

It is clear that the Government does not need the consent of the assignee to release funds to the surety, and any inference in this regard in the FAR should be revised, as it is contrary to law.

Exhibit 8.2

Takeover Agreement

RELATING ______________________________
PROJECT ________________________________
CONTRACT NUMBER ____________________

THIS AGREEMENT is made and entered into this ___ day of ________, 19___, between the United States of America ["Agency"] (hereinafter called "Government"), and ____ (hereinafter called "Surety").

WHEREAS, on or about ______________, Government entered into a Contract No. _____________ with _____________________ (hereinafter called "Contractor"), for construction of a project defined as ___________ for ____, and, including any change orders hereto (hereinafter called the "Contract").

WHEREAS, surety [or its subsidiary, ________________________, as Surety for the Contractor, executed a Performance Bond and a Payment Bond (No. __________________), copies of which are attached hereto, required by the Government in connection with said contract. Performance Bond is in the sum of $_______, and Payment Bond is in the sum of $_______, respectively, except as modified by change orders consented to by Surety increasing or decreasing said amount.

WHEREAS, on _______, the Government has held the Contractor in default and has terminated the rights of the Contractor to proceed under the Contract and the Government has made demand upon Surety, to arrange for completion of said contract, and

WHEREAS, the Government desires to effect the completion of the work covered by the Contract in order to expedite completion and to avoid the delay and inconvenience of reletting; and

WHEREAS, Surety is willing and desires to complete or to procure the completion of the Contract in accordance with the terms of this Agreement, as a measure of cooperation with Government and as a measure to minimize excess costs, subject to the monetary limitation of its Performance Bond; and

WHEREAS, under its Performance Bond, Surety is willing to cause the Contract to be completed in accordance with the provisions of this Agreement, provided that in so doing it will receive the Contract balances as hereinafter set forth;

NOW, THEREFORE, in reliance upon the matters set out above and in consideration of Surety, agreeing to complete through [Completion Contractor),

Exhibit 8.2 (continued)

the work required by said contract in accordance with the terms and conditions of the contract, including all plans and specifications referred to therein and all Change Orders issued pursuant thereto, and in consideration of the mutual covenants set out below, the Government and Surety agree as follows:

1. Surety agrees to undertake to cause performance of all the duties and obligations of Contractor, as contained in said contract, including all contract documents as described therein, and all Change Orders issued pursuant thereto, to have the work of Contractor completed in strict accordance with the terms and conditions of said contract, pursuant to the Performance Bond provisions.

2. The Government agrees that it will pay direct to Surety, as the same shall become progressively payable in accordance with the payment provisions of the Contract, all sums now due and payable and to become due and payable upon the Contract, including all unearned Contract balances, all earned retainage percentages, all earned but unpaid estimates and any and all money contracted to be paid hereunder, as would be or would have been payable to the Original Contractor if there had been no declared default, provided however, that:

(a) The amount paid to Surety shall not be in excess of Surety's costs and expenses incurred in the performance of the work including its payments and obligations under the payment bond given in connection with the contract; and

(b) Any unpaid earnings of the defaulting contractor, including retained percentages and progress estimates for work accomplished before termination, shall be subject to debts due the Government by the Contractor, except to the extent that such unpaid earnings may be required to permit payment to Surety of its actual costs and expenses incurred in the completion of the work, exclusive of its payments and obligations under the payment bond given in connection with the contract; however, nothing in this Agreement shall prevent payments of the claims consented to be paid for in paragraph 2(e).

(c) FAR § 49.404 (e) (3) provides that:

> If the contract proceeds have been assigned to a financing institution, the Surety may not be paid from unpaid earnings, unless the assignee consents to the payment in writing.

For an assignment to have occurred, it must comply with the Assignment of Claims Act of 1940 as amended and its implementing regulations found in FAR § 32.8. The Government is aware of Surety's position that the conditions set forth in FAR § 32.802 have not been satisfied by any alleged assignee, and that under applicable case law, not assignment could be effectuated after knowledge by [Agency] of the Principal's alleged [default or abandonment of the project] without the discharge of Surety's obligations *pro tanto* and that Surety under the

Exhibit 8.2 (continued)

present circumstances has a priority to unpaid earnings over any alleged assignee. The Government is aware of Surety's position that the above quoted language from FAR § 49.404(e) (3) is in applicable and contrary to law and no consent to payments from unpaid earnings shall be required of any alleged assignee before payment to Surety. The Government, by acknowledging its awareness of Surety's position as stated in this subparagraph 2(c) does not admit that the facts and/or legal theories asserted by Surety are correct.

(d) This agreement shall not waive or release the Government's right to claim liquidated damages for delays in completion of the work, except to the extent that such delays, if any, may be excused under the provisions of the Contract; and surety is likewise entitled to such extensions of contract time as are provided for under the contract and is to be relieved of any delays excused under the contract.

(e) In no event shall Surety be entitled to be paid any amount in excess of its total expenditures necessarily made in completing the work and discharging any liabilities it may have, if any, under the payment bond of the Original Contractor. Those claims under the payment bond paid to date and claims not paid to date are listed in Exhibit ________ to this Agreement. Surety is entitled to be paid for all such amounts eventually paid. Proof of actual payment will be provided to the Government.

3. Notwithstanding anything herein to the contrary, Surety shall remain liable to the Government under the bond issued by Surety, provided, however, nothing contained in this Agreement shall be deemed to enlarge Surety's obligation under the bond issued by it on behalf of the Original Contractor and under no circumstances shall Surety be held liable to the Government for any amount in excess of the Penal Sum of $________, as set forth in the bond.

4. All payments and notices to Surety shall be delivered to Surety at the following address:

Surety

____

____

5. Administration and inspection of the Project will remain with the Government and its agents/engineers in accordance with the terms of the Original Contract.

6. Insofar as they comply with the provisions of the Contract, the Government agrees that all materials, appliances and plants presently on the project site are available to Surety and its designated independent contractors without cost for use in the completion of the remainder of the Contract.

Exhibit 8.2 (continued)

7. The Government acknowledges that Surety, in entering into this Agreement does not acknowledge the validity of the Government's termination of the Contractor's (the Principal's) Contract, the assessment of liquidated damages by the Government or any other action taken by the Government, except as provided herein. Furthermore, in entering into this Agreement, Surety does not thereby waive, prejudice, or in any way adversely affect any claim that it, as Surety, or the Contractor (the Principal), might have against the Government.

8. The Government agrees that it will give Surety notification of any problem that occurs in respect to the remaining work in the completion of the Contract.

9. The Government agrees that Surety's right to proceed to complete the Contract shall not be terminated nor Surety charged additional liquidated damages if further delay in completing the work arises from conditions or events which are excusable under the original Contract documents.

10. Surety expressly reserves all prior rights, equitable liens and rights to subrogation that would be the United States', the laborers' of materialmen's or the Contractor's (the Principal's) under the Contract or at law or equity, as well as its own rights dating back to the execution of the performance and payment bonds, including but not limited to those rights and remedies that may accrue during the completion of the Contract. No waiver of such rights is agreed to or implied or intended regardless of any provisions of this Takeover Agreement to the contrary. Any disagreement between the Government and Surety shall be considered a dispute within the Disputes Clause contained within the Contract and Surety shall be entitled to exercise such rights as are afforded by the Disputes Clause and the Contracts Disputes Act Of 1978, as amended.

11. All terms and conditions of the Original Contract shall be and remain the same.

12. The parties hereto do not intend by any provision of this Agreement to create any third-party beneficiaries nor to confer any benefit upon or enforceable rights or otherwise upon any one other than the parties hereto.

13. It is understood and agreed that this Agreement constitutes the whole of the understanding, discussions and agreements by and between the parties, and the written or oral discussion prior to the effective date hereof shall not in any way vary or alter the terms of this Agreement.

14. This Agreement shall not in any way be amended or modified without the written consent of both parties.

15. This Agreement shall extend to and be binding upon the parties hereto and their respective successors and assigns.

IN WITNESS HERETO, all parties to this Agreement have caused to be Bet their hands and seals this day and year first above written.

Exhibit 8.2 (continued)

	UNITED STATES OF AMERICA
	[AGENCY]
Date Signed: ____________	By: ____________
Attest: ____________	Title: ____________
	SURETY
Date Signed: ____________	By: ____________
Attest: ____________	Title: ____________

Exhibit 8.3

Forms for Tendering a Contractor

SOLICITATION, OFFER, AND AWARD (*Construction, Alteration, or Repair*)	1. SOLICITATION NO. N/A	2. TYPE OF SOLICITATION ☐ SEALED BID (*IFB*) ☐ NEGOTIATED (*RFP*)	3. DATE ISSUED N/A	PAGE OF PAGES 1 of 3

IMPORTANT – The "offer" section on the reverse must be fully completed by offeror.

4. CONTRACT NO.	5. REQUISITION/PURCHASE REQUEST NO.	6. PROJECT NO.
N62477-92-C-0213	NAVFAC SPECIFICATION NO:	21-90-0070

7. ISSUED BY CODE	8. ADDRESS OFFER TO
Chesapeake Division Naval Facilities Engineering Command Building 212, Washington Navy Yard Washington, D.C. 20374-2121	N/A

9. FOR INFORMATION CALL:	A. NAME	B. TELEPHONE NO. (*Include area code*) (*NO COLLECT CALLS*)
	Sandra K. Soderston	(202)433-5804

SOLICITATION

NOTE: In sealed bid solicitations "offer" and "offeror" mean "bid" and "bidder".

10. THE GOVERNMENT REQUIRES PERFORMANCE OF THE WORK DESCRIBED IN THESE DOCUMENTS (*Title, identifying no., date*):

THIS CONTRACT IS FOR COMPLETION OF DEFAULTED CONTRACT N62477-90-C-0040.

Old Republic Surety Company in its capacity as Surety under the defaulted contract, have tendered this contractor to enter into this contract with the Navy to complete performance of the defaulted contract for a price not in excess of the unpaid balance of the defaulted contract. Any amount in excess of $100,026.00, the unpaid balance of the defaulted contract, is for resolution solely between the Contractor and Old Republic Surety Company.

11. The Contractor shall begin performance within 15 calendar days and complete it within 90 calendar days after receiving ☒ award, ☐ notice to proceed. This performance period is ☒ mandatory, ☐ negotiable. (*See* ______.)

12A. THE CONTRACTOR MUST FURNISH ANY REQUIRED PERFORMANCE AND PAYMENT BONDS? (*If "YES," indicate within how many calendar days after award in Item 12B.*)	12B. CALENDAR DAYS
☒ YES ☐ NO	10

13. ADDITIONAL SOLICITATION REQUIREMENTS: N/A

A. Sealed offers in original and ______ copies to perform the work required are due at the place specified in Item 8 by ______ (*hour*) local time ______ (*date*). If this is a sealed bid solicitation, offers will be publicly opened at that time. Sealed envelopes containing offers shall be marked to show the offeror's name and address, the solicitation number, and the date and time offers are due.

B. An offer guarantee ☐ is, ☐ is not required.

C. All offers are subject to the (1) work requirements, and (2) other provisions and clauses incorporated in the solicitation in full text or by reference.

D. Offers providing less than ______ calendar days for Government acceptance after the date offers are due will not be considered and will be rejected

NSN 7540-01-155-3212 1442-102 STANDARD FORM 1442 (REV. 4-85) Prescribed by GSA FAR (48 CFR) 53.236-1(e)

Exhibit 8.3 (continued)

OFFER *(Must be fully completed by offeror)*

...ME AND ADDRESS OF OFFEROR *(Include ZIP Code)*

...orter Contracting Company, Inc.
7413 McWhorter Place
Annandale, Virginia 22003

Taxpayer ... No. ____________

15. TELEPHONE NO. *(Include area code)*

16. REMITTANCE ADDRESS *(Include only if different than Item 14)*

CODE FACILITY CODE

17. The offeror agrees to perform the work required at the prices specified below in strict accordance with the terms of this solicitation, if this offer is accep... by the Government in writing within ______ calendar days after the date offers are due. *(Insert any number equal to or greater than the minimum ...quirement stated in Item 13D. Failure to insert any number means the offeror accepts the minimum in Item 13D.*

AMOUNTS ▶ $100,026.00

18. The offeror agrees to furnish any required performance and payment bonds.

19. ACKNOWLEDGMENT OF AMENDMENTS
(The offeror acknowledges receipt of amendments to the solicitation — give number and date of each)

AMENDMENT NO.									
DATE									

20A. NAME AND TITLE OF PERSON AUTHORIZED TO SIGN OFFER *(Type or print)*

20B. SIGNATURE

20C. OFFER DATE

AWARD *(To be completed by Government)*

21. ITEMS ACCEPTED:

Completion of all items of owrk for defaulted contract N62477-90-C-0070, NAVFAC Specification No. 21-90-0070 including correction and repair of all defective work.

CONTRACT COMPLETION DATE: 05 NOV 92

22. AMOUNT

$100,026.00

23. ACCOUNTING AND APPROPRIATION DATA

AA1711106.2790 000 67353 0 067353 20 000000
1087015SP14Q RCP#M6735391RCOSP14 $100,026.00

24. SUBMIT INVOICES TO ADDRESS SHOWN IN *(4 copies unless otherwise specified)* ▶ ITEM 26

25. OTHER THAN FULL AND OPEN COMPETITION PURSUANT TO

☐ 10 U.S.C. 2304(c) ( ) ☐ 41 U.S.C. 253(c) ( )

26. ADMINISTERED BY CODE

Resident Officer in Charge of Construction
Naval District Washington
Building 142
Washington Navy Yard
Washington, D. C. 20374

27. PAYMENT WILL BE MADE BY

UIC N62583
Refeence No:

CONTRACTING OFFICER WILL COMPLETE ITEM 28 OR 29 AS APPLICABLE

☐ 28. NEGOTIATED AGREEMENT *Contractor is required to sign this document and return ______ copies to issuing office.)* Contractor agrees to furnish and deliver all items or perform all work requirements identified on this form and any continuation sheets for the consideration stated in this contract. The rights and obligations of the parties to this contract shall be governed by (a) this contract award, (b) the solicitation, and (c) the clauses, representations, certifications, and specifications incorporated by reference in or attached to this contract.

☐ 29. AWARD *(Contractor is not required to sign this document.)* Your offe... on this solicitation is hereby accepted as to the items listed. This award con... summates the contract, which consists of (a) the Government solicitation an... your offer, and (b) this contract award. No further contractual document... necessary.

30A. NAME AND TITLE OF CONTRACTOR OR PERSON AUTHORIZED TO SIGN *(Type or print)*

31A. NAME OF CONTRACTING OFFICER *(Type or print)*

30B. SIGNATURE

30C. DATE

31B. UNITED STATES OF AMERICA

BY

31C. AWARD DATE

☆ U.S. GOVERNMENT PRINTING OFFICE: 1987 ...

Exhibit 8.3 (continued)

N62477-92-C-0213
Page 3 of 3

NOTE - SOME WORK WAS PERFORMED UNDER DEFAULTED CONTRACT N62477-92-C-0213, THEREFORE, ALL WORK IS TO BE PERFORMED UNDER THIS COMPLETION CONTRACT IS REQUIRED TO CORRECT ANY DEFECTIVE WORK FROM THE DEFAULTED CONTRACTOR'S EFFORT AS WELL AS ANY INCOMPLETE WORK REQUIRED TO FURNISH A COMPLETE AND USEABLE FACILITY.

The following changes shall be made to Defaulted Contract N62477-90-C-0070:

Section 01011, paragraph 1.4 PROJECT SCHEDULE AND TIME CONSTRAINTS;

1.4.1 Commencement, prosecution, and completion of Work (APR 84): The Contractor shall be required to (a) commence work under this contract within 15 calendar days after the date the Contractor receives the notice to proceed, (b) prosecute the work diligently, and (c) complete the entire work ready for use not later than 90 calendar days after the required commencement of work. The time stated for completion shall include final cleanup of the premises. (FAR 52.212-3)

Contract Clauses - Construction Contract Clauses dated DEC 1991 are incorporated into this completion contract.

Department of Labor, Wage Determination No. DC91-1 with Modifications 1 through 10, Building Contract will be applicable to this completion contract.

Exhibit 8.3 (continued)

CONTRACT CONTENTS

This contract N62477-92-C-0213 consists of the following documents:

(1) SF 1442 Solicitation, Offer and Award (Rev. 4-85)

(2) Construction Contract Clauses dated DEC 1991

(3) Labor Standard Provisions dated May 1990

(4) Department of Labor, Wage Determination No. DC91-1 including Modifications 1 through 10, Building Construction

Exhibit 8.3 (continued)

AGREEMENT

WHEREAS, Old Republic Surety Company ("Surety") executed the performance and payment bonds required by the Miller Act in connection with a contract between Mancine, Inc. and the United States (Contract No. N62477-90-C-0070) for work at Henderson Hall, Arlington, Virginia; and

WHEREAS, the united States terminated Contract No. N62477-90-C-OO7O for default and made a demand upon Surety under its performance bond; and

WHEREAS, Porter contracting Company, Inc. ("Porter") submitted an offer to Surety to complete the work required by Contract No. N62477-90-C-0070, subject to certain conditions as set forth in said offer, for a price off $87,445.00; and

WHEREAS, Surety tendered, and the United States accepted, Porter as a completing contractor and Porter has entered into a contract, Contract No. N62477-92-C-0213, with the United States to perform the Henderson Hall project for $100,026.00.

NOW THEREFORE, it is agreed by and between Surety and Porter on this 28 day of August, 1992, that:

1. Copies of the Invitation for Bids (Sections 1-9) sent to Porter on June 8, 1992, and Porter's offer to Surety in response to said Invitation are attached hereto and incorporated as a part of this Agreement.

2. Porter shell submit to Surety a line item breakdown of its bid of $87,445.00 using the same line items as are approved by the Navy for Contract No. N62477-92-C-0213. Upon receipt of each payment from the Navy under the completion contract, Porter shall pay to Surety the difference between the amount paid and the amount due for the same percentage of completion per the line item breakdown submitted to the Surety.

3. Any Change Orders issued under Contract No. N62477-92-C-0213 shall be a matter between Porter and the Navy and shall not affect Surety.

4. If Porter discovers possible latent defects in work performed by Mancine, Porter shall notify Surety and provide an estimate of the cost to correct the allegedly defective work. Surety shall have the option:

(a) to authorize Porter to correct the defects at on agreed upon sum to be paid by surety to Porter upon acceptance of the corrective work; or

(b) to direct Porter to correct the detects on a Cost-Plus basis as described in Article 3lC, page 16 of the Invitation for Bids; or

(c) to arrange for the corrections to be made by someone other than Porter. If Surety makes such an arrangements, Porter shall subcontract with the entity chosen by Surety (but Surety shall make all parents for the corrective work) or otherwise cooperate to allow the corrective work-to be performed; or

Exhibit 8.3 (continued)

(d) to contest the existence of a latent defect by pursuing any administrative or judicial remedy afforded by the Navy contracts. Porter will cooperate to allow Surety to pursue such administrative remedies but Surety shall bear the costs involved.

PORTER CONTRACTING COMPANY, INC.

By: ______________________________

OLD REPUBLIC SURETY COMPANY

By: ______________________________

Exhibit 9.1

IN THE BANKRUPTCY COURT FOR THE
DISTRICT OF DESPAIR
EASTERN DIVISION

In re Buford T. Hawgjowles	§	
Construction Co., Inc.	§	
	§	No. 1,000,000
Debtor.	§	(Chapter 11)

MOTION TO LIFT THE AUTOMATIC STAY
TO TERMINATE CONTRACT

The Grand Interstate Barbecue Hickory Pit ("Obligee")[1] moves this Court in accordance with Sections 362(d)(1) and 363(d)(2) of the Bankruptcy Code to lift the automatic stay to allow Obligee to terminate the contract between it and the Debtor for construction of a four story smokehouse and tatoo parlor. In further support of this motion, Obligee states:

1. Debtor entered into a general contract with Obligee for construction of a smokehouse and tatoo parlor to be completed four months after the execution of the general contract.

2. Debtor filed a petition seeking relief under Chapter 11 sixty days ago. Since filing that petition, the Debtor has failed to perform the general contract work, failed to pay parties who furnished materials for the project and has taken no action to formally assume the obligations of the general contract under Section 365 of the Bankruptcy Code.[2]

3. Obligee has declared the Debtor in default but cannot terminate the contract by reason of the automatic stay in effect by operation of Section 362(a).

4. The projected cost of completing all contract work now exceeds the amount held by the Obligee for the work.

---

1 The motion to lift the stay to cancel a contract must be brought by the party empowered to terminate the contract—the obligee. The surety and obligee should work together where this action is necessary to enable the obligee to terminate the contract in order to go forward with the takeover by the surety or the tender of a new contractor.

2 One should recite the termination clause of the contract in the motion.

Exhibit 9.1 (continued)

5. Obligee has notified Surety of the defaults. The Surety cannot take action to replace Debtor on the project until the Debtor's contract with Obligee is terminated.

6. Debtor's inaction will increase the cost to complete and the losses related to the completion of the work. The stay should be lifted for cause, because of the Debtor's failure to perform, and because the Debtor and the estate have no equity in the contract consideration remaining to be paid. Grounds exist for lifting the stay under either Section 363(d)(1) or 362(d)(2).[3]

For the foregoing reasons, The Grand Interstate Barbecue Hickory Pit prays the Court order the stay lifted pursuant to Sections 362(d)(1) and 362(d)(2) of the Bankruptcy Code so that the contract for the construction of the four story smokehouse and tatoo parlor between Obligee and Debtor can be terminated in accordance with the terms of that contract.

THE GRAND INTERSTATE
BARBECUE HICKORY PIT

By: ______________________________
H. "Rocky" Milktoast, One of the
Attorneys for Obligee

---

3 This motion asserts both cause under § 363(d)(1) and lack of equity in the contract under § 363(d)(2) as grounds for the court to lift the stay. In some instances, the Debtor may have equity in the contract if it performed but refuses to perform because of the risk and the marginal profitability of the contract. If this motion is subject to a contested proceeding, the surety and obligee must be able to demonstrate the default justifying termination and/or the debtor's lack of equity in the contract consideration.

Exhibit 9.2

Pre-Petition Agreement Regarding Executory Contracts

AGREEMENT RELATING TO THE USE OF CONTRACT FUNDS AND PAYMENT OF BONDED OBLIGATIONS

This agreement is between Buford T. Hawgjowles Construction Co., Inc. ("Hawgjowles") and Pure of Heart Surety Company ("Surety").

Surety issued performance and payment bonds securing the obligation of Hawgjowles to perform work and pay for labor and materials on a number of projects with the United States Government.

Hawgjowles executed a General Agreement of Indemnity in favor of the Surety by which Hawgjowles agreed to make all payments required under the bonds and to indemnify Surety from losses, including fees and expenses, incurred by reason of the execution of the bonds.

Hawgjowles has requested that Surety provide financial assistance to satisfy accounts payable that Hawgjowles is presently unable to pay, that are due on projects bonded by Surety, and that could be payment obligations under Surety's bonds in the event these accounts remain unpaid.

Surety wants to assure the contract funds on bonded projects are used to perform the work and reduce the accounts payable on those projects prior to Hawgjowles using those funds for any other purpose.

AGREEMENT FOR SPECIAL ACCOUNT FOR BONDED CONTRACT FUNDS

1. **Payment of Accounts Payable.** Surety agrees to pay the accounts payable identified in the list attached as Exhibit "A" of this Agreement. Payment will be made through Special Account(s) described below in paragraph 3.

2. **Deposit of Contract Funds into Special Account(s).** Hawgjowles agrees that all contract payments[1] (extras or claims), progress payments and retained funds due and not yet paid to Hawgjowles and due Hawgjowles in the future on any project for which Surety provided performance and payment bonds will be deposited into the Special Account(s) provided for in this Agreement. Hawgjowles

---

1 The term "contract funds" will sometimes be used in this Agreement. "Contract funds" shall refer to all consideration due and to be paid for performance of bonded contracts, including, but not limited to, extras, claims, progress payments and retained funds.

Exhibit 9.2 (continued)

and Surety will notify each obligee of this arrangement and obtain their consent for direct payment of these funds in to the Special Account. In the event the obligees will not consent to the direct deposit of funds to the account, Hawgjowles will provide any endorsement, signature(s) or document(s) required to ensure deposit of the funds to the Special Account(s). Hawgjowles acknowledges that all contract funds (extras, claims, progress payments, retained funds) paid to it from contracts bonded by Surety are trust funds to be deposited into the Special Account(s) and disbursed in accordance with the priorities set forth in paragraph 3 below.

3. **Establishment of Special Account(s).** The Special Account(s) shall be established at The Worthless Bank and be designated Surety Special Trust Account. Surety shall designate the authorized signatories for the account(s).

A. **Funds Deposited into Account(s)**. The funds deposited into the account shall consist of all contract receivables (extras, claims, progress payments and retained funds) due and not yet paid and due Hawgjowles in the future on any project or contract bonded by Surety. Funds deposited in this account will be held in trust and disbursed in accordance with the priority set forth below.

B. **Disbursements from Account and Application of Funds Held in Trust.** Hawgjowles acknowledges that the funds deposited into the Hawgjowles Surety Special Account are held in trust for the benefit of Surety, and are to be applied for the benefit of Surety to first reduce obligations that Surety would be liable for under the terms of the performance and payment bonds. Disbursements will be made from the Special Account for deposits received on bonded contracts in accordance with the following priority scheme:

First, funds received through each payment from a project or contract will be disbursed to satisfy accounts payable that might otherwise be obligations of Surety under the performance of payment bonds for that project or contract;

Second, percent (%) of the amount of the payment deposited to the account will be held by Surety to cover future performance and payment claims and to cover any shortfalls between the payments received on a project and the amount required to satisfy all accounts payable due at the time of the payment;

Third, amounts in excess of the first and second priority will be paid to Hawgjowles for its own use.

4. **Rights Under this Agreement are in Addition to the Rights Granted Under the General Agreement of Indemnity.** Hawgjowles affirms its obligations to Surety under the General Agreement of Indemnity dated ________________

Exhibit 9.2 (continued)

and acknowledges that this Agreement in no way affects the obligations of Hawgjowles to Surety under the indemnity agreement.

5. **Surety's Rights in the Event of Default(s) by Hawgjowles on Bonded Contract(s).** In the event Hawgjowles is in default or is declared in default of any contract(s) after the date of this Agreement, Surety can take any action provided for under the General Agreement of Indemnity and which Surety is entitled to take by virtue of its status as surety to protect its interest in the contract or contracts then in default or declared in default, including, but not limited to, stopping all payments to Hawgjowles from the contract of contracts in question, instructing the obligee or obligees to hold funds to be paid or due on such contracts and making arrangements for the performance or payment of contract obligations. Nothing in this Agreement shall be construed as limiting the rights and remedies afforded Surety by law or under the General Agreement of Indemnity to protect their interests in contracts and contract funds in default or declared in default.

6. **Surety's Rights in the Event of a Hawgjowles Insolvency Proceeding.** Hawgjowles acknowledges that it is experiencing cash flow difficulties and requests Surety's financial assistance to satisfy the payables identified in Exhibit "A" which should enable Hawgjowles to obtain the release of additional contract funds. Hawgjowles recognizes Surety possesses equitable rights in and to contract funds, and is subrogated to the rights of the obligees to use the contract funds to pay for performance and payment obligations under the contracts.

A. **Lifting of the Automatic Stay.** Hawgjowles agrees that in the event it is subject to any insolvency proceeding, bankruptcy, receivership, dissolution, reorganization or similar proceeding, state or federal, voluntary or involuntary, Surety is entitled to the automatic and absolute lifting of any automatic stay that might apply to the Surety's right to take control of contracts or contract funds, specifically, but not limited to, the stay imposed by Section 362 of the Bankruptcy Code, as amended; Hawgjowles hereby consents to the lifting of the automatic stay to enable Surety or the obligees to terminate the contract(s) and apply any remaining contract funds towards the completion of the contracts and payment of contract obligations, and will not contest any motion by Surety to lift the stay in the event Hawgjowles is unable within ten (10) days after the filing of the petition or event commencing an insolvency proceeding to file a motion under Section 365 of the Bankruptcy Code for the assumption of such contracts, which motion is filed with the consent and approval of the obligee(s) to such assumption, or, in an insolvency proceeding other than under the Federal Bankruptcy Code, to otherwise arrange for the performance and payment of contract obligations, with the consent of the obligee(s), within ten (10) days of the

Exhibit 9.2 (continued)

event or act initiating the insolvency proceeding. With respect to any contract that Hawgjowles is unable to move to assume within 10 days of the filing of a bankruptcy petition, or is unable to arrange for completion and payment of obligations within 10 days of the event or act commencing some other insolvency proceeding, or if Hawgjowles is unable to obtain the consent of the obligee(s) to the motion to assume or arrangement to complete, Hawgjowles expressly acknowledges: A) it possesses no equity in the contract after the contract funds are applied to the performance and payment of outstanding contract obligations and B) the contract is not necessary to any plan of reorganization of any type.

B. **Adequate Protection of Surety's Rights to Contract Funds.** The Special Account(s) are intended to protect Surety's equitable rights in and to contract funds to secure it from losses and to assure that contract obligations are paid and performed. Hawgjowles acknowledges that Surety's interest in and to contract funds can only receive adequate protection, as that term is used in the Federal Bankruptcy Code, by Hawgjowles's assumption under Section 365 of the Code of bonded contracts *and* by disbursement of the contract funds to satisfy performance and payment obligations on the assumed contracts that would otherwise be obligations under the Surety's bonds, or by disbursement of the contract funds in accordance with the First priority of disbursement provided for in paragraph 3A above.

7. **Severability of Provisions of this Agreement.** The provisions of this Agreement are severable, and the unenforceability of any one provision shall not affect the enforceability or render unenforceable the other provisions of this Agreement.

8. **Applicable Law.** The law of the State of Despair shall govern the terms of this Agreement.

9. **Execution and Acknowledgement.** This Agreement is executed this _____ day of ____________________, 1995 by Pure of Heart Surety Company and Buford T. Hawgjowles Construction Co., Inc.

BUFORD T. HAWGJOWLES
CONSTRUCTION CO., INC.

By: ________________________________

Attest: ______________________________
Secretary For Hawgjowles

Exhibit 9.2 (continued)

PURE OF HEART SURETY COMPANY

By: ______________________________

Attest: ____________________________
Secretary For Surety

Exhibit 9.3

Subordination Agreement

SUBORDINATION AND ASSIGNMENT OF RIGHTS
TO CONTRACT RIGHTS AND CLAIM ASSERTED BY
BUFORD T. HAWGJOWLES CONSTRUCTION CO., INC.

This Agreement is between The Worthless Bank ("Worthless Bank") and Pure of Heart Surety Company ("Surety") in connection with their respective rights in and to assets in which Buford T. Hawgjowles Construction Co., Inc. ("Hawgjowles") has rights by virtue of contracts entered into between Hawgjowles and the State of Despair Highway Commission ("Commission").

Worthless Bank claims a perfected blanket security interest in all of Hawgjowles' contracts and contract rights by virtue of its perfection of the assignment of these rights in document no. ______________ filed with the Secretary of State of the State of Despair;

Worthless Bank claims its interest in the contract rights and claims of Hawgjowles is a first perfected security interest superior and prior to all other parties claiming a perfected interest in such rights and claims under Article 9 of the Uniform Commercial Code;

Surety claims that its rights arising by virtue of equitable subrogation and setoff are superior and prior to any right Worthless Bank claims under its perfected assignment of contract rights and claims;

Hawgjowles has requested Surety to advance funds to pay contract payables on contracts that Surety bonded that are or would be claims under Surety's payment bonds on these projects;

To facilitate the payment of these payables and to clarify the rights of Worthless Bank and Surety with respect to certain assets of Hawgjowles, Worthless Bank and Surety enter into this Agreement providing for the subordination of certain of the Worthless Bank's rights and assignment of certain of the Worthless Bank's rights to Surety.

AGREEMENT

1. The parties agree that the foregoing recitals are incorporated into this Agreement.

2. The parties agree that there is consideration for the terms of this Agreement, insofar as the payment of payables by Surety will permit Hawgjowles to continue its operations and reduce its indebtedness to Worthless Bank and to complete projects bonded by Surety.

Exhibit 9.3 (continued)

3. Hawgjowles is prosecuting a claim against the Commission for extra compensation due to differing site conditions encountered at Old Geyser mine. With respect to any recoveries on that claim and with respect to any other contract consideration due and not yet paid by the Commission to Hawgjowles on that contract, Worthless Bank and Surety agree that the respective claims shall be as follows:

A. With respect to the contracts bonded by Surety, to the extent that Surety incurs losses under the bonds, Surety has a superior and prior right to recover the losses paid on the bonds from any remaining contract consideration (progress payments, retainages or claims) held by or recovered from the Commission on the contracts on which Surety sustains a loss or losses[1];

B. After payment of the claims arising out of Surety's equitable subrogation rights acknowledged above in subparagraph A, Worthless Bank shall be entitled to recover by virtue of its perfected assignment the first $ 1 million recovered by Hawgjowles (after payment of all costs of recovery including attorney fees incurred by Hawgjowles and, Worthless Bank and Surety should they incur fees and costs in prosecuting the claim) on its claim against the Commission on Old Geyser mine;

C. After payment of $1 million to Worthless Bank as provided in subparagraph B of this paragraph, Surety is entitled to the next $500,000 in recoveries from the Old Geyser claim;

D. All recoveries in excess of the first $ 1 million Worthless Bank recovers and the next $500,000 Surety recovers under subparagraph B and C above shall be divided between Worthless Bank and Surety based on a ratio allocating % of the recoveries to Surety and % of the recoveries to Worthless Bank, until Surety is fully compensated all losses for which it can seek recovery from Hawgjowles under the Indemnity Agreement between Hawgjowles and Surety, and until Worthless Bank's full indebtedness under its loan agreements with Hawgjowles is repaid;

---

1 The Worthless Bank does not acknowledge in this Agreement Surety's claim that it is subrogated to the right of the obligee to setoff payments due on one project to cover losses on other projects. Surety does not agree to waive its claim that it can assert as subrogee the right of an obligee to setoff payments on one project to cover losses on others, and expressly reserves the right to assert such rights. Except for the express acknowledgement of Surety's rights in Paragraph 3.A., this Agreement neither acknowledges nor waives any other subrogation rights of Surety as a surety.

Exhibit 9.3 (continued)

E. Hawgjowles shall be entitled to collect any recoveries in excess of the amounts due Worthless Bank and Surety.

4. Worthless Bank agrees that the secured interest it claims in Commission contracts identified above, and its interest in any other contracts, is subordinate and inferior to any claim against the contracts, the contract rights and proceeds provided for under this Agreement; and to the extent required to effect the distribution to the parties provided for under this Agreement, Worthless Bank assigns to Surety all of its rights to recoveries from the contracts and claims, except for the recoveries expressly granted Worthless Bank under this Agreement. Any perfected secured interest of Worthless Bank to the contract consideration and claims is subordinate to the rights of the parties expressly acknowledged and granted under this Agreement.

5. As assignees of the contract claims, Worthless Bank and Surety may elect to prosecute the claims should Hawgjowles fail or be unable to prosecute the claims. Surety and Worthless Bank will select counsel to prosecute the claim by mutual agreement. Surety and Worthless Bank must both consent to settlement of the claim. The consent for retention of counsel and settlement cannot be unreasonably withheld. In the event there is a firm settlement offer, that one of the parties to this agreement wants to accept and the other does not, the party desiring to accept the settlement can cease contributing to the costs of the prosecution of the claim after giving written notice to the other party of the desire to accept the settlement offer. The party dissenting from the settlement is free to continue prosecution of the claim at its own expense. The party dissenting from settlement and prosecuting the claim shall be entitled to all recoveries above the amount offered in settlement. In the event of a recovery in excess of a prior settlement offer, expenses and fees incurred up to the date of the offer shall be pro-rated and distributed in accordance with the priorities and terms of this Agreement. In the event a recovery is less than the amount previously offered in settlement, the dissenting party who prosecuted the claim must bear the fees and costs incurred after the date of the offer, and must pay the party who wanted to accept the settlement offer the difference between what that party received from any recoveries and what that party would have received had the settlement been accepted on the date offered. Attorney's fees for recovery efforts shall be apportioned on an interim basis between Worthless Bank and Surety based on the percentages of recoveries.

6. Worthless Bank and Surety agree to execute any documents required for the implementation and enforcing of the terms of this Agreement.

7. Worthless Bank and Surety agree that the terms of this Agreement may be specifically enforced by either party to implement its terms.

Exhibit 9.3 (continued)

8. The law of the State of Despair shall apply to the terms of this Agreement.

AGREED TO IN FORM AND SUBSTANCE:

PURE OF HEART SURETY COMPANY

By:__________________________

Title:_________________________

Date:_________________________

THE WORTHLESS BANK

By:__________________________

Title:_________________________

Date:_________________________

Acknowledged By:

____

On Behalf of Buford T.
Hawgjowles Construction Co., Inc.

Exhibit 9.4

Sample Notice to Obligee

Re:	PRINCIPAL:	Buford T. Hawgjowles Construction Co.
	BOND NO.:	007
	PROJECT:	Four Story Smokehouse and Tatoo Parlor
	OBLIGEE:	The Grand Interstate Barbecue Hickory Pit

Dear Sir/Ms:

My firm represents the interests of Pure of Heart Surety Co. in connection with the bankruptcy of Buford T. Hawgjowles Construction Co., Inc. ("Hawgjowles"), Pure of Heart Surety is the surety on the above referenced bond for Hawgjowles. On May 9, 1995, Hawgjowles filed a petition seeking relief under Chapter 11 of the Bankruptcy Code.

As you are probably aware, Hawgjowles, as a debtor-in-possession, is protected by the automatic stay provision of the Bankruptcy Code, 11 U.S.C., Sec. 362, from legal proceedings by its creditors. In addition, Pure of Heart Surety and your company, are subject to the terms of the Bankruptcy Code in determining the disposition of Hawgjowles' contract. Because Hawgjowles is protected under the automatic stay provision and may elect to assume your company's contract, any action undertaken by your company with respect to Hawgjowles' rights under the contract probably requires the approval of the Bankruptcy Court. Should you terminate, relet or assume performance of the contract without compliance with the provisions of the Bankruptcy Code you risk court imposed sanctions.

Either as result of direct communication with you or through written notice from claimants, Pure of Heart Surety has become aware that there are either claims for payment, uncompleted work under Hawgjowles' contract, or both, on the project. Pure of Heart Surety may be liable for any valid claims against its bond for sums due for material and supplies required for the execution of its contract work. Moreover, in the event Hawgjowles rejects this contract, Pure of Heart Surety, under the terms of its bond, may be liable for performance of the work or the cost incurred in completion.

Accordingly, Pure of Heart Surety asserts that any contract funds from your contract with the debtor that you are presently holding are trust funds for the payment of outstanding supplier and material bills as well as other completion costs, incurred both prior and subsequent to the filing of the petition. In the event any funds are disbursed on the project prior to the assumption of the contract by

Exhibit 9.4 (continued)

Hawgjowles, and without Pure of Heart Surety's approval, Pure of Heart Surety will consider its obligation discharged to the extent the contract funds are insufficient to cover claims and completion costs.

Representatives of Hawgjowles may contact you and demand payment of the contract progress payments that Hawgjowles claims it has earned to date. Hawgjowles does not have an unconditional right to payment. Under the Bankruptcy Code, Hawgjowles must provide adequate protection as a condition for demanding turnover of the contract funds.

Pure of Heart Surety looks to the remaining contract funds as security for the performance and payment of the contract obligations. You have a secured interest in these contract funds by virtue of possession. Pure of Heart Surety demands that before any contract funds are released that an order be entered affording you adequate protection under the Bankruptcy Code. By demanding adequate protection, you can assure that the contract funds will be used to satisfy contract obligations, and thus reduce the risk to my client. The court can provide adequate protection by requiring assumption of the contract, segregation of the contract funds and the grant of an administrative priority to cover losses should Hawgjowles fail to perform. Pure of Heart Surety will regard the release of contract funds by you without a demand for adequate protection as a release of security. Such a release of security can result in the discharge of Pure of Heart Surety as a surety. If you have any questions regarding this demand, please contact the undersigned.

We have been unable to meet with representatives of Hawgjowles to discuss the status of your contract or to verify the existence of claims. We would also like to verify the amount remaining in the contract to be paid the debtor. We therefore ask that you furnish the following information:

1) The last paid request and any pending pay requests or estimates on the project from Hawgjowles.
2) Any progress schedules of the work to be performed.
3) Any documentation or correspondence pertaining to unpaid material or labor costs incurred by Hawgjowles on the project.
4) Any documentation for backcharges or change orders resulting in an adjustment of the contract price.

Your cooperation would assist us in concluding our investigation.

The filing of the Chapter 11 petition itself cannot not be regarded as an act of default of the contract. Nevertheless, the initial notices regarding Hawgjowles' failure to pay suppliers and subcontractors is a cause for concern, and may require further action in the future.

Exhibit 9.4 (continued)

Pure of Heart Surety continues to investigate potential claims under its bonds. This letter, and the investigation by Pure of Heart Surety, should not be construed by you as an admission of any liability.

If you have any questions, please contact the undersigned. Your cooperation and assistance would be appreciate.

Very truly yours,

Sedgwick, Detert, Moran & Arnold

T. Scott Leo

Exhibit 9.5

IN THE BANKRUPTCY COURT FOR THE
DISTRICT OF DESPAIR
EASTERN DIVISION

In re Buford T. Hawgjowles	§	
Construction Co., Inc.	§	
	§	No. 1,000,000
Debtor.	§	(Chapter 11)

MOTION OF PURE OF HEART SURETY COMPANY
TO PROHIBIT USE OF CASH COLLATERAL

Pure of Heart Surety Co. ("Surety") moves this Court for an order pursuant to Section 363(e) of the Code prohibiting the use of cash collateral by the Debtor. In support of this motion, Surety states:

1. Surety bonded contracts that the Debtor has yet to assume.
2. The contract receivables due the Debtor constitute cash collateral within the meaning of Section 363(a).
3. Surety has an interest in the contract receivables as the subrogee of the obligees on the bonds and as the party that will be compelled to perform the contract obligations in the event the debtor rejects the contracts.[1]
4. Debtor has failed to assume the contracts within the meaning of Section 365. On some of the contracts it is likely the Debtor must reject those contracts because it is presently in default of performance and payment obligations on those contracts.

---

1 In cash collateral litigation the most hotly contested issue for a surety will be its standing to object to the debtor's use of cash collateral. The surety can circuitously demand the owner assert its right to adequate protection and threaten the owner that any later claim for performance will be barred or discharged because the owner failed to assert its rights in the bankruptcy proceeding. The uncertainty the surety faces in the bankruptcy proceeding on this issue is obvious if one compares the holdings in *In re Pacific Marine Dredging and Const.*, 79 Bankr. 924 (Bankr. D. Or. 1987), which strongly recognized the surety's equitable rights, with *In re Universal Builders, Inc.*, 53 Bankr. 183 (Bankr. M.D. Tenn. 1985), which rejected any basis for the surety asserting adequate protection independently of the obligee.

Exhibit 9.5 (continued)

5. The contract receivables held by the obligees on the bonds, the owners of the projects, serve to reduce the loss to the Surety in the event of the failure of the Debtor to perform.

6. As of the date of this motion, the Debtor has failed to provide adequate protection by assuming the contracts and curing defaults and providing adequate assurance of future performance.

For the foregoing reasons, Pure of Heart Surety Company prays for an order pursuant to Section 363(e) prohibiting the debtor from using bonded contract receivables unless and until the Debtor assumes such contracts under Section 365 and provides other assurances that the Surety's interest in the contract receivables is adequately protected within the meaning of Section 361 of the Bankruptcy Code.

PURE OF HEART SURETY CO.

By: ______________________________

T. Scott Leo, One of the Attorneys
for Pure of Heart Surety Co.

T. Scott Leo
Sedgwick, Detert, Moran & Arnold
209 S. LaSalle St., 7th Floor
Chicago, IL 60604
(312) 641-9050

Exhibit 9.6

IN THE BANKRUPTCY COURT FOR THE
DISTRICT OF DESPAIR
EASTERN DIVISION

In re Buford T. Hawgjowles	§	
Construction Co., Inc.	§	
	§	No. 1,000,000
Debtor.	§	(Chapter 11)

MOTION FOR AN ORDER TO SET DATE CERTAIN BY WHICH THE DEBTOR MUST ASSUME OR REJECT AN EXECUTORY CONTRACT

Pure of Heart Surety Co. ("Surety") by its attorneys T. Scott Leo moves this Court in accordance with Section 365(d)(2) and Section 105[1] of the Bankruptcy Code to a set a date certain by which the Debtor must assume an executory contract for [contract description]. In further support of this motion Surety states:

1. The Debtor entered into a contract for [description] with [party to the contract] on [date].

2. As of the date of filing the petition initiating this cause under Chapter 11, [date], substantial work remained to be performed on the project [give the percentage to complete if appropriate], and work remains to be performed on the contract as of the date of this motion [provide amount or percent to complete if appropriate].

3. As of the date of filing this motion, the Debtor has yet to assume or reject the contract pursuant to Section 365.

4. The Debtor has ceased work and abandoned the project, which is a continuing default by the Debtor under the terms of the contract. Surety will need to take steps to replace the debtor or otherwise arrange for the conclusion of the

---

1 Note: In this motion, reference is added to Section 105 as additional authority for this motion in the event either the debtor or another party argues that Section 365(d)(2) only gives standing to a party to the contract to move to set a time frame to assume or reject. Section 105 is the provision of the Code that grants the bankruptcy court general powers to issue orders to preserve and administer the estate. If continued inaction will result in a loss to the estate and the creditors, the court should be authorized to take action under Section 105.

Exhibit 9.6 (continued)

contract work unless the Debtor takes steps to promptly assume and complete the contract.

5. Surety requests that the Court give the debtor until [insert date] to move to assume the contract and to bring that matter for hearing. In the event that the Debtor fails to move for the assumption of the contract by that date, Surety requests that an order be entered deeming the contract rejected, granting relief from the automatic stay, and enabling Surety to take appropriate action to relet the contract or otherwise conclude the work.

6. Further delay in the Debtor's taking action on this project will result in increased cost to complete, compelling the rejection of the contract, increasing the loss related to completion of the work for the Surety and increasing the Surety's unsecured claim against the Debtor's estate.

7. In light of the increasing loss to the estate arising out of the failure of the Debtor to assume or reject the contract in question, this court possesses authority under either Section 362(d)(2) or Section 105 of the Bankruptcy Code to set a definite date by which the Debtor must assume or reject this contract.

For the foregoing reasons, Pure of Heart Surety Company prays the Court enter an order in accordance with Section 365(d)(2) and Section 105 of the Bankruptcy Code requiring the Debtor to assume the contract for [description] by [date] and to order that the contract be deemed rejected if not assumed by the Debtor on or before that date.

PURE OF HEART SURETY CO.

By: ______________________________
T. Scott Leo, One of the Attorneys
for Pure of Heart Surety Co.

T. Scott Leo
Sedgwick, Detert, Moran & Arnold
209 S. LaSalle St., 7th Floor
Chicago, IL 60604
(312) 641-9050

Exhibit 9.6 (continued)

IN THE BANKRUPTCY COURT FOR THE
DISTRICT OF DESPAIR
EASTERN DIVISION

In re Buford T. Hawgjowles	§	
Construction Co., Inc.	§	
	§	No. 1,000,000
Debtor.	§	(Chapter 11)

MOTION FOR SECTION 105 STATUS CONFERENCE

Pure of Heart Surety Co. ("Surety") moves this court in accordance with § 105(d)(1) to hold a status conference for the express purpose of setting a time frame for the assumption and rejection of executory contracts and to establish an expedited procedure for hearing the motion to assume filed by the debtor, Buford T. Hawgjowles Construction Co., Inc. ("Debtor") and the objections filed by The Worthless Bank ("Bank"). In further support of this motion Surety states:

1. This motion is brought pursuant to amended § 105(d)(1), effective October 22, 1994, which provides that any party in interest can request a status conference at which the court can prescribe conditions and limitations for the expeditious handling of issues in the bankruptcy proceeding including setting "a date by which the debtor, or trustee must assume of reject an executory contract." 11 U.S.C. § 105(d)(1)(A).

2. Surety issued bonds securing the performance and payment of contract obligations by Debtor. Some of these contracts Debtor now proposes to assume.

3. Surety's bonds are financial accommodations that Hawgjowles cannot assume. *In re Sun Runner Marine, Inc.*, 945 F.2d 1089 (9th Cir. 1991); *In re Matter of Edward's Mobile Home Sales, Inc.*, 119 Bankr. 857 (Bankr. N.D. Fla. 1990); *In re Adana Mortgage Bankers, Inc.*, 12 Bankr. 977 (Bankr. N.D. Ga. 1980); *In re Wegner Farms*, 49 Bankr. 440 (Bankr. N.D. Iowa 1985). Surety may consider extending the financial accommodation issued on behalf of Debtor to cover post petition performance provided Debtor can prove that it can perform and pay the contract obligations and the order approving assumption of the contract protects Surety from potential losses.

4. Bank has objected to the assumption of certain bonded contracts by Hawgjowles, requesting a hearing to determine the benefit of the assumption of the contracts to the estate and the creditors. Surety concurs with some of the points raised in Bank's objections and asks the court to arrange for a prompt determination of these issues.

Exhibit 9.6 (continued)

The Contracts Must be Promptly Assumed or Rejected

5. Surety is receiving notices of claims on contracts that Hawgjowles proposes to assume. *Debtor is defaulting on contracts it proposes to assume.* If Debtor does not take prompt action to assume the contracts and cure defaults, the increase in the cost to complete from further delay will render assumption of the contracts impossible.

6. So that the estate does not lose the profit on valuable contracts that Debtor could perform, and so that the losses due to delay do not increase on the contracts Debtor ought to reject, Surety asks the court to hold a status to set a time frame by which contracts must be assumed or be deemed rejected, and to arrange for an expedited hearing procedure for the motions to assume the contracts that Debtor proposes to assume. This procedure will enable the estate to realize the benefit of any contracts that might be assumed and will reduce the losses to parties like Surety who must perform and pay the contract obligations on the contracts that Debtor rejects.

For the foregoing reasons, Pure of Heart Surety Company prays the court promptly schedule a status hearing to address the following issues:

A. A date by which contracts must be assumed by the debtor or be deemed rejected;

B. An expedited procedure for hearing the motion(s) to assume and any objections;

C. The scope of the issues and financial and other information needed for the hearing on the motion(s) to assume.

PURE OF HEART SURETY CO.

By: ____________________________

T. Scott Leo, One of the Attorneys
for Pure of Heart Surety Co.

T. Scott Leo
Sedgwick, Detert, Moran & Arnold
209 S. LaSalle St., 7th Floor
Chicago, IL 60604
(312) 641-9050

Exhibit 9.7

Cancellation of Surety Bonds

IN THE BANKRUPTCY COURT FOR THE
DISTRICT OF DESPAIR
EASTERN DIVISION

In re Buford T. Hawgjowles	§	
Construction Co., Inc.	§	
	§	No. 1,000,000
Debtor.	§	(Chapter 11)

NOTICE BY THE SURETIES OF CANCELLATION OF
SURETY BONDS THAT ARE FINANCIAL ACCOMMODATIONS

Pure of Heart Surety Co. ("Surety") moves this court pursuant to Section 362(d)(2) to lift the automatic stay to permit Surety to cancel performance and payment bonds issued by it on behalf of the Debtor and also notifies the parties in the Hawgjowles bankruptcy proceeding of the following:

1. **Cancellation of License and Regulatory Bonds.** The Surety will issue notices of cancellation to the obligees to cancel the license, permit and other administrative bonds listed on Exhibit A. These bonds are financial accommodations within the meaning of § 365(c)(2) that cannot be assumed by Debtor. Surety will not extend surety credit to Debtor post-petition.

2. **Performance and Payment Bond Credit Will Not be Extended By Surety for Debtor's Post-Petition Operations.** With respect to contracts that Debtor seeks to assume, Surety provides notice that it will not extend surety credit to Debtor post-petition and will not agree to continue to keep the bonds in effect post-petition. Surety issues this notice to advise the parties and the Debtor that new surety obligations must be obtained by Debtor for its post-petition performance and to provide adequate assurance of future performance on the contracts it seeks to assume.

3. **The Court Should Lift the Stay to Permit Cancellation of the Bonds.** The surety bonds are financial accommodations within the meaning of Section 365(c) and are not property of the Debtor's estate. The stay should be lifted to permit the cancellation of the bonds under Section 362(d)(2) as the Debtor has

Exhibit 9.7 (continued)

no equity in the bonds and the Surety has elected not to extend the financial accommodations on behalf of the Debtor post-petition.[1]

For the foregoing reasons, Pure of Heart Surety Company prays the Court enter an order lifting the automatic stay pursuant to Section 362(d)(2) of the Bankruptcy Code so that the bonds identified above can be canceled.

PURE OF HEART SURETY CO.

By: ______________________________
T. Scott Leo, One of the Attorneys
for Pure of Heart Surety Co.

T. Scott Leo
Sedgwick, Detert, Moran & Arnold
209 S. LaSalle St., 7th Floor
Chicago, IL 60604
(312) 641-9050

---

1 At least one case holds that a financial accommodation simply cannot be assumed by a debtor and therefore there is no reason to lift the stay to cancel the bonds. *In re Sun Runner Marine, Inc.*, 945 F.2d 1089 (9th Cir. 1991). For this reason, the sample form provided notifies the parties of the cancellation and alternatively requests the stay be lifted. One could opt to simply send a notice stating the intention of the surety not to extend financial accommodations to the debtor post-petition. At any later hearing to assume a contract, the surety could appear and reiterate that the bond securing the contract will not extend to post-petition performance.

Exhibit 9.8

Granting of Secured Status For Extension of New Credit

IN THE BANKRUPTCY COURT FOR THE
DISTRICT OF DESPAIR
EASTERN DIVISION

In re Buford T. Hawgjowles	§	
Construction Co., Inc.	§	
	§	No. 1,000,000
Debtor.	§	(Chapter 11)

APPLICATION TO GRANT PURE OF HEART SURETY COMPANY SECURED STATUS UNDER SECTION 364

Debtor, Buford T. Hawgjowles Construction Co., Inc. ("Debtor")[1] presents this application to approve the granting of secured status to Pure of Heart Surety Company ("Surety") in exchange for the issuance of new surety bonds required for the Debtor's continued operations. Debtor seeks approval of secured status for the following reasons and upon the following terms and conditions:

1. Debtor requested Surety to provide certain bonds necessary for its continued business operations.

2. These bonds include the following license and permit bonds required for the debtor to continue to do business as a contractor in this state:[2]

[LIST BONDS]

3. Each of the bonds are required for the Debtor to be able to continue its performance of executory contracts. Debtor has attempted to obtain this type of extension of credit in the ordinary course of business and has been unable to secure such credit.

4. Surety is willing to issue these new bonds and to keep some existing bonds in effect provided that Debtor, to the extent Surety incurs any losses on these bonds and to the extent the Debtor fails to pay premiums, grants a first,

---

1 The motion is brought by the debtor. 11 U.S.C. § 364(b).

2 The motion refers to permit and license bond but there is no reason a performance and payment bond surety could not demand the same type of security for the issuance of new bonds.

Exhibit 9.8 (continued)

valid, enforceable perfected and senior security interest and lien in favor of the Surety pursuant to the provisions of Sections 364(c) and 364(d) in and to the following property of the debtor: [list specific property or categories of property, e.g., equipment, inventory]. Debtor also requests that Surety be granted and administrative priority pursuant to Section 364(c)(1) over any and all administrative expenses of the kind specified in Section 503(b) and 507(b) of the Bankruptcy Code including priority over and above all costs of administration of this Chapter 11 proceeding and any ensuing Chapter 7 proceeding for protection and security for losses arising out of the issuance of bonds by Surety on behalf of Debtor.[3]

For the foregoing reasons, Buford T. Hawgjowles Construction Co., Inc. prays the court enter an order approving the obtaining of the bonds from Surety and approving the allowance of the administrative expense claim and priority lien requested pursuant to Sections 364(c) and 364(d) of the Bankruptcy Code.

BUFORD T. HAWGJOWLES
CONSTRUCTION CO., INC.

By: ______________________________
Slim Pickens, One of the Attorneys
for Debtor

3 Because the debtor's financing bank will object to granting a blanket super-priority as will debtor's counsel, whose claim for fees will be primed by such a lien, most financing under these circumstances involve specific assets the debtor can pledge as security as opposed to blanket liens. It is far easier to obtain approval for a request that does not ask for a blanket administrative claim that primes all other administrative claims.

Exhibit 9.9

Sample "Back Door" Financing Agreement

AGREEMENT ADJUSTING CONTRACT
PRICE AND FOR ASSUMPTION AND COMPLETION
OF REMAINING CONTRACT WORK

RECITALS

Buford T. Hawgjowles Construction Co., Inc. ("Hawgjowles") is a party to a contract dated June 9, 1994 ("Contract") with Grand Interstate Hickory Barbecue Pit ("Barbecue Pit") for the construction of a four story smokehouse and tatoo parlor ("Project");

Hawgjowles is presently in default on the Contract;

Hawgjowles is a debtor-in-possession under Chapter 11 of the Bankruptcy Code, No. 1,000,000, filed on May 9, 1995 in the Bankruptcy Court for the District of Despair, Eastern Division;

Pure of Heart Surety Co. executed as surety for Hawgjowles a performance bond in connection with the Contract which names Barbecue Pit as obligee;

The parties to this agreement desire to have Hawgjowles complete the Project as promptly as possible and to resolve certain issues in dispute.

NOW THEREFORE, the parties agree:

1. **Incorporation of Recitals.** The recitals are incorporated into and made a part of this Agreement.

2. **Assumption of Contract.** Hawgjowles agrees to assume the contract in accordance with Section 365 of the Bankruptcy Code, to perform in accordance with the terms of the Contract, except as expressly modified by this Agreement. Pure of Heart Surety agrees to keep its performance bond in effect to secure Hawgjowles' post petition performance. Barbecue Pit agrees to the modification of the original Contract set forth in this Agreement.

3. **Modification of Contract Terms.** Hawgjowles, Barbecue Pit and Pure of Heart Surety assent to the following modification of the Contract terms:

a. Hawgjowles shall maintain a normal construction progress in accordance with the schedule attached.[1]

---

1 The Agreement can include any number of items the parties negotiate regarding scheduling: waiver of liquidated damages, incentives for completion, etc.

Exhibit 9.9 (continued)

b. Hawgjowles will provide complete access to Pure of Heart Surety and Barbecue Pit to information regarding work performed, materials purchased, equipment used on the Project, fabrication of items for incorporation in the Project.
c. The Contract price shall be increased from $1,000,000 to $1,200,000. This increase is contingent upon timely and proper performance by Hawgjowles.
d. The unpaid balance of the Contract, as increased in this Agreement, is $700,000. That balance shall be paid to Hawgjowles in accordance with the following schedule:

$________	receipt of structural steel
$________	pouring of foundation
$________	completion of electrical work
$________	installation of rotary smokehouse devices
$________	acceptance of project by Barbecue Pit

e. Hawgjowles grants to Barbecue Pit a security interest in all materials ordered or purchased for incorporation into the Project. The order approving assumption will provide for this first secured interest in favor of Barbecue Pit, which will be valid whether or not it is properly perfected.

4. **Release of Surety and Reduction of Penal Sum of Performance Bond.** Upon acceptance of the Project by Barbecue Pit, Barbecue Pit will release Pure of Heart Surety of all liability on the performance bond and return the original bond to Pure of Heart Surety. Barbecue Pit acknowledges the payment of the additional $200,000 for performance of the Contract, set forth in paragraph 3 above, by Pure of Heart Surety reduces the penal sum of the performance bond by that amount.

5. **Acknowledgement and Assumption of General Agreement of Indemnity.** Hawgjowles and the undersigned indemnitors acknowledge the General Agreement of Indemnity in favor of Pure of Heart Surety remains in effect. Hawgjowles will take the appropriate action to obtain approval of the assumption of the obligations of the Indemnity Agreement by Hawgjowles as debtor-in-possession in the Bankruptcy Court.[2]

---

2 Hawgjowles can either assume the Indemnity Agreement or have the obligation of that agreement approved as administrative expense obligations of the debtor. The indemnity agreement cannot be assumed if it is not deemed executory. The standard test for executory obligations is whether

Exhibit 9.9 (continued)

6. **Approval of Court.** This Agreement is subject to approval of the Bankruptcy Court in the Hawgjowles Chapter 11 case by a final order, after expiration of all appeal periods or resolution of any appeal taken.

Wherefore, we execute this Agreement this _____ day of _____________, 19___.

GRAND INTERSTATE HICKORY
BARBECUE PIT

By:_______________________________

BUFORD T. HAWGJOWLES
CONSTRUCTION CO., INC.

By:_______________________________

PURE OF HEART SURETY COMPANY

By:_______________________________

---

performance remains on the part of both parties. *In re Evans Products Co.*, 91 B.R. 1003 (Bankr. S.D. Fla. 1988) (bond and indemnity obligation treated as executory).

Exhibit 9.9 (continued)

ASSENTED TO:

____
Indemnitor

____
Indemnitor

Creditors' Committee

By: ______________________________
Counsel for the Committee

Exhibit 12.1

Excerpt from Model Rules of Professional Conduct Rules (1.4, 1.6-1.10)

1. Rule 1.4 Communication

(a) A lawyer shall keep a client reasonably informed about the status of a matter and promptly comply with reasonable requests for information.
(b) A lawyer shall explain a matter to the extent reasonably necessary to permit the client to make informed decisions regarding the representation.

2. Rule 1.6 Confidentiality of Information

(a) A lawyer shall not reveal information relating to representation of a client unless the client consents after consultation, except for disclosures that are impliedly authorized in order to carry out the representation, and except as stated in paragraph (b).
(b) A lawyer may reveal such information to the extent the lawyer reasonably believes necessary:

(1) to prevent the client from committing a criminal act that the lawyer believes is likely to result in imminent death or substantial bodily harm; or

(2) to establish a claim or defense on behalf of the lawyer in a controversy between the lawyer and the client, to establish a defense to a criminal charge or civil claim against the lawyer based upon conduct in which the client was involved, or to respond to allegations in any proceeding concerning the lawyer's representation of the client.

3. Rule 1.7 Conflict of Interest: General Rule

(a) A lawyer shall not represent a client if the representation of that client will be directly adverse to another client, unless:

(1) The lawyer reasonably believes the representation will not adversely affect the relationship with the other client; and

(2) each client consents after consultation.

(b) A lawyer shall not represent a client if the representation of that client may be materially limited by the lawyer's responsibilities to another client or to a third person, or by the lawyer's own interests, unless:

(1) the lawyer reasonably believes the representation will not be adversely affected; and

Exhibit 12.1 (continued)

(2) the client consents after consultation. When representation of multiple clients in a single matter is undertaken, the consultation shall include explanation of the implications of the common representation and the advantages and risks involved.

4. *Rule 1.8 Conflict of Interest: Prohibited Transactions*

(a) A lawyer shall not enter into a business transaction with a client or knowingly acquire an ownership, possessory, security or other pecuniary interest adverse to a client unless:

(1) the transaction and terms on which the lawyer acquires the interest are fair and reasonable to the client and are fully disclosed and transmitted in writing to the client in a manner which can be reasonably understood by the client;

(2) the client is given a reasonable opportunity to seek the advice of independent counsel in the transaction; and

(3) the client consents in writing thereto.

(b) A lawyer shall not use information relating to representation of a client to the disadvantage of the client unless the client consents after consultation, except as permitted or required by Rule 1.6 or Rule 3.3.

(c) A lawyer shall not prepare an instrument giving the lawyer or a person related to the lawyer as parent, child, sibling, or spouse any substantial gift from a client, including a testamentary gift, except where the client is related to the donee.

(d) Prior to the conclusion of representation of a client, a lawyer shall not make or negotiate an agreement giving the lawyer literary or media rights to a portrayal or account based in substantial part on information relating to the representation.

(e) A lawyer shall not provide financial assistance to a client in connection with pending or contemplated litigation, except that:

(1) a lawyer may advance court costs and expenses of litigation, the repayment of which may be contingent on the outcome of the matter; and

(2) a lawyer representing an indigent client may pay court costs and expenses of litigation on behalf of the client.

(f) A lawyer shall not accept compensation for representing a client from one other than the client unless:

(1) the client consents after consultation;

(2) there is no interference with the lawyer's independence of professional judgment or with the client-lawyer relationship; and

Exhibit 12.1 (continued)

(3) information relating to representation of a client is protected as required by Rule 1.6

(g) A lawyer who represents two or more clients shall not participate in making an aggregated settlement of the claims of or against the clients, or in a criminal case an aggregate agreement as to guilty or *nolo contendere* pleas, unless each client consents after consultation, including disclosure of the existence and nature of all the claims or pleas involved and of the participation of each person in the settlement.

(h) A lawyer shall not make an agreement prospectively limiting the lawyer's liability to a client for malpractice unless permitted by law and the client is independently represented in making the agreement, or settle a claim for such liability with an unrepresented client or former client without first advising that person in writing that independent representation is appropriate in connection therewith.

(i) A lawyer related to another lawyer as parent, child, sibling or spouse shall not represent a client in a representation directly adverse to a person whom the lawyer knows is represented by the other lawyer except upon consent by the client after consultation regarding the relationship.

(j) A lawyer shall not acquire a proprietary interest in the cause of action or subject matter of litigation the lawyer is conducting for a client except that the lawyer may:

(1) acquire a lien granted by law to secure the lawyer's fee or expenses; and

(2) contract with a client for a reasonable contingent fee in a civil case.

5. ***Rule 1.9 Conflict of interest: Former Client***

(a) A lawyer who has formerly represented a client in a matter shall not thereafter represent another person in the same or a substantially related matter in which that person's interests are materially adverse to the interests of the former client unless the former client consents after consultation.

(b) A lawyer shall not knowingly represent a person in the same or a substantially related matter in which a firm with which the lawyer formerly was associated had previously represented a client

(1) whose interests are materially adverse to that person; and

(2) about whom the lawyer had acquired information protected by Rules 1.6 and 1.9(c) that is material to the matter;

unless the former client consents after consultation.

Exhibit 12.1 (continued)

(c) A lawyer who has formerly represented a client in a matter or whose present or former firm has formerly represented a client in a matter shall not thereafter:

(1) use information relating to the representation to the disadvantage of the former client except as Rule 1.6 or Rule 3.3 would permit or require with respect to a client, or when the information has become generally known; or

(2) reveal information relating to the representation except as Rule 1.6 or Rule 3.3 would permit or require with respect to a client.

6. Rule 1.10 Imputed Disqualification: General Rule

(a) While lawyers are associated in a firm, none of them shall knowingly represent a client when any one of them practicing alone would be prohibited from doing so by Rules 1.7, 1.8(c), 1.9 or 2.2.

(b) When a lawyer has terminated an association with a firm, the firm is not prohibited from thereafter representing a person with interests materially adverse to those of a client represented by the formerly associated lawyer and not currently represented by the firm, unless:

(1) the matter is the same or substantially related to that in which the formerly associated lawyer represented the client; and

(2) any lawyer remaining in the firm has information protected by Rules 1.6 and 1.9(c) that is material to the matter.

(c) A disqualification prescribed by this rule may be waived by the affected client under the conditions stated in Rule 1.7.

Exhibit 12.2

Sample Letter to Claimant

[Date]

Mr. Relentless Advocate
Advocate & Do Right
Last Ditch, NM 8000

File No.:	074-91-0001
Principal:	Faulty Towers, Inc.
Project:	U.S. Observatory Tower
Obligee:	U.S. Department of the Interior
Lawsuit:	*Concrete Supply v. Faulty Towers, Inc. Bossy Concrete Co., Reliable Surety Co.*

Dear Mr. Advocate:

This will acknowledge receipt of the Summons and Complaint you served upon Reliable Surety Company. Please note that our acknowledgment of receipt of the Summons and Complaint should not be construed as an admission of liability under our bond, nor as waiver or estoppel of any rights or defenses of Reliable Surety Company under its bond, or applicable law.

However, pending the appearance of counsel in the above litigation, please feel free to submit any additional documentation you believe is necessary for us to review your client's claim, other than that which was attached to the Summons and Complaint. We will review this litigation with our Principal in order to ascertain its position and intentions. After we have done so, we will be in touch with you through the attorneys we anticipate appearing to represent us in the above litigation, in order to advise you of our position.

Pending the appearance of counsel in the above litigation, please feel free to furnish any documentation or information you believe supports your position, if you are willing to do without formal discovery.

Very truly yours,

RELIABLE SURETY COMPANY

Bond Claim Department

Exhibit 12.3

Sample Letter to Principal

[Date]

Mr. Faulty Towers
Faulty Towers, Inc.
Last Ditch, NM 80000
Mr. Howard Learnright
Learnright & Doolittle
Last Ditch, NM 80000

File No.:	074-91-00001
Principal:	Faulty Towers, Inc.
Project:	U.S. Observatory Tower
Obligee	U.S. Department of the Interior
Lawsuit:	*Concrete Supply v. Faulty Towers, Inc. Bossy Concrete Co., Reliable Surety Co.*

Gentlemen:

Reliable Surety Company has been served with a Summons and Complaint on July 31, 1991 in an action brought by Concrete Supply, a supplier to your subcontractor, Bossy Concrete Co. According to our calculation, the Answer date for this Company is August 20, 1991. A copy of the Summons and Complaint is enclosed.

In accordance with the terms and conditions of our Agreement of Indemnity and generally accepted Surety law, we hereby tender the defense of this litigation to our Principal, Faulty Towers, Inc., and Indemnitors, to protect and save harmless this Surety from any loss, cost or expense connected with the above-referenced lawsuit.

We tender the defense for a number of reasons, including the knowledge that your office is closer to the situation factually and were it necessary for this Company to hire its own counsel at this time, it would result in attorneys' fees for which we would be required to seek reimbursement under the terms of the aforementioned Indemnity Agreement.

To assist us in investigating this claim, please furnish all documentation or information you have concerning this claim including copies of subcontracts, notices and correspondence with either Concrete Supply or Bossy Concrete Co.

We also request copies of the responsive pleadings filed on our behalf for our approval prior to filing as well as any other documents pertinent to the suit.

Exhibit 12.3 (continued)

If this tender of defense is acceptable, please acknowledge such acceptance by signing the enclosed copy of this letter and returning it immediately. In the event the tender of defense is not acceptable, please notify me at the number indicated above. If we do not receive this executed letter from you or otherwise hear from you by August 10, we will assume that the tender of our defense has been refused, and Reliable Surety Company will undertake its own defense in this action, and will seek reimbursement for all costs, fees, and expenses under the Indemnity Agreement.

Our tender of defense is not intended, nor should it be construed to be a waiver of any conflict of interest, nor of our right at our sole discretion to retain counsel to represent this firm's interest, at any time during the pendency of this claim, and to seek reimbursement for all costs, fee and expenses under the Indemnity Agreement.

Sincerely,

RELIABLE SURETY COMPANY

Bond Claim Department

cc: (*Company Attorney*)
Enc.

Tender of Defense Accepted by:

FAULTY TOWERS, INC.

____

Faulty Towers, President

Exhibit 12.4

Sample Letter to Joint Counsel

[Date]

Mr. Howard Learnright
Learnright & Doolittle
Last Ditch, NM 80000

File No.:	074-91-00001
Principal:	Faulty Towers, Inc.
Project:	U.S. Observatory Tower
Obligee:	U.S. Department of the Interior
Lawsuit:	*Concrete Supply v. Faulty Towers, Inc. Bossy Concrete Co., Reliable Surety Co.*

Dear Mr. Learnright:

From Mr. Tower, of Faulty Towers, it is our understanding you have been retained to represent our interests at the expense of our Principal and Indemnitors. Please find enclosed our form Case Management Plan Flow Chart. Please call us upon receipt of this letter to review the Case Management Flow Chart so we may jointly complete the chart. Also, we would ask that you copy us on all correspondence and pleadings, and provide us with a draft copy of the Answer for our approval prior to filing it with the court.

The surety defenses you should raise on our behalf should include but not be limited to Concrete Supply's failure to satisfy the 90-day notice provision of the Miller Act. Please also raise all of our Principal's defenses on our behalf as well.

Notable facts which our investigation has revealed are that Concrete Supply last furnished material to the job site on or before April 1, 1991, but did not furnish written notice of the claim to our Principal until July 17, 1991. Copies of the invoice and delivery tickets showing the date of last delivery are enclosed, along with other pertinent parts of our claim file.

We also request that you keep us advised of the progress of the litigation and that you undertake discovery regarding the surety defenses and issues mentioned above in addition to the defenses of our Principal. Also, please provide status reports when each phase of discovery is completed, e.g., when Answers to Interrogatories are received, depositions are completed, etc.

Exhibit 12.4 (continued)

As you are aware, a surety may have an independent duty to investigate claims, and, by this letter, we are asking for your assistance in discharging this obligation.

If you have any questions, please advise.

Very truly yours,

RELIABLE SURETY COMPANY

cc: (*Principal*)
Enc.

Exhibit 13.1

Notice of Claims to Indemnitors

[Surety's Letterhead]

[Date]

VIA REGULAR AND
CERTIFIED MAIL, RETURN
RECEIPT REQUESTED

[Names and Addresses of Principal and All Indemnitors]

RE: Surety:
Principal:
Bond No.:
Obligee:
Project:
Bond No.:
Obligee:
Project:
NOTICE

Dear Ms. , Mr. , Ms. , Mr. :

_________________ *[Surety]* is Surety on the above referenced bonds issued on behalf of _________________ as Principal. You may recall that _____________ *[Surety]* issued such bonds for _______________ *[Principal]* pursuant to a General Indemnity Agreement executed by each of you. We enclose a copy of the General Indemnity Agreement for your information.

_________________ *[Surety]* has received _________________ *[identification of particular bond]* claims and demands from ____________ *[names of Claimants or Obligee]*. [[In addition, _______________ *[Principal]* has advised *[Surety]* that it has experienced financial difficulties which have created a serious cash flow problem, placing completion of current projects in jeopardy.]] On behalf of the surety, [[and with the cooperation of _________ _______________ *[Principal]*,]] we have begun an investigation of these claims and demands and the status of completion of the bonded projects.

To date surety has made payment of the following sums to claimants: __________ *[for each bond, amounts and names of Claimants paid]*. A more

Exhibit 13.1 (continued)

complete report of the claims and costs will be available as soon as we complete our investigation.

Under the General Indemnity Agreement, each of you, individually, jointly and severally, agreed to hold ______________ *[Surety]* harmless from all liability, loss, costs, damages, fees of attorneys and other expenses, and to indemnify the surety for all loss, costs, damages, fees of attorneys and other expenses it sustained or incurred by reason of having executed those bonds.

The purpose of this letter is to notify you of these pending claims and to invite your participation in resolving them with the least possible expense. To the extent that surety expends funds for the payment of claims, for completion of the project, and for the investigation, evaluation, negotiation or defense of such claims, surety will, in turn, seek full reimbursement from each of you of all amounts expended on account of the bonds for which you provided your agreement or indemnity, together with all attorneys' fees, consulting fees, costs and expenses incurred in that connection.

Please contact the undersigned to discuss these matters further.

Nothing herein shall be deemed to be an estoppel, waiver or modification of any of Surety's rights or defenses and Surety hereby reserves all of its rights and defenses under any general agreement of indemnity, contracts, agreements, bonds, or applicable law.

Very truly yours,

____________________________ *[Surety]*

____________________________ *[Name]*

____________________________ *[Title]*

Exhibit 13.2

Notice of Claims to Principal

[Surety's Letterhead]

[Date]

VIA REGULAR AND
CERTIFIED MAIL, RETURN
RECEIPT REQUESTED

[Principal's Name and Address]

RE: Surety:
Principal:
Bond No.:
Obligee:
Project:
Claimant:
NOTICE

Dear ___________:

We enclose to you herewith a copy of _______________ *[Claimant's]* letter of _____________ *[Date]*, including the attachments thereto. Would you Please verify and immediately confirm back to us in writing (1) that the amounts are properly due and owing, (2) that you agree with the amounts due, and (3) that there are no back-charges, offsets, damages, or other defenses to the alleged claim. Please send to us a copy of all documents in support of your position.

Should you have any questions, please call.

Nothing herein shall be deemed to be an estoppel, waiver or modification of any of Surety's rights or defenses and Surety hereby reserves all of its rights and defenses under any general agreement of indemnity, contracts, agreements, bonds, or applicable law.

Exhibit 13.2 (continued)

Sincerely

_______________________________ *[Surety]*

_______________________________ *[Name]*

_______________________________ *[Title]*

cc: w/o enc.
[Indemnitors]

Exhibit 13.3

Acknowledgment of Receipt of Claim to Claimant

[Surety's Letterhead]

[Date]

[Claimant Name and Address]

RE: Surety:
Principal:
Bond No.:
Obligee:
Project:
Claimant:

Dear ___________:

On behalf of _________ *[Surety]* ____________, we have been asked to respond to your letter of _________________. To assist in our review, would you please complete and execute the enclosed Proof of Loss forms and send us copies of all contracts and/or purchase orders which evidence your agreement with *[Principal]* to furnish the labor, materials, or equipment forming the basis of your claim. Also, please provide a copy of all invoices, signed delivery receipts, summaries, letters to and from Principal, engineer or others, and back-up documentation in support of your claim.

We have also directed an inquiry to _______________ *[Principal]* concerning this matter; after receiving their response, we will be in a position to more fully respond to your claim.

Please note, Surety is pursuing its investigation of your claim under a full and complete reservation of all rights and defenses; nothing herein shall be deemed to be an estoppel, waiver or modification of any of Surety's rights or defenses and Surety hereby reserves all of its rights and defenses under any general agreement of indemnity, contracts, agreements, bonds, or applicable law.

Exhibit 13.3 (continued)

Sincerely

______________________________ *[Surety]*

______________________________ *[Name]*

______________________________ *[Title]*

cc: *[Principal]*

Exhibit 13.4

Demand for Collateral Security to Indemnitors

[Surety's Letterhead]

[Date]

VIA REGULAR AND
CERTIFIED MAIL, RETURN
RECEIPT REQUESTED

[Names and Addresses of Principal and All Indemnitors]

RE: Surety:
Principal:
Bond No.:
Obligee:
Project:
Bond No.:
Obligee:
Project:
DEMAND FOR COLLATERAL

Dear Ms. , Mr. , Ms. , Mr. :

___________________ *[Surety]* is Surety on the above referenced bonds issued on behalf of ____________________, as Principal. Under the General Indemnity Agreement dated ____________ which each of you signed and agreed to, you agreed, among other things, to jointly and individually:

> "indemnify and hold the Surety harmless from and against any and all demands, liabilities, losses, costs, damages, attorneys' fees and expenses of whatever kind or nature which arise by reason of, or in consequence of, the execution by the Surety of any bond on behalf of the Principal..."

Exhibit 13.4 (continued)

Based upon a review of the documents thus far made available the following appears:

Bond No. ________

____________ *[Project]*. The Surety has received notice of the following alleged unpaid amounts:

______________	*[Sub-Subcontractor]*	$
______________	*[Subcontractor]*	$

The Surety has not been provided any information as to payables due vendors or subcontractors, nor contract balances remaining. This may leave a shortfall and exposure to Surety under this Bond of ($______). However to __________ *[Date]* $_______ has been paid out under this Bond.

[OR]

Bond No. ________

__________ *[Project]*. The Surety has received the following claim which has been negotiated to a settlement:

______________	*[Subcontractor]*	$

The Surety has not been provided information as to the amounts which may be owing to subcontractors. There appears to be $_________ contract balances remaining. This leaves a shortfall and exposure to the Surety under this Bond of ($_________).

[OR]

Exhibit 13.4 (continued)

Bond No. ________

______________ *[Project]*. The Surety has received and paid the following claims:

______________ *[Subcontractor]* $
______________ *[Material Supplier]* $
______________ *[Sub-Subcontractor]* $
______________ *[Equipment Supplier]* $

The Surety has received notice of the following alleged unpaid amounts:

______________ *[Subcontractor]* $
______________ *[Supplier]* $

Also, a suit had been filed by ______________ *[Subcontractor]* v. Principal and Surety, in the Circuit Court of ___________ County, ___________ *[State]* in pursuit of its alleged $_________ claim.

The Surety has not been provided any information as to payables due other vendors or subcontractors. Contract balances remaining equal $_________. This may leave a shortfall and exposure to the Surety under this Bond of ($_________)

[OR]

Bond No. ________

______________ *[Project]*. The Surety has received and paid the following claims:

______________ *[Subcontractor]* $
______________ *[Supplier]* $

The Surety has not been provided information as to any other amounts which may be owing to subcontractors. There appears to be a remaining contract balance of $_________. This leaves a positive balance under this one Bond of $_________.

[OR]

Exhibit 13.4 (continued)

Bond No. ________

____________ *[Project]. Under the Payment Bond:*

The Surety has received notice of the following alleged unpaid amounts:

____________	*[Subcontractor]*	$
____________	*[Subcontractor]*	$
____________	*[Subcontractor]*	$____________
		$

The Surety has received and paid the following claims:

____________	*[Supplier]*	$
____________	*[Subcontractor]*	$____________
		$

Payment Bond claims paid from the Trust Account funds:

____________	*[Subcontractor]*	$
____________	*[Subcontractor]*	$____________
		$

Under the Performance Bond:

The Surety has received notice of the following amounts due:

____________	*[Subcontractor]*	$
____________	*[Subcontractor]*	$____________
		$

The Surety has not been provided information as to any other amounts which may be owing to subcontractors. There was a contract balance of $_______. This leaves a shortfall and exposure to the Surety under this Bond of at least ($_________).

Exhibit 13.4 (continued)

The Surety has incurred consulting costs through _____________ *[Date]* of $______ and estimates future consulting costs of $_____________, the total anticipated consulting costs are $__________.

And, the Surety has incurred legal fees and expenses of $_________ through __________ *[Date]*. Additional legal fees and expenses may be incurred and must also be due from the indemnitors.

[On each of the above Bonds, the Surety had written the Principal on numerous occasions requesting information and has not received any complete response.] [The Surety for many months had requested and was refused entry to review, examine and copy all of the Principal's books and records.] [Even to this date, the Surety has not been provided full and complete documents and information.]

The Surety has established a reserve for potential claims. In accordance with your indemnity agreement to the Surety, the Surety hereby demands that you jointly or severally deposit with the Surety $_________ cash or other property acceptable to the Surety, as collateral security, to protect the Surety from all of the above losses on the above projects bonded on behalf of _______________ *[Principal]*.

In an effort to reach an amicable resolution of this matter, the Surety requests that each of you immediately contact the undersigned in order to make arrangements for the payment of the above and the satisfaction of your obligations to the Surety. If we have not heard from you and not received a reasonable settlement proposal in writing to the Surety's satisfaction within the next thirty (30) days, we shall assume that you are not interested in reaching an amicable settlement of your obligations and we shall undertake whatever action is necessary to fully protect the Surety's interests.

Also, nothing herein shall be deemed to be an estoppel, waiver or modification of any of Surety's rights or defenses and Surety hereby reserves all of its rights and defenses under any general agreement of indemnity, contracts, agreements, bonds, or applicable law.

Should you have any questions, please call me. We look forward to receiving your prompt attention to this matter.

Exhibit 13.4 (continued)

Sincerely

______________________________ *[Surety]*

______________________________ *[Name]*

______________________________ *[Title]*

cc: ________________, Esquire

Exhibit 13.5

Acknowledgment of Default by Principal and Indemnitor

WHEREAS, ________________, as Surety, provided certain payment and performance bonds on behalf of ____________________, as Principal, including the following:

Obligee:
Project:
Bond No.:
Amount of Bond:

WHEREAS, ____________ *[Principal]* has also executed a General Agreement of Indemnity in favor of the Surety, under which it issued these bonds; and

WHEREAS, ____________ *[Principal]* is now financially unable to perform its obligations under the contract and bonds and is in default under the bonds.

NOW, THEREFORE, ____________, as Principal and Indemnitor, acknowledges its defaults under the concerned bond obligations to the Surety, and further agrees as follows:

1. __________________ *[Principal]* affirms its assignment to the Surety of all rights under the above described contracts in accordance with the terms of the General Indemnity Agreement executed by it. In order to provide for the payment of all further monies due under the above contracts, ____________ *[Principal]* agrees to execute forms directing the obligees and owners to make all further payments under those contracts to Surety.

2. The Principal and Indemnitor will immediately make available to Surety all of its books and records, including all bills and invoices for work performed and materials and equipment provided in the performance of the project, and assist Surety and its representatives in preparing technical and accounting reviews of such projects.

3. __________________ *[Principal]* acknowledges that it is in default under its bond obligations to Surety, but further acknowledges that the execution of this document is not induced by any promise or agreement of the Surety to furnish any financial assistance to the Principal or to forbear from the enforcement of any rights, legal or equitable, which the Surety may have against Principal and Indemnitor, and that nothing contained in this Acknowledgment of Default shall waive, alter, amend, modify, or estop any of the obligations of

Exhibit 13.5 (continued)

Principal and Indemnitor to Surety under any General Agreement of Indemnity, Contract, Agreements, or applicable law.

Executed this _____ day of ________________, 19____.

____________________ *[Principal]*

ATTEST:

(SEAL)

By: __________________________

Its: __________________, President

____

Secretary

Exhibit 13.6

Acknowledgment of Default and Transfer of Collateral Security and Subcontracts

CERTIFIED COPY OF RESOLUTIONS OF
SPECIAL MEETING OF BOARD OF DIRECTORS OF

____
[Principal]

I hereby certify that I am the duly elected and qualified Secretary of __________________, a ____________________ corporation, and the keeper of the records and corporate seal of said corporation, and that the following are true and correct excerpts of resolutions duly adopted at a special meeting of the Directors of the Corporation held in accordance with the Bylaws of the Corporation on the ______ day of _____________, 19___.

WHEREAS, this Corporation has encountered financial difficulties which make it impossible for it to pay for or complete its obligations under certain construction contracts with the ________________________ *[Obligee]* identified as ___________________________ *[Contract No.]* __________________ *[Project]*; and

WHEREAS, ____________________, as Surety, previously issued its payment and performance bonds at the request of this Corporation, as Principal and Indemnitor; and

WHEREAS, this Corporation has acknowledged to ____________ *[Surety]* its default and inability to pay for or complete the bonded contracts; and

WHEREAS, __________________ *[Surety]* has demanded that this Corporation execute and deliver to it certain collateral security to indemnify ______________________ *[Surety]* against claims, losses, costs and expenses which it has and will incur in the future by reason of the execution of the bonds;

NOW, THEREFORE, BE IT RESOLVED, that this Board of Directors deems it to be in the best interest of the Corporation to execute and deliver certain collateral security to ___________________ *[Surety]* on account of the claims, losses, costs and expenses which have been and will be incurred by _________________ *[Surety]* by reason of the issuance of any performance and payment bonds and that this Corporation acknowledges and reaffirms that all of the provisions of any General Agreement of Indemnity shall remain in full force and effect; and

Exhibit 13.6 (continued)

BE IT FURTHER RESOLVED, that this Corporation should execute and deliver to ____________________ *[Surety]* the forms of Acknowledgement of Default by Principal and Indemnitor, Assignments of all contact proceeds under said contracts, Assignment of all rights under any subcontract Agreements with ____________________ *[Subcontractors]*, letters to ______________ *[Obligee]* acknowledging the Corporation's inability to pay for or complete the contracts, and Security Agreements covering inventory, accounts receivable, and equipment, all of which were presented to the meeting; and

BE IT FURTHER RESOLVED, that the officers of this Corporation are authorized and directed to execute and deliver all of those instruments and documents to __________________ *[Surety]*, and to do such other acts and things as may be necessary and proper to carry out the intent of the foregoing resolution and to satisfy all of the obligations of this Corporation to ________________ *[Surety]*.

I further state that there is no provision in the Charter or Bylaws of this Corporation limiting the powers of the Corporation to pass the foregoing resolutions and that they are in full conformity with the provisions of the Chapter and Bylaws.

IN WITNESS WHEREOF, I have set my hand and affixed the corporate seal of the Corporation, this _____ day of ________________, 19___.

____

____________________, Secretary

Corporation

(SEAL)

I, __________________________, ________________________ of ____________________ *[Principal]*, certify that the foregoing is a true and correct copy of the foregoing resolutions adopted as above set forth.

________________ ________________

____

Exhibit 13.7

Notice of Principal's Default to Obligee and Direction Not to Pay

[Surety's Letterhead]

[Date]

VIA REGULAR AND
CERTIFIED MAIL, RETURN
RECEIPT REQUESTED

[Obligee's Name and Address]

RE: Surety:
Principal:
Bond No.:
Obligee:
Project:
NOTICE

Dear __________:

________________________ *[Surety]* is the payment and performance bond surety for ________________________ *[Principal]* with regard to the above-referenced construction project. It is our understanding that ______________ [identify facts of actual of impending default, e.g.:]

1. Subcontractors and suppliers of Principal have asserted numerous claims for payment asserted against the Payment Bond; **[OR]**
2. Surety has received a notice of default from Obligee concerning the Principal; **[OR]**
3. Principal has admitted to Surety that it is financially unable to pay for the completion or proceed with its contract for the project or pay the outstanding claims for payment of its subcontractors and suppliers; **[OR]**
4. Surety has been required to make payment upon certain claims for payment of subcontractors or suppliers of Principal under Surety's Payment Bond furnished for the Project; **[OR]**]

As a consequence of the above, __________________ *[Surety]* is exposed to *[actual or potential]* losses under its *[payment and performance]* bonds furnished for this project.

Exhibit 13.7 (continued)

We are attempting to communicate with the appropriate representatives of ____________________ *[Principal]* to investigate the facts concerning this matter. *[to be used when P'rincipal not in bankruptcy]*. As of this time, however, we demand, on behalf of ____________________ *[Surety]* that you release no further funds under the above-referenced contract without the in-advance written consent and direction of ________________ *[Surety]*. We make this demand on the basis of and to protect the Surety's rights of subrogation end to enable the Surety to protect its interests under its Bonds furnished for this Project. *[Optional]*: Please note that any failure or refusal to observe this demand *[may or will]* be prejudicial to the surety, and result in serious legal consequences. *[OR, to be used when Principal in bankruptcy]* As of this time, we wish to advise you that the Surety claims an interest in any remaining contract funds and suggest that you may wish to consider holding the funds pending a bankruptcy court determination of the party's rights to those funds. We make this suggestion on the basis of and to protect the Surety's rights of subrogation and to enable the Surety to protect its interests under its Bonds furnished for this project.

If you have any questions with regard to this notice, please contact the undersigned as soon as possible. We will be contacting you shortly to discuss this matter further as our investigation proceeds. Thank you in advance for your cooperation in this matter.

Nothing herein shall be deemed to be an estoppel, waiver or modification of any of Surety's rights or defenses and Surety hereby reserves all of its rights and defenses under any general contracts, agreements, bonds, or applicable law.

Very truly yours,

______________________________ *[Surety]*

______________________________ *[Name]*

______________________________ *[Title]*

cc: *[Principal]*
[Indemnitors]

Exhibit 13.8

Principal's Voluntary Default and Direction To Obligee to Pay Funds to Surety

[Principal's Letterhead]

[Date]

VIA REGULAR AND
CERTIFIED MAIL, RETURN
RECEIPT REQUESTED

[Owner's Name and Address]

RE: Surety:
Principal:
Bond No.:
Project:
Contract No.:

Dear __________:

___________________, as contractor on the project mentioned above, acknowledges its inability to pay for the completion of or perform the contract between ____________________, as owner, and __________________ as contractor, dated ________________, because of financial difficulties.

Accordingly, ______________ *[Principal]* notifies you of its voluntary default on this construction contract. You are at liberty to call upon the surety to arrange for the completion of the performance of the construction project.

___________________ *[Principal]* hereby irrevocably directs that all contract funds be paid to _________________ *[Surety]* at __________________ *[Address]* to the attention of ___________________ *[Name]* and that this direction to pay shall be irrevocable without the in-advance express written consent of the Surety.

Exhibit 13.8 (continued)

Very truly yours,

___________________________ *[Principal]*

By: ______________________________
Its: __________________________, President

cc: *[Surety]*